smithdar
deidrea

www.swcollege.com/tax/raabe/rabbe.html

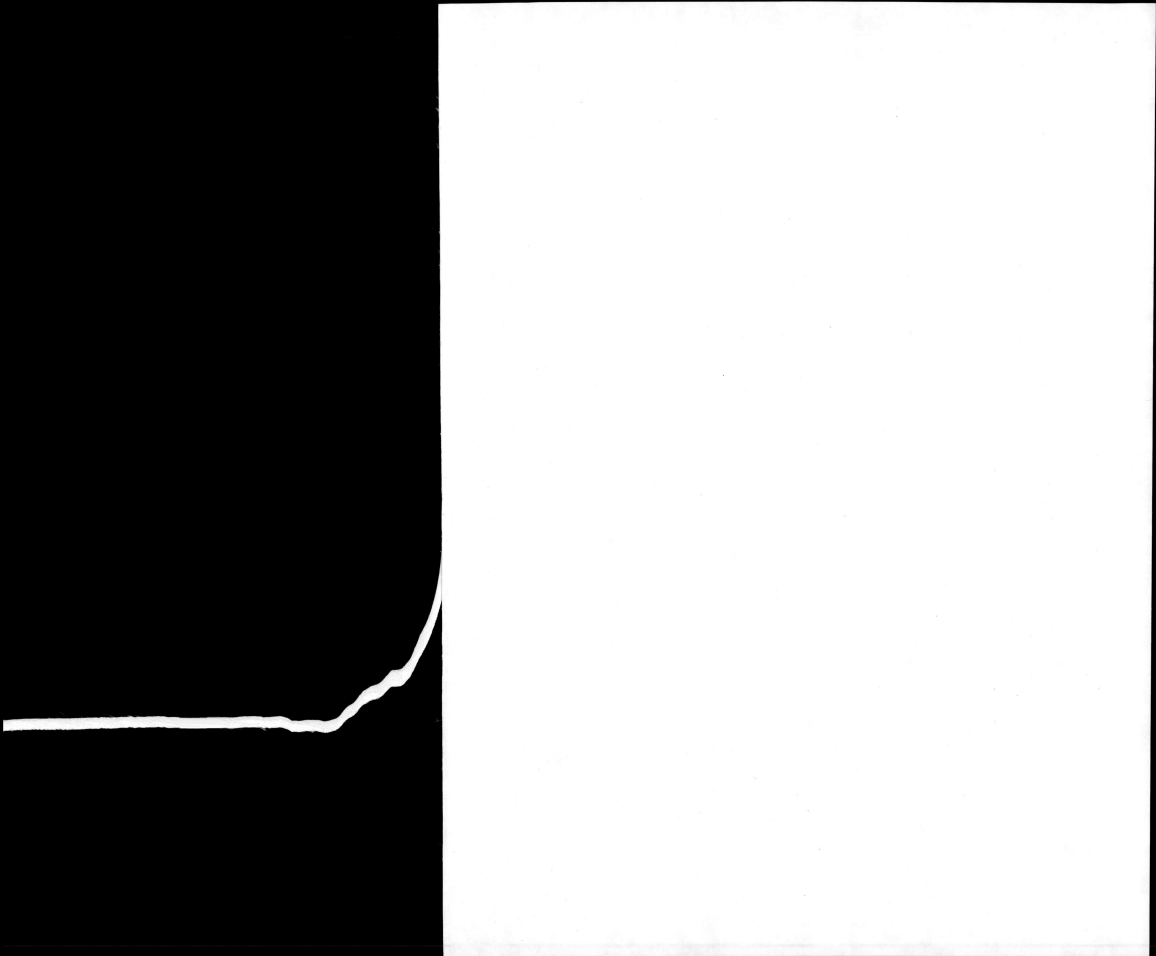

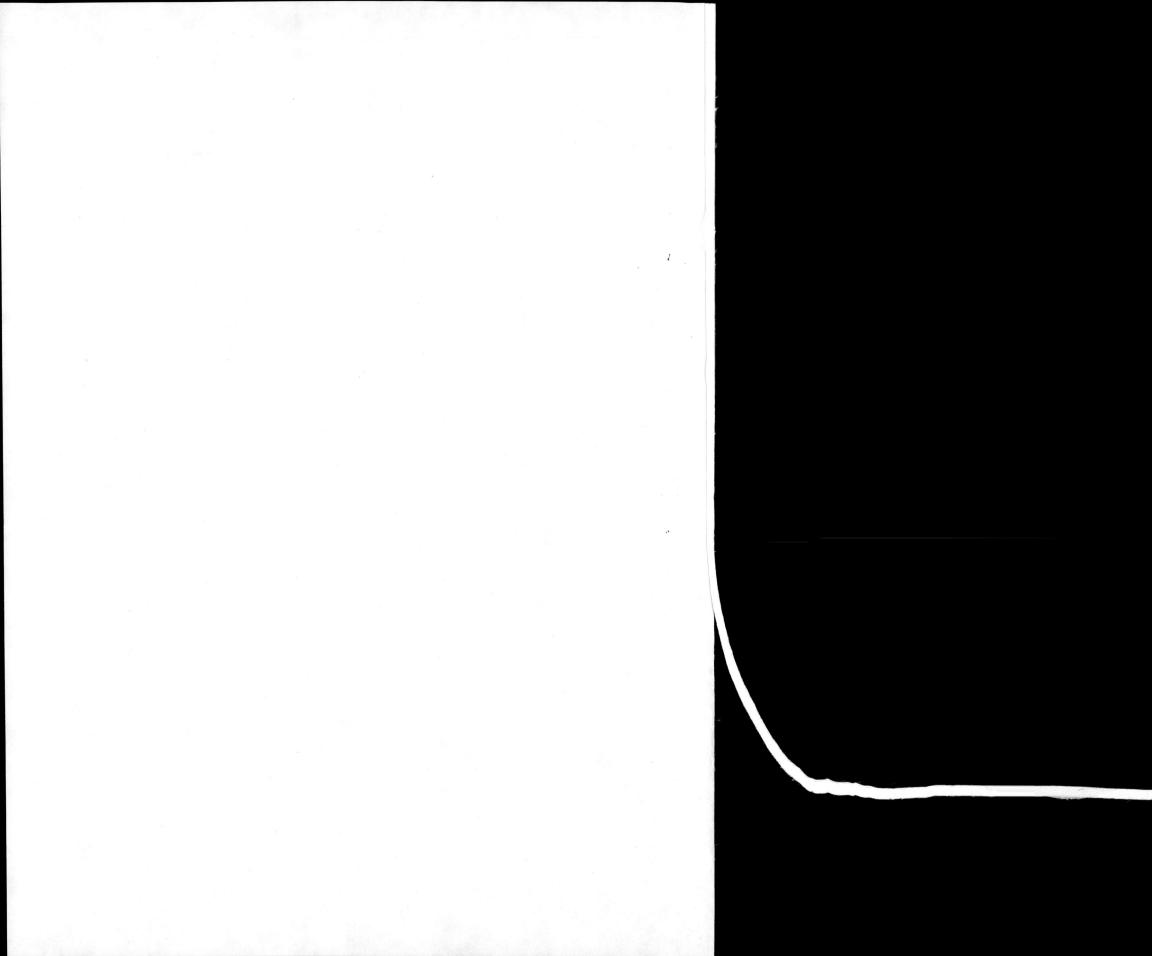

West's
Federal Tax Research

Fifth Edition

West's
Federal Tax Research

Fifth Edition

William A. Raabe Ph.D., C.P.A.
Samford University

Gerald E. Whittenburg Ph.D., C.P.A.
San Diego State University

John C. Bost J.D.
San Diego State University

Debra L. Sanders Ph.D., C.P.A.
Washington State University

South-Western College Publishing
an International Thomson Publishing company I(T)P®

Cincinnati • Albany • Boston • Detroit • Johannesburg • London • Madrid • Melbourne • Mexico City
New York • Pacific Grove • San Francisco • Scottsdale • Singapore • Tokyo • Toronto

Publishing Team Director: Rick Lindgren
Acquisitions Editor: Alex Von Rosenberg
Developmental Editor: Esther Craig
Production Editor: Sandra Gangelhoff
Marketing Manager: Maureen Riopelle
Manufacturing Coordinator: Gordon Woodside
Cover Designer: Rick Moore
Composition: Parkwood Composition Services, Inc.
Copyediting: Lorretta Palagi

1 2 3 4 5 6 7 8 9 WST 7 6 5 4 3 2 1 0 9

Library of Congress Cataloging-in-Publication Data

West's federal tax research / William A. Raabe . . . [et al.]. — 5th ed.
    p.   cm.
    Rev. ed. of: West's federal tax research / William A. Raabe,
Gerald E. Whittenburg, John C. Bost. 4th ed. 1997.
    Includes index.
    ISBN 0-324-00491-5 (hardcover : alk. paper)
    1. Taxation—Law and legislation—United States—Legal research.
I. Raabe, William A. II. Raabe, William A. West's federal tax research.
KF241.T38W47 2000   98-46491
343.7304'072—dc21   CIP

Printed in the United States of America.

I(T)P® International Thomson Publishing
South-Western College Publishing is an ITP Company.
The ITP trademark is used under license.

This book is dedicated to our parents
William A. and Shirley Raabe
Irene M. Whittenburg
Warren L. and Sara L. Bost
Dola and Jack Cairo
who first taught us to respect and question authority

About the Authors

William A. Raabe, PhD, CPA, is the Director of Accounting Programs in the Samford University School of Business. He is a leader among business school tax faculty in incorporating developments in technology into curricula for the educational development of tax professionals.

Dr. Raabe's teaching and research interests focus on multijurisdictional taxation and financial planning, and he is recognized as the leader among business-school academics in the fields of state and local income, sales, and property taxation. Dr. Raabe is the author or editor of approximately twenty book titles, including *West's Federal Taxation,* and the *Multistate Corporate Tax Guide.* He has received university-wide recognition as the winner of the AMPCO Foundation Award for Teaching Excellence, and the Wisconsin Institute of CPAs named him the Educator of the Year.

Gerald E. Whittenburg, PhD, CPA, CMA, is a Professor in the School of Accountancy at San Diego State University. A graduate of the University of Houston, Dr. Whittenburg's teaching and research interests include individual and corporate taxation, pension plans, and tax research methodology.

Dr. Whittenburg is also an author of West's *Income Tax Fundamentals.* In addition, he has published articles in such journals as the *Journal of Taxation, Taxation for Accountants, Taxes, Journal of Taxation of Investments, Journal of Taxation of Employee Benefits,* and *Journal of Accounting Education.* Professor Whittenburg's professional designations include Certified Public Accountant (CPA) and Certified Management Accountant (CMA). He has received numerous teaching awards, including the Trustee's Outstanding Faculty Award for the entire California State University System.

Debra L. Sanders, PhD, CPA, is a professor in the Washington State University School of Accounting, Information Systems and Business Law. She has received numerous awards for outstanding teaching, research, and service including the Boeing Distinguished Faculty Research Award, the Shell Corporation Outstanding Teacher Award, and the College of Business and Economics Outstanding Service Award.

Dr. Sanders, a graduate of Arizona State University, publishes in both academic and professional journals. Articles written by her have appeared in the academic journals *Behavioral Research in Accounting, National Tax Journal, The Journal of the American Taxation Association, Advances in Taxation,* and *The International Journal of Accounting.* The professional journals that have published her articles include *Taxation for Accountants, Taxation for Lawyers, The Review of Taxation of Individuals, Taxes, The Tax Advisor,* and *Journal of Financial Planning.*

John C. Bost, JD, MST, is an Associate Professor at San Diego State University, where he teaches courses in transfer taxation and the legal environment of business. A graduate of the University of California—Hastings College of the Law, Professor Bost is a certified specialist in Taxation Law, and Probate, Estate Planning, and Trust Law.

Articles written by Professor Bost have appeared in *Taxation for Accountants, Taxation for Lawyers,* the *Community Property Journal,* and the *Journal of Agriculture Taxation and Law.*

Contents in Brief

Contents

13 Tax Practice and Administration: Sanctions, Agreements, and Disclosures   410

Preface

We are pleased to offer the fifth edition of this popular text, which has been prepared as a comprehensive, stand-alone reference tool for the reader who wishes to become proficient in the practice of federal tax research. It is written for readers who are familiar with the fundamentals of the federal income and transfer tax law, at a level that typically is achieved on the completion of two comprehensive introductory courses in taxation in either (1) the accounting program in a business school or (2) second- or third-year courses in a law school.

Accordingly, the text is most appropriate for (1) upper-level accounting students in a business school (i.e., seniors in a four-year program or those in the fifth year of a 150-hour program) who desire additional information concerning the practice of taxation; (2) those who are enrolled in a nontax graduate program in business administration (e.g., an MBA or MS—management program) and would like further practical training in the functions of taxation in today's business environment; (3) second- or third-year law school students, especially those who desire a more detailed and pragmatic introduction to a specialized tax practice; (4) those who are commencing a graduate degree program in taxation, in either a business school or a law school, and require a varied and sophisticated introduction to the procedures of tax research and to the routine functions and implications of a tax practice; and (5) practicing accountants and attorneys who need an introduction, updating, or refresher relative to tax practice and research as an element of their career paths.

Structure and Pedagogy

Sensing that existing textbooks too often ignore the detailed, pragmatic approach that today's students require in developing effective and efficient tax research skills, the authors have employed an unprecedented degree of "hands-on" tax research analysis throughout the text. This book does not stop, as do so many others, with a *discussion* of tax research procedures or of the sources of the federal tax law; nor does it try to satisfy with a mere sampling of the pertinent tax reference materials. Rather, its pedagogy reflects the authors' conviction that the reader must be engaged in a series of exercises that require individualize experience with the most important elements of the federal tax law.

This conviction is evident in the most important aspects of the structure of the book.

▶ An extremely readable style encourages the student to complete and understand even the most complex aspects of tax research and practice.

▶ Hundreds of exercises and discussion questions are provided that require the reader personally to explore the reference materials of the well-developed tax library in developing solutions. About 100 such items are new to this edition.

▶ Assignments require the reader to construct case briefs, file memos, client letters, and other elements of a comprehensive client file.

▶ Hundreds of pages of reproductions and illustrations have been excerpted from the most important tax reference materials.

▶ Summary charts, diagrams, and other study aids are interspersed throughout the text that summarize the elements of the primary and secondary sources of the federal tax law and allow for development of the reader's own research routines and techniques.

▶ Dozens of real-life research cases offer the reader a chance to do extensive hands-on research. Appropriate applications of inductive and deductive reasoning are encouraged to help the reader develop conclusions.

▶ An extensive introduction is provided that details the necessary aspects of tax practice, including preparer penalties, statutes of limitation, interest conventions, and return selection for IRS audit.

▶ A tax planning orientation to tax practice is developed in a manner that is unequaled in other texts of this sort.

▶ A thorough and comprehensive examination is provided of electronic tax research tools, including computerized databases and Internet applications. An introduction to the structure and procedures of the most popular such resources is given, and they integrated throughout the book from the very first chapters of the text.

▶ Extensive coverage is given to materials that keep the practitioner current with respect to changes in tax-related law.

▶ Attention is paid to other developments that affect those who conduct tax research, including revisions to codes of ethics, IRS organizational structure and enforcement functions, and other principles that control tax practice.

Computer Orientation

The unprecedented coverage in earlier editions of this text relative to the computer-oriented tools available to tax researchers was extremely well received. Accordingly, and in light of the growing importance of these tools for the practitioner, the discussion of such materials has been expanded yet again in this edition, and now takes perhaps equal footing with our discussions of the traditional paper-based resources. This orientation is demanded by our audience, and its remains the greatest innovation of this text to the tax literature. Our extensive review involves a close look at Internet and CD-ROM-based research, and other developments that have extended the boundaries of tax research.

Using the Text

Although various instructors may wish to alter the specific sequence in which the chapters of the text are examined, several comments relative to the effective use of the book are in order.

The text's exercises, cases, and advanced cases offer enough variety in both difficulty and subject matter that they may be assigned to individual readers, or to student groups of two or three, for their optimal use. The instructor also should consider giving each student in the course a different research case to complete, thereby both discouraging joint work and reducing the strain on the pertinent library resources.

Given both the nature of the tax research process and the limited tax library resources that are available to most firms and universities, the instructor must take care (1) to assign discussion materials for which the necessary resources are available and (2) to work through the assignment him- or herself, to ascertain that one's target solution to the assignment reflects the very latest in the development of the federal tax law.

Deliberation relative to several of the research cases could be delayed until the discussion concerning a specific electronic research service, which will provide additional illustrations. Alternatively, the reader could be encouraged to rework a previous assignment once the computerized tax reference tools have been introduced.

Other pedagogical support for the text will help to maintain this text's preeminence in providing instructors with teaching tools that assist in delivering this difficult course.

▶ Up-to-date solutions to the various chapter-end questions, exercises, cases, and advanced cases.
▶ Lecture notes and outlines, augmented by professional-quality transparency masters.
▶ An extensive test bank and an expanded set of in-class quizzes for use in classroom discussion.
▶ PowerPoint slides, additional support and update material provided at the text's home page (tax.swcollege.com) on the World Wide Web.

Acknowledgements and Thanks

The authors welcome your comments and suggestions for further improvements to this text. Please feel free to use the following addresses to convey these remarks.

William A. Raabe
Samford University School of Business
Birmingham, AL 35229
(205) 870-2446
E-mail: waraabe@samford.edu
Web page: http://waraabe.samford.edu

Gerald E. Whittenburg
San Diego State University
San Diego, CA 92182-8221
E-mail: gwhitten@mail.sdsu.edu

Debra L. Sanders
Department of Accounting and Business Law
Washington State University
Pullman, WA 99164-4729
E-mail: dsanders@wsu.edu

The authors are grateful to the many instructors and students who assisted in the development of this text, both by their use thereof and by their resulting constructive criticisms. In addition, we have benefited from the contributions of the professional reviewers of the text, listed below, for their numerous contributions of both substance and style. Any errors, of course, are the sole responsibilities of the authors.

Glenn S. Freed, University of Alabama at Birmingham
Roger L. Lirely, Western Carolina University
Frank M. Messina, University of Alabama at Birmingham
Janet Trewin, Drexel University
Donald T. Williamson, American University

The Tax Research Environment

CHAPTER ONE

An Introduction to Tax Practice

LEARNING OBJECTIVES

► Describe the elements of modern tax practice in the United States

► Distinguish between open and closed transactions

► Identify sources of legal and ethical standards that guide those who engage in tax practice

► Examine in detail the major collections of ethical standards that bear upon tax practitioners today

► Place tax issues in a broader context of ethics and morality

► Understand the limitations on tax research by CPAs and other nonattorneys

CHAPTER OUTLINE

In simple terms, taxation is the process of collecting revenue from citizens to finance government activities. In a modern technological society such as that of the United States, however, taxation comprises an interaction among several disciplines that is far from simple. The tax system is derived from law, accounting, economics, political science, and sociology (Exhibit 1–1). Principles of economics, sociology, and political science provide the environment, while law and accounting precepts are applied in a typical tax practice.

Tax policy questions concerning the effects that a specified tax law change will have on economic growth, the effects of projected inflation on the implementation of the tax law and vice versa, and the effects of the tax law on the United States' balance of payments are addressed by economists. Political scientists, economists, and sociologists, alternatively, examine issues such as who bears the ultimate burden of a tax, how a tax bill becomes law (including practical effects of the legislative process), the social equity of a tax, and whether a tax is discriminatory. Attorneys interpret (and often create) taxation statutes, and accountants apply the tax laws to current or prospective economic transactions.

Elements of Tax Practice

The tax laws of a democratic country such as the United States are created by a political process. In recent years, the result of this political process has been a law that levies taxes on income, sales, estates, gifts, and other items that usually are reflected by the accounting process. Thus, tax practice can be described as the application of tax legislation to specific accounting situations. The elements of modern tax practice can be separated into four (admittedly overlapping) categories: compliance, planning, litigation, and research.

Tax Compliance

In general, **tax compliance** consists of the gathering of pertinent information, evaluation and classification of such information, and the filing of necessary tax returns.

EXHIBIT 1–1   Elements of taxation

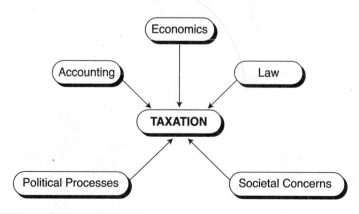

Tax compliance also includes other functions necessary to satisfy government requirements, such as representation at a client's Internal Revenue Service (IRS) audit. Commercial tax preparers, enrolled agents, attorneys, and certified public accountants (CPAs) all perform tax compliance to some extent. Noncomplex individual, partnership, and corporate tax returns often are completed by commercial tax preparers. Enrolled agents, attorneys, and CPAs usually are involved in the preparation of more complex tax returns; in addition, they provide tax planning services and represent their clients before the IRS. The elements of tax compliance and administration are examined in more detail in later chapters.

Tax Planning

Tax planning is the process of arranging one's financial affairs to optimize tax liabilities. There is nothing inherently illegal or immoral in the avoidance of taxation according to the tax system's rules. The eminent jurist Learned Hand best expressed this doctrine in the dissenting opinion of *Commissioner v. Newman*[1]:

> Over and over again, courts have said that there is nothing sinister in so arranging one's affairs as to keep taxes as low as possible. Everybody does so, rich or poor, and all do right, for nobody owes any public duty to pay more than the law demands: taxes are enforced extractions, not voluntary contributions.

However, whereas **tax avoidance** is the legitimate object of much of modern tax practice, **tax evasion** constitutes the illegal nonpayment of a tax and cannot be condoned. Fraudulent acts of this sort are unrelated to the professional practice of tax planning.

Tax planning can be divided into two major categories: **open transactions** and **closed transactions.** In an open transaction the tax practitioner maintains some degree of control over the attendant tax liability because the transaction is not yet completed; for example, the title to an asset that has not yet passed. If desired, some modifications to an incomplete transaction can be made to receive more favorable tax treatment. In a closed transaction, however, all of the pertinent actions have been completed; therefore, tax planning may be limited to the presentation of the facts to the government in the most favorable, legally acceptable manner possible.

In recent years, the use of computers has greatly enhanced tax planning. By using electronic spreadsheets and other programs, the tax practitioner can perform a "what if" sensitivity analysis of an open-fact transaction.

Tax Litigation

A specialized area within the practice of law is the concentration on **tax litigation.** Litigation is the process of settling a dispute with another party (here, usually the IRS) in a court of law (here, a federal court). Typically, a tax attorney handles tax litigation that progresses beyond the initial appeal of an IRS audit result. Accountants and other financial advisors also can serve in a support capacity. Chapters 5, 10, and 13 contain additional discussions of the various opportunities and strategies available in tax litigation.

[1]159 F.2d 848 (CA-2, 1947).

Tax Research

Tax research is undertaken to answer taxation questions. The tax research process includes the (1) identification of pertinent issues, (2) determination of proper authorities, (3) evaluation of the appropriateness of these authorities, and (4) application of these authorities to specific facts. Tax research techniques are examined in Chapters 2 through 10 of this text.

Rules and Ethics in Tax Practice

A person who prepares tax returns for monetary or other compensation, or who is licensed to practice in the tax-related professions, is subject to various statutes, rules, and codes of professional conduct. All tax practitioners are regulated by IRS ***Circular 230*** (reprinted in Appendix A), *Regulations Governing the Practice of Attorneys, Certified Public Accountants, Enrolled Agents, Enrolled Actuaries, and Appraisers before the Internal Revenue Service.* The ethical conduct of an attorney is also governed by the laws of the state(s) in which he or she is licensed to practice. Most states have adopted, often with some modification, guidelines that are based on the **American Bar Association (ABA)** *Model Code of Professional Responsibility* or the newer *ABA Model Rules for Professional Conduct.* CPAs who are members of the **American Institute of Certified Public Accountants (AICPA)** must follow its *Code of Professional Conduct* (reprinted in Appendix B), and any other rules generated by the state board(s) of accountancy. The AICPA has also produced a series of *Statements on Responsibilities in Tax Practice* (reprinted in Appendix C), which contain advisory guidelines for CPAs who prepare tax returns.

Although CPAs who are not members of the AICPA are not bound by the *Code of Professional Conduct* and the *Statements on Responsibilities in Tax Practice,* those rules and standards are a useful source of guidance for all members of the profession. Statutory tax law also specifies certain penalties and other rules of conduct that apply to everyone (e.g., to attorneys, CPAs, and enrolled agents) in addition to their respective professional standards, and also to commercial tax preparers who are not attorneys, CPAs, or enrolled agents. Chapter 13 addresses these rules. The basic sources of rules and ethics for tax practitioners are summarized in Exhibit 1–2.

EXHIBIT 1–2   Sources of rules and ethics for tax practitioners

Source	Issued By	Binding Upon
ABA Model Code of Professional Responsibility	American Bar Association	Attorneys at law
AICPA Code of Professional Conduct	American Institute of CPAs	Certified public accountants who are AICPA members
Circular 230	Internal Revenue Service	Those in practice before the IRS
Statements on Responsibilities in Tax Practice	American Institute of CPAs	Certified public accountants who are AICPA members
Internal Revenue Code	U.S. Congress	Tax preparers

Circular 230

Circular 230, which constitutes Part 31 of the Treasury Department Regulations, is designed to provide protection to taxpayers and the IRS by requiring tax preparers to be technically competent and to adhere to ethical standards. *Circular 230* contains the following definition of **practice before the IRS** in Section 10.2 of Subpart A.

> . . . matters connected with presentation to the Internal Revenue Service or any of its officers or employees relating to a client's rights, privileges, or liabilities under laws or regulations administered by the Internal Revenue Service. Such presentations include the preparation and filing of necessary documents, correspondence with and communications to the Internal Revenue Service, and the representation of a client at conferences, hearings and meetings.

Under this definition, practice before the IRS consists primarily of the representation of clients during audit procedures, such as a meeting with a revenue agent on behalf of a client to establish the correctness of a taxpayer's return. The preparation of tax returns or the furnishing of information to the IRS in response to a request for such information is not considered practice before the IRS. (Tax return preparation rules are addressed by various statutes discussed in Chapter 13.) *Circular 230* also states who may conduct such a practice, and sets forth the disciplinary procedures that apply.

Who May Practice Under Section 10.3, Subpart A, of *Circular 230,* the following individuals may practice before the IRS.

► Attorneys
► Certified public accountants
► Enrolled agents
► Enrolled actuaries

To qualify under this rule, an attorney must be a member in good standing of the bar of the highest court in any state, possession, territory, commonwealth, or the District of Columbia. Likewise, CPAs and enrolled actuaries must be qualified to practice in any state, possession, territory, commonwealth, or the District of Columbia. No further substantive examination is required.

Enrolled Agents Individuals who are not attorneys or certified public accountants can qualify to practice before the Internal Revenue Service by becoming an enrolled agent (EA). An **enrolled agent** is someone who has either passed a special Internal Revenue Service examination (currently given once a year, in September) or worked for the IRS for five years. The procedures for becoming an enrolled agent are detailed in *Circular 230,* Subpart A, § 10.4, § 10.5, and § 10.6. Enrolled agents have the same rights as attorneys and certified public accountants to represent clients before the Internal Revenue Service. Under *Circular 230,* an enrolled agent must renew his or her enrollment card on a three-year cycle. For each enrollment cycle, enrolled agents, like attorneys and CPAs, must meet certain continuing education requirements as defined in Subpart A, § 10.6. For an EA's enrollment card to be renewed, he or she must complete seventy-two hours (i.e., an average of twenty-four hours per year) of qualifying continuing education for each three-year enrollment period. In addition, a minimum of sixteen hours of continuing education credit must be completed during each year of an enrollment cycle. Subpart A, § 10.6(f) defines what qualifies as continuing education for enrolled agents.

Circular 230 allows an individual to be an attorney or CPA and an enrolled agent simultaneously. Being both an EA and an attorney or CPA might be useful to certain tax practitioners who practice across state lines. For example, a CPA in Texas who is also an enrolled agent can practice in any state: The enrolled agent's card effectively is a national license to practice before the Internal Revenue Service anywhere in the United States (including territories). In addition, most state taxing agencies grant an enrolled agent the right to practice before that state agency.

Limited Practice without Enrollment   In *Circular 230,* the Internal Revenue Service has authorized certain individuals to practice without being an attorney, CPA, or enrolled agent. Individuals (with proper identification) can represent themselves under § 10.7(a) and participate in Internal Revenue Service rule making as provided for under § 10.7(b). In addition, under § 10.7(c), individuals (with proper identification and authorization, IRS Form 2848) are allowed to represent taxpayers in the following special situations.

▶ An individual may represent a member of his or her immediate family.
▶ A regular full-time employee of an individual employer may represent the employer.
▶ A general partner or regular full-time employee of a partnership may represent the partnership.
▶ A bona fide officer or regular full-time employee of a corporation (including a parent, subsidiary, or other affiliated corporation), an association, or organized group may represent the corporation, association, or organized group.
▶ A trustee, receiver, guardian, personal representative, administrator, executor, or regular full-time employee of a trust, receivership, guardianship, or estate may represent the trust, receivership, guardianship, or estate.
▶ An officer or regular employee of a governmental unit, agency, or authority may represent the governmental unit, agency, or authority in the course of his or her official duties.
▶ An individual may represent any individual or entity before personnel of the Internal Revenue Service who are outside the United States.

Tax Return Preparers   Any person who signs a tax return as having prepared it for a taxpayer is authorized to conduct "limited practice" before the Internal Revenue Service (with proper taxpayer authorization) under § 10.7(c)(viii). *Circular 230* requires that such person must not be disbarred or suspended from practice before the Internal Revenue Service or his or her profession. A tax return preparer can make an appearance as the taxpayer's representative only before the Examination Division of the IRS. A return preparer may not represent a taxpayer before any other Internal Revenue Service division, including the Appeals and Collection Divisions [IRS Publication 947]. In addition, the following actions are outside the authority of an unenrolled preparer [Rev. Proc. 81-38, 1981-1 C.B. 386].

▶ Executing a claim for refund for the taxpayer
▶ Receiving checks in payment of any refund of taxes, penalties, or interest for the taxpayer

▶ Agreeing to later assessment or collection of taxes than is provided for by the applicable statute of limitations

▶ Executing closing agreements with respect to tax liability or other specific matters for the taxpayer

▶ Executing waivers of restriction on assessment or collection of a tax deficiency

Conduct before the IRS   Subpart B of *Circular 230* provides the rules of conduct for those individuals authorized to practice before the Internal Revenue Service. Attorneys, CPAs, and enrolled agents must observe the following rules of conduct when practicing before the IRS.

▶ A tax practitioner must furnish information, on request, to any authorized agent of the Internal Revenue Service, unless the practitioner has reason to believe the request is of doubtful legality or the information is privileged [§ 10.20(a)].

▶ A tax practitioner must provide the Director of Practice of the IRS, on request, any information concerning the violation of any regulation pertaining to practice before the Internal Revenue Service. The tax practitioner must testify in a disbarment or suspension proceeding, unless there is reason to doubt the legality of the request or the information is privileged [§ 10.20(b)].

▶ A tax practitioner who knows of client noncompliance, error, or omission with regard to the tax laws must advise the client of that noncompliance, error, or omission [§ 10.21].

▶ A practitioner must exercise due diligence in preparing tax returns and other documents submitted to the Internal Revenue Service [§ 10.22].

▶ Practitioners must not unreasonably delay matters before the Internal Revenue Service [§ 10.23].

▶ Practitioners must not accept assistance from or employ a disbarred or suspended person or a former Internal Revenue Service employee disqualified from practice under another rule or U.S. law [§ 10.24].

▶ Partners of government employees cannot represent anyone for which the government employee-partner has (or has had) official responsibility [§ 10.25]. For example, a CPA firm with an IRS agent as a partner could not represent any taxpayer that is (or was in the past) assigned to the IRS agent/partner.

▶ No former government employee shall, subsequent to his or her government employment, represent anyone in any matter administered by the Internal Revenue Service if such representation would violate other U.S. laws [§ 10.26].

▶ No tax practitioner may act as a notary public for his or her clients [§ 10.27].

▶ Fees for tax work must not be contingent or unconscionable [§ 10.28], and a practitioner must not negotiate a taxpayer refund check [§ 10.31].

▶ No practitioner can represent conflicting interests before the Internal Revenue Service unless he or she has the express consent of the directly interested parties [§ 10.29].

▶ Tax practitioners who issue tax shelter opinion letters must comply with the complex requirements of § 10.33 of *Circular 230*.

Due Diligence   Section 10.22 of *Circular 230* requires tax practitioners to use due diligence in preparing tax returns and in their practice before the IRS. Due diligence is not defined in *Circular 230*. However, the Second Circuit[2] has held that due dili-

---

[2]*Harary v. Blumenthal,* 555 F.2d 1113 (CA-2, 1977).

gence requires that the tax practitioner be honest with his or her client in connection with all IRS-related matters. In the view of the IRS, the failure to exercise due diligence involves conduct that is more than a simple error, but less than willful and reckless misconduct.[3] In determining if a practitioner has exercised due diligence, the IRS uses several factors, including the nature of the error, the explanation of the error, and other standards that apply (for example, the *AICPA Statements on Responsibility in Tax Practice* that are discussed later in this chapter). In essence, due diligence means a tax practitioner should use reasonable effort to comply with the tax laws.

> **Example 1–1** Judy is a CPA who fails to include rental income on a tax return she completed for a client. The omitted rental income was from a new rental property purchased by the client this year and therefore had not been reported on prior years' tax returns. The taxpayer did not mention the new rental property to Judy in any communications with her. Under these circumstances, Judy has exercised due diligence in preparing the tax return. However, if Judy also kept the rental income records for the new rental property and still omitted the income from the tax return, she would not be exercising due diligence.

Contingent and Unconscionable Fees Tax practitioners are prohibited from charging **contingent fees** on an original tax return by § 10.28(b) of *Circular 230*. Examples of contingent fees include a fee that is based on a percentage of the refund on a tax return, or a fee that is a percentage of tax "saved." Although contingent fees are prohibited for the preparation of an original return, a practitioner may charge a contingent fee for an amended return or a claim for refund (other than a claim for refund made on an original return). The tax practitioner must reasonably anticipate, at the time of the fee arrangement, that the amended return will receive a substantive review by the IRS.

> **Example 1–2** Oak Corporation has been audited by the IRS for its tax return filed two years ago. The controller of the company completed the original return. The IRS is asserting that Oak underpaid its taxes by $100,000. Oak contacted Joe, a CPA, and engaged him to handle the appeals process with the IRS. In this situation, Joe can use a contingent fee arrangement. (For instance, Joe's fee could be 30 percent of any amount by which he could get the IRS to reduce the assessment.)

Section 10.28(a) also prohibits a tax practitioner from charging an unconscionable fee. This term is undefined in *Circular 230*. If a tax practitioner charges a fee that is out of line with some measure of the value of the service provided to a client, then the fee would be unconscionable. For example, a CPA could not charge a fee of $10,000 to an unsophisticated taxpayer (such as an elderly person) for simple tax work that most CPAs would complete for less than $500.

Solicitation and Advertising An attorney, CPA, or enrolled agent may use public communication to obtain clients under § 10.30 of Subpart B. Types of public communications allowed by this provision include billboards, telephone books, and advertisements in newspapers, on radio, and on television. However, such public communications must not contain false, fraudulent, unduly influencing, coercive, or unfair statements or claims. If done in a dignified manner, examples of items that a

---

[3]*Referrals to the Director of Practice,* Coursebook (Training 994-102), IRS, December 1992.

practitioner may communicate to the public include (1) his or her name, address, and telephone number, (2) names of individuals associated with the practitioner, (3) a factual description of services offered, (4) credit cards accepted, (5) foreign language ability, (6) membership in professional organizations, (7) professional licenses held, and (8) a statement of practice limitations. Attorneys, CPAs, and enrolled agents also must observe any applicable standards of ethical conduct adopted by the American Bar Association (ABA), the American Institute of CPAs (AICPA), and the National Association of Enrolled Agents (NAEA).

Tax Return Positions Tax practitioners under *Circular 230* must meet certain standards with respect to advice given to clients on tax return positions. Under § 10.34, a practitioner must not sign a tax return if he or she determines that the return contains a position that does not have a **realistic possibility** of being sustained on its merits if challenged by the Internal Revenue Service. The realistic possibility standard is met if analysis of the tax return position by a reasonable and well-informed person knowledgeable in the tax law(s) would lead such person to conclude that the position has approximately a one in three (or greater) likelihood of being sustained on its merits [§ 10.34(a)(4)].

A practitioner may recommend a position on a tax return that does not meet the realistic possibility standard if the position is not frivolous and the position is *disclosed* on the tax return. A frivolous position is one that is patently improper under the tax law. When analyzing the merits of a tax return position, the authorities applicable under IRC § 6662 and Reg. § 1.6662 should be used to decide if the realistic possibility standard has been met. See Chapter 13 for further discussion of pertinent restrictions on tax return positions.

AICPA Code of Professional Conduct

Members of the American Institute of Certified Public Accountants (AICPA) are subject to the Institute's *Code of Professional Conduct*. The Code is relevant to all of the professional services performed by CPAs, including those services provided in the practice of public accounting, private industry, government, or education. It was previously referred to as the *AICPA Code of Ethics*. Changes adopted in 1988 were believed necessary to reflect the significant changes in the profession and the environment in which CPAs practice, although the basic tenets of ethical and professional conduct remained the same. One of the most significant changes was the expansion of the rules to apply to all members in all fields of practice, except where the wording of the rule limits the application to a specified field of practice. Under the prior *Code of Ethics,* only members engaged in the practice of public accounting were required to observe all of the rules. Other members, such as those in the fields of education, government, and industry, were subject only to the rules requiring integrity and objectivity and the rule prohibiting members from performing acts discreditable to the profession.

In addition, the rule prohibiting a CPA in public practice from engaging in a business or an occupation concurrently with the practice of public accounting, which would create a conflict of interest in rendering professional services, was deleted from the *Code of Professional Conduct.* The members of the Institute felt that such conflicts of interest are effectively prohibited under new Rule 102, Integrity and Objectivity. (See Appendix B for the complete text of the Code.)

The *Code of Professional Conduct* was designed to provide its members with the following:

▶ A comprehensive code of ethical and professional conduct
▶ A guide for all members in answering complex questions
▶ Assurance to the public concerning the obligations and responsibilities of the accounting profession

The *AICPA Code of Professional Conduct* consists of two integral sections: the *principles* and the *rules.* The principles provide a foundation on which the rules are based. The principles suggest that a CPA should strive for behavior above the minimal level of acceptable conduct required by law and regulations. In addition to expressing the basic tenets of ethical and professional conduct, the principles are intended to provide a framework for the certified public accountant's responsibilities to the public, clients, and colleagues. Included are guidelines concerning the member's responsibility to perform professional services with integrity, objectivity, and independence.

The rules consist of a set of enforceable ethical standards that have been approved by a majority of the members of the AICPA. These rules are broad in nature and apply to all of the professional services that a CPA performs, whether in the practice of public accounting or in the fields of education, industry, or government. The only exceptions to the rules occur when their wording indicates that their application is limited to a specified field of practice only, or with respect to certain activities of those who are practicing in another country. In the latter case, however, the CPA must adhere to the ethical standards of the foreign country.

Any failure to follow the rules under the *Code of Professional Conduct* may result in the offender's receiving admonishment, suspension, or expulsion from membership in the AICPA. The rules apply not only to the CPA, but also to those employees who are under his or her supervision, partners or shareholders in the practice of the CPA, and any others who act on the CPA's behalf (even if they are not compensated for their activities). As previously discussed, the *Code of Professional Conduct* is applicable to all of the professional services performed by a CPA, including services rendered in the fields of public accounting, such as tax and management advisory services, education, industry, and government.

In addition to the principles and rules, the *Code of Professional Conduct* provides for three additional promulgations. These are interpretations of rules, ethics rulings, and "ethics features." *Interpretations of Rules* are issued by the Division of Professional Ethics of the AICPA. They provide additional detailed guidelines for the scope and application of the rules. These guidelines are enforceable, and the CPA must be prepared to justify any departure from them.

The Division of Professional Ethics of the AICPA also issues *ethics rulings* to further explain the application and interpretation of the rules of conduct and interpretations of the rules in specific circumstances. A member who in similar circumstances departs from the findings of these ethics rulings must be prepared to justify such departure. In addition, the Division of Professional Ethics publishes a column in the *Journal of Accountancy* dealing with issues of professional ethics. These informal articles are intended to address issues raised in questions submitted by members of the AICPA. The questions and answers contained in the articles are not considered formal rulings by the AICPA.

Rule 101: Independence

Under Rule 101, a CPA (or CPA firm) in public practice must be independent of the enterprise for which professional services are being provided. **Independence** is required not only for opinions on financial statements, but also for certain other reports and services where a body of the AICPA has promulgated standards requiring independence. A CPA is not independent if one or more financial relationships exist with a client during the period of professional engagement, or at the issuing of the opinion. Thus, independence is impaired if a CPA

- ▶ has any direct or indirect material financial interest in the client's enterprise;
- ▶ has any jointly held material investment with the client, or with its officers, directors, or principal stockholders;
- ▶ has any loan to or from the client, an officer of the client, or any principal stockholder of the client, except for loans, such as home mortgages, that were obtained under normal lending procedures;
- ▶ is an officer, director, employee, or underwriter of the client during the period that is covered by the financial statements, during the period of the professional engagement, or at the time of expressing an opinion; or
- ▶ is related as a trustee, executor, or administrator of any estate that holds a direct or material indirect financial interest in the client.

These independence standards also apply to a CPA who is restricted to doing tax work in a partnership with other CPAs who are examining related financial statements. For instance, a tax partner in a CPA firm should not own stock in a client whose financial statements are audited by her partners in the firm, even though she may have nothing to do with auditing that client's statements.

Rule 102: Integrity and Objectivity

All professional services by a CPA should be rendered with objectivity and integrity, avoiding any conflict of interest. A CPA should not knowingly misrepresent facts or subordinate his or her judgment to that of others in rendering any professional services. For example, in a tax practice, the CPA may be requested to follow blindly the guidelines of a government agency or the demands of an audited client. Rule 102 prohibits such blind obedience. Prior to the most recent revision of Rule 102, a CPA in tax practice could resolve doubt in favor of the client. This phrase was omitted in the revised language because resolving doubt in favor of a client in an advocacy engagement is not considered to impair integrity or objectivity and thus need not be specifically "allowed."

Rule 201: General Standards

The CPA must comply with the following general standards, as well as any interpretations of such standards, of the *AICPA Code of Professional Conduct*.

- ▶ The CPA must be able to complete all professional services with professional competence.
- ▶ The CPA must exercise due professional care in the performance of all professional services.
- ▶ The CPA shall adequately plan and supervise the performance of all professional services.
- ▶ The CPA must obtain sufficient relevant data to afford a reasonable basis for any conclusion or recommendation in connection with the performance of any professional services.

The standard requiring "professional competence" recognizes the need for members of the profession to commit to a program of professional development, learning, and improvement. Such a program of professional continuing education is also recognized in the standard of "due professional care."

Rule 202: Compliance with Standards   A CPA, whether providing tax, management advisory, auditing, review, compilation, or other professional services, must comply with all standards promulgated by bodies designated by the AICPA Council.

Rule 203: Accounting Principles   A CPA is prohibited from expressing an opinion that financial data of an entity conform with Generally Accepted Accounting Principles if those statements or other financial data contain any material departure from the profession's technical standards. In some cases, where a departure is present but the financial statement or other financial data would have been misleading without that departure, a member may be able to comply with this rule by describing the departure, the effect of the departure, and the justification for it.

Rule 301: Confidential Client Information   A CPA in the practice of public accounting must not disclose confidential client data without the specific consent of the client. Rule 301 does not, however, apply

- ▶ if there is a conflict with Rules 202 (Compliance with Standards) and 203 (Accounting Principles) as set forth by the *AICPA Code of Professional Conduct;*
- ▶ if the CPA is served with an enforceable subpoena or summons, or must comply with applicable laws and government regulations;
- ▶ if there is a review of a CPA's practice under AICPA or state society authorization; or
- ▶ if the CPA is responding to an inquiry of an investigative or disciplinary body of a recognized society, or where the CPA is initiating a complaint with a disciplinary body.

In connection with this rule, members of the investigative bodies who may be exposed to confidential client information are precluded from disclosing such information.

Rule 302: Contingent Fees   A CPA in public practice cannot charge or receive a contingent fee for any professional services from a client for whom the CPA or the CPA's firm performs audit, review, or compilation work. For example, a fee schedule of $5,000 for a qualified audit opinion and $35,000 for an unqualified opinion would not be allowed. Rule 302 also prohibits a CPA from preparing an original or amended tax return or claim for a tax refund for a contingent fee.

A contingent fee is defined here as a fee established for the performance of any service pursuant to an arrangement in which no fee will be charged unless a specified finding or result is attained, or in which the amount of the fee is otherwise dependent on the finding or result of such service. Solely for purposes of this rule, fees are not regarded as being contingent if fixed by courts or other public authorities, or, in tax matters, if determined based on the results of judicial proceedings or the findings of governmental agencies.

Rule 501: Acts Discreditable   A CPA must not commit an act that is discreditable to the profession. This rule is not specific as to what constitutes a discreditable act; however, violations have been found when the CPA committed a felony, failed to return client records after a client requested them, signed a false tax return, or issued a misleading audit opinion.

Rule 502: Advertising and Other Forms of Solicitation   A CPA in public practice cannot seek clients by false, misleading, or deceptive advertising or other forms of solicitation. In addition, solicitation by the use of coercion, overreaching, or harassing conduct is not allowed. The Institute has placed no restrictions as to the type, media, or frequency of a CPA's advertisements, or on the artwork that is associated with them. Under Rule 502, an activity would be prohibited

▶ if it created false or unjustified expectations of favorable results;

▶ if it implied the ability to influence any court, tribunal, regulatory agency, or similar body or official;

▶ if it contains a representation that specific professional services in current or future periods will be performed for a stated fee, estimated fee, or fee range when it was likely at the time of the representation that such fees would be substantially increased and the prospective client was not advised of that likelihood, or

▶ if it contains any other representations that would be likely to cause a reasonable person to misunderstand or be deceived.

For example, a radio spot that states a CPA firm "can beat the IRS every time" would be in violation of Rule 502.

Rule 503: Commissions and Referral Fees

A CPA in public practice cannot charge or receive a commission or referral fee from a client for whom the CPA or the CPA's firm performs audit, review, or compilation work. Thus, under Rule 503, a CPA who does only tax or other nonaudit work for a client may accept or pay a commission. The CPA must, however, disclose the commission to the client or other party in the transaction. In addition, a member who accepts or pays a referral fee for recommending or referring any service of a CPA must disclose that fact.

Rule 505: Form of Organization and Name

CPAs may practice public accounting only in the form of organization permitted by state law or regulation whose characteristics conform to resolutions of the AICPA Council. Under Rule 505, a CPA cannot practice under a firm name that is misleading. The names of one or more past owners may be included in the firm name of a successor organization. In addition, all partners or members of a firm must be members of the AICPA if a firm is to designate itself as "Members of the AICPA."

Statements on Responsibilities in Tax Practice

To assist CPAs, the AICPA has issued a series of statements as to what constitutes appropriate standards of tax practice. These *Statements on Responsibilities in Tax Practice* (SRTP) (see Appendix C) delineate a CPA's responsibilities to his or her clients, the public, the government, and the profession. They are intended to address specifically the problems inherent in the tax practitioner's dual role in serving the client and the public. The statements are intended to supplement, rather than replace, the *AICPA Code of Professional Conduct*. They are designed to address the development of tax practice as an integral part of a CPA's practice and the changing environment in which tax practitioners must operate, including the rapidly changing tax laws. The principal objectives of the SRTPs are

▶ to recommend appropriate standards for the CPA's responsibilities in tax practice;

▶ to encourage an increased understanding of the CPA's responsibilities by the Treasury Department and the IRS; and

▶ to foster an increased public understanding of, compliance with, and confidence in the tax system through awareness of the recommended standards of responsibilities of CPAs.

The SRTP's primary effect is educational. Unlike the regulations under *Circular 230,* the provisions of the *Internal Revenue Code,* and the *AICPA Code of Professional Conduct,* the statements do not have formal administrative authority, but instead depend for their authority on general acceptance by practitioners and the public.

SRTP No. 1: Tax Return Positions

In preparing a tax return, a CPA should have a *good-faith belief* that a recommended position has a *realistic possibility* of being sustained if challenged; otherwise such a position should not be recommended by the CPA. A CPA may reach a conclusion that a position is warranted based on existing law and regulations, as well as on other sources such as well-reasoned articles by tax specialists, treatises, IRS General Counsel Memoranda and written determinations, and explanations of revenue acts as prepared by the Joint Committee on Taxation. The tax professional should be aware that in this statement the members of the AICPA have adopted a standard that is similar to the *substantial authority* standard of IRC § 6662; however, the statement specifically states that the CPA may reach a conclusion based on authority as specified in the statement without regard to whether such sources are treated as "authority" under IRC § 6662. Thus, a CPA who is in compliance with SRTP No. 1 may still lack substantial authority for taking a position under § 6662. In cases where a client insists on a specific position, a CPA may sign the return even though the position does not meet the above standard, provided that (1) the position is adequately disclosed on the return by the client, and (2) the position is not "frivolous." Under no circumstances should a CPA recommend a tax return position that is exploitative or frivolous.

In cases where the CPA believes that the taxpayer may have some exposure to a penalty, the statement suggests that the CPA advise the client of such risk. Where disclosure of a position on the tax return may mitigate the possibility of a taxpayer penalty under the *Internal Revenue Code,* the CPA should consider recommending that the client disclose the position on the return.

SRTP No. 2: Answers to Questions on Returns

Before signing a return as the preparer, a CPA should make a reasonable effort to obtain from the client appropriate answers to all questions on the taxpayer's tax return. Where the taxpayer leaves a question on the return unanswered and reasonable grounds exist for not answering the question, the CPA need not provide an explanation for the omission. The possibility that an answer to a question may prove disadvantageous to the taxpayer, however, does not justify omitting the answer.

Reasonable grounds may exist for omitting an answer to a question on a return. For example, such an omission is acceptable where

▶ the pertinent data are not readily available and are not significant to the determination of taxable income (or loss) or the tax liability;

▶ the taxpayer and CPA are genuinely uncertain as to the meaning of the question on the return; or

▶ an answer to a question is voluminous (however, assurance should be given on the return that the data can be supplied upon examination).

In relying for reasonable grounds on the fact that an answer is voluminous, the taxpayer and CPA should be aware of a relevant IRS district newsletter, which states that a notation on Form 1120 and related schedules that information will be provided on request is *not* considered acceptable.[4]

SRTP No. 3: Certain Procedural Aspects of Preparing Returns

In preparing or signing a return, the CPA ordinarily may rely without verification on information that the client or a third party has provided, unless such information appears to be incorrect, incomplete, or inconsistent. A more formal audit-like review of documents or supporting evidence is generally not required for a CPA to sign the tax return. Where material provided by the client appears to be incorrect or incomplete, however, the CPA should obtain additional information from the client. In situations where the statutes require that specific conditions be met, the CPA should determine, by inquiry, whether the conditions have been met. For example, the Code and Regulations impose substantiation requirements for the deduction of certain expenditures. In such a case, the CPA has an obligation to make appropriate inquiries.

Although CPAs are not required to examine supporting documents, they should encourage the client to provide such documents when deemed appropriate, for example, in the case of deductions or income from a pass-through entity, such as a partnership.

The CPA should make proper use of the prior year's tax return when feasible to gather information about the client and help to avoid omissions and errors with respect to income, deductions, and credit computations.

SRTP No. 4: Use of Estimates

A CPA may prepare tax returns that involve the use of the taxpayer's estimates if it is impractical to obtain exact data and if the estimated amounts appear reasonable to the CPA. In all cases, the estimated information must be supplied by the taxpayer; however, the CPA may provide advice in connection with the estimate. When the taxpayer's estimates are used, they should be presented in such a manner as to avoid the implication of greater accuracy than exists. Situations where the use of estimates may be appropriate include cases where the keeping of precise records for numerous items of small amounts is difficult to achieve, where data are not available at the time of filing the tax return, or when certain records are missing.

The use of estimates in making pertinent accounting judgments where such use is not in conflict with the *Internal Revenue Code* is not prohibited under this statement; such judgments are acceptable and expected. For example, the income tax Regulations permit the use of a reasonable estimate for accruals if exact amounts are not known.

Although in most cases the use of estimates does not necessitate that the item be specifically disclosed on the taxpayer's return, disclosure should be made where failure to do so would result in misleading the IRS about the accuracy of the return. For example, disclosure may be necessary where the taxpayer's records have been destroyed in a fire or where the taxpayer has not received a Schedule K-1 from a pass-through entity at the time the return is filed. Tax practitioners should make their clients aware that the tax law does not allow estimates of certain income and expenditure items, and that more restrictive substantiation requirements apply in cases of certain expenditures, such as travel and entertainment expenses.

---

[4]*IRS Brooklyn District Newsletter No. 47,* 10/89.

SRTP No. 5: Departure from a Position Previously Concluded in an Administrative Proceeding or Court Decision   The recommendation by a CPA as to the treatment of an item on a tax return should be based on the facts and the law as they are evaluated at the time during which the return is prepared or signed by the CPA. Unless the taxpayer is bound by the IRS to the treatment of an item in later years, such as by a closing agreement, the disposition of an item in a prior year's audit or as part of a prior year's court decision, the CPA is not prevented from recommending a different treatment of a similar item in a later year's return. Thus, a CPA may sign a return that contains a departure from a treatment required by the IRS in a prior year, provided that the standards in SRTP No. 1 are adhered to.

In most cases, a CPA's recommendation as to the treatment of an item on a tax return will be consistent with the treatment of a similar item consented to in a prior year's **administrative proceeding** or as a result of the prior year's court decision. In deciding whether a recommendation contrary to the prior treatment is warranted, the CPA should consider the following.

- ▶ Neither the IRS nor the taxpayer is bound to act consistently with respect to the treatment of an item in a prior proceeding; however, the IRS tends to act consistently in similar situations.
- ▶ The standards under SRTP No. 1, Tax Return Positions, must be followed. In determining whether such standards can be met, the CPA must consider the existence of an unfavorable court decision and the taxpayer's consent in an earlier administrative proceeding.
- ▶ In some cases, the taxpayer's consent to the treatment of an item in a prior administrative or judicial proceeding may have been due to a desire to settle the issue or a lack of supporting data, whereas in the current year these factors no longer exist.
- ▶ The tax climate may have changed for a given issue since the prior court decision was reached or the prior administrative hearing concluded.

SRTP No. 6: Knowledge of Error: Return Preparation   The CPA must advise the client promptly, whether or not the CPA prepared or signed the return in question, when he or she learns of an error in a previously filed tax return, or becomes aware that a required return was not filed. Such advice should include a recommendation for appropriate measures the client should take. However, the CPA is neither obligated to inform the IRS of the situation, nor may he or she do so without the client's permission, except as provided by law.

If the CPA is requested to prepare the current year's return, and the client has not taken action to correct an error in a prior year's return, the CPA should consider whether to proceed with the preparation of the current year's return. If the current year's return is prepared, the CPA should take reasonable steps to ensure the error is not repeated.

A CPA may advise a client, either orally or in writing, as to the correction of errors in the prior year's return. In a case where there is a possibility the client may be charged with fraud, the client should be referred to an attorney. If a CPA discovers the error during an audit or other nontax engagement, he or she should refer the client to the tax return preparer. If the item in question has an insignificant effect on the client's tax liability, the item should not be considered an "error" under this statement. In addition, the term "error" does not include a situation where the client's position satisfied the standards under SRTP No. 1 at the time the return was filed.

SRTP No. 7: Knowledge of Error: Administrative Proceedings When a CPA represents a client in an administrative proceeding (such as an audit), and the CPA is aware of an error other than one that has an insignificant effect on the taxpayer's tax liability, the CPA should request the client's agreement to disclose the error to the IRS. Lacking such an agreement with the client, the CPA may be under a duty to withdraw from the engagement and may consider terminating the professional relationship with the client. Disclosure, once agreed on, should be made in a timely manner to avoid misleading the IRS.

SRTP No. 8: Form and Content of Advice to Clients In providing tax advice to clients, the CPA must use judgment that reflects professional competence and serves the client's needs. The CPA must assume that any advice given will be used to determine the manner of reporting items on the client's tax return; therefore, the CPA should ensure that the standards under SRTP No. 1 are satisfied. When providing advice that will be relied on by third parties, the CPA's responsibilities may differ. Neither a standard format nor guidelines have been issued or established that would cover all situations and circumstances involving written or oral advice from a CPA. When giving such advice to clients, in addition to exercising professional judgment, the CPA should consider each of the following.

- ► The importance of the transaction and the amounts involved
- ► The specific or general nature of the client's inquiry
- ► The time available to develop and submit the advice
- ► The technical complications that are presented
- ► The existence of authority and precedents
- ► The tax sophistication of the client
- ► The possibility of seeking legal advice

Written communication is recommended in important, unusual, or complicated transactions, while oral advice is acceptable in more typical situations. In the communication, the CPA should advise the client that the advice reflects his or her professional judgment based on the current situation and that subsequent developments may affect previous advice, such as stating that the position of authorities is subject to change. See Chapter 10.

When subsequent developments affect the advice that a CPA has previously communicated to a client, the CPA is under no obligation to initiate further communication of such developments to the client unless a specific agreement has been reached with the client, or the CPA is assisting in the application of a procedure or plan relative to such advice.

Exhibit 1–3 summarizes the main topic of each of the *AICPA Statements on Responsibilities in Tax Practice.*

ABA Model Code of Professional Responsibility

In 1969, the American Bar Association (ABA) adopted a revised set of guidelines for professional conduct, the *Model Code of Professional Responsibility.* The Code includes nine *canons,* which may be thought of as statements of principles. Canon 6, for instance, requires an attorney to represent a client competently. Each canon is followed by a series of *ethical considerations* (ECs), which in turn are supported by *disciplinary rules* (DRs). The ethical considerations are aspirational in character, setting forth objectives toward which all attorneys are to strive. The disciplinary rules

EXHIBIT 1–3   Summary of *AICPA Statements on Responsibilities in Tax Practice*

Statement	Summary of Contents
1	Enumerates the standards for recommendations of tax return positions by tax practitioners and the preparation and signing of tax returns
2	Tells how a CPA should handle answering questions on a tax return
3	Describes procedural aspects of preparing tax returns
4	Defines when a CPA can use the taxpayer's estimates in preparing a tax return
5	Explains what a CPA should do about items on a current return when similar items were audited on a prior year's return or were the subject of a judicial hearing
6	States what a CPA should do upon learning about an error in a prior year's tax return
7	Gives the procedure to follow if an error is discovered during an audit
8	Establishes standards for the giving of tax advice to clients

set forth minimum standards of conduct. Any failure to abide by the disciplinary rules may subject the attorney to disciplinary procedures and punishment.

In nearly all jurisdictions, the ABA Model Code was adopted by the appropriate policy agency, although sometimes modifications were made. In August 1983, the ABA adopted the *Model Rules for Professional Conduct,* which in a majority of the states have substantially replaced the Model Code as the guide for attorney professional conduct.

The ABA has a Standing Committee on Ethics and Professional Responsibility that answers questions concerning ethics and professional conduct. Requests for opinions from the committee should be directed to the American Bar Association Center for Professional Responsibility in Chicago.

Neither the ABA Model Code nor the Model Rules have the force of law. Each was designed to be adopted by the appropriate agencies that govern the practice of law in the states. In many jurisdictions, the state supreme court is charged with policing the practice of law; in other states, the legislature bears this responsibility. Attorneys should consult their own jurisdiction's ethical guidelines to determine whether the provisions of the ABA Model Code or the Model Rules, or some modification of these doctrines, have been adopted. This text discusses only some of the rules that the authors believe to be the most relevant to a tax practice.

Rule 1.1 requires the attorney to be competent. A competent attorney possesses the legal knowledge, skill, thoroughness, and preparedness that is reasonably necessary for the representation undertaken. It is clear that adequate representation may be given, even in a novel field, through study and/or association with an attorney already familiar with the appropriate area of law. *Horne v. Peckham* held malpractice was committed when documents were prepared that resulted in adverse tax consequences, although the attorney had advised the clients that he was not well versed in taxation matters.[5] Rule 1.8(h) prohibits an attorney from requiring a client to enter into an agreement that prospectively would limit the attorney's liability for

[5]158 Cal. Reptr. 714 (1979).

malpractice, unless such an arrangement is permitted by local law, and then only if the client also receives an independent review of the agreement.

Rule 1.3 requires the attorney to act with reasonable diligence and promptness in carrying out matters of client representation. In taxation, the procedural time limits that must be met to protect the client's interests often are very short, so this rule can present difficulties for the attorney.

Rule 1.4 requires the attorney to keep the client reasonably informed as to the status of a matter, and to make explanations with appropriate frequency and sophistication so the client can make informed decisions.

Rule 1.6 binds the attorney to keep confidential any information related to the representation, unless the client's permission to disclose has been given or can be inferred by the nature of the representation. Obviously, information furnished for the purpose of the attorney's preparation of a tax return is expected to be revealed to proper agencies, whereas conversations in preparation for a tax audit conference may be strictly confidential.

Rule 1.6(b) allows the attorney to reveal confidential information when necessary to prevent a criminal act that is likely to result in substantial bodily harm, or to establish a defense for the attorney in a civil or criminal action wherein the attorney is accused of complicity in wrongful conduct. Seldom would a client's intended actions with regard to tax matters involve criminal bodily harm to another; nonetheless, client requests for aid in subverting the tax law are not uncommon.

Rule 1.2 warns that an attorney should not counsel a client to engage in criminal conduct, nor assist a client in criminal or fraudulent conduct. An attorney would be deemed to have furthered the criminal or fraudulent purpose by suggesting how such conduct might be concealed, for example, in shielding gross income from the tax authority. The practitioner must admonish the client to refrain from further illegal conduct and, perhaps, may need to withdraw from an engagement if the wrongful conduct does not cease. However, nothing in the rules should be interpreted as discouraging an attorney from being an advocate for a person who is charged with a crime.

Rule 3.1 prohibits frivolous defenses and claims, but it also states that the attorney for one who is charged with a crime may require the prosecution to establish every element of the case. Rule 3.3 requires candor toward a tribunal. This rule prohibits the knowing use of a false statement, the failure to disclose a material fact, or the failure to disclose a legal authority in the controlling jurisdiction, even when such authority is adverse to the client's position. Of course, as an advocate for the client, the attorney may be able to argue successfully that the cited authority is inapplicable. For instance, a case might have been decided wrongly, a Treasury Regulation may misinterpret the Code Section that it attempts to clarify, or a Code Section may be unconstitutional, in which case the precedent need not be followed.

Under Rule 4.1, the attorney cannot knowingly make false statements of material fact or law to third persons. This rule also prohibits the failure to disclose a material fact if such failure assists the client in a criminal or fraudulent act, unless disclosure is prohibited under the general confidentiality of Rule 1.6. Attorneys are prohibited, under Rule 5.4, from sharing legal fees with nonattorneys, and from forming partnerships to practice law with nonattorneys, or with professional corporations that have nonattorney shareholders. Thus, an attorney cannot form a partnership with a CPA to perform general financial and estate planning services for their clients.

The last thirty years have seen a trend among the states to recognize taxation as a field of specialization in the practice of law. Rule 7.4 forbids an attorney to state or imply that he is a specialist, unless the practitioner has obtained such designation through the state's specialization procedures. To become a state bar-certified specialist in taxation usually requires demonstration by the attorney that she has engaged in a variety of tax matters and has taken or taught numerous continuing education courses in the tax field. In addition, the attorney may be required to take an examination and submit to a background investigation of her reputation. The investigation is generally conducted by an independent committee that contacts other attorneys, as well as judges, in the jurisdiction where the attorney seeking certification has a tax practice. The investigation centers on the attorney's reputation for expertise and a high level of competence in the area of taxation.

The designation of taxation as a formal specialty among CPAs has met with little approval to date, and as yet no major professional body has officially created a corresponding specialty area within public accounting.

An attorney is permitted to indicate an area of practice. However, unless the attorney has been recognized formally by the state licensing authority as a specialist, he is not allowed to claim to be a "specialist," nor to assert that his or her practice is "limited to" or "concentrated in" a specific field of law, such as taxation.

The American Bar Association has not amended the Model Rules in more than twenty years. A commission called "Ethics 2000" has been established by the ABA to review the rules and to propose any needed adjustments. The specific charge of the Ethics 2000 Committee is to (1) conduct a comprehensive study and evaluate the ethical and professionalism precepts of the legal profession; (2) examine and evaluate the *ABA Model Rules for Professional Conduct* and the rules governing professional conduct in state and federal jurisdictions; (3) conduct original research, surveys, and hearings; and (4) formulate recommendations for action. The report of the Ethics 2000 Committee is due in the year 2000.

Nonregulatory Ethics

There is substantially more to ethical behavior than just following the rules of ethics or conduct of professional organizations such as the AICPA or ABA. Professional ethical behavior is the result of the interaction of personal morality, social responsibility, business ethics, and other general **ethical standards.** See Exhibit 1–4.

Morality

The subject of morality fills tens of thousands of books. Publications as diverse as the Bible and popular novels examine morality in one way or another. When something is judged to be morally right or wrong (or good or bad), the underlying standards on which such judgments are based are called moral standards.

According to some people's moral standards, cheating "just a little" in computing a tax liability is morally acceptable. Most people in the United States believe that everyone cheats a little on their taxes. Cheating significantly may be viewed differently, but where is the dividing line between morally "okay" tax cheating and morally wrong *tax evasion*? Under the self-assessed tax system in the United States, different moral standards provide different answers—from complete honesty to various degrees of dishonesty. The tax practitioner must be ready to work with clients holding various systems of morality and to accept the consequences of the moral

EXHIBIT 1–4 Ethical behavior sources

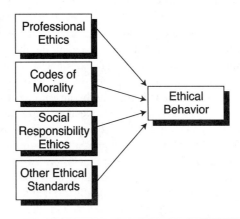

choices made, including the possibility of losing a client, paying fines and penalties to the IRS, or even going to jail.

Social Responsibility

The tax practitioner must be aware of social responsibility in areas such as environmental protection, equal opportunity, and occupational safety. Since World War II, society has held the business world increasingly responsible for meeting certain noneconomic standards. In 1970, Milton Friedman, the Nobel Prize-winning economist, said that the "social responsibility" of business is merely to increase profits. But the prevailing sentiment today is that business and the professions should return something to society to make it better, not just to make a profit. For the tax practitioner, this could mean going beyond the minimum legal responsibility to provide equal opportunity in the hiring of employees by making special recruitment efforts, or it could mean volunteering time to help charitable organizations with their tax problems.

Business Ethics

In recent years, one of the major topics in the business world has been the question of business ethics. There are many people who think that ethics has application only in the personal life, not in the business or professional life. Like Milton Friedman, they think the business of business is to make a profit. This view is popular because (1) people who work in business or professions must concern themselves with producing goods and services to earn a profit, and (2) it is easier to measure profit than to make value judgments. People are more comfortable discussing problems in terms of profits, not the ethical impact of the entity and its actions. Few business and professional people are trained in ethical analysis, and therefore they usually are not familiar with how to evaluate a problem in terms of ethics.

That business and professional organizations have ethical responsibilities is readily apparent to anyone who reads the popular press. The lawsuits brought on by the savings and loan failures of the late 1980s and against the Big Five accounting firms in the last two decades are prime examples of society holding business to a standard of ethical conduct. Most of the Big Five will settle lawsuits against them for millions of dollars for what was, in part, a business ethics failure.

Other Ethical Standards

The study of nonregulatory ethics could be expanded to cover such other issues as public policy, religious beliefs, and cultural values, issues that are beyond the scope of this text. Most of such topics would be addressed in a university course on ethics or business ethics. A tax practitioner can expand his or her understanding of the application of ethics to accounting and business situations by referring to the books on the following reading list:

▶ Armstrong, Mary Beth, *Ethics and Professionalism for CPAs* (Cincinnati: South-Western Publishing Co., 1993).

▶ Brooks, Leonard J., *Professional Ethics for Accountants* (Minneapolis/St. Paul: West Publishing Co., 1995).

▶ Bucholz, Rogene, *Fundamental Concepts and Problems in Business Ethics* (Englewood Cliffs, NJ: Prentice Hall, 1989).

▶ Collins, Denis, and Thomas O'Rourke, *Ethical Dilemmas in Accounting* (Cincinnati: South-Western Publishing Co., 1994).

▶ Donaldson, Thomas, *Corporations and Morality* (Englewood Cliffs, NJ: Prentice Hall, 1983).

▶ Velasquez, Manuel, *Business Ethics*, 2d ed. (Englewood Cliffs, NJ: Prentice Hall, 1988).

The following are examples of nonregulatory ethics dilemmas that could arise in a business, accounting, or tax setting:

Example 1–3 Hilary is a CPA who is a sole practitioner. This year, one of her clients, Gold Corporation, opened a new division in Europe. This is a long-time client of Hilary's and she is anxious to keep it. However, Hilary has no experience in international tax and would not be able to give Gold the kind of tax advice needed for the new division. The ethical question is whether Hilary should inform the client of her lack of knowledge in this area and risk losing the client, or should she remain silent and "wing it" on the international tax issues. What should Hilary do in this situation?

Example 1–4 Patrick is a CPA who is a partner in a successful local CPA practice. The state in which Patrick lives has a forty-hour annual continuing professional education (CPE) requirement. If the CPE requirement is not met, a CPA will have his or her license suspended and will not be able to practice. Patrick is approached by the Flight-by-Night CPE company about signing up for some of their CPE courses. The company representative tells Patrick that they will report that Patrick attended the courses so that he gets the CPE credit, even if he does not attend. Because Patrick is overloaded with work, he considers this a "low hassle" way to get his CPA license renewed. Would it be ethical for Patrick to obtain his CPE credit this way?

Example 1–5 Devona is an auditor for a large international CPA firm working in the Boston office. She is sent on an inventory observation for a new client of the Houston office of the firm. The Houston office gives her a six-hour budget for the job. When she arrives at the client's office, Devona discovers that the Houston office has substantially underestimated the size of inventory observation. The client has a $20,000,000 inventory comprised of more than 6,000 different items. The client plans to take twenty hours to complete the count. Devona is up for promotion and she does not want to have a negative personnel review because she overran the budget on this job. Therefore, she considers spending the budgeted six hours on the observation, and signing off in the audit work papers that she completely observed the inventory. Devona thinks this would be OK since she perceives there is only a small risk of a material misstatement of the inventory. Would it be ethical for Devona to do this?

Example 1–6 Last year, one of Andy's clients, Trout Corporation, had a significant tax problem. Andy needed thirty-five hours of research time to arrive at an answer to Trout's problem. This year, another of Andy's clients, Bass Corporation, had the same problem. Because of his experience with Trout, Andy could solve Bass's tax problem in three hours. The ethical question is whether Andy should bill Bass for three hours or thirty-five hours of professional consulting time. There are two ways to look at this situation. Andy only spent three hours on the job, so he should only bill for three hours of time. Yet, there is "value" in Andy already knowing the approach to take on the Bass matter, so perhaps he should bill for that knowledge, and not just for the actual time spent working on the problem. What should Andy do in this situation?

Example 1–7 Betty is negotiating a transaction on the behalf of one of her clients, John Carp. During the process, Betty becomes aware that the other party to the transaction does not adequately understand the tax consequences of the proposed transaction, which are highly favorable to Carp. In fact, if the transaction were completed as proposed, the other side would suffer significant negative tax consequences. Ethically, should Betty inform the other party of the potential negative tax consequences of the proposed transaction?

As shown in the above examples, the application of ethics to business situations is not clear-cut. In many situations, doing what is right may not be possible. The tax practitioner constantly is faced with challenges on how to apply proper business ethics on a daily basis.

Tax Research by Certified Public Accountants

Over the years, the tax community has addressed the issue of whether the practice of tax by a CPA or other nonattorney constitutes the **unauthorized practice of law.** The problem stems from the tax law itself, passed in 1913. The provisions of early tax law called for an income tax, but the statute was not specific about the accounting methods to be used in implementing it. In fact, not until 1954 was a formal statutory effort made to address accounting issues in the computation of taxable income. For this reason, many attorneys avoided tax work, allowing CPAs to fill the void and provide taxpayers with most of the professional-quality tax work.

When a CPA resolves an issue in most nonroutine tax situations, he or she is, to some extent, solving a legal problem. The issue is not whether the CPA is rendering legal service, but, rather, how much legal service is provided. When does the CPA cross the mythical boundary and begin an unauthorized practice of law? Neither these professions nor the courts have promulgated binding guidelines on this issue. Instead, the federal agencies seem to have taken the lead in attempting to solve this problem.

Historical Developments

Lowell Bar Association v. Loeb addressed the issue of the unauthorized practice of law by nonattorneys engaged in tax practice.[6] The Lowell Massachusetts Bar Association sued Birdie Loeb, a commercial tax preparer, for her preparation of simple wage-earner tax returns. On appeal, the court held that the preparation of "simple" tax returns did not constitute the unauthorized practice of Massachusetts law because tax return preparation could not be identified as strictly within the legal discipline. Tax practice includes interaction among various disciplines, including law, accounting, economics, political science, and others.

Subsequent courts attempted to adopt the *Lowell* "wholly within the field of law" test in other jurisdictions, but they found that definition of the boundaries of the legal profession was so difficult, and the 1943 opinion was so general and vague, that the *Lowell* precedent was of little value in other situations.

Probably the best known case concerning a tax accountant's unauthorized practice of law is *Bercu*.[7] Bercu was an accountant who consulted with a client concerning whether sales taxes that were accrued, but not yet paid, could be deducted on a tax return. The taxpayer who requested this advice was not one of Bercu's regular clients. Bercu advised the client that the sales tax could be deducted when it was paid. Bercu presented a bill to the client and, when it was not paid, he sued the client to collect the fees.

Ultimately, the State Court of New York held that it was not proper for Bercu to render services in such a situation. The Court indicated that Bercu could have provided this type of service and answered the sales tax question had it been incidental to the tax return work he regularly performed for his clients.

This "incidental to accounting practice" test became the chief issue in several subsequent cases concerning the unauthorized practice of law. In a Minnesota case, *Gardner v. Conway,* a person who was neither an attorney nor a CPA attempted to answer difficult and substantial questions of law.[8] The court held that the practitioner improperly gave advice to the client and rejected the "incidental to practice" test as an approach to providing guidelines for the definition of tax practice.

In a California case, *Agran v. Shapiro,* CPA Agran prepared returns, performed research, and represented his clients before the IRS.[9] Agran's preparation of Shapiro's return involved extensive research—including more than 100 court cases, Code sections, and Regulations—concerning a question involving the proper treatment of a net operating loss. Upon completion of the work, the CPA presented his bill and, when he was not paid, sued Shapiro to collect. Agran was found by the court to have engaged in the unauthorized practice of law and, therefore, was unable to collect his fees. In its decision, the California Superior Court relied on *Gardner v. Conway* and rejected the "incidental to practice" test that Agran used in his defense. The Court did not decide, however, whether the authorization to practice before the IRS preempted the right of the state to regulate tax practice.

In *Sperry v. Florida,* the U.S. Supreme Court held that a federal statute that admitted nonattorneys to practice before federal agencies (in this case, the Patent Office)

---

[6]315 Mass. 176, S2 N.E.2d 27 (1943).
[7]In re *Bercu,* 299 N.Y. 728, 87 N.E.2d 451 (1949).
[8]234 Minn. 468, 48 N.W.2d 788 (1951).
[9]127 Cal. App.2d Supp. 807, 273 P.2d 619 (1954).

took precedence over state regulation.[10] In late 1965, Congress enacted Public Law 89-332, amending prior law and allowing CPAs to practice before the IRS. Although this law added to the force of the *Sperry* decision as it applied to CPAs, *Sperry* still provides for the preemption of federal regulations and statutes in matters of practice before other federal agencies.

In 1981, the AICPA and the ABA held a conference for attorneys and CPAs to address some of these definitional questions relative to tax practice and the unauthorized practice of law. The stated purpose of this session was to "promote understanding between the professions in the interests of the clients and the general public." This National Conference of Lawyers and CPAs issued a statement in November 1981, reaffirming that clients are best served when attorneys and CPAs work together in tax practice. The text of the statement identifies eight areas related to income taxation and three areas related to estate and gift planning in which such professional cooperation should be encouraged. The statement lacks any form of exclusionary language. Indeed, it asserts the following.

> Frequently, the legal and accounting phases (of tax practice) are so intertwined that they are difficult to distinguish. This is particularly true in the field of income taxation, where questions of law and accounting are often inextricably intertwined.[11]

Attorneys Employed in a CPA Firm

In the 1990s, the issue of unauthorized practice of law arose again in a new context. This time the issue was raised because the Big Five accounting firms had been hiring licensed attorneys or buying law firms and going into the practice of law. In 1997, a complaint was filed against Arthur Andersen in Texas for the unauthorized practice of law.[12] The complaint stated that Arthur Andersen lawyers offered broad legal services such as forming legal entities (including drafting corporate and partnership organizational document), doing estate planning, writing compensatory agreements, and filing petitions in the tax court. In addition, another complaint, filed about the same time, stated that Arthur Andersen's property tax valuation service should be considered the unauthorized practice of law.

The fundamental question in this new unauthorized practice of law situation is how far a nonlegal firm can go in providing legal services to its clients. If Arthur Andersen is allowed to practice general law, then other nonlegal entities, such as banks, also can be expected to employee attorneys and enter the general practice of law. The question of whether CPA firms and other nonlegal firms can employ attorneys to practice general law has yet to be resolved.

CPAs and Other Nonattorneys

Currently, CPAs and other nonattorneys who practice tax law before the IRS are in little danger of entering into the unauthorized practice of law provided they avoid providing general legal services. This can be accomplished if CPAs and other nonattorneys do not themselves engage in the following kinds of general law activities.

---

[10]373 U.S. 379, 83 S.Ct. 1322 (1963).

[11]For a complete discussion of this conference statement, see the *Journal of Accountancy,* August 1982, p. 122.

[12]"Texas Investigates Unauthorized Practice of Law by Big Six Firm," *Tax Notes Today* (September 19, 1997).

- ▶ Expressing a legal opinion on any nontax matter
- ▶ Drafting wills or trust instruments
- ▶ Drafting contracts
- ▶ Drafting incorporation papers
- ▶ Drafting partnership agreements

Taxpayers can draft any of these documents themselves without the services of an attorney. If a CPA's client wishes to handle personal legal affairs in this manner, the CPA (exercising caution) can render professional advice without running afoul of the case law concerning the unauthorized practice of law.

As long as CPAs and other nonattorneys stay within the practice of tax, and do not cross over into the practice of general law, the control exercised by *Circular 230* and the code should ensure that virtually all tax compliance, planning, and research activities that are provided by adequately trained nonattorney CPAs constitute the "authorized practice of law."

▶ Summary

In addition to the tax return preparation statutes that are discussed in Chapter 13, CPAs, attorneys, enrolled agents, and others who practice before the IRS are faced with various sets of overlapping rules of conduct. *Circular 230* applies to anyone who practices before the IRS. In addition, members of the legal and public accounting professions are subject to codes of ethics and conduct. Similarly, cultural codes of morality and social responsibility form general boundaries relative to acceptable behavior by a taxpayer or tax professional. When engaged in tax practice, one always must be aware of the appropriate rules of conduct that apply and conduct themselves in accordance with those rules.

▶ Key Words

By the time you complete this chapter, you should be comfortable discussing each of the following terms. If you need additional review of any of these items, return to the appropriate material in the chapter or consult the glossary to this text.

Administrative Proceeding	Open Transaction
American Bar Association (ABA)	Practice before the IRS
American Institute of Certified	Realistic Possibility
Public Accountants (AICPA)	Tax Avoidance
Circular 230	Tax Compliance
Closed Transaction	Tax Evasion
Contingent Fees	Tax Litigation
Enrolled Agent	Tax Planning
Ethical Standards	Tax Research
Independence	Unauthorized Practice of Law

▶ Discussion Questions

1. In a modern, industrial society, the tax system is derived from several disciplines. Identify the disciplines that play this role in the United States. Explain how each of them affects the U.S. tax system.
2. The elements of tax practice fall into what four major categories?

3. What is tax compliance as practiced in the United States? Give several examples of activities that can be classified as tax compliance.

4. Several groups of individuals do most of the tax compliance work in the United States. Identify these groups and describe briefly the kind of work that each group does. In this regard, be sure to define the term "enrolled agent."

5. What is tax planning? Explain the difference between tax evasion and tax avoidance, and the role of each in professional tax planning.

6. Tax planning falls into two major categories, the "open" transaction and the "closed" transaction. Discuss each type of transaction, and describe how each affects tax planning.

7. What is tax litigation? What type of tax practitioner typically handles tax litigation on a client's behalf?

8. Define tax research. Briefly describe the tax research process.

9. Who issues *Circular 230?* Which tax practitioners are regulated by it?

10. CPAs must follow the rules of *Circular 230.* In addition, CPAs in tax practice are subject to two other sets of ethical rules. Give the name and the issuer of both of these sets of rules.

11. The term "practice before the IRS" includes the representation of clients in the United States Tax Court for cases being handled under the "small tax case procedure." True or false? Explain your answer. (IRS adapted)

12. The rules that govern practice before the IRS are found in *Circular 230.* Discuss what entails practice before the IRS, and state which section of *Circular 230* contains the definition.

13. Leigh, who is not an enrolled agent, attorney, or CPA, is employed by Rose, a CPA. One of Rose's clients has been notified that his 1997 income tax return has been selected for audit by the IRS. Rose had prepared the return and signed it as preparer. Rose has been called out of town on a family emergency and would like for Leigh to represent the client. Leigh cannot represent the client even if she has Rose's written authority to do so and has the client's power of attorney. True or false? Explain your answer. (IRS adapted)

14. Regular full-time employees are allowed to represent certain organizations before the Internal Revenue Service without being an attorney, CPA, or enrolled agent. Name the organizations that can be represented by full-time employees, and cite where you found that authority in *Circular 230.*

15. A practitioner could be suspended from practice before the IRS if the practitioner employs, accepts assistance from, or shares fees with any person who is under disbarment or suspension from practice before the IRS. True or false? Explain your answer. (IRS adapted)

16. Tax practitioners must not sign a tax return under *Circular 230* if the return takes a position that does not have a "realistic possibility" of being sustained by the Internal Revenue Service.

   a. What is a realistic possibility as defined by the Internal Revenue Service?

   b. Is it possible for a tax practitioner to sign a tax return that takes a position that does not meet the realistic possibility standard? If so, what must be done to allow the tax practitioner to sign the tax return?

17. Under *Circular 230,* may an attorney, CPA, or enrolled agent advertise on television? On the Internet? If so, what standards are applied to the advertisements?

18. Can a tax practitioner who is a CPA form a CPA partnership with an IRS agent who is also a CPA? What limits (if any) would be placed on such a partnership?

19. If a tax practitioner finds an error in a prior year's tax return, what action must he or she take (if any) under *Circular 230?* What subpart and section addresses this situation?

20. Practicing CPAs generally are subject to the *AICPA Code of Professional Conduct.* What is its stated purpose?

21. The rules under the *AICPA Code of Professional Conduct* are a group of enforceable ethical standards. Broad in nature, they generally apply to all of the services that are performed by a CPA who is an AICPA member. Identify the two situations in which the application of the rules may be limited.

22. In what situation may a CPA under the *AICPA Code of Professional Conduct* accept a commission?

23. Under Rule 101 (Independence), a CPA (or CPA firm) in public practice must be independent of the enterprise for which professional services are being provided. Discuss situations in which the CPA's independence may be impaired.

24. Under Rule 102 (Integrity and Objectivity), a CPA who is engaged in tax practice may resolve a doubtful area in favor of his or her client. Explain.

25. A CPA must meet certain qualitative standards under Rule 201 (General Standards). Discuss the four general standards of this rule.

26. In each of the following independent situations, state which *AICPA Code of Professional Conduct* (if any) is violated by a CPA in public practice.

    a. The CPA opens a tax practice and names the new firm "Jill's Super Tax."

    b. In return for recommending a certain investment to an *audit* client, a CPA receives a 5 percent commission from the broker who sells the investments.

    c. A taxpayer is being assessed by the IRS for an additional $100,000 of tax. The CPA offers to represent the taxpayer for a fee that is equal to 25 percent of any amount by which he can get the IRS to reduce its assessment.

    d. A CPA places an advertisement in the local newspaper that states that she is the "Best CPA in the Western World." The advertisement further states that, because of her great skill, the CPA has considerable influence with the IRS and the United States Tax Court.

    e. A CPA partnership has eight partners, six of whom are members of the AICPA. On its letterhead, the firm designates itself as "Members of the AICPA."

    f. A CPA who is not in public practice is convicted of helping to run a large illegal drug operation.

27. Under Rule 301 of the *AICPA Code of Professional Conduct,* a CPA must not disclose confidential client data without the specific consent of the client. Under what conditions might a disclosure of confidential information without the client's consent be appropriate?

28. What are the *Statements on Responsibilities in Tax Practice?* Who issues them? Discuss their principal objectives.

29. What guidelines does SRTP No. 1 provide for a tax practitioner regarding tax return positions?

30. According to SRTP No. 2, a tax return should be signed by a CPA only after reasonable effort has been made to answer all of the questions on the return that apply to the taxpayer. What are some of the reasonable grounds under which a CPA may sign a return as the preparer even though some of the pertinent questions remain unanswered?

31. What guidelines are provided by SRTP No. 3 as to the reliance by a CPA on

information supplied by the taxpayer for use in preparing the taxpayer's return?

32. A CPA may use estimates in completing a tax return according to SRTP No. 4. When might the use of estimates be considered appropriate?

33. Last year a client was audited by the IRS and an item of deduction on the tax return was disallowed. On this year's tax return, the client would like to deduct a similar item. Discuss the circumstances under which a CPA may allow the taxpayer to take the deduction on the current year's return and still be in compliance with SRTP No. 5. Under what conditions must special disclosure be made by the CPA?

34. When a CPA learns of an error in a previously filed tax return or learns of an error during an audit, how is he or she to respond and still be in compliance with SRTP No. 6 and No. 7?

35. What situations are addressed by SRTP No. 8?

36. Differentiate between the *ABA Model Code of Professional Responsibility* and that organization's *Model Rules for Professional Conduct.*

37. Who sets ethical rules for attorneys in the various states?

38. Under what circumstances may an attorney reveal confidential client information according to Rule 1.6(b)?

39. Rule 1.1 requires that an attorney be competent. How does that rule define this term?

40. What is an attorney prohibited from doing under each of the following rules as they pertain to a tax practice?

    a. Rule 3.1
    b. Rule 4.1
    c. Rule 5.4

41. When can an attorney state or imply that he or she is a "specialist" in a specific area of the law?

42. Identify the types of nonregulatory ethics discussed in the text. Why should a tax practitioner be concerned with such items?

43. How does the term "the unauthorized practice of law" apply to CPAs?

44. If a CPA firm hires attorneys to offer general legal services to its clients, what kind of problems might the CPA firm face?

45. List several services or products that a CPA or enrolled agent purposely should not make a part of a tax practice, so as to minimize exposure to a charge of the unauthorized practice of law.

► _____ Exercises

46. Summarize what is discussed in each of the following sections of *Circular 230.*

    a. Subpart A, § 10.4(b)
    b. Subpart B, § 10.21
    c. Subpart B, § 10.26
    d. Subpart B, § 10.32

47. Summarize what is discussed in each of the following sections of *Circular 230.*

    a. Subpart C, § 10.51(b)
    b. Subpart A, § 10.6(e)
    c. Subpart A, § 10.2(e)
    d. Subpart B, § 10.28

48. Which subpart and section of *Circular 230* discusses each the following topics?

   a. Solicitation

   b. Negotiation of a taxpayer's refund checks

   c. Depositions

   d. Authority to disbar or suspend from practice before the Internal Revenue Service

49. Which subpart and section of *Circular 230* discusses each the following topics?

   a. Conflicting interests

   b. Tax shelter opinions

   c. Disreputable conduct

   d. Assistance from disbarred or suspended persons

50. Summarize what is discussed in each of the following rules of the *AICPA Code of Professional Conduct*. Give a simple example of a transaction or an action relevant to each rule.

   a. Article VI, ¶ .01

   b. Rule 201, ¶ .02 201-1

   c. Rule 502, ¶ .03 502-2

   d. Rule 504, ¶ .01

51. Summarize what is discussed in each of the following *Statements on Responsibilities in Tax Practice.*

   a. SRTP No. 1

   b. SRTP No. 4

   c. SRTP No. 6

52. What is the precedent setting-value of each of the following cases?

   a. *Lowell Bar Association v. Loeb*

   b. *Bercu*

   c. *Sperry v. Florida*

53. Inclusion of which of the following statements in a CPA's advertisement is *unacceptable* under the *AICPA Code of Professional Conduct?* Explain your answer.

   a. Julie Adams
      Certified Public Accountant
      Fluency in Spanish and French

   b. Julie Adams
      Certified Public Accountant
      MBA, Big State University, 1992

   c. Julie Adams
      Certified Public Accountant
      Free Initial Consultation

   d. Julie Adams
      Certified Public Accountant
      I Always Win IRS Audits

54. Which of the following situations would most likely result in a violation of the practitioner's ethical standards? Explain your answer.

    a. A CPA is controller of a bank and grants permission to the bank to use his "CPA" title in the listing of the bank officers in the bank's publications.

    b. A CPA who is also a member of the bar represents on her letterhead that she is both an attorney and a CPA.

    c. A CPA, the sole shareholder in a professional accountancy corporation, uses the term "and company" in his firm's title.

    d. A CPA who writes a newsletter on financial management topics grants permission to the publisher to solicit subscriptions.

55. Which of the following situations would provide an acceptable case for using a client's estimated figure in the preparation of a federal income tax return? Explain your answer.

    a. The client has the necessary data available, but is busy with a pressing public offering and has not had the time to look through her records for the information.

    b. The data are not available at the time of filing the return, and the estimated amounts appear reasonable to the CPA.

    c. The client has the data available at the time for filing the return, but feels that the data do not fairly represent the results of her business operation and therefore desires to use an "estimate."

    d. The client, relying on the income tax regulations that allow the use of reasonable estimates under certain circumstances, desires to use an estimate to determine the amount of his deduction for entertainment expenses.

56. According to the *AICPA Code of Professional Conduct,* CPAs in tax practice who are representing a client in a formal controversy with the government are permitted to receive contingent fees because

    a. this practice establishes fees that are commensurate with the value of the services rendered.

    b. attorneys who are in tax practice customarily set contingent fees.

    c. determinations by tax authorities are a matter of judicial proceedings that do not involve third parties.

    d. the consequences are based on the findings of judicial proceedings or the findings of a government agency.

57. The *AICPA Code of Professional Conduct* states that a CPA shall not disclose any confidential information in the course of a professional engagement, except with the consent of the client. This rule should be understood to preclude a CPA from responding to an inquiry that is received from

    a. an investigative body of a state CPA society.

    b. the Trial Board of the AICPA.

    c. a CPA-shareholder of the client corporation.

    d. an AICPA voluntary quality review body.

58. A taxpayer's records are destroyed by fire. A CPA prepares the tax return based on estimates and other indirect information she has obtained. Under the *Statements on Responsibility in Tax Practice,* she should

    a. disclose the use of estimates to the IRS.

    b. not disclose the use of estimates to the IRS.

    c. charge the taxpayer a double fee.

     d.   not prepare a return based on estimates.

     e.   have an attorney prepare the return.

59. With regard to the categories of individuals who may practice before the IRS under *Circular 230,* which of the following statements is correct? Explain your answer.

     a.   Only enrolled agents, attorneys, or CPAs may represent trusts and estates before any officer or employee of the IRS.

     b.   An individual who is not an enrolled agent, attorney, or CPA and who signs a return as having prepared it for the taxpayer may, with proper authorization from the taxpayer, appear as the taxpayer's representative, with or without the taxpayer, at an IRS Appeals Office conference with respect to the tax liability of the taxpayer for the taxable year or period covered by the return.

     c.   Under the limited practice provision in *Circular 230,* only general partners may represent a partnership.

     d.   Under the limited practice provision in *Circular 230,* an individual who is under suspension or disbarment from practice before the IRS may not engage in limited practice before the IRS. (IRS adapted)

60. If an enrolled agent, attorney, or CPA knows that a client has not complied with the revenue laws of the United States with respect to a matter administered by the IRS, the enrolled agent, attorney, or CPA is required under *Circular 230* to

     a.   do nothing until advised by the client to take corrective action.

     b.   advise the client of the noncompliance.

     c.   immediately notify the IRS.

     d.   advise the client and notify the IRS. (IRS adapted)

▶ _____ ## Research Cases

61. You are a CPA in practice who has just obtained a new client. Another CPA did the tax returns for the prior three years. The client has operated his business as an S corporation during the three-year period. After starting work on this year's tax return, you notice the S corporation has an October 31 fiscal year-end. After examining the file, you discover that three years ago, when the S corporation adopted the fiscal tax year, a § 444 election was not made. In addition, the S corporation has not maintained the proper required "minimum deposit account" with the IRS.

    The client wants your advice on what to do now. You determine that there are three options: (1) you can do nothing and hope the IRS doesn't find out, (2) you can notify the IRS of the mistake and pay any interest and penalties, or (3) you can elect a calendar year and hope the IRS doesn't notice the current invalid fiscal year. What potential nonregulatory ethical issues do you see in this situation that could influence your decision on any recommendation?

62. You are a CPA in practice and have a long-term client who is involved in a nasty divorce proceeding with her husband. The client has assets she deposited in a bank account in the Grand Cayman Islands. There is U.S.-taxable interest on the deposits. Because she doesn't want her husband to know about the deposits, she asks you to report the interest on her tax return in such a way that it will not "tip off" her husband to the existence of the account. You can handle this request by reporting the interest through the Schedule C (instead of Schedule B) on her tax return and thus avoid making the source of the income known. What potential nonregulatory ethics issues do you see in this situation?

63. Ahi Corporation is one of your clients in Hawaii. The company had a good year last year and owes the IRS $100,000,000, due on March 15. There are no penalties or interest due to the IRS. One of Ahi Inc.'s employees approaches you with the following plan to benefit from the so-called "float" on the large payment due to the government. First, Ahi Inc. will courier its tax return and payment to the U.S. Virgins Islands. There, the tax return will be mailed to the IRS Service Center in Fresno by certified mail on the return's due date, March 15. By doing this, the employee thinks it will take at least six days for the tax return to reach the IRS and for them to cash the $100,000,000 check. Ahi can earn 7 percent after tax on its money, so the interest earned during these six days because of the float is $19,178 per day [($100,000,000 × .07) / 365 days]. Thus, the total interest earned on the float for six days would be $115,068 ($19,178 × 6 days).

    a. Would you recommend Ahi complete this transaction?
    b. What potential ethics issues do you see in this situation?

64. John Haddock owns 75 percent of Haddock Corporation. The other 25 percent of the stock is held by John's wife, Marsha. You are a tax manager assigned to prepare the corporate tax return for Haddock. While working on the return, you note that Haddock Inc. pays rent to John for a building he owns with his son, John, Jr. The rent being paid is at least three times the normal rate for rentals of similar property in that area of town. You report this observation to the partner on the engagement. She tells you that it is all right to deduct the payments because Haddock Corp. has been doing it for several years. Under your firm's policy, managers sign the tax return for clients.

    a. Would you sign this tax return?
    b. What potential ethics issues do you see in this situation?

65. You are negotiating a transaction for your client, Shark Corporation. Parties on the other side of the deal ask you for information about the structural stability of a building, which is a significant part of the transaction. Coleman, Shark's tax director, tells you to say "everything is OK," when, in reality, the building has substantial hidden damage. Coleman tells you to say this because it would be more favorable to Shark's position in the transaction.

    a. How do you respond to Coleman's request?
    b. What if you have already told the other side that the building is OK when you learn about the problems?
    c. What other potential ethics issues do you see with this situation?

66. Big CPA Firm has many partners in one of its local offices. Two of these partners are Tom, a tax partner, and Alice, an audit partner. Because of the size of the office, Tom and Alice do not know each other very well.

    Tom has a tax client, Anchovy Corporation, that is in severe financial trouble and may have to file for bankruptcy. Anchovy is a customer of Sardine Corporation, one of Alice's audit clients. Accounts receivable on Sardine's books from Anchovy are significant. If Anchovy goes bankrupt, it could cause serious problems for Sardine. Alice is unaware of the bad financial condition of Anchovy.

    a.   Can Tom disclose to Alice the problems at Anchovy?

    b.   What if Anchovy goes under and takes Sardine with it?

    c.   What potential ethics issues do you see with this situation?

67.   You are the tax manager in a CPA office. One of your clients, Snapper Corporation, is also an audit client of the firm. The CFO of Snapper invites you and the audit manager for a one-week deep-sea fishing trip to Mexico, all expenses to be paid by Snapper. The audit manager says that you both should go and just not tell your supervisor at the CPA firm any details (like who paid the expenses) about the trip.

    a.   Would you go on the trip?

    b.   Would you tell your supervisors at the CPA firm if the audit manager went on the trip without you?

    c.   What other potential ethics issues do you see in this situation?

68.   Clara comes to an attorney's office in need of assistance with her husband's estate. Her husband, Phil, a factory worker, had been a saver all his life and owned approximately $1,500,000 in stocks and bonds. Clara is relatively unsophisticated in financial matters, so the attorney agrees to handle the estate for 17 percent of the value of the estate. The normal charge for such work is 3–5 percent of the estate. The widow agrees to the 17 percent arrangement. The attorney then hires CPA Charles for $10,000, to compute Phil's estate tax on Form 706, and to prepare other appropriate documents.

    a.   Does Charles have any responsibility to inform the widow that she is being significantly overcharged by the attorney?

    b.   What potential ethics issues do you see with this situation?

69.   Darlene works for Big CPA Firm. When she was being interviewed, Darlene was told by a partner in the firm that she was not to underreport her time spent on various engagements. However, after working for a few months, she discovers that everyone in her office "eats time." Because she is not eating time like everyone else, Darlene is always overbudget. She is beginning to get a reputation as a "budget buster." As a result, none of the senior tax staff wants her on their engagements. She is getting the worst clients and bad reviews from the people she works for. It appears that unless she starts eating time, Darlene's future with the firm is limited.

    a.   What would you recommend Darlene do?

    b.   What potential ethics issues do you see with this situation?

70.   Freya is an accountant working on the tax return of a High-Tech client. After reviewing the work papers, she discovers that there is a pattern of double billing the U.S. Navy for various projects done by the tax client. She brings this to the attention of her manager on the job, and he tells her that it is not the CPA firm's business what the client does since this is not an audit engagement.

    a.   What would you recommend Freya do at this point?

    b.   What potential ethics issues do you see with this situation?

Tax Research Methodology

LEARNING OBJECTIVES

▶ Recognize the importance of a systematic approach to tax research

▶ Delineate and elaborate on the steps of the tax research process

▶ Appreciate the importance of gathering pertinent facts and identifying research issues

▶ Discuss the sources of the federal tax law

▶ Identify how computer resources affect the conduct of tax research

CHAPTER OUTLINE

Outline of Tax Research Process
Step 1: Establish the Facts
Step 2: Identify the Issues
 Tax Research as an Iterative Process
Step 3: Locate Authority
Step 4: Evaluate Authority
Step 5: Develop Conclusions and
  Recommendations
Step 6: Communicate the Recommendations
Computerized Tax Research
Online Systems
CD-Based Systems

Benefits of Using a Computerized Tax Service
Factors in Choosing a Computer Tax Service
Using a Computer in Tax Research
Step 1: State the Issue as a Question
Step 2: Identify the Key Words
Step 3: Construct a Computer Research Query
Step 4: Select a Database and Execute the Search
Step 5: Interpret and Refine the Search

The overriding purpose of tax research is to find solutions to the tax problems of one's clients or employer. The process is similar to that of traditional legal research. The researcher must find authority, evaluate the usefulness of that authority, and apply the results of the research to a specific situation.

One can identify two essential tax research skills. The first is the ability to use certain mechanical techniques to identify and locate the tax authorities that relate to solving a problem. The second entails a combination of reasoning and creativity and is more difficult to learn. A tax researcher must begin with native intelligence and imagination and add training and experience properly to apply the information found. Creativity is necessary to explore the relevant relationships among the circumstances and problems at hand to find a satisfying (and defensible) solution. In many cases, no legal authority will exist that is directly on point for the problem. If such a situation exists, the researcher must combine seemingly unrelated facts, ideas (including those that he or she has derived from previous research work), and legal authority to arrive at a truly novel conclusion. This creative ability of the researcher often spells the difference between success and failure in the research process.

Outline of the Tax Research Process

As the tax problems of the client become more significant, the related tax research can become time consuming and thus expensive to the client. A moderate tax research problem often takes up to eight or ten hours of research time, and the bill for these services may approach or even exceed $2,000. Because of the costs that are involved, the tax researcher must work as efficiently as possible to obtain the solution to the client's problem. The researcher needs a framework for the research process, so that he or she does not waste time and effort in arriving at a solution to the problem.

The tax research process can be broken down into six major steps (Exhibit 2–1). Tax researchers (especially those without a great amount of experience at the task) must approach the resolution of a tax problem in a structured manner, so that the analysis of the problem will be thorough and the solution complete.

Step 1: Establish the Facts

All tax research begins with an evaluation of the client's factual situation. To find the solution to a problem, the researcher must understand fully all of the facts that could affect the related tax outcome. Many beginning tax researchers make the mistake of attempting to research a problem before they completely understand all of the relevant facts and circumstances.

Moreover, a tax researcher may approach the tax research process so rigidly that he or she ignores new factual questions that arise during the other steps of the research task. As Exhibit 2–1 illustrates, the tax researcher may engage in several rounds of fact gathering, including those necessitated by additional tax questions that arise as he or she is searching for or evaluating pertinent tax authority. These research "feedback loops" are not endless, although they might appear to be. The best tax researcher is one who can balance the need for efficiency against the need for thoroughness.

EXHIBIT 2–1 Steps in tax research

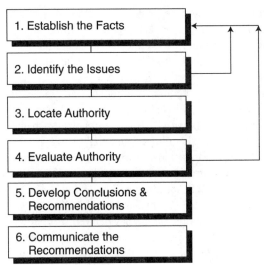

Significant tax facts that often influence the client's situation include

▶ the client's tax entity, for example, individual, corporation, trust;
▶ the client's family status and stability;
▶ the client's past, present, and projected marginal tax rates;
▶ the client's place of legal domicile and citizenship;
▶ the client's motivation for the transaction;
▶ relationships among the client and other parties who are involved in the transaction;
▶ whether special tax rules apply to the taxpayer due to the type of business in which the taxpayer is engaged, (he or she is a farmer, fisherman, or long-term contractor); and
▶ whether the transaction is proposed or completed.

Fact gathering can present many practical problems for the researcher. Often, the client will (wittingly or not) omit information that is vital to a solution. He or she may not believe that the information is important, or may have personal reasons for not conveying the information to the practitioner. In such cases, the researcher must persist until all of the available information is known. In some cases, facts that initially appear to be irrelevant may prove to be important as the research project progresses. The researcher, therefore, should pay attention to and record all details that the client discloses. Efficient tax research cannot be completed until the fact situation is clear; without all of the facts at hand, the researcher could make costly false starts that, when additional pertinent facts become known, must be discarded or redone, often at the client's (or, worse, at the researcher's!) expense.

In gathering facts relative to a research problem, the researcher also must be aware of the nontax considerations that are pertinent to the client's situation. For example, the client may have economic constraints (such as cash flow problems) that could preclude the implementation of certain solutions. In addition, the client may have personal preferences that will not accommodate the best tax solution to the problem. For instance, assume that the client could reduce his own income and estate tax liability by making a series of gifts to his grandchildren. However, because the client does not trust the financial judgment of the grandchildren, he does not want to make any such gifts to them during his lifetime. Accordingly, the researcher must look for alternative methods by which to reduce the client's total family tax burden.

Step 2: Identify the Issues

A combination of education, training, and experience is necessary to enable the researcher to identify successfully all of the issues with respect to a tax problem. In some situations, this step can be the most difficult element of a tax research problem.

Issues in a closed-fact tax research problem often arise from a conflict with the IRS. In such a case, one can easily ascertain the issue(s). Research of this nature usually consists of finding support for an action that the client has already taken.

In most research projects, however, the researcher must develop the list of issues. Research issues can be divided into two major categories, namely, fact issues and law issues. **Fact issues** are concerned with information having an objective reality, such as the dates of transactions, the amounts involved in an exchange, reasonableness, intent, and purpose. **Law issues** arise when the facts are well established, but it is not clear which portion of the tax law applies to the issue. The application of the law might not be clear because of an apparent conflict among code sections, because a genuine uncertainty as to the meaning of a term as used in the *Internal Revenue Code* may exist, or because there are no provisions in the law that deal directly with the transaction at hand.

When undertaking a research project where the issue may end up being challenged in court, the researcher must be sure to address all of the issues in the tax return. The legal concept of *collateral estoppel* bars relitigation on the same facts or the same issues. Therefore, the practitioner must make sure that his or her case is researched fully, and that no issues that could be resolved in the client's favor have been overlooked. If such an issue is not addressed in the original case, it may be lost forever.

In many situations, a research project may encompass several tax years. The researcher must be aware of any fact or law changes that occur during the period that might affect the results of the research project. The pertinent facts or law may be subject to changes that will cause the researcher to arrive at different conclusions and recommendations, depending on the tax year involved. For example, at one time, the question of whether property qualified for the regular investment credit was a common problem encountered by the tax practitioner. Since the investment credit was repealed for most property placed in service after 1985, subject to transitional rules for certain property, defining "qualified property" is no longer an issue for most taxpayers. Because the transitional rules and the recapture rules still apply where the investment credit was claimed, though, the researcher must still be aware of the provisions.

Seemingly simple situations can often generate many tax research issues. In the process of identifying tax issues, the researcher might discover that additional facts are necessary to provide sufficient answers for the new questions. The taxpayer in the following example is used to illustrate the potential for complexities in merely identifying tax research issues.

Example 2–1 The KML Medical Group of Houston would like to hire a new physician from Atlanta. However, the new physician owns a home in Georgia on which she will sustain a loss if it is sold in the current housing market. KML approached the Happy Care Hospital, the institution at which the group practices, and asked whether they would reimburse the new physician for the loss to facilitate her move to Texas. The hospital agreed to reimburse the physician this year for her $20,000 realized loss.

► A tax researcher might address or clarify at least the following issues in making recommendations concerning tax treatment of the reimbursement:

► Why did the hospital reimburse the physician?

► Is there any parent-subsidiary relationship between the hospital and the KML Medical Group?

► Do any members of the KML Medical Group have an equity or debt interest in the hospital?

► Does the reimbursement constitute gross income to the physician?

► If the reimbursement does constitute gross income to the physician, is it treated as active, passive, or investment income?

► Is the new physician classified as an employee of the hospital?

► Should the hospital report the payment to the physician on a Form 1099 or W-2?

► Should the hospital withhold any income or FICA tax on the reimbursement?

► Can the hospital deduct the reimbursement as a trade or business expense?

► Should the physician consider the reimbursement and/or the loss on the sale of her residence in computing her moving expense deduction?

► If the reimbursement is considered gross income to the physician, when should the amount be included in the physician's income?

► Is the reimbursement subject to any restrictions such as the physician's continued employment? For how long?

► Is the reimbursement to the physician considered an additional amount realized on the sale of her residence?

► Can the reimbursement be considered a gift from the hospital to the physician?

Imagine how the question concerning whether the physician's gross income (if any) was ordinary income might lead to the further questions concerning her potential employee status, income tax and FICA withholding, and reporting issues.

Tax Research as an Iterative Process   The process of tax research is iterative in the sense that, once an answer is found, it often causes a new issue to appear and thus requires the gathering of more information. In other words, the tax research process is not strictly linear. This relationship between facts, issues, and answers is illustrated in Exhibit 2–2. The linear tax research process requires *mechanical skills* and *critical thinking*. Mechanical techniques are gained and sharpened through both knowledge and experience. *Knowledge* is usually gained through education in universities and other formal class work. *Experience* is obtained through working in the field and dealing with real tax problems on a recurring basis. Critical thinking is the hardest skill for the researcher to develop. To some extent it depends on native ability, but a person can be taught the elements of logical analysis and can learn to watch for common pitfalls in evaluating information. Being able to analyze and solve a problem is something the tax researcher must master if he or she is to earn a living in this field. Knowledge is useless when it cannot be applied to solve the problem at hand. The following example illustrates how both mechanical skills and critical thinking are used to solve a tax research problem.

EXHIBIT 2–2   Interactions among research facts, issues, and solutions

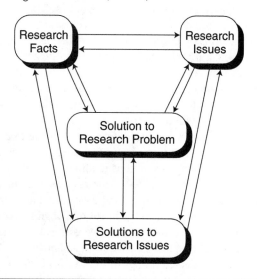

Example 2–2 This year, Chris Lee, a client of your CPA firm, sold stock in Slippery Bank (a publicly traded company with a limited market) to Kolpin Corporation for $100,000. Chris has records that show the stock was acquired ten years ago and has a basis of $135,000. He personally owns 30 percent of Kolpin Corporation. On first glance, the tax researcher would conclude that Chris would have a capital loss of $35,000, which would be deductible against his current-year long-term capital gains of $50,000. This situation appears to be very straightforward.

The problem could become complex, though, if someone at the CPA firm asked questions about the other owners of Kolpin. What if Chris's wife, Judy Lee, owns Kolpin stock? The researcher must back up in the research process and gather more facts to determine how many shares she owns.

Suppose Judy Lee owns 25 percent of the Kolpin stock. Now the tax practitioner (you) is faced with new facts and issues; § 267 of the *Internal Revenue Code* suggests that the loss might be disallowed. By looking at § 267(b)(2), you would find that losses between an individual and a corporation are disallowed if "more than 50 percent in value of the outstanding stock of which is owned directly or indirectly, by or for such individual." You then need to know what is "indirect ownership." Looking further in the Code, you would find in § 267(c), "An individual shall be considered as owning the stock owned, directly or indirectly, by or for his family." Finally, in § 267(c)(4), you would discover, "The family of an individual shall include only his brother and sisters (whether by whole or half blood), spouse, ancestors, and lineal descendants."

Armed with this new information, it becomes clear that Chris is a related party to Kolpin Corporation within the meaning of § 267. He owns more than 50 percent of the stock, 30 percent directly and 25 percent indirectly through his wife. As a result, the $35,000 capital loss is not allowed to Chris and he cannot use it to offset his other capital gains.

Step 3: Locate Authority

Once facts have been gathered and the issues defined, the tax researcher must locate legal authority that relates to the issue(s). Authority comes from many sources, including Congress, the courts, and the IRS. Since the inception of the 1913 tax law, several hundred thousand pages of such authority have been produced. To solve a given problem, the researcher must find the appropriate authority in this massive amount of information.

In general, tax authority can be classified as either primary or secondary authority. **Primary authority** comes from statutory, administrative, and judicial sources. **Statutory sources** include the U.S. Constitution, tax treaties, and tax laws passed by Congress. Statutory authority is the basis for all tax provisions. The Constitution grants Congress the power to impose and collect taxes, and also authorizes the creation of treaties with other countries. The power of Congress to implement and collect taxes is summarized in the *Internal Revenue Code*, the official title of U.S. tax law. The *Internal Revenue Code* constitutes the basis for all tax law and, therefore, the basis for arriving at solutions to all tax questions.

The other primary sources of the tax law, administrative and judicial authority, function primarily to interpret and explain the application of the provisions of the *Internal Revenue Code* and the intent of Congress. **Administrative sources** include the various rulings of the Treasury Department and the IRS. These are issued in the form of Regulations, Revenue Rulings, and other pronouncements. **Judicial sources** consist of the collected rulings of the various courts on federal tax matters. The primary sources of the tax law will be discussed in greater detail in Chapters 3, 4, and 5. **Secondary authority** consists of unofficial sources of tax information. Examples of secondary authority include tax services, journals, textbooks and treatises, and newsletters. The distinction between primary and secondary sources of authority has become more important since the enactment of IRC § 6662, which imposes a penalty on substantial understatements of tax, except where the taxpayer has "substantial authority" for the position taken on the return. The regulations under § 6662 specify the sources of "substantial authority" to include the provisions of the *Internal Revenue Code*, temporary and final Regulations, court cases, administrative pronouncements, tax treaties, and congressional intent as reflected in committee reports. This list was expanded by the Committee Report for the Revenue Reconciliation Act of 1989 to include Proposed Regulations, Private Letter Rulings, Technical Advice Memoranda, Actions on Decisions, General Counsel Memoranda, Information or Press Releases, Notices, and any other similar documents published by the IRS in the *Internal Revenue Bulletin*. Treatises and articles in legal periodicals, however, are not considered substantial authority under this statute.

Secondary authority is useful when conflicting primary authority exists, when there appears to be no extant primary authority, or when the researcher needs an explanation or clarification of the primary authority. During the past fifteen years, as the support staffs of government agencies and (especially) federal courts have decreased in number or otherwise become inadequate, more dependence has been placed on the secondary authorities of the tax law, even by the IRS, the Treasury Department, and the court system. The beginning researcher must be careful, though, not to rely too heavily on secondary authority, and always to read any pertinent primary authority that is referred to in the secondary sources.

Because of the vast amount of tax authority that is available, the tax researcher would have a tremendous problem in undertaking a tax research problem for a client if it were not for commercial **tax services** and treatises. Several publishers have produced coordinated sets of reference materials that organize the tax authority into a usable format, making the *Internal Revenue Code* much more accessible. These commercial tax services are useful in that they often provide simplified explanations with footnote citations, as well as examples illustrating the application of the law. These tax services may lead the tax researcher, via the footnote references, to the primary source that is pertinent to the question at hand.

Traditionally, tax services have been classified as either annotated or topical. The annotated services are organized in *Internal Revenue Code* section order, and the topical services are arranged by topic, as defined by the publisher's editorial staff. However, the use of computers has significantly blurred the differences between the organization of commercial tax services. With computer hypertext linking, any of the tax services can be used from a Code or topical orientation. Exhibit 2–3 includes a listing of the current major commercial tax services. The tax services are discussed in greater detail in later chapters.

Court decisions are published in sets of bound volumes called *court reporters.* Depending on the court involved, the reporters are produced by the Government Printing Office (GPO), West Publishing Company, Research Institute of America (RIA), and Commerce Clearing House (CCH). Exhibit 2–4 lists the common court reporters that contain tax cases frequently used in tax research. Chapter 5 discusses in greater detail the means by which to find court cases in these reporters.

Both CCH and RIA provide "citators" as part of their tax services. A citator is a reference source that enables the researcher to follow the judicial history of court cases. The citators are discussed in detail in Chapter 6. The GPO prints many of the pronouncements of the IRS. The primary publication for IRS authority is in a set of bound volumes titled the *Cumulative Bulletin.* Chapter 4 includes a detailed discussion concerning the use of this authority.

Tax journals are another source of information that can be useful. By reading tax journals, a tax practitioner can become aware of many current problem areas in taxation. She can also increase her awareness of recent developments in the tax law, tax compliance matters, and tax planning techniques and opportunities. Numerous journals, ranging from law reviews to *Cosmopolitan,* publish articles on current tax matters. The tax researcher typically is interested in publications devoted to scholarly

---

EXHIBIT 2–3 Major tax services

Publisher	Title of Tax Service	Orientation
Research Institute of America (RIA)	*Tax Coordinator 2d*	Topic
Research Institute of America (RIA)	*United States Tax Reporter*	Code
Commerce Clearing House (CCH)	*Standard Federal Tax Reporter*	Code
Commerce Clearing House (CCH)	*Federal Tax Service*	Topic
Bureau of National Affairs (BNA)	*Tax Management Portfolios*	Topic
West Group	*Mertens Law of Federal Income Taxation*	Topic

Note: In 1992, Prentice Hall (and Maxwell Macmillan, an associated publisher) sold its annotated tax reporter and other research items to the Research Institute of America (RIA). RIA has renamed and continued the former annotated Prentice Hall tax reporter, as well as its original topical reporter (Tax Coordinator). As the new products are phased into existing shelf space, some of the items mentioned in this book as produced by RIA, especially older material, still may appear in tax libraries as Prentice Hall or Maxwell Macmillan publications.
Note: The major tax publishers have plans to phase out some of the paper tax services and other published material. In the future, only the high-demand tax material is likely to remain available in printed form.

EXHIBIT 2–4   Common court reporters used in tax research

Publisher	Court Reporter Title
Research Institute of America	*American Federal Tax Reports (AFTR)*
Research Institute of America	*TC Memorandum Decisions*
West Publishing Co.	*Federal Supplement*
West Publishing Co.	*Federal Reporter*
West Publishing Co.	*Supreme Court Reporter*
Commerce Clearing House	*United States Tax Cases (USTC)*
Commerce Clearing House	*Tax Court Memorandum Decisions*
Government Printing Office	*Tax Court of the U.S. Reports*
Government Printing Office	*Tax State Reports*

and professional discussions of tax matters. Among these publications, each tax journal usually is written for a specific group of readers. Chapter 9 further examines the major tax journals and explains how to locate articles of interest to the tax practitioner. Exhibit 2–5 lists several useful tax journals, their publishers, and the target readership of each.

Step 4: Evaluate Authority

After the researcher has located authority that deals with the client's problem, he or she must evaluate the usefulness of that authority. All tax authority does not carry the same precedential value. For example, the Tax Court could hold that an item should be excluded from gross income at the same time that an outstanding IRS Revenue Ruling asserts the item is taxable. The tax researcher must evaluate the two authorities and decide whether to recommend that his or her client report the disputed item.

EXHIBIT 2–5   Selected tax journals

Journal	Publisher	Target Readership
Journal of Taxation	Warren, Gorham, and Lamont	Sophisticated tax practitioners
Taxation for Accountants	Warren, Gorham, and Lamont	Accountants in general practice
Journal of International Taxation	Warren, Gorham, and Lamont	Multinational taxpayers and their advisers
Estate Planning	Warren, Gorham, and Lamont	Practitioners who are interested in estate and gift tax matters
The Tax Adviser	American Institute of CPAs	Members of AICPA and other tax practitioners
TAXES	Commerce Clearing House	General tax practitioners

In the process of evaluating the authority for the issue(s) under research, new issues not previously considered by the researcher may come to light. If this is the case, the researcher may be required to gather additional facts, find additional pertinent authority, and evaluate the new issues. This loop is illustrated in Exhibit 2–1.

Step 5: Develop Conclusions and Recommendations

After several iterations of the first four steps of the tax research process, the researcher must arrive at his or her conclusions for the tax issues raised. Often, the research will not have resulted in a clear solution to the client's tax problems, perhaps because of unresolved issues of law or incomplete descriptions of the facts. In addition, the personal preferences of the client must also be considered. The "ideal" solution for tax purposes may be entirely impractical because of other factors that are integral to the tax question. In any of these cases, the tax practitioner must use professional judgment in making recommendations based on the conclusions drawn from the tax research process.

Where unresolved issues exist, the researcher might inform the client about alternative possible outcomes of each disputed transaction, and give the best recommendation for each. If the research involved an open-fact situation, the recommendation might detail several alternative courses of future action (e.g., whether to complete the deal, or how to document the intended effects of the transaction). In many cases, the researcher may find it appropriate to present his or her recommendation of the "best" solution from a tax perspective, as well as one or more alternative recommendations that may be much more workable solutions. In any case, the researcher will want to discuss with the client the pros and cons of all reasonable recommendations and the risks associated with each course of action.

Step 6: Communicate the Recommendations

The final step in the research process is to communicate the results and recommendations of the research. The results of the research effort usually are summarized in a memorandum to the client file and in a letter to the client. Both of these items usually contain a restatement of the pertinent facts as the researcher understands them, any assumptions the researcher made, the issues addressed, the applicable authority, and the practitioner's recommendations. An example of the structure of a simple tax research memo is shown in Exhibit 2–6. The memorandum to the file usually contains more detail than does the letter to the client.

In any event, the researcher must temper his or her communication of the research results so that it is understandable by the intended reader. For instance, the researcher should use vastly different jargon and citation techniques in preparing an article for the *Journal of Taxation* than in preparing a client memo for a businessperson or layperson who is not sophisticated in tax matters. Chapter 10 provides additional guidelines and formats for client memoranda and other means of delivering the results of one's research.

Computerized Tax Research

The body of knowledge that encompasses the field of taxation has been growing at a phenomenal pace for the past fifteen years. Since 1975, Congress has enacted more

EXHIBIT 2–6 Tax research memo format example

Over & Short CPAs
San Francisco, CA

Relevant Facts:

_____

_____

_____

Specific Issues:

_____

_____

_____

Conclusions:

_____

_____

_____

Support:

_____

_____

_____

Actions to be Taken:

_____ Discuss with client.   Date discussed: _____

_____ Prepare a memo or letter to the client.

_____ Explore other fact situations.

_____ Other action. Describe _____

Preparer: _____

Reviewer: _____

than a dozen major tax and revenue bills that have had a significant effect on U.S. taxpayers. In addition, each year hundreds of new Treasury Regulations, court decisions, Revenue and Private Letter Rulings, Revenue Procedures, and Technical Advice Memoranda are issued.

The avalanche of tax-related information is not expected to decrease during the foreseeable future. The abundance of available information, as well as the complexity of the tax laws that have been enacted since 1975, has made it even more difficult and time consuming to conduct thorough and effective research concerning a tax-related issue.

Whenever a diligent tax professional is providing advice or other services to a client, he or she must be cognizant of the latest legislative changes and judicial decisions. Furthermore, he or she must be able to draw upon, and sort through, the vast body of established tax knowledge, and to apply statutes and administrative and judicial rulings to the current tax issue

Computers have significantly changed how tax research is conducted. The vast amount of storage available on a computer, coupled with the computer's fast retrieval of information, has made it an invaluable tool for tax research. The tax practitioner has three chief ways to find computer information for tax research purposes: (1) online subscription systems, (2) online nonsubscription **Internet** sites, and (3) CD-based systems. In an **online system,** the user telephones a remote data location and uses resources that remain in the central computer. In a **CD-based system,** the publisher sends one or more plastic disks to the practitioner, who then reads from the disk whenever necessary.

Online Systems

Computerized tax online services are accessible through the Internet and several public telecommunications networks. The materials that are available through the use of these services are contained in databases that are stored at centralized computer locations. These databases may be accessed from remote locations with the use of a variety of compatible video display terminals and keyboards. Usually they can be accessed via compatible commercial (including personal) computers that the user already owns. The personal computer's (PC) function keys typically perform all of the services that are required by the search software. Some popular online subscription systems are shown in Exhibit 2–7 and examples of online nonsubscription Internet sites are shown in Exhibit 2–8.

Electronic online tax research systems are relatively simple to operate. Normally, the user will have no trouble utilizing the system after he or she has devised an effective search command or query. Once the user is satisfied with the composition of his or her search query in an online system, it is transmitted over a telecommunications network to a central computer, where it is processed, and documents are identified that satisfy the search request. The texts of the retrieved documents then are transmitted to the user and displayed on his or her terminal. After the documents are received, the user must evaluate them and decide whether further research is required. Any documents that are displayed on the terminal may be printed in the researcher's office or saved as a file on a PC and retained for future reference.

CD-Based Systems

Since the late 1980s, CD-based technology has been a viable participant in the field of computerized tax research. This technology uses compact discs (CDs) similar to those previously popularized for conveying musical recordings; each disc carries information equivalent to at least 250,000 pages of documents. CD-ROM systems allow for an efficient review of voluminous data collections, where such data can be stored in electronic format. Thus, early applications of the technology involved text-oriented (such as legal and taxation, insurance, encyclopedia and dictionary, and book library holdings) materials, and graphic-oriented (such as geographical maps, two-dimensional art, and musical scores) settings. In a tax research context, a few discs can hold the text of an entire tax library, from the Code and Regulations to Revenue Rulings, case opinions, Committee Reports, publisher's commentary, textbooks, and treatises. Some of the popular CD-ROM systems are shown in Exhibit 2–9.

CD-ROM systems employ plastic discs as the medium of information storage. A CD typically is fed into a device that can read its contents, using logical commands

EXHIBIT 2–7 Online subscription systems

Name	Description
RIA CheckPoint	A web-based computer tax research service that contains all the RIA material on federal, state, local, and international taxation. CheckPoint contains all RIA analytical material such as the *Tax Coordinator 2d* and the *United States Tax Reporter*. All public domain information such as the code and regulations, U.S. tax treaties, IRS publications and pronouncements, and court cases are available on CheckPoint.
Westlaw	Offered by the major legal publisher, this system contains all federal and state legal sources including court cases, administrative releases, and statutory information. All government documents (IRS publications, court cases, etc.) are also available on this system. Also available on CD-ROM.
Lexis-Nexis	The largest of the commercial computer-based information systems. Besides containing all federal and state legal and tax research material, Lexis has extensive libraries of newspapers, magazines, journals, patent records, and medical, economic, and accounting databases.
CCH Tax Research Network	A web-based Internet system that contains all of CCH's tax services and other federal and state legal and tax information. All government documents (IRS publications, court cases, etc.) are available on this system.
CCH Access	A non-Internet online system that contains all of CCH's tax services and other federal and state legal and tax information. All government documents (IRS publications, court cases, etc.) are available on this system. Also available on CD-ROM.

similar to those discussed throughout this chapter, but cannot write on the disc or otherwise modify its contents, because the discs utilize read-only memory (ROM). The CD-ROM reader is attached to or built into a personal computer, where it acts as an additional disk drive. Indeed, perhaps the best way to describe CD-ROM technology is to note that it offers both the storage capacity of a hard disk and the portability of a floppy disk, in that the CDs allow entire hard drives to be interchanged and updated. Thus, the tax researcher can use this technology both to ensure the timeliness of the data and to expand the number of available documents in the library.

Vendor-provided software prompts the user to enter search queries pertinent to the task; this may include reporting on the list of documents that satisfy the queries and allowing for a review of the documents and further modifications of the search, printing the identified documents, and perhaps downloading to another disk or word-processing program. For this purpose, in some systems, logical queries can be entered, whereas others allow a menu-oriented or natural-language search sequence. Accordingly, the user may not need to learn yet another set of queries and commands to begin CD-ROM research on an installed and functioning system.

EXHIBIT 2–8   Examples of online nonsubscription Internet sites

Site Name	Internet Address	Description
Will Yancey's Home Page	http://www.willyancey.com	One of the best indexes available to other tax, accounting, and legal web sites. There are hundreds of links to commercial, federal government, state, local, and international web sites.
Internal Revenue Service	http://www.irs.ustreas.gov	A site where taxpayers can communicate with the IRS and download tax forms, documents, and other IRS information.
Thomas	http://thomas.loc.gov	Legislative information from the Library of Congress.
Practitioner's Publishing Co.	http://www.ppcinfo.com	An excellent site that contains a free newsletter, free common tax forms, and an index to other Internet tax resources.
Ernst & Young	http://www.ey.com/home.asp	A web site that contains a large amount of tax and accounting information from the staff of E&Y.
Deloitte & Touche	http://www.dtonline.com	The D&T web site contains a large amount of tax and accounting information from the staff of D&T.

Benefits of Using a Computerized Tax Service

Traditional tax research usually begins with the consultation of topical and annotated tax services or tax-related texts. In most instances, the user first must consult a topical index to locate the appropriate page or pages on which to begin his or her research. However, any time that a printed tax service is accessed by way of its topical index, the user is relying on someone else's judgment (i.e., the service's editors) or performance (e.g., the filing staff of the library for proper treatment of update material) as to what is important with respect to the specific topic. Moreover, the desired information may not be located, even if it exists and has been filed properly, because the key word for which the user is looking is not the same word that was used by the editor in the index to discuss the issue that is the subject of the search. It is also possible that, when the index was prepared, the topic of the search was ignored because it was not as important a topic as it is today.

The primary benefit of using a computerized tax service is that such a resource makes it possible for the *user* to index any significant term, that is, by using it as a

EXHIBIT 2-9 CD-ROM tax services

Name	Description
RIA OnPoint	RIA's tax service(s) and other RIA publications. The user can subscribe to any (or all) of the primary authority sources (complete court reporters, *Cumulative Bulletins,* etc.). Multiple CD-ROM disks. RIA CheckPoint is a similar service that is available on the Internet.
Westlaw	The Code, the Regulations, *Cumulative Bulletins,* and all of West's published legal and tax research information. Also available online.
Kleinrock's Tax Library	The Code, the Regulations, *Cumulative Bulletins* (since 1954), Tax Court Regular decisions (since 1954), Tax Court Memo decisions and other court cases (since 1987), and all IRS publications. One CD-ROM disk. Monthly or quarterly subscriptions available.
Infotax (Tax Analysts)	The Code, the Regulations, *Cumulative Bulletins* (since 1954), Tax Court Regular decisions (since 1954), Tax Court Memo decisions and other court cases (since 1985), *Circular 230,* and all IRS publications. One CD-ROM disk. Monthly or quarterly subscriptions available.
CCH Access	CCH's tax service(s) and other CCH publications. The user can subscribe to any (or all) of the primary authority sources (complete court reporters, *Cumulative Bulletins,* etc.). Multiple CD-ROM disks. Also available online.

search term in a query. By creating his or her own indexes, the researcher is not bound by the limitations that are imposed in manually accessing tax materials through a printed service or text. Once the central computer or CD is accessed with a proper search request, the service's software will electronically scan the designated files and retrieve all of the documents that contain the word or words included in the query. Thus, the user is able to bypass the predefined list of topics that constitute the subject's index and perform his or her search directly on the documents themselves.

Another benefit of using a computerized tax research system is that the user can tailor his or her query to fit the requirements of a specific tax problem. Because the user defines the precise specifications of the query, computerized research is exceptionally flexible. Each search request can be made as specific or as broad as desired, depending on the issue to be researched. If they are properly structured, computerized search queries can result in the research process being conducted with greater speed and thoroughness, and they can reduce the amount of time spent on that phase of the research task.

Such speed and flexibility is best realized as the researcher moves among pertinent tax documents. Most of the electronic services allow this capability through **hypertext** linking. Generally, when a hypertext link is indicated, typically through a different color for the text or a special character like a caret, the user can move to the related document so indicated with a click of the mouse or keyboard. For instance, the researcher could be reading a court case that refers to § 2032A. By clicking on the hypertext link character, he or she is taken directly to the text of the code section, for direct perusal of the statutory language. Similarly, links can be made to pertinent regulations, or to similar court documents in a manner that has no parallel in the traditional paper-oriented world of tax research. As the underlying documents become more voluminous, the importance of moving among the documents quickly is met only with an electronic research base.

Online services are updated much faster than printed tax services. A researcher generally is able to retrieve recent court decisions and administrative rulings from a computerized service one or more weeks before his or her library will receive updated print material containing the same case or ruling. In addition, the computerized services include one or more of the daily tax news summaries, including those written by the editorial staff of the producer of the service itself, or by other tax service organizations, such as BNA's *Daily Tax Report* or Tax Analysts' *Tax Notes Today*. In this regard, a computerized tax service allows a tax researcher to stay on top of the late news and developments without incurring additional subscription costs for the stand-alone services.

Computerized services are particularly useful in researching case law. Every word that is contained in a case is included in the database of the computerized service. Thus, the user can save time by directly accessing only those cases that contain the key terms of his or her search. For example, all of the cases that deal with unreasonable compensation can be accessed within minutes, simply by using *unreasonable compensation* as a search request. In addition, the research is probably more thorough this way than it would be by traditional methods because the user will be able to retrieve all of the cases that are included in the library that is accessed, not just those that are included in a legal index or digest.

An additional benefit of using a computerized tax service is that certain documents may be obtained only from the central computer library. For example, full printed transcripts of Actions on Decision and slip opinions normally are not published. However, these documents often may be obtained from the databases of computerized commercial tax services.

A computerized research service also can be used to obtain regularly published documents to which the researcher does not have access. For example, the full text of Private Letter Rulings is available on most computerized tax research databases. Thus, by using a computerized service, a tax practitioner can obtain only the ruling needed, without subscribing to an expensive loose-leaf service for the entire year.

Factors in Choosing a Computer Tax Service

In *Computer-Assisted Legal and Tax Research* (Prentice-Hall), Thomas and Weinstein propose that a potential subscriber consider the following factors when choosing a computerized tax database:

▶ *Database contents:* Does the service provide specialty libraries that will be important in the researcher's work and that are unavailable elsewhere?

▶ *Search capabilities:* While the search commands and requirements are similar among the commercial tax services, some of the electronic services allow direct reviews of editorial information, and others encompass the Shepard's citations service.

▶ *Training:* Each of the services offers some level of educational training, either at the user's office or at a regional training center. The proximity, depth, and quality of such seminars may differ among services and across the country.

▶ *Customer support:* Other forms of contact with the user, such as to develop more sophisticated search techniques or to provide necessary repair services, should be available to the subscriber.

▶ *Price:* One must consider the cost of the time required to perform the research itself, as well as that of necessary equipment or special software.

In the past, tax practitioners were faced with a choice of either a variable-cost online computer service (e.g., Lexis, Westlaw) or a fixed-cost CD-ROM tax service (e.g., RIA OnPoint). Recently, however, the advent of the **World Wide Web**-based fixed-cost tax service (e.g., RIA CheckPoint) has changed what is the optimal computer tax subscription for many tax practitioners. With a web-based tax service, tax practitoners have all the features (e.g., fast updates, large databases) of the variable-cost online system with the fixed-cost structure of a CD-ROM system. In addition, a web-based computer tax service does not require any additional hardware since most tax practitioners already have the hardware for tax return preparation and word processing. Because of all its inherit advantages, the web-based tax service will probably become the standard source for current and archival tax research material.

Using a Computer in Tax Research

In the first part of this chapter, we presented a model of the tax research process. In this model, steps 1 and 2 of the tax research model are to (1) establish the facts and (2) identify the issues related to the research question(s). The next step in the research model is to locate tax authority with which to solve the research question. In most situations, the tax researcher is going to use a computer to find the required authority (or to conclude that there is no authority on the subject). The process of finding tax authority using a computer can be broken down into several steps, as shown in Exhibit 2–10.

EXHIBIT 2–10   Steps in the computer research process

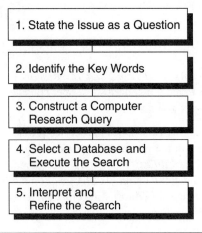

1. State the Issue as a Question

2. Identify the Key Words

3. Construct a Computer Research Query

4. Select a Database and Execute the Search

5. Interpret and Refine the Search

Step 1: State the Issue as a Question

After the tax researcher has established the facts and identified the issues that he or she needs to resolve, the issues should be stated as a question to be answered. For example, suppose the researcher has a client who is a self-employed attorney. As part of her trade or business, the attorney incurs substantial travel expenses during the year. She has learned that if she buys airline tickets in advance and extends her visit over a Saturday night, she will receive a large savings on airfare. Usually, an extra day of meals and lodging can save many hundreds of dollars in her airfare travel expenses. In the current year, she has spent $4,000 in extra Saturday night expenses to save $12,000 in airfare. The research question in this situation could be stated as:

> Are the additional travel costs (primarily meals and lodging) of staying over a Saturday night deductible in order to save substantial amounts on the business airfare?

Step 2: Identify the Key Words

Once the research question has been stated, the researcher must next identify the key words to construct a proper query in the next step. In the above research question the key words would be as follows:

- ▶ travel
- ▶ meals and lodging
- ▶ Saturday
- ▶ deductible
- ▶ airfare

The researcher is looking for words that, when entered into a computer, will find tax authority that is "on point." If the correct key words are not identified, tax researchers cannot find the authority needed or they could be led down blind alleys.

Step 3: Construct a Computer Research Query

Computer tax research systems use a **query** in order to begin the search for the authority needed by the researcher. The construction of the query varies for each commercial computer tax research system, however, that are many similarities between the systems. All tax computer research systems recognize various types of connectors to construct a research query. For example, the RIA **CheckPoint** system uses drop-down menus for basic searches, however, it also supports Boolean and plain English search connectors for more complex searches. The connectors in CheckPoint are shown in Exhibit 2–11.

Other computer tax services use similar methods to construct tax research queries. For example, the CheckPoint "&" and "|" are not available in Lexis. The words "and" and "or" must be used in constructing a Boolean search. For a proximity connector, Lexis uses "w/n" where "n" is the number of words in proximity. Thus, in Lexis, the CheckPoint proximity query *"travel Saturday"@25* would be *travel w/25 Saturday*. In addition, the end-of-a-root-word wildcard in Lexis is an exclamation point (!) instead of an asterisk (*) as in CheckPoint.

EXHIBIT 2-11 CheckPoint search syntax

Boolean Search Syntax

Search Connector	Use This Symbol	Example
AND	(&)	funding deficiency funding & deficiency
OR	(I)	reimbursement or proceeds reimbursement I proceeds
NOT	(^)	reimbursement not proceeds reimbursement ^ proceeds
Word endings	*	deprecia*
Exact phrase	" "	"charitable contributions"
Unordered proximity	" "@#	"charitable contributions"@10
Ordered proximity	" "/#	"charitable contributions"@/10
Stemming	%	run% finds runs, running
Thesaurus	$	child$ finds children, youth, etc.

Note: # refers to the number of words in proximity.

Plain English Search Syntax

Choose one of the following plain English search connectors on the General Search screen:

All of these key words searches for documents containing all of the key words in any order.

Any of these key words searches for documents containing any key words.

This exact phrase searches for all key words in the exact order that they are entered. To perform a proximity search use one of the following:

Within 5 words of each other searches for key words that are within 5 words of each other.

Within 10 words of each other searches for key words that are within 10 words of each other.

Computer tax services are continually being updated. Users should check the appropriate help menu of whichever computer tax service is being used to determine how to construct a query and to find other new features.

Step 4: Select a Database and Execute the Search

Once the query is constructed, the researcher must log on to and choose a database to search. Each computer tax research system contains numerous databases. As an example, CheckPoint contains the following databases (among many others):

- ► *The Federal Tax Coordinator 2d* (a tax service)
- ► *Federal Taxes Weekly Alert* (a newsletter)
- ► *Internal Revenue Code*
- ► The Final and Temporary Regulations
- ► IRS Rulings and Releases (e.g., Revenue Rulings, notices, announcements, Private Letter Rulings, etc.)

► Federal Court Tax Decisions
► *Citator 2d* (a judicial history index)

Continuing our example of the deductibility of Saturday night expenses we could choose to search the IRS databases using one of the queries above. For example, we could choose the IRS Rulings and Releases database and use the search query "travel Saturday." See Exhibit 2–11. If we executed this search on CheckPoint, we would find that the IRS has issued Private Letter Ruling 9237014 that states the extra expenses for staying over a Saturday to get a lower airfare are deductible as part of the expenses of the business trip. See Exhibit 2–12.

Step 5: Interpret and Refine the Search

After executing a computer tax search, often the research is going to have too little or too much information. If there is too little information, the search query has to be broadened. For example, other keywords may have to be used, or proximity connectors may have to be relaxed. On the other hand, if the researcher has too much information, the search query has to be tightened. For example, more unique key words may have to be used, or proximity connectors may have to be used or narrowed.

Computer tax services (e.g., Lexis, Westlaw, Kleinrock's, CCH Tax Research Network) have their own format for conducting tax searches. However, they all use

EXHIBIT 2–12   CheckPoint query and database selection screen

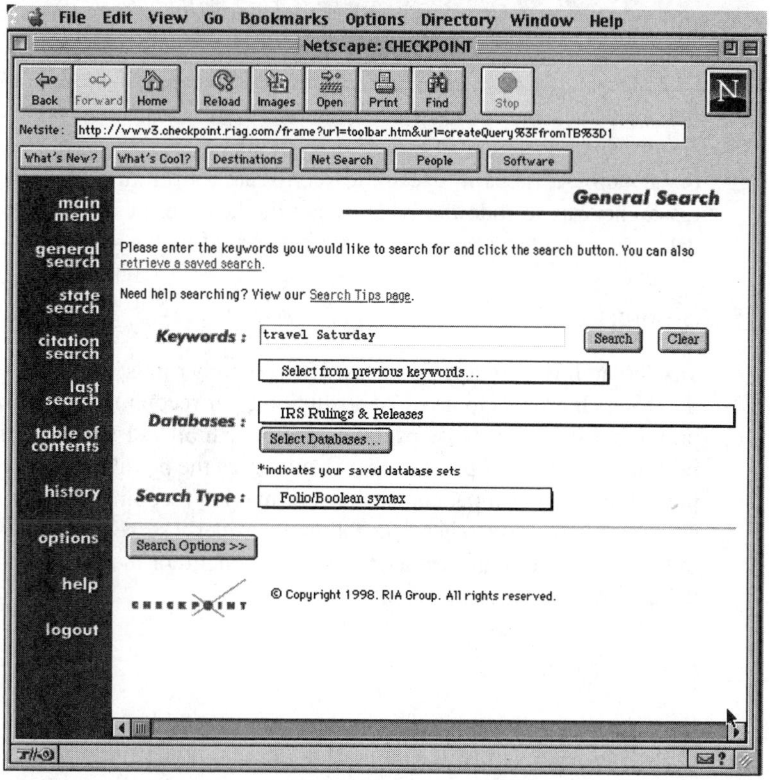

EXHIBIT 2–13 CheckPoint search results

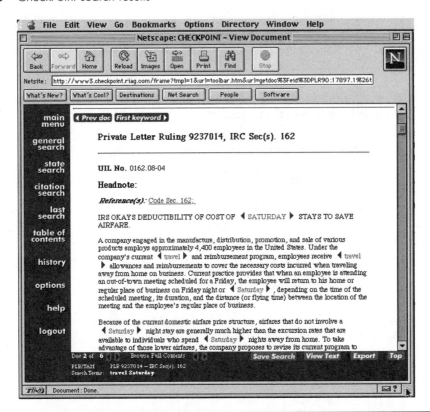

the same basic steps in executing such searches. In all computer tax systems, the researcher has to state the issue, select the key words, construct a query, choose a database, execute a search, and interpret and refine the search.

▶ Summary

Tax research is a complex process. The researcher must complete all of the steps in the research process to arrive at a solution to or recommendation for the client's tax problem. Moreover, the steps delineated in Exhibit 2–1 (or iterations of them) must be completed in their proper order to minimize the possibility of errors in evaluating the authority, arriving at conclusions, or making recommendations. If the process is abbreviated, the researcher risks failure to properly serve the client. This could result in the payment of unnecessary taxes by the client, or in the payment of damages by the tax practitioner to the client.

▶ Key Words

By the time you complete this chapter, you should be comfortable discussing each of the following terms. If you need additional review, return to the material in the chapter or consult the glossary to this text.

Administrative Sources
CD-Based System
CheckPoint
Collateral Estoppel
Fact Issue
Hypertext
Internal Revenue Code
Internet
Judicial Sources
Law Issue

Lexis
Online System
Primary Authority
Query
Secondary Authority
Statutory Sources
Tax Journal
Tax Service
World Wide Web

▶ ———————————   Discussion Questions

1. What is the purpose of tax research?
2. What are the basic steps in conducting tax research? Briefly discuss each step in the tax research process.
3. What are the two chief tax research skills, as identified in this text? Explain the importance of each basic skill.
4. The tax researcher must find the facts as the first step in tax research. Give examples of the kind of factual information that a tax practitioner might want to obtain.
5. What are some of the potential pitfalls in the first step of the tax research process?
6. In each of the following independent situations, indicate whether the item generally would be a tax (T) or a nontax (NT) consideration in solving a tax research or tax planning problem.

    a. The taxpayer would like to set up a private foundation to reduce her annual income tax liability.
    b. The taxpayer has a very poor cash flow because of prior investments; therefore, he has a limited ability to make "tax-advantaged" investments.
    c. The taxpayer wants to transfer as much of her property to her grandchildren as possible. However, she does not want any of the property to fall into the hands of the grandchildren's mother (her daughter-in-law).
    d. The taxpayer lived through the Great Depression of the 1930s and does not like investments with any risk, such as owning stocks or bonds.
    e. The taxpayer likes to maintain highly liquid investments, such as money market funds and certificates of deposit in insured banks and savings and loan institutions.
    f. The taxpayer hates to pay federal taxes. He will take any legal action to avoid paying any federal income, estate, or gift taxes.

7. Identify and briefly describe the two major types of tax research issues.
8. What is *collateral estoppel?* How does it affect tax research and planning?
9. Tax law provisions tend to change over time. Explain how this might affect tax research and planning.
10. In the tax research process, the researcher has an obligation to the client to evaluate authority. Do the precedents in all tax authority carry the same value? Explain.
11. Primary tax authority can be classified as statutory, administrative, or judicial. Briefly describe each.

12. Classify each of the following items as primary (P) or secondary (S) tax research authority.

   a. The *Internal Revenue Code*
   b. A Tax Court case
   c. A textbook on corporate taxation
   d. Treasury Regulations
   e. An IRS Revenue Ruling
   f. An article in *Taxation for Accountants*
   g. *Taxes on Parade* a newsletter
   h. A Supreme Court decision on a tax matter

13. Briefly characterize and distinguish between annotated tax services and topical tax services.

14. Classify each of the following commercial tax services as either an annotated service (A) or a topical service (T).

   a. CCH's *Standard Federal Tax Reports*
   b. RIA's *Tax Coordinator*
   c. BNA's *Tax Management Portfolios*
   d. *Mertens Law of Federal Income Taxation*
   e. CCH's *Federal Tax Service*
   f. RIA's *United States Tax Reporter*

15. Where can one find published court decisions?

16. Who publishes each of the following court reporters?

   a. *Tax Court Memorandum Decisions*
   b. *United States Reports*
   c. *TC Memorandum Decisions*
   d. *Federal Reporter*
   e. *Supreme Court Reporter*
   f. *Federal Supplement*
   g. *American Federal Tax Reports*
   h. *Tax Court of the U.S. Reports*
   i. *United States Tax Cases*

17. What kind of information can be found in a citator?

18. Name the primary bound publication where IRS pronouncements can be found.

19. Tax practitioners use the term "tax service" all the time. What is a tax service?

20. What is the target readership of each of the following tax journals?

   a. *TAXES*
   b. *Journal of State Taxation*
   c. *Taxation for Accountants*
   d. *The Tax Adviser*
   e. *Estate Planning*

21. Specific items of tax authority have different "values" in helping the tax researcher to solve his or her problem. Explain this statement and describe how it applies to the tax research process.

22. Step 5 in the tax research process is concerned with reaching a conclusion or

making a recommendation. If one has not found a clear answer to a tax research problem, how is a conclusion or recommendation to be reached?

23. The final step in the research process typically involves a memorandum to the client file and/or a letter to the client communicating the results of the research. List the items that should be found in the body of both of these documents.

24. It has been said that the tax research process is more circular than linear. Do you agree with this statement? Explain your answer.

25. What is deemed to be substantial authority under the § 6662 Regulations? Why is this important?

26. Describe a CD-based tax research system. What are two advantages of such a system over a standard printed tax service?

27. What is the difference between an online and a CD-ROM computer tax research system? What is the advantage of an online system over a CD-ROM system and over a printed tax service? Are there any disadvantages of online systems?

28. What is the Internet address of the Internal Revenue Service's server?

29. What is computerized tax research, and why is it necessary for the tax professional to be able to use computerized techniques to conduct tax research?

30. Describe how an online computerized tax service operates.

31. Describe how a CD-ROM computerized tax database operates.

32. Under what circumstances would a tax professional be most likely to consult a computerized tax research service?

33. What are the disadvantages of using a computerized tax service?

34. List four benefits of using a computerized service to conduct your tax research.

35. What are the major steps in developing an effective computerized tax research query?

36. If you were researching an issue and the computer informed you that it had located 1,000 pertinent documents, what would you do to reduce the number of retrieved documents to a more reasonable number?

▶ _____ Exercises

37. Use your university's tax library (or other library assigned by your instructor) to discover the breadth of tax journal offerings. List any five tax journals and the publisher of each.

38. The purpose of this exercise is for you to locate publications that frequently are used in tax research. Give the call number and location (i.e., floor, room, stack, etc.) in your library, and the major color of the binding of the publication, for each of the following references. If a publication is not available, state that it is not.

    a. RIA's *United States Tax Reporter*
    b. *Bender's Tax Service*
    c. CCH's *Standard Federal Tax Reports*
    d. BNA's *Tax Management Portfolios*
    e. *Mertens Law of Federal Income Taxation*
    f. RIA's *Tax Coordinator*

39. Find out whether each of the following court reporters is available in your library. Give the call number and location (i.e., floor, room, stack, etc.) for each reference. If a reporter is not available, state that it is not.

    a. *American Federal Tax Reports*
    b. *United States Tax Cases*
    c. *Tax Court of the U.S. Reports*
    d. *Tax Court Memorandum Decisions*
    e. *United States Reports*
    f. *Federal Reporter, 3d Series*

40. Determine if each of the following tax journals is available in your library. What is the most current issue in your library? List the author(s) and title of any two articles from the most recent issue.

    a. *Journal of Taxation*
    b. *Taxation for Accountants*
    c. *Journal of International Taxation*
    d. *The Tax Adviser*
    e. *TAXES*

41. Is the *Internal Revenue Code* found in separate volumes in each of the following tax services? If so, in how many volumes?

    a. CCH's *Standard Federal Tax Reports*
    b. BNA's *Tax Management Portfolios*
    c. RIA's *Tax Coordinator 2d*

42. Find a copy of the *Cumulative Bulletin* in your university's library. By looking in a volume, list three different tax research sources published in a *Cumulative Bulletin*.

43. Locate a copy of the *American Federal Tax Reports* in your library. List two courts that have decisions published in this court reporter.

44. Locate a copy of CCH's *United States Tax Cases* in your library. List two courts which have decisions published in this court reporter.

45. In your university's library, locate the CCH and RIA citators. How many volumes does each contain?

46. Determine if your campus has any of the following CD-ROM tax research services available for student use. If a service is available on your campus, describe how you would gain access to that system for research projects in your tax classes. If a service is not available on your campus, state where you might be able to find it.

    a. Kleinrock's
    b. InfoTax
    c. RIA OnPoint
    d. Westlaw
    e. CCH Access

47. Log on to Lexis. How many computer screens does it take to show all the libraries available on Lexis?

48. Determine if your campus has any of the following online tax research services available for student use. If a service is available on your campus, describe how you would gain access to that system for research projects in your tax classes. If a service is not available on your campus, state where you might be able to find it.

    a. RIA CheckPoint

    b. Lexis

    c. CCH Access

49. What is the Internet address of the White House in Washington, D.C.? Log on to the Internet and send a message to the President of the United States, stating your opinion on some current tax, political topic, or other item of interest to you. Print a copy of the message you sent and turn it into your instructor. If you do not want anyone to see your message, just turn in the "Internet routing portion" of your message.

50. Log on to the Internet and find the IRS forms page. Download and print any IRS form numbered from 8,000 to 8,999. You may first need to download the Adobe Acrobat Reader (© Adobe Systems) software to be able to view or print the form. The software is provided free by Adobe through a link on the IRS page.

51. Jennifer owns 200 acres of land on which she grows flowers for sale to local nurseries. Her adjusted basis in the land is $30,000. She receives condemnation proceeds of $20,000 from the state for ten acres of her land where there will be a new freeway. The state also pays her $30,000 for the harmful effects that the increased auto exhausts might have on her flowers. List as many tax research issues as you can to determine the tax consequences of these transactions. Do not attempt to answer any of the questions you raise. Simply identify the research issues.

52. Joey parked his car on the top of a hill when he went to watch the X games in San Diego. He did not properly set his brakes or curb the wheels when he parked the car. When he returned from the games, he found his car had rolled down the hill, smashed into Nick's house, and injured Nick, who was watching TV in his den. Joey does not have car insurance. List as many tax research issues as you can to determine the tax consequences of this accident. Do not attempt to answer any of the questions you raise. Simply identify the research issues.

53. John and Marsha are married and filed a joint return for the past year. During that year, Marsha was employed as an assistant cashier at a local bank and, as such, was able to embezzle $75,000, none of which was reported on their joint return. Before the defalcation was discovered, Marsha disappeared and has not been seen or heard from since. List as many tax research issues as you can to determine the tax consequences of this crime. Do not attempt to answer any of the questions you raise. Simply identify the research issues.

54. In the current year, Dave receives stock worth $125,000 from his employer. The stock is restricted and cannot be sold by Dave for seven years. Dave estimates the stock will be worth $300,000 after the seven years. List as many tax research issues as you can to determine the tax consequences of this transaction. Do not attempt to answer any of the questions you raise. Simply identify the research issues.

55. On December 1, 19x1, Ericka receives $18,000 for three months' rent (December, January, and February) of an office building. List as many tax research issues as you can to determine the tax consequences of this transaction. Do not attempt to answer any of the questions you raise. Simply identify the research issues.

56. Formulate a search query to determine whether your client is required to include in gross income the proceeds from a redemption of a tax-exempt bond, purchased in 1988 and called by the school district this year. Redemption proceeds were $90,000, and the 1988 purchase price on the secondary market was $76,000. Give an example of both a CheckPoint and a Lexis query.

57. Formulate a query to determine the provisions of the United States' treaty with Germany relative to fellowship income received by a business student during a summer internship with the German Department of Price Controls. Give an example of both a CheckPoint and a Lexis query.

58. Formulate a search query to determine whether your client is required to capitalize fringe benefits and general overhead that is attributable to employees who are building an addition to your client's factory during a "slack time" at work. Give an example of both a CheckPoint and a Lexis query.

59. Formulate a search query to determine whether your client can retroactively elect to change its accounting method. Give an example of both a CheckPoint and a Lexis query.

60. Formulate a search query to find all of the cases in which the word *constructive* occurs within ten words of the word *dividend*. Give an example of both a CheckPoint and a Lexis query.

► _____ Research Cases

61. Sam Manuel has been employed on a full-time basis as an electrical engineer for the past three years. Prior to obtaining full-time employment, he was self-employed as an inventor of complex electronic components. During this period of self-employment, most of his projects produced little income, although several produced a significant amount of revenue.

   Due to the large expenditures necessary and the failure of the majority of the products to produce a profit, Sam was forced to seek full-time employment. After obtaining full-time employment, he continued to work long hours to perfect several of his inventions. He continued to enjoy relatively little success with most of his products, but certain projects were successfully marketed and generated a profit. For the last two years, Sam's invention activity has generated a net loss.

   a. List as many possible tax research issues as you can to determine whether the losses may be deducted.
   b. After completing your list of tax research issues, list the key words you might use to construct a computer tax research query.

62. Matthew Broadway was a partner in the law firm of Johnson and Smith, a partnership of twenty partners, for the past ten years. Without the knowledge or consent of the other partners, Matthew worked on a highly complicated acquisition and merger project for six months, at all times using the resources of the law firm. Several months later, the firm for which Matthew provided the professional services made out a check for $300,000 to the firm of Johnson and Smith. Matthew insisted that the fee should rightly be his, while the firm disputed his claim. As a result of the dispute, the fee was held in escrow until the following year when the dispute was settled.

The dispute was settled with Matthew agreeing to withdraw from the partnership. Included as part of the withdrawal agreement was a clause that specified he would receive $45,000 of the $300,000 fee, with the law firm retaining the remainder. Six months later, Matthew received a total payment of $125,000, which included the $45,000 fee, from Johnson and Smith.

   a. List as many possible tax research issues as you can to determine the tax treatment of the $125,000 payment received by Matthew.

   b. After completing your list of tax research issues, list the key words you might use to construct a computer tax research query.

63. Juanita Sharp purchased a large parcel of property for $120,000. A short time after purchasing the property, Sharp submitted plans for the division of the parcel into six lots and the construction of three single-family residences on three of the lots. The city permits required that the property be divided into six lots and that street improvements and water and sewer access be provided. Sharp spent $22,000 for the street, water, and sewer improvements. As a result of the improvements, the value of each of the three vacant lots increased by $1,000, based on an appraisal completed subsequent to the completion of the improvements. The costs of constructing the three single-family residences totaled $200,000.

   a. List as many possible tax research issues as you can to determine how the original purchase price of $120,000, the $22,000 cost of the improvements, and the $200,000 cost of the construction of the homes should be allocated to the basis of each of the lots for purposes of determining gain or loss on the sale of the lots.

   b. After completing your list of tax research issues, list the key words you might use to construct a computer tax research query.

64. Tom and Donna were divorced three years ago. At the time of their divorce, they owned a highly appreciated residence. Tom remained half-owner of the house, but moved out and allowed Donna to continue living in the house. In the current year, Tom and Donna sold the house for $300,000. Last year, Tom purchased a new house for $190,000.

   a. List as many possible tax research issues as you can to determine tax treatment(s) available to Tom on the sale and purchase of the residence.

   b. After completing your list of tax research issues, list the key words you might use to construct a computer tax research query.

65. Your client, Barney Green, and his wife, Edith, attended a three-day program in Honolulu, entitled "Financial, Tax, and Investment Planning for Investors." The Greens went to Hawaii several days early, so that they could get adjusted to jet lag and be ready for the seminar. The $3,000 cost of the trip included the following expenses.

First-class air fare	$1,200
Hotel (7 days)	800
Program fee	300
Meals and other expenses	700

The Greens have records to substantiate all of the above expenditures in a manner that is acceptable under IRC § 274.

    a. List as many possible tax research issues as you can to determine whether the Greens can deduct any or all of the $3,000 of expenditures on their current-year tax return.

    b. After completing your list of tax research issues, list the key words you might use to construct a computer tax research query.

    c. Execute a computer search using your query. For simplicity, select the IRS Taxpayer Information Publications (TIPS) database from whichever computer tax service you use. Summarize your findings.

66. Ban Vallew was divorced in 1981. He has a son, Katt, by this marriage, who is in the custody of his ex-wife. Katt Vallew has a history of emotional disturbance. He has been sent to a psychiatrist for several years for this problem. This year he has become so disturbed, manifesting violence at home and school, that he had to be sent to a special school in Arizona for problem children. This school is very expensive ($2,000 per month), the cost of which Ban pays for. Ban would like to determine whether he is entitled to the medical-expenses deduction (over 7.5 percent of adjusted gross income) for the cost of this special school.

    a. List as many possible tax research issues as you can to determine tax treatment(s) available to Ban on the payments to the special school.

    b. After completing your list of tax research issues, list the key words you might use to construct a computer tax research query.

    c. Execute a computer search using your query. For simplicity, select the IRS Taxpayer Information Publications (TIPS) database from whichever computer tax service you use. Summarize your findings.

67. Linda Larue suffered from arthritis. Her chiropractor advised her that she needed to swim daily to alleviate her pain and other symptoms. Consequently, Linda and her husband, Philo, purchased for $100,000 a new home that had a swimming pool, after selling their old home for $85,000. If the Larues had constructed a pool at their former residence, it would have cost $15,000 to build, and it would have increased the value of their home by $8,000.

    a. List as many possible tax research issues as you can to determine whether the Larues can deduct any of their current-year expenditures for Linda's arthritis.

    b. After completing your list of tax research issues, list the key words you might use to construct a computer tax research query.

    c. Execute a computer search using your query. For simplicity, select the IRS Revenue Rulings database from whichever computer tax service you use. Summarize your findings.

Primary Sources of Federal Tax Law

Constitutional and Legislative Sources

LEARNING OBJECTIVES

► Outline the primary and secondary sources of the federal tax law

► Describe in detail the nature and structure of the statutory sources of the tax law, including the Constitution, tax treaties, and the *Internal Revenue Code*

► Delineate how statutory tax law is created and how tax research resources are generated in this process

► Determine how to locate the statutory sources of the tax law

► Discuss how the tax researcher can carefully interpret the *Internal Revenue Code*

CHAPTER OUTLINE

Sources of Federal Tax Law
History of U.S. Taxation
U.S. Constitution
Tax Treaties
The Legislative Process
   Where to Find Committee Reports

Internal Revenue Code
   Organization of the *Internal Revenue Code*
   Where to Find the *Internal Revenue Code*
Interpreting the *Internal Revenue Code*

In Chapter 2, we provided an overview of tax research methodology, presenting the steps that are necessary to complete a federal tax research project in a timely manner. In addition, we presented an introductory discussion concerning the materials used in conducting research.

In this chapter, we take a closer look at the tax research process. We will outline the primary and secondary sources of federal tax law, examine in some detail the primary statutory sources of federal tax law, learn how to locate selected provisions thereof, and find out how these laws may pertain to a client's problem. Following a short look at the history of the federal tax law, we will examine the statutory sources of income tax laws, including the U.S. Constitution, tax treaties, and other revenue laws that Congress has passed.

Sources of Federal Tax Law

The sources of the federal tax law can be classified as **primary authorities** or **secondary authorities.** Chapters 3 through 9 of this text include detailed examinations of these various sources, discussing their nature, location, and use in the tax research process. The sources of the federal tax law to be examined here are presented in outline form in Exhibit 3–1. In particular, we will examine the **statutory sources** of the U.S. Constitution, tax treaties, and the *Internal Revenue Code*. The

---

EXHIBIT 3–1   Primary and secondary sources of federal tax law

Primary Sources	Secondary Sources
Statutory sources	Tax services
U.S. Constitution	Annotated services
Tax treaties	Topical services
Internal Revenue Code	Tax journals and newsletters
Language of the statute	Tax textbooks and treatises
Legislative history and intent	
Administrative sources	
Treasury Regulations	
Revenue Rulings	
Revenue Procedures	
Other written determinations	
Miscellaneous IRS publications	
Judicial sources	
Supreme Court	
Courts of Appeals	
Entry-level courts	
Tax Court	
Tax Court, Small Cases Division	
Claims Courts	
District Courts	

reader should refer to this outline while reading this text to maintain perspective as to the relationships between each of the sources discussed.

History of U.S. Taxation

Although the Massachusetts Bay Colony enacted an income tax law in 1643, the first U.S. income tax was not created until the Civil War. An income tax law was passed at that time to help the North pay for the cost of fighting the war. This federal income tax law was passed on August 5, 1861. Although the tax was not generally enforced, some limited collections were made under the law.

This first federal income tax was levied at the rate of a modest 3 percent on income between $600 and $10,000, and 5 percent on marginal incomes in excess of $10,000. Later, in 1867, the rate was a flat 5 percent of income in excess of $1,000. The Civil War income taxes were allowed to expire in 1872. In 1894 another income tax act was passed by Congress. By this time, however, the income tax had become an important political issue. The southern and western states generally favored the tax and the eastern states generally opposed it, because the tax had developed into an important element of the Populist political movement. In *Pollock v. Farmers' Loan and Trust Co.,* the Supreme Court held that the income tax was unconstitutional because it was a constitutionally prohibited "direct tax."[1]

The supporters of the income tax decided to amend the Constitution, so that there would be no question as to the constitutionality of a federal income tax. The proposed amendment was sent to the states on July 12, 1909, by the Sixty-first Congress; it was ratified on February 3, 1913. The new Sixteenth Amendment to the Constitution stated:

> The Congress shall have the power to lay and collect taxes on incomes, from whatever source derived, without apportionment among the several States, and without regard to any census or enumeration.

Before the Sixteenth Amendment was ratified, Congress passed a corporate income tax in 1909. This tax also was challenged at the Supreme Court level, in *Flint v. Stone Tracy Co.*[2] The Court held that this tax was constitutional, because it was a special form of excise tax, using income as its base, rather than a (prohibited) direct income tax.

In recent years, the income tax has been attacked in the courts on the basis that it is unconstitutional. For instance, some protesters have asserted that, since the U.S. currency no longer is based on the gold standard, the Sixteenth Amendment's measure of income, and therefore the tax itself, is invalid. Others have asserted that the federal income tax law forces the taxpayer to surrender his or her Fifth Amendment rights against self-incrimination. Federal courts, however, have denied virtually all of the protesters' challenges.

As a result of inflation and other economic turbulence of the 1970s and early 1980s, such tax protests increased rapidly, and Congress passed several new laws to discourage them. For instance, a taxpayer is subject to a $500 fine if he or she files a "frivolous" tax return as a form of protest against the IRS or the U.S. budgetary

[1] 157 U.S. 429, 15 S.Ct. 673 (1895).
[2] 220 U.S. 107, 31 S.Ct. 342 (1911).

process. This fine would be levied, for example, when the taxpayer files a blank tax return accompanied by a note suggesting that the federal income tax is unconstitutional or that the taxpayer wishes to protest against tax revenues going to create nuclear weapons. To date, a number of lower courts have upheld the constitutionality of this fine.[3]

The Tax Court can impose a penalty, not to exceed $25,000, if the taxpayer brings a "frivolous" matter before the Court. A frivolous matter is where the intent is to delay the revenue collection process and where the proceedings are found to be groundless, or where the taxpayer unreasonably failed to pursue available administrative remedies.[4] Sanctions can also be imposed against tax practitioners.

U.S. Constitution

The Constitution of the United States is the source of all of the federal laws of the country, including both tax and nontax provisions. In addition to the Sixteenth Amendment, however, the Constitution contains other provisions that bear upon the taxation process. For example, the Constitution provides that Congress may impose import taxes but not export taxes. Moreover, the constitutional rights of due process and of the privacy of the citizen apply in tax, as well as nontax, environments.

The Constitution also requires that taxes imposed by Congress apply uniformly throughout the United States. For instance, it would be unconstitutional for Congress to impose one federal income tax rate in California and another rate in Vermont. Moreover, except as provided by the Sixteenth Amendment, the Constitution still bars per capita and other direct taxes, unless the revenues that are generated from these taxes are apportioned to the population of the states from which they were collected.

The federal courts have upheld the constitutionality of the estate and gift taxes because they are in the form of excise taxes on (the transfer of) property, rather than direct taxes on individuals. Thus, one can conclude that, for better or worse, most future judicial challenges to the constitutionality of the elements of the federal tax structure probably will be fruitless.

One can find copies of the U.S. Constitution in many textbooks, encyclopedias, dictionaries, and in publications such as *The World Almanac* and the *Information Please Almanac.* The Constitution also is reproduced in Volume One of the *United States Code,* as published by the Government Printing Office, and in Appendix D of this text.

The U.S. Constitution can also be found at various nonsubscription Internet sites. Examples (see Exhibit 3–2) of such sites would be.

> http://www.nara.gov/exhall/charters/constitution/conmain.html
> http://lcweb2.loc.gov/const/const.html

Tax Treaties

Tax treaties are agreements negotiated between countries concerning the treatment of entities subject to tax in both countries. The United States has entered into treaties with most of the major Western countries of the world. The overriding purpose of such treaties (also known as *tax conventions*) is to eliminate the "double taxation"

---

[3]E.g., *Schull,* 84 2 USTC ¶ 9529 (D.C., Va.).
[4]§§ 6673 and 6702.

EXHIBIT 3–2   Example of U.S. Constitution from the Internet

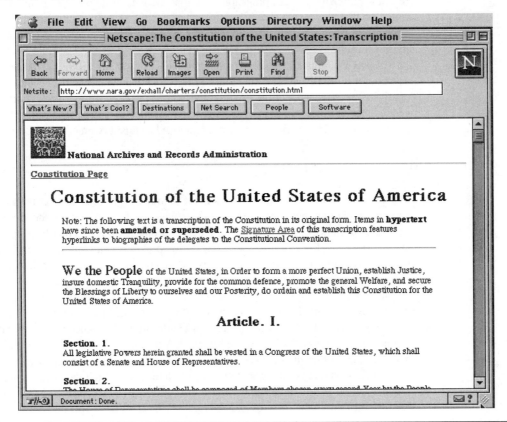

that the taxpayer would face if his or her income were subject to tax in both countries. In such a case, a U.S. citizen who has generated income from an investment in
the United Kingdom (U.K.) usually would be allowed a credit on her U.S. income
tax return to the extent of any related U.K. taxes that she paid.

Any tax matter can be covered in a tax treaty with another country. Many times
there are multiple tax treaties with a given country. For example, one treaty will
address income tax issues, while another treaty covers estate tax, and a third treaty
addresses excise taxes. An example of a portion of a tax treaty is shown as Exhibit
3–3. In addition to the tax treaties, the U.S. government enters into nontax international agreements that are not formal tax treaties; however, in many respects they
function like one. Along with other provisions, these agreements address tax issues
involving the parties associated with the agreement. Examples of such international
agreements include the North American Free Trade Agreement (NAFTA) and the
General Agreement on Tariffs and Trade (GATT).

The Constitution provides that "Laws of the United States which shall be made
in pursuance thereof; and all Treaties made, or which shall be made, under the
Authority of the United States, shall be the supreme Law of the Land." An *Internal*

EXHIBIT 3–3   Tax treaty excerpt

CONVENTION BETWEEN THE GOVERNMENT OF THE UNITED STATES OF
AMERICA AND THE GOVERNMENT OF THE REPUBLIC OF ITALY FOR THE
AVOIDANCE OF DOUBLE TAXATION WITH RESPECT TO TAXES ON INCOME
AND THE PREVENTION OF FRAUD OR FISCAL EVASION

[Signed 4/17/84]

The Government of the United States of America and the Government of the Republic
of Italy, desiring to conclude a convention for the avoidance of double taxation with
respect to taxes on income and the prevention of fraud or fiscal evasion, have agreed as
follows:

ARTICLE 1: PERSONAL SCOPE

1. Except as otherwise provided in this Convention, this Convention shall apply to
    persons who are residents of one or both of the Contracting States.
2. Notwithstanding any provision of this Convention except paragraph 3 of this Article, a
    Contracting State may tax:
    a) its residents (as determined under Article 4 (Resident)); and
    b) its citizens by reason of citizenship as if there were no convention between the
        Government of the United States of America and the Government of Italy for the
        avoidance of double taxation with respect to taxes on income and the prevention
        of fraud or fiscal evasion.
3. The provisions of paragraph 2 shall not affect:
    a) the benefits conferred by a Contracting State under paragraph 3 of Article 18
        (Pensions, etc.), and under Articles 23 (Relief from Double Taxation), 24
        (Non-Discrimination), and 25 (Mutual Agreement Procedure); and
    b) the benefits conferred by a Contracting State under Articles 19 (Government
        Service), 20 (Professors and Teachers), 21 (Students and Trainees), and 27
        (Diplomatic Agents and Consular Officials), upon individuals who are neither
        citizens of, nor have immigrant status in, that State.

ARTICLE 2: TAXES COVERED

1. This Convention shall apply to taxes on income imposed on behalf of a Contracting
    State.
2. The existing taxes to which this Convention shall apply are:
    a) in the case of the United States: the Federal income taxes imposed by the *Internal
        Revenue Code* and the excise taxes imposed on insurance premiums paid to
        foreign insurers and with respect to private foundations, but excluding
        (notwithstanding paragraph 5 of Article 10 [Dividends]) the accumulated earnings
        tax and the personal holding company tax, (hereinafter referred to as "United
        States tax");
    b) in the case of Italy:
        i)   the individual income tax (l'imposta sul reddito delle persone fisiche);
        ii)   the corporation income tax (l'imposta sul reddito delle persone giuridiche); and
        iii) the local income tax (l'imposta locale sui redditi) except to the extent
              imposed on cadastral income; even if they are collected by withholding taxes
              at the source (hereinafter referred to as "Italian tax").

Revenue Code provision and a provision under a treaty will sometimes conflict. In such a case, both of the provisions cannot represent the law; the one adopted later in time generally controls.

> **Example 3–1** Treaty Override. Prior to 1980, the United States negotiated treaties with several countries that allowed foreign taxpayers to sell U.S. real estate and not pay tax on gains. Under these treaties, nonresident aliens and foreign corporations could avoid U.S. taxes on real estate if the gains were treated as capital gains and were not effectively connected with the conduct of a U.S. business. Because of this favorable treatment for foreign investors, many U.S. farmers felt foreign investors were bidding up the price of farmland in the United States. This and other concerns led Congress to pass the Foreign Investment in Real Property Tax Act (FIRPTA) of 1980. Under § 897, FIRPTA makes gains and losses by nonresident aliens and foreign corporations taxable by treating such transactions as effectively connected with a U.S. trade or business. This provision overrides any treaties in effect at that time, by making foreign capital gains on real property taxable for transactions after 1984. If an existing treaty was renegotiated prior to 1985, the new treaty could designate a different effective date for § 897; however, the designated effective date could not be more than two years after the signing of the renegotiated treaty.

This later-in-time rule appears to be a simplistic approach to the complex interaction of the Code and treaty provisions. The courts have presented interpretive guidelines to be used in resolving interstatutory conflicts. One such guideline is that, where possible, equal effect should be given to both statutes; congressional intent to repeal a statute should not be assumed. A significant judicial history also exists for the interaction of treaties and the Code. In fact, as with conflicts between statutes, courts usually attempt to reconcile the apparent conflict, in a way that gives consideration to both the treaty and the Code provisions.

The equality of the two types of provisions is indicated in the Code, which provides that neither a treaty nor a law shall be given preferential status by reason of its being a treaty or a law.[5] The language of both the Code and the Constitution make this clear. The only codified exception to this rule is that treaty provisions in effect in 1954 and which conflicted with the 1954 Code as originally enacted are given precedence over the existing provisions of the 1954 Code, but not over later amendments to the Code. Section 894 states that due regard shall be given to any treaty obligation of the United States that applies to the taxpayer, when applying the provisions of the *Internal Revenue Code*.

Treaties are authorized by the Constitution. In Article II, Section 2, of the Constitution, the President of the United States is allowed to enter into treaties with other countries after receiving the advice and consent of the Senate. The President may also enter into other international agreements that have effects on the federal tax structure. Such agreements need not be ratified by the Senate, however; they are implemented by Congress in accordance with existing federal laws.

Treaties may be terminated in several ways. They may expire because of a specific Congressional time limitation, be superseded by a newer treaty, or be terminated by the countries' mutual actions.

Tax researchers often find it necessary to examine the provisions of tax treaties. Exhibit 3–4 shows where to find tax treaties in a traditional tax library.

---

[5] § 7852(d).

EXHIBIT 3–4   Examples of where to find tax treaties

Title	Publisher
Computer Sources:	
RIA CheckPoint Internet	Research Institute of America
RIA OnPoint CD-ROM	Research Institute of America
Westlaw CD and online	West Publishing Co.
CCH Tax Research Network	Commerce Clearing House
CCH Access CD and online	Commerce Clearing House
Kleinrock's CD-ROM	Kleinrock Publishing Co.
Infotax CD-ROM	Tax Analysts
Printed Sources:	
Tax Coordinator 2d	Research Institute of America
Tax Treaties Service	Commerce Clearing House
Tax Treaties Service	Warren, Gorham, & Lamont
United States Code Annotated	West Publishing Co.

Treaties are an important source of federal law, including tax law. When dealing with a research problem that has international connotations, the researcher must locate, read, and evaluate any tax treaty that applies to the client's problem. The researcher cannot rely on the more typical sources of tax research information, because these references usually address only domestic tax precedents.

The Legislative Process

To understand how to research tax issues, the tax researcher must have a grasp of the federal legislative process. The tax law of the United States, like automobiles and hot dogs, is created in a multistep process. At each stage in the creation of a tax law, Congress generates additional items of information, each of which may be useful in addressing a client's tax problem.

Most tax legislation begins in the House of Representatives. In the House, tax law changes are considered by the Ways and Means Committee. Upon approval by this committee, the bill is sent to the full House of Representatives for its approval. The bill then is sent to the Senate, where it is referred to the Finance Committee. When the Finance Committee approves the bill, the proposal is considered by the entire Senate.

If any differences between the House and Senate versions of the tax bill exist (which is almost always the case), the bill is referred to a Joint Conference Committee, where these differences are resolved. The compromise bill must be approved by both houses of Congress before it is forwarded to the President. If the President signs the bill, the new provisions are incorporated into the ***Internal Revenue Code.*** If the bill is vetoed by the President, however, it is not enacted, unless Congress overrides the veto with a sufficient revote. Exhibit 3–5 summarizes the usual steps of the legislative process as it is encountered relative to tax legislation.

At each step in the legislative process, the appropriate committee of Congress produces a **Committee Report,** which explains the elements of the proposed changes and the reasons for each of the proposals. These Committee Reports are an important tool for tax researchers. In many situations where the tax law is unclear,

EXHIBIT 3–5 Legislative process to amend the tax law

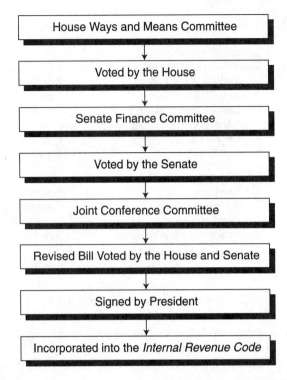

| House Ways and Means Committee |
| Voted by the House |
| Senate Finance Committee |
| Voted by the Senate |
| Joint Conference Committee |
| Revised Bill Voted by the House and Senate |
| Signed by President |
| Incorporated into the *Internal Revenue Code* |

or when recent legislation has been passed, they can provide insight concerning the meaning of a specific phrase of the statute or of the intention of Congress concerning a certain provision of the law. Committee Reports typically result from the deliberations of the Ways and Means Committee, the Finance Committee, and the Joint Conference Committee. A "General Explanation" of tax legislation occasionally is prepared by the Joint Committee on Taxation (the "Blue Book"). Exhibit 3–6 reproduces a portion of such a Committee Report.

Committee Reports generally are referred to by public law number. Every bill that Congress passes is assigned such a number. For example, the Tax Reform Act of 1986 was designated as P.L. 99-514. Public Law is abbreviated as "P.L." in this context. The prefix of the numerical designation (here, 99) refers to the session of Congress that passed the law. The suffix of the Public Law number (here, 514) indicates that this was the 514th bill that this session of Congress adopted.

Congressional sessions last for two years; therefore, the researcher may find it useful to construct a method by which to identify the two-year period in which a tax law was passed. The recent sessions of Congress are identified as follows.

Congressional Sessions	Years
One-hundred-sixth	1999–2000
One-hundred-seventh	2001–02
One-hundred-eighth	2003–04
One-hundred-ninth	2005–06
One-hundred-tenth	2006–08

EXHIBIT 3–6   Committee Report excerpt

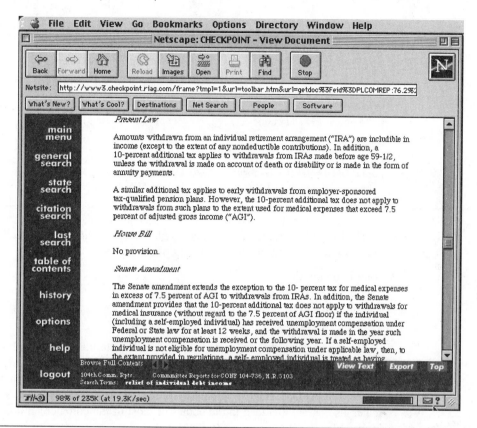

Through 1999, to convert a session number into the second year of the applicable congressional session, multiply the session number by 2 and subtract 112 (the number of years from 1788 to 1900). Thus, the second year of the One-hundredth Congress was 1988 [(100 × 2) - 112 = 88]. For the year 2000 and after, substitute 212 (the number of years from 1788 to 2000) for 112 in the formula. For example, the second year of the One-hundred-eighth Congress is 2004 [(108 × 2) - 212 = 04].

Where to Find Committee Reports

When a new tax law is passed, the pertinent Committee Reports are printed in the Internal Revenue Service's weekly *Internal Revenue Bulletin.* The weekly IRS reports are reorganized and published every six months in the *Cumulative Bulletin.* However, the texts of the 1954 Committee Reports relative to the *Internal Revenue Code* are found not in the *Cumulative Bulletin,* but in the *United States Code Congressional and Administrative News.* Finally, all of the pre-1939 Revenue Act Committee Reports are reprinted in the 1939 *Cumulative Bulletin.* Exhibit 3–7 summarizes the locations and publishers of the most important tax-related Committee Reports.

EXHIBIT 3–7 Location of Committee Reports

Publication	Publisher
Computer Sources:	
RIA CheckPoint Internet	Research Institute of America
RIA OnPoint CD-ROM	Research Institute of America
Westlaw CD and online	West Publishing Co.
CCH Tax Research Network	Commerce Clearing House
CCH Access CD and online	Commerce Clearing House
Printed Sources:	
Cumulative Bulletin	Government Printing Office
Public Law Legislative History	Commerce Clearing House
Primary Sources (since 1968)	Bureau of National Affairs

The Committee Reports and other legislative items can also be found at various nonsubscription Internet sites. Examples of such sites would be:

http://thomas.loc.gov
http://www.house.gov/jct
http://www.house.gov/ways_means/
http://www.senate.gov/~finance/

Commerce Clearing House and the Research Institute of America both publish, usually in paperback form, a collection of Committee Reports (or excerpts thereof) whenever a major new tax law is passed. If a tax researcher wants to find the Committee Reports that underlie a statutory provision, he or she also can use reference materials that are included in the bodies of most of the commercial tax services or in the index to the *Cumulative Bulletin.*

Exhibit 3–8 gives examples of the Committee Reports, by Public Law (P.L.) number, that have amended Code § 117. The Committee Reports Findings List in Commerce Clearing House's *Citator,* Volume M–Z, is a good place for the tax researcher to locate a Committee Report(s) by P.L. number. See Chapter 6 of this text for a detailed review of the use of citators.

In addition to the Committee Reports, the Floor Debate Report may be of value to the tax researcher. The Floor Debate Report includes a summary of what was said from

EXHIBIT 3–8 Committee Reports for Code § 117 (Qualified Scholarships) since 1980

P.L. 100-647, §§ 1011, 4001
   Joint Conference Committee, 1988-3 C.B. 473.
P.L. 99-514, §§ 123, 1114, 1151
   Joint Conference Committee, 1986-3 C.B. (Vol. 4) 1.
   Senate Finance Committee, 1986-3 C.B. (Vol. 3) 1.
   House Ways and Means Committee, 1986-3 C.B. (Vol. 2) 1.
P.L. 98-369, § 532
   Joint Conference Committee, 1984-3 (Vol. 2) C.B. 1.
P.L. 96-541, § 5
   Senate Finance Committee, 1980-2 C.B. 599.

the floor of the House or Senate concerning the proposed bill. It may include some detailed or technical information that is excluded from the Committee Report. The Floor Debate Report is included in the *Congressional Record* for the day of the debate.

Internal Revenue Code

After the Sixteenth Amendment was ratified in 1913, Congress passed a series of self-contained revenue acts, each of which formed the entire income tax law of the United States. For about two decades, Congress passed such a free-standing revenue act every year or two. By the 1930s, however, this series of revenue acts, and the task of rewriting the entire tax statute so often, had become unmanageable. Thus, in 1939, Congress replaced the revenue acts with the *Internal Revenue Code of 1939,* the first fully organized federal tax law.

Although the concept of a free-standing tax code, as part of the entire *United States Code,* was a good idea, the organization of the *Internal Revenue Code of 1939* left little room to accommodate subsequent changes to the law. Accordingly, the 1939 Code was replaced with a reorganized, more flexible codification in 1954. Due to extensive revisions to the Code that were made as part of the Tax Reform Act of 1986, the statute was renamed the *Internal Revenue Code of 1986.* Thus, although the statute still follows the 1954 numbering system and organization, the official title of the extant U.S. tax law is the *Internal Revenue Code of 1986, as Amended.*

The principal sources of tax laws of the United States since 1913, then, have been identified as follows.

Period	Principal U.S. Tax Law
1913–39	Periodic Revenue Acts
1939–54	*Internal Revenue Code of 1939*
1954–86	*Internal Revenue Code of 1954*
1986–Present	*Internal Revenue Code of 1986*

Many provisions of the 1939 Code were carried over into the *Internal Revenue Code of 1954* without substantive change; some of these sections were adopted into the Code verbatim, although all of the sections were renumbered as part of the 1954 reorganization.

The *Internal Revenue Code* is part of the *United States Code,* which is a codification of all of the federal laws of the United States. The elements of the *United States Code* are organized alphabetically and assigned title numbers. Accordingly, the *Internal Revenue Code* constitutes Title 26 of the *United States Code;* its neighbors in the *U.S. Code* include "Insane Asylums" and "Intoxicating Liquors."

Organization of the *Internal Revenue Code*

The *Internal Revenue Code* is organized into several levels or subdivisions, as follows.

1. Subtitles
2. Chapters
3. Subchapters
4. Parts
5. Subparts
6. Sections
7. Subsections

Subtitles of the Code are assigned a capital letter to identify them (currently A through I are used). Generally, each subtitle contains all of the tax provisions that relate to a well-defined area of the tax law. Exhibit 3–9 identifies the subtitles of the current Code. The tax researcher spends most of his or her time working with Subtitles A, Income Taxes; B, Estate and Gift Taxes; and F, Procedure and Administration. The other subtitles typically are used only from time to time for special research problems.

Each subtitle contains a number of chapters, numbered, although not continuously, from 1 through 98. These chapter numbers do not start over at each subtitle; rather, they are used in ascending order throughout the Code. Thus, for example, there is only one Chapter 11 in the *Internal Revenue Code*, not nine of them. Each chapter contains the tax provisions that relate to a more narrowly defined area of the tax law than is addressed by the subtitles. Most of the subtitles include several chapters. Exhibit 3–10 examines the numbering system of the chapters of the *Internal Revenue Code*, concentrating on selected important chapters.

The chapters of the *Internal Revenue Code* are further divided into subchapters. Typically a subchapter contains a group of provisions that relates to a fairly specific area of the tax law. Subchapters sometimes are divided into parts, which may be divided into subparts. Letters are used to denote subchapters, and the lettering scheme starts over with each chapter. Thus, there may be a Subchapter A in each chapter.

Many times, tax practitioners use the subchapter designation as a shorthand reference to identify a certain area of taxation. For example, Subchapter C of Chapter 1 of Subtitle A of the *Internal Revenue Code* includes many of the basic corporate income tax provisions. Thus, when a tax practitioner wants to refer to a corporate tax matter, he or she often simply identifies it as a "Subchapter C" issue. Exhibit 3–11 identifies the subchapters of Chapter 1 (Income Taxes) of the Code.

Most of the Code's subchapters are divided into parts. The parts provide a natural grouping of provisions that address essentially the same issue. Not all subchapters are divided into parts, and occasionally the parts are not numbered consecutively. For instance, the parts of Chapter 1, Subchapter A (i.e., normal income taxes), are

Part I	Tax on Individuals
Part II	Tax on Corporations
Part III	Changes in Rates during a Taxable Year
Part IV	Credits against Tax
Part VI	Alternative Minimum Tax
Part VII	Environmental Tax

EXHIBIT 3–9 Subtitles of the *Internal Revenue Code*, as amended

Subtitle	Tax Law Included
A	Income Taxes
B	Estate and Gift Taxes
C	Employment Taxes
D	Miscellaneous Excise Taxes
E	Alcohol; Tobacco; Miscellaneous Excise Taxes
F	Procedure and Administration
G	Joint Committee on Taxation
H	Presidential Election Campaign Financing
I	Trust Funds

EXHIBIT 3–10   Key chapters of the *Internal Revenue Code*

Chapter	Subjects Included
1	Normal Taxes and Surtaxes
2	Self-Employment Tax
6	Consolidated Returns
11	Estate Taxes
12	Gift Taxes
61	Administration/Information
79	Definitions

The most important division of the *Internal Revenue Code* for the tax researcher is the section, because the Code is arranged so that its primary unit is the section number. The sections currently are numbered 1 through 9602, although not all of the numbers are used. Each section number is used only once in the Code. The researcher can refer to a specific provision of the *Internal Revenue Code* by its section number, and not be concerned about duplication in another part of the law. Indeed, the most common element of the jargon of the tax practitioner community is the Code section number, and tax researchers *must* learn to identify important tax provisions merely by the corresponding section number.

Code sections can be divided into various smaller elements for the convenience of the drafter or user of the section. A section can contain subsections, paragraphs,

EXHIBIT 3–11   Subchapters of Chapter 1 (Normal Taxes), Subtitle A (Income Taxes), *Internal Revenue Code*

Subchapter	Topic(s) Included
A	Determination of Tax Liability
B	Computation of Taxable Income
C	Corporate Distributions and Adjustments
D	Deferred Compensation
E	Accounting Periods and Methods
F	Tax-Exempt Organizations
G	Corporate Accumulations/Personal Holding Companies
H	Banking Institutions
I	Natural Resources
J	Income Taxation of Estates and Trusts
K	Partnerships and Partners
L	Insurance Companies
M	Mutual Funds
N	International Taxation
O	Property Transactions
P	Capital Gains and Losses
Q	Readjustment of Tax between Years and Special Limitations
R	[Repealed]
S	S Corporations and Shareholders
T	Cooperatives and Patrons
U	[Repealed]
V	Bankruptcy Effects

subparagraphs, and clauses. Sections are denoted by numbers (1, 2, etc.), subsections by lowercase letters (a, b, etc.), paragraphs by numbers, subparagraphs by capital letters (A, B, etc.), and clauses by lowercase roman numerals (i, ii, etc.). In citing a Code section, one uses parentheses for each division that occurs after the section number. Exhibit 3–12 provides a specific interpretation of a Code section citation.

Although there are thousands of Code sections, certain ones contain basic principles that affect most tax situations (Exhibit 3–13). The tax researcher should be familiar with this group of Code sections for efficient analysis of his or her clients' tax problems.

Where to Find the *Internal Revenue Code*

The amended *Internal Revenue Code* can be found in several places. National publishers such as Research Institute of America (RIA), West, and Commerce Clearing House (CCH) publish paperback versions of the Code for use by tax practitioners. In addition, the text of the Code may be found in most commercial tax services and as Title 26 of the *United States Code.*

The type of tax service will indicate the probable location of the original language of the Code in the service. Typically, an annotated tax service (refer to Chapter 2 to review this definition) will include the text of the Code with the related section's discussion. On the other hand, a topical tax service typically reproduces the text of the Code in an appendix to pertinent chapters or volumes of the service.

The *U.S. Code* and the *Internal Revenue Code* (which is Title 26 of the *U.S. Code*) can also be found at various nonsubscription Internet sites. An example of such site would be:

http://law.house.gov/uscsrch.htm

Occasionally, a tax researcher needs to refer to a source that originated from the *Internal Revenue Code of 1939.* Many of the provisions of the 1986 (and 1954) Code can be found in the 1939 Code. Exhibit 3–14 gives examples of 1986 Code sections and their 1939 Code equivalents.

Other useful indices to the Code itself are provided by the editors of the tax services. For example, several useful tables are included in the Code volumes of the Commerce Clearing House tax service. In Cross-Reference Table 1, 1939 Code sections are cross-referenced to their 1954 (and 1986) counterparts. In Table 2 of the CCH service, current Code sections are cross-referenced to the 1939 Code.

Table III of this feature cross-references the Code sections within the current Code. These three tables can be useful to the tax researcher when he or she needs to find a 1939 Code section number, perhaps in interpreting a court case that addresses a pre-1954 Code issue, or in identifying situations where a Code section is referred to elsewhere in the current Code, or perhaps to find out whether other Code sections provide information bearing on the section being reviewed.

Most tax services also contain information about the history of each Code section. Typically, at the end of the text of each Code section, the editors include a list of the Public Laws that have altered or amended the section. This listing generally includes a reference to the section as it existed prior to amendment, as well as the effective date of the amendment to the law. The tax researcher must be careful to consider the impact of any such amendments. Exhibit 3–15 illustrates the Public Law history with respect to a specific Code section.

One other publication will prove to be valuable if the researcher is addressing issues that predate the 1954 Code. *Seidman's Legislative History of Federal Income*

EXHIBIT 3–12   Interpreting a Code section citation

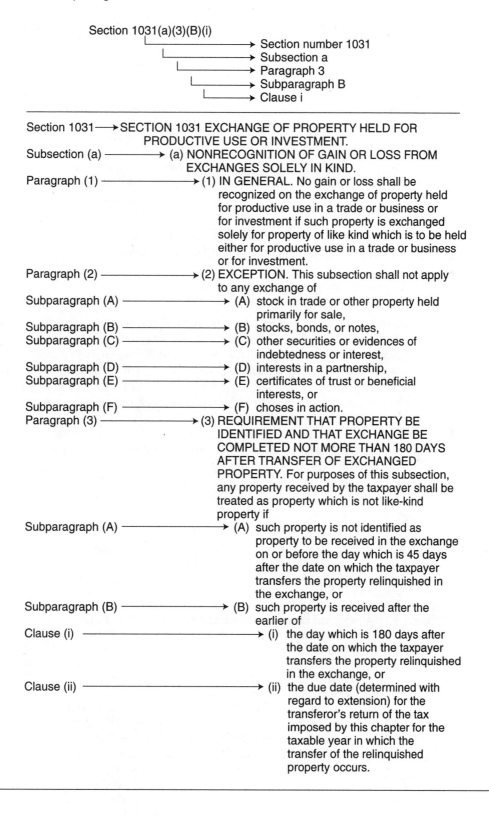

EXHIBIT 3–13 Some important Code sections

Section Number	Contents
1	Individual Tax Rates
11	Corporate Tax Rates
61	Definition of Gross Income
62	Deductions for Adjusted Gross Income
162	Trade or Business Deductions
163	Interest Deduction
164	Deduction for Taxes
165	Losses
167, 168	Depreciation, Cost Recovery
212	Production-of-Income Expenses

Tax Laws details the historical evolution of the early tax law. It explains how certain provisions evolved into their current form in the Code.

Interpreting the *Internal Revenue Code*

One of the greatest problems for a tax researcher is the interpretation of the *Internal Revenue Code*. Often, Code provisions are long, interrelated, and confusing. For example, several sentences in the Code exceed 300 words; one of them exceeds 400 words. In researching a client's tax problem, one must read each Code section that might apply. Many times, a single phrase or clause in the section may prevent the client from being subject to the provision, or may contain other unexpected implications for the client's situation.

A researcher, in his or her initial review, may find the topical index, which is included by most publishers of the Code, a useful tool in locating a starting point or the relevant Code section. In reading, interpreting, and evaluating a selected Code section, the tax researcher must be especially critical of the language used through-

EXHIBIT 3–14 Examples of 1986 Code sections derived from the 1939 Code

1986 Code Section	1939 Code Section
§ 61, Gross income defined	§ 22(a)
§ 71, Alimony and separate maintenance payments	§ 22(k)
§ 103, Interest on state and local bonds	§ 22(b)(4)
§ 151, Allowance of deductions for personal exemptions	§ 25(b)
§ 162, Trade or business expenses	§ 23(a)(1)
§ 172, Net operating loss deduction	§ 122
§ 212, Expenses for production of income	§ 23(a)(2)
§ 301, Distributions of property	§ 22(e), 115(a), (b), (d), (e), and (j)
§ 316, Dividends defined	§ 115(a) and (b)
§ 701, Partners, not partnership, subject to tax	§ 181

EXHIBIT 3–15   1984–1997 P.L. Amendments to Section 1031

1997

> Subsection (h). -- Pub. L. 105-34, Section 1052(a), amended subsection (h). [Effective for transfers after June 8, 1997, in taxable years ending after such date, for special rules see "Effective Date for 1997 Amendment" below.]
>
> Prior to its amendment, subsection (h) read as follows:
>
> (h) SPECIAL RULE FOR FOREIGN REAL PROPERTY
>
> For purposes of this section, real property located in the United States and real property located outside the United States are not property of a like kind.

1990

> Subsection (a)(2). -- Pub. L. 101-508, Section 11703(d)(1), inserted attend "For purposes of this section, an interest in a partnership which has in effect a valid election under section 761(a) to be excluded from the application of all of subchapter K shall be treated as an interest in each of the assets of such partnership and not as an interest in a partnership."
>
> Subsection (f)(3). -- Pub. L. 101-508, Section 11701(h), substituted "section 267(b) or 707(b)(1)" for "section 267(b)".

1989

> Subsections (f) to (h). -- Pub. L. 101-239 added subsecs. (f) to (h).

1986

> Subsection (a)(3)(A). -- Pub. L. 99-514 substituted "on or before the day" for "before the day".

1984

> Subsection (a). -- Pub. L. 98-369, Section 77(a), in amending subsect. generally, designated existing provisions as par. (1), substituted "No gain or loss shall be recognized on the exchange of property held for productive use in a trade or business or for investment if such property is exchanged solely for property of like kind which is to be held either for productive use in a trade or business or for investment" for "No gain or loss shall be recognized if property held for productive use in trade or business or for investment (not including stock in trade or other property held primarily for sale, nor stocks, bonds, notes, choses in action, certificates of trust or beneficial interest, or other securities or evidences of indebtedness or interest) is exchanged solely for property of a like kind to be held either for productive use in trade or business or for investment", and added pars. (2) and (3).

out the section. Many, if not most, Code sections contain a general rule, followed by specific conditions that must be satisfied in order to apply the provision, and situations under which the taxpayer is excepted from the general rule. In some cases, the exceptions to the general rule are further modified to provide for exceptions to the general exceptions. Moreover, some exceptions to a Code section are addressed not within the same section, but in another section of the Code. Therefore, all relevant provisions must be read carefully.

In addition to being aware of the required conditions for application of a section, as well as the exceptions thereto, the researcher must be aware of the definitions of terms used in the section; pertinent definitions may be given within the section or in some other provision of the Code. These definitions may be significantly different from the common use of the term.

In § 7701, the text defines many of the terms used throughout the Code, but these definitions may be superseded by material contained within the applicable Code section. In addition, the researcher may need to look beyond the Code such as to the Regulations or other authority, to determine the conditions that a specific term may encompass. In all cases, the researcher should avoid jumping to premature conclusions until a thorough analysis of all relevant Code sections has been completed.

The tax researcher must be careful not to overlook words that connect phrases, such as "and" and "or." These words have very different logical meanings, and, even when the words are "hidden" at the end of the previous clause or subparagraph, they may significantly change the outcome of a research project. The word "and" is conjunctive; the word "or" is disjunctive. If the word "and" lies between two phrases, both of them must be true for the provision to apply to the client's problem. However, if the word "or" lies between two phrases, then only one of them must be true for the provision to apply.

The researcher also must be careful with words that modify percentage or dollar amounts. The phrases "less than 50%," "more than 50%," and "not less than 50%" have very different meanings in determining whether the provisions of a section apply. The researcher also must distinguish between such terms as "30 days" and "one month," because they usually identify different time periods.

> **Example 3–2** Conflicting Code Sections. Paul is a roofing contractor and has a truck he uses 100 percent of the time in his business. The truck cost $35,000 three years ago, and Paul has claimed ACRS of $24,920 on the truck, which leaves him an adjusted basis of $10,080. Paul sells the truck for $22,080 resulting in a gain of $12,000 on the truck. How is he to treat this gain for tax purposes?
>
> In the *Internal Revenue Code*, Paul finds that when depreciable property used in a trade or business [§ 1231(b)] is sold, the gain is treated as a long-term capital gain [§ 1231(a)]. Thus, he might report the gain on his tax return as a long-term capital gain. However, in § 1245(a), Paul discovers that gain on depreciable personal property (in this case, the truck) is ordinary income to the extent of depreciation claimed since 1961. Thus, § 1245 would indicate the gain is ordinary, not long-term, capital.
>
> How is the problem resolved? In § 1245(d), Paul finds a directive that the recapture provision "shall apply notwithstanding any other provision of this subtitle [of the Code]." As a result, he must report the gain as ordinary income on his tax return, not long-term capital gain.
>
> If Paul had read only § 1231 of the Code and not § 1245, he would have arrived at a different conclusion about the gain. In many situations, when Code sections conflict, the resolution of the conflict may not be as easy as in this example.

When analyzing a provision that recently has been changed by Congress, a researcher must be very careful to cross-reference all of the uses of terms whose definitions have been affected by the new law. Often, Congress does not use the care necessary to ascertain that all of the "loose ends" of the new provisions have been tied up. In recent years, almost every major change in the tax law has been followed by a "technical corrections act," to remove errors in implementing and interpreting the new provisions of the law, as well as to clarify problems that arise in integrating the new provisions with the existing provisions of the Code. Most of these corrections are identified by practitioners whose clients' situations are adversely affected by a given reading of the amended law; thus, the typical technical corrections act testifies as much to the thoroughness of the practitioners' research as to shoddy drafting of the law by Congress.

Because the provisions of the *Internal Revenue Code* change frequently, the researcher must be aware of the effective dates of the various changes to the law. A provision may not go into effect immediately upon its adoption by Congress. The date of the act with which the change in law is passed is not always indicative of the effective date of the provision. Often, various provisions under the same tax law will become effective on different dates and, in fact, may have effective dates that precede the date of the tax act. Similarly, when a provision of the tax law is deleted from the Code, the provision may be left in effect for a designated period of time before it actually expires. Transitional rules may also apply. The effective date for a change in the tax law usually may be found in the explanation of the Public Laws, which follows the pertinent Code section (see, for example, Exhibit 3–15). In some cases, the researcher may need to look to the explanation under another Code section for the effective date of a provision. The researcher must be careful to align the client's facts with the effective law at the pertinent dates, or a serious mistake could be made in the research conclusion.

Finally, the tax researcher must be aware that not *all* of the answers to a tax question will be found in the Code. The Code may be silent concerning the problem at hand, the application of Code language to the fact situation at hand may not be clear, or Code sections may appear to be in conflict. Thus, the researcher must look for an answer from other sources, such as tax treaties, administrative rulings (see Chapter 4), judicial decisions (see Chapter 5), or secondary sources of the law (see Chapters 6 through 9). Alternatively, the controlling law may be found in other parts of the Code, such as tariff or bankruptcy laws. Exhibit 3–16 lists examples of federal laws other than the Code that affect specific tax matters.

▶ _____ Summary

The three major sources of statutory tax law are the Constitution, tax treaties, and the *Internal Revenue Code*. The tax researcher must thoroughly understand each of these sources and the interrelationships among them. The Constitution is the basis for all federal laws. The tax treaties are agreements between countries, negotiated by

---

EXHIBIT 3–16   Examples of federal laws other than the *Internal Revenue Code* that may affect a tax transaction

Administrative Procedure Act
Alaska Native Claims Settlement Act
Atomic Energy Act Tax Provision
Bank Holding Company Act of 1956
Civil Rights Attorneys' Fees Awards Act of 1976
Financial Institutions Reform, Recovery, and Enforcement Act of 1989
Metric Conversion Act of 1975
Merchant Marine Act: Capital Construction Fund
New York City Pension Act
Organic Act of Guam

the President and approved by the Senate, that cover taxpayers subject to the tax laws of both countries. Tax treaties generally have a lesser or complementary authority compared to the *Internal Revenue Code*. The greatest volume of tax statutes is found in the *Internal Revenue Code*, which is Title 26 of the *United States Code*. The Code contains the tax laws that Congress has passed, and it is the basic document for most U.S. tax provisions.

► Key Words

By the time you complete this chapter, you should be comfortable discussing each of the following terms. If you need additional review of any of these items, return to the appropriate material in the chapter or consult the glossary to this text.

Committee Report   Secondary authority
Internal Revenue Code   Statutory sources
Primary authority   Tax treaty

► Discussion Questions

1. What are the three primary statutory sources of U.S. federal tax law?
2. Discuss the effect of *Pollock v. Farmers' Loan and Trust Co.* on the development of U.S. income tax laws.
3. The Sixteenth Amendment to the Constitution had a significant effect on the U.S. income tax. What was it?
4. What did the U.S. Supreme Court hold in *Flint v. Stone Tracy Co.* in 1911?
5. Tax protestors who file "frivolous" tax returns or bring "frivolous" proceedings before the U.S. Tax Court are subject to certain fines or other penalties. What are the grounds for imposing each penalty? What is the maximum amount of each penalty?
6. Discuss the powers of taxation that are granted to Congress by the U.S. Constitution. Are any limits placed on the powers of Congress to so tax?
7. Have the federal courts ever held federal estate and gift taxes to be unconstitutional?
8. What is a tax treaty? Explain the purpose of a tax treaty. What matters generally are covered in a tax treaty?
9. How is a tax treaty terminated?
10. When an *Internal Revenue Code* section and a tax treaty provision appear to conflict, which usually prevails?
11. Describe the ratification process for a tax treaty between the United States and another country.
12. The tax researcher must be able to find descriptions of tax treaties to solve certain tax problems. List at least five different publications and their publishers that provide this information. State whether each publication gives the complete text of the treaty or just a summary.
13. Briefly summarize the usual steps of the legislative process for development of federal tax legislation.
14. As a bill proceeds through Congress, various Committee Reports are generated. List the three Committee Reports that typically are prepared for a new tax law.
15. When are Committee Reports useful to a tax researcher?

16. What is a Public Law number? In P.L. 100-203, what do the "100" and the "203" indicate?

17. Where would a tax researcher find pertinent Committee Reports? List at least four publications and their publishers that include tax-related Committee Reports. Is there an index that would help a tax researcher locate a specific Committee Report? If so, where might such an index be found?

18. In addition to the Committee Reports, which are a by-product to the development of tax legislation, what other report may be of value to the tax researcher analyzing a new provision of the tax law? Why?

19. Discuss the evolution of today's *Internal Revenue Code.*

20. The *Internal Revenue Code* is Title 26 of the *United States Code.* How is the *Internal Revenue Code* subdivided?

21. How are the subtitles of the *Internal Revenue Code* identified? What generally is contained in a subtitle?

22. In the citation § 101(a)(2)(B), what does the "a" stand for? What do the "2" and the "B" indicate to a tax researcher?

23. Not all statutory tax laws are found in the *Internal Revenue Code.* Is this statement true or false? Discuss briefly.

24. Discuss briefly the events leading to the passage of the Sixteenth Amendment to the U.S. Constitution.

▶ _____ Exercises

25. What is found in each of the following subtitles of the *Internal Revenue Code?*

    a. Subtitle B
    b. Subtitle F
    c. Subtitle A
    d. Subtitle C

26. Each subtitle of the *Internal Revenue Code* contains several chapters. How are chapters identified? What generally is included in a chapter of the Code?

27. Identify the general content of each of the following chapters of the *Internal Revenue Code.*

    a. Chapter 11
    b. Chapter 61
    c. Chapter 1
    d. Chapter 12

28. Chapters of the *Internal Revenue Code* are subdivided into subchapters. How are subchapters identified? What generally is contained in a subchapter?

29. What is the general content of each of the following subchapters of the *Internal Revenue Code?*

    a. Subchapter C
    b. Subchapter K
    c. Subchapter S
    d. Subchapter E

30. Subchapters of the *Internal Revenue Code* sometimes contain parts. How are such parts identified? What is contained in a typical part?

31. The most important division of the *Internal Revenue Code* is the section. Sections usually are subdivided into various smaller elements. Name several of these elements and state how they are denoted.

32. Do section numbers repeat themselves, or is each one unique?

33. Identify the general contents of each of the following *Internal Revenue Code* sections.

    a. § 61
    b. § 162
    c. § 1
    d. § 212

34. Use a computer tax service (e.g., RIA CheckPoint, Lexis, Kleinrock's, etc.) to answer the following questions.

    a. Which computer service did you use?
    b. What is the general content of *Internal Revenue Code* § 28?
    c. What is the general content of *Internal Revenue Code* § 141?
    d. What is the general content of *Internal Revenue Code* § 166?
    e. Print a copy of any one of the above Code sections and attach it to your assignment.

35. Use a computer tax service (e.g., RIA CheckPoint, Lexis, Kleinrock's, etc.) to answer the following questions.

    a. Which computer tax service did you use?
    b. What is the general content of *Internal Revenue Code* § 117?
    c. What is the general content of *Internal Revenue Code* § 165?
    d. What is the general content of *Internal Revenue Code* § 304?
    e. Print a copy of any one of the above Code sections and attach it to your assignment.

36. Name several locations where a tax researcher would find the text of the current *Internal Revenue Code*.

37. If a tax researcher wants to know if there is an equivalent 1939 Code section for a specific 1986 Code section, how would he or she locate it?

38. One important problem that faces a tax researcher is interpretation of the *Internal Revenue Code*. Comment on each of the following interpretation problems.

    a. Exceptions to a Code section
    b. Words that connect phrases, such as "and" and "or"
    c. Recent changes in the Code
    d. Effective dates
    e. Words that modify percentages, dollar amounts, or time

39. Comment on the statement, "All tax questions can be answered using the *Internal Revenue Code*."

40. Does the United States have an income tax treaty with any of the following countries? If it does, in what year was the treaty signed? State where you found this information.

    a. Japan
    b. United Kingdom

    c. Egypt

    d. Germany

41. Does the United States have an estate tax treaty with any of the following countries? If it does, in what year was the treaty signed? State where you found this information.

    a. Canada

    b. Finland

    c. Hungary

    d. Italy

42. Give the number of the first paragraph in the CCH's *Standard Federal Tax Reports* and RIA's *Tax Coordinator* that addresses the tax treaty between the United States and each of the following countries.

    a. Germany

    b. Italy

    c. Japan

    d. Korea

    e. Brazil

43. In a printed copy of the *Internal Revenue Code*, read Section 119.

    a. How many subsection(s) does § 119 include?

    b. How many paragraph(s) does § 119(b) include?

    c. How many subparagraph(s) does § 119(b)(3) include?

    d. In which subtitle of the Code is § 119 found?

    e. In which chapter of the Code is § 119 found?

    f. In which subchapter of the Code is § 119 found?

44. Use a computer tax service (e.g., RIA CheckPoint, Lexis, Kleinrock's, etc.) to locate § 117 of the *Internal Revenue Code*. Answer the following questions.

    a. Which computer tax service did you use?

    b. How many subsection(s) does § 117 include?

    c. How many paragraph(s) does § 117(b) include?

    d. How many subparagraph(s) does § 117(d)(2) include?

    e. Print a copy of this section and attach it to your assignment.

45. Use a computer tax service (e.g., RIA CheckPoint, Lexis, Kleinrock's, etc.) to locate § 385 of the *Internal Revenue Code*. Answer the following questions.

    a. Which computer tax service did you use?

    b. How many subsection(s) does § 385 include?

    c. How many paragraph(s) does § 385(b) include?

    d. Print a copy of this section and attach it to your assignment.

46. When was each of the following sections originally enacted? State how you obtained this information.

    a. § 843

    b. § 131

    c. § 469

    d. § 263A

47. In which subtitle, chapter, and subchapter of the 1986 Code are each of the following sections found?

    a. § 32
    b. § 172
    c. § 2039
    d. § 6013

48. List the first three section numbers and titles of each of the following subchapters of Chapter 1 of the *Internal Revenue Code*.

    a. Subchapter B
    b. Subchapter E
    c. Subchapter J
    d. Subchapter S

49. What is the title and section number of the first two sections of each of the following subchapters (of Chapter 1) of the *Internal Revenue Code*?

    a. Subchapter A
    b. Subchapter C
    c. Subchapter F
    d. Subchapter W

50. What is the title and section number of the second and third section of each of the following subchapters (of Chapter 1) of the *Internal Revenue Code*?

    a. Subchapter A
    b. Subchapter C
    c. Subchapter D
    d. Subchapter K

51. Use the Findings List in Code Volume I of the CCH tax service and give the popular name (if any) and the enactment date for each of the following laws.

    a. P.L. 98-369
    b. P.L. 94-455
    c. P.L. 91-172
    d. P.L. 97-354

52. Use Cross-Reference Table III of the CCH Code volumes to list which other Code sections refer to the following 1986 sections. If no other sections refer to the named section number, say so.

    a. § 1
    b. § 61
    c. § 212
    d. § 280A

53. Identify the equivalent section of the 1954 Code for each of the following sections of the 1939 Code. If there is no equivalent section, say so.

    a. § 1
    b. § 113(a)
    c. § 22(a)

    d. § 115(a)

    e. § 181

54. Use a computer tax service (e.g., RIA CheckPoint, Lexis, Kleinrock's, etc.) to locate the following Code sections. What other Code sections reference each of the sections you found? State which computer tax service you used to complete this assignment.

    a. § 72

    b. § 307

    c. § 446

55. Name the article and section of the U.S. Constitution that gives Congress the power to tax.

56. Enumerate the Code sections that contain the chief tax law provisions on the following topics.

    a. S corporations

    b. Personal holding company tax

    c. Gift tax

    d. Tax accounting methods

57. Use a nonsubscription Internet site to determine how many Senators are on the Senate Finance Committee. Who is the Chair of the Finance Committee? State where you found this information.

58. Use a nonsubscription Internet site to determine how many Representatives are on the House Ways and Means Committee. Who is the Chair of the Ways and Means Committee? State where you found this information.

59. Use a nonsubscription Internet site to determine what is contained in each of the following. State where you found this information.

    a. U.S. Const. art. I, § 9 cl. 3

    b. U.S. Const. art. I, § 8 cl. 1

    c. U.S. Const. art. II, § 2 cl. 2

60. Locate and print the first page of a House Way and Means Committee Report using only a nonsubscription Internet site. State where you found this information.

▶ _____ Research Cases

61. Private G.I. Jane was a soldier in the Gulf War. Her salary was $1,300 per month, and she was in the war zone for eight months. How much of her salary is taxable for the eight months? In answering this case, use only the *Internal Revenue Code* for your research. *Computer search key words:* combat, pay, officers, enlisted

62. Carol received a gift of stock from her favorite uncle. The stock had a fair market value of $30,000 and a basis to the uncle of $10,000 at the date of the gift. How much is taxable to Carol from this gift? In answering this case, use only the *Internal Revenue Code* for your research. *Computer search key words:* gift, gross income, exclusion

63. Maria is an independent long-haul trucker. She receives a speeding ticket for $125, which she pays. Can Maria deduct the ticket on Schedule C? In answering this case, use only the *Internal Revenue Code* for your research. *Computer search key words:* fines, penalties, deduction

64. Julie loaned her friend Nathan $2,500. Nathan did not repay the debt and skipped town. Can Julie claim any deduction? In answering this case, use only the *Internal Revenue Code* for your research. *Computer search key words:* loss, bad debt, worthless

65. In December of 19x1, Ann's twelve-year-old cousin, Susan, came to live with her after Susan's parents met an untimely death in a car accident. In 19x2, Ann provided all normal support (e.g., food, clothing, education) for Susan. Ann did not formally adopt Susan. If Susan lived in the household for the entire year, can Ann claim a dependency exemption for her cousin for the 19x2 tax year? In answering this case, use only the *Internal Revenue Code* for your research. *Computer search key words:* dependent, household, support

66. John and Maria support their twenty-one-year-old son, Bill. The son earned $10,500 last year working in a part-time job. Bill went to college part time in the spring semester of the current year. To complete his degree, Bill started school full time in the fall. The fall semester at Bill's college runs from August 20 to December 20. Can John and Maria claim Bill as a dependent on the current year's tax return, even if Bill earns $9,000 gross income? Assume any dependency test not mentioned has been met. In answering this case, use a computer tax service with only the *Internal Revenue Code* database selected. State your key words and which computer tax service you used to arrive at your answer.

67. George and Linda are divorced and own a house from the marriage. Under the divorce decree, Linda pays George $3,000 per month alimony. Since the real estate market has collapsed in the area where they live, George and Linda cannot sell the house. Since they are still friends, they decide to live in separate wings of the house until the real estate market recovers. If George and Linda live together for the entire current year, can Linda claim a deduction for the alimony paid to George? In answering this case, use a computer tax service with only the *Internal Revenue Code* database selected. State your key words and which computer tax service you used to arrive at your answer.

68. Juan sold IBM stock to Richard for a $10,000 loss. Richard is the husband of Juan's sister. How much of the loss can Juan deduct in the current year, if Juan's taxable income is $55,000 and he has no other capital transactions? In answering this case, use a computer tax service with only the *Internal Revenue Code* database selected. State your key words and which computer tax service you used to arrive at your answer.

69. Tex is a rancher. This year her herd of cattle was infested with hoof-and-mouth disease and had to be destroyed. Tex's insurance policy reimburses her for an amount in excess of the tax basis in the cattle, thereby creating an "insurance gain." After receiving the insurance proceeds, Tex buys a new herd of cattle. Can Tex defer the recognition of this insurance gain on the destroyed herd? In answering this case, use a computer tax service with only the *Internal Revenue Code* database selected. State your key words and which computer tax service you used to arrive at your answer.

70. Betty owed Martha $5,000. In payment of this debt, Betty transferred to Martha a life insurance policy on Betty, with a cash surrender value of $5,000. The face value of the policy is $100,000. Martha names herself as beneficiary of the policy and continues to make the premium payments. After Martha has paid $15,000 in premiums, Betty dies and Martha collects $100,000. Is any of the $100,000 Martha received taxable? In answering this case, use a computer tax service with only the *Internal Revenue Code* database selected. State your key words and which computer tax service you used to arrive at your answer.

71. On May 1, Rick formed a new corporation, Red, Inc. He spent $3,000 in legal fees and paid the state $600 in incorporation fees to set up Red Corporation. Red Corporation started operating its business on May 10. Can Rick or Red Corporation deduct either of these organizational fees? In answering this case, use a computer tax service with only the *Internal Revenue Code* database selected. State your key words and which computer tax service you used to arrive at your answer.

72. This year, there were massive brush fires in the interior of Mexico. Amy gave $10,000 to the Mexican Relief Foundation, which is located in Mexico City. The funds were used to provide food, clothing, and shelter to the victims of the Mexican fires. Is Amy's charitable contribution deductible for income tax purposes? In answering this case, use a computer tax service with only the *Internal Revenue Code* database selected. State your key words and which computer tax service you used to arrive at your answer.

73. Curtis is fifty years old and has an IRA with substantial funds in it. His son, Curtis, Jr., was accepted to Yale University upon graduating from high school. Curtis had not planned for this and needs to draw $25,000 per year out of his IRA to help pay the tuition and fees at Yale. What are the tax consequences of the withdrawals from the IRA? In answering this case, use a computer tax service with only the *Internal Revenue Code* database selected. State your key words and which computer tax service you used to arrive at your answer.

74. Dennis is an executive of Gold Corporation. He receives a one-for-one distribution of stock rights for each share of common stock he owns. On the date of distribution the stock rights have a fair market value of $2 per right and the stock has fair market value of $20 per share. Dennis owns 10,000 shares of the stock with a basis of $5 per share. If Dennis does not make any special elections with regards to the stock rights, what is his basis in the rights? In answering this case, use a computer tax service with only the *Internal Revenue Code* database selected. State your key words and which computer tax service you used to arrive at your answer.

Administrative Regulations and Rulings

The Treasury Department is charged with administering the tax laws of the United States. In accomplishing this task, it makes various pronouncements to explain the *Internal Revenue Code*. Administrative pronouncements of this type constitute one of the major categories of primary tax authority. Thus, to properly research a client's tax problem, the tax researcher must understand what the various rulings represent, their significance, and their location.

The Secretary of the Treasury has the general responsibility for administering the tax law. The Secretary is a member of the President's cabinet and is not to be confused with the Treasurer of the United States. The Treasurer is another official in the Treasury Department, but is not concerned directly with tax matters.

The Internal Revenue Service is a division of the Treasury Department. It is assigned to manage day-to-day operations associated with administration of the provisions of the *Internal Revenue Code*. The chief operating official of the IRS is the Commissioner of Internal Revenue, a presidential appointee. The Treasury Secretary delegates most of the administrative responsibilities for the tax law to the IRS Commissioner.

To facilitate the IRS's administration of the tax laws, the Code authorizes the Treasury Secretary (or his or her delegate) to prescribe the Rules and Regulations necessary to administer the Code. According to § 7805(a),

> Except where such authority is expressly given by this title to any person other than an officer or employee of the Treasury Department, the Secretary shall prescribe all needful rules and regulations for the enforcement of this title, including all rules and regulations as may be necessary by reason of any alteration of law in relation to internal revenue.

This section gives the IRS general authority to issue binding Rules and Regulations concerning Title 26 of the *United States Code*. In practice, most of the IRS's pronouncements are written by IRS staff or by the office of the Chief Counsel of the IRS, who is an assistant General Counsel of the Treasury Department.

The tax researcher must be especially familiar with the four major types of pronouncements that may be forthcoming under this authority, namely, Regulations, Revenue Rulings, Revenue Procedures, and Letter Rulings. Each of these categories of rulings is issued for a different purpose and carries a different degree of authority. The first three of these categories generally are published by the IRS, while the Letter Rulings (and other pronouncements) typically are not published by any government agency. The remainder of this chapter addresses the nature and location of each of these administrative pronouncements.

Regulations

The **Regulations** constitute the IRS's and, thereby, the Treasury's official interpretation of the *Internal Revenue Code*. Regulations are issued in the form of **Treasury Decisions (TDs),** which are published in the *Federal Register* and, sometime later, in the *Internal Revenue Bulletin,* discussed later in this chapter. At least thirty days before a TD is published in final form, however, it must be issued in proposed form, allowing interested parties time to comment on it. As a result of the comments received during this process of public hearings, the IRS may make changes in the TD before its final publication.

Before and during the hearings process, the TDs are referred to as **Proposed Regulations** and, unlike Final Regulations, do not have the effect of law. After the hearings are completed, and changes (if any) have been made to the text of the TD, the TD is published in final form. Final Regulations are integrated with previously approved TDs and constitute the full set of IRS Regulations. After this integration has occurred, the TD designation usually is dropped, and the pronouncement simply is referred to as a "Regulation."

Observers have identified two distinct categories of Regulations, general and legislative. **General Regulations** are issued under the general authority granted to the IRS to interpret the language of the Code, usually under a specific Code (or Committee Report) directive of Congress, and with specific congressional authority. An example can be found under § 212, Expenses for the Production of Income. This short Code section has many pages of interpretive Regulations, providing taxpayers with operational rules for applying this provision to tax situations.

With respect to **Legislative Regulations,** the IRS is directed by Congress to fulfill effectively a law-making function and to specify the substantive requirements of a tax provision. Regulations that are ordered by the Code in this manner essentially carry the authority of the statute itself and are not easily challenged by taxpayers. Such authority is granted because, in certain (especially technical) areas of the tax law, Congress cannot or does not care to address the detailed or complex issues that are associated with an otherwise-defined tax issue. Accordingly, Congress directs the IRS to pronounce Regulations on the matter. For example, Congress delegated to the IRS the authority to prescribe Regulations necessary to carry out the provisions of § 135, which grants an exclusion for interest on certain U.S. savings bonds used for higher education expenses, including Regulations requiring record keeping and information reporting. Another example of this legislative authority is found in § 385, which directs the IRS to prescribe Regulations to distinguish debt from equity in "thinly capitalized" corporations. Legislative Regulations bear the greatest precedential value of any IRS pronouncement.

Temporary Regulations

In addition to Proposed and Final Regulations, the IRS periodically issues **Temporary Regulations** in response to a Congressional or judicial change in the tax law or its interpretation. Temporary Regulations are not subject to the public-hearings procedure that typifies the development of a Final Regulation, and they are effective immediately upon publication. Although they are effective immediately, the IRS must simultaneously issue the Regulations in proposed form; the Temporary Regulations expire three years after issuance pursuant to the statute (IRC § 7805). Temporary Regulations are issued to provide the taxpayer with immediate guidance concerning a new provision of the law, perhaps concerning filing requirements that must be satisfied immediately or the clarification of definitions and terms.

Until a Temporary Regulation is replaced with the Final Regulation under a Code section, the tax researcher should treat the Temporary Regulation as though it were final. Thus, Temporary Regulations are fully in effect and must be followed until they are superseded, whereas Proposed Regulations, having been issued only to solicit comments and to expose the IRS's proposed interpretation of the law, need not be followed as if they were law.

Effective Date of Regulations

In general, under § 7805(b), a new Regulation can be effective on the date on which such Regulation is filed with the *Federal Register*. However, there are certain situations in which a Regulation can be effective retroactively. These are:

1. The Regulation is filed or issued within 18 months of the date of the enactment of the statutory provision to which the regulation relates.
2. The Regulation is designed to prevent abuse by taxpayers.
3. The Regulation corrects a procedural defect in the issuance of a prior Regulation.
4. The Regulation relates to internal Treasury Department policies, practices, or procedures.
5. The Regulation may apply retroactively by congressional directive.
6. The Commissioner also has the power to allow taxpayers to elect to apply new Regulations retroactively.

In situations where a Regulation applies retroactively, it technically can apply starting with the date of the underlying Code section to which it relates. However, the statute of limitations may limit the application of a retroactive Regulation in many situations.

Citing a Regulation

Tax practitioners use a uniform system for citing specific Regulations. Each Regulation is assigned a unique number by the Treasury, which is broadly based on the Code section being interpreted in that Regulation. An example of this citation system appears in Exhibit 4–1. The number to the left of the period in a Regulation citation indicates the type of issue that is addressed in the pronouncement. The most commonly encountered types of Regulations include the following.

1. Income Tax
20. Estate Tax
25. Gift Tax
31. Employment Tax
301. Procedural Matters

By being familiar with this arbitrary numbering system used by the Regulations, the tax researcher immediately can identify the general issue that is addressed in a pronouncement. Note that these numbers indicating the type of issue addressed in the Regulation do not necessarily correspond to the chapter numbers of the Code sections that address the same issues.

The number to the immediate right of the period in the citation of a Regulation indicates the Code section to which the Regulation relates. In the Exhibit 4–1 example of a full citation, one can determine that this is an income tax Regulation dealing with § 262 of the *Internal Revenue Code*. The numbers and letters to the right of the section number denote the Regulation number and smaller divisions of the pronouncement. Regulation numbers typically are consecutive, starting with 0 or 1, and

EXHIBIT 4–1 Interpreting a Regulation citation

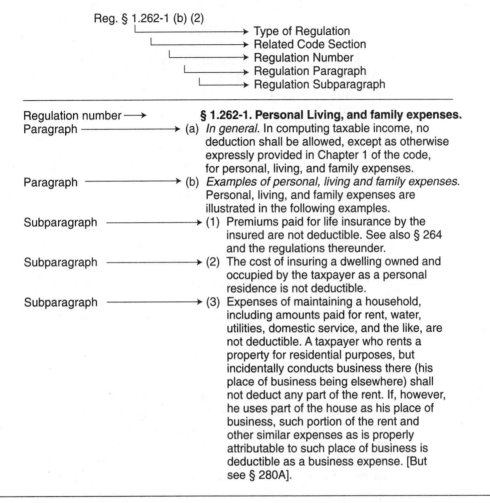

Reg. § 1.262-1 (b) (2)
→ Type of Regulation
→ Related Code Section
→ Regulation Number
→ Regulation Paragraph
→ Regulation Subparagraph

Regulation number →
Paragraph →
Paragraph →
Subparagraph →
Subparagraph →
Subparagraph →

§ 1.262-1. Personal Living, and family expenses.

(a) *In general.* In computing taxable income, no deduction shall be allowed, except as otherwise expressly provided in Chapter 1 of the code, for personal, living, and family expenses.

(b) *Examples of personal, living and family expenses.* Personal, living, and family expenses are illustrated in the following examples.

(1) Premiums paid for life insurance by the insured are not deductible. See also § 264 and the regulations thereunder.

(2) The cost of insuring a dwelling owned and occupied by the taxpayer as a personal residence is not deductible.

(3) Expenses of maintaining a household, including amounts paid for rent, water, utilities, domestic service, and the like, are not deductible. A taxpayer who rents a property for residential purposes, but incidentally conducts business there (his place of business being elsewhere) shall not deduct any part of the rent. If, however, he uses part of the house as his place of business, such portion of the rent and other similar expenses as is properly attributable to such place of business is deductible as a business expense. [But see § 280A].

follow the general order of the issues that are addressed in the corresponding Code section. The Regulation numbers, paragraphs, and so on, do not necessarily correspond, however, to the subsection or other division designations of the underlying Code section.

The numbering system for Temporary Regulations is similar to the numbering system for the Final and Proposed Regulations; however, usually the reference to or citation of a Temporary Regulation will include a "T" designating the temporary nature of the Regulation. An example of a citation for a Temporary Regulation under Code Section 280H is:

Reg. Sec. 1.280H-1T(b)(3).

Assessing Regulations

In the course of tax practice, the researcher occasionally will be faced with a question concerning the validity of a Regulation. If the practitioner disagrees with the scope or language of the Regulation, he or she bears the burden of proof to show the Regulation is improper. This can be difficult. Many Regulations simply restate the Code or Congressional Committee Reports; they are known as "hard and solid" Regulations. Moreover, because of the authority delegated to the IRS, Legislative Regulations have the full force and effect of law. Finally, the Supreme Court views General Regulations as also having the force and effect of law, unless they conflict with the statute.[1] Thus, a taxpayer challenge to a Regulation typically must assert an improper exercise of IRS power, or an overly broad application of a rule.

In questioning the provisions of a Regulation, the tax researcher must be aware of several accuracy penalties Congress has enacted in the *Internal Revenue Code*. For example, § 6662 assesses a penalty equal to 20 percent of any underpayment of tax where the underpayment is found to be due to "negligence," which includes any failure to make a reasonable attempt to comply with the Code or any evidence of disregard of Treasury Rules or Regulations. Thus, if a practitioner chooses to ignore an administrative element of the tax law, he or she must possess substantial authority to do so to avoid this penalty or others of its kind. See Chapter 13 for a more detailed examination of these provisions.

Locating Regulations

When Treasury decisions are final, they are published in the ***Internal Revenue Bulletin*** (IRB), a weekly newsletter of the IRS. Twice a year, the IRBs, reorganized by Code section, are bound into a set of volumes titled the ***Cumulative Bulletin,*** which becomes the permanent IRS location of the Regulations.

Most commercial tax services also reproduce the Regulations in their materials; annotated services usually include the text adjacent to the language of the Code and the related court case notes, and topical services usually provide an appendix that includes the edited Regulations for the volume or chapter that discusses the pertinent issue. Paperback or hardbound editions of the tax Regulations also are available from several commercial publishers, including Research Institute of America (RIA), West Publishing Company, and Commerce Clearing House (CCH) typically as a companion to a similar edition of the Code.

Exhibit 4–2 shows common places where the tax researcher can find the Regulations and most other sources of administrative tax research material.

Revenue Rulings

Revenue Rulings are second to Regulations as important administrative sources of the federal tax law. A Revenue Ruling is an official pronouncement of the National Office of the IRS; it deals with the application of the Code and Regulations to a specific factual situation, usually one that has been submitted by a taxpayer. Thus, most Revenue Rulings indicate how the IRS will treat a given taxpayer transaction. Revenue Rulings do not carry the force and effect of Regulations.

Revenue Rulings provide excellent sources of information; in fact, they are published chiefly for the purpose of guiding taxpayers. Therefore, even for a tax researcher whose client did not submit the original request for the Ruling, the result of the Ruling is of value if it concerns a transaction similar in nature, structure, or

---

[1]*Maryland Casualty Co. v. United States,* 251 U.S. 342, 40 S.Ct. 155 (1920).

EXHIBIT 4–2 Sources of administrative tax law

Computer Sources:

RIA CheckPoint Internet	Research Institute of America
RIA OnPoint CD-ROM	Research Institute of America
Westlaw CD and online	West Publishing Co.
CCH Tax Research Network	Commerce Clearing House
CCH Access CD and online	Commerce Clearing House

Printed Sources:

Tax Coordinator 2d	Research Institute of America
United States Code Annotated	West Publishing Co.
Standard Federal Tax Reports	Commerce Clearing House
Cumulative Bulletin	Government Printing Office
Public Law Legislative History	Commerce Clearing House
Primary Sources (since 1968)	Bureau of National Affairs

---

effect to the client's situation. Reliance should, however, not be placed on a Revenue Ruling if it has been affected by subsequent legislation, Regulations, Rulings, or court decisions.

Revenue Rulings adhere to a general internal structure, as illustrated in Exhibit 4–3. The typical structure is as follows.

1. *Issue:* A statement of the issue in question.
2. *Facts:* The facts on which the Revenue Ruling is based.
3. *Law and analysis:* The IRS's application of current law to the issue in the Revenue Ruling.
4. *Holding:* How the IRS will treat the transaction.

Multiple Revenue Rulings (e.g., 57 in 1997 and 65 in 1996) are released by the IRS each year. Each is identified by the year in which it was released and the number for that year. The IRS publishes them in the weekly *Internal Revenue Bulletin* and, later, in the *Cumulative Bulletin.*

Revenue Ruling Citations

Revenue Rulings bear both a temporary and a permanent citation. The temporary citation is structured as follows.

Rev. Rul. 96-58, 1996-50 I.R.B. 4

where:

96-58 is the Revenue Ruling number (the 58th Revenue Ruling of 1996).
1996-50 is the weekly issue of the *Internal Revenue Bulletin* (the 50th week of 1996).
I.R.B. is the abbreviation for the *Internal Revenue Bulletin.*
4 is the page number.

The permanent citation for the same Revenue Ruling would be as follows.

Rev. Rul. 96-58, 1996-2 C.B. 6

EXHIBIT 4–3   Revenue Ruling

REV. RUL. 97-55

ISSUE

Are the Wetlands Reserve Program, the Environmental Quality Incentives Program, and the Wildlife Habitat Incentives Program substantially similar to the type of programs described in Section 126(a)(1) through (8) of the *Internal Revenue Code* so that cost-share payments made under such programs and in connection with small watersheds are within the scope of Section 126(a)(9) and, thereby, cost-share payments received under the programs are eligible for exclusion from gross income to the extent permitted by Section 126?

FACTS

The Wetlands Reserve Program (WRP), authorized by Title XII of the Food Security Act of 1985, Pub. L. No. 99-198, 99 Stat. 1504, reauthorized by the Federal Agriculture Improvement and Reform Act of 1996 (the 1996 Farm Act), Pub. L. No. 104-127, 110 Stat. 995, is a voluntary wetlands conservation program to restore and protect wetlands on private property. Landowners who participate in the WRP may sell a conservation easement or enter into a restoration cost-share agreement with the Department of Agriculture to restore and protect wetlands. Under a restoration cost-share agreement, a landowner agrees to undertake approved conservation-related improvements on the property in return for a cost-share payment, generally between 75 and 100 percent of the costs for restoring the wetland. A conservation easement and a restoration cost-share agreement may be combined in one agreement with the Department of Agriculture but separate payments are made for the easement and for the cost-share agreement.

* * *

LAW AND ANALYSIS

Under Section 126(a), gross income does not include the excludible portion of payments made to taxpayers by federal and state governments for a share of the cost of improvements to property under certain conservation programs set forth in Section 126(a)(1) through (8). Under Section 126(a)(9), programs affecting small watersheds are eligible for Section 126 treatment if they are administered by the Secretary of Agriculture and are determined by the Secretary of the Treasury or the Secretary's delegate to be substantially similar to the type of programs described in Section 126(a)(1) through (8). Even if the Secretary of the Treasury determines that a particular program is within the scope of Section 126(a)(9), not all cost-share payments under such program will qualify for the exclusion under Section 126. In addition to the determination requirement, the specific project must be with respect to a small watershed and then only the "excludible portion" of any payment can qualify for exclusion. See Sections 126(b)(1), 16A.126-1(b)(5) and 16A.126-1(d)(3) for the definitions of "excludible portion" and "small watershed."

HOLDING

The Commissioner has determined that WRP, EQIP, and WHIP are substantially similar to the type of programs described in Section 126(a)(1) through (8) so that cost-share payments made under such programs and in connection with small watersheds are within the scope of Section 126(a)(9) and, thereby, cost-share payments received under the programs are eligible for exclusion from gross income to the extent permitted by Section 126. See Section 16A.126-1 to determine what portion, if any, of the cost-share payments are excludible from gross income under Section 126.

where:

> 96-58 is the Revenue Ruling number (the 58th Revenue Ruling of 1996).
> 1996-2 is the volume number of *Cumulative Bulletin* (volume 2 of 1996).
> C.B. is the abbreviation for the *Cumulative Bulletin.*
> 6 is the page number.

Once the pertinent *Cumulative Bulletin* is published, the temporary citation is normally no longer used.

Locating Revenue Rulings

Generally, the tax researcher must examine every applicable Revenue Ruling before a tax research project is complete. Revenue Rulings can be found at most of the locations (i.e., tax services, the *Cumulative Bulletin,* CD-ROM services, online services, and some Internet sites) shown in Exhibit 4–2. Prior to 1953, Revenue Rulings were known by different names, including Appeals and Review Memorandum (ARM), General Counsel's Memorandum (GCM), and Office Decision (OD). These early rulings still may have some application in client situations if the IRS has not revoked them or modified them in any way. A tax researcher cannot ignore such rulings simply because they are old.

The current status of a Revenue Ruling or other IRS ruling can be checked in the most current index to the *Cumulative Bulletin.* In addition, several of the commercial tax services, including *Mertens* and Commerce Clearing House (CCH), present a variety of finding lists and other references with which to examine the status of a ruling. Later chapters of this text demonstrate the use of a tax service with respect to subsequent developments concerning IRS rulings.

Revenue Rulings can also be located with computer tax services.

Example 4–1 Sid is a retired CPA who helps out each year with the IRS Volunteer Income Tax Assistance (VITA) program in his community. This program helps senior citizens, low-income taxpayers, and other who need help with their taxes free of charge. Sid would like to know if he is entitled to any charitable deduction under § 170 for his time and expenses in participating in this program. Exhibits 4–4 and 4–5 show the results of a computer tax search of a Revenue Ruling database addressing this question.

Revenue Procedures

Revenue Procedures deal with the internal practice and procedures of the IRS in the administration of the tax laws. They constitute the IRS's way of releasing information to taxpayers. For example, when the IRS releases specifications for facsimile tax forms generated by a computer service, or informs the public about areas in which it will no longer issue Revenue Rulings, it issues a Revenue Procedure to that effect. Although a Revenue Procedure may not be as useful as a Regulation or a Revenue Ruling in the direct resolution of a tax research problem, the practitioner still should be familiar with all of the pertinent Procedures.

Revenue Procedures are issued in a manner similar to that for Revenue Rulings. They first are published in the weekly *Internal Revenue Bulletin* and later are

EXHIBIT 4–4   VITA search query

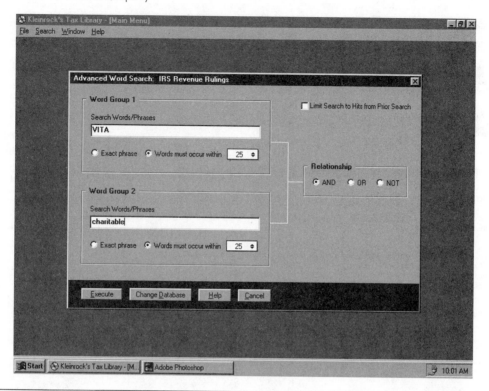

included in the bound edition of the *Cumulative Bulletin.* The IRS issues approximately 50 to 60 Revenue Procedures per year (e.g., there were 61 in 1997).

A Revenue Procedure is cited using the same system as that for Revenue Rulings, that is, adopting first a temporary and then a permanent citation. In this regard, the temporary citation refers to the location of the Procedure in the *Internal Revenue Bulletin,* and the permanent citation denotes its location in the *Cumulative Bulletin.* Thus, a typical Revenue Procedure would have the following permanent citation.

Rev. Proc. 94-11, 1994-1 C.B. 557

A Revenue Procedure is reproduced in Exhibit 4–6. Revenue Procedures can be found in the same publications in which Revenue Rulings are located.

Letter Rulings

The tax researcher is also interested in the *letter rulings* that are issued by the IRS in several forms, including Private Letter Rulings, Determination Letters, and Technical Advice Memoranda. The IRS does not publish these items in any official collection, but they are available from several commercial sources, as will be discussed later in this chapter.

EXHIBIT 4–5 VITA search query results

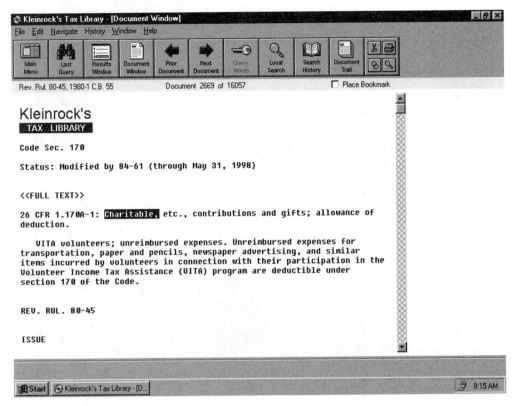

Private Letter Rulings

The National Office of the IRS issues **Private Letter Rulings** in response to a tax-payer's request for the IRS's position on a specified tax issue. The IRS has authority to decline to issue Letter Rulings under certain conditions, such as where the problem is one of an inherently factual nature. The content, format, and procedures that are used for Revenue Rulings apply with respect to Private Letter Rulings. The IRS does not publish its reply in the *Internal Revenue Bulletin* or *Cumulative Bulletin,* however. Rather, it sends its response only to the taxpayer who submitted the request. An example of a Private Letter Ruling is shown in Exhibit 4–7.

The process is as follows. The taxpayer asks the IRS to disclose its interpretation of the Code, Regulations, and pertinent court cases for a transaction the taxpayer describes; the description should include a statement of the business purpose for the transaction. For instance, if two corporations plan to merge, one of them might request a Private Letter Ruling to find out whether the IRS believes that the Code's tax-favored reorganization provisions will apply to the anticipated merger. In many cases, if the IRS asserts that the transaction will not receive a treatment favorable to the taxpayer, it will suggest means by which the transaction could be restructured to obtain the favorable treatment.

EXHIBIT 4–6   Revenue Procedure

REV. PROC. 98-20

SECTION 1. PURPOSE

This revenue procedure sets forth the acceptable form of the written assurances (certification) that a real estate reporting person must obtain from the seller of a principal residence to except such sale or exchange from the information reporting requirements for real estate transactions under Section 6045(e)(5) of the *Internal Revenue Code*.

SECTION 2. BACKGROUND

.01 Section 6045(e) and Section 1.6045-4 of the Income Tax Regulations generally require a real estate reporting person (as defined in Section 6045(e)(2) and Section 1.6045-4) to file an information return regarding a real estate transaction and to furnish a payee statement to the seller regarding that transaction. The information return and statement must include the name, address, and taxpayer identification number (TIN) of the seller, and the gross proceeds of the real estate transaction. This information is reported on Form 1099-S, Proceeds From Real Estate Transactions.

.02 Section 312 of the Taxpayer Relief Act of 1997 (the Act), Pub. L. No. 105-34, 111 Stat. 788 (August 5, 1997), effective for sales or exchanges after May 6, 1997, amended Section 6045(e) by adding a new paragraph (5), which excepts a sale or exchange of a residence from the Section 6045(e) information reporting requirements if the seller provides the real estate reporting person with a certification setting forth certain written assurances, including an assurance that the residence is the seller's principal residence (within the meaning of Section 121) and an assurance that the full amount of the gain on the sale or exchange of the principal residence is excludible from gross income under Section 121.

.03 Section 312 of the Act also amended Section 121 to provide new rules for the exclusion of gain on certain sales or exchanges of a principal residence. Section 121, as amended, provides that a taxpayer may exclude from gross income up to $250,000 of gain on the sale or exchange of a principal residence if certain conditions are met. In certain circumstances, a married individual filing a joint return for the taxable year of the sale or exchange may exclude from gross income up to $500,000 of gain. This exclusion also applies to the sale or exchange of stock held by a tenant-stockholder in a cooperative housing corporation (as defined in Section 216) and may apply to the sale or exchange of a remainder interest in a principal residence if the taxpayer so elects.

SECTION 3. SCOPE

This revenue procedure applies to the information reporting requirements under Section 6045(e) for a sale or exchange of a principal residence.

As mentioned, a Private Letter Ruling is issued only to the taxpayer who requested the ruling. Of interest, however, is the recent inclusion of Private Letter Rulings on the list of authorities constituting "substantial authority" upon which a taxpayer may rely to avoid certain statutory penalties.[2] Previously, Letter Rulings could not be cited as precedent by other than the person requesting the Ruling.[3] It is thought that this broadening of the list of authorities is not intended to expand the use of Letter Rulings in determining a taxpayer's treatment of an item in a tax return. Letter Rulings are, in any case, an important source of information, since they indicate how the IRS may treat a similar transaction.

[2]Reg. § 1.6662-4(d)(3)(iii).
[3]IRC § 6110(j)(3) and Reg. § 1.6661-3(b)(2).

EXHIBIT 4–7 Private Letter Ruling

PRIVATE LETTER RULING 9536031

[Annual cost-of-living Adjustment for § 72(t) IRA Distributions]

This letter is in response to your request, dated December 28, 1994, for a ruling on behalf of Taxpayer G as to whether certain proposed distributions from an individual retirement account (IRA) owned by Taxpayer G are part of a series of substantially equal periodic payments and are therefore not subject to the 10% additional tax imposed under section 72(t) of the *Internal Revenue Code* (Code) on early distributions. The request was modified in telephone calls with our office on June 5, June 6, and June 7, 1995.

According to the facts as stated, Taxpayer G, currently age 49, received a distribution from a plan described in Section 401(k) of the Code on July 8, 1994, following termination of employment. This distribution was subsequently rolled over into an existing IRA (IRA A), the sole IRA owned by Taxpayer G. Taxpayer G decided to start receiving annual distributions in 1994 from IRA A. The annual distribution amount for 1994 was calculated by amortizing the account balance of IRA A as of August 1, 1994, over a number of years equal to Taxpayer G's life expectancy (obtained from Table V in Section 1.72-9 of the Income Tax Regulations, using the age attained by Taxpayer G in 1994), using an assumed interest rate of earnings equal to 5.95%. Thereafter, the annual distribution amount will be increased each year by a 3 percent cost-of-living adjustment. That is, the annual distribution amount for 1995 and subsequent years will equal 103 percent of the prior year distribution amount.

* * *

Notice 89-25 was published on March 20, 1989, and provided guidance, in the form of questions and answers, on certain provisions of the Tax Reform Act of 1986 (TRA '86). In the absence of regulations on Section 72(t) of the Code, this notice provided guidance with respect to the exception to the tax on premature distributions provided under Section 72(t)(2)(A)(iv). Q&A-12 of Notice 89-25 provides three methods for determining substantially equal periodic payments for purposes of Section 72(t)(2)(A)(iv) of the Code. Two of these methods involve the use of an interest rate assumption which must be an interest rate that does not exceed a reasonable interest rate on the date payments commence.

The proposed method for determining annual periodic payments described in the ruling request, as modified, is to determine an annual distribution amount for 1994 by amortizing the account balance of IRA A as of August 1, 1994, over a number of years equal to Taxpayer G's life expectancy (obtained from Table V in Section 1.72-9 of the Income Tax Regulations, using the age attained by Taxpayer G in 1994), assuming an interest rate of earnings equal to 5.95 percent. This annual distribution amount will be increased by a 3 percent cost-of-living factor for each year after 1994. Thus, the annual distribution amount for 1995 will equal 103 percent of the 1994 distribution amount, and for years subsequent to 1995 the annual distribution amount will equal 103 percent of the prior year annual distribution amount.

The life expectancy and the interest rate used are such that they do not result in the circumvention of the requirements of Sections 72(t)(2)(A)(iv) and 72(t)(4) of the Code (through the use of an unreasonable high interest rate or an unreasonable life expectancy).

Accordingly, we conclude that the proposed method (as modified) of determining periodic payments satisfies one of the methods described in Notice 89-25 and results in substantially equal periodic payments within the meaning of Section 72(t)(2)(A)(iv) of the Code, and such payments will not be subject to the additional tax of Section 72(t) unless the requirements of Section 72(t)(4) are not met.

Private Letter Rulings also constitute an important IRS stimulus for new Revenue Rulings. When the IRS comes across an unusual transaction that it believes to be of general interest, or when it receives a flurry of Letter Ruling requests concerning very similar fact situations, a Private Ruling may be converted into Revenue Ruling form and published in official administrative sources. The IRS must notify the taxpayer of its intention to disclose the ruling, and the taxpayer has the right to protest such disclosure. Before publication, all aspects of the new ruling, including the statement of facts, are purged of any reference to the taxpayer's name or other identifying information.

Technical Advice Memoranda

A **Technical Advice Memorandum** is issued by the IRS's National Office, making it similar in this regard to the Private Letter Ruling and different from the Determination Letter. The Technical Advice Memorandum, however, concerns a completed transaction. Whereas a Private Letter Ruling typically is requested by a taxpayer prior to completing a transaction or filing a tax return, a Technical Advice Memorandum usually is requested by an agent when a question arises during an audit than cannot be answered satisfactorily by the local office.

Similar to the Private Letter Ruling, a Technical Advice Memorandum applies strictly to the taxpayer for whose audit it was requested, and it cannot be relied on by other taxpayers. However, again, the information that is contained in the memorandum may be useful to the tax researcher for the insight that it gives concerning the thinking of the IRS relative to a given problem area in taxation.

These memoranda are not included in any official IRS publication, but they are open for public inspection, as we will discuss next. If the facts or the holding of a Technical Advice Memorandum are felt by the IRS to be of general interest, the memorandum may be converted into Revenue Ruling format and published by the IRS in the *Internal Revenue Bulletin* and the *Cumulative Bulletin*.

Determination Letters

A **Determination Letter** is similar in purpose and nature to a Private Letter Ruling, except that it is issued by the office of the local IRS district director, rather than by the National Office of the IRS. Because a Determination Letter is issued by a lower-level IRS official, it usually deals with issues and transactions that are not overtly controversial. For instance, the trustee of a pension plan might request a Determination Letter to ascertain whether the plan is qualified for the Code's tax-favored deferred compensation treatment.

Determination Letters usually relate to completed transactions rather than to the proposed transactions that typically lead to the issuance of a Private Letter Ruling. Determination Letters are not included in any official IRS publication, but they may be available to the tax researcher from other sources.

Public Inspection of Written Determinations

The public can receive copies of any unpublished IRS Letter Rulings.[4] Included under this provision are Private Letter Rulings, Determination Letters, and Techni-

[4] § 6110(f).

cal Advice Memoranda.[5] Before any public inspection is allowed, however, the IRS must remove the taxpayer's name and any other information that might be used by a third party to identify the taxpayer. In addition, the IRS is required to purge the document of any items that could affect national defense or foreign policy, trade secrets, financial information, data relative to the regulation of financial institutions, geographical data, and items that could invade personal privacy.[6] If the taxpayer opposes the disclosure of the written determination, he or she can bring the matter before the IRS and the Tax Court prior to the scheduled disclosure under § 6110(f).

Once all of the required data have been removed from the written determination, it must be open for public inspection at such places as the Treasury Secretary designates in the Regulations. Information of this type is available in Washington, D.C., and at selected other locations.

IRC § 6110 specifically limits the precedential value of any of these written determinations. Overall, such pronouncements may not be cited as authority in a tax matter by either the taxpayer or the IRS. However, Letter Rulings can be used as "examples" of IRS treatment of similar fact patterns when dealing with the IRS. For example, the tax practitioners could suggest that a Letter Ruling be used as guidance in an instant situation. However, keep in mind that an IRS agent does not have to follow a Letter Ruling issued to a different taxpayer since under § 6110 it has limited precedential value.

In 1989, Congress expanded the list of authorities on which taxpayers may rely to avoid certain understatement of tax penalties to include Private Letter Rulings, Technical Advice Memoranda, Actions on Decisions, General Counsel Memoranda, and other similar documents published by the IRS in the *Internal Revenue Bulletin.* The Committee Report expressed a general intent to broaden the list of authorities on which a taxpayer may rely to avoid penalties; however, it does not appear that Congress intended to change the general precedential value of these pronouncements with respect to determining a taxpayer's tax liability.

Written Determination Numbering System

Because the IRS issues approximately 2,000 Letter Rulings per year, it assigns a seven-digit document number to each written determination for identification purposes. The first two digits indicate the year in which the ruling was issued, the next two numbers denote the week, and the last three digits indicate the number of the ruling for the week. Thus, a lengthy but unique identifier is created for each pronouncement. For example, the number of a Letter Ruling can be interpreted as follows.

Ltr. Rul. 9915026

where:

99 is the year of the Ruling is issued.
15 is the week of the year the Ruling is issued.
026 indicates that this is the 26th Ruling issued that week.

---

[5]§ 6110(b)(1).
[6]§ 6110(c).

Locating Written Determinations

The tax researcher needs access to written determinations to complete many tax research projects. Selected written determinations can be found in summary form in the major tax services. However, if the tax researcher needs access to the full text of written determinations, a computer tax database is the best approach. Consult Exhibit 4–2 for the computer tax databases (both CD-ROM and online systems) that contain the full text of IRS written determinations.

Other IRS Pronouncements

The IRS issues several other types of information that can be of value to the tax researcher, including acquiescences and nonacquiescences, the *Internal Revenue Bulletin,* the *Bulletin Index-Digest System,* Chief Counsel Memoranda, and other miscellaneous publications.

Acquiescences and Nonacquiescences

When the IRS loses an issue or decision in court, the Commissioner may announce an acquiescence or nonacquiescence to the decision. An **acquiescence** indicates that the court decision, although it was adverse to the IRS, will be followed in similar situations. The Commissioner determines, at his or her own discretion, the degree of similarity required before the IRS will follow the result that is unfavorable to itself.

A **nonacquiescence** indicates that the IRS disagrees with the adverse decision in the case and will follow the decision only for the specific taxpayer whose case resulted in the adverse ruling. If the IRS wishes to express agreement with only part of the decision that is settled in the taxpayer's favor, the Commissioner may nonacquiesce with respect to certain issues. Finally, an acquiescense or nonacquiescence is not issued if the IRS prevails in a court case, since it likely agrees with all pertinent holdings.

Nonacquiescence may indicate to the tax practitioner that the IRS is likely to challenge a similar decision for the taxpayer in a case that has a similar fact situation. However, the issuance of an acquiescence does not necessarily mean that the IRS agrees with the adverse decision, but only that it will not pursue the matter in a (similar and) subsequent case. Each of these items of information can be useful when the practitioner prepares for, or anticipates, a court challenge to the client's position in a tax matter.

As mentioned, if the IRS has acquiesced to a case, then the taxpayer can rely on that decision as precedence that will be followed by agents for similar fact patterns. However, if the IRS has nonacquiesced, the taxpayer must evaluate whether to purse a similar fact pattern in court. Such items as the cost of litigation plus the probability of winning must be appraised before proceeding with a case similar to one with which the IRS has nonacquiesced.

Occasionally, the IRS changes (with an attendant retroactive effect on taxpayers) its acquiescence or nonacquiescence position by withdrawing the original pronouncement.[7] This may occur after only a short time passes or many years later.

---

[7]In *U.S. v. City Loan and Savings,* 287 F.2d 612 (CA-6, 1961), the court allowed the IRS to withdraw an acquiescence on an issue-by-issue, but not taxpayer-by-taxpayer, basis.

Such a change in the IRS's position typically is accompanied by a brief explanation of the reason for the change—for example, because of a contrary holding in a subsequent court case or a change in the agency's policy concerning the issue.

IRS acquiescence decisions are driven by related litigation costs, revenue effects, and administrative and policy directives. IRS acquiescences and nonacquiescences are published in the *Internal Revenue Bulletin* and thereafter in the *Cumulative Bulletin*. Exhibit 4–8 reproduces an acquiescence from the *Cumulative Bulletin* in which the IRS indicates its position on a case. A citator (see Chapter 6) also can be used to locate acquiescence and nonacquiescence decisions.

EXHIBIT 4–8 Action on Decision

ACTION ON DECISION CC-1997-010

November 10, 1997

Subject: *Sun Microsystems, Inc. v. Commissioner,* T.C. Memo 1995-69.

Issue: Whether the spread income realized from a disqualifying disposition of stock purchased through the taxpayer's incentive stock option ("ISO") plan constitutes wages under Section 41(b)(2)(D) in determining whether certain qualified research expenses qualify for the credit for increasing research activities under Section 41.

Discussion: Under the taxpayer's ISO plan, employees engaged in qualified services from April 1983 to July 1986 were granted ISOs meeting the requirements of former Section 422A of the Code. During the 1987 tax year, the taxpayer's employees sold shares of stock they had acquired through the exercise of ISOs before the expiration of the holding periods under Section 422A. These "disqualifying dispositions" under Section 421(b) generated income to the taxpayer's employees equal to the difference between the fair market value of the shares on the exercise date and the amount paid for the shares ("spread income"). The taxpayer claimed a credit for increasing research activities under Section 41 on its 1987 return, including as "wages" the spread income attributable to the disqualifying dispositions of ISO stock. The Service issued a notice of deficiency, proposing to reduce the taxpayer's qualified research expenses by the income attributable to the disqualifying dispositions, thereby reducing the taxpayer's credit for increasing research activities under Section 41 for 1987.

Under Section 41(b)(2)(D), wages—a research expense used in calculating the research credit—means the same as wages under Section 3401(a). Relying on Rev. Rul. 71-52, 1971-1 C.B. 278, the Service argued that the spread income from disqualifying dispositions of ISO stock was not wages under Section 3401. In Rev. Rul. 71-52, the Service ruled that spread income attributable to disqualifying dispositions of stock purchased under a qualified stock option plan was ordinary income but not wages requiring a corporation to withhold employment taxes (although the Service later announced it was reconsidering this position in Notice 87-49, 1987-2 C.B. 355). The Tax Court rejected the Service's argument, relying on *Apple Computer, Inc. v. Commissioner,* 98 T.C. 232 (1992), acq., 1992-2 C.B. 1. In *Apple Computer, Inc.,* the court held that the spread income attributable to the exercise of a nonqualified stock option was wages under Section 3401(a) and, therefore, wages under Section 41 for purposes of the research credit.

Finding neither support for the Service's position in Rev. Rul. 71-52, nor a basis for distinguishing *Apple Computer, Inc.,* the court held that the spread income attributable to disqualifying dispositions of ISO stock constitutes wages for determining the credit for increasing research activities under Section 41

Recommendation: Acquiescence.

The index to the *Internal Revenue Bulletin* lists acquiescences and nonacquiescences alphabetically and in Code section order. After the IRS issues such a pronouncement, any reference to the citation for the case includes either the abbreviation "Acq" or "Nonacq" (or, occasionally, "NA") to indicate the subsequent development.

Internal Revenue Bulletin

The IRS's official publication for its pronouncements is the *Internal Revenue Bulletin* (IRB). Most IRS Revenue Rulings and Revenue Procedures, and the agency's acquiescences and nonacquiescences to regular Tax Court decisions, first are published in the IRB. This reference bulletin also includes the following information, all of which can be useful to the tax researcher.

▶ New tax laws, issued by Congress as Public Laws
▶ Committee Reports underlying tax statutes
▶ Procedural rules
▶ New tax treaties
▶ Treasury Decisions (which become Regulations)
▶ Other notices

Interested parties can subscribe to the *Internal Revenue Bulletin* by contacting the Internal Revenue Service. Alternatively, some of the commercial tax services include subscriptions to, or reproductions of, all of the issues of the *Internal Revenue Bulletin.*

Bulletin Index-Digest System

The IRS also produces the **Bulletin Index-Digest System,** a comprehensive index of matters that it has published since 1952 in the *Internal Revenue Bulletin.* This resource is available from the Government Printing Office on a subscription basis and contains a variety of finding lists that accommodate alternate methods of IRB research. The *Bulletin Index-Digest System* consists of four separate services.

Service #1. Income Tax, Publication 641
Service #2. Estate and Gift Taxes, Publication 642
Service #3. Employment Taxes, Publication 643
Service #4. Excise Taxes, Publication 644

Each of these services consists of a basic volume and the latest cumulative supplement. The cumulative supplements are issued quarterly for the Income Tax service, and semiannually for the other three services. About every two years a new basic volume is published to consolidate the materials of the existing basic volume and the ever-increasing supplemental materials.[8]

Contents of the System   The *Bulletin Index-Digest System* contains separate finding lists for Revenue Rulings, Revenue Procedures, Public Laws that amend the *Internal Revenue Code*, and Treasury Decisions that amend the pertinent

---

[8]*Internal Revenue Manual,* § (11)(10)(30).

Regulations. In addition, the system includes a number of special lists to identify other items that may be of interest to the tax researcher, such as the following.

► Supreme Court decisions
► Certain Tax Court decisions
► Revenue Rulings and Revenue Procedures issued under tax conventions
► Miscellaneous items that are published in the IRB
► Lists of Revenue Rulings and Revenue Procedures
► Actions relative to published Revenue Rulings and Revenue Procedures
► Public Laws that have been published in the IRB
► Tax conventions and related items that have been published in the IRB

A major portion of the *Bulletin Index-Digest System* consists of digests, that is, brief summaries, of (1) Revenue Procedures and Revenue Rulings, arranged alphabetically under topical headings and subheadings; (2) Supreme Court decisions and adverse-to-the-government Tax Court decisions to which the Commissioner has announced acquiescence or nonacquiescence; and (3) executive orders, Treasury Department orders, delegation orders, and certain other miscellaneous items that have been published in the *Cumulative Bulletin*. Each such digest is preceded by descriptive "key words" that further identify the subject matter of the item, and each digest is followed by a citation to both the Code and/or Regulations section under which the item was published and the *Cumulative Bulletin* in which the full text of the cited item may be found.

This arrangement of digests under topical headings allows the practitioner to use a "subject matter" approach to find Revenue Rulings and most other items that are pertinent to the research task. Public Laws, Treasury Decisions, and tax conventions are not digested in this publication. Thus, the user can employ only the system's finding lists for determining whether any such items are relevant to the taxpayer's tax issue.

The *Bulletin Index-Digest System* does not contain a Code section finding list for Revenue Rulings, Revenue Procedures, Supreme Court decisions, or Actions on Decisions of the Tax Court that relate to the 1939 Code. One must use a commercial tax service, or some other available resource, to cross-reference the section numbers of the 1939 Code to those of the current edition. Digests of such items, however, include citations to the relevant 1939, 1954, and 1986 Code and Regulation material.

Again, in using the *Bulletin Index-Digest System,* one always must be sure to examine the most recent cumulative supplement to the service. The release dates of both the basic volume and the supplement itself are printed on the front cover of the publication.

Chief Counsel Memoranda

The office of the IRS's Chief Counsel periodically generates memoranda that may be of use to the tax researcher. Although the IRS does not publish these memoranda in any official document, they are available from commercial publishers. A **Technical Memorandum** (TM) is prepared in the production of a Proposed Regulation. A **General Counsel's Memorandum** (GCM) is generated upon the request of the IRS, typically as a means to assist in the preparation of Revenue Rulings and Private Letter Rulings. An **Action on Decision** (AOD) is prepared when the IRS loses a case in a court. The text of the AOD recommends the action, if any, that the IRS should take in response to the adverse decision (see Exhibit 4–8).

The commercial tax services discuss the most important of the GCMs. If the practitioner requires one of these documents that is not included in any of the commercial or computerized tax services, it is available from the IRS Freedom of Information Act Reading Room in Washington, D.C.

Announcements and Notices

The IRS issues **Announcements and Notices** concerning items of general importance to taxpayers. For example, at year-end, the IRS will issue a Notice to announce the mailing of the new tax-form packages to taxpayers, or changes on the Forms 1040, 1040A, and 1040EZ. Exhibit 4–9 reproduces a typical Notice. Notices are generally considered more important than Announcements by the IRS, and thus they are published in the permanent, bound volumes of *Cumulative Bulletins*. Announce-

---

EXHIBIT 4–9   IRS Notice

NOTICE 97-53

PENALTY-FREE WITHDRAWALS FROM IRAs FOR HIGHER EDUCATION EXPENSES

Section 203 of the Taxpayer Relief Act of 1997 provides that the 10-percent additional tax on early distributions from individual retirement arrangements (IRAs) does not apply to certain distributions for educational expenses after 1997. This Notice provides guidance concerning the effective date of this provision.

In general, Section 72(t) of the *Internal Revenue Code* imposes an additional 10-percent tax on amounts withdrawn from a qualified retirement plan (including an IRA) before age 59 1/2 subject to certain exceptions. Section 203 of the Taxpayer Relief Act of 1997 added certain educational expenses to the list of exceptions to the 10-percent additional tax. The exception for educational expenses is limited to the qualified higher education expenses of the taxpayer, the taxpayer's spouse, or any child or grandchild of the taxpayer or spouse.

Section 203 is effective for IRA distributions made after December 31, 1997, with respect to expenses paid after that date, for education provided in academic periods beginning after that date. An "academic period" includes a semester, trimester, quarter, or other academic term designated by the educational institution. For this purpose, an academic period begins on the first day of classes, and does not include periods of orientation, counseling or vacation.

For example, assume the 1997-1998 schedule of a college or university divides the academic year into two semesters; the first semester begins in September 1997, and the second semester begins in January 1998. The benefits are not available for the September semester. The benefits of Section 203 would be available, however, for the qualified expenses for the semester that begins in January 1998, provided the IRA distribution is made after December 31, 1997, and the expenses are paid after that date. This result applies to students who are enrolled in both semesters as well as to students whose enrollment begins only with the January semester.

ments are not published in the *Cumulative Bulletin;* however, they are published in the weekly *Internal Revenue Bulletin.*

Notices also are used to announce new provisions of the tax law that may affect a large number of taxpayers. For example, several Notices were issued in 1984 concerning the requirement that tax shelter partnerships obtain registration numbers from the IRS. Similarly, Notices regularly are used to announce the standard mileage rate that is used to compute taxpayers' deductions for the business use of automobiles. Important Notices are reproduced in the body of most of the commercial tax services' publications.

Miscellaneous Publications

The IRS publishes numerous general and specialized documents to help taxpayers. Some of the more common ones include the following.

Publication 17, *Your Federal Income Tax*
Publication 225, *Farmer's Tax Guide*
Publication 334, *Tax Guide for Small Business*
Publication 519, *U.S. Tax Guide for Aliens*
Publication 589, *Tax Information on S Corporations*

Each of these documents is available directly from the IRS, both in print and electronic formats. In addition, several of the commercial tax publishers offer copies of these lay-oriented *Publications.* Furthermore, any library that is designated as a government depository receives all of these documents. Finally, many of the above Publications can be ordered from the IRS in Spanish-language editions.

Although the IRS Publications contain useful information, the tax researcher must be careful when relying on them. IRS Publications typically do not cite the Code, Regulations, or other authority on which the information included therein is based. In fact, the IRS disclaims any responsibility for damages that the taxpayer may suffer in erroneously relying on its Publications, and it may, in fact, take positions that are contrary to those that are included in the Publications in certain court cases or appeals hearings.

These documents are prepared from the government's point of view. For instance, if a lower court has ruled against the IRS on a given matter that is addressed in a Publication, the text of the document probably will not mention the possibility that the IRS's official position will be found to be incorrect on appeal. Although IRS Publications can be the source of some basic information that is useful for laypersons, or in a tax compliance context, the tax researcher should not rely on or cite such a reference in a professional research report.

The IRS Internet Site

The Internal Revenue Service maintains a notable World Wide Web site on the Internet that can be of significant value to the tax professional and the average taxpayer. This site gives the user access to items such as IRS forms, IRS Publications, the Regulations (full text or in plain English), and a daily IRS newsletter. The forms and other items can be downloaded and printed on the user's computer. The address of the IRS home page is as follows (Exhibit 4–10).

EXHIBIT 4–10   "The Digital Daily"

http://www.irs.ustreas.gov/basic/cover.html

When using the IRS Internet site, the tax researcher has several ways to access the information provided. First, one can connect to the IRS home page Site Tree (http://www.irs.ustreas.gov./basic/search/site_tree.html) and get an outline listing of all the documents available. On this page, the user can browse the entire site table of contents for the needed information. Secondly, the user could use the search engine (http://www.irs.ustreas.gov./basic/search/index.html) provided by the IRS. By typing in key words, the user can search the IRS Internet site for any desired material.

> **Example 4–2** Farmer John would like to know if he can deduct prepaid farm supplies. By clicking on the search button on the IRS Digital Daily, John will go to the IRS site search engine (Exhibit 4–11). He can enter his search request and he would be referred to the IRS Publication 225, section that contains the rules for deducting prepaid farm supplies (see Exhibit 4–12).

The IRS's Web site is an excellent choice for taxpayers to use. In the future, Internet users can expect this site to expand rapidly the government-source information available to taxpayers and practitioners.

EXHIBIT 4–11   IRS search engine

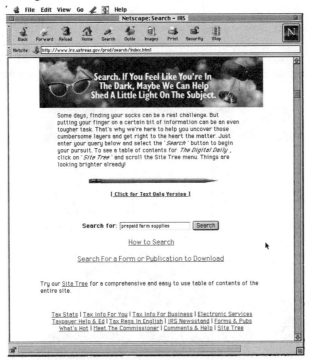

EXHIBIT 4–12   IRS search engine results

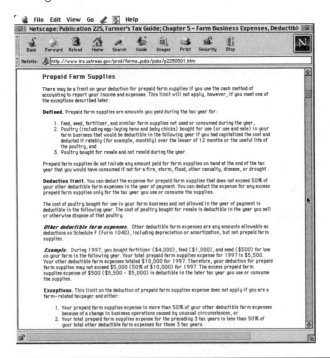

EXHIBIT 4–13 Common IRS pronouncements

Pronouncement	Purpose
Regulation	The official Treasury or IRS interpretation of a portion of the *Internal Revenue Code*
Revenue Ruling	The IRS's application of the tax law to a specific fact situation
Revenue Procedure	A statement of IRS practice or procedure that affects taxpayers or the general public
Private Letter Ruling	Statement issued by the National Office of the IRS at a taxpayer's request, applying the tax law to a proposed transaction
Determination Letter	Statement issued by the District Director in response to a taxpayer request, concerning the application of the tax law to a specific completed transaction
Acquiescence	Acceptance by the IRS of a Tax Court decision
Treasury Decision	The means by which a Regulation is promulgated or amended
Technical Advice Memorandum	A letter ruling issued on a completed transaction, usually during an audit

▶ Summary

Administrative pronouncements provide the tax researcher with a significant amount of information from and about the IRS. The primary IRS pronouncements that are of interest to the tax researcher include the Regulations, Revenue Rulings, Revenue Procedures, and Letter Rulings. The tax practitioner who performs competent research must be aware of the content and format of each of these items, know how to locate them, appreciate the precedential value of each, and understand how each might affect the client's tax problem. Exhibit 4–13 summarizes the most commonly encountered IRS pronouncements.

▶ Key Words

By the time you complete this chapter, you should be comfortable discussing each of the following terms. If you need additional review of any of these items, return to the appropriate material in the chapter or consult the glossary to this text.

Acquiescence	Nonacquiescence
Action on Decision	Private Letter Ruling
Announcements and Notices	Proposed Regulation
Bulletin Index-Digest System	Regulation
Cumulative Bulletin	Revenue Procedure
Determination Letter	Revenue Ruling
General Counsel's Memorandum	Technical Advice Memorandum
General Regulation	Technical Memorandum
Internal Revenue Bulletin	Temporary Regulation
Legislative Regulation	Treasury Decision

► _____ Discussion Questions

1. What department and agency of the U.S. government has the responsibility to administer the federal tax laws?

2. Section 7805(a) of the *Internal Revenue Code* authorizes the IRS to perform what activities?

3. The IRS issues numerous pronouncements. Name the four that are the most important in conducting federal tax research.

4. Define the terms *Regulation* and *Treasury Decision.* Where are Treasury Decisions published so that interested parties can comment on them?

5. "A tax researcher should not ignore Proposed Regulations." Comment on this statement.

6. Define and distinguish between *General* and *Legislative* Regulations.

7. In the citation, Reg. § 1.212-3, what do the "1," the "212," and the "3" indicate?

8. Give the number that is associated with each of the following categories of Regulations.

   a. Estate tax Regulations
   b. Income tax Regulations
   c. Gift tax Regulations
   d. Procedural Regulations
   e. Employment tax Regulations

9. What are Temporary Regulations? What weight do they carry in the tax researcher's analysis?

10. The burden of proof is on the taxpayer to prove that a provision of the Regulations is improper. How could this affect one's tax research?

11. In general, what is the effective date of a new Regulation?

12. Give at least three locations where a tax researcher can find the complete text of a Regulation.

13. What is a Revenue Ruling?

14. Describe the structure of a typical Revenue Ruling.

15. Where are Revenue Rulings initially published by the IRS? Where are the rulings permanently published in hardbound editions?

16. Explain each of the elements of this citation: Rev. Rul. 95-123, 1995-1 C.B. 321.

17. What resources are available to help the tax researcher who wishes to check the current status of a Revenue Ruling?

18. Of what relevance to the tax practitioner is a Revenue Procedure?

19. Where can a tax researcher find copies of Revenue Procedures?

20. Construct the permanent citation for the third Revenue Procedure of 1996, which was published on January 17. It is published on pages 345–347 of the appropriate document.

21. Identify three types of letter rulings that are of interest to the tax researcher. Indicate whether each of these rulings is published by the IRS.

22. Which office of the IRS issues Private Letter Rulings? Who requests such a ruling? What kinds of issues are addressed therein?

23. Sometimes a Private Letter Ruling is generalized and included in an official IRS publication. What form does this recast private ruling take?

24. What is a Determination Letter? Which office of the IRS issues Determination Letters? What kinds of issues are addressed therein?

25. What is a Technical Advice Memorandum? Who requests it? What kinds of issues are addressed therein? Does the IRS include Technical Advice Memoranda in any official publication?

26. Discuss the precedential value of Private Letter Rulings, Determination Letters, and Technical Advice Memoranda. What role do these items play in conducting tax research?

27. Which IRS documents are open to public inspection under § 6110?

28. What is the precedential value of an IRS written determination under § 6110?

29. Explain each of the elements of this citation: Ltr. Rul. 9615032.

30. Where can a tax researcher find copies of written determinations?

31. The most important IRS publications are the *Internal Revenue Bulletin* and the *Cumulative Bulletin.* How often is each of these documents published? Name six items that typically are published in the *Cumulative Bulletin.*

32. Explain each of the elements of this citation: Rev. Proc. 96-39, 1996-1 CB 123.

33. Answer the following questions about this citation: Reg. § 20.2039-1(a).

    a. What does the "20" stand for?
    b. What does the "2039" stand for?
    c. What does the "1" stand for?
    d. What does the "(a)" stand for?

34. Distinguish between a citation with "IRB" in it and one with "CB" in it.

35. Discuss the difference between a Revenue Ruling and a Revenue Procedure.

36. In what publication(s) would a tax researcher find the official listing of the IRS acquiescences and nonacquiescences to a Tax Court decision?

37. Can the IRS change its mind on acquiescences or nonacquiescences?

38. The IRS's *Bulletin Index-Digest System* consists of four separate services. What are they?

39. What is the purpose of each of the following?

    a. Technical Memorandum (TM)
    b. General Counsel's Memorandum (GCM)
    c. Action on Decision (AOD)

40. Describe each of the following.

    a. Publication 17
    b. Publication 225
    c. Publication 589

41. What is an IRS Notice? When is it used? In your opinion, could a tax practitioner rely on an IRS Notice as authority for a tax return position?

42. Why should the tax researcher exercise caution in relying on an IRS publication, such as published instructions to tax forms, in undertaking a research project?

▶ _____ Exercises

43. Locate Revenue Ruling 74-385. Explain the effect of that ruling on previous Treasury Department pronouncements.

44. Briefly describe the subject of each of the following Private Letter Rulings.

    a. 8450028
    b. 8921017
    c. 8817032
    d. 8449005

45. Locate the Committee Reports for the Revenue Reconciliation Act of 1989. What was the reasoning, as expressed in the Committee Reports, for the increase in the maximum penalty under § 6673?

46. What is the current status of each of the following IRS pronouncements?

    a. Notice 89-92
    b. Revenue Ruling 90-103
    c. Revenue Procedure 89-31
    d. Announcement 91-20

47. What is the subject of each of the following IRS Notices?

    a. 89-114
    b. 91-37
    c. 92-44

48. Give the page and volume number in the *Cumulative Bulletin* where each of the following Revenue Procedures can be found.

    a. 71-19
    b. 86-41
    c. 91-23

49. What is the subject matter of each of the following Technical Advice Memoranda?

    a. 9015001
    b. 9145004
    c. 9242002

50. Briefly describe the subject matter of each of the following Treasury Decisions.

    a. 8346
    b. 8433
    c. 8443

51. For each of the following Code sections, how many Treasury Regulations have been issued? Give the total number of such Regulations and the number of the last Regulation. Use a computer tax service (RIA CheckPoint, Lexis, Kleinrock's, etc.) to complete this exercise. State which computer tax service you used.

    a. § 102
    b. § 143
    c. § 301
    d. § 385

52. Use a computer tax service (RIA CheckPoint, Lexis, Kleinrock's, etc.) to complete this exercise. What is the current status of each of the following Revenue Rulings?

    a. Rev. Rul. 95-5

    b. Rev. Rul. 94-10

    c. Rev. Rul. 90-131

53. Use a computer tax service (RIA CheckPoint, Lexis, Kleinrock's, etc.) to complete this exercise. What is the current status of each of the following Revenue Rulings?

    a. Rev. Rul. 95-35

    b. Rev. Rul. 94-17

    c. Rev. Rul. 87-34

54. Use traditional published sources to complete this exercise. What is the subject matter of each of the following Letter Rulings?

    a. 9441010

    b. 9332004

    c. 9008013

55. Use a computer tax service (RIA CheckPoint, Lexis, Kleinrock's, etc.) to complete the prior exercise. State which computer tax service you used.

56. What is the subject matter of each of the following Letter Rulings? Use traditional published sources to complete this exercise.

    a. 9549021

    b. 9333008

    c. 8940004

57. Use a computer tax service (RIA CheckPoint, Lexis, Kleinrock's, etc.) to complete the prior exercise. State which computer tax service you used.

58. Locate the pronouncement at 1989-1 C.B. 76. Use traditional published sources to complete this exercise.

    a. What is the number assigned to this written determination?

    b. What is the issue(s) addressed in this written determination?

    c. What is the holding in this written determination?

59. Use a computer tax service (RIA CheckPoint, Lexis, Kleinrock's, etc.) to complete the prior exercise. State which computer tax service you used.

60. Locate the pronouncement at 1992-1 C.B. 673. Use traditional published sources to complete this exercise.

    a. What is the number assigned to this written determination?

    b. What is the subject matter discussed in this written determination?

61. Use a computer tax service (RIA CheckPoint, Lexis, Kleinrock's, etc.) to complete the prior exercise. State which computer tax service you used.

62. A member of a tax-exempt business league makes deposits into a strike fund. The contribution reverts to the taxpayer if the fund is terminated. Are these deposits tax-deductible?

Database to search: IRS Letter Rulings
Key words: business, league, strike, fund

63. Can proceeds from a life insurance policy be included in a decedent's gross estate if the policy was purchased by an S corporation for an employee-shareholder?

Databases to search: the Code and IRS letter Rulings
Key words: Sec. 2042, life, insurance, estate, inclusion

64. Is a veterinary medical corporation a "personal service corporation" for purposes of the required use of the flat 34 percent tax rate?

Database to search: Revenue Rulings
Key words: veterinary, personal, service, corporation

65. Are homeowners who claim an itemized deduction for interest paid on adjustable rate mortgages (ARMs) and then receive refunds in a later year required to show the refunds as taxable income?

Database to search: Notices
Key words: adjustable, rate, mortgage, refund

66. Are points paid by home buyers on VA and FHA loans deductible in the year the house is purchased?

Database to search: Revenue Procedures
Key words: loan, origination, fees, VA, FHA

► _____

Research Cases

67. Lance asks you to explain why his employer, the Good Food Truck Stop, an establishment that employs more than thirty waiter/waitresses, included $2,400 in tip income on his Form W-2 for the year. Lance always has kept track of the tips he actually received, and he has reported them in full on his tax return.

Partial list of research material: § 6053; Rev. Proc. 86-2, 1986-1 C.B. 560

68. Joe incurred $38,000 of investment interest expense in the current year. He also generated $35,000 in dividend income and had a $65,000 passive loss for the year. What is the amount of Joe's interest deduction?

Partial list of research material: § 163; Reg. § 1.163-8T; Announcement 87-4, 1987-3 I.R.B. 17

69. Georgia won the Massachusetts lottery, which means that she will receive $28,000 a year for the next thirty years. Georgia purchased the lucky ticket in March 1997, and it was selected the winner in June. Georgia regularly spent $100 a month on lottery tickets, one-third from Massachusetts and two-thirds for Vermont's lottery program.

   a. What is Georgia's gross income from this prize?
   b. Is there any corresponding deduction for 1997?

Partial list of research material: § 74; Rev. Rul. 78-140, 1978-1 C.B. 27

70. Dieter won the lottery this year, which means that he will receive $400,000 a year for the next thirty years. The present value of Dieter's prize is about $3,750,000. Conscious of the tax benefits of income shifting, Dieter irrevocably assigned one-fifth of every annuity payment to his daughter Heidi. What are the effects of these events on Dieter's taxable income?

Partial list of research material: § 74; Rev. Rul. 58-127, 1958-1 C.B. 42

71. Ace High and Lady Luck live together and have pooled their funds for several months to purchase food and other household necessities, and to buy an occasional state lottery ticket. Ace used part of these pooled funds to buy a lottery ticket that won $3,000,000. When they discovered that the lottery proceeds could be paid only to one recipient under state law, Ace and Lady executed a "separate ownership agreement." The agreement created an equal interest in the ticket for both Ace and Lady. Must Ace pay gift tax on the transfer of a one-half interest in the ticket to Lady? What is the value of the gift?

List of research material: Ltr. Rul. 9217004.

72. Shaky Savings & Loan has a depositor named Olive who opened an account last year. At that time, Olive gave Shaky her Social Security number as a tax-payer identification number (TIN). The IRS notified Shaky that Olive's Social Security number was invalid. This year, Shaky asked Olive for a corrected number, which she provided. Later this year, the IRS notified Shaky that the new Social Security number also was invalid. What should Shaky do at this point about backup withholding on Olive's account? Prepare (in good form) a research memorandum to the file.

73. Alpine Corporation is a qualified small business corporation eligible to elect S corporation status. Albert is a shareholder in Alpine. On February 1 of the current year, Albert dies before signing the proper S corporation election form. The stock passes to Albert's estate. Ellen is appointed executor of Albert's estate on May 1 of the current year. On March 10 of the current year, Alpine filed Form 2553, the election forum to be an S corporation, properly signed by all March 10 shareholders, and Ellen (the executrix) on behalf of Albert. Is this a valid S corporation election? Prepare (in good form) a research memorandum to the file.

74. Joe Bacillus, owns Bacillus's Italian Restaurant. A friend of Joe's who owns a sports bar comes to Joe and wants to form a partnership with Joe to buy an old building, renovate it, and then move both the restaurant and the sports bar into it along with other tenants. Joe would like to make this investment. He needs approximately $200,000 for his share of the buy-in of the partnership that will purchase, renovate, and manage the building. However, because of other recent large expenses, Joe finds himself cash short at the present time. His only large liquid asset is his self-directed IRA, which currently owns $225,000 in stock and bonds. Joe proposes that he direct the IRA to sell the securities and to use the proceeds to invest in the building renovation partnership. Conduct appropriate research (including a computer search) to determine if Joe's plan is workable. Prepare (in good form) a research memorandum to the file.

Judicial Interpretations

LEARNING OBJECTIVES

► Describe the structural relationship among the federal courts that hear taxation cases

► Detail the constitution of, and procedures concerning, each element of the federal court system hearing tax cases

► Use proper citation conventions for each of the courts that hear tax cases

► State where tax court cases are published for use by tax researchers

► Describe conditions under which the practitioner might choose each of the trial-level courts for a client's litigation

► Work with the format and content of a court case brief

► Use the Internet to locate a court case

CHAPTER OUTLINE

Since the adoption of the Sixteenth Amendment to the Constitution in 1913, more than 50,000 federal court decisions have been rendered concerning litigation between taxpayers and the Internal Revenue Service. These cases constitute the third primary source of federal tax law. Such court cases are of special interest to the tax researcher because they typically are concerned with controversial areas of taxation. In this chapter, we will examine the federal court system, learn to locate various federal tax judicial decisions, and discuss the use of those decisions in solving tax research problems.

Federal Court System

When a taxpayer and the Internal Revenue Service cannot reach an agreement concerning a specific tax matter using the administrative review process (i.e., audits and appeals, which are discussed in Chapter 12), the dispute may be settled in the federal courts. Either the taxpayer or the IRS may initiate legal proceedings in the federal court system. A taxpayer may decide to initiate proceedings as a final attempt to recover an overpayment of tax the IRS refuses to refund, or to reverse a deficiency assessment determined by the IRS. Alternatively, the IRS may initiate proceedings to assert its claim to a deficiency, to enforce collection of taxes, or to impose civil or criminal penalties on the taxpayer.

Judicial decisions are the third primary source of the tax law. The *Internal Revenue Code* is the basis for federal tax laws, and the administrative pronouncements of the IRS interpret provisions of the Code and explain their application. Frequently, however, additional issues and questions arise regarding the proper interpretation or intended application of the law that are not answered either in the law itself or in the administrative pronouncements. The judicial system is left with the task of resolving these questions. In this process, additional tax law is generated that can carry the full force of the statute itself. Often, recurring litigation in an area of innovative or unexpected judicial decisions regarding tax matters will result in Congress enacting legislation codifying certain judicial decisions. The practitioner must be familiar with the workings of this judicial system, which has the ability to stimulate tax laws and influence future legislative developments. In addition, in the event an issue is litigated in the court system, the tax practitioner must be familiar with the precedential value of court cases and the process for review of the court's decision.

Most disagreements with the Internal Revenue Service are resolved through the administrative process of appeals. Judicial decisions should be given significant weight in arriving at a conclusion or recommendation to a tax problem; however, caution should be exercised when it is apparent from the IRS's prior actions that a given position is almost certain to result in litigation. The costs of litigation, in terms of both money and time, may be prohibitive for certain taxpayers.

All litigation between a taxpayer and the government begins in a trial court. If the decision of the trial court is not satisfactory to one of the parties, the trial court decision may be appealed to an appellate court. The appellate court will review the trial court decision, often hear new evidence and arguments, and then either uphold the trial court's decision, modify it in some way, or reverse it.

The federal court system consists of three trial courts and two levels of appellate courts. The three trial courts are the U.S. Tax Court, the U.S. District Courts, and the U.S. Court of Federal Claims. The two appellate courts are the U.S. Court of Appeals and the U.S. Supreme Court. Each of the trial courts has different attributes and is designed to serve in a different capacity in the federal judicial system. Exhibit 5–1 diagrams the existing federal court system. An appeal from any of the three trial courts is to the appropriate U.S. Court of Appeals. The parties have no direct access to the Supreme Court.

Legal Conventions

Burden of Proof   In most litigation, the party initiating the case has the burden of convincing the court that he is correct with respect to the issue. Historically, however, in most civil tax cases, the *Internal Revenue Code* placed the burden of proof on the taxpayer, whether or not he or she initiated the case, except in cases of such items as hobby losses, fraud with intent to evade tax, and the accumulated earnings tax.

In 1998, the tax law was changed to shift the burden of proof to the IRS in a few situations. The IRS now has the burden of proof in any court proceeding on income, gift, estate, or generation-skipping tax liability with respect to factual issues, provided the taxpayer (1) introduces credible evidence of the factual issue, (2) maintains records and substantiates items as presently required under the Code and Regulations, and (3) cooperates with reasonable IRS requests for meetings, interviews, witnesses, information, and documents. For corporations, trusts, and partnerships with net worth exceeding $7 million, the burden of proof remains on the taxpayer. The new rules apply only those IRS–taxpayer disputes arising in connection with audits that began after the IRS Restructuring and Reform Act of 1998 was signed into law.

The burden of proof also automatically shifts to the IRS in two situations:

► If the IRS uses statistics to reconstruct an individual's income, or
► If the court proceeding against an individual taxpayer involves a penalty or addition to tax.

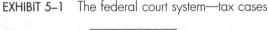

EXHIBIT 5–1   The federal court system—tax cases

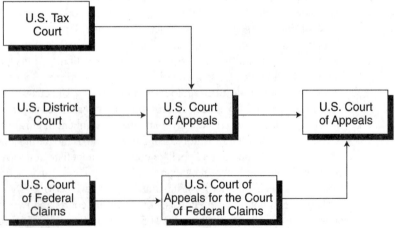

When reading a published opinion, the tax researcher should note whether the decision was based on the IRS's or the taxpayer's failure to meet a needed evidentiary burden, or whether the IRS or the taxpayer established his or her position with sufficient proof. The first situation should be considered a weaker precedent than the second. Understanding the "strength" of a court decision is an important part of tax research.

Tax Confidentiality Privilege   The IRS Restructuring and Reform Act of 1998 extends the existing attorney–client privilege of confidentiality in tax matters to nonattorneys authorized to practice before the IRS (e.g., CPAs and enrolled agents), as identified in Chapter 1. The nonattorney–client privilege may be asserted only in a *noncriminal tax* proceeding before the IRS or federal courts. The nonattorney–client privilege does not extend to written communications between a tax practitioner and a corporation in connection with the promotion of any tax shelter.

Certified public accountants and enrolled agents need to understand the rules regarding tax confidentiality as they have been applied to lawyers so as to be aware of the privilege limits. For example, privileged communication usually does not apply to the preparation of tax returns, the giving of accounting or business advice, or tax accrual workpapers. Unlike the attorney–client privilege, the nonattorney–client privilege does not automatically apply to state tax situations.

Common Legal Terminology   Some of the common legal terms likely to be encountered by the tax researcher follow.

ad hoc For one particular or special purpose; for example, an ad hoc committee might be formed to solve a certain problem.

ad valorem According to value; used in taxation to designate an assessment of taxes based on property value.

appellant The party who appeals a decision, usually to a higher court.

bona fide In good faith and without fraud or deceit.

certiorari (writ of) The process by which the U.S. Supreme Court agrees to hear a case, based on the appeal of a lower court decision by one of the parties involved in that decision.

collateral estoppel When an issue of fact has been determined by valid judgment, that issue cannot be litigated again by the same parties in future litigation.

covenant An agreement or promise to do or not to do something.

de jure In law or lawful; legitimate.

de facto In fact or reality; by virtue of accomplishment or deed.

defendant In civil proceedings, the party who is responding to the complaint; usually the one who is being sued in some matter.

deposition A written statement of a witness under oath, normally taken in question-and-answer form.

dictum (dicta) A statement or remark in a court opinion that is not necessary to support the decision.

en banc A decision by all the judges of a court instead of a single judge or a selected set of judges.

enjoin To command or instruct with authority; a judge can enjoin someone to do or not to do some act.

habeas corpus (writ of) The procedure for determining if the authorities can hold an individual in custody.

nolo contendere A party does not want to fight or continue to maintain a defense; the defendant will not contend a charge made by the government; "no contest."

non obstante veredicto (n.o.v.) Notwithstanding the verdict; a judgment that reverses the determination of a jury.

nullity Something in law that is void; an act having no legal force.

parol evidence The doctrine that renders any evidence of a prior understanding of the parties to a contract invalid if it contradicts the terms of a written contract.

plaintiff The one who initially brings a lawsuit.

per curiam A decision of the whole court, instead of just a limited number of judges.

prima facie At face value; something that is obvious and does not require further support.

res judicata The legal concept that bars relitigation on the same set of facts. Because of this concept, taxpayers must make sure that all of the issues they want (or don't want) to be litigated are included in a case. Once the case is decided, it cannot be reopened.

slip opinion An individual court decision published separately shortly after the decision is rendered.

vacate A reversal or abandonment of a prior decision of a court.

Tax Court

The U.S. **Tax Court** is a specialized trial court that hears only federal tax cases. Established under § 7441 of the *Internal Revenue Code*, its jurisdiction is limited to cases concerning the various *Internal Revenue Code*s and Revenue Acts that were adopted after February 26, 1926. Before 1943 the Tax Court was known as the **Board of Tax Appeals** (BTA); it was an administrative board of the Treasury Department rather than a true judicial court. In 1943 the BTA became the U.S. Tax Court, an administrative court, and in 1969 its status was upgraded to that of a full judicial court, with enforcement powers.

Nineteen judges hear Tax Court cases. Each judge is appointed to a fifteen-year term by the President of the United States, with the advice and confirmation of the Senate. This appointment must be based solely on the grounds of the judge's fitness to perform the duties of the office. A Tax Court justice may be removed from his or her position by the President, after notice and opportunity for public hearing, because of inefficiency, neglect of duty, or malfeasance in office, but for no other reason.

To alleviate the heavy case load of the appointed Tax Court judges, the Chief Judge of the Court periodically designates additional special trial judges to hear pertinent cases for a temporary period. Limited primarily by the budget granted by Congress, these temporary appointments are useful in decreasing the waiting period for taxpayers who wish to be heard before the Court. The decisions of these special judges carry the full authority of the U.S. Tax Court.

Tax Court judges are tax law specialists, not generalists. Typically, they have acquired many years of judicial or tax litigation experience before being appointed to the Tax Court. Thus, if a taxpayer wants to argue a technical tax issue with the IRS, the Tax Court usually is the best trial-level forum in which to try the case. Tax

Court judges are better able to understand such issues than would a judge in a more general court.

The U.S. Tax Court is a national court, based in Washington, D.C. Its jurisdiction is not limited to a specific geographical region, though, as is the case with some other federal courts. Taxpayers need not travel to Washington, D.C., to have a case tried before the Tax Court because some of its judges travel throughout the country and are available to hear taxpayer cases in every major city of the United States several times every year. See Exhibit 5–2 for a list of cities where the Tax Court holds trials.

EXHIBIT 5–2   Tax Court trial locations

ALABAMA:
  Birmingham
  Mobile
ALASKA:
  Anchorage
ARIZONA:
  Phoenix
ARKANSAS:
  Little Rock
CALIFORNIA:
  Los Angeles
  San Diego
  San Francisco
COLORADO:
  Denver
CONNECTICUT:
  Hartford
DISTRICT OF
    COLUMBIA:
  Washington
FLORIDA:
  Jacksonville
  Miami
  Tampa
GEORGIA:
  Atlanta
HAWAII:
  Honolulu
IDAHO:
  Boise
ILLINOIS:
  Chicago
INDIANA:
  Indianapolis
IOWA:
  Des Moines

KENTUCKY:
  Louisville
LOUISIANA:
  New Orleans
MARYLAND:
  Baltimore
MASSACHUSETTS:
  Boston
MICHIGAN:
  Detroit
MINNESOTA:
  St. Paul
MISSISSIPPI:
  Biloxi
  Jackson
MISSOURI:
  Kansas City
  St. Louis
MONTANA:
  Helena
NEBRASKA:
  Omaha
NEVADA:
  Las Vegas
  Reno
NEW JERSEY:
  Newark
NEW MEXICO:
  Albuquerque
NEW YORK:
  Buffalo
  New York City
  Westbury
NORTH CAROLINA:
  Winston-Salem

OHIO:
  Cincinnati
  Cleveland
  Columbus
OKLAHOMA:
  Oklahoma City
OREGON:
  Portland
PENNSYLVANIA:
  Philadelphia
  Pittsburgh
SOUTH CAROLINA:
  Columbia
TENNESSEE:
  Knoxville
  Memphis
  Nashville
TEXAS:
  Dallas
  El Paso
  Houston
  Lubbock
  San Antonio
UTAH:
  Salt Lake City
VIRGINIA:
  Richmond
WASHINGTON:
  Seattle
  Spokane
WEST VIRGINIA:
  Charleston/Huntington
WISCONSIN:
  Milwaukee

Note: The Court sits in about fifteen other cities to hear Small Tax Cases. A list of such cities is contained in a pamphlet entitled "Election of Small Tax Case Procedure and Preparation of Petitions," a copy of which may be obtained from the Clerk of the Court.

When a case is heard before the Tax Court, it almost always is presented before only one of the nineteen Tax Court judges. Taxpayers cannot request jury trials before this court. After the judge hears the case, he or she prepares a decision that is reviewed by the Chief Judge of the court. In most instances, the trial judge's opinion stands, but the Chief Judge can designate the opinion for review by the other members of the Tax Court. Upon their agreement with the decision, the opinion is released.

If the case involves an unusual, important, or novel issue, more than one judge, or the entire Tax Court, might hear the case. This rare occurrence is identified as an *en banc* sitting of the court.

For a case to be heard, the taxpayer must petition the Court within ninety days of the IRS's mailing of a notice and demand for payment of the disputed amount. The taxpayer need not pay the disputed tax liability before the case is heard.

Tax Court Decisions   The Tax Court issues two kinds of decisions: regular and memorandum. A **Regular decision** (50–70 cases per year) generally involves a new or unusual point of law, as determined by the Chief Judge of the court. If the chief judge believes that the decision concerns only the application of existing law or an interpretation of facts, the decision is issued as a **Memorandum decision** (500–600 cases per year). Over the years, however, this classification scheme has not always been strictly followed by the Court. Many of its Memorandum decisions address significant points of law or other issues important to the tax researcher. Accordingly, one should not ignore Memorandum decisions. If issues or points of law pertinent to the problem at hand are addressed, both Regular and Memorandum decisions of the Tax Court should be considered by the taxpayer.

Because the Tax Court is a national court, it hears cases that may be appealed to Courts of Appeals (discussed later in this chapter) in different geographical regions, or *circuits*. Because these Courts of Appeals occasionally disagree on tax issues, the Tax Court is faced with a dilemma. For example, one Court of Appeals may have held that a specific item is deductible in computing taxable income, while another has held against such a deduction. Which precedent should the Tax Court follow? Under *Golsen,* 54 T.C. 742 (1970), the Tax Court will follow the Court of Appeals that has direct jurisdiction over the taxpayer in question. If the Court of Appeals that has jurisdiction over the taxpayer has not ruled on the matter, the Tax Court will decide the case on the basis of its own interpretation of the disputed provision. This *Golsen* **rule** means the Tax Court may reach opposite decisions, based on identical facts, for taxpayers differentiated solely by the geographical area in which they live. The tax researcher must be aware of the *Golsen* rule in analyzing cases that may be affected by it.

Small Cases Division   The Tax Court maintains a **Small Cases Division,** which is similar to a small claims court. If the amount of a disputed deficiency, including penalties, or claimed overpayment does not exceed $50,000, a taxpayer may be heard before the Small Cases Division, upon approval of the Tax Court. The hearing is conducted as informally as possible, and the taxpayer may represent him- or herself, that is, acting *pro se.* (Of course, the taxpayer may be represented by an attorney if he or she so desires.) Neither elaborate written briefs nor formal oral arguments are required in the Small Cases Division.

At any time before a decision is final, the Tax Court may interrupt a Small Cases hearing and transfer the case to the regular Tax Court for trial. This might occur, for example, when important facts or issues of law, more suitably heard in the more formal Tax Court context, become apparent only after the Small Cases proceedings have begun.

Small Cases decisions are not published. Thus, they are not available for review by tax researchers or for use as precedent by any other taxpayer. The decision of the Small Cases judge is final and may not be appealed by the taxpayer or the government.

Locating Tax Court Decisions   Tax Court regular decisions are published by the Government Printing Office (GPO) in a set of bound reporters called the *Tax Court of the United States Reports.* These volumes are cited as "T.C." The Board of Tax Appeals had its own reporter, called the *United States Board of Tax Appeals,* cited as "B.T.A."

Memorandum decisions are not published by the GPO. They are included in special-decision reporters that are published by Commerce Clearing House (CCH) and by Research Institute of America (RIA). The CCH reporter is titled *Tax Court Memorandum Decisions,* cited as "TCM," and the RIA reporter is known as *RIA Tax Court Memorandum Decisions,* cited as "RIA T.C. Memo." The Tax Court reporter is published twice a year, and both of the memorandum-case reporters are published once a year.

Because many months may elapse between the release of a Tax Court decision and its publication in a bound reporter, such decisions receive both a temporary and a permanent citation. The **temporary citation** is structured as follows.

DeCou, Charles H., 103 T.C. _____, No. 6 (1994), where:

103 is the volume number.
T.C. is the abbreviation for the Tax Court Reporter.
_____ indicates the page number, which is to be determined later.
No. 6 is the number of the case.
(1994) is the year of the decision.

The temporary citation includes no page number for the case, because the opinion has not yet been published. All proper citations either italicize or underline the name of the court case; major elements of the citation are separated by commas. The **permanent citation** for the same case is reported as follows.

DeCou, Charles H., 103 T.C. 80 (1994), where:

103 is the volume number.
T.C. is the abbreviation for the Tax Court Reporter.
80 is the page number.
(1994) is the year of the decision.

Most court case citations include the names of both parties involved. This convention is ignored for most Tax Court citations, however, because all such cases involve the taxpayer bringing suit against the government to avoid payment of disputed tax liabilities. Thus, a traditional citation for the above case would be *DeCou v. U.S.* (or, more precisely, *Charles H. DeCou v. Commissioner*). Nonetheless, common practice allows the tax researcher to omit the reference to the defendant in the action (i.e., the government), because such reference could be inferred from the notation for the court in which the lawsuit is heard.

Once the GPO publishes the decision in the permanent bound edition of the regular Tax Court cases, the temporary citation becomes obsolete. The same citation procedure is used with respect to Board of Tax Appeals cases, substituting "B.T.A." for the "T.C." identification. Indeed, this procedure for disclosing the citation for a case (i.e., Name–Volume Number–Reporter–Page Number–Year) is common among all American courts. Exhibit 5–3 is an example of a regular Tax Court decision, reproduced from the GPO Tax Court reporter.

EXHIBIT 5–3 Tax Court opinion

JOHN D. and KAREN BEATTY, Petitioners v. COMMISSIONER OF INTERNAL REVENUE, Respondent.
(106 T.C. 268)

Docket No. 8273-94. Filed April 17, 1996.

P, an Indiana county sheriff, was required by State statute to provide meals to the prisoners incarcerated in the county jail. The costs of providing the meals were borne by P. P received a meal allowance from the county on a per meal basis at a specified rate established by the State. P claims that he provided the meals to the county prisoners as an independent contractor, and reported the meal allowances received and costs incurred on a Schedule C. R contends that P provided the meals to the county prisoners as an employee of the county and must deduct such costs on a Schedule A as employee business expenses. Held: The costs of the meals constitute costs of goods sold and are taken into account in the determination of P's gross income. Consequently, under the circumstances of this case, it makes no difference for Federal income tax purposes, whether P provided the meals to the prisoners as an independent contractor or county employee.

Stephen E. Arthur and Ronald M. Soskin, for petitioners.

Ronald T. Jordan, for respondent.

DAWSON, Judge: This case was assigned to Special Trial Judge Lewis R. Carluzzo pursuant to the provisions of Section 7443A(b)(4) and Rules 180, 181, and 183. The Court agrees with and adopts the Special Trial Judge's opinion, which is set forth below.

OPINION OF THE SPECIAL TRIAL JUDGE

CARLUZZO, Special Trial Judge: Respondent determined a deficiency in petitioners' 1991 Federal income tax in the amount of $3,627. All of the issues that result from adjustments made in the notice of deficiency have been resolved by the parties. The issues that remain in dispute were raised in two amendments to answer filed by respondent in connection with her claim for an increased deficiency in the amount of $15,062. The primary issue argued by the parties is whether petitioner John D. Beatty, as the elected sheriff of Howard County, Indiana, provided certain services to the county as an employee of the county or as an independent contractor. This issue will sometimes be referred to as the classification issue. The alternative issue, raised by petitioner, is whether the costs of the meals constitute costs of goods sold and are taken into account in determining petitioner's gross income.

FINDINGS OF FACT

Some of the facts have been stipulated and are so found. The stipulation of facts and the exhibits attached thereto are incorporated herein by this reference. During the year in issue, petitioners were husband and wife and filed a joint Federal income tax return. At the time the petition was filed, petitioners resided in Greentown, Indiana. References to petitioner are to John D. Beatty.

In 1986, petitioner was elected for a 4-year term, to commence in 1987, to the position of county sheriff for Howard County, Indiana. In 1990, petitioner was reelected to a second 4-year term which commenced in 1991. Prior to being elected county sheriff, petitioner had

EXHIBIT 5–3   *Continued*

been employed by Howard County in various positions, including deputy sheriff, since 1971.

In addition to other responsibilities, a county sheriff in the State of Indiana is required to take care of the county jail and the prisoners incarcerated there. Ind. Code Ann. Section 36-2-13-5(a)(7) (Burns 1989). Included in this statutory obligation is the sheriff's duty to feed the county prisoners, which a county sheriff is required to do at his or her expense. In return for feeding the county prisoners, a county sheriff is entitled to receive a meal allowance from the county at a rate not to exceed a statutory maximum amount per meal. Ind. Code Ann. Section 36-8-10-7 (Burns 1989). The specific allowance per meal is determined on an annual basis by the State Examiner of the Indiana State Board of Accounts. Id. For the year 1991, this amount was $1.05 per meal.

Beginning in 1987, petitioner assumed responsibility for a prisoner meal program (the program) that had been established by one of his predecessors several years earlier. Petitioner continued to operate the program as it had been operated in the past, making no substantive changes to the administration of the program. The program was managed by a kitchen supervisor/cook who was an employee of, and paid by, Howard County. The kitchen supervisor/cook was responsible for preparing menus, ordering food and supplies from vendors, receiving and inspecting deliveries of food and supplies, cooking meals, serving meals to prisoners, and keeping account of the number of meals served to prisoners.

The number and the nutritional quality of meals served to county prisoners were governed by standards established by the Indiana Department of Corrections. The sanitary quality of the kitchen facilities, food preparation techniques, and the food provided to county prisoners were subject to standards imposed by the Howard County Department of Health. Petitioner's duties in connection with the program included approving menus, paying vendors, and signing the required claim forms necessary to receive payment of the meal allowances.

In order to receive the meal allowances, petitioner, on a monthly basis, provided the county auditor with a statement listing the names of prisoners incarcerated in the jail and the number of meals served to each prisoner. Once the statements were certified as correct by the county auditor, the governing Board of Commissioners authorized payment to be made to petitioner. Because he was not required to do so, petitioner did not provide the county auditor with substantiation or verification of the actual costs incurred in feeding county prisoners. Pursuant to the Indiana statutory scheme in effect during the year in issue, petitioner was entitled to retain the difference between the meal allowances he received from the county for feeding the county prisoners and the costs he incurred to do so.

In 1991, as county sheriff, petitioner received a $30,566 salary that was appropriately reported as wages on petitioners' 1991 Federal income tax return. In addition to his salary, petitioner also received $109,952 as meal allowances from Howard County for providing meals to the prisoners incarcerated in the county jail.

Petitioner reported the $109,952 as gross receipts on a Schedule C included with petitioners' 1991 Federal income tax return. The Schedule C reflected that petitioner incurred cost of goods sold in the amount of $68,540. It appears from the Schedule C that the entire amount of the cost of goods sold was composed of purchases made during the year, a conclusion that is also supported by reasonable inferences drawn from petitioner's testimony. After reducing the gross receipts by the cost of goods sold, petitioner computed his gross profit and gross income from the prisoner meal program to be $41,412 and reported that amount on the appropriate lines of the Schedule C. Because no expense deductions were claimed on the Schedule C, $41,412 was also reported as net profit. Petitioners included this $41,412 amount in the amount reported as business income on line 12 of Form 1040 of their 1991 Federal income tax return.

OPINION

In her amendments to answer respondent has taken the position that petitioner improperly reported the meal allowances as income from a trade or business separate and

EXHIBIT 5-3 *Continued*

apart from his employment as Howard County sheriff. According to respondent, by providing meals to the county prisoners, petitioner was discharging a duty imposed upon him as a county employee, not as the proprietor of a separate trade or business. Consequently, respondent contends that the $109,952 received by petitioner as meal allowances should be considered additional compensation paid to petitioner as an employee of Howard County, and includable in his income as such. Respondent further contends that any costs incurred by petitioner in connection with the program should be considered employee business expenses, deductible only as miscellaneous itemized deductions on petitioners' Schedule A. Respondent goes on to argue that if the meal allowances are considered additional employee compensation, and the costs petitioner incurred in connection with the program are deductible as employee business expenses, the provisions of Section 67 (2-percent floor on miscellaneous itemized deductions) and Section 55 (alternative minimum tax) result in the increased deficiency now claimed by respondent.

Petitioner maintains that he did not receive the meal allowances in return for services provided to Howard County as an employee, but rather as an independent contractor. According to petitioners, the income and costs attributable to the program are properly reportable, and were properly reported, on a Schedule C. As an alternative, petitioners also argue that even if the meal allowances were received by petitioner "in an employee capacity, only the net profit earned * * * constituted gross income."

Although the parties paid some attention to the alternative position advanced by petitioners, almost the entire record and major portions of the briefs relate to the classification issue. In their respective briefs, the parties discussed at length the relevant factors that are usually considered in resolving such issues. Judging from the way that the issues were framed and the arguments presented, it is clear that the parties expect that the classification issue must first be resolved before petitioners correct 1991 Federal income tax liability can be determined.

The parties have proceeded in this case upon the apparent assumption that the costs petitioner incurred in connection with the program constitute, within the meaning of Sections 62 and 162(a), either trade or business expenses (if the classification issue were resolved in petitioners' favor), or employee business expenses (if the classification issue were resolved in respondent's favor). After carefully considering their arguments in the context of the record, it would appear that the parties' views of the forest have been blocked by the trees.

Both parties have ignored the simple fact that petitioner did not claim any Section 162(a) deductions with respect to the program. Petitioner did report cost of goods sold on the Schedule C. However, the elements included in a computation of a taxpayer's cost of goods sold do not fall within the category of expenses deductible pursuant to Section 162(a). This Court has consistently held that the cost of goods sold is not a deduction (within the meaning of Section 162(a)), but is subtracted from gross receipts in the determination of a taxpayer's gross income. *Max Sobel Wholesale Liquors v. Commissioner,* 69 T.C. 477 (1977), affd. 630 F.2d 670 (9th Cir. 1980); *Sullenger v. Commissioner,* 11 T.C. 1076, 1077 (1948); see sec. 1.61-3(a), Income Tax Regs. With respect to the determination of petitioners' 1991 Federal income tax liability, the critical question is not how petitioner must treat deductions allowable under Section 162(a) after the classification issue has been resolved, but rather what petitioner's gross income from the program was in the first instance.

Limiting our inquiry in this manner, the parties' arguments with respect to the classification issue and treatment of the related Section 162(a) deductions simply have no application because no such deductions were claimed. Because Section 162(a) deductions are not involved, and because the parties agree that the tax imposed by Section 1401 (additional tax imposed upon earnings from self-employment) is not applicable, it makes no difference in this case whether petitioner reports the income from the program as an

EXHIBIT 5–3   *Continued*

independent contractor or as an employee of Howard County. Consequently, we decline to address the question whether petitioner acted as an employee or independent contractor of Howard County with respect to the program. Under the circumstances of this case, such a distinction gives rise to no Federal income tax consequences.

As we view the case, the determination of petitioner's 1991 gross income from the program is all that is necessary to resolve the controversy between the parties, and that income is easily determined. It is $41,412, computed by subtracting cost of goods sold from the gross receipts petitioner received with respect to the program. That was the amount petitioner was required to report, and did report, on his 1991 Federal income tax return. To reflect the foregoing and the settled issues,

Decision will be entered under Rule 155.

Using the same citation conventions, the general and permanent citations, respectively, for a Tax Court memorandum decision would appear as follows.

General
Nicholls, Walter J., T.C. Memo 1995–291, where:
   T.C. Memo is a reference to a Tax Court Memorandum decision.
   1995 is the year of the decision.
   291 is the decision number.

Permanent RIA
Nicholls, Walter J., RIA T.C. Memo. ¶ 95,291, where:
   RIA T.C. Memo is the RIA Tax Court Memorandum reporter.
   ¶ 95,291 is the paragraph number.

Permanent CCH
Nicholls, Walter J., 69 TCM 3042 (1995), where:
   69 is the volume number.
   TCM is the CCH Tax Court Memorandum reporter.
   3042 is the page number.
   (1995) is the year of the decision.

One can observe from the RIA citation that the opinion was issued in 1995 because all of the Tax Court Memorandum Decisions for that year are included in the RIA reporter using paragraph numbers that begin with "95."

As we observed with respect to the regular Tax Court decisions, the temporary citation becomes obsolete when the permanent bound edition of the memorandum reporter is published.

Besides the traditional published sources for Tax Court decisions, these items also are available on computer tax services such as RIA CheckPoint, Lexis, Kleinrock's, etc. All the computer services reference the general citation and most give the parallel RIA and CCH reporter citations.

Tax Court Rule 155   When a court reaches a tax decision, it normally will not compute the tax that is due to the government or the refund that is due to a taxpayer.

The computation of this amount is left to be determined by the IRS and the taxpayer. The court will compute the tax only if the government and the taxpayer cannot agree. When the Tax Court reaches a decision without calculating the tax, the decision is said to be entered under *Rule 155*. See *Estate of Wayne-Chi Young v. Commissioner,* 110 T.C. 24, for an example of when the Tax Court will enter a decision under Rule 155. For Tax Court decisions prior to 1974, this practice was referred to as *Rule 50.*

Scope of Tax Court Decisions   The Tax Court may examine an entire tax return for a taxpayer whose case it is hearing. On the other hand, the District Court and Court of Federal Claims can address only the specific issue or issues that are involved in the case. If a taxpayer wants only a specific issue (or issues) litigated in a case, then the District Court or Court of Federal Claims may be a better forum for him than the Tax Court.

District Courts   ncmd.uscourts.gov/crtmap.htm

The U.S. **District Courts** are another trial-level forum that hears tax cases. Unlike the Tax Court, however, the District Courts hear cases involving legal issues based on the entire United States Code, not just the *Internal Revenue Code*. District Court judges typically are generalists, rather than specialists in federal tax laws. The same District Court judge might render opinions concerning matters of tax law, civil rights, bank robbery, interstate commerce, kidnapping, and fraud.

The District Courts are further distinguished from the Tax Court in that a taxpayer who disagrees with the IRS may take his or her case to the appropriate District Court only after paying the disputed tax liability; thus, in the typical District Court taxation case, the taxpayer sues the government for a refund of the disputed tax liability.

Numerous District Courts are located throughout the United States, each assigned a geographical area. The designated district can be as small as one city (New York City) or as large as the largest state (Alaska). Typically, the taxpayer will request a hearing before the District Court that has jurisdiction in the location in which he or she lives or conducts business.

District Court cases are heard before one judge, not a panel of judges. In the appropriate District Court, the taxpayer can request a jury trial concerning a tax case (or certain other federal matters). This opportunity may be useful if the taxpayer wants to argue an "emotional" issue rather than a technical one, or if the taxpayer or his or her associates are particularly credible witnesses (and thus have a good chance of winning a jury trial). Limited to decisions concerning questions of fact, juries apparently occasionally can be persuaded in a tax case to hold for the taxpayer when a judge might not be so inclined.

Because the District Courts are general in nature and do not specialize in tax matters, over time, their decisions can vary significantly among the districts. Some of their decisions have important precedential value and can be relied on by the tax researcher; however, many of these decisions are poorly structured or poorly conceived from a technical standpoint, and represent candidates for overturn on appeal. The tax researcher must examine these decisions carefully to assess their probable use as a precedent before using them to help solve a client's tax problem.

Locating District Court Decisions   District Court tax decisions are published in three different reporters. West Publishing includes such cases in its *Federal Supplement Series;* citations for these cases include the "F.Supp." abbreviation. The series contains all decisions of the District Courts designated for publication, including those for the numerous nontax cases. Most university and law school libraries subscribe to the *Federal Supplement Series.* However, it is a waste of money for the tax researcher to subscribe to this series to obtain just the tax decisions that are rendered in the District Courts. Instead, the tax researcher can use special tax case reporters that include only tax decisions selected from all of the decisions of the federal courts except Tax Court. (As we discussed earlier, the Tax Court's Regular and Memorandum Decisions are published in specialized reporters, so they do not present a budgeting problem of this sort.)

RIA's specialized tax reporter is titled *American Federal Tax Reports,* abbreviated in citations as **"AFTR."** Currently, the second series of this reporter is in use, with "2d" added to indicate that the cases therein usually relate to the current *Internal Revenue Code.* Accordingly, the abbreviation AFTR2d is commonly used. CCH's specialized federal tax case reporter is known as *United States Tax Cases,* which is abbreviated as **"USTC"** in traditional citations. Do not confuse this abbreviation with that for the U.S. Tax Court, which we have identified as "T.C." Occasionally, the West citation (F.Supp.) is referred to as the primary citation for a case, and the CCH and RIA reporters are used for secondary citations. The AFTR2d and USTC reporters each publish 1,200–1,500 tax cases per year from courts other than the U.S. Tax Court.

Besides the traditional published primary and secondary court reporters, several electronic court reporters are available. Both Kleinrock's and Infotax publish tax decisions as part of their computer services. The computer-based reporters have their own citations, and they usually cross-reference one or more of the standard printed reporters (West, RIA, CCH). An illustration of the various citations for a District Court case follows.

Published Court Reporters

West reporter:	*Ruhland, Kenneth,* 839 F.Supp. 993 (N.D.N.Y., 1993)
CCH reporter:	*Ruhland, Kenneth,* 94-1 USTC ¶ 50,047 (N.D.N.Y., 1993)
RIA reporter:	*Ruhland, Kenneth,* 73 AFTR2d 94-502 (N.D.N.Y., 1993)

Computer Court Reporters

Kleinrock's:	*Ruhland, Kenneth,* KTC 1993-256 (N.D.N.Y., 1993)
Infotax:	*Ruhland, Kenneth,* 94 TNT 20-66 (N.D.N.Y., 1993)

Note: RIA CheckPoint and CCH Tax Research Network use their respective published court reporter citations.

Each of these citations indicates both the specific District Court that heard the case and the year in which the opinion was issued. Given publication time lags, however, this may not match the year in which the reporter volume was published. Unless necessitated by such a delay, a proper citation need not include in the parentheses the year in which the opinion was issued, in all but a West citation.

Notice that more than one volume of the USTC reporter was published by CCH in 1994, as indicated by the volume number, and that this reporter uses paragraph numbers to organize the opinions. Other elements of the citations are familiar. A complete citation for this case, using traditional form, would appear as follows.

Ruhland, Kenneth, 839 F.Supp. 993; 94-1 USTC ¶ 50,047; 73 AFTR2d 94-502; 94 TNT 20-66; KTC 1993-256 (N.D.N.Y. 1993)

Court of Federal Claims

The U.S. **Court of Federal Claims** is the newest of the trial-level courts. It was created as of October 1, 1982, by the Federal Courts Improvement Act (P.L. 97-164). In this act, the U.S. Court of Claims and the U.S. Court of Customs and Patent Appeals were reorganized into two new courts. The trial division of the U.S. Court of Claims became the new U.S. Claims Court, and the remaining divisions of both courts became the new Court of Appeals for the Federal Circuit, discussed later. The forum was renamed the U.S. Court of Federal Claims in 1992. Sixteen judges are appointed to the Court of Federal Claims. Its jurisdiction lies in hearing cases concerning all monetary claims against the federal government, only one type of which is in the form of tax refunds. Thus, the taxpayer must pay the disputed tax and sue the government for a refund in order for the case to be heard in the Court of Federal Claims. Similarly, like the District Court but unlike the Tax Court, the Court of Federal Claims is composed of judges who, with only a few exceptions, are not specialists in technical tax law. The Court of Federal Claims does not allow jury trials on any matter.

The U.S. Court of Federal Claims is a national court located in Washington, D.C. However, because the Court of Federal Claims judges periodically travel to the major cities of the country and hear cases in these various locations, in a manner similar to that of the Tax Court, one need not go to Washington, D.C., to present a case before the Court of Federal Claims.

Moreover, because the Court of Federal Claims is a national court that must follow the decisions only of the Federal District of the Court of Appeals, it is not bound by the geographical Circuit Courts of Appeals that have ruled on similar cases, nor by the Court of Appeals for the circuit in which the taxpayer works or resides. This may be important to a taxpayer whose circuit has held adversely to his or her position on the disputed issue: If the case were presented to the appropriate District Court, or to the Tax Court (recall the *Golsen* rule), the precedent of the adverse ruling would be adopted by those trial courts, but the Court of Federal Claims is not so bound.

Locating Court of Federal Claims Decisions   Before October 1982, all U.S. Court of Claims decisions concerning both tax and nontax issues were published in West's *Federal Reporter,* second series (this reporter now is in its third series). Citations to the reporter use the abbreviations "F.2d" or "F.3d," as the case may be. Current decisions of the U.S. Court of Federal Claims can be found in West's primary reporter, *U.S. Court of Federal Claims,* which can be cited by using the abbreviation "Fed. Cl." In addition, tax decisions of the old U.S. Court of Claims and the new U.S. Court of Federal Claims are available through several secondary published and electronic reporters. U.S. Court of Federal Claims decisions are published in CCH's *United States Tax Cases* (USTC), RIA's *American Federal Tax Reports 2d* (AFTR2d), and by the various CD-ROM services.

Examine the following proper primary and secondary citations for decisions of the U.S. Court of Federal Claims. All of the elements of these citations are familiar to us. As is most often the situation, when a decision is issued and published in the same year, one need not be redundant in identifying the given year in the body of the citation, because the reader can infer the year from other aspects of the listing. A complete citation of the case would include references to all of the publications, in the form indicated previously.

Published Court Reporters

West reporter: *Bennett, Courtney,* 30 Fed. Cl. 396 (1994)
CCH reporter: *Bennett, Courtney,* 94-1 USTC ¶ 50,044 (Fed. Cl., 1994)
RIA reporter: *Bennett, Courtney,* 73 AFTR2d 94-534 (Fed. Cl., 1994)

Computer Court Reporters

Infotax CD-ROM: *Bennett, Courtney,* 95 TNT 30-9 (Fed.Cl., 1994)
Kleinrock's CD-ROM: *Bennett, Courtney,* KTC 1994-647 (Fed. Cl., 1994)

Note: RIA CheckPoint and CCH Tax Research Network use their respective published court reporter citations.

As a general tax court, the U.S. Court of Federal Claims has generated decisions that cannot easily be anticipated. Practitioners usually should pursue a case in the U.S. Court of Federal Claims when the applicable U.S. District and U.S. Tax Court decisions are adverse to the taxpayer, or when a nontechnical matter lies at the heart of the taxpayer's case.

Courts of Appeals

The first level of federal appellate courts is the U.S. **Courts of Appeals.** Like the District Court and Court of Federal Claims, the Courts of Appeals consider issues in both tax and nontax litigation, although the Courts of Appeals generally will hear only cases that involve a question of law. Seldom will a Circuit Court of Appeals challenge the trial court's findings as to the facts.

Congress has created thirteen Courts of Appeals: Eleven are geographical, in that they are responsible for cases that originate in designated states; one is assigned to Washington, D.C.; and one is known as the Court of Appeals for the Federal Circuit. This last court hears tax and other cases that originate only in the Court of Federal Claims. The other Courts of Appeals consider tax and nontax issues brought from the Tax Court or a District Court for an assigned geographical region.

The eleven geographical Courts of Appeals are organized into geographical *circuits,* each of which is assigned a number. Practitioners commonly refer to the circuit courts by this number. For example, the Court of Appeals designated to hear cases that originate in Seattle typically is referred to as the Ninth Circuit Court of Appeals. Exhibit 5–4 shows the jurisdiction of each of the Courts of Appeals. Approximately twenty judges have been appointed to each of the circuit courts. Typically, a three-judge panel hears a Court of Appeals case. Jury trials are not available in these courts.

A Court of Appeals decision carries precedential weight because each circuit is independent of the others and must follow only the decisions of the U.S. Supreme Court. Because the Supreme Court hears only about a dozen tax cases annually, the Court of Appeals, in most situations, represents the final authority in federal tax matters. Thus, a researcher generally must follow the holding of a tax decision issued by the Court of Appeals for the circuit in which the client works or resides if the controlling facts or issues of law are sufficiently similar.

Decisions by the circuit court in which the taxpayer works or resides should be given great consideration, even if the researcher has found that another circuit court has held in the taxpayer's favor in a similar case. For example, if a taxpayer lives in

EXHIBIT 5–4 Circuit court jurisdictions

Circuit	Assigned Jurisdiction
First	Maine, Massachusetts, New Hampshire, Puerto Rico, Rhode Island
Second	Connecticut, New York, Vermont
Third	Delaware, New Jersey, Pennsylvania, Virgin Islands
Fourth	Maryland, North Carolina, South Carolina, Virginia, West Virginia
Fifth	Canal Zone, Louisiana, Mississippi, Texas
Sixth	Kentucky, Michigan, Ohio, Tennessee
Seventh	Illinois, Indiana, Wisconsin
Eighth	Arkansas, Iowa, Minnesota, Missouri, Nebraska, North Dakota, South Dakota
Ninth	Alaska, Arizona, California, Guam, Hawaii, Idaho, Montana, Nevada, Oregon, Washington
Tenth	Colorado, Kansas, New Mexico, Oklahoma, Utah, Wyoming
Eleventh	Alabama, Florida, Georgia
D.C.	Washington, D.C.
Federal	U.S. Court of Federal Claims

San Antonio, and the Fifth Circuit has held that an item similar to the taxpayer's does not qualify as a deduction, the deduction most likely should not be claimed, even if the Seventh or Eighth Circuit has held that the deduction is available. Under the *Golsen* rule, the unfavorable Fifth Circuit decision will apply to the taxpayer at the trial-court level, even though the U.S. Tax Court will be forced in this example to render opinions that are inconsistent among taxpayers.

If, in the same example, however, the Fifth Circuit had not yet ruled on the issue, and the favorable Seventh Circuit ruling is available, the researcher may be more comfortable in following the decision of the "outside" circuit. Prior decisions of Courts of Appeals are of great importance in the construction of subsequent decisions by another circuit, and the researcher rightly can place precedential value on the holdings of other circuits in anticipating the proper position for a client.

So, in general, the Court of Appeals decisions most important to a given taxpayer are those issued by the circuit in which he or she works or resides. In addition, however, these observations can be made: Second, Ninth, and D.C. Circuit decisions are especially important, because of numerous innovative, unusual, and controversial judicial interpretations of the tax laws, and because their jurisdictions include the two most populous states in the nation and the nation's capital.

Locating Court of Appeals Decisions   Court of Appeals decisions are reported in several general and specialized tax publications. All of the decisions of the various Courts of Appeals designated for publication are included in West's *Federal Reporter* (F.2d or F.3d). Most tax cases from the Courts of Appeals are published in the *United States Tax Cases* service (USTC), and in the *American Federal Tax Reports*. The familiar citation conventions are used in the following examples of primary and secondary citations for a Court of Appeals decision.

Published Court Reporters

West reporter: *Home of Faith,* 39 F.3d 263 (CA-10, 1994)
CCH reporter: *Home of Faith,* 94-2 USTC ¶ 50,570 (CA-10, 1994)
RIA reporter: *Home of Faith,* 74 AFTR2d 94-5608 (CA-10, 1994)

Computer Court Reporters

Kleinrock's: *Home of Faith,* KTC 1994-564 (CA-10, 1994)
Infotax: *Home of Faith,* 94 TNT 225–18 (CA-10, 1994)

Note: RIA CheckPoint and CCH Tax Research Network use their respective published court reporter citations.

Exhibit 5–5 reproduces a tax decision from the Court of Appeals, as it appears in the AFTR2d service.

EXHIBIT 5–5   Court of Appeals decision

UNITED STATES OF AMERICA, PLAINTIFF-APPELLEE, v.
STEPHEN W. BENTSON, DEFENDANT-APPELLANT

UNITED STATES COURT OF APPEALS FOR THE NINTH CIRCUIT No. 90-10460. 10/16/91, 947 F.2d 1353. Affirming an unreported District Court Decision. October 16, 1991, filed .

Edward Brookhart, for the plaintiff-appellee.
William A. Cohan, for the defendant-appellant.

JUDGES: Herbert Y. C. Choy and Joseph T. Sneed, Circuit Judges, and Robert J. Kelleher,* District Judge. Opinion by Judge Sneed.

SNEED, *Circuit Judge:* Stephen W. Bentson appeals his conviction for willful failure to file tax returns for the years 1983 and 1984. Bentson argues inter alia that the Internal Revenue Service's alleged failure to comply with the Paperwork Reduction Act (PRA) precludes his being penalized for failing to file a return, and that the charges against him must be dismissed because the IRS did not publish the 1040 tax return form as a rule in the *Federal Register* pursuant to the Administrative Procedure Act (APA). For reasons substantially the same as those given in our opinion today in *United States v. Hicks,* 947 F.2d 1356, 68 A.F.T.R.2d (P-H) 5762 (9th Cir. 1991), we find Bentson's arguments meritless, and affirm the judgment below.

I.
FACTS AND PROCEEDINGS BELOW

For the tax year 1982, Bentson filed a so-called protest tax return, in which he refused to supply information other than his name, address, social security number, and signature. He filled the remaining blanks of his Form 1040 with asterisks, and stated in an attachment that any requirement that he supply additional information violated his constitutional rights under the Fifth Amendment. No tax returns have been located for Bentson for the tax years 1983 and 1984. Bentson was charged with three counts of willful failure to file tax returns, one for each for the years 1982 through 1984, in violation of the 26 U.S.C. § 7203. Bentson filed a timely pretrial motion for dismissal on the ground that the IRS violated the PRA by its failure to display Office of Management and Budget (OMB) control numbers on the instructions and regulations associated with tax return Form 1040. He also filed an untimely pretrial motion for dismissal on the ground that the IRS violated the APA by failing to publish Form 1040 and associated instructions in the *Federal Register.* The District Court denied both motions.

A bench trial was held. After the close of the government's case in chief, Bentson moved for judgment of acquittal, relying on this court's initial decision in *United States v. Kimball,* 896 F.2d 1218, vacated, 925 F.2d 356 (9th Cir. 1991) (en banc). The trial court granted Bentson's motion as to the first count only. Ultimately, the court found Bentson guilty on

EXHIBIT 5–5 *Continued*

the other two counts, and sentenced him to eight months incarceration followed by three years' probation, along with a $2000 fine.

Bentson filed a post-trial motion for a judgment of acquittal, arguing that the government had failed to offer evidence sufficient to prove beyond a reasonable doubt that he did not file protest returns for 1983 and 1984. His theory was that under the *Kimball* rule, if protest returns had indeed been filed, he could not be convicted under 26 U.S.C. § 7203. The District Court denied the motion.

On appeal, Bentson renewed his PRA and APA arguments, asserting that the judgment against him should be reversed as a matter of law. In his opening appellate brief, Bentson also renewed his contention that the government failed to prove he did not file protest returns for 1983 and 1984. After the brief was submitted, this court, sitting en banc, reheard the Kimball case and reversed its decision therein. 925 F.2d 356 (9th Cir. 1991). In his reply brief, Bentson has altered his stance. He now asserts that the government failed to prove he did not file valid returns for 1983 and 1984.

II.

JURISDICTION AND STANDARD OF REVIEW

We have jurisdiction pursuant to 28 U.S.C. § 1291. With respect to his APA and PRA arguments, Bentson raises only issues of law, which we review de novo, see *United States v. McConney,* 728 F.2d 1195, 1201 (9th Cir.) (en banc), cert. denied, 469 U.S. 824, 83 L. Ed. 2d 46, 105 S.Ct. 101 (1984). With respect to the government's alleged failure of proof, we must determine whether, after viewing the evidence in the light most favorable to the prosecution, any rational trier of fact could have found the essential elements of the crime beyond a reasonable doubt. *United States v. Marchini,* 797 F.2d 759, 766 (9th Cir. 1986), cert. denied, 479 U.S. 1085, 94 L.Ed.2d 145, 107 S.Ct. 1288 (1987).

III.

ANALYSIS

A. Form 1040: Compliance with the Paperwork Reduction Act

Bentson argues that the IRS failed to comply with the PRA in that it failed to obtain OMB control numbers for the regulations and instructions associated with tax return Form 1040. In support he cites the decisions of this court in *United States v. Hatch,* 919 F.2d 1394 (9th Cir. 1990), and *United States v. Smith,* 866 F.2d 1092 (9th Cir. 1989).

In today's decision in *United States v. Hicks,* 947 F.2d 1356 (9th Cir. 1991), we held that the public protection provision of the PRA, 44 U.S.C. § 3512, constitutes no defense to prosecution under 26 U.S.C. § 7203. Bentson's PRA argument is essentially the same as the argument we rejected in *Hicks,* and we find no merit in it. Bentson points to dicta in *United States v. Collins,* 920 F.2d 619, 630-31, nn. 12-13 (10th Cir. 1990), that suggests that persons charged with criminal violations of the *Internal Revenue Code* might in some circumstances legitimately raise a PRA defense. For reasons given in *Hicks,* we believe that the PRA was not intended to provide such a defense, and therefore we disagree with the *Collins* court's dicta.

B. Form 1040: Compliance with the Administrative Procedure Act

Bentson argues that Form 1040 and its instructions constitute a "rule" for purposes of the APA and therefore must be published in the *Federal Register*. Without publication, he argues, the statute providing for penalties for willful failure to file a tax return, 26 U.S.C. § 7203, has no legal effect, and he cannot be prosecuted under it.

The District Court denied Bentson's motion for dismissal based on the APA as untimely. Whether or not it was untimely, the legal theory on which the motion was based has no merit. *Hicks,* supra.

EXHIBIT 5–5   *Continued*

C. Failure of Proof

Bentson asserts in his reply brief that the government failed to offer evidence sufficient to prove that he did not file valid tax returns for 1983 and 1984. Legal issues raised for the first time in reply briefs are waived. Eberle v. City of Anaheim, 901 F.2d 81, 818 (9th Cir. 1990). However, even assuming that Bentson's new theory raised no new legal issue, we reject it, because we find that Bentson made a binding judicial admission to the contrary.

In his closing statement before the District Court, Bentson's counsel said:

> The defense is not suggesting that returns were filed for 1983 and '84, which the Internal Revenue Service would consider to be valid documents. The defendant submits rather that the government's evidence fails to show that protest documents were not filed for 1983 and 1984.

Our review of Bentson's closing statement convinces us that the language quoted above was a straightforward judicial admission, not merely a concession for the sake of argument. It was a binding concession that Bentson did not file valid returns for the years 1983 and 1984. See *United States v. Wilmer,* 799 F.2d 495, 502 (9th Cir. 1986) (attorney's statement during oral arguments constitutes judicial admission), cert. denied, 481 U.S. 1004, 107 S.Ct. 1626, 92 L.Ed.2d 200 (1987); *Magallanes-Damian v. INS,* 783 F.2d 931, 934 (9th Cir. 1986) (deportation case) (absent egregious circumstances, parties are generally bound by admission of attorney); 9 J. Wigmore, *Evidence* §§ 2588, 2594 (Chadbourn revision, 1981) (oral judicial admission is binding). A judicial admission is binding before both the trial and appellate courts. *American Title Ins. Co. v. Lacelaw Corp.,* 861 F.2d 224, 226 (9th Cir. 1988). Having stated in open court that he was not claiming that he filed valid tax returns, Bentson may not now claim that the government failed to prove he did not file valid tax returns.

AFFIRMED.

Complete citations of decisions rendered by an appellate court (the Courts of Appeals and the Supreme Court) often include a history of the case through the lower courts. In this more elaborate citation, each of the lower court citations is modified to indicate whether the present case affirmed, reversed, or modified the prior decision. We will discuss each of these modifications further in Chapter 6.

Supreme Court

The U.S. **Supreme Court** is an appellate court and the highest court in the nation. Article III of the Constitution created the Supreme Court and extended to it judicial power "to all cases of law and equity, arising under this Constitution, the laws of the United States, and treaties. . . ." Thus, concerning all areas of federal law, the Supreme Court is the final level of appeal and the sovereign legal authority.

The Supreme Court meets and hears cases only in Washington, D.C. If a taxpayer wants to have his or her case heard by the Supreme Court, the taxpayer and counsel must travel to the nation's capital to present the arguments. The Supreme Court is a nine-justice panel; all nine judges hear every case that the Court agrees to consider. The Court does not conduct jury trials.

A U.S. citizen does not have an automatic right to have his or her case heard by the Supreme Court. Permission to present the case must be requested by a **writ of certiorari.** If the Court decides to hear the case, the "certiorari is granted"; if it refuses, the "certiorari is denied." One must treat a Supreme Court decision as having the full force of the law; although Congress might repeal the challenged statute, or the federal administration might refuse to fund or enforce the underlying law and related activities, neither the citizen nor the government can appeal a Supreme Court decision.

As we have discussed, however, certiorari is granted in very few tax cases. Only about a dozen appeals relating to tax issues—state, local, and federal; income, property, sales, estate, and gift; individual, corporate, and fiduciary—are heard by the Supreme Court in a typical year. In most cases, those petitions granted involve an issue at conflict among the federal circuits or a tax issue of major importance. For instance, the Court might hear a client's case concerning the inclusion in gross income of life insurance proceeds, if many similar cases had been brought before the various federal courts and tremendous tax liabilities were under dispute, or if two or more of the circuits had issued inconsistent holdings on the matter.

In denying the petition for certiorari, the Supreme Court is not "upholding," or in any way confirming, a lower court decision. Rather, the Court simply does not find the appealed case to be interesting or important enough to consider during its limited sessions. The lower court's decision does stand, but one cannot infer that the decision necessarily is correct or that it should be followed in the future by other taxpayers whose situations are similar. These matters of open-fact tax planning must be analyzed using the tax researcher's professional judgment.

Locating Supreme Court Decisions   At least five different general and specialized reporters publish all of the tax-related Supreme Court decisions. CCH includes such cases in the *United States Tax Cases* service (USTC), and RIA publishes them in the *American Federal Tax Reports* (AFTR, AFTR2d, or AFTR3d). The Government Printing Office publishes the *United States Supreme Court Reports,* which contains all of the tax and nontax decisions of the Court. In common citation convention, references to this service are abbreviated as "U.S." In addition, West Publishing includes all Supreme Court decisions in the *Supreme Court Reporter* (S.Ct.).

In the following examples of proper citations, one can infer from the GPO and West citations that the case was heard by the Supreme Court, and any further reference to that forum (e.g., as USSC) would be redundant. In addition, if a case involves an issue of pre-1954 Code tax law, the first series of the AFTR service would be cited. Exhibit 5–6 is an example of a tax decision of the Supreme Court, reproduced from the USTC reporter.

Published Court Reporters

GPO reporter:	*Indianapolis Power & Light,* 493 U.S. 203 (1990)
West reporter:	*Indianapolis Power & Light,* 110 S.Ct. 589 (1990)
CCH reporter:	*Indianapolis Power & Light,* 90-1 ¶ 50,007 (USSC, 1990)
RIA reporter:	*Indianapolis Power & Light,* 65 AFTR2d 90-394 (USSC, 1990)

Computer Court Reports

Kleinrock's:	*Indianapolis Power & Light,* KTC 1990-53 (USSC, 1990)
Infotax:	*Indianapolis Power & Light,* 90 TNT 8-4 (USSC, 1990)

Note: RIA CheckPoint and CCH Tax Research Network use their respective published court reporter citations.

EXHIBIT 5-6   Supreme Court decision syllabus

SUPREME COURT OF THE UNITED STATES

Syllabus

O'GILVIE et al., Minors v. UNITED STATES

Certiorari to the United States Court of Appeals for the Tenth Circuit

Docket: 95-966, 95-977 - Decided December 10, 1996

519 U.S. 79; 117 S.Ct. 452

Petitioners, the husband and two children of a woman who died of toxic shock syndrome, received a jury award of $1,525,000 actual damages and $10 million punitive damages in a tort suit based on Kansas law against the maker of the product that caused decedent's death. They paid federal income tax insofar as the award's proceeds represented punitive damages, but immediately sought a refund. Procedurally speaking, this litigation represents the consolidation of two cases brought in the same Federal District Court: the husband's suit against the Government for a refund, and the Government's suit against the children to recover the refund that the Government had made to the children earlier. The District Court found for petitioners under 26 U.S.C. Section 104(a)(2), which, as it read in 1988, excluded from "gross income," the "amount of any damages received . . . on account of personal injuries or sickness." (Emphasis added.) The court held on the merits that the italicized language includes punitive damages, thereby excluding such damages from gross income. The Tenth Circuit reversed, holding that the exclusionary provision does not cover punitive damages.

Held:

1. Petitioners' punitive damages were not received "on account of" personal injuries; hence the gross-income-exclusion provision does not apply and the damages are taxable. Pp. 2–11.

(a) Although the phrase "on account of" does not unambiguously define itself, several factors prompt this Court to agree with the Government when it interprets the exclusionary provision to apply to those personal injury lawsuit damages that were awarded by reason of, or because of, the personal injuries, and not to punitive damages that do not compensate injury, but are private fines levied by civil juries to punish reprehensible conduct and to deter its future occurrence. For one thing, the Government's interpretation gives the phrase "on account of" a meaning consistent with the dictionary definition. More important, in *Commissioner v. Schleier,* 515 U.S. 323, this Court came close to resolving the statute's ambiguity in the Government's favor when it said that the statute covers pain and suffering damages, medical expenses, and lost wages in an ordinary tort case because they are "designed to compensate . . . victims" id., at ____, n. 5, but does not apply to elements of damages that are "punitive in nature," id., at ____. The Government's reading also is more faithful to the statutory provision's history and basic tax-related purpose of excluding compensatory damages that restore a victim's lost, nontaxable "capital." Petitioners suggest no very good reason why Congress might have wanted the exclusion to have covered these punitive damages, which are not a substitute for any normally untaxed personal (or financial) quality, good, or "asset" and do not compensate for any kind of loss. Pp. 2–8.

(b) Petitioners' three arguments to the contrary—that certain words or phrases in the original, or current, version of the statute work in their favor; that the exclusion of punitive damages from gross income may be justified by Congress' desire to be generous to tort victims and to avoid such administrative problems as separating punitive from compensatory portions of a global settlement or determining the extent to which a punitive damages award is itself intended to compensate; and that their position is supported by a 1989 statutory amendment that specifically says that the gross income exclusion does not apply to any punitive damages in connection with a case not involving physical injury or sickness—are not sufficiently persuasive to overcome the Government's interpretation. Pp. 8–11.

EXHIBIT 5–6 *Continued*

2. Petitioners' two case-specific procedural arguments—that the Government's lawsuit was untimely and that its original notice of appeal was filed a few days late—are rejected. Pp. 12–14.

66 F. 3d 1550, affirmed.

BREYER, J., delivered the opinion of the Court, in which REHNQUIST, C.J., and STEVENS, KENNEDY, SOUTER, and GINSBURG, JJ., joined. SCALIA, J., filed a dissenting opinion, in which O'CONNOR and THOMAS, JJ., joined.

* * *

Case Briefs

Tax researchers have found that the construction of a concise **case brief** is of great value to them, both when they return to a client's research problem or planning environment after a period of time passes, and in using the given case in constructing a research analysis for another client. The reader should be careful, though, to distinguish this concise research tool from the case briefs required as part of the procedure of most court hearings. The latter is a lengthy document that includes a detailed analysis of all parts of the litigants' arguments.

A proper tax research case brief presents in summary fashion, ideally not exceeding one page, the facts, issue(s), holding, and analysis of the chosen court case. From such a brief, the researcher can discover in a very short period of time whether the full text of the case is of further use in the present analysis. If the briefed case does warrant further examination, the researcher can locate it (or any other cases that are cited in the brief itself) very quickly.

Study carefully the format of the case brief in Exhibit 5–7. Notice that the indicated tax research issues correspond with each of the analyses and holdings of the court, as indicated by the numbers of the brief's outline format. Finally, notice that citations to other cases, or to administrative proclamations, are complete and somewhat detailed, helping to facilitate further research.

The Internet and Judicial Sources

The Internet and the World Wide Web provide a new way for tax researchers to access judicial sources of tax law. Many law schools, journals, tax publishers, and individuals have set up their own home pages (web sites) on the Internet. While not as user friendly as a commercial CD-ROM or online service, these home pages allow anyone with access to the Internet to locate many court decisions. Examples of some of these home pages that have links to other judicial sources are as follows.

Emory U. School of Law	http://www.law.emory.edu/
Cornell U. School of Law	http://www.law.cornell.edu/
U. of Texas School of Law	http://www.utexas.edu/law
Law Journal Extra	http://www.ljextra.com/
Practitioner's Publishing Co.	http://www.ppcinfo.com/
Will Yancey's Home Page	http://www.willyancey.com/

EXHIBIT 5–7   Court case brief illustrated

CITATION	*U.S. v. Stephen W. Bentson,* 947 F.2d 1353; 92-1 USTC ¶ 50,048; 68 AFTR2d 5773 (CA-9, 1991).
ISSUE(S)	(1) Does the IRS's failure to comply with the Paperwork Reduction Act (PRA) preclude a taxpayer from being penalized for failing to file a tax return and cause charges against him to be dismissed?
	(2) Could the IRS penalties be avoided because the Form 1040 had not been published in the *Federal Register*?
	(3) Could the IRS penalties be avoided because of a lack of proof that Bentson had failed to file returns?
FACTS	For the tax year 1982, Bentson filed a "protest tax return." He refused to supply information other than his name, address, social security number, and signature. The rest of his Form 1040 was filled with asterisks, and he attached a statement asserting that to supply other information violated his Fifth Amendment constitutional right. No tax returns could be located for 1983 and 1984. Bentson was charged by the IRS with three counts of willful failure to file tax returns. A District Court bench trial was held. After the close of the government's case Bentson moved for dismissal, relying on *U.S. v. Kimball,* 896 F.2d 1218, vacated, 925 F.2d 356 (CA-9, 1991).
HOLDING	The District Court granted Bentson's motion as to the first count only. He was found guilty on two counts and sentenced to eight months incarceration followed by three years' probation, and a $2,000 fine. The Ninth Circuit affirmed the lower court's decision.
ANALYSIS	(1) Bentson argued the IRS failed to comply with the Paperwork Reduction Act and relied on the original *U.S. v. Kimball.* This decision was reversed in 1991 (see 925 F.2d 356). The Ninth Circuit held that the public protection provision of the Paperwork Reduction Act is not a defense to prosecution under IRC § 7203 (willful failure to file a return, supply information, or pay tax).
	(2) Bentson argued that Form 1040 and the instructions constitute a "rule" for purposes of the Administrative Procedures Act (APA) and therefore must be published in the *Federal Register* to be valid. The Ninth Circuit ruled this argument had no merit.
	(3) Bentson argued the IRS had not proved he did not file tax returns for 1983 and 1984. This argument was rejected because Bentson had already made a binding judicial admission to the contrary.

How might the Internet be used to find the published opinion relating to a court case? Suppose a tax researcher wanted to obtain a copy of a certain Court of Appeals decision from the Fifth Circuit in New Orleans. First, the user should connect to a tax research site, such as the Emory U. School of Law home page (see example in Exhibit 5–8). The user then would click on the line for Federal Courts Finder. A new Internet page is presented, showing a map of the United States and a set of links to the various Courts of Appeal (see Exhibit 5–9). Because the user is looking for a Fifth Circuit Court of Appeals decision, he or she would click on the link for the Fifth Circuit. The user would then be transferred to the database for decisions of the Fifth Circuit in New Orleans (see Exhibit 5–10). This web page allows the user to search for a case by user-selected criteria, such as a date, a citation, parties involved, or key words. Once the case is found, a copy can be printed by the user.

EXHIBIT 5–8 Emory University School of Law web page

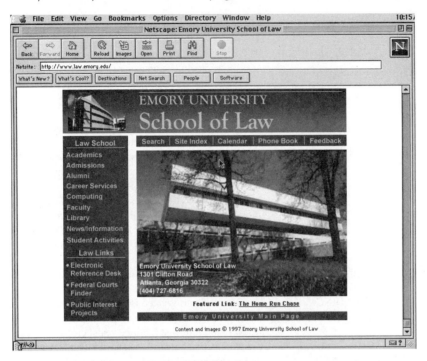

EXHIBIT 5–9 U.S. Federal Courts Finder

EXHIBIT 5–10   Fifth Circuit Court of Appeals web page

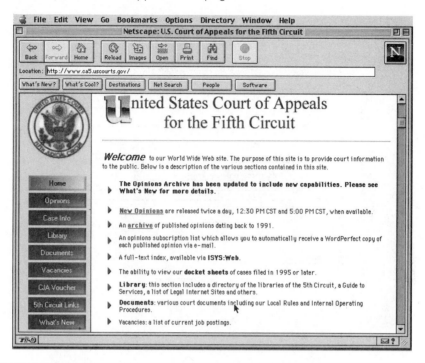

This methodology can be used by a legal researcher to locate many federal and state court cases. In the future, improvements in the reliability and user friendliness of the Internet should make the World Wide Web an even more effective means of locating judicial sources involving tax issues.

Computer Tax Service Example

The tax researcher can use an online computer tax service to find court cases of interest. If the researcher knows the case name or citation, he or she can enter it directly and obtain a copy of the case. However, if the case name or citation is not known, the researcher can use a computer query to find cases that have addressed the issue at hand.

> **Example 5–1** Your client is involved in a dispute with the IRS over the valuation for estate tax purposes of a closely held business. In the process of getting ready to go to the Tax Court on this matter, you have to hire an expert witness to justify the client's valuation of the business. During the interviews, one of the experts says that she will use the Capital Asset Pricing Model (CAPM) as the basis for her valuation. You are not sure what the CAPM is and how the courts will react to it. You therefore execute a computer search using RIA CheckPoint to see if there is any information available on the use of the CAPM in tax valuation. Exhibit 5–11 shows an example of a search query that could be used to find any court cases that have discussed the CAPM. Exhibit 5–12 shows a portion of a Tax Court Memorandum Decision (*Furman v. Comm.*, T.C. Memo. 1998-157) you found in which the Tax Court rejected the use of the CAPM in

EXHIBIT 5-11 CheckPoint CAPM search query

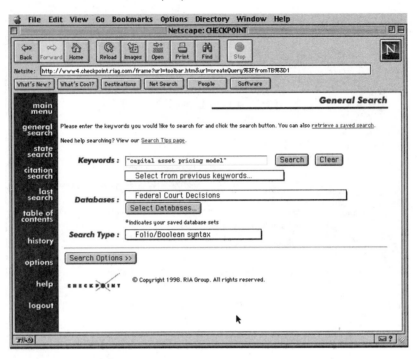

EXHIBIT 5-12 CheckPoint CAPM search query

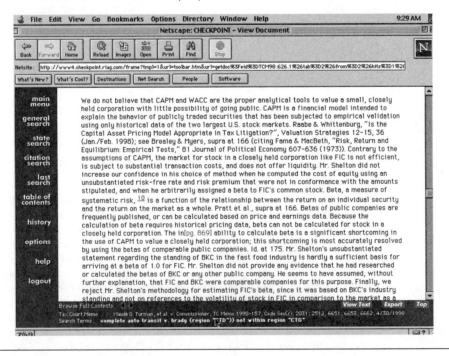

favor of another method. Thus, you decide to hire an expert familiar with the other method of valuation.

▶_____ Summary

The tax practitioner must possess a working knowledge of the federal court system in order to address tax research problems. The researcher must understand the role of the courts in generating federal tax law, the relationship of the courts to one another, the constitution and jurisdiction of each court, where to locate an appropriate decision, and how to interpret that decision.

Exhibit 5–13 offers a summary of some of the attributes of the trial-level and appeals courts discussed in this chapter. Because of differences among courts, the tax adviser may be inclined to choose one of the trial-level courts over the others to accommodate the special needs or circumstances of the client.

Exhibit 5–14 summarizes the decisions available in each of the tax case reporter services discussed in this chapter, in more detail than presented in Exhibit 2-4. With the variety of tax publications available, choices can be made so that the practitioner's tax research budget can be used effectively, without sacrifice of his or her ability to solve the client's problems.

Finally, a number of observations concerning citation conventions can be made. Review the citation examples given in this chapter to verify the list shown in Exhibit 5–15 and to add your own observations to it.

▶_____ Key Words

By the time you complete this chapter, you should be comfortable discussing each of the following terms. If you need additional review of any of these items, return to the appropriate material in the chapter or consult the glossary to this text.

EXHIBIT 5–13   The judicial obstacle course: selected attributes of trial-level courts

Item	Tax Court	District Court	Court of Federal Claims
Jurisdiction	Tax cases only	Legal issues based on entire *U.S. Code*	Monetary claims against U.S. government
Judges	Tax law specialists	Tax law generalists	Tax law generalists
Domain	National court, but judges travel	Limited geographical area	National court, but judges travel
Jury trial available?	No	Yes, if question of fact	No
Number of judges hearing case	One, reviewed by chief judge; *en banc* hearing for certain issues	One	One to five
Small Cases division available?	Yes	No	No
Payment of tax	Trial, then payment	Payment, then trial	Payment, then trial
Precedents court must follow	Supreme Court; pertinent circuit court; Tax Court	Supreme Court; pertinent circuit court; own District court	Supreme Court; Federal Circuit Court; Court of Federal Claims

AFTR	Permanent Citation
Board of Tax Appeals	Regular Decision
Case Brief	Small Cases Division
Court of Federal Claims	Supreme Court
Courts of Appeals	Tax Court
District Court	Temporary Citation
En Banc	USTC
Golsen Rule	Writ of Certiorari
Memorandum Decision	

► _____ Discussion Questions

1. Who can initiate a court case that deals with a tax matter—the taxpayer or the IRS?
2. Explain the general organization of the federal court system for cases concerning federal tax issues.
3. May a taxpayer take his or her tax case directly to the Supreme Court?
4. Who has the burden of proof in most cases involving the tax law? Why?
5. The U.S. Tax Court hears only certain types of cases. Identify those cases.

EXHIBIT 5–14 Court decision reporter summary

I. By Reporter

Reporter, Common Abbreviation	Publisher, Common Abbreviation	Decisions Included
Primary Reporters		
T.C. (B.T.A.)	GPO	Regular Tax Court (BTA) decisions
TCM	CCH	Tax Court Memorandum decisions
RIA T.C. Mem. Dec.	RIA	Tax Court Memorandum decisions
F.Supp	West	District court decisions
Fed. Cl.	West	Court of Federal Claims decisions
F.3d (F.2d)	West	Court of Appeals and pre-1982 Court of Claims decisions
U.S.	GPO	All Supreme Court decisions
S.Ct.	West	All Supreme Court decisions
Secondary Reporters		
USTC	CCH	Tax cases from all federal courts except the Tax Court
AFTR series	RIA	Tax cases from all federal courts except the Tax Court
Electronic Reporters		
TNT	Infotax	Tax cases from all federal courts except the Tax Court
KTC	Kleinrock's	Tax cases from all federal courts except the Tax Court

EXHIBIT 5–14   *Continued*

II. By Court

Court	Publisher	Citation Abbreviation	Reporter
Supreme Court			
▶ All cases	West	S.Ct.	*Supreme Court Reports*
	GPO	U.S.	*U.S. Supreme Court Report*
▶ Tax only	CCH	USTC	*U.S. Tax Cases*
	RIA	AFTR series	*American Federal Tax Reports*
	Infotax	TNT	*Tax Notes Today*
	Kleinrock's	KTC	*Kleinrock's Tax Cases*
Court of Appeal			
▶ All cases	West	F.3d (F.2d)	*Federal Reporter,* 3d (2d) series
▶ Tax only	CCH	USTC	
	RIA	AFTR series	
	Infotax	TNT	
	Kleinrock's	KTC	
Tax Court			
▶ Regular	GPO	T.C.	*Tax Court of the U.S. Reports*
▶ Memo	CCH	TCM	*Tax Court Memorandum Decisions*
	RIA	RIA T.C.	*RIA Tax Court*
		Mem.Dec.	*Memorandum Decisions*
	Infotax	TNT	
	Kleinrock's	T.C. Memo	
District Courts			
▶ All cases	West	F.Supp.	*Federal Supplement Series*
▶ Tax only	CCH	USTC	
	RIA	AFTR series	
	Infotax	TNT	
	Kleinrock's	KT C	
Court of Federal Claims			
▶ All cases pre-1982	West	Fed. Cl.	*U.S. Court of Federal Claims*
	West	F.2d.	*Federal Reporter*
▶ Tax only	CCH	USTC	
	RIA	AFTR series	
	Infotax	TNT	
	Kleinrock's	KTC	

6. The U.S. Tax Court has undergone an evolution since it was founded. What happened to its structure in 1926, 1943, and 1969, respectively?

7. How many judges sit on the U.S. Tax Court? What is the length of time of the appointment of each judge?

8. The U.S. Tax Court is a national court that meets in Washington, D.C. Does this mean that the taxpayer and his or her attorney must travel to Washington to have a case heard?

9. May a taxpayer have a jury trial in the U.S. Tax Court?

EXHIBIT 5–15 Citation conventions and observations

The common form of a citation is as follows: case name–volume number–reporter–page number–court–year

The AFTR second series began with 1954 IRC cases.

The B.T.A. became the U.S. Tax Court in 1943.

The U.S. Court of Claims became the U.S. Claims Court in 1982, and the U.S. Court of Federal Claims in 1992.

Unless the case was published in a year different from that in which it was heard, the USTC volume number (and many AFTR page numbers) includes a reference to the year, so the year need not be repeated in the citation.

The S.Ct. and U.S. citations imply that the case was heard in the Supreme Court, so the court abbreviation need not be repeated in the citation.

The government need not be mentioned in a typical Tax Court citation.

10. What does the term sitting *"en banc"* mean?

11. Distinguish between a Regular and a Memorandum decision of the Tax Court.

12. The U.S. Tax Court is a national court that hears cases of taxpayers who may appeal to various geographical Courts of Appeals. How does the Tax Court reconcile the opposite holdings of two or more of these Courts of Appeals for taxpayers who work or reside in different parts of the country?

13. What is the Small Cases Division of the U.S. Tax Court? What is the maximum amount of the deficiency that can be the subject of a Small Cases hearing? Comment on the trial procedures in the Small Cases Division.

14. Where are regular Tax Court decisions published? Illustrate the elements of both a temporary and a permanent regular Tax Court citation. Explain what each part of the citation means.

15. Tax Court Memorandum decisions are not published by the federal government. However, commercial reporters include these decisions. Illustrate the elements of both a temporary and a permanent citation for a Tax Court Memorandum decision, using both the CCH and RIA reporters. Explain what each part of the citation means.

16. What is the jurisdiction of a U.S. District Court?

17. Must the taxpayer pay the disputed tax deficiency to the government before his or her case will be heard in a District Court? In the U.S. Court of Federal Claims? In the U.S. Tax Court?

18. Which of the trial courts is most appropriate for a taxpayer who wishes to limit the judicial review of the relevant year's tax return to the specific issue(s) involved in the case?

19. Which of the trial courts would best serve a taxpayer litigating an issue of a technical tax nature? Why?

20. Is a Federal District Court a national court? How many judges hear a case brought before a Federal District Court?

21. Name the three court case reporters that publish tax and nontax District Court decisions. Illustrate the elements of a citation that might be found in each reporter. Explain what each part of the citation means.

22. Differentiate between a primary and a secondary case citation.
23. What type of cases are heard by the U.S. Court of Federal Claims?
24. How many judges are appointed to the U.S. Court of Federal Claims?
25. Is the U.S. Court of Federal Claims a national court? Must a taxpayer go to Washington, D.C., to present a case to this U.S. court?
26. Name the three court case reporters that publish U.S. Court of Federal Claims decisions. Illustrate the elements of a citation that might be found in each reporter. Explain what each part of the citation means.
27. Are the U.S. Courts of Appeals national courts? What type of cases do they hear?
28. Identify the circuit court that would hear the case of a taxpayer who lives or works in each of the following areas.

   a. Texas
   b. New York
   c. California
   d. Colorado
   e. Illinois
   f. A case that is appealed from the U.S. Court of Federal Claims

29. Each Court of Appeals has approximately twenty judges. How many of these judges hear a typical case?
30. Name the three court case reporters that publish Court of Appeals decisions. Illustrate the elements of a citation that might be found in each reporter. Explain what each part of the citation means.
31. Can a taxpayer have a jury trial before a Court of Appeals?
32. What is the highest court in the United States? What is its jurisdiction? Where does it hear cases?
33. How does one petition the Supreme Court to hear one's tax case?
34. How many justices are appointed to the Supreme Court? How many hear each case?
35. Why does the Supreme Court hear so few tax cases?
36. Differentiate between the Supreme Court's overturning of a lower court's decision, and its denial of a writ of certiorari.
37. Name the five court case reporters that publish Supreme Court decisions. Illustrate the elements of a citation that might be found in each reporter. Explain what each part of the citation means.
38. Is it possible for a taxpayer to have a jury trial before any of the trial courts? Before a Court of Appeals? Before the U.S. Supreme Court?
39. Discuss the precedential value of a Court of Appeals decision. Which Court of Appeals decisions are most important to a specific taxpayer?
40. In the (fictitious) citation *Gomez v. U.S.,* 102 T.C. 123 (1999), what does the "102" stand for? The "T.C."? The "123"?
41. Which court would have issued the (fictitious) *O'Dell v. U.S.,* 66 TCM 86 (2000) decision? What does each element in the citation mean?
42. In the citation *Simons-Eastern v. U.S.,* 354 F.Supp. 1003 (D.Ct., Ga, 1972), the "F.Supp." tells the tax researcher the decision is from which court?
43. *By using only the citation,* state which court issued each of the following decisions. If you cannot determine which court by looking at the citation only, say so.
   a. *Ambrose v. U.S.,* 4 Cl.Ct. 352 (1984)

    b. *D.C. Crummey v. U.S.,* 68-2 USTC ¶ 12,541

    c. *Helvering v. Clifford,* 23 AFTR 1077

    d. *James v. U.S.,* 81 S.Ct. 1052 (1961)

▶ _____ Exercises

44. Use a published court reporter to find the court decision located at 50 T.C. 630.

    a. Who was the trial judge?

    b. In what year was the case tried?

    c. What were the issues involved?

    d. Identify the party whose arguments prevailed.

45. Use a published court reporter to find the court decision located at 1994 RIA T.C. Memo. ¶ 94,523.

    a. What court heard the case?

    b. Who was the judge(s)?

    c. In what year was the case decided?

    d. What was the issue(s) involved?

46. Use a published court reporter to find the court decision located at 68-1 USTC ¶ 9145.

    a. What court heard the case?

    b. Name the judge(s) who heard the case.

    c. What were the issues involved?

    d. Identify the party whose arguments prevailed.

47. Use a published court reporter to find the court decision located at 7 AFTR2d 1361.

    a. What court heard the case?

    b. Name the judge(s) who heard the case.

    c. What were the issues involved?

    d. Identify the party whose arguments prevailed.

48. Find the court decision located at 100 T.C. 32. Use a computer tax service (RIA CheckPoint, Lexis, Kleinrock's, etc.) to complete this exercise. State which computer service you used.

    a. What court heard the case?

    b. Who was the judge(s)?

    c. In what year was the case decided?

    d. What was the issue(s) involved?

49. Find the court decision located at T.C. Memo. 1994-514. Use a computer tax service (RIA CheckPoint, Lexis, Kleinrock's, etc.) to complete this exercise. State which computer service you used.

    a. What court heard the case?

    b. Who was the judge(s)?

    c. In what year was the case decided?

    d. What was the issue(s) involved?

50. Find the court decision located at 81-1 USTC ¶ 9479. Use a computer tax service (RIA CheckPoint, Lexis, Kleinrock's, etc.) to complete this exercise. State which computer service you used.

   a. What court heard the case?
   b. Who was the judge(s)?
   c. In what year was the case decided?
   d. What was the issue(s) involved?

51. Find the court decision located at 79-1 USTC ¶ 9407. Use a computer tax service (RIA CheckPoint, Lexis, Kleinrock's, etc.) to complete this exercise. State which computer service you used.

   a. What court heard the case?
   b. Who was the judge(s)?
   c. In what year was the case decided?
   d. What was the issue(s) involved?

52. Find the court decision located at 67 AFTR2d 91-718. Use a computer tax service (RIA CheckPoint, Lexis, Kleinrock's, etc.) to complete this exercise. State which computer service you used.

   a. What court heard the case?
   b. Who was the judge(s)?
   c. In what year was the case decided?
   d. What was the issue(s) involved?

53. If your last name begins with the letters A–L, read and brief each of the following cases.

   a. *Sorensen,* T.C. Memo. 1994-175
   b. *Keller,* 84-1 USTC ¶ 9194

   If your last name begins with the letters M–Z, read and brief each of the following cases.

   c. *Washington,* 77 T.C. 601
   d. *Tellier,* 17 AFTR2d 633

54. If your last name begins with the letters A–L, read and brief each of the following cases.

   a. *Rownd,* T.C. Memo. 1994-465
   b. *Arnes,* 93-1 USTC ¶ 50,016

   If your last name begins with the letters M-Z, read and brief each of the following cases.

   c. *Willie Nelson Music Co.,* 85 T.C. 914
   d. *Independent Contracts, Inc.,* 73 AFTR2d 94-1406

55. Read and brief each of the following cases.

   a. *Gregory v. Helvering,* 55 S.Ct. 266 (1935)
   b. *Hunt,* T.C. Memo 1965–172

56. Read and brief each of the following cases.

    a. *Cohan v. Comm.,* 39 F.2d 540; 8 AFTR 10552; 42-1 USTC ¶ 489 (CA-2, 1930) (Limit the brief to the travel and entertainment issue.)

    b. *Allen, 16 T.C. 163 (1951)*

57. Read and brief each of the following cases.

    a. *Thor Power Tool Co. v. Comm.,* 99 S.Ct. 773, 79-1 USTC ¶ 9,139, 43 AFTR2d 79-362

    b. *Clark v. Comm.,* 40 B.T.A. 333 (1939)

58. Can a newspaper depreciate the value allocated to existing subscribers of an acquired newspaper, where the calculation of the value of the newspaper was made by determining the present value of the future profits from the subscribers?

59. Fernando owns a newspaper. The newspaper has a clipping service that has millions of historic articles in it. The basis of the clipping collection is zero, but its fair-market value is very high. Fernando donates the collection to a state historical society (a qualified charitable organization). Is he entitled to a charitable deduction? If so, for how much?

60. Can a corporation utilizing a "White Knight" to discourage a hostile takeover deduct the costs (investment banker's fee, legal fees, SEC filing fee, etc.) of the takeover defense?

61. In 1989, Clete received a $100,000 back-wages settlement of a discrimination suit brought under the Civil Rights Act. Is the $100,000 taxable to him?

62. Doris went to the post office to mail her tax return to the IRS. A friend went with her, and they both saw the postal clerk postmark the return and place it in a mail pouch. The tax return was not received by the IRS. Is the sworn testimony of Doris and her friend sufficient proof of filing the tax return?

▶ _____ ## Research Cases

63. Snidely Limited spent $1 million this year to upgrade its manufacturing plant, which had received several warnings from the state environmental agency about releasing pollution into the local river. Late in the year, Snidely received an assessment of $700,000 for violating the state's Clean Water Act. After he negotiated with the State, which cost $135,000 in legal fees, Snidely promised to spend another $200,000 next year for more pollution control devices, and the fine was reduced to $450,000. How much of these expenditures can Snidely Limited deduct for tax purposes?

Partial list of research material: § 162; Rev. Rul. 76-130, 1976-1 C.B. 16; *Tucker,* 69 T.C. 675.

64. Last year, only four of thirty-two professional basketball teams turned a nominal accounting profit. Betty purchased such a team this year. Her taxable loss therefrom properly was determined to be $950,000. Can she deduct this loss?

Partial list of research material: § 183; Reg. § 1.183-2; *Brannen,* 722 F.2d 695.

65. Herbert, a collector of rare coins, bought a 1916 Spanish Bowlero for $2,000 in 1984. He sold the coin for $4,500 in January 1997. Herbert retired from his loading dock job in June 1997 and began actively buying and selling rare coins. By December 1997, Herbert's realized gain from such activities was $21,500. What type of taxable income was January's $2,500 gain?

Partial list of research material: § 1221; Rev. Rul. 68-634, 1968-2 C.B. 46; *Frankel,* 56 TCM 1156 (1989).

66. Steve is an usher at his local church. Can he deduct commuting expenses for the Sundays that he is assigned to usher for church services?
Partial list of research material: § 170; Rev. Rul. 56-508, 1956-2 C.B. 126; *Churukian,* 40 TCM 475 (1980).

67. A new member of the San Diego Chargers wants the team to transfer $1,000,000 into an escrow account, in his name, for later withdrawal. The player suggests this payment in lieu of the traditional signing bonus. When is this income taxable to him?
Partial list of research material: § 451; Rev. Rul. 70-435, 1970-2 C.B. 100; *Drysdale,* 277 F.2d 413.

68. Professor Stevens obtained tenure and promotion to full professor status many years ago. Yet, he continues to publish research papers in scholarly journals to satisfy his own curiosity and to maintain his professional prestige and status within the academic community. Publications are also necessary in order for Professor Stevens to receive pay raises at his university. This year, Dr. Stevens spent $750 of his own funds to travel to southern Utah to collect some critical pieces of data for his work. What is the tax treatment of this expenditure?
Partial list of research material: § 162; Zell, 85–2 USTC ¶ 9698; *Smith,* 50 TCM 904.

69. The local electric company requires a $200 refundable deposit of new customers, in lieu of a credit check. Landlord Pete pays this amount for all of his new-to-town tenants. Can he deduct the $200 payments on his tax return?
Partial list of research material: § 162; *Hopkins,* 30 T.C. 1015; *Waring Products,* 27 T.C. 921.

70. High-Top Financing charges its personal loan holders a 2 percent fee if the full loan principal is paid prior to the due date. What is the tax effect of this year's $50,000 of prepayment penalties collected by High-Top?
Partial list of research material: § 61; *Hort,* 41-1 USTC ¶ 9354.

71. Cecilia died this year, owning mutual funds in her IRA worth $120,000. Under the terms of the IRA, Cecilia's surviving husband, Frank, was the beneficiary of the account, and he took a lump-sum distribution from the fund. Both Cecilia and Frank were age 57 at the beginning of the year.

   a. How does Frank account for the inheritance, assuming that he rolls it over into his own IRA in a timely manner?
   b. Would your answer change if Frank were Cecilia's brother?

   Partial list of research material: § 408; Rev. Rul. 92-47, 1992-1 C.B. 198; *Aronson,* 98 T.C. 283 (1992).

72. During a properly declared U.S. war with Outer Altoona, Harriet, a single taxpayer, was killed in action. Current-year federal taxable income to the date of Harriet's death totaled $19,000, and federal income tax withholding came to $2,300.

   a. What is Harriet's tax liability for the year of her death?
   b. What documentation must accompany her final Form 1040?

   Partial list of research material: § 692; Rev. Proc. 85–35, 1985–2 C.B. 433; *Hampton,* 75–1 USTC ¶ 9315.

73. Jerry Baker and his adorable wife Hammi believe in the worship of the "Sea God." This is a very personal religion to Jerry and Hammi. To practice their beliefs, the Bakers want to take a two-week trip to Tahiti this year to worship their deity. The cost (airfare, hotels, etc.) of this religious "pilgrimage" is $5,250. Jerry wants to know if he can deduct the cost of this trip as a charitable deduction on the joint Form 1040, Schedule A.
   Partial list of research material: § 170 and *Kessler,* 87 T.C. 1285 (1986).

74. Willie Waylon is a famous country and western singer. As an investment, Willie started a chain of Bar-B-Q restaurants called Willie's Wonderful Ribs. Willie's friends and associates invested $500,000 in this venture. The restaurant chain failed, and the investors lost all their money. Because of his visibility and status in the entertainment community, Willie felt that he personally had to make good on the losses suffered by the investors, so he paid $500,000 to reimburse them all. What are Willie's tax consequences?
   Partial list of research material: § 162 and *Lohrke,* 48 T.C. 679.

75. Paul Preppie is an accountant for the Very Big (VB) Corporation of America, located in Los Angeles, California. When Paul went to work for VB, he did not have a college degree. VB required that Paul earn a B.S. degree in accounting, so he enrolled in a local private university's night school and obtained the degree. VB Corporation does not reimburse employees for attending night school, and since Paul attended a private university, the tuition and other costs were relatively expensive. Can Paul deduct any of the $5,500 he paid in tuition and other costs during the current tax year? Prepare (in good form) a research memorandum to the file. (See Exhibit 2–6 in Chapter 2 for an illustration of the structure of a tax memo.)

76. Several years ago, Carol Mutter, a cash-basis taxpayer, obtained a mortgage from Weak National Bank to purchase a personal residence. In December 1999, $8,500 of interest was due on the mortgage, but Carol had only $75 in her checking account. On December 31, 1999, she borrowed $8,500 from Weak Bank, evidenced by a note, and the proceeds were deposited in her checking account. On the same day, Carol issued a check in the identical amount of $8,500 to Weak Bank for the interest due. Is the interest expense deductible for the 1999 tax year? Prepare (in good form) a research memorandum to the file. (See Exhibit 2–6 in Chapter 2 for an illustration of the structure of a tax memo.)

77. Phyllis maintained an IRA account at the brokerage firm ABC. On February 11 of the current year, she requested a check for the balance of her account. She received the check made out in her name and deposited it the same day in a new IRA account at the brokerage firm XYZ. Phyllis then requested a check on May 8 from XYZ, which was deposited in another new IRA account 35 days later. Is the May 8 distribution taxable to Phyllis? Prepare (in good form) a research memorandum to the file. (See Exhibit 2–6 in Chapter 2 for an illustration of the structure of a tax memo.)

78. Crystal Eros is a devout Pyramidist and a member of the Religious Society of Yanni, a Pyramidist organization. She adheres to the fundamental tenets of Pyramidist theology, including the belief that the Spirit of God is in every person and that it is wrong to kill or otherwise harm another person. Crystal's faith dictates that she not voluntarily participate, directly or indirectly, in military activities. Because federal income taxes fund military activities, Crystal

believes that her faith prohibits her from paying such taxes. Is there any legal substantiation for Crystal's position? Prepare (in good form) a research memorandum to the file. (See Exhibit 2–6 in Chapter 2 for an illustration of the structure of a tax memo.)

79. Sally Sweet is a shareholder who owns all the stock in one S corporation and more than 50 percent of the stock of two other S corporations. Two of the corporations own and operate restaurants and the third owns and operates a motel. She devoted substantial time to the business activities of the S corporations. The shareholder considered herself an independent contractor who provided services to the S Corporations on a contractual basis. The S corporations paid Sally consulting fees which, along with other fees, were reported on Schedule C. For the last three years, because of losses generated by two of the S corporations, Sally reported she had negative earnings from self-employment and therefore had no self-employment tax liability. Are the S Corporation losses self-employment income? Prepare (in good form) a research memorandum to the file. (See Exhibit 2–6 in Chapter 2 for an illustration of the structure of a tax memo.)

Using Secondary Sources as Research Tools

Citators and Other Finding Devices

LEARNING OBJECTIVES

▶ Understand the function of the citator in the tax research process

▶ Become adept at using the indexing systems in each of the most popular tax citators

▶ Know the abbreviation and reference conventions used by the most popular tax citators

▶ Efficiently use the update materials in the most popular tax citators

▶ Know the comparative strengths and weaknesses of the most popular tax citators

▶ Become familiar with the basic and advanced citator functions of online and Internet resources

CHAPTER OUTLINE

The first chapters of this text discussed the tremendous amount of legislative, administrative, and judicial sources of the tax law. This body of law is constantly changing because new laws are passed, administrative pronouncements are issued, judicial opinions are released, and old laws are superseded or overruled on a daily basis. This chapter addresses how tax practitioners can find the most up-to-date tax laws, cases, and administrative material, in both published and computerized forms.

The Evolving Nature of Tax Research

The current quantity and variety of research aids available to the practitioner are impressive. These research tools are evolving rapidly due to the phenomenal technological advancements in computerization. As an example, computers have revolutionized the capacity to manipulate and store information in a minimal amount of space. What used to be stored on scores of bookshelves can now be held on a single CD. The updating of tax services has gone from monthly or weekly to daily and continuous through online or Internet access.

It is very easy to be mesmerized by computer technology, but remember, it is the research techniques that produce efficient and effective results, not the medium in which the research is performed. It is crucial for the tax researcher to assess which medium, and which service within each medium, is best for the particular research project at hand. The research methodology must then be tailored to the service and medium selected. Choosing the wrong aid or methodology is inefficient and may produce a less than optimum solution to a client's tax problem. No one universal tax service or medium is superior to all others in all situations. With this in mind, this and the following chapters provide a foundation for evaluating the strengths and weaknesses of the various published and computerized tax research tools.

Basic Research Goals

The goals of tax research are to define the research problem, to find tax law that addresses the problem, to apply the law to the problem, to reach a conclusion about how the tax law affects the client, and to communicate the findings to the client. Research serves different functions at different points in this process. In the beginning, the researcher is trying to obtain a basic understanding of the tax law pertaining to the client's problem. Reading journal articles or other authoritative explanations of the law, such as those found in tax services, is helpful at this stage. Next the researcher wants to determine how *the* primary source of tax law, the *Internal Revenue Code,* applies to the client's situation. Once the applicable Code sections are identified, they must be interpreted. Remember, if the Code is clear, what it says applies because it is of the highest authority. However, in most cases the Code is not clear and practitioners turn to other primary tax law sources such as Regulations, rulings, or court cases to seek clarification. In this phase, the tax law is searched to find primary sources that interpret specific Code sections or contain facts resembling those in the client's case. This process is frequently one in which the practitioner tries various interpretations of the client's facts to see how they fit with the applicable Code and primary law. Finally, once an opinion is formed as to the optimum application of the law to the client's situation, the practitioner needs to confirm that the primary tax law being relied on has not been affected by subsequent developments. The conclusions of the practitioner, based on the results from the research, can then be communicated to the client.

Both published and computerized tax research systems can be used to meet these goals with varying degrees of effectiveness; the researcher should be familiar with both. Some materials may only be accessible to the researcher in one system or the other because either the publisher or the researcher's library supports only one type.

Citators

Law relies heavily on precedent, and tax law is no exception. Virtually every time a case is decided, the judge who writes the opinion refers to other cases and administrative rulings for guidance. The law attempts to maintain continuity so that people know what to expect. Each appellate opinion sets a precedent that applies to later cases.

What Is a Citator?

The law is constantly in a state of flux and, again, tax law is no exception. A case decided at one level may be appealed by one or both parties. The higher court may overrule the lower court. Infrequently, a court may see a flaw in the reasoning it or another (equal or lower) court used to decide an earlier case and use a different reasoning to reach a distinct decision. When a court takes some action that relies on or rejects or affects the holding of another case, it refers to that case in its opinion. All of this results in a tangle of inter-references among vast numbers of cases.

Along with statutory and administrative law, tax practitioners rely on court decisions to determine or argue the appropriate treatment of their clients' tax situations. They must be able to determine if subsequent events have affected the validity of the law on which they rely. Thus, they need a tool to help them ascertain which cases are strong precedents and which have been overruled. One way would be to follow the reference threads from case to case, but this would be extremely tedious and would only identify earlier cases. Fortunately, there is a way to access subsequent cases. Citators do much of this work of following the threads in subsequent cases and summarizing, in shorthand form, where the threads lead and what they mean.

A citator is a tool through which a tax researcher can learn the history of a case and evaluate the strength of its holdings. Before a researcher relies on the holding in a case, it is important to ascertain how later cases and rulings treated that holding. Thus, when a case relevant to a client's tax situation is found, this case's listing in the citator will indicate what later cases and rulings have said about its opinion. Many citators include administrative rulings as well as cases in their lists of cited holdings. Some secondary sources such as law review articles that refer to cases may be included as well.

To avoid confusion, it is important to learn the specific terminology that describes references between cases. When one case refers to another case, it **cites** the latter case. The case referring to the other case is called the **citing case.** The case that is referred to is the **cited case.** The citing case will contain the name of the cited case and where it can be found. The reference is called a **citation.** A **citator** is a service, in either published or computerized form, that indexes cited cases, gives full citations, and lists the citing cases and where each citing case can be found. A significant older case, one that establishes an important principle, may be cited in hundreds of other cases. Thus, its entry in a citator would be extremely long and complex. A very recent or narrow case would have been cited very few times and thus have a short entry.

The various commercial citators manipulate and organize the lists of citing cases in distinctive ways. Depending on the researcher's purpose, one citator may be more helpful than another. For example, one citator may only list citations that have a major impact on the logic or holding of the cited case. Another may list all citations. A researcher, initially checking to make sure a case has not been overruled, would prefer the former. The citations may be annotated in some way to indicate the type of impact the citing case has. A case may be considered at the trial and appellate levels, and generate a decision at each level. Because each level of decision in a case may be cited in other cases, the case may be organized by decision level. As each citator is discussed in this chapter, you should consider its suitability for specific research applications.

It is important for the practitioner to consider a case in context, to trace its judicially derived tax law point of view, and to monitor the reaction of subsequent court cases. This is even more important when the opinion is innovative. By using a citator properly, the practitioner reviews subsequent courts' reactions and determines the strength of the precedent established by the opinion. The first step in this review is an examination of the citator's lists of subsequent citing cases. Given the massive number of court cases issued annually, the citator is a vital element in the practitioner's tax research process.

For instance, say that a tax researcher has identified the case *Hirshon's Estate* (a 1957 Second Circuit Court of Appeals holding) as pertinent to a research project, because the facts are similar to the researcher's situation. The holding in the case might help or hurt the client's case. The task then is to find out how strong the holding in the *Hirshon* case is. The researcher must determine whether that case was appealed to the Supreme Court and, if so, what the ruling was. In addition, the researcher should consider the comments of subsequent court cases concerning the reasoning and holding of the *Hirshon* decision.

Commercial Citators

The three commercial citators that exclusively cover tax cases are updated frequently and on a regular schedule to keep their information current. The Commerce Clearing House (CCH) and Research Institute of America (RIA) citators are organized alphabetically by the case names. *Shepard's Federal Tax Citator* is organized by reference to the case reporter and volume number in which the case is found. The CCH citations are *general,* directing the researcher to the first page of the citing case, whereas the other two citators have citations which are *local,* directing the researcher to the exact page where the cited case is mentioned in the citing case. For example, *Richard W. Drake* (52 TC 842) is cited in *Nammack* (56 TC 1379) on page 1383. The CCH citing is *Nammack,* 56 TC 1379, whereas the RIA citator has *Nammack,* 56 TC 1383.

These three commercial citators are available in published or computerized formats. CCH provides its citator as part of its *Standard Federal Tax Reports* tax services, whereas the RIA citator is offered separately from its tax services. Both of these are available on CDs and through the Internet from each company's web site as well as in published form. *Shepard's Federal Tax Citator* is offered online and through the Internet by WESTLAW and LEXIS. Each of these services provides access to Shepard's as part of their overall offerings. *Shepard's Federal Tax Citator* is also available in print from its publisher, McGraw-Hill.

The discussion of citators begins with the published versions of the three major citators because these give a sense of the origins and evolution of citators, as well as some concept of the physical scope of the information contained in citators. While each of the citators can still be perused in published form, they may be offered exclusively in computerized formats in the near future. In the meantime we can still experience the musty charm of such books as the well-worn original Prentice-Hall *Citator,* published in 1941.

RIA *Citators*

The **Research Institute of America** *PH Citator* and *Citator 2nd Series* were formerly published by Prentice-Hall and then Maxwell Macmillan. Many practitioners still refer to this service as the *PH Citator,* however, we will use the term RIA *Citators* to refer to the entire citator series. The RIA *Citators* are divided into two series. The first series, the *PH Citator,* consists of three bound volumes that cover all of the federal tax cases dated between 1863 and 1953. The second series, *Citator 2nd Series,* consists of three bound volumes, 1954–1977, 1978–1989, and 1990–1996, plus paperback cumulative supplements that cover from 1997 to the present. The name "Prentice Hall" was eliminated from the *Citator 2nd Series* as of Volume 3. Along with cases, Treasury Decisions and Rulings (administrative pronouncements) are also analyzed at the back of each volume.

Each bound volume provides the history of cases that were decided during the period for which the volume covers. The volume also includes updates for cited cases that first appeared in previous volumes. Within each volume, the cases are arranged in alphabetical order. Hence, *Corn Products Refining Co.* (350 US 46), decided in 1955, first appears in Volume 1 of the *Citator 2nd Series.* Its entry in this volume includes its judicial history and a listing of citing cases through the end of 1977. Exhibit 6–1 shows only a small portion of these citing cases. Actually there are nearly four pages of citing cases for *Corn Products.* In the subsequent volumes of the *Citator 2nd Series,* the *Corn Products* case name appears in alphabetical order, followed by a listing of more recent citing cases (see Exhibit 6–1). Notice that each citator volume and supplement issued since Volume 1 of *Citator 2nd Series* must be examined to develop a complete list of citing cases for *Corn Products.*

Exhibit 6–2 shows which volumes of the RIA *Citators* to consult, depending on when a case was decided. One exception to this general organization scheme should be noted. Because Tax Court Memorandum decisions originally were not included in the *PH Citator,* none of them are found in Volume 1 of the First Series. Initial entries for decisions issued during the period 1934–1941 are found in Volume 2 of the *PH Citator.*

RIA *Citators* Conventions   When the plaintiff in a tax case is the U.S. Government, Commissioner of Internal Revenue, Secretary of the Treasury, or the taxpayer's IRS District Director, the RIA *Citators* do not list the case under the plaintiff's name as is the traditional legal convention. This is because there are a

EXHIBIT 6–1 *Citator 2nd Series, Corn Products* case

Volume 1

CORN PRODUCTS REFINING CO. v COMM., 350 US 46, 76 S Ct 20, 100 L Ed 29, 47 AFTR 1789, 1955-2 CB 512 (11-7-55); reh. den., 350 US 943, 76 S Ct 297, 100 L Ed 823, 1-9-56

sa—Corn Products Refining Co. v Comm., 215 F2d 513, 46 AFTR 528 (USCA 2)

s—Windle, W. W., Co. v Comm., 39 AFTR2d 77-784, 550 F2d 44 (USCA 1)

s—Frasher, Norville & Mabel, 1973 P-H TC Memo 73-1220

s—Capell, John F., Est. of, 1977 P-H TC Memo 77-1675

e—Electric Materials Co., The v Comm., 242 F2d 949, 50 AFTR 2111 (USCA 3)

e—Standard Hosiery Mills, Inc. v. Comm., 249 F2d 471, 52 AFTR 887 (USCA 4)

Helms Bakeries v Comm., 3 AFTR2d 646, 263 F2d 644 (USCA 9)

Haggard, Jr. v Wood, 9 AFTR2d 351, 298 F2d 27 (USCA 9) [See 350 US 52, 47 AFTR 1793]

f—Cinelli, Ferdinand v Comm., 34 AFTR2d 74-5782, 74-5783, 502 F2d 697, 699 (USCA 6)

q—Monfort of Colo., Inc v. U.S., 40 AFTR2d 77-5541, 77-5542, 561 F2d 194, 195 (USCA 10) [See 350 US 51-53, 47 AFTR 1793-1794]

f—Boone, Ralph, Adm. C.T.A. v U.S., 33 AFTR2d 74-542, 374 F Supp 116 (DC Md) [See 350 US 47, n. 1, 47 AFTR 1790]

f—Sicanoff Vegetable Oil Corp., 27 TC 1066, 27-1957 P-H TC 619

e—Shea, John F., Est. of, 57 TC 22, 57 P-H TC 15

e—Chemplast, Inc., 60 TC 629, 60 P-H TC 385 [See 350 US 52, 47 AFTR 1793]

n—Pfeifer, Ella, Est. of, 69 TC 307, 69 P-H TC 172-173 Old Dominion Plywood Corp., 1966 P-H TC Memo 66-787 [See 350 US 52, 47 AFTR 1793]

f—Carpenter, William L. & Helen W., 1966 P-H TC Memo 66-1089 [See 350 US 50, 47 AFTR 1792]

f—Simplot, J. R., Co., 1967 P-H TC Memo 67-533 [See 350 US 52, 47 AFTR 1793]

e—Datamation Services, Inc., 1976 P-H TC Memo 76-1086, 76-1087 [See 350 US 52, 47 AFTR 1793]

f—Bell Fibre Products Corp., 1977 P-H TC Memo 77-187 [See 350 US 52, 47 AFTR 1793]

Internat. Flavors & Fragrances, Inc., 1977 P-H TC Memo 77-259

f—Bush, Gerson A., 1977 P-H TC Memo 77-349, 77-350 [See 350 US 52, 47 AFTR 1793]

e—Rev. Rul. 62-141, 1962-2 CB 184 [See 350 US 52, 47 AFTR 1793]

g-1—Rogers; U.S. v, 7 AFTR2d 560, 286 F2d 280 (USCA 6)

n-1—Rogers; U.S. v, 7 AFTR2d 562, 286 F2d 282 (USCA 6)

g-1—Weaver, Nelson, Realty Co. v. Comm., 10 AFTR2d 5574, 307 F2d 902 (USCA 5)

g-1—Flora v U.S., 142 F Supp 605, 49 AFTR 1854 (DC Wyo)

1—Weiler v U.S., 6 AFTR2d 5682, 187 F Supp 746 (DC Penn)

f-1—Kurtin, Albert & Patricia Bristol, 26 TC 962, 26-1956 P-H TC 552

g-1—Shea, John F., Est. of, 57 TC 26, 57 P-H TC 18

g-2—Martin, Execx. v U.S., 230 F2d 106, 49 AFTR 206 (USCA 7)

g-2—Faroll, Exec. v Jarecki, 231 F2d 283, 49 AFTR 425 (USCA 7)

g-2—Hightower, Jr.; Patterson v, 245 F2d 768, 51 AFTR 800 (USCA 5)

2—Allen v Comm., 6 AFTR2d 5844, 283 F2d 790 (USCA 7)

n-2—Rogers; U.S. v, 7 AFTR2d 562, 286 F2d 282 (USCA 6)

Volume 2

• **CORN PRODUCTS REFINING CO. v COMM., 350 US 46, 47 AFTR 1789**

f—Cline Herbert B., Jr. v Comm., 45 AFTR2d 80-1095, 617 F2d 194 (USCA 6) [See 350 US 51-52, 47 AFTR 1793]

e—Cleveland Electric Illuminating Co., The v U.S., 54 AFTR2d 84-6256, 6 Cl Ct 716 [See 350 US 53, 47 AFTR 1793-1794]

f—Minn. Power & Light Co. v U.S., 55 AFTR2d 85-1611, 6 Cl Ct 567 [See 350 US 52-53, 47 AFTR 1793-1794]

e—Buono, George v., 74 TC 198, 204, 74 PH TC 109, 112 [See 350 US 52, 47 AFTR 1793]

e—Smith, Harry Lee & Patricia Ann, 78 TC 350, 364, 378, 386, 78 PH TC 185, 192, 199, 203

e—Mariani Frozen Foods, Inc., 81 TC 450, 479, 81 PH TC 234, 249 [See 350 US 52, 47 AFTR 1793]

f—Warsaw Photographic Associates, Inc., 84 TC 43, 84 PH TC 22 [See 350 US 52, 47 AFTR 1793]

g—Foy, James E. & Nancy L., 84 TC 65, 84 PH TC 34 [See 350 US 51-52, 47 AFTR 1792-1793]

e—New Mexico Timber Co., 84 TC 1303, 84 PH TC 676 [See 350 US 47, 47 AFTR 1791]

e—Recklitis, Christopher P., 91 TC 907, 91 PH TC 452

f—Long, William R., 93 TC 10, 93 PH TC 6 [See 350 US 52, 47 AFTR 1793]

Volume 3

• **CORN PRODUCTS REFINING CO. v COMM., 350 US 46, 76 S Ct 20, 100 L Ed 29, 47 AFTR 1789, 1955-2 CB 512, 55-2 USTC ¶ 9746, (11-7-55), reh. den., 350 US 943, 76 S Ct 297, 100 L Ed 823, 1-9-56**

Azar Nut Co. v Comm., 67 AFTR 2d 91-988, 931 F2d 316, (CA5)

k—Blazek, Loren Lee, In re, 71A AFTR 2d 93-3942, (DC KS)

f—Circle K Corp. v U.S., 67 AFTR 2d 91-1059, 23 Cl Ct 165, [See 350 US 51-52, 47 AFTR 1793]

Circle K Corp. v. U.S., 68 AFTR 2d 91-5461, 23 Cl Ct 664

k—Circle K Corp. v. U.S., 68 AFTR 2d 91-5466, 23 Cl Ct 670, [See 350 US 51-53, 47 AFTR 1793-1794]

Kraft, Inc. v. U.S., 73 AFTR 2d 94-978, 30 Fed Cl 820, (Cl Ct)

f—Butcher, C. H. Jr., In re, 65 AFTR 2d 90-1063, 90-1064, 90-1067, (Bktcy Ct TN), [See 350 US 50-52, 47 AFTR 1792-1793]

inap—Carmel, Richard J., In re, 69 AFTR 2d 92-569, (Bktcy Ct IL)

k—Fed. Nat. Mortgage Assn., 100 TC 569, 571, 100 TCR 303—307

f—Flint, Clarence A. & Jeannette E., 1991 TC Memo 91-2041, [See 350 US 52, 47 AFTR 1793]

First Chicago Corp & Affiliated Corporations, 1995 RIA TC Memo 95-661-95-662

TD 8493, 1993-2 CB 256

k-4—Dial, Don D. v Comm., 70 AFTR 2d 92-5131, 968 F2d 901, (CA9)

k-4—Michelson, Douglas J., 1990 PH TC Memo 90-130

k-4—Tway, Jack C. & Phyllis, 1993 RIA TC Memo 93-1019

n-5—Hoover Co., The, 72 TC 251, 72 PH TC 136

f-5—Botai Corp., N.V., 1990 PH TC Memo 90-2284

f-5—English, Jesse W. & Betty J., 1993 RIA TC Memo 93-499, [Cited at 17 AFTR2d 605, 383 US 572]

k-5—Fortner, James D., 1993 RIA TC Memo 93-914

1997

• **CORN PRODUCTS REFINING CO. v COMM., 47 AFTR 1789, 350 US 46, 76 S Ct 20, 100 L Ed 29, 55-2 USTC ¶ 9746, 1955-2 CB 512, (US, 11/7/55), reh. den., 350 US 943, 76 S Ct 297, 100 L Ed 823, 1-9-56**

Cenex Inc v. U.S., 80 AFTR 2d 97-5003, 38 Fed Cl 334, (Ct Fed Cl)

l—Marrin, Stephen & Jane, 1997 RIA TC Memo 97-161

Cullin, Edward S., 1997 RIA TC Memo 97-1912

4—Israel, Leon Jr., Estate of, 108 TC 218, 108 TCR 128, [Cited at 80 TC 409]

5—Drummond, Thomas B., 1997 RIA TC Memo 97-419, [Cited at 17 AFTR 2d 605, 383 US 572]

EXHIBIT 6–2   RIA *Citators* organization

| For Decisions Dated | Consult Volumes | |
	PH Citator	*Citator 2nd Series*
1863–1941	1, 2, 3	1, 2, 3, and supplements
1942–1947	2, 3	1, 2, 3, and supplements
1948–1953	3	1, 2, 3, and supplements
1954–1977	None	1, 2, 3, and supplements
1978–1989	None	2, 3, and supplements
1990–1996	None	3 and supplements
1997–present	None	Supplements

massive number of cases in which Eisner, Helvering, Burnet, or other Commissioners or Secretaries of the Treasury initiated the litigation. Rather, the RIA *Citators* list all cases by the first taxpayer's name who is party to the suit. This convention greatly facilitates the researcher's search for specific cases.

The case name is followed by its citation in various court reporters and the judicial history of the case. Notations regarding the holdings of the other courts that have heard this case are indicated by symbols, such as "sa" for affirming the earlier case, and "r" for reversing a lower court's decision on appeal. For instance, the *Corn Products* citation in Exhibit 6–1 is:

> Corn Products Refining Co. v Comm., 350 US 46, 76 S Ct 20,
> 100 L Ed 29, 47 AFTR 1789, 1955-2 CB 512 (11-7-55);
> reh. den., 350 US 943, 76 S Ct 297, 100 L Ed 823, 1-9-56

> sa- Corn Products Refining Co. v Comm., 215 F2d 513,
> AFTR 528 (USCA 2)

Exhibit 6–3 lists the judicial history symbols for the cited case itself. The abbreviations in Exhibit 6–4 apply to the citing case and indicate how the citing cases evaluated the cited case.

The RIA *Citators* first list the citations for cases that are in agreement with the cited case. Complete agreement is indicated by the abbreviation "iv," short for the legal idiom "on all fours." Next, citing cases are listed that discuss the holdings or reasoning of the cited case but do not refer to a specific paragraph or **headnote.** Headnotes are the paragraphs in which the editors of the court reporter summarize the court's holdings on each issue. The headnotes number each court issue separately and headnotes appear in the court reporters before the text of the actual court case.

Following the general citing cases are the cases that refer to specific headnote issues. These citing cases are organized by the headnote numbers to which they refer. The RIA editors use the evaluation symbols in Exhibit 6–4 to indicate how the citing case relates to the cited opinion. Hence, "g-1," followed by the name and citation of a citing case (see *Rogers* in Exhibit 6–1 as an example) means that the citing case distinguished either the rule of law or the facts that were discussed in the first headnote to the cited case.

Within any of these groupings—all fours, no specific headnote, Headnote 1, Headnote 2, and so on—citing cases and rulings are listed in the following order.

EXHIBIT 6–3   RIA *Citators* symbols for cited cases

SYMBOLS USED IN CITATOR
COURT DECISIONS
Judicial History

a	affirmed by a higher court (Note: When available, the official cite to the affirmance is provided; if the affirmance is by unpublished order or opinion, the date of the decision and the court deciding the case are provided.)
App auth	appeal authorized by the Treasury
App	appeal pending (Note: Later volumes may have to be consulted to determine if the appellate case was decided.)
cert gr	petition for certiorari was granted by the U.S. Supreme Court
d	appeal dismissed by the court or withdrawn by the party filing the appeal
(G)	following an appeal notation, this symbol indicates that it was the government filing an appeal
m	the earlier decision has been modified by the higher court, or by a later decision.
r	the decision of the lower court has been reversed on appeal
rc	related case arising out of the same taxable event or concerning the same taxpayer
reh den	rehearing has been denied by the same court in which the original case was heard
reinst	a dismissed appeal has been reinstated by the appellate court and is under consideration again
remd	the case has been remanded for proceedings consistent with the higher court decision
remg	the cited case is remanding the earlier case
revg & remg	the decision of the lower court has been reversed and remanded by a higher court on appeal
s	same case or ruling
sa	the cited case is affirming the earlier case
sm	the cited case is modifying the earlier case
sr	the cited case is reversing the earlier case
sx	the cited case is an earlier proceeding in a case for which a petition for certiorari was denied
(T)	an appeal was filed from the lower court decision by the taxpayer
vacd	the lower court decision was vacated on appeal or by the original court on remand
vacg	a higher court or the original court on remand has vacated the lower court decision
widrn	the original opinion was withdrawn by the court
x	petition for certiorari was denied by the U.S. Supreme Court
•	Supreme Court cases are designated by a bold-faced bullet (•) before the case line for easy location

Certain notations appear at the end of the cited case line. These notations include:

(A)	the government has acquiesced in the reasoning or the result of the cited case
(NA)	the government has refused to acquiesce or to adopt the reasoning or the result of the cited case, and will challenge the position adopted if future proceedings arise on the same issue
on rem	the case has been remanded by a higher court and the case cited is the resulting decision

EXHIBIT 6–4   RIA *Citators* symbols for citing cases

Evaluation of Cited Cases

c   the citing case court has adversely commented on the reasoning of the cited case, and has criticized the earlier decision

e   the cited case is used favorably by the citing case court

f   the reasoning of the court in the cited case is followed by the later decision

g   the cited and citing cases are distinguished from each other on either facts or law

inap   the citing case court has specifically indicated that the cited case does not apply to the situation stated in the citing case.

iv   on all fours (both the cited and citing cases are virtually identical)

k   the cited and citing case principles are reconciled

l   the rationale of the cited case is limited to the facts or circumstances surrounding that case (this can occur frequently in situations in which there has been an intervening higher court decision or law change)

n   the cited case was noted in a dissenting opinion

o   the later case directly overrules the cited case (use of the evaluation is generally limited to situations in which the court notes that it is specifically overturning the cited case, and that the case will no longer be of any value)

q   the decision of the cited case is questioned and its validity debated in relation to the citing case at issue

The evaluations used for the court decisions generally are followed by a number. That number refers to the headnoted issue in the American Federal Tax Reports (AFTR) or Tax Court decision to which the citing case relates. If the case is not directly on point with any headnote, a bracketed notation at the end of the citing case line directs the researcher to the page in the cited case on which the issue appears.

▶ U.S. Supreme Court

▶ U.S. Courts of Appeal

▶ U.S. Court of Federal Claims (or predecessor court)

▶ U.S. District Court

▶ U.S. Tax Court (or predecessor court—BTA, regular and memorandum decisions)

▶ State courts

▶ Treasury Rulings and Decisions

Citing cases in any court or ruling group are arranged in chronological order. The abbreviated listings for *Corn Products* in Exhibit 6–1 illustrate this organization scheme.

In their listings, the RIA *Citators* include all of the citing cases that mention the cited opinion. Therefore, the listings for important cases containing many issues can be several pages long. The headnote number references allow researchers to restrict their search to only those citing cases with issues that are relevant to their client's factual situation. Thus, if the researcher is interested in the issue described in the first headnote of *Corn Products* only cases designated with a 1 (from *Rogers* to *Shea*) need to be reviewed.

Many researchers prefer to start their analysis of a case with the most recent volume of the RIA *Citators* and work backward through the earlier volumes. In this way, they can quickly identify the present status of the cited case. For example, a steady stream of favorable references probably indicates that the precedent of the original case is still valid, whereas either a list of negative comments or a scarcity of references may indicate a weak or overruled precedent. The citator portion of a research project is complete when the researcher is satisfied that the status of the case is sufficiently confirmed. At this point some of the citing cases should be examined because the facts of a client's situation are rarely identical to the cases initially located.

If the cases found initially support the client's position, but the facts are somewhat different, the search should continue for a supportive case with more similar facts. Hence, those citations marked "k," indicating that their facts or opinions are different from those of the cited case, also should be consulted. If the initial cases found have holdings adverse to a client's position, the practitioner should search for cases marked "g," indicating that the citing case is distinguished from the cited case. These cases may reason that the facts in the taxpayer's case are actually different from those of the cited case, thus supporting a different holding. Some of these facts may resemble the facts of the practitioner's client and provide the desired support. Similarly, a case marked "l," which limits the holding of the cited case to a narrow set of facts, may make the holding inapplicable to the client's fact situation.

RIA *Citators* Case Example   We use the 1981 Supreme Court case *Upjohn Company* to illustrate the most commonly encountered features of the RIA *Citators*. The *Upjohn* case generated three separate opinions and its course through the courts is one frequently encountered by other cases. It was first decided in 1978 by the U.S. District Court (41 AFTR2d 78-796), which found for the IRS. The taxpayer appealed to the U.S. Court of Appeals for the Sixth Circuit. This case, decided in 1979 (44 AFTR2d 79-5179), found for the IRS on most issues. The taxpayer appealed again, this time to the U.S. Supreme Court. The Supreme Court decided the case in the taxpayer's favor in 1981 (47 AFTR2d 81-523). Consequently, there are three separate entries for this case in the *Citator 2nd Series:* the trial court, the appellate court, and the Supreme Court. Each of these courts wrote an opinion that can be cited by other cases. The Supreme Court opinion is the most likely to be cited, because it is the final decision on the issues. There is little reason for future decisions to cite the trial or appellate cases, since they were reversed.

Begin a review of *Upjohn* by examining the two headnotes to the opinion, as they appear in the tax case reporter, at 47 AFTR2d 81-523 (see Exhibit 6–5). This case addresses the issue of attorney–client privilege where the client is a publicly traded corporation. Headnote 1 summarizes the holding of the case concerning the attorney–client privilege for statements to corporate counsel by employees outside the control group. Headnote 2 summarizes the holding of the case concerning whether the *work-product doctrine* protects memoranda of corporate counsel, prepared in an internal investigation, from IRS scrutiny.

Since the District Court case was decided in 1978 and the Supreme Court case was decided in 1981, the three courts' citations all first appear in Volume 2 of the *Citator 2nd Series,* which reports cases from 1978–1989. The researcher would start

EXHIBIT 6–5 Headnotes for *Upjohn* Supreme Court Case

UPJOHN CO., ET AL., PETITIONERS v. U.S., ET AL., RESPONDENTS. U.S. Supreme Court, No. 79-886, Jan. 13, 1981. Court of Appeals, (6th Cir.) 44 AFTR 2d 79-5179, reversed. Decision for taxpayer. 101 S.Ct. 677.

1. INTERNAL REVENUE SERVICE—Discovery of liability and enforcement of tax—authority in general—privileged communications. Attorney-client privilege attached to employee statements made to counsel during internal investigation of possible illegal payments. Privilege didn't apply to statements which weren't responses to questionnaires or interview questions. Communications were made by employees beyond control group, not taxpayer's officers and agents, but narrow interpretation of control group frustrated privilege. Privilege attached since information was furnished by employees acting within scope of employment and was otherwise unavailable from upper-echelon management. *Reference:* 1981 P-H Fed. ¶39,650(15). Sec. 7602.

2. INTERNAL REVENUE SERVICE—Discovery of liability and enforcement of tax—authority in general—privileged communications. Work-product doctrine applied to IRS summons seeking memoranda prepared by taxpayer's general counsel during internal investigation of illegal payments. Government's substantial need or inability to locate equivalent information by questioning taxpayer's employees wasn't enough to mandate disclosure of attorney's mental processes. And memoranda based on employees' oral statements were otherwise protected by attorney-client privilege. *Reference:* 1981 P-H Fed. ¶39,650(50). Sec. 7602.

---

here and continue with Volume 3 and each paperback supplement. Exhibit 6–6 is the portion of page 2829 from Volume 2 that includes references for *Upjohn*. Using this Exhibit and the list of abbreviations from Exhibit 6–3, determine the history of *Upjohn* from the RIA *Citator 2nd Series*. The first set of citations in bold refers to the Sixth Circuit case. The citations given are to RIA's AFTR2d series followed by a parallel citation to an official reporter such as F2d. Citations to the USTC series, published by RIA's main competitor, CCH, are not provided until the 1990 volume of *Citator 2nd Series*.

The first reference with the "r" is to the Supreme Court case, which reversed the Sixth Circuit decision. The next citing is to the District Court case. Its decision was remanded by the Sixth Circuit for proceedings consistent with the Sixth Circuit's findings. Using the symbols in Exhibit 6–4, we can determine that the *Davis* citing

EXHIBIT 6–6   *Citator 2nd Series, Upjohn case*

➔   **UPJOHN CO., THE; U.S. v, 44 AFTR2d 79-5179, 600 F2d 1223 (USCA 6, 6-28-79)**
  r—Upjohn Co. v. U.S., 47 AFTR2d 81-523, 449 US 383, 101 S Ct 677, 66 LEd2d 584
  remg—Upjohn Co.; U.S. v, 41 AFTR2d 78-796 (DC Mich)
  Davis, Craig E.: U.S. v, 47 AFTR2d 81-948, 636 F2d 1039 (USCA 5) [See 44 AFTR2d 79-5182, 600 F2d 1228, n. 13]
  q—El Paso Co., The; U.S. v, 50 AFTR2d 82-5536, 682 F2d 538 (USCA 5) [See 44 AFTR2d 79-5182, 600 F2d 1228, n. 12]
  n—El Paso Co., The; U.S. v, 50 AFTR2d 82-5546, 682 F2d 550 (USCA 5) [See 44 AFTR2d 79-5182, 600 F2d

  q-1—Amerada Hess Corp.; U.S. v, 45 AFTR2d 80-589, 619 F2d 987 (USCA 10)
  e-1—Bonnell, Harold; U.S. v, 45 AFTR2d 80-730, 483 F Supp 1079 (DC Minn) [See 44 AFTR2d 79-5182, 600 F2d 1228, n. 13]

➔ • **UPJOHN CO. v U.S., 47 AFTR2d 81-523, 449 US 383, 101 S Ct 677, 66 LEd2d 584 (1-13-81)**
  sr—Upjohn Co., The; U.S. v, 44 AFTR2d 79-5179, 600 F2d 1223 (USCA 6)
  f—Zolin, Frank S.; U.S. v, 63 AFTR2d 89-1487 (US) 109 S Ct 2625 [See 47 AFTR2d 81-526, 449 US 389]
  n—Young, Arthur, & Co.; U.S. v, 49 AFTR2d 82-1115, 82-1117, 677 F2d 222, 224 (USCA 2)
  e—Grand Jury 83-2, In re; U.S. v, 55 AFTR2d 85-367 (USCA 4) [See 47 AFTR2d 81-526, 449 US 389]
  e—Klein, Lee J., In re, 56 AFTR2d 85-6167 (USCA 7) [See 47 AFTR2d 81-530, 449 US 399]
  f—Aronson, Mitchell; U.S. v, 56 AFTR2d 85-6369, 610 F Supp 220 (DC Fla) [See 47 AFTR2d 81-526, 449 US 398]
  k—Hartz Mountain Industries, Inc. & Subs, 93 TC 525, 93 PH TC 264 [See 47 AFTR2d 81-526, 449 US 389]
  Mulvania, Richard L., 1984 PH TC Memo 84-369 [See 47 AFTR2d 81-526, 449 US 389]
  k-1—Doe, John v U.S., 62 AFTR2d 88-5750, 487 US 214, 108 S Ct 2350
  l—Wyatt, Oscar S., Jr.; U.S. v, 47 AFTR2d 81-789, 637 F2d 295 (USCA 5)
  l—Moody, Shearn, Jr. v I.R.S., 48 AFTR2d 81-5172, 654 F2d 798 (CADC)

  l—Riewe, Daryl; U.S. v, 49 AFTR2d 82-1205, 676 F2d 420 (USCA 10)
  e-1—El Paso Co., The; U.S. v, 50 AFTR2d 82-5535—82-5536, 682 F2d 538 (USCA 5) [See 47 AFTR2d 81-526, 449 US 389]
  n-1—El Paso Co., The; U.S. v, 50 AFTR2d 82-5546, 682 F2d 550 (USCA 5)
  n-1—El Paso Co., Co.; U.S. v, 50 AFTR2d 82-5546, 682 F2d 551 (USCA 5)
  l—Sealed Case, In re, 50 AFTR2d 82-5646, 82-5647, 82-5648, 82-5649, 676 F2d 808, 810, 811 (CADC)
  l—Newton, Willis H., In re, 52 AFTR2d 83-6309, 718 F2d 1021 (USCA 11)
  e-1—Liebman, Emanuel; U.S. v, 54 AFTR2d 84-5939, 84-5940, 742 F2d 809, 810 (USCA 3) [See 47 AFTR2d 81-526, 449 US 389]
  k-1—Olson, Robert G. v U.S., 63 AFTR2d 89-1170, 872 F2d 822 (USCA 8)
  g-1—Firestone Tire & Rubber Co., The v Dept. of Justice, 50 AFTR2d 82-5490 (DC DC)
  f-1—LSB Industries, Inc. & Subsidiaries v Comm., 51 AFTR2d 83-344, 556 F Supp 42 (DC Okla)
  e-1—Kilpatrick, William A.; U.S. v, 56 AFTR2d 85-6086, 85-6092—85-6093, 594 F Supp 1342, 1350 (DC Colo)
  g-1—Parker, Lyndon J.; U.S. v, 58 AFTR2d 86-5368 (DC Pa)
  f-1—Isherwood, Hunter & Diehm; Olive, Anthony P. v, 60 AFTR2d 87-5044, 656 F Supp 1173 (DC Virgin Islands)
  k-1—Holifield, Dallas L. v U.S., 62 AFTR2d 88-5764, 689 F Supp 867 (DC Wis)
  f-2—Young, Arthur, & Co.; U.S. v, 49 AFTR2d 82-1113, 677 F2d 219 (USCA 2)
  f-2—Delaney, Migdail & Young, Chartered v I.R.S., 60 AFTR2d 87-5515, 826 F2d 127 (CADC)
  e-2—Schenectady Svgs. Bk.; U.S. v, 49 AFTR2d 82-1056, 525 F Supp 650 (DC NY)

➔   **UPJOHN CO.; U.S. v, 41 AFTR2d 78-796 (DC Mich, 2-23-78)**
  remd—Upjohn Co., The; U.S. v, 44 AFTR2d 79-5179, 600 F2d 1223 (USCA 6)

case was in general agreement with the Sixth Circuit, but the *El Paso* citing case questioned the holding of the Sixth Circuit in its majority opinion and mentioned it in the dissenting opinion. The *Amerada Hess* opinion also questioned the holding with respect to the issue in the first headnote. The *Bonnell* decision explained the same issue in generally favorable terms but not to the degree of fully following it.

The Supreme Court citation of *Upjohn* appears next, designated by a bold black bullet. The first reference (marked "sr") notes that the Supreme Court case reverses the Sixth Circuit decision. The Supreme Court's citing cases are listed in the order previously described for RIA *Citators*. First are the cases that cite the Supreme Court case but do not reference a particular headnote paragraph. When a citing discussion does not relate directly to any of the numbered headnote issues, a bracketed local citation of the cited case is given. For example, the *Zolin* case follows the reasoning presented on page 81-526 of the *Upjohn* case. Notice that the cases in this section are listed with the Courts of Appeal cases first, then the District Court decisions, and lastly Tax Court Regular and Memorandum cases.

Starting with *John Doe,* the citing cases are listed in headnote groupings. Several citing cases address the issue in Headnote 1, whereas only a few are concerned with Headnote 2. The Fifth Circuit *El Paso* decision cites the Supreme Court decision

EXHIBIT 6–7 *Citator 2nd Series* supplements, *Upjohn* case

Volume 3

- **UPJOHN CO. v U.S., 47 AFTR 2d 81-523, 449 US 383, 101 S Ct 677, 66 L Ed 2d 584, 81-1 USTC ¶ 9138, (1-13-81)**
  f—Holifield, Dallas L. v U.S., 66 AFTR 2d 90-5413, 909 F2d 203, (CA7), [See 47 AFTR2d 81-529, 449 US 396]
  f—Adlman, Monroe; U.S. v., 76 AFTR 2d 95-7191, (CA2), [See 47 AFTR2d 81-526, 449 US 389]
  f—Aramony, William; U.S. v., 78 AFTR 2d 96-5756, 88 F3d 1389, (CA4), [See 47 AFTR2d 81-526, 449 US 389]
  e—LeMaine, Reynald D. v. I.R.S., 71A AFTR 2d 93-4256, (DC MA), [See 47 AFTR2d 81-529, 449 US 395-396]
  f—Buckner, Roger C. v U.S., 76 AFTR 2d 95-6656, (DC ID), [See 47 AFTR2d 81-526, 449 US 389]
  f—Palmer, Fred R.; U.S. v., et al, 76 AFTR 2d 95-6680, (DC ID), [See 47 AFTR2d 81-526, 449 US 389]
  f—Scott Paper Co v. U.S., 78 AFTR 2d 96-5670, 943 F Supp 499, (DC PA), [See 47 AFTR2d 81-526, 449 US 389]
  f—Matz, Jeffrey A. v. U.S., 78 AFTR 2d 96-6416, (DC AZ), [See 47 AFTR2d 81-526, 449 US 398]
  e—Fu Investment Co., Ltd., 104 TC 414, 104 TCR 247, [See 47 AFTR2d 81-526, 449 US 389]
  e—Bernardo, Bradford C. & Marybeth B., 104 TC (No. 33), 104 TCR 411, [See 47 AFTR2d 81-526, 449 US 389, cited at 93 TC 525]
  e-1—Mobil Corp., U.S. v, 71 AFTR 2d 93-1876—93-1877, (DC TX)
  e-1—Kinney, Michael, M.D. v. U.S., 77 AFTR 2d 96-554, (DC FL)
  e-1—Chevron Corp; U.S. v., 77 AFTR 2d 96-1551, (DC CA)
  f-2—Rockwell Internat.; U.S. v, 65 AFTR 2d 90-840, 90-841, 897 F2d 1264, 1265, (CA3)
  e-2—Bell, Jack; U.S. v., 74 AFTR 2d 94-7273, 94-7275, (DC CA)

1997 Supplement

- **UPJOHN CO. v U.S., 47 AFTR 2d 81-523, 449 US 383, 101 S Ct 677, 66 L Ed 2d 584, 81-1 USTC ¶ 9138, (US, 1/13/81)**
  e—Massachusetts Institute of Technology; U.S. v., 80 AFTR 2d 97-7983, (CA1), [See 47 AFTR 2d 81-526, 449 US 389-390]
  e—Massachusetts Institute of Technology ;U.S. v., 79 AFTR 2d 97-596, (DC MA), [See 47 AFTR 2d 81-526, 449 US 389]
  e—Pribble, William C., Jr.; U.S. v., 79 AFTR 2d 97-1085, (DC MN), [See 47 AFTR 2d 81-530, 449 US 398]
  e—Hanna, John J. v. U.S., 80 AFTR 2d 97-7092, (Ct Fed Cl), [See 47 AFTR 2d 81-526, 449 US 389, cited at 63 AFTR 2d 89-1487, 491 US 562]

June 1998 Supplement

- **UPJOHN CO. v U.S., 47 AFTR 2d 81-523, 449 US 383, 101 S Ct 677, 66 L Ed 2d 584, 81-1 USTC ¶ 9138, (US, 1/13/81)**
  e—Adlman, Monroe; U.S. v., 81 AFTR 2d 98-822, 98-823, (CA2), [See 47 AFTR 2d 81-526, 449 US 389]
  e—R.M. Dolgin, Inc; U.S. v., 81 AFTR 2d 98-808, (DC MO), [See 47 AFTR 2d 81-526, 449 US 389]
  e—Toliver, George T.; U.S. v., 81 AFTR 2d 98-543, 972 F Supp 1041, (DC VA), [See 47 AFTR 2d 81-526, 449 US 389]

three times, in both the majority and dissenting opinions. This case was also a citing case under the Sixth Circuit decision. Examine these three *El Paso* citations closely to verify that the citations are "local"; that is, that they refer the researcher to specific pages in the citing opinion.

The last citation for *Upjohn* is the District Court case. This citation indicates that the District Court adjudicating the original case was located in Michigan and decided the case on 2-23-78. The cite also shows that this case was remanded by the Sixth Circuit case. There are no citing cases for the District Court case.

To complete the citator review of a case, it is necessary to consult all subsequent bound volumes and paperback supplements. Exhibit 6–7 shows the citing cases in Volume 3 of the *Citator 2nd Series,* the 1997 supplement, and the June 1998 supplement. Most of these cases do not distinguish which issues in the *Upjohn* case they address. All of these citing cases either follow or explain the Supreme Court case. From the number and support of citing cases we have reviewed, it is safe to conclude that the precedent of the *Upjohn* is well established and the case is still good law.

RIA *Citators* Ruling Example   It is equally important for a researcher to determine if a Revenue Ruling that appears to be on point with a client's tax situation is still in effect as it is to ascertain the precedence of a court case. Therefore, RIA *Citators* include cites for Treasury Decisions and Rulings (referred to here after as rulings) in the back of each of its volumes. The steps in checking the validity of a ruling are the same as with a court case; however, the abbreviations and citation organization in the RIA *Citators* are somewhat different. Exhibit 6–8 shows the symbols used in describing the judicial history of rulings. These abbreviations are employed in addition to symbols for cited and citing cases given in Exhibits 6–3 and 6–4.

The rulings contained in the Treasury Decision and Ruling section of the RIA *Citators* are presented in alphabetical order by type of ruling. The section starts with Announcements and ends with Treasury Decisions. Within each type of ruling, the cited pronouncements and the citing rulings are in chronological order. Citing cases follow the citing rulings. Exhibit 6–9 demonstrates this organization. Page 3110 of *Citator 2nd Series,* Volume 3, starts with Revenue Ruling 94-81 and ends with Revenue Ruling 95-71. The rulings made obsolete by Revenue Ruling 95-56 start with Revenue Ruling 84-152 and end with Revenue Ruling 87-89. This ruling is also cited in the Tax Court Memorandum *Gaw* case on four different pages. If this ruling applied to a client's tax situation, the practitioner would want to check the 1997 and 1998 citator supplements to determine the validity of the ruling. Because neither of the supplements has listings for this ruling, the practitioner can assume for the present that the ruling is still valid.

EXHIBIT 6–8   RIA *Citators* symbols for cited rulings

SYMBOLS USED IN CITATOR

TREASURY DECISIONS AND RULINGS

Judicial History

The symbols and evaluations used for the treasury decisions and rulings are similar to those used for the court decisions, which are shown in pages v and vi, with some additions:

ampfd	amplified
ampfg	amplifying
clfd	clarified
clfg	clarifying
impmd	implemented
impmg	implementing
inap	inapplicable
ob	the cited boldface ruling has been declared obsolete by a later ruling, or has declared an earlier ruling obsolete
rescd	rescinded
rescg	rescinding
revkd	the IRS has revoked the cited ruling in light of its later position
revkg	the cited ruling is revoking the earlier ruling
supmd	supplemented
supmg	supplementing
supsd	the cited ruling has been superseded by a later ruling
supsdg	the cited ruling supersedes the earlier ruling
susp	the operation of the cited ruling is temporarily suspended

Note: Whenever possible, the rulings contain their official cites in the Cumulative Bulletins. Because of the proliferation of material, however, not all material is contained in that source. If there is no official location in the government's material, the cited ruling contains a reference to the United States Tax Reporter paragraph at which the ruling is reproduced.

EXHIBIT 6–9 RIA *Citator 2nd Series* rulings citations

3110   **Rev Rul 94-81—Rev Rul 95-71**

Rev Rul 94-81, 1994-2 CB 412
   e—Fond Du Lac Reservation Business Committee; U.S. v., 76 AFTR 2d 95-6568, 95-6570, 906 F Supp 526, (DC MN)
Rev Rul 95-1, 1995-1 CB 108
Rev Rul 95-2, 1995-1 CB 220
   supsdg—Rev Rul 94-2, 1994-1 CB 311
   supsdg—Rev Rul 94-10, 1994-1 CB 316
Rev Rul 95-3, 1995-1 CB 160
Rev Rul 95-4, 1995-1 CB 141
   supmg—Rev Rul 92-19, 1992-1 CB 227
   supmd—Rev Rul 96-2, 1996-1 CB 141
   e—Rev Rul 97-2, 1997 USTR 86.159
Rev Rul 95-5, 1995-1 CB 100
Rev Rul 95-6, 1995-1 CB 80
   e—Announc 96-25, 1996 USTR 86.359
   e—Rev Rul 95-29, 1995-1 CB 82
   e—TD 8591, 1995-1 CB 87
Rev Rul 95-7, 1995-1 CB 185
Rev Rul 95-8, 1995-1 CB 107
   e—Rev Rul 95-26, 1995-1 CB 132
   e—Rev Rul 95-45, 1995-1 CB 53
Rev Rul 95-9, 1995-1 CB 222
Rev Rul 95-10, 1995-1 CB 168
   supmg—Rev Rul 96-4, 1996 USTR ¶ 86.001
   supsdg—Rev Rul 96-4, 1996 USTR ¶ 86.001
Rev Rul 95-11, 1995-1 CB 224
   supmg—Rev Rul 96-5, 1996 USTR ¶ 86.002
   supsdg—Rev Rul 96-5, 1996 USTR ¶ 86.002
Rev Rul 95-12, 1995-1 CB 101
Rev Rul 95-13, 1995-1 CB 162
Rev Rul 95-14, 1995-1 CB 169
Rev Rul 95-15, 1995-1 CB 212
   sm—Rev Rul 94-78, 1994-2 CB 276
   supsdg—Rev Rul 94-78, 1994-2 CB 276
   rc—Rev Proc 95-17, 1995-1 CB 556
Rev Rul 95-16, 1995-1 CB 9
   revkg—Rev Rul 86-70, 1986-1 CB 83
Rev Rul 95-17, 1995-1 CB 10
   rc—Rev Rul 95-15, 1995-1 CB 212
   supmg—Rev Rul 94-14, 1994-1 CB 72
Rev Rul 95-18, 1995-1 CB 102
Rev Rul 95-19, 1995-1 CB 143
Rev Rul 95-20, 1995-1 CB 163
Rev Rul 95-21, 1995-1 CB 131
   ob—Rev Rul 71-301, 1971-2 CB 256
Rev Rul 95-22, 1995-1 CB 145
Rev Rul 95-23, 1995-1 CB 3
Rev Rul 95-24, 1995-1 CB 14
Rev Rul 95-25, 1995-1 CB 103
Rev Rul 95-26, 1995-1 CB 131
   e—Rev Rul 95-45, 1995-1 CB 53
Rev Rul 95-27, 1995-1 CB 164
Rev Rul 95-28, 1995-1 CB 74
   e—Announc 96-4, 1996 USTR 86.078
   e—Rev Rul 96-7, 1996 USTR 86.037
Rev Rul 95-29, 1995-1 CB 81
   clfd—Rev Rul 95-29A, 1995-1 CB 85, 1995-2 CB 66
Rev Rul 95-29A, 1995-1 CB 85, 1995-2 CB 66
   clfg—Rev Rul 95-29, 1995-1 CB 81
Rev Rul 95-30, 1995-1 CB 72
Rev Rul 95-31, 1995-1 CB 76
   ob—Notice 89-52, 1989-1 CB 692
Rev Rul 95-32, 1995-1 CB 8
   e—Letter Ruling 9544001, 1995 USTR 87,000
   e—Letter Ruling 9607016, 1996 USTR 86,255
Rev Rul 95-33, 1995-1 CB 214
   s—IR- 95-27, 1995 USTR ¶ 86.128
Rev Rul 95-34, 1995-1 CB 224
   ob—Rev Proc 79-53, 1979-2 CB 578

Rev Rul 95-39, 1995-1 CB 165
Rev Rul 95-40, 1995-1 CB 195
Rev Rul 95-41, 1995-1 CB 132
Rev Rul 95-42, 1995-1 CB 167
Rev Rul 95-43, 1995-1 CB 105
Rev Rul 95-44, 1995-1 CB 3
Rev Rul 95-45, 1995-1 CB 53
Rev Rul 95-46, 1995-1 CB 217
   s—IR- 95-46, 1995 USTR ¶ 86,225
Rev Rul 95-47, 1995-1 CB 106
Rev Rul 95-48, 1995-2 CB 125
Rev Rul 95-49, 1995-2 CB 7
Rev Rul 95-50, 1995-2 CB 71
Rev Rul 95-51, 1995-2 CB 127
Rev Rul 95-52, 1995-2 CB 27
   rc—Rev Proc 95-38, 1995-2 CB 397
   e—ABC Rentals of San Antonio, Inc. et al v. Com., 78 AFTR 2d 96-6637, 97 F3d 396, (CA10)
Rev Rul 95-53, 1995-2 CB 30
   clfg—Rev Rul 79-41, 1979-1 CB 124
   supsdg—Rev Rul 79-41, 1979-1 CB 124
Rev Rul 95-54, 1995-2 CB 6
Rev Rul 95-55, 1995-2 CB 313
Rev Rul 95-56, 1995-2 CB 322
   ob—Rev Rul 84-152, 1984-2 CB 381
   ob—Rev Rul 84-153, 1984-2 CB 383
   ob—Rev Rul 85-163, 1985-2 CB 349
   ob—Rev Rul 87-89, 1987-2 CB 195, [See situations 1 and 2]
   e—Gaw, Anthony Teong-Chan, Transferee, 1995 RIA TC Memo 95-3362, 95-3363, 95-3397, 95-3399
Rev Rul 95-57, 1995-2 CB 62
Rev Rul 95-58, 1995-2 CB 191
   revkg—Rev Rul 79-353, 1979-2 CB 325
   revkg—Rev Rul 81-51, 1981-1 CB 458
   revkg—Rev Rul 77-182, 1977-1 CB 273
   e—Letter Ruling 9607008, 1996 USTR 19,595, 19,597
Rev Rul 95-59, 1995-2 CB 266
   s—IR- 95-51, 1995 USTR ¶ 86,301
Rev Rul 95-60, 1995-2 CB 78
   e—Indianapolis Life Insurance Co v. U.S., 78 AFTR 2d 96-6147, 940 F Supp 1376, (DC IN)
Rev Rul 95-61, 1995-2 CB 72
Rev Rul 95-62, 1995-2 CB 129
Rev Rul 95-63, 1995-2 CB 85
   supsdg—Rev Rul 92-63, 1992-2 CB 195
   sm—Rev Rul 92-63, 1992-2 CB 195
Rev Rul 95-64, 1995-2 CB 7
Rev Rul 95-65, 1995-2 CB 73
Rev Rul 95-66, 1995-2 CB 11
   m—Rev Rul 96-25, 1996 USTR ¶ 86,191
   sm—Rev Rul 95-35, 1995-1 CB 4
Rev Rul 95-67, 1995-2 CB 130
Rev Rul 95-68, 1995-2 CB 272
Rev Rul 95-69, 1995-2 CB 38
Rev Rul 95-70, 1995-2 CB 124
Rev Rul 95-71, 1995-2 CB 323
   ob—Rev Rul 54-171, 1954-1 CB 282
   ob—Rev Rul 54-257, 1954-2 CB 429
   ob—Rev Rul 56-171, 1956-1 CB 179
   ob—Rev Rul 56-286, 1956-1 CB 172
   ob—Rev Rul 57-243, 1957-1 CB 116
   ob—Rev Rul 57-490, 1957-2 CB 231
   ob—Rev Rul 58-9, 1958-1 CB 190
   ob—Rev Rul 58-241, 1958-1 CB 179
   ob—Rev Rul 58-391, 1958-2 CB 139
   ob—Rev Rul 63-125, 1963-2 CB 146
   ob—Rev Rul 64-100, 1964-1 CB 130
   ob—Rev Rul 64-239, 1964-2 CB 93
   ob—Rev Rul 64-257, 1964-2 CB 91

CCH *Citator*

The **Commerce Clearing House *Citator*** (CCH *Citator*) is offered as an integral part of CCH's *Standard Federal Tax Reports.* (The *Standard Federal Tax Reports* is an annotated tax service that discusses and explains the Code in great detail. This tax service is discussed in detail in Chapter 7.) This citator differs from the RIA *Citators* in that it is a two-volume, loose-leaf series with no bound volumes. The loose-leaf volumes are A to L and M to Z with a Finding List for Rulings in the back of the M to Z volume. It also covers only the federal income tax decisions that have been issued since 1913. Federal estate and gift tax cases are cited in a separate volume. Court decisions that are obsolete, because of a change in the statute they interpret, are marked with a dagger symbol and no citing cases are listed.

CCH *Citator* Example   Examine the excerpt in Exhibit 6–10 from the CCH *Citator.* It is also for the *Upjohn* case. The names of cited cases are set in bold print, followed by paragraph number references to the *Standard Federal Tax Reports* compilations. Thus, the *Upjohn* decision is discussed in ¶¶ 43,727.5028 and 43,727.5068 of the CCH service. These cites are a useful method of entering into the CCH tax service. The tax service contents will help the researcher evaluate the case in the context of relevant Code sections, Regulations, and administrative sources of tax law.

Notice that the list of cases in the CCH *Citator* is much shorter than that in the RIA *Citators.* This is because only those citing cases that the CCH editors believe will serve as a useful guide to the value of the cited case as a precedent are listed. Thus, the tax researcher is directed to those cases that may be most likely to develop, explain, criticize, or otherwise evaluate a rule of law. This is in contrast to the RIA and Shepard's citators, which list all of the cases that have mentioned the cited case. Although the latter practice provides a level of thoroughness that may be useful in some situations, the CCH editorial screening procedure guards against the possibility that the researcher will be overwhelmed by the sheer volume of citing cases presented. The more selective CCH approach, of course, forces the researcher to rely on an editor's evaluation concerning the usefulness of the citing cases.

The bold black bullets under the case name in Exhibit 6–10 designate the court levels that have addressed a case. Unlike the RIA *Citators,* the highest level court to address the case is listed first, and the trial-level court is listed last. Hence, the citation for the *Upjohn* Supreme Court case is listed first followed by its citing cases, then the Sixth Circuit case followed by its citing cases, and lastly the District Court case. The advantage of this organization is that the researcher can easily determine the highest court that heard the case and the bullet headings clearly identify the levels of the courts cases. The citing cases under each court decision are listed in reverse chronological order with any Revenue Rulings addressing the case completing the citation entry. This allows the researcher to identify quickly the most recent cases that have cited the case of interest, but this ordering makes it more difficult to identify which cases are by the highest courts.

The CCH *Citator* like the RIA *Citators* provides information about the judicial history of the case. The reference for the Supreme Court case denotes that it reversed the Sixth Circuit's holding and remanded the case. The Sixth Circuit reference indicates it affirmed some holdings of the District Court decision and reversed and remanded on other issues. However, the CCH *Citator* does not supply the useful symbols utilized in the RIA *Citators* for the citing cases. Thus, the researcher cannot determine if the *Bell* case followed, or explained, or distinguished itself from the *Upjohn* case.

EXHIBIT 6-10 CCH *Citator, Upjohn* case

```
Upjohn Co. . . . . . . . . . ¶43,727.5028, 43,727.5068
  ● SCt—(rev'g & rem'g CA-6), 81-1 USTC ¶9138; Ct
    D 2003; 1981-1 CB 591; SupCt
Bell, DC-Calif, 95-1 USTC ¶50,006
Mobil Corp., DC-Tex, 93-1 USTC ¶50,335
Fu Investment Co., Ltd., TC, Dec. 50,563, 104 TC —
  , No. 20
Bernardo, TC, Dec. 50,705, 104 TC 677
Massachusetts Institute of Technology, DC-Mass,
  97-1 USTC ¶50,269
Dolgin, Inc., DC-Mo, 97-2 USTC ¶50,806
Zolin, Frank S., SCt, 89-1 USTC ¶9380, 491 US 554,
  109 SCt 2619
Doe, SCt, 88-2 USTC ¶9545, 487 US 201, 108 SCt
  2341
Holifield, CA-7, 90-2 USTC ¶50,423, 909 F2d 201
Rockwell International, CA-3, 90-1 USTC ¶50,151,
  897 F2d 1255
Olson, Robert G., CA-8, 89-1 USTC ¶9339, 872 F2d
  820
Klein, CA-7, 85-2 USTC ¶9701
Liebman, CA-3, 84-2 USTC ¶9790, 742 F2d 807
El Paso Co., CA-5, 82-2 USTC ¶9534, 682 F2d 530
Riewe, CA-10, 82-1 USTC ¶9338, 676 F2d 418
Sealed Case, CA-DC, 82-1 USTC ¶9335, 676 F2d 793
Young & Co., CA-2, 82-1 USTC ¶9320, 677 F2d 211
Moody, CA, 81-2 USTC ¶9484, 654 F2d 795
Wyatt, CA-5, 81-1 USTC ¶9211, 637 F2d 293
Holifield, DC-Wis, 88-2 USTC ¶9472, 689 FSupp 865
Isherwood, Hunter & Diehm Olive v., DC-V.I., 88-1
  USTC ¶9131
Hartz Mountain Industries, Inc., TC, Dec. 46,126, 93
  TC 521
  ● CA-6—(aff'g, rev'g & rem'g DC), 79-2 USTC
    ¶9457; 600 F2d 1223
Rockwell International, CA-3, 90-1 USTC ¶50,151,
  897 F2d 1255
El Paso Co., CA-5, 82-2 USTC ¶9534, 682 F2d 530
Davis, CA-5, 81-1 USTC ¶9193, 636 F2d 1028
Amerada Hess Corp., CA-3, 80-1 USTC ¶9160, 619
  F2d 980
Bonnell, DC-Minn, 80-1 USTC ¶9170, 483 FSupp
  1070
  ● DC-Mich—78-1 USTC ¶9437
  ● DC-Mich—78-1 USTC ¶9277
Upjohn Est., William E., Exr. . . . . . . . . . ¶24,808.966
  ● CA-6—(aff'g BTA memo), 41-2 USTC ¶9792; 124
    F2d 73
Beeghly Fund. CA-6, 63-1 USTC ¶9101, 310 F2d 756
Jordan Foundation, CA-7, 54-1 USTC ¶9269, 210
  F2d 885
Citizens & Southern Nat'l Bank, CA-5, 45-1 USTC
  ¶9182, 147 F2d 977
Boston Safe Deposit & Trust Co., DC-Mass, 55-1
  USTC ¶9303. 129 FSupp 616
Danz, TC, Dec. 19,013, 18 TC 454
Baer, TC, Dec. 13,185(M), 2 TCM 29
  ● BTA—Dec. 11,257-D; July 9, 1940
Upjohn, William J. . . . . . . . . . . . . . . . . (Estate Tax)
  ● DC-Mich—72-2 USTC ¶12,888
```

One of the major advantages of the CCH *Citator* being loose-leaf is that it can be updated by adding or replacing the pages in the binders. This eliminates the need to search numerous citator volumes when the practitioner wants to develop a thorough list of citing cases. Because the main Citator Table is updated on an annual basis, the practitioner should check whether there are recent citing cases that might change the status of the initial cases identified as pertinent. The Current Citator Table, updated quarterly, gives citations of cases that have been decided since the last annual revision. The "[current year] Case Table" and the "Latest Additions to [current year] Case Table" located in the New Matters volume of the *Standard Federal Tax Reports* tax service give the most recent case information. This is updated on a weekly basis.

CCH *Citator* Conventions   Cases are listed alphabetically with acronyms treated as separate words. Even business names that begin with a number are listed alphabetically as if the number were spelled out. For example, the 123 Corporation would be listed under "O" for "one." The ampersand and connectors such as "and," "of," and "to," and legal conventions like "in re" and "in the matter of" are ignored. Alphabetical order is maintained within the group of businesses whose names begin with the letter. If the taxpayer in the case has the letter "A" in front of its name, such as *A. & P. Production Co.*, it will precede all cases with double "A" such as *A.A. Electric Supply Co.*, which would itself precede *AAA Exterminators,* which in turn would precede *Aab, Raymond J.* Notice in the excerpt in Exhibit 6–11 that *A. P. Family Trust* comes before *A to Z Welding,* which in turn is listed ahead of *Aagaard, Robert W.* Because the CCH *Citator* lists cases in what it calls "strict" alphabetical order, when you don't find a case listed where you expect it, be sure you are looking in the right place.

The CCH *Citator* gives citations to CCH's own *United States Tax Cases* series, followed by the parallel citation to an official reporter. It does not give citations for the RIA court reporter services such as AFTR2d. This can sometimes be a problem when a journal article gives an AFTR2d cite, for example, but the practitioner has access only to the CCH *Citator* and CCH court reporters.

Shepard's *Citator*

Shepard's was the first to introduce the citator as an aid to legal research. It has developed citators for virtually every case reporter series, as well as for specialized areas of the law, such as taxation. Because of its early entry into the citator market, and the breadth of its coverage, legal researchers often refer to the process of evaluating the validity of a case and locating additional authority via a citator as **Shepardizing** the case.

Shepard's is the only major tax citator that is organized by case reporter series. Within each court reporter division, the cases are arranged in chronological order by volume rather than in alphabetical order by the case name. Presently, ***Shepard's Federal Tax Citator*** (Shepard's *Citator*) 1995 edition has eight bound volumes, plus two paper-bound volumes through 1997. Part 1a of the paper-bound volumes is for cases and Part 1b is rulings and statutes. Paperback supplements update these bound

---

EXHIBIT 6–11   CCH *Citator* case order

A. P. Family Trust (See Wolan, Margaret, Trustee)
A. & P. Production Co. . . . . ¶ 29,626.409
  ● CA-5—(aff'g BTA), 41-2 USTC ¶ 9651; 122 F2d 192
  ● BTA—Dec. 11,010-A; Feb. 9, 1940
A & P Water & Sewer Supplies, Inc. (See Tidewater
  Plumbing & Heating, Inc.)
A. & R. Concrete Co. (See Gilcrest Co., J. K. v. A. & R.
  Concrete Co.)
A. to Z. Equipment Corp.: Fidelity & Deposit Co. of
  Maryland v. (See Fidelity & Deposit Co. of
  Maryland v. A. to Z. Equipment Corp.)
A to Z Welding & Mfg. Co., Inc. . . . . ¶ 40,580.21,
  42,283.738, 42,283.781
  ● CA-8—(aff'g DC per curiam), 87-1 USTC ¶ 9109;
  803 F2d 932
  Buildwright Homes, Inc., BC-DC-Ohio, 95-1 USTC
  ¶ 50,173
  Goldsby, BC-DC-Ark, 92-1 USTC ¶ 50,118
  LaSalle Rolling Mills, Inc., CA-7, 87-2 USTC ¶ 9592,
  832 F2d 390
  Upton Printing Co., Inc., BC-DC-La, 90-2 USTC
  ¶ 50,392, 116 BR 66
  Frazier, DC-Va, 89-2 USTC ¶ 9495
  Casa Garcia, Inc., DC-La, 89-2 USTC ¶ 9426
  Condel, Inc.,, BAP-9, 88-2 USTC ¶ 9555
  Young, Ltd., DC-Nev, 88-2 USTC ¶ 9397, 87 BR 635
  Heritage Village, DC-SC, 88-1 USTC ¶ 9234
  Cambridge Machined Products Corp., DC-Mass,
  87-2 USTC ¶ 9649
  ● DC-Ark—86-1 USTC ¶ 9112; 58 BR 138
  LaSalle Rolling Mills, Inc., DC-Ill, 86-2 USTC ¶ 9723
  Gay Fire Equipment Co., Inc., DC-Ga, 86-1 USTC
  ¶ 9267

A.A. Electric Supply Co. (See Board of Education v.
  Bruce Electric Co.)
AAA Cycles (See Richman, R.R.)
AAA Delivery, Inc. (See Atkins, Everett W. v. Wells, Jr.,
  C.V.)
AAA Exterminators (See Lieb, Jr., William C.)
Aab, Raymond J. . . . . ¶ 14,854.502
  ● TC—Dec. 38,376(M); 42 TCM 1519; TC Memo.
  1981-620
  Storzer, TC, Dec. 39,099(M), 44 TCM 100, TC
  Memo. 1982-328
AABCO Building and Janitorial Services, Inc. . . .
  . . . . ¶ 39,060.78
  ● DC-Ky—89-2 USTC ¶ 9604
Aagaard, Carl M. . . . . ¶ 3100.095, 40,551G.36
  ● TC—Dec. 42,043(M); 49 TCM 1278; TC Memo.
  1985-194
  Metcalf, TC, Dec. 42,388(M), 50 TCM 1077, TC
  Memo. 1985-487
Aagaard, Robert W. . . . . ¶ 9604.10, 10,001.43,
  31,515A.079, 31,562.42, 31,562.47,
  32,263.3965
  ● TC—Dec. 30,755; 56 TC 191; A. 1971-2 CB 1
  Richards, TC, Dec. 49,276(M), 66 TCM 707, TC
  Memo. 1993-422
  Delk, TC, Dec. 50,697(M), 69 TCM 2908, TC Memo.
  1995-265
  Thomas,, TC, Dec. 45,460, 92 TC 206
  DeNiro Est., TC, Dec. 41,962(M), 49 TCM 1004, TC
  Memo. 1985-128
  Andrews, TC, Dec. 37,916(M), 41 TCM 1533, TC

volumes every other month in February, April, June, August, October, and December. Every three or four years, the publisher issues a new bound volume to incorporate this update material. Shepard's includes cases reported in all of the court case reporter series discussed in Chapter 5 and pertinent sections of the Code and Regulations.

To use the Shepard's *Citator,* the practitioner must know the court reporter citation for the case. This can be a problem if only the name of a case is known. In locating a citation, first find the division of the *Citator* for the court reporter of the case. Within the court reporter division, the volume numbers for each reporter appear at the upper outside corners of each page. For each such volume, the *Citator* lists, in bold print, the first page number of the cited cases. If more than one court opinion begins on the same page of the reporter volume, the *Citator* distinguishes them as "Case 1" and "Case 2." After the page number, the case name and the year of the decision are given. The other reporter locations, known as parallel citations, follow in parentheses. These features can be identified by examining Exhibit 6–12. The

---

EXHIBIT 6–12 Shepard's *Citator* 1995 bound volume, *Upjohn* case

Vol. 101   **SUPREME COURT REPORTER (Tax Cases)**

Colo	d 63AF2d1169	103FRD³66	563FS⁷830	143FRD¹⁰511	142FRD¹269
707 P2d353	f 63AF2d1483	103FRD⁵66	567FS⁵1360	f 143FRD¹⁰518	142FRD¹411
Conn	65AF2d833	f 104FRD464	580FS⁵1098	145FRD¹301	f 143FRD¹66
487 A2d1089	66AF2d5413	106FRD204	580FS⁶1099	145FRD¹630	143FRD⁵66
D C	71AF2d1876	106FRD¹205	587FS¹58	145FRD¹⁰630	144FRD232
642 A2d118	71AF2d1877	118FRD¹⁰247	589FS¹451	f 145FRD634	144FRD⁶268
Fla	71AAF2d4256	139FRD¹8	589FS²451	148FRD¹⁰102	154FRD¹101
537 So2d647	74AF2d7273	139FRD⁳8	598FS¹990	13BRW¹57	154FRD²101

472 NW498	[50335	139FRD557	102FRD³9	513FS¹522	805FS⁷1305
	118FRD196	144FRD³604	102FRD⁹11	557FS¹⁰1058	805FS⁵1306
—677—	133FRD324	152FRD³3	102FRD¹⁰11	562FS³441	110FRD¹513
Upjohn Co. v	Cir. DC	d 40BRW57	103FRD¹122	619FS¹1046	110FRD⁵517
United States	654F2d¹⁰798	d 79BRW98	106FRD⁵38	619FS⁷1047	114FRD¹695
1981	665F2d¹1220	Cir. 2	106FRD⁶38	656FS⁶1173	e 114FRD⁵696
(47AF2d523)	665F2d⁵1220	670F2d386	110FRD¹⁰690	d 692FS⁵493	116FRD¹210
(81UTC¶ 9138)	676F2d⁸808	675F2d484	111FRD¹79	728FS¹1102	116FRD³210
(449US383)	f 676F2d¹⁰810	675F2d¹487	111FRD⁵79	764FS¹343	118FRD⁵587
(66L𝕰584)	686F2d²32	675F2d²487	111FRD⁶80	766FS⁵265	126FRD¹⁰506
s 44AF2d5179	686F2d³33	d 675F2d³488	112FRD103	766FS⁴270	f 136FRD¹426
s 79UTC¶ 9457	737F2d¹98	d 675F2d⁶488	112FRD391	766FS⁵271	142FRD126
s 600F2d1223	737F2d⁵99	675F2d¹⁰492	113FRD⁵560	809FS¹363	144FRD¹70
103SC¹1621	737F2d²101	677F2d¹219	114FRD⁶644	815FS¹814	148FRD¹538
103SC³1621	738F2d⁵1369	f 677F2d⁴220	117FRD¹525	834FS¹707	150FRD³545
e 105SC¹⁵1990	738F2d⁶1369	j 677F2d222	121FRD10	841FS1398	152FRD80
108SC2350	826F2d127	700F2d⁵827	121FRD¹200	848FS566	Cir. 5
f 109SC2625	f 838F2d⁵1302	731F2d¹1037	121FRD³203	858FS54	637F2d295
f 109SC¹2626	856F2d¹⁰273	731F2d²1037	121FRD¹⁰639	858FS¹55	682F2d¹538
47AF2d789	h 861F2d⁸735	731F2d³1037	125FRD386	859FS¹766	682F2d²538
48AF2d5170	861F2d¹⁰736	j 781F2d260	d 125FRD¹387	93FRD⁴141	682F2d³538
49AF2d1054	518FS¹680	825F2d679	128FRD35	103FRD³409	682F2d⁶539
49AF2d1204	518FS²680	828F2d¹100	f 130FRD¹31	d 103FRD¹425	682F2d¹⁰542
j 50AF2d5530	e 518FS⁵681	828F2d³100	f 131FRD¹377	103FRD⁶430	682F2d⁸544
50AF2d5530	e 518FS⁷681	888F2d¹⁰12	f 131FRD³377	f 109FRD687	j 682F2d550
51AF2d343	571FS⁵506	892F2d243	f 131FRD⁵377	115FRD517	693F2d⁶1242
d 52AF2d5537	f 654FS³1364	926F2d¹1292	f 131FRD¹398	115FRD³518	722F2d¹177
52AF2d5537	d 654FS1365	926F2d⁶1294	f 131FRD⁵404	125FRD⁹615	822F2d¹524
52AF2d6304	f 672FS⁴	979F2d³944	f 131FRD¹⁰654	127FRD⁶654	h 854F2d¹785
54AF2d5938	d 672FS⁵5	992F2d452	f 131FRD⁶405	130FRD¹570	927F2d875
d 56AF2d6073	705FS⁴676	9F3d⁷236	e 136FRD360	131FRD¹66	972F2d620
e 56AF2d6367	744FS⁸1185	507FS⁵112	137FRD¹⁰644	132FRD¹395	f 43F3d⁹970
56AF2d6367	857FS⁵104	521FS¹640	140FRD¹⁰304	f 134FRD⁵123	556FS1155
58AF2d5368	100FRD⁶24	525FS⁸650	140FRD³305	f 134FRD⁶123	647FS118
60AF2d5042	100FRD⁶438	553FS⁵50	140FRD⁷306	135FRD¹98	841FS1428
60AF2d5513	100FRD⁹439	553FS⁹51	143FRD³46	139FRD¹⁰614	f 89FRD⁶600
62AF2d5764	101FRD439	f 561FS1253	143FRD⁵501	142FRD⁶268	f 91FRD⁴417

1997 paper-bound volumes and the 1998 supplemental updates do not repeat the case name, year of decision, or other parallel citations (see Exhibit 6–13).

Citing cases follow the citation and history for the cited case. The judicial history of the cited case is given, indicating affirmation, reversals, dismissals, and so on. Citing cases are divided between those of *treatment,* in which the cited case is criticized, distinguished, explained, followed, overruled, etc., and those of *operation,* in which the cited case has been amended, extended, limited, revoked, superseded, etc. Shepard's *Citator* does not furnish the names of the citing cases, just their citation. However, Shepard's *Citator* does include references to selected law review articles and a listing of citations to federal statutes and Regulations.

Abbreviation Conventions for Shepard's *Citator*   Shepard's *Citator* uses its own set of letter abbreviations, which precede the citation for the citing case, to evaluate the treatment of the cited case. For instance, as indicated in Exhibit 6–14 "a" indicates that the case was affirmed, "r" that it was reversed, "c" that it was criticized, and "j" means that the case was cited in the dissenting opinion. The practitioner must take care not to mix up the symbols used by the RIA *Citators* with those of the Shepard's *Citator.* For example, the symbol "d" in the RIA *Citators* means that the appeal was dismissed or withdrawn, whereas in the Shepard's *Citator* "d" means that the citing case is distinguished from the cited case.

A small superscript number appears immediately to the left of the page number in a citing reference. This number indicates the headnote paragraph to which the citing court's analysis relates. The headnote numbering identification is available only for federal tax cases appearing in the West court reporter series, the *Lawyers' Cooperative Edition,* and the *United States Supreme Court Reports,* but not for the Shepard's listing of the USTC and AFTR court reporters.

Because headnote paragraphs represent a summary and analysis of the law by the editors of a given court reporter, the numbered headnotes for a specific case do not necessarily correspond among the various reporters. Thus, when using headnote numbers to limit a citator search, the researcher must be cognizant of which court reporter headnote numbers are pertinent to each citator service. Compare the headnotes in Exhibit 6–15, taken from West's *Supreme Court Reports* for the *Upjohn* case, with the headnotes for the case in the AFTR2d series reproduced in Exhibit 6–5. The editors of these two court reporters analyzed the judicial opinions to different degrees of detail. The drafting of headnotes and the breadth of the issue that each headnote addresses are a matter of the style and editorial policy of the entity that publishes the reporter. The AFTR2d evaluation of the *Upjohn* case required just two headnotes, compared to the ten headnotes from West's *Supreme Court Reporter.* In further contrast, the *Lawyers' Cooperative Edition* coverage of the same case includes five headnotes.

Notice the small keys and numbers in the headnotes in Exhibit 6–15. The West headnote system has a particularly valuable feature for finding tax law, the West Key Number System. The points of law articulated in a case are editorially classified into Key Numbers that fit into an extensive system for organizing case law. West publishes a series of digests that organize the holdings of cases by Key Numbers. For example, if researchers want to find cases that cover certain tax transactions, they can go to a West digest and look under the Key Number for that point of law. The Key Number would furnish a list of cases addressing the issue. In fact, a researcher could start with the Taxation section in the West digest to initially find cases covering the tax issue. This service is offered online and on the Internet

EXHIBIT 6–13 Shepard's *Citator* 1997 and 1998 supplements, *Upjohn* case

Vol. 100   **SUPREME COURT REPORTER (Tax Cases)**

Cir. 2
94F3d[13]792
Cir. 3
78AF2d5582
79AF2d1234
96UTC¶
[50633
89F3d1064
910FS1060
910FS[1]1062
966FSP343
Cir. 4
55F3d[2]930
927FS[2]948
Cir. 7
47F3d184
77F3d[2]1013
928FS739
Cir. 8
888FS[2]972
888FS[14]973
948FS[1]829
955FS1175
Cir. 9
80AF2d5350
Cir. 10
67F3d[10]1512
84F3d[10]1294
Cir. 11
j 66F3d1584
44MJ465
j 44MJ474
Ariz
914P2d1331
Ark
933SW368
Calif
41CaR2d642
41CaR2d648
895P2d884
895P2d890
Colo
888P2d307
Conn
663A2d331
D C
f 653A2d866
689A2d538
694A2d864
Kan
891P2d322
Wash
886P2d132

Vol. 101

—549—
110SC2252
114SC[4]2021
114SC2025
Cir. 2
79AF2d1458
96UTC¶
[50494
955FS[5]29

Cir. 3
80AF2d5143
Cir. 6
79AF2d[5]1830
Ala
668So2d792
672So2d799
N Y
647NE748
623NYS2d536

—677—
116SC[1]1929
USDk 95-266[1]
Cir. DC
107F3d49
952FS842
161FRD226
168FRD446
168FRD[9]447
170FRD[2]70
170FRD[3]70
Cir. 1
79AF2d596
97UTC¶
[50269
57F3d[6]36
60F3d[8]883
918FS509
918FS[1]510
918FS[3]510
936FS[5]56
936FS[5]57
957FS[1]303
e 159FRD[10]364
171FRD14
173FRD[3]16
Cir. 2
76AF2d[3]7191
95UTC¶
[50579
68F3d39
68F3d[1]499
117F3d87
879FS[8]233
879FS[11]233
882FS[1]43
920FS[3]364
938FS[4]1130
948FS[3]330
961FS[1]670
157FRD[1]168
159FRD[1]388
161FRD[10]279
161FRD[3]282
164FRD333
168FRD165
168FRD468
169FRD561
171FRD64
172FRD[5]55
172FRD643
173FRD[3]94
f 173FRD95
173FRD[5]95
173FRD[1]372
173FRD[7]372

199BRW97
199BRW[10]98
199BRW448
199BRW[1]449
Cir. 3
78AF2d5670
96UTC¶
[50396
103F3d1152
110F3d961
892FS110
914FS[1]1090
914FS[7]1090
914FS[3]1091
d 914FS1098
914FS[10]1098
932FS117
943FS[1]499
943FS[8]499
960FS[10]843
156FRD[9]594
156FRD[10]594
156FRD[6]599
160FRD34
172FRD[6]150
Cir. 4
78AF2d5756
88F3d[1]1389
88F3d[3]1389
102F3d[3]750
106F3d[1]600
f 106F3d601
106F3d[3]601
106F3d[6]603
f 106F3d[9]608
908FS[1]322
910FS1119
910FS[1]1120
910FS[6]1120
965FSP751
158FRD[1]584
Cir. 5
d 48F3d[5]904
891FS[1]363
168FRD[4]559
Cir. 6
78F3d[1]254
951FS[3]684
162FRD296
Cir. 7
96F3d976
883FS[6]1208
909FS1121
919FS1257
961FS210
168FRD640
172FRD[3]397
f 172FRD[5]397
204BRW[10]964
Cir. 8
79AF2d1085
112F3d915
112F3d[5]918
d 112F3d920
112F3d[1]920
j 112F3d930
875FS[5]648

922FS243
956FS[6]1510
156FRD[2]176
168FRD[6]646
Cir. 9
76AF2d6656
76AF2d6680
77AF2d1551
78AF2d6416
95UTC¶
[50006
96UTC¶
[50201
96F3d1296
e 96F3d[3]1297
99F3d1500
99F3d[1]1502
109F3d[1]550
Cir. 10
902FS[1]1362
912FS505
f 912FS506
162FRD[1]689
162FRD[2]689
162FRD[3]689
f 162FRD690
167FRD[6]200
170FRD[1]484
170FRD[6]484
Cir. 11
77AF2d555
113F3d1556
959FS[10]1536
d 161FRD473
169FRD697
196BRW[7]599
Cir. Fed.
101F3d1391
Ala
677So2d1172
Ariz
920P2d299
Calif
37CaR2d855
Conn
691A2d32
f 691A2d34
696A2d340
Del
653A2d261
694A2d432
D C
657A2d290
Fla
659So2d1161
678So2d417
Mass
d 677NE145
Mich
f 528NW781
Nev
891P2d1184
f 891P2d1185
N J
661A2d823
678A2d286

691A2d334
694A2d267
696A2d567
N Y
674NE671
651NYS2d962
Ohio
664NE532
Ore
942P2d265
Tex
904SW646
904SW647
904SW648
Wash
905P2d370
916P2d425
W Va
459SE146
460SE684
460SE688
484SE209

—836—
116SC[2]1077
j 116SC1081
USDk 94-1471
[²
j USDk
[94-1471
Ltr#9651047
Ltr#9714011
Ltr#9716021
Ltr#9721031
Ltr#9722042
Ltr#9726020
Ltr#9738038
TAM#9542002
Cir. 3
77AF2d1955
95UTC¶
[50393
96UTC¶
[60230
925FS[1]270
Cir. 4
75AF2d2508
77AF2d2554
95UTC¶
[50286
96UTC¶
[50323
86F3d1333
88F3d1336
Cir. 6
j 89F3d1284
Cir. 8
76AF2d[7]7970
96UTC¶
[50072
Cir. 11
77AF2d[2]344
96UTC¶
[50023
71F3d[2]811
ClCt
32FedCl[1] 282

976FS[6]764
f 976FS766
Cir. 8
130F3d[4]819
Cir. 11
1998USApp
[LX[5]3248
135F3d[5]1405
Ariz
949P2d48

—2439—
Cir. 3
971FS[3]868
984FSP342
Cir. 4
982FS[1]382
982FS[10]382
Cir. 5
127F3d[4]460
Cir. 11
e 117F3d[9]1214
117F3d[14]1214
117F3d[4]1215
117F3d[10]1215

Vol. 101

—549—
La
701So2d1307

—677—
Cir. DC
124F3d234
124F3d[10]236
j 124F3d237
124F3d1307
Cir. 1
1998USApp
[LX[6]1944
80AF2d[3]7983
97UTC¶
[50955
129F3d[2]684
136F3d[6]1
174FRD228
176FRD[3]13
176FRD[6]13
176FRD[7]13
Cir. 2
f 81AF2d[10]830
f 98UTC¶
[50230
134F3d1196
f 134F3d[10]1204
1998USDist
[LX546
1998USDist
[LX1181
1998USDist
[LX4200
1998USDist
[LX5155
969FS[1]883

973FS[1]140
984FS[3]824
175FRD[9]11
175FRD[1]21
175FRD[6]21
Cir. 3
174FRD[6]632
Cir. 4
81AF2d543
1998USDist
[LX429
972FS[1]1041
Cir. 5
121F3d[1]974
174FRD[5]62
174FRD[7]62
216BRW[3]591
Cir. 6
128F3d[5]437
128F3d[10]437
j 128F3d442
134F3d[5]356
j 134F3d359
Cir. 8
81AF2d808
97UTC¶
[50806
216BRW14
Cir. 9
132F3d[1]510
969FS[5]598
175FRD655
Cir. 10
1998USApp
[LX[10]2032
129F3d1368
129F3d[3]1370
133F3d1356
136F3d[10]695
Cir. 11
d 1998USDist
[LX4801
ClCt
80AF2d7092
97UTC¶
[50993
Calif
69CaR2d145
Fla
697So2d1252
Ky
957SW726
La
703So2d1

—836—
Ltr#9750062
Ltr#9752064
Ltr#9814039

—1037—
Cir. 4
124F3d[2]648
ClCt
80AF2d7587
81AF2d[2]373

through the WESTLAW service. Exhibit 6–16 contains a list of the Key Number topics for Taxation.

Shepard's *Citator* Example   Because Shepard's is organized by case reporter, the researcher must locate the division for the court reporter in which the case is found. The edited excerpt from *Shepard's Federal Tax Citator* in Exhibit 6–12 was taken from the 1995 bound volume, Part 5, page 1612, for the *Supreme Court Reporter* division. The case Shepardized is *Upjohn Company* (101S Ct 677). Reporter volume 101 is indicated in bold type, as is the page number for the first page of the case (677). The case name is given just below the bold page number. Note the parallel citations, in parentheses, that follow are to the RIA's AFTR2d series (abbreviated at AF2d) and to CCH's USTC series as well as other tax court reporters. Confirm that *Upjohn* was cited twice on page 1621 of volume 103 of the *Supreme Court Reporter*. These citations relate to headnotes 1 and 3 of *Upjohn* as published in the *Supreme Court Reporter*.

For each cited case, the Shepard's analysis begins with Supreme Court citations and continues with tax cases reported in the AFTR and USTC series. Then, by cir-

---

EXHIBIT 6–14   Shepard's *Citator* symbols for cited cases and citing cases

ABBREVIATIONS—ANALYSIS

History of Case

a	(affirmed)	The citing case affirms or adheres to the case you are Shepardizing.
cc.	(connected case)	The citing case is related to the case you are Shepardizing, arising out of the same subject matter or involving the same parties.
Corr	(correction)	Error in prior treasury decision, revenue ruling or procedure pointed out and rectified.
D	(dismissed)	Same case or appeal therefrom dismissed.
m	(modified)	As a result of rehearing or appeal, the citing case modifies (changes in some way, including affirmance in part and reversal in part) the decision in the case you are Shepardizing.
PLR	(Prior Letter Ruling)	Prior Letter Ruling with same text reissued under a new letter ruling number.
r	(reversed)	The citing case reverses the case you are Shepardizing.
s	(same case)	The cited case involves the same litigation as the case you are Shepardizing, but at a different stage of the proceedings.
S	(superseded)	The decision in the citing case supersedes (has been substituted for) the case you are Shepardizing.
v	(vacated)	The citing case vacates (withdraws) the case you are Shepardizing.
US cert den in		Certiorari denied by U.S. Supreme Court.
US cert dis in		Certiorari dismissed by U.S. Supreme Court.
US cert gran in		Certiorari granted by U.S. Supreme Court.
US reh den in		Rehearing denied by U.S. Supreme Court.
US reh dis in		Rehearing dismissed by U.S. Supreme Court.
US app pndg		Appeal pending before the U.S. Supreme Court.

(continued)

EXHIBIT 6–14 *Continued*

Treatment of Case

Acq	(acquiescence)	Acquiescence by Commissioner in reasoning or result of the cited case.
AcqR	(acquiescence, result only)	Acquiescence by Commissioner in result only, and not in the reasoning employed to reach such a result.
Amp	(amplified)	Previous revenue ruling or procedure expanded or extended to different factual situation.
c	(criticized)	The citing case disagrees with the reasoning/result of the case you are Shepardizing, although the citing court may not have the authority to materially affect its precedential value.
Clr	(clarification)	Clarification of prior revenue rule or procedure.
d	(distinguished)	The citing case is diferent from the case you are Shepardizing, involving either a dissimilar fact situation or a different application of the law.
e	(explained)	The citing case interprets or clarifies the case you are Shepardizing in a significant way.
f	(followed)	The citing case relies on the case you are Shepardizing as controlling or persuasive authority.
h	(harmonized)	The citing case is different from the case you are Shepardizing, but the citing court relies on the cited case after reconciling the difference or inconsistency.
j	(dissenting opinion)	The case you are Shepardizing is cited in a dissenting opinion.
L	(limited)	The citing case restricts the application of the case you are Shepardizing, finding that its reasoning applies only in limited, specific circumstances.
Noacq	(nonacquiescence)	Nonacquiescence by Commissioner in reasoning or result of the cited case.
o	(overruled)	The citing case expressly overrules all or part of the case you are Shepardizing.
p	(parallel)	The citing case relies on the case you are Shepardizing by describing it as "on all fours" or "parallel" to the citing case.
q	(questioned)	The citing case questions the continuing validity or precedential value of the case you are Shepardizing because of intervening circumstances, including legislative or judicial overruling.
SLR	(subsequent Letter Ruling)	Subsequent Letter Ruling issued in same case.

cuit, the service analyzes cases decided by the federal appeals courts, followed by the U.S. Court of Claims and various state courts. Within each of these citing groups, the citations are listed in chronological order. When the cited case is an opinion of the Supreme Court, the Court of Appeals case generally follows the indicated parallel citations; it is accompanied by an "s," to signify that this is the same case. There may be several "s" citations if the case has been remanded more than once, or if it also appears in the *Federal Supplement*.

When using the Shepard's *Citator,* begin with the bound volume in which the case first appears, then consult the bound supplements. Finally, examine the most recent

EXHIBIT 6–15   Shepard's *Citator* headnotes for *Supreme Court Reporter*

1. Witnesses ☞198(1)

Purpose of attorney–client privilege is to encourage full and frank communication between attorneys and their clients and thereby to promote broader public interests in observance of law and administration of justice. Fed.Rules Evid. Rule 501, 28 U.S. C.A.

2. Witnesses ☞198(1)

Attorney–client privilege rests on need for advocate and counselor to know all that relates to client's reasons for seeking representation if professional mission is to be carried out. ABA Code of Professional Responsibility, EC4–1.

3. Witnesses ☞198(1)

Attorney–client privilege exists to protect not only giving of professional advice to those who can act on it but also the giving of information to lawyer to enable him to give sound and informed advice. Fed.Rules Evid. Rule 501, 28 U.S.C.A.; ABA Code of Professional Responsibility, EC4–1.

4. Witnesses ☞199(2)

District court's test, of availability of attorney–client privilege, was objectionable as frustrating very purpose of privilege, insofar as test restricted availability of privilege to those corporate officers who played "substantial role" in deciding and directing corporation's legal response. Fed. Rules Evid. Rule 501, 28 U.S.C.A.

5. Witnesses ☞199(2)

Where communications at issue were made by corporate employees to counsel for corporation acting as such, at direction of corporate superiors in order to secure legal advice from counsel, and employees were aware that they were being questioned so that corporation could obtain legal advice, such communications, consistently with underlying purposes of attorney–client privilege, were protected against compelled disclosure. Fed.Rules Evid. Rule 501, 28 U.S. C.A.

6. Witnesses ☞198(1)

Attorney–client privilege only protects disclosure of communications, and it does not protect disclosure of underlying facts by those who communicated with attorney. Fed.Rules Evid. Rule 501, 28 U.S.C.A.

7. Witnesses ☞198(1)

Application of privilege, such as attorney–client privilege, is determined on case-by-case basis. Fed.Rules Evid. Rule 501, 28 U.S.C.A.

8. Internal Revenue ☞1451

Obligation imposed by tax summons remains subject to traditional privileges and limitations, and work–product doctrine does apply to IRS summonses. Fed.Rules Evid. Rule 501, 28 U.S.C.A.; Fed.Rules Civ.Proc. Rules 26(b)(3), 81(a)(3), 28 U.S.C.A.; 26 U.S. C.A. §§ 7402(b), 7602, 7604(a).

9. Federal Civil Procedure ☞1600.2

Forcing attorney to disclose notes and memoranda of witness' oral statements is particularly disfavored, and rule accords special protection to work product revealing attorney's mental processes. Fed.Rules Civ. Proc. Rules 26, 26(b)(3), 28 U.S.C.A.

10. Federal Civil Procedure ☞1600.2

Notes and memoranda sought by government were work products based on oral statements of witnesses, and where, if they revealed communications, protected by attorney–client privilege, and to extent they did not reveal communications, they revealed attorney's mental processes in evaluating the communications, and disclosure would not be required simply on showing of substantial need and inability to obtain equivalent without undue hardship, and stronger showing of necessity and unavailability by other means than was made by government or applied by magistrate would be necessary to compel disclosure. Fed.Rules Evid. Rule 501, 28 U.S.C.A.; 26 U.S.C.A. § 7602; Fed.Rules Civ.Proc. Rule 26(b)(3), 28 U.S.C.A.

EXHIBIT 6–16   Key Number Service for Taxation

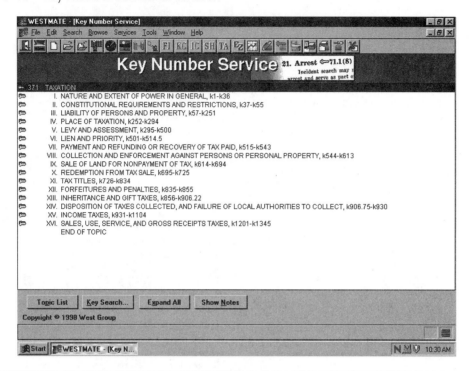

paperback bimonthly supplement. An absence of the page number for the cited case in any supplement after the case's first appearance indicates that the case has not been cited within the dates covered by the supplement.

Comparing the Published Citators

Compare the entries for *Upjohn* in RIA *Citators,* CCH *Citator,* and Shepard's *Citator* in Exhibits 6–6, 6–7, 6–10, 6–12, and 6–13. In making this comparison, keep in mind that the publishers of the citators have made editorial decisions concerning the scope of their coverage, the organization, and that the CCH and RIA citators are intended to relate primarily to their own court reporters and tax services. The comparison of the citators presented in Exhibit 6–17 includes how each citator treats the following issues.

▶   Order of cited cases, as listed (i.e., trial level first or highest appeal first)
▶   Completeness of listing of citing cases
▶   Extent of information concerning citing cases
▶   Reporters included in citations of cited and citing cases
▶   References in citator to general tax service

EXHIBIT 6–17   Comparing published citators

Item	CCH *Citator*	RIA *Citators*	Shepard's *Citator*
Organization number	Cited case name—alphabetical	Cited case name—alphabetical	Case reporter reporter—volume
Cited cases selection	Selected by editors	All tax cases	All tax cases
Citation location	General	Local	Local
Order of cited cases	Highest appeal first	No consistent order	Not applicable
Researcher first needs to know	Case name only	Case name, approximate year of decision	Citation of cited case
Headnote analysis	Not used	Used	Used
Location of current matter	Cases at front of A–L volume; Finding Lists at end of M–Z volume	Paperback supplements and advance sheets	Separate volumes, plus paperback supplement and advance sheets
Miscellaneous	Dagger symbol and no citing cases indicate obsolete case law; bold dots indicate judicial history; ties into CCH *Standard Federal Tax Reports*	AFTR series, 3 volumes (1863–1954 law) AFTR2d series, two bound volumes, plus supplements; bold dot indicates Supreme Court; bold-print citation indicates new level of case	8 volumes; also cites the Code, Regulations, Revenue Rulings, selected law journals, and annotations

Computerized Citators

Computerized tax citators are available on CD-ROM, through online services, and over the Internet. Each of these could be considered as separate mediums and discussed individually, but it may be more productive to think of them in terms of their common features. At the heart of these systems is the ability to store huge amounts of information in a small physical space and then to find, organize, and display the information very quickly. Further, the computerized citators can also link citations to the text of the case, thus making retrieval of the relevant cases as easy as clicking on the cite.

WESTLAW Citator System

WESTLAW is a computerized legal research service equipped with several citator systems that automate much of the tedious work of using a published citator. It is available online and over the Internet. One of the advantages of computerized services like WESTLAW is their ability to find and display instantly the citation's specific location within a citing case. The citation will be highlighted each time it appears in the citing case. To facilitate in the search of citing cases, WESTLAW provides a computerized version of the Shepard's *Citators*. Further, WESTLAW itself can be used as a citator by performing a text search for a citation. In total, WESTLAW offers six citator services: Key-Cite (KC), Insta-Cite (IC), Shepard's Citations

(SH), Shepard's PreView (SP) , QuickCite (QC), and CCH Tax Citator (see Exhibit 6–19). As discussed in the following paragraphs, each of these citators was developed to address different aspects of the citing process.

To access WESTLAW via the Internet or from an online service, the **WEST-MATE** software must be used. The **PREMISE** software may also be used to access WESTLAW online. From the Internet "Welcome to WESTLAW" screen, reproduced in Exhibit 16–18, the citators can be accessed either through the "check a citation" picture bar on the left side of the screen, or the "IC" or "SH" button at the top of the screen. After selecting a citator the researcher enters the citation to be Shepardized. The system for entering citations has been designed to be flexible. Most citation formats are accepted as long as the general form of "volume–reporter–page" is used. The process works whether the citation is in capital or lowercase letters. Interior spaces and periods are optional as well. One quick way to enter citations is in lowercase letters with spaces but no periods. For example, the case *Upjohn Co. v. U.S.,* 101 S.Ct. 677, would be entered as "101 s ct 677." Other formats, such as 101 S.Ct. 677, 101 sct 677, or 101 s.ct. 677, also would work.

Insta-Cite   The **Insta-Cite** citator is a powerful tool that provides a direct history of a case within three to eighteen hours of West Publishing receiving a copy of the decision. Direct history of a case includes only lower or higher court decisions on

---

EXHIBIT 6–18   Welcome to WESTLAW screen

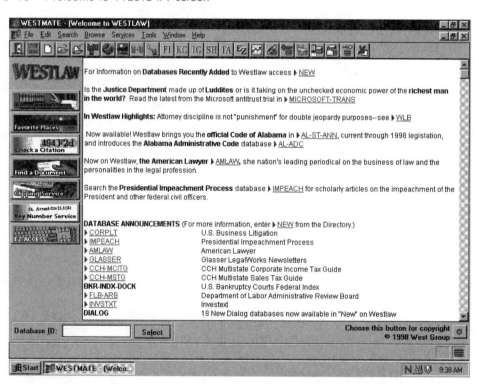

EXHIBIT 6–19   WESTLAW Citators Service screen

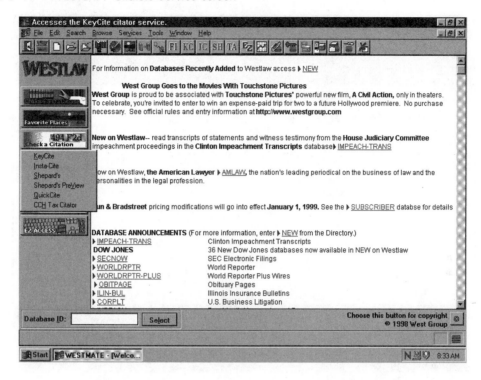

this same case. For example, *Upjohn*'s direct history would include only the District Court case, the Sixth Circuit case, and the Supreme Court case. This information is useful in verifying whether a case is still valid law. While the direct history indicates whether there is a more recent decision for the particular case, it does not identify citing cases that might affect the holdings of the case.

Given a few more days for editorial work, Insta-Cite will also provide a negative indirect history of the case. A negative indirect history includes any citing cases that adversely affect the precedent value of the case of interest. Such cases would be those that criticize, limit, question, or overrule its logic or holding. Insta-Cite provides negative indirect history with full-text links for cases decided from 1972 to the present. Further, Insta-Cite is useful for verifying the spelling, court of decision, date, and parallel citations the researcher has collected are correct. Depending on the version of WESTLAW available to the researcher, Insta-Cite may be accessed through the "IC" button at the top of the screen or through KeyCite as indicated in Exhibit 6–20. While Insta-Cite only provides citations of cases with a negative impact on the case of interest, KeyCite provides both positive and negative citing cases. Thus, as Exhibit 6–20 states, KeyCite provides the same information as Insta-Cite but not as timely.

Shepard's Citations   The full coverage of Shepard's citators including *Shepard's Federal Tax Citator* are available through WESTLAW. These citators provide the

EXHIBIT 6–20 WESTLAW Insta-Cite

same comprehensive judicial history of the cited document—whether direct or indi-rect, positive, negative, or neutral—as the printed versions. Besides cases, Shepard's references law reviews, legal treatises, *American Law Reports,* and *Lawyer' Edition 2d.* Parallel citations to other reporters and citations to secondary sources such as articles also are provided. The completeness of the references has its cost, however. Like the printed versions, the WESTLAW *Federal Tax Citator* is updated only bimonthly. Thus, the data obtained through the computerized version of *Federal Tax Citator* is no more up to date than the published version. The other WESTLAW cita-tors were created to address the timeliness issue.

Exhibit 6–21 summarizes the information generated by a **Shepard's Citations** request. This screen has six main elements organized in two lines at the top and in four columns below. The lines at the top summarize information about the search. The "Citations to" line indicates the case for which the information is provided and the "Coverage" line reveals how current the results are by identifying the most recent supplement searched. The four columns at the bottom part of the screen give the following information about each citing case found: retrieval number, abbrevia-tion and description of the analysis of the case by the citing case, citing case's cita-tion, and headnote number addressed by the citing case. The texts of the citing cases are linked to their citations for easy retrieval of their full text.

EXHIBIT 6–21   WESTLAW Shepard's Citations references

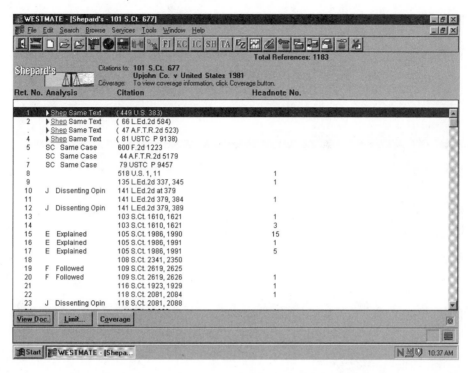

Shepard's PreView   Due to Shepard's editorial classification of new cases, there is some lag time between when a case is decided and when Shepard's information reaches WESTLAW. **Shepard's PreView,** a joint service of Shepard's and West, was created to provide more current case information with only a four- to six-week lag. It is as current as the National Reporter System and West Advance Sheets. Cases in Shepard's PreView that have not yet been entered into the regular Shepard's Citations do not include the usual editorial analysis. The PreView screen is similar to the regular Shepard's Citations screen except that there is no analysis or headnote number (see Exhibit 6–22). Citing cases can be retrieved by clicking on the citation.

QuickCite   For the most current citations not provided by Shepard's PreView and access to all types of documents, use the **QuickCite** citator. This citator actually uses WESTLAW's document search capabilities. The database for the QuickCite search can be the same as for the Shepard's search or a different database can be specified. QuickCite also allows a date restriction; only documents added to WESTLAW after the specified date are retrieved (see Exhibit 6–23). Thus, the researcher could specify that only databases that have been added to WESTLAW since the date of the last Shepard's PreView update be reviewed. This would ensure that only cases not previously available are located.

EXHIBIT 6–22 WESTLAW Shepard's PreView citator references

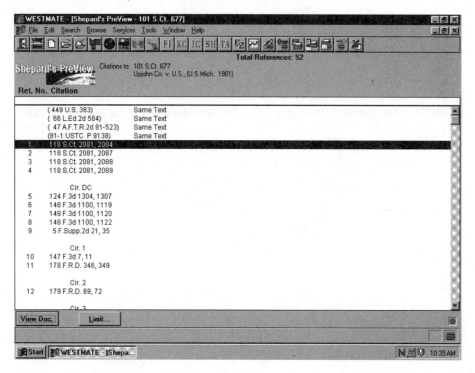

KeyCite   The **KeyCite** citator furnishes a comprehensive direct and indirect history for cases. The indirect history includes secondary materials that have the cited case in their text. KeyCite allows the researcher to select a full history, negative history, or omit minor cases. This last option is a very useful filter for reducing the quantity of citing cases retrieved by WESTLAW. It is not available with the other citators. The KeyCite information is also integrated with the Key Number Service, which was discussed earlier in the Shepard's Citator section of this chapter. A screen for the KeyCite service is shown in Exhibit 6–24. Note the stars at the end of the negative history citing cases. These indicate the importance of the cases to the cited case.

Table of Authorities   The **Table of Authorities** is not like the previously discussed five citator services. Citators provide a history of a particular case and a list of cases citing it. The Table of Authorities, on the other hand, lists cases that are cited within the case of interest. This is useful for finding deficiencies in a relevant case that does not support the client's preferred tax position. If the relevant case relies on other cases with negative or weak histories, the reasoning in a relevant case may be flawed. A partial list of the Table of Authorities for the *Upjohn* case is contained in Exhibit 6–25.

EXHIBIT 6-23   WESTLAW QuickCite screen

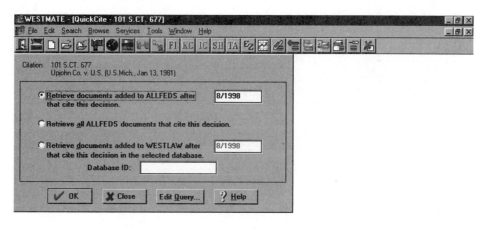

LEXIS Citator Systems

LEXIS is another computerized legal research service with two citators, Shepard's and Auto-Cite, and two search systems, LEXCITE and LEXIS, that can function like citators. All of these features have their counterparts in the WESTLAW service. Each of these features will be discussed separately and the WESTLAW counterpart identified.

Shepard's Citations   This citator is exactly like the WESTLAW Shepard's Citations. A feature that is available through LEXIS is the ability to restrict the Shepardizing search to specific histories or treatment analyses. Any of the History of Case or Treatment of Case abbreviations found in Exhibit 6–14 can be used to restrict the search. Thus, the researcher can have only the criticizing and the distinguishing citing cases retrieved if so desired.

To Shepardize from any point in LEXIS, transmit "sh" or "shep" followed by the citation for the case of interest. Like WESTLAW, the Shepard's service is flexible about how the citation is entered. If Shepardizing from within the case, simply transmit "sh" without a citation. LEXIS will assume the citation of the current case and provide its Shepardized reference list of cases. The full text of any case on the reference list can be retrieved by clicking on its citation.

EXHIBIT 6–24 WESTLAW KeyCite

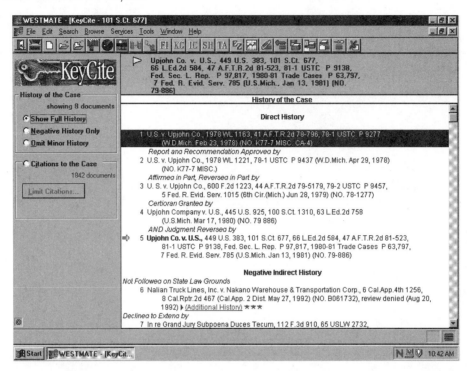

Auto-Cite   The **Auto-Cite** citator is very similar to WESTLAW's Insta-Cite service. This service was designed and is maintained by Lawyers Cooperative Publishing. Since Auto-Cite originally was conceived to help their editors check the validity of citations, its primary objectives are to provide accuracy of citations that are as current as possible, and to do so within 24 hours of receipt of each case. As with Insta-Cite, researchers use Auto-Cite to determine whether their case is still good law. Auto-Cite is also useful for determining the standing of Revenue Rulings and Revenue Procedures.

The information Auto-Cite retrieves includes the correct spelling of the case name and its official citation, the year of the decision and its jurisdiction, parallel cites, appellate and prior history, treatment history of the case, and lists of articles. The treatment history of the cases focuses on cases with jurisdictionally relevant precedential value. Thus, Auto-Cite's focus is on cases that impact the strength of the cited case's holding, whereas Shepard's focus is to provide a comprehensive history of the case. Auto-Cite can be accessed in the same manner as Shepard's by using "ac" as the abbreviation for Auto-Cite.

A special feature of Auto-Cite is that it identifies cases to which the citated case makes negative references. This feature is not available with other citators. The Table of Authorities of WESTLAW has a similar feature in that it produces a list of cases discussed by the cited case, but it does not classify the treatment of the cases by the cited case.

EXHIBIT 6–25   WESTLAW Table of Authorities

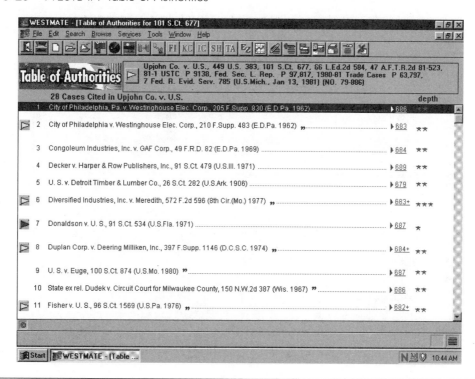

LEXCITE   The LEXIS service also features **LEXCITE,** a search methodology designed to understand the "volume–reporter–page" format of citation. It is similar to QuickCite in its function. For the case citation entered, LEXCITE ascertains parallel citations and then searches for all of the cites in the case law documents. This is very useful in that it saves having to perform a separate search on each court reporter citation for the same case. LEXCITE will find embedded references to a variety of documents such as cases, law reviews, journals, *Federal Register,* and Revenue Rulings. However, unlike LEXIS Shepard's and Auto-Cite and WESTLAW QuickCite, LEXCITE will only search case law files. Also, it will not find references to case names only; the court reporter citation must be present for LEXCITE to identify the document as a source.

Although you can use LEXCITE in any case library and file you choose, the library called CITES was designed to be used with LEXCITE. The broadest file in that library, MEGA, covers all federal and state cases. A less inclusive file of more interest to tax practitioners is FED, which limits the search to federal cases. Another library useful to tax practitioners is FEDTAX and the file CASES would be compatible with the LEXCITE search requirements.

An advantage of using LEXCITE is that the practitioner can customize the search to cases that address only a particular point of law in the cited case by using other search terms in addition to the citation. Terms can also be added to cause date restrictions on the search. For example, if you wanted cases that address the *Upjohn* case's

EXHIBIT 6–26 CCH CITATOR screen

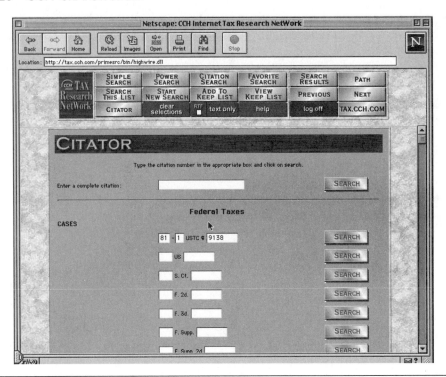

effects on corporate counsel that occurred after 1990 you could use "lexcite (101 sct 677) and corporate counsel and date aft 12/90." LEXCITE requires the citation to be in parentheses with the word "lexcite" preceding it. The "volume–reporter–page" convention must be followed but capitalization, internal spaces, and periods are optional, as long as the citation follows the basic format.

LEXIS as a Citator A researcher would want to use LEXIS as a citator when only the name of a case and not its citation is known. A regular LEXIS search on the case name will locate every occurrence of the name within the chosen library and file. If it is a common name, there may be many irrelevant references retrieved by LEXIS. If the case name is long, it is best to use essential parts of the name, so the search won't miss an occurrence because the case name has been shortened in the documents. Further, the search can be tailored by using other search terms in combination with the name, as can be done with LEXCITE. Unlike LEXCITE, there is no restriction on the libraries and files that can be accessed. Thus, references to the case of interest can be found in journal articles, newspapers, and numerous other documents besides cases.

CCH and RIA Citators

Both CCH and RIA provide the equivalent of their published citators through their computerized tax services. These citators function in a manner very similar to the

EXHIBIT 6–27   CCH CITATOR list of cases

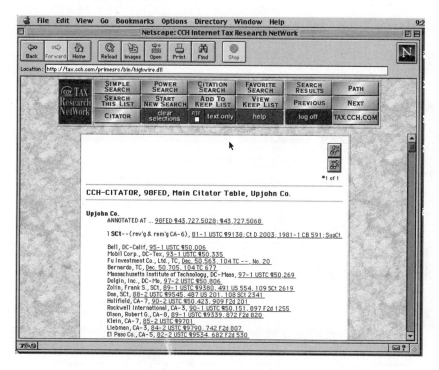

WESTLAW and LEXIS citators. Through its *Tax Research Network* Internet site (http://tax.cch.com/network) the CCH *Citator* may be accessed by selecting CITATOR at the initial screen after the folders to be searched are designated. The CITATOR allows the researcher to type in a citation for a case free style or use templets, based on the possible court reporters, to enter the citation (see Exhibit 6–26). A partial list of the results from a search on *Upjohn* is shown in Exhibit 6–27. CCH, as does RIA, furnishes full-text links to each reference produced by the citator search.

The RIA *CheckPoint* Internet service (http://checkpoint.riag.com) requires that a database, such as *Citator 2,* be specified before a citation for the case can be entered (see Exhibit 6–28). The next screen allows the researcher to identify the case to be cited. Unlike most of the other citators, RIA allows the name of the case or a court reporter citation to be entered. It also furnishes templates for the case citation based on the court reporters. The search can be designated to yield a direct history for the cited case, an indirect hist ory of citing cases, or both. The researcher indicates what type of search by choosing "Cited," "Citing," or "Both" at the top part of the screen presented in Exhibit 6–29. The results of the search for the cited case will appear on the next screen. Click on the citation for the case and the list of citing cases will appear along with the citation for the cited case. The format of the results of the search is similar to that provided by the CCH search.

The computerized services automate virtually all of the tedious mechanical aspects of ensuring that the citations in written communications are valid, formally

EXHIBIT 6–28   RIA *Citators* database selection screen

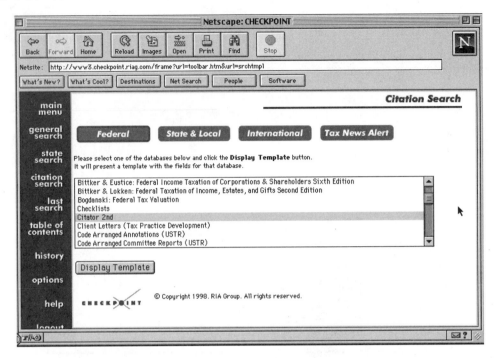

correct, and good law. Further, they make the retrieval of the full text of the cited or a citing case almost effortless. This brief discussion has attempted to present an overview of these services to inform you that they are available and encourage you to learn to use them.

► Summary

The tax researcher's job of sorting through the thousands of potentially pertinent federal tax court cases is facilitated by citators, which can be either published or computerized. When familiar with these research tools, the current status and precedential value of a specific case or ruling can be determined effectively and quickly. This determination is necessary for the researcher to evaluate the judicial and administrative sources of the tax law that could affect the client's tax research issue.

► Key Words

By the time you complete your work in this chapter, you should be comfortable discussing each of the following terms. If you need additional review of any of these items, return to the appropriate material in the chapter or consult the glossary at the end of this text.

EXHIBIT 6–29   RIA *Citators* screen

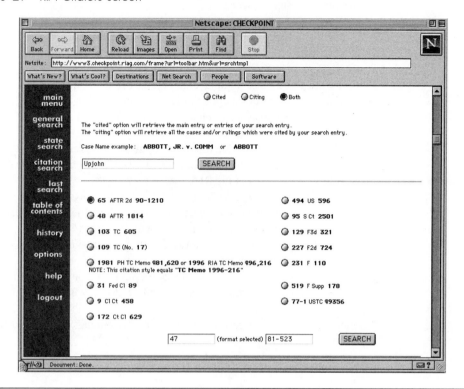

Auto-Cite
CCH *Citator*
Citator
Citator 2nd Series
Cited Case
Cites
Citing Case
Headnote
KeyCite
Insta-Cite
LEXCITE
LEXIS

PH Citator
PREMISE
QuickCite
RIA *Citators*
Shepardizing
Shepard's Citations
Shepard's Federal Tax Citator
Shepard's PreView
Table of Authorities
WESTLAW
WESTMATE

▶ _____ Discussion Questions

1. Describe some of the advantages of computerized tax research tools. Are computerized research tools better than published services?
2. What is the typical updating schedule of online and Internet tax services?
3. What are the goals of tax research?
4. Describe the different functions of research.

5. Describe the authority of the Code. What do practitioners do if the Code is not clear on an issue?

6. Why are subsequent cases important to the value of a prior case?

7. Describe the function of a citator in the tax research process.

8. Distinguish between the terms *cited case* and *citing case*.

9. Distinguish between the terms *citation* and *a cite*.

10. Name the three most popular commercial tax citators, and indicate whether they are sold as part of a commercial tax service.

11. Explain the difference between a general directing and a local cite. Which service uses local directing cites?

12. In what formats (media) are the most popular commercial tax citators offered?

13. What publishers have been associated with the *Citator* and *Citator 2nd Series*?

14. How are the volumes in the RIA *Citators* arranged?

15. The case *Corn Products Refining Co.* (350 US 46) was decided in 1955, therefore a researcher need only examine Volume 1 of the *Citator 2nd Series* to citate this case. Comment on this statement.

16. What is the special treatment of Tax Court Memorandum decisions in Volume 2 of the *PH Citator*? What is the reason for this treatment?

17. The RIA *Citators* do not follow the traditional legal convention of listing cases under the plaintiff's name. What convention do they use? Why are the cases listed in this manner?

18. State which citator uses the following abbreviations/symbols and what each means.

    a. d
    b. r
    c. g
    d. h
    e. iv
    f. n
    g. p
    h. q
    i. remd

19. The RIA *Citators* list citations in what order?

20. List in what order the following types of cases would be given under the "no specific headnotes" category of citations for a case.

    U.S. Courts of Appeal
    Board of Tax Appeals
    U.S. District Court
    U.S. Court of Federal Claims
    State courts
    U.S. Supreme Court
    U.S. Tax Court
    Treasury Rulings and Decisions

21. To utilize fully the RIA *Citators,* one must use the service with which court reporter?

22. Why are Revenue Rulings included in the RIA *Citators*? Where are they located in the RIA *Citators*?

23. How many volumes are there in the CCH *Citator*? How are the volumes arranged?

24. How are Court decisions that are obsolete designated in the CCH *Citator*?

25. What do the bold bullets indicate in the CCH *Citator*?

26. In the CCH *Citator*, what is the ordering of the citations for the courts hearing the same cited case?

27. What is the CCH *Citator* convention for listing citing cases?

28. What is the advantage of the CCH *Citator* being loose-leaf rather than bound?

29. What does "Shepardizing" mean?

30. Compare the coverage Shepard's provides with its citator series versus RIA and CCH citator series.

31. With the Shepard's *Citator*, a researcher can located a case either by the case name or by its citation. Comment on this statement.

32. How is Shepard's *Citator* organized? In what order are the citing cases listed?

33. What is the significance of the superscript number appearing immediately to the left of the page number in a citing reference in the Shepard's *Citator*?

34. What is the West Key Number System used for?

35. What are the different citators available through WESTLAW?

36. How is the Table of Authorities different from the other WESTLAW citators?

37. What are the different citators available through LEXIS?

38. Which computerized citator allows the name of the case to be used in searching a case?

39. What company was the first to introduce citators as legal aids?

▶ _____   Exercises

40. In the CCH *Citator*, find *Algernon Blair, Inc.* under the letter "A" and under the letter "B."

    a. Are these two the same case?

    b. Give the judicial history for *Algernon Blair, Inc.* listed under the letter "B."

    c. What is the citation of the *Algernon Blair, Inc.* case that is cited by Revenue Rulings?

    d. List the Revenue Rulings that cite this case.

41. In the RIA *Citators*, find *Algernon Blair, Inc.* under the letter "A" and under the letter "B."

    a. In what volume of what series do the cases initially appear?

    b. What reference does the Tax Court case listed under the Letter "A" make?

    c. Give the Prentice Hall (PH) citation for the *Algernon Blair, Inc.* case listed under letter "B."

    d. "[See 29 TC 1211]" is listed after the citing case of *Holmes Enterprises, Inc.* What does "See 29 TC 1211" mean?

42. Use both the CCH *Citator* and the RIA *Citators* to answer the following questions regarding the Tax Court case *Algernon Blair, Inc.*

    a. Which citator made it easier to identify how many Revenue Rulings were citing this case?

b. What was the most recent citing case for each citator service? In which service was it easier to determine the most recent citing case?

c. What year was the Eastwood Mall Inc. citing case decided? How did it evaluate *Algernon Blair, Inc.* in its discussion? From which citator was it easier to obtain this information?

d. Which citator provides the most extensive list of citing cases and Revenue Ruling for *Algernon Blair, Inc.*?

43. Determine the alphabetical order, from first to last, in which the following cases appear in the CCH *Citator.*

Byron H. Gaar, Jr., 43 TCM 1425
GBG, Inc., 43 TCM 169
G. C. Services Corp., 73 TC 406
William H. George, 26TC 396
G & G Records, Inc., 46 TCM 430

44. Locate *John Doe,* 74-1 USTC ¶9344, and answer the following questions.

a. In what year was this decision rendered?
b. What is the citation for *John Doe* in the F2d court reporter?
c. What is the citation for *John Doe* in the AFTR2d court reporter?
d. What was the court of original jurisdiction for this case?

45. Locate *New Britian,* 98 L Ed 520, in *Shepard's Federal Tax Citator.*

a. What are the parallel citations for this case?
b. In what year was this case decided?
c. How many different headnotes are discussed by citing cases?
d. Look up this case in the *Supreme Court Reporter* section of *Shepard's Federal Tax Citator.* How many different headnotes are discussed by citing cases?

46. Using WESTLAW and the Insta-Cite citator, locate the case *Holland* 46 AFTR 943.

a. What is the most recent citing case listed for *Holland*?
b. What is the highest court that heard *Holland*? Give the direct history for *Holland.*
c. Change to the Table of Authorities. How many cases are cited within *Holland*?

47. Locate *Tank Truck Rentals, Inc.,* 78 S. Ct. 507, on LEXIS. Answer the following questions about this case using only the Shepard's *Citator.*

a. What is the most recent Supreme Court case to cite the *Tank Truck* case? Give the complete citation for this citing case.
b. Give the complete citations in proper form for the trial and appeals court opinions for the case.
c. Are there any court cases that cite the trial court decision of this case? If so, approximately how many?

48. Locate *Kerry W. Illes,* 71 AFTR 2d 93-1724, in the citator of your choice and answer the following questions.

a. From what court of original jurisdiction was this case appealed?

    b. Was a petition for certiorari filed with the Supreme Court? If a petition was filed, was certiorari granted?

    c. What is the most recent citing case of *Illes*?

    d. What point of law does Headnote 3 of the *Illes* case address? (The actual case must be located to answer this question.)

    e. Locate a 1997 Seventh Circuit Appeals case that cites the *Illes* case with respect to Headnote 3. On what page does the cite appear? Find the cite and describe the context in which the *Illes* case is discussed.

49. Using WESTLAW or LEXIS, locate the citation for *Winstead,* 97-1 USTC ¶50,322.

    a. What is the AFTR2d citation and the F3d citation for *Winstead*?

    b. What are the citing cases listed by Shepard's Citations?

    c. What is the case name for the case citing *Winstead* at 38 Fed. Cl 458?

    d. In what context is *Winstead* at 38 Fed. Cl 458?

▶ _____ Research Cases

For each of the research problems locate court cases or administrative pronouncements (Revenue Rulings, Revenue Procedures, etc.) that support your position. Provide a list of cases or administrative pronouncements citing your authority that demonstrate your authority is still good law.

50. Mark is a pitcher for a major league baseball team. His pitching colleagues "encourage" each other to better performances via the "gopher-ball club." The "club" levies fines for various types of home runs that are given up by its members; for example, it levies a $25 fine for a home run by Sammy Sosa and a $150 fine for a home run by any other Chicago Cub. At the end of the season, one-third of the collected fines are used to fund a club party, while the balance is given to the local chapter of the Cancer Research Fund. Mark contributed $300 of the club's $1,800 collections this year. Can he deduct any portion of this amount?

51. Jamie's adjusted gross income is $21,000. During the year, she spent $250 of her own funds on birthday treats for the students in the second-grade class that she teaches. She bought these presents during a seventy-five-mile round trip to a specialty educational toy store. Can she deduct any portion of these amounts?

52. Rachel suffers from arthritis. Her physician suggested that macarena dance lessons would be useful therapy to relax her tensions and relieve her pain. Are the lessons deductible?

53. Peggy had been a drug abuser until she entered the Norwood Detoxification Program. After intensive therapy during a hospital stay, Peggy was allowed to return home. The counseling sessions continued weekly, but, because of the distance between Peggy's home and her psychiatrist's office, long-distance telephone calls were made. Can Peggy deduct the incremental cost of these calls?

54. Sally sells her home to Bob and pays the $9,000 in points by offsetting this amount against her sales proceeds. Determine the tax effects on both parties.

55. Ethel and Rick spent $4,500 in allocable interest and taxes, and $1,100 in advertising and maintenance, for their "bed and breakfast" inn. This year's rental income from the inn came to $4,900. Determine the tax effects of conducting the B&B as a one-third part of Ethel and Rick's residence.

56. The parents of this year's "Annie" (she is age 8) spent $8,000 in travel expenses for auditions and rehearsals of the popular play. When she got the part, her parents were designated in the Broadway contract to receive one-half of her total earnings. Discuss the proper recognition of gross income and related deductions concerning this arrangement.

57. Barbara's psychologist recommended that Barbara divorce her husband, Tom. Tom's dress and eating habits had led to Barbara's serious neuroses. Are the costs of the divorce deductible to Tom? To Barbara?

58. Newark Marine Food Service sells hot lunches and snacks to the crews of ships that dock at the Port of Newark. According to custom, the officers of the visiting ships receive a 5 percent "commission" from all sales, so that Marine can retain its "exclusive rights" to the seamen's business. Are the commissions deductible by the shipping firms?

59. Judy was reimbursed $850 for her business dinners with her employer's clients. The bills came to $1,065, split equally between Judy's dinners and that of the clients' dinners. Judy's dinners at home usually cost her about $10 each. What is Judy's tax treatment concerning this meal; that is, can the taxpayer deduct the cost of her own meal?

60. Joy accompanied her husband on a business trip to San Diego because he had been injured in a subway accident and could no longer drive an automobile. Joy was not associated with his business directly, but she did perform as his chauffeur on the trip. What is the tax treatment of Joy's incremental expenses for the trip?

61. After his divorce, Brown paid the expenses of maintaining the family home, which continued to be the principal residence of his ex-wife and their three daughters. He owned the house but never lived there. Instead, he maintained another home as his principal residence. Can he claim head of household status, assuming that he is assigned the dependency exemptions for the daughters?

62. Laura is a lay teacher at St. William's Catholic School. The school requires that all of its faculty members hold a high school diploma. Laura completed her Bachelor of Arts degree in primary education this year. What items associated with Laura's education will be deductible, assuming that she receives no reimbursements for any of them?

63. Carl is enrolled in a graduate taxation program. His professors have criticized his speaking and writing abilities, so he is taking an English Department course in business communications for degree credit as an allowable elective. Can Carl deduct his incremental costs that are associated with this communications course?

64. Vandals caused $1,250 damage to Tricia's fully depreciated rental property. Determine her casualty loss or other deduction.

65. Buddy was injured by Matt in an automobile accident. The court awarded Buddy $30,000 in damages, but Matt was able to raise (and paid to Buddy) only $12,000. They both then considered the matter closed. Compute the amount of gross income to Buddy, and to Matt, from these transactions.

66. Con man Floyd sold Larry the Library of Congress for $15,000. Larry had embezzled the $15,000 he used to make the purchase from his employer.

    a. How much gross income should Larry and Floyd report as a result of these transactions?

b. What is the tax treatment for Larry when he repays his (former) employer?

67.   Reverend Ruth received an annual salary of $15,000 and a parsonage allowance of $6,000. She paid $4,000 rent on the home, and she spent $1,100 on housing-related purchases. What is her gross income from these items?

68.   Jill received a research grant from the University of Minnesota in amounts of $10,000 for her time and $3,000 for related supplies and expenses. She purchased a $28,000 Audi the day after depositing the state's check. Jill is a candidate for a master's degree in philosophy and ethics. What is her gross income from the grant?

69.   CPA Jerry receives "supper money" of $12 for any night that he works overtime. What is his gross income from these payments?

70.   To what extent should Professor Dodd include in gross income the value of examination copies of books that he receives without charge from book publishers?

71.   The Forestry Care District provides Ranger Wilson with groceries so that she may prepare her meals in the ranger's tower. What is her gross income with respect to the groceries?

72.   Holly is on her deathbed. She sells the family estate to a relative, the $3,000,000 proceeds being placed in escrow to be used to pay Holly's $880,000 death taxes. The balance of the escrow account is designated for the creation of a chaired professorship in taxation at State University. Thus, Holly gets no financial benefit from the sale. How much gross income must she recognize from the sale?

Published Tax Services

Every tax researcher must have access to one or more commercial tax services. By organizing the vast array of primary and secondary sources of the tax law, these tax services make the practitioner's research tasks more efficient and comprehensive.

Tax services can be classified into two general types, annotated and topical. **Annotated tax services** are organized by *Internal Revenue Code* section number. **Topical tax services,** on the other hand, divide the tax law into its functional components, with underlying principles and issues as an organizing format. Two of the most well-known annotated services and two of the several topical services will be examined in detail in this chapter.

The Research Process: Illustrative Example

To facilitate your understanding of the research process when using tax services, an actual research problem will be used to illustrate each of the steps. It is important that **you go to your library** and follow the research in the actual volumes of the services. The procedural knowledge necessary for the development of tax research skills can only be required through hands-on practice. The following illustrations are designed to aid you in finding the correct material in the services and are *not* a substitute for you actually using the services.

The illustrative research project concerns the following fact situation.

> **Example 7–1** Our client, Terry, owns and operates an auto body repair shop. Typically, Terry pays a "referral fee" of 10 percent of the final repair charges to the party who suggested that the repair customer work through our client's shop. The most frequent recipients of the referral fees that Terry pays are insurance claim adjusters. Under applicable state law, such payments to adjusters are illegal, but criminal prosecution is quite rare. The payments are very common and body shops that do not pay them find their referrals substantially curtailed. Our client wants to deduct this year's $25,434 expense for referral fees.

> As part of your reading to maintain your knowledge of tax law, you have seen summaries of the *Car-Ron Asphalt Paving* and *Raymond Bertolini Trucking* cases and think they may be pertinent to our client's fact situation.

Annotated Tax Services

The annotated services explored in this chapter are the *Standard Federal Tax Reports* published by Commerce Clearing House (CCH) and the *United States Tax Reporter* published by Research Institute of America (RIA). The volumes of these services are called **Compilations** because they provide an editor's explanation and evaluation of the Code section compiled with its recent committee reports, Regulations, and annotations of related court cases and administrative rulings. CCH also includes as part of the *Standard Federal Tax Reports* two separate volumes containing just the *Internal Revenue Code* and a two-volume citator series. While RIA also includes a two-volume *Internal Revenue Code*, its multivolume citator series is available as a separate service.

Approaching the Research Problem

The starting point in approaching any tax research problem is to formulate the tax question being asked. One way of framing the question Example 7–1 presents is: Are the illegal referral fee payments deductible as a business expense when many businesses pay them and a business that does not pay referrals suffers? This first formulation of the research question should not be considered its final version. As research is performed, other issues will probably be identified that will require the question to be refined. Recall that the iterative process of tax research was discussed in Chapter 2 relative to Exhibits 2–1 and 2–2.

Gradually the research question is refined into its final state. However, this refinement does not guarantee that a definite answer to the tax question, substantiated by controlling law, will be found. The final conclusion may be that one solution appears more supportable than another, or that the IRS or the courts will interpret the facts and circumstances in a particular manner when making a decision. Remember that in most tax decisions professional judgment is required because the controlling law is imprecise and can be interpreted by the taxpayer and the IRS differently.

The facts that are important in deciding what to recommend to our client in Example 7–1 are whether the payments are ordinary and necessary business expenses, and, if they are, whether their illegality has some effect on their deductibility. The fact that the law forbidding kickbacks to insurance claim adjusters is rarely enforced may be relevant.

Entering Compilation Volumes

Finding the relevant material needed to resolve a tax question is the key to tax research. How the Compilation volumes are entered will determine how quickly and efficiently the pertinent material is found. Use of the annotated services often follows the sequence indicated in Exhibit 7–1. The Compilation volumes lead the researcher to primary sources of the tax law. The Codes sections and Regulations are reproduced in full text in the Compilations, whereas cases and rulings are found in the annotated services only in summary form, unless they were issued in the current year. The research including court cases and rulings will continue by referring to the court case reporter series, the *Cumulative Bulletins,* or a Private Letter Ruling collection. Finally, the researcher should consult a citator to evaluate the status and precedential value of the court cases or rulings relevant to the tax problem.

Thus, the most appropriate view of the function of the commercial tax services is as *an index to the collection of primary and secondary sources of the tax law mate-*

EXHIBIT 7–1   Using the Compilations effectively

1. Efficiently enter the Compilation volumes and locate paragraphs that may be appropriate.
2. Skim the material, identifying the most pertinent elements of the primary tax law for the research.
3. Carefully read the paragraphs that apply directly to the research.
4. Find and analyze the relevant update materials and *Citator* materials.
5. Find and read all the primary materials (Code, Regulations, court cases, rulings, etc.) identified by the research.

EXHIBIT 7–2   Accessing the Compilation volumes

```
      KEY WORD              CODE SECTION NUMBER              CASE NAME
              "Spine Scan"          "Spine Scan"

    ┌──────────────────┐                          ┌──────────────────────┐
    │ Index            │                          │ CCH Citator Volume   │
    │ CCH Index Volume │                          │ USTR Volume 2        │
    │ USTR Volume 1    │                          │ Table of Cases       │
    └──────────────────┘                          └──────────────────────┘

                    ┌─────────────────────────┐
                    │ Compilation Volumes     │
                    │ Spine shows: year, code │
                    │ range, volume number,   │
                    │ broad topic description,│
                    │ paragraph range         │
                    │ CCH Volumes 1–15        │
                    │ USTR Volumes 3–15       │
                    └─────────────────────────┘

┌──────────────────────────────────┐      ┌──────────────────────┐
│ New Matter/Recent Developments   │      │ Primary Sources      │
│ CCH Volume 16, USTR Volume 16    │ ──►  │ Full text of         │
│ Corresponding paragraph numbers  │      │ cases, rulings       │
│ point to any new cases or        │      └──────────────────────┘
│ pending legislation              │                 ▲
└──────────────────────────────────┘                 ▼
                                          ┌──────────────────────┐
                                          │ Use citators to      │
                                          │ assess status        │
                                          └──────────────────────┘
```

rials, not as an end in themselves. Generally, only reckless (or inadequately trained) tax researchers will confine their analysis to the tax services. The tax services should efficiently direct the researcher to the germane primary sources of the controlling tax law. It is the professional duty of the researcher to undertake an evaluation of such sources. Furthermore, quality research is not completed until the latest developments in the relevant areas of the law have been assessed.

Exhibit 7–2 shows that the three major methods of finding materials in the compilations consist of searching by key word, Code section, and case name. How to use each method will be illustrated using the CCH *Standard Federal Tax Reports.* In those situations where the services differ, both services will be presented to help you compare the CCH *Standard Federal Tax Reports* and RIA *United States Tax Reporter.*

Key Word Searches

The Compilation volumes of an annotated service can always be entered by Code section number, because the section numbers are printed on the spines of the volumes. However, if the tax topic is narrow or unfamiliar, it usually is more efficient to begin directly with a key word search in the service's Topical Index.

When making a list of key words, select a variety of terms that are directly related to the tax question. This will increase the odds of finding the most relevant material related to the tax issue. Nevertheless, the selection should be limited so that the search does not become inefficient. In preparing to undertake the tax research project of Example 7–1, the following key words come to mind (from the broad to the specific): *business deduction, illegal payments,* and *kickbacks.*

The Topical Index provides great variety and specificity of key word entries, thus using the index often requires significant research time and effort to examine its great number of entries. However, time spent in a thorough examination of the index to identify all relevant material will pay off once the researcher moves into the Compilation volumes. To avoid false starts, Volume 16, New Matters Index, (Volume 16, Recent Developments Index, in RIA) should always be checked before investing a substantial amount of time on a specific research path. This will ensure that the information found in the Compilations is read in light of any recent changes in the tax law.

Using the excerpt in Exhibit 7–3a, the CCH Topical Index provides references for "kickbacks, deductibility" as a subheading under "Business Expenses," with an

---

EXHIBIT 7–3a CCH Topical Index

Topical Index
References are to paragraph (¶) numbers.   **10,309**

BUSINESS EXPENSES—continued
. golf course greens upkeep 8471.124
. golf professional................ 8471.124
. government's loss of records 8470.579
. graft payments................ 8808.5657
. guarantor payments . 8470.4084—8470.4089
. hair styling and grooming 8474.2508
. hall of fame, construction of ... 13,709.1537
. hearing aid upkeep 13,603.266
. hedging transactions .... 32,226.01—

. investors................... 8471.1475
. irrigation assessments 13,709.585
. janitor service 8470.682; 8470.687
. judgments 8476.44
➤ . kickbacks, deductibility ... 8808.01; 8808.564
. Kiwanis club dues 8803.20
. labels worthless 8470.3995
. labor unions, payments to 8803.025
. land donated to city........... 8803.0554
. law student................... 8471.1295
. lawyer...................... 8471.13
. lease cancellation payment 8470.405;
                                      8704.06
. lease of equipment 8470.2825
. lease v. purchase of property ... 11,274.01—
                                     11,274.66
. . disqualifying event 11,274.30
. lease with option to purchase v. sale
  .... 8704.022—8704.0226

KICKBACKS 8450
. agent recipient 2150.045
. audit questions................ 8808.5623
. claim of right doctrine 21,005.1215
➤ . deductibility 8808.01; 8808.564

KICKBACKS—continued
. failure to report
. . fraud penalty 40,558.826
. foreign officials .... 8450; 8807—8808.50;
                                         8808.40
. . deferral of tax on income produced,
      prohibition against 29,040; 29,046.09
. gross income, inclusion in . 5600.103; 5901.50
. illegal political contributions ... 12,523.1315

"Kiddie tax"—see Minors: unearned income
  of, tax on

EXHIBIT 7–3b   RIA Topical Index

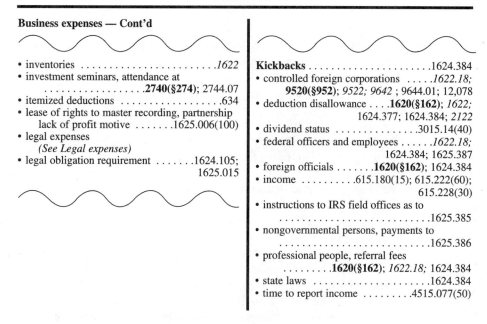

Business

Business expenses — Cont'd

- inventories *1622*
- investment seminars, attendance at
  ....**2740(§274)**; 2744.07
- itemized deductions 634
- lease of rights to master recording, partnership
  lack of profit motive ....1625.006(100)
- legal expenses
  (See Legal expenses)
- legal obligation requirement 1624.105;
  1625.015

Kickbacks 1624.384
- controlled foreign corporations *1622.18;*
  9520(§952); *9522; 9642* ; 9644.01; 12,078
- deduction disallowance .... **1620(§162)**; *1622;*
  1624.377; 1624.384; *2122*
- dividend status ....3015.14(40)
- federal officers and employees *1622.18;*
  1624.384; 1625.387
- foreign officials ....**1620(§162)**; 1624.384
- income ....615.180(15); 615.222(60);
  615.228(30)
- instructions to IRS field offices as to
  ....1625.385
- nongovernmental persons, payments to
  ....1625.386
- professional people, referral fees
  ....**1620(§162)**; *1622.18;* 1624.384
- state laws 1624.384
- time to report income ....4515.077(50)

accompanying reference to ¶¶ 8808.01 and 8808.564 found in Volume 2 of the service. These paragraphs appear to contain the material most relevant to our client's tax problem. "Kickbacks" also appears as a heading in the index with "deductibility" as a subheading. Interestingly, "illegal payments" is neither a heading or a subheading under "Business Expenses." This demonstrates the value of thinking of several alternative key words before starting an index search.

Using the edited RIA Topical Index in Exhibit 7–3b, the general entry "Business Expenses" provides no direct reference that would apply to the facts in our research case. Turning to the other key terms, there is also no separate heading for "Illegal payments," but the entries under "Kickbacks" appear promising. This heading gives the researcher much more detail, which then guides the subsequent search to concentrate on the paragraphs following the subheadings "deduction disallowance," "professional people, referral fees," and "state laws." All of these paragraph references direct the user to materials that are located in Compilation Volume 4 for Code § 162.

To help the researcher identify specific types of Compilation material, the RIA Topical Index uses abbreviation conventions. Parenthesized numbers, as in ¶ 4515.077(50) under "Kickbacks, time to report income," indicates the references are to **annotations,** a brief summary of relevant court cases, Letter Rulings, or administrative procedures. Boldface entries, such as the **1620** **(§162)** after "Kickbacks, deduction disallowance," are references to the *Internal Revenue Code*. The italicized entries, like the *1622* also after "Kickbacks, deduction disallowance," are references to the Regulations.

Code Section Searches

Frequently, seasoned tax researchers will know the numbers of the *Internal Revenue Code* sections that apply to a client's fact situation. They can find the appropriate Compilation material simply by using this Code section number. Both CCH and RIA print each volume's Code section ranges on the spines of the Compilation binders. Because Regulation numbers correspond with their controlling Code sections, a Regulation can also lead the researcher directly to the appropriate Compilation materials. Code and Regulation section numbers are a prominent part of the Compilation pages also.

Another manner of entry into the Compilations is through a **spine scan,** scanning the volume contents listed on the spines of the service's binders. The broadest term on our key word list for the Example 7–1 tax question, *business deduction,* appears on the spine of CCH's Volume 2 (RIA's Volume 4) as a major division heading. Therefore, you could determine where to enter the Compilation volumes by performing a spine scan.

After opening a binder, the researcher will notice the tab guides that delineate the major divisions of the volume. The Table of Contents found immediately after each tab guide furnishes a good overview of the Compilation paragraphs that follow. Further, it can lead the researcher to relevant Compilation materials. In the CCH Table of Contents, the Code sections included in the division appear in the first column. Subsequent columns address Regulations, topical headings, and paragraph references, respectively. The elliptical CCH symbol indicates editorial analysis by the CCH staff. The abbreviated Table of Contents for § 162 is reproduced in Exhibit 7–4. For our illustrative research problem, Regulation §1.162-18, "Illegal bribes and kickbacks . . 8807" and the CCH explanation of the regulation that follows at ¶ 8808 are appropriate places to continue our research.

The RIA division Table of Contents is also helpful to review before consulting specific paragraphs of Compilation material. This table of contents provides narrower paragraph headings for a more direct entry to the most relevant materials. The excerpt from the RIA Table of Contents (Exhibit 7–5) shows that ¶ 1624.377 is an overview of expenditures against public policy, and that ¶ 1624.384 includes material concerning bribes, kickbacks, and other illegal payments.

The final introductory material for the CCH Compilation division is an Overview. Positioned immediately after the division's Table of Contents, this presentation of the high points of the division's contents may yield the researcher specific paragraph references for already-identified key words (see Exhibit 7–6). For our research problem, notice that the Overview summarizes illegality, fines, and penalties, but it does not directly address the narrow issues in our case as might be expected from an "overview."

Code Volumes   The *Internal Revenue Code* language appears twice in both the CCH and RIA services. It appears once in the Compilation volumes and again in its basic form in the separate Code volumes. These separate volumes allow the researcher to examine the Code itself more quickly than is possible using the lengthier Compilation materials. Although the Compilation materials are excellent for in-depth analysis of Code sections, the statutory language is interspersed with excerpts from corresponding committee reports, Regulations, and editorial commentary.

The Code volumes support strict reference and cross-section functions. In addition, the volumes include historical notes that help trace the evolutionary develop-

EXHIBIT 7–4 CCH division Table of Contents

Business Deductions ● Travel and Entertainment ● Legal Expenses ● Repairs ● Rentals

. . . Code Secs. 161, 162 . . . business expenses . . . dues . . . entertainment . . . employees' expenses . . . traveling expenses . . . fines and penalties . . . repairs . . . reasonable compensation . . . bonuses . . . pensions . . . rents paid . . . farmers' expenses . . . reporting for employees' expenses

Table of Contents

'86 Code Sec.	Reg. § / CCH Expl'n		Paragraph
		Overview	8401
161		**Allowance of deductions**	8402
	§ 1.161-1	Allowance of deductions......	8403
162		**Trade or business expenses** ..	8450
	§ 1.162-1	Business expenses	8451
	CCH	Trade or business expenses .	8470
	CCH	What is a "business"?	8471
	CCH	Insurance premiums	8472
	CCH	Entertainment and meals ..	8473
	CCH	Employees' expenses	8474
	CCH	Legal and litigation-related expenses	8476
	§ 1.162-17	Reporting and substantiation of certain business expenses of employees	8805
	CCH	Substantiation of employees' expenses	8806
	→ § 1.162-18	Illegal bribes and kickbacks ..	8807
	CCH	Illegal bribes, kickbacks and other payments	8808
	§ 1.162-19	Capital contributions to Federal National Mortgage Association	8809

EXHIBIT 7–5   RIA division Table of Contents

EXHIBIT 7–6   CCH division Overview

[¶ 8401]   Overview   **21,505**

BUSINESS DEDUCTIONS ● TRAVEL AND ENTERTAINMENT ● LEGAL EXPENSES ● REPAIRS ● RENTALS

A preliminary discussion introducing the subjects covered in this division. Use it for quick review of the high points of the detailed "compilation" of law, regulations, decisions, rulings and comment following.

Business Expenses   A taxpayer engaged in business can deduct all ordinary and necessary business expenses that are incurred in that business (¶ 8470.013). An individual's personal expenses (¶ 12,540 et seq.) and expenses for the production of income (¶ 12,520) are not deductible as business expenses. Business deductions for capital expenditures must generally be claimed over a number of years (¶ 13,709.01).

Cohan Rule   If business deductions are not substantiated, difficulties may arise in proving the actual amount of an expense. To overcome this difficulty, the *Cohan* rule was devised by the courts. Under the *Cohan* rule, a court may allow an amount which it believes represents business expenses incurred by the taxpayer when little or no corroborating evidence is presented (¶ 8470.586 and ¶ 8470.5861).

However, the *Cohan* rule cannot be used for traveling, entertainment and gift expenses, or expenses associated with listed property as defined under Code Sec. 280F(d). Therefore, in the absence of required substantiation, business deductions for these types of expenses may not be approximated (¶ 14,417.01 et seq.).

"Trade or Business" Defined   The term "trade or business" is generally defined as an activity undertaken with the expectation of making a profit (¶ 8471.01). The definition includes services rendered as an employee. Thus, business expenses incurred by an employee may be deducted if they meet specific requirements. Generally, an employee's unreimbursed business expenses are required to be deducted as miscellaneous itemized deductions (¶ 8474.01 and ¶ 8500.026). This means that most unreimbursed expenses, along with other miscellaneous itemized deductions, are deductible only if the total of such expenses exceeds two percent of the employee's adjusted gross income. However, special rules control the employee business deductions of "statutory employees," disabled individuals and certain performing artists (¶ 8474.012).

Illegality, Fines and Penalties   A business may generally deduct ordinary and necessary business expenses even though its activities are illegal. However, a specific exception to this rule exists for illegal trafficking in drugs (¶ 15,051.01). Fines and penalties for violation of state and federal statutes in connection with a trade or business (such as parking fines or fines for overloaded trucks) may not be deducted (¶ 8904.316).

Legal Expenses   Legal expenses paid or incurred as a result of some business transaction, or made primarily to preserve "existing" business, reputation or good will, are ordinarily deductible. However, in cases of legal expenses incurred in acquiring property, the expense is a capital expenditure. Legal expenses incurred in criminal proceed-

ment of the Code. They also contain cross-reference tables that facilitate the matching of current Code section numbers to their 1939 Code counterparts.

The Code volumes for both services include a topical index and a listing of tax legislation that has amended the Code. In its Code Volume II, the CCH service also reproduces portions of selected laws that are not part of the *Internal Revenue Code* but that might have an incidental effect on tax liabilities. Code sections that address estate and gift taxes and federal excise taxes also are included in the services' Code volumes, but are not in the Compilations. Both publishers sell estate and gift and excise tax services separately from their standard annotated income tax services.

Case Name Searches

The last method of entering the Compilation material is through a case name. Recall from Example 7–1 that there were two known court case opinions that might have some bearing on our client's tax research issue. Both of these cases involved Ohio construction companies that sought to deduct kickback payments they made to a general contractor. Case names and IRS rulings often provide effective means of accessing compilation materials.

The CCH *Citator* is included as part of the *Standard Federal Tax Reports* service. As discussed in Chapter 6, the citations in this services are listed alphabetically by case name. In addition to formal citations, there are references to the Compilation paragraphs where the case is mentioned plus a list of other cases in which the case is cited. The Exhibit 7–7 selection from the CCH *Citator* shows that the *Bertolini* case is mentioned in four Compilation paragraphs, the two of interest in our research being ¶¶ 8808.35 and 8808.564. A decimal point in a CCH citation indicates that the reference is to an annotation paragraph in the Compilation. We cannot tell from this listing whether the original taxpayer prevailed in the trial-level case, although the citations of the history of the case indicate that the Sixth Circuit overturned the Tax Court's decision. The *Car-Ron* case entry (Exhibit 7–7) also refers to annotations at ¶¶ 8808.35 and 8808.564. It has been cited in one Tax Court Regular decision and four Memorandum decisions.

Since RIA does not include its multivolume *Citator* as part of its *United States Tax Reporter* service, it furnishes a tax-case **Finding List** in Volume 2. The Finding List presents court cases alphabetically and provides the Compilation paragraphs in which the cases are mentioned. It also gives the reporter location where the full text of the case may be found. A supplemental table of recent cases precedes the main table of cases. Keep in mind that the Finding List cannot be used in lieu of a citator. It provides neither a detailed judicial history of the case nor a list of other cases in which the case is cited. It merely serves as an entry to the Compilations.

Excerpts from the RIA case Finding List for the *Bertolini* and *Car-Ron* cases are reproduced in Exhibit 7–8. The case name is followed by reporter and Compilation paragraph locations for the case. An asterisk indicates a reference to the publisher's Tax Court Memorandum case reporter. The *Bertolini* and *Car-Ron* decisions are discussed in the annotations at ¶¶ 1625.028(90) and 1625.386(7). The Tax Court's Memorandum decisions concerning both cases are mentioned at the same paragraphs.

Other Pathways into the Compilations

Both of the annotated tax services provide a series of helpful finding lists. Each has finding list tables that correlate Regulations, Revenue Rulings, Treasury Decisions,

EXHIBIT 7–7   CCH *Citator*

```
──────CCH──────                    92,613
```

BER

Bertin, Michel J. A.
- ● TC—Dec. 12,916; 1 TC 355; NA. 1943 CB 27
  Swent, TC, Dec. 13,665(M), 2 TCM 1186
  Evans, TC, Dec. 13,213(M), 2 TCM 117
  Wilson, TC, Dec. 13,176(M), 2 TCM 12
  Levy, TC, Dec. 12,923-E, 1 TCM 316
Bertino, Eugene G.
- ● TC—Dec. 37,401; 75 TC 284; A. 1981-2 CB 1
Bertoli, John E. ¶42,981.05
- ● TC—Dec. 50,198; 103 TC 501
  Swanson, TC, Dec. 51,155, 106 TC 76
➤ Bertolini Trucking Co., Raymond . . . . . . ¶8470.244,
      8808.35, 8808.564, 40,375.23
- ● CA-6—(rev'g TC), 84-2 usтc ¶9591; 736 F2d
      1120
  Leanse, TC, Dec. 49,677(M), 67 TCM 2198, TC
      Memo. 1994-68
  Car-Ron Asphalt Paving Co., Inc., CA-6, 85-1 usтc
      ¶9298, 758 F2d 1132
  Brizell, TC, Dec. 45,911, 93 TC 151
  Greater Display & Wire Forming, Inc., TC, Dec.
      44,802(M), 55 TCM 922, TC Memo. 1988-231
  United Title Ins. Co., TC, Dec. 44,552(M), 55 TCM
      34, TC Memo. 1988-38
- ● TC—Dec. 39,474(M); 45 TCM 44; TC Memo.
      1982-643
Bertolino, Rudolph J. . . . . ¶42,343.60
- ● CA-9—(aff'g unreported TC), 91-1 usтc ¶50,201;
      930 F2d 759
  Hanson, CA-5, 92-2 usтc ¶50,554, 975 F2d 1150
  Merchant III, Est., CA-9, 91-2 usтc ¶50,543, 947
      F2d 1390
  Ferrel v. Brown, DC-Wash, 93-2 usтc ¶50,613, 847
      FSupp 1524
  Bothwell, TC, Dec. 50,592(M), 69 TCM 2403, TC
      Memo. 1995-170
  Oak Knoll Cellar, TC, Dec. 50,047(M), 68 TCM 412,
      TC Memo. 1994-396
  Holmes, CA-9, 91-2 usтc ¶50,350, 937 F2d 481
Bertollini, Barbara (See Kinnie, William A.)
                                          ¶33,878.644

CAR   92,880

Carroll-McCreary Co., Inc.—continued ·
  Walsh Holyoke Steam Boiler Works, Inc., CA-1, 47-1
      usтc ¶5908, 160 F2d 185
  Chenango Textile Corp., CA-2, 45-1 usтc ¶9241,
      148 F2d 296
  United Grocers, DC-Calif, 60-2 usтc ¶9718, 186
      FSupp 724
  Berger, TC, Dec. 25,382, 37 TC 1026
  Crean Brothers, Inc., TC, Dec. 17,993, 15 TC 889
  Midland Tailors, TC, Dec. 13,297(M), 2 TCM 281
  Hall Corp., George, TC, Dec. 12,935, 1 TC 471
- ● BTA—Dec. 11,281-C; July 31, 1940
Carrollo, Charles V. . . . . ¶39,060.021, 42,018.0965
- ● CA-8—(aff'g DC denial of taxpayer's motion to
      vacate judgment), 44-1 usтc ¶9294; 141 F2d 997
  Ausmus, Jr., CA-6, 85-2 usтc ¶9742, 774 F2d 722
  Palermo, DC-Pa, 57-2 usтc ¶9771, 152 FSupp 825
- ● DC-Mo—41-1 usтc ¶9164
➤ Car-Ron Asphalt Paving Co., Inc. . . . . ¶8808.35,
      8808.564
- ● CA-6—(aff'g TC), 85-1 usтc ¶9298; 758 F2d
      1132
  DeLorean, TC, Dec. 50,722(M), 69 TCM 3027, TC
      Memo. 1995-287
  Brizell, TC, Dec. 45,911, 93 TC 151
  McCormick Contracting Co., Inc., T.D., TC, Dec.
      44,967(M), 55 TCM 1522, TC Memo. 1988-365
  Greater Display & Wire Forming, Inc., TC, Dec.
      44,802(M), 55 TCM 922, TC Memo. 1988-231
  United Title Ins. Co., TC, Dec. 44,552(M), 55 TCM
      34, TC Memo. 1988-38
- ● TC—Dec. 40,434(M); 46 TCM 1314; TC Memo.
      1983-548 ·
```

Private Letter Rulings, and other references to the Compilation paragraphs. CCH's Finding Lists are located in *Citator* Volume M–Z. The RIA ruling Finding Lists are in Volume 2 along with the case Finding List. If you wanted, for instance, to follow up on a suggestion by a fellow tax researcher that Revenue Ruling 74-323, 1974-2 CB 40, may apply to our client's tax situation in Example 7–1, a Revenue Ruling Finding List is an efficient means for locating the appropriate Compilation paragraphs.

The CCH Revenue Ruling Finding List not only leads to the applicable Compilation paragraphs, it also shows the history of the ruling and gives citations for court cases and other rulings that have cited it. Thus, it performs many of the same functions as the Revenue Rulings section of the RIA *Citator.* The excerpts from the CCH Finding List in Exhibit 7–9 illustrate the search chain that can be followed, starting with the 1974 Revenue Ruling. The columns are printed together here for illustration. Each column is actually found on different pages in the CCH Revenue Ruling Finding List.

Using Exhibit 7–9, you discover that the ruling of interest, Revenue Ruling 74-323, discussed at Compilation ¶ 8088.5626, was subsequently cited in Revenue Ruling 77-243. This latter ruling was then cited in Revenue Ruling 77-244, and was later modified by Revenue Ruling 82-149, the 1982 ruling that revoked Revenue Ruling 77-244. After examining Compilation ¶ 8088.5626, you should read the full text of either or both of the 1974 and 1982 rulings if they seem relevant from the
```

EXHIBIT 7–8 RIA Case Finding List

MAIN TABLE OF CASES

BERTUCCI

Berthold, Paul W. v Comm., (1968, CA6) 22 AFTR 2d 5872, 404 F2d 119, 68-2 USTC ¶9670 ..3015.06(5); 3015.14(50)

Bertin, Michael J. A., (1942) 1 TC 355 (NA, 1944 CB 33) ..9115.11(90)

Bertino, Eugene G., (1980) 75 TC 284 ..448.50(10)

Bertolini, Raymond, Trucking Co., *82,643 ..1625.028(90); 1625.386(7); 66,515.14(5)

➤ Bertolini, Raymond, Trucking Co. v Comm., (1984, CA6) 54 AFTR 2d 84-5413, 736 F2d 1120, 84-2 USTC ¶9591 ..1625.028(90); 1625.386(7)

Bertolino, Rudolph L. v Comm.,(1991, CA9) 67 AFTR 2d 91-905, 930 F2d 759, 91-1 USTC ¶50,201 ..74,305.01(45)

Bertram, Kathleen E., *68,195 ..14,025.09(133)

Bertram, William S., *78,247 ..2635.04(85)

Bertrams, H. A., *68,281 ..1655.463(65)

Bertsch, John M., *83,646 ..74,536.1427(30)

Bertucci, Frank E. v U.S., (1957) 50 AFTR 1277, 137 Ct Cl 323, 146 F Supp 949, 57-1 USTC ¶9325 ..60,135.01(20)

CARATAN

Caputo, Richard, *83,359 ..13,055.03(5)

Car Color, Inc.; PPG Industries, Inc. v (See PPG Industries, Inc. v Hartford Fire Insurance Co., The)

Car-Ron Asphalt Paving Co., Inc., *83,548 .. 1625.028(90); 1625.386

➤ Car-Ron Asphalt Paving Co., Inc. v. Comm., (1985, CA6) 55 AFTR 2d 85-1258, 758 F2d 1132, 85-1 USTC ¶9298 ..1625.028(90); 1625.386(7)

Carabbia, Ronald; U.S. v, (1967, CA6) 20 AFTR 2d 5362, 20 AFTR 2d 5365, 381 F2d 133, 67-2 USTC ¶9647, 67-2 USTC ¶15,765 ..73,447.504(5)

Carabbia, Ronald; U.S. v, (1967, CA6) 20 AFTR 2d 5362, 20 AFTR 2d 5365, 381 F2d 133, 67-2 USTC ¶9647, 67-2 USTC ¶15,765 ..73,447.504(5)

Compilation paragraph summaries. Notice that the CCH Finding List provides formal citations for the rulings and that the CCH list also points to the annual Compilation volume in which the full text of the ruling initially was published. Verify from the Finding List that Revenue Ruling 74-323 initially was examined in Compilation ¶ 6740 of the 1974 edition of the CCH service, if your library has kept the 1974 service.

The excerpt in Exhibit 7–10 is from the RIA Finding List. The Compilation reference for Revenue Ruling 74-323, is ¶ 1625.386. Notice that this entry does not provide any evaluation of the value of the ruling as precedent. This type of information is found in the RIA *Citator* rather than in the Finding List.

It is apparent from our review of the CCH and RIA Compilations that they include an immense amount of information useful to a tax researcher. Thus, it is important that the practitioner become familiar with the manner in which the services are organized and also be comfortable with the terminology employed by these services.

The CCH Annotated Service

The CCH *Standard Federal Tax Reports* is a twenty-two-volume service whose binders are replaced each year. The Index volume is unnumbered and contains the Topical Index, a tax calendar, rate tables and schedules, tax planning information, checklists, definitions, and special tables. The other volumes not numbered are the two-volume *Internal Revenue Code* volumes and the two-volume *Citator.*

Each compilation volume is organized into several divisions with tab guides separating each division. As previously mentioned, at the beginning of each division is

EXHIBIT 7–9   CCH Revenue Ruling Finding List

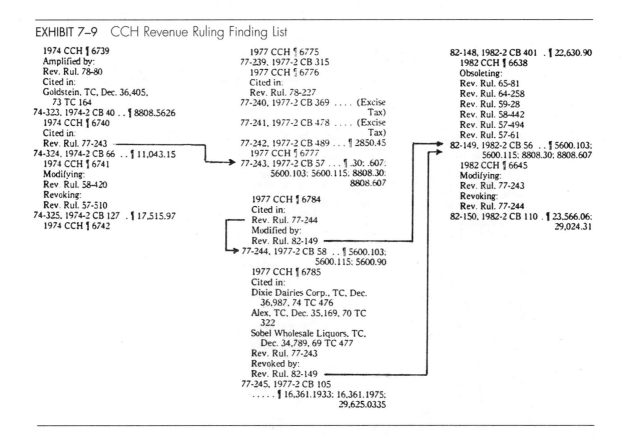

1974 CCH ¶ 6739
Amplified by:
Rev. Rul. 78–80
Cited in:
Goldstein, TC, Dec. 36,405,
  73 TC 164
74-323, 1974-2 CB 40 . . ¶ 8808.5626
1974 CCH ¶ 6740
Cited in:
Rev. Rul. 77-243 ——
74-324, 1974-2 CB 66 . . ¶ 11,043.15
1974 CCH ¶ 6741
Modifying:
Rev. Rul. 58–420
Revoking:
Rev. Rul. 57-510
74-325, 1974-2 CB 127 . ¶ 17,515.97
1974 CCH ¶ 6742

1977 CCH ¶ 6775
77-239, 1977-2 CB 315
1977 CCH ¶ 6776
Cited in:
Rev. Rul. 78-227
77-240, 1977-2 CB 369 . . . . (Excise Tax)
77-241, 1977-2 CB 478 . . . . (Excise Tax)
77-242, 1977-2 CB 489 . . . ¶ 2850.45
1977 CCH ¶ 6777
77-243, 1977-2 CB 57 . . . ¶ .30; .607;
  5600.103; 5600.115; 8808.30;
    8808.607

1977 CCH ¶ 6784
Cited in:
Rev. Rul. 77-244
Modified by:
Rev. Rul. 82-149 ——
77-244, 1977-2 CB 58 . . ¶ 5600.103;
  5600.115; 5600.90
1977 CCH ¶ 6785
Cited in:
Dixie Dairies Corp., TC, Dec.
  36,987, 74 TC 476
Alex, TC, Dec. 35,169, 70 TC
  322
Sobel Wholesale Liquors, TC,
  Dec. 34,789, 69 TC 477
Rev. Rul. 77-243
Revoked by:
Rev. Rul. 82-149 ——
77-245, 1977-2 CB 105
  . . . . . ¶ 16,361.1933; 16,361.1975;
    29,625.0335

82-148, 1982-2 CB 401 . ¶ 22,630.90
1982 CCH ¶ 6638
Obsoleting:
Rev. Rul. 65-81
Rev. Rul. 64-258
Rev. Rul. 59-28
Rev. Rul. 58-442
Rev. Rul. 57-494
Rev. Rul. 57-61
82-149, 1982-2 CB 56 . . ¶ 5600.103;
  5600.115; 8808.30; 8808.607
1982 CCH ¶ 6645
Modifying:
Rev. Rul. 77-243
Revoking:
Rev. Rul. 77-244
82-150, 1982-2 CB 110 . ¶ 23,566.06;
  29,024.31

a summary paragraph, a table of contents for the division, and an Overview commentary. The full text of each Code section is reproduced, usually followed by historical notes concerning its legislative evolution. Typically, this notation includes the relevant portion of Committee Reports from recent bills and citations for older underlying Committee Reports. Following the Code section materials are the related final and temporary Regulations reproduced in full text. Proposed Regulations and proposed amendments to the existing Regulations are next. For each Code section and many of the Regulations, the CCH editors write easy-to-read explanations and analyses of the law. Lastly, annotations of court cases and rulings are reported by topic. The annotations can be voluminous because there may be numerous cases and rulings that have addressed each area of the law. Therefore, a detailed alphabetical index organizes the annotation entries. As can be seen in Exhibit 7–11, each of the components of the Compilation has a distinctive format for ease of recognition.

The broad subject of our research project is the deduction of trade or business expenses. Our client in Example 7–1 seeks to deduct kickbacks to insurance claims adjusters that referred clients to him. We start our analysis of the CCH Compilation materials with Code § 161 and § 162, which control the deduction of trade or business expenses. Regulation § 1.162-18, "Illegal bribes and kickbacks," is on point with our research. The editors' explanation of Regulation §1.162-18 consists of three pages. This material is followed by the index to the annotations (Exhibit 7–12).

EXHIBIT 7–10   RIA Finding List

RevRul 74-307—RevRul 74-392

74-307, 1974-2 CB 126 .... 4015.13(20),(30)	74-350, 1974-2 CB 139 .... 4045.04(75)
modifying and clarifying RevRul 68-453; RevRul 73-501	74-351, 1974-2 CB 144 .... 1625.405(140); 4515.155(5),(25); 9055.01(95)
74-308, 1974-2 CB 168 .... 5015.15(25)	modified by RevRul 81-290
74-309, 1974-2 CB 203 .... 8725.04(15)	superseding IT 4037; Mim 6475; Mim 6494; Mim 6584
superseding TD 4299	74-352, 1974-2 CB 197 .... 8565.12(5)
74-310, 1974-2 CB 205 .... 9025.01(50)	74-353, 1974-2 CB 200 .... 8565.03(20)
74-311, 1974-2 CB 211 .... 9015.03(35),(40)	74-354, 1974-2 CB 326 .... 34,015.47(70)
74-312, 1974-2 CB 320 .... Estate	74-355, 1974-2 CB 339 .... 34,015.42(50)
74-313, 1974-2 CB 351 .... Excise	74-356, 1974-2 CB 359 .... Excise
74-314, 1974-2 CB 360 .... Excise	74-357, 1974-2 CB 359 .... Excise
obsoleted by RevRul 92-18	74-358, 1974-2 CB 43 ... 1625.095(25); 1675.022(80); 4615.23(20)
74-315, 1974-2 CB 386 .... 49,425.01(5)	
74-316, 1974-2 CB 389 .... 49,445(15)	amplifying RevRul 62-20
74-317, 1974-2 CB 13 ...... 555.01(40); 6425.02(75)	74-359, 1974-2 CB 129 .... 4015.13(10)
74-318, 1974-2 CB 14 .... 615.241(5); 2775	74-360, 1974-2 CB 130 .... 4015.13(10)
superseding RevRul 58-209	74-361, 1974-2 CB 159 ... 1705.25(65); 5015.07(245); 5015.13(5),(30); 5135.011(5)
74-319, 1974-2 CB 15 .... 615.241(5); 2775; 77,015.07(17)	superseding RevRul 66-221
74-320, 1974-2 CB 404 .... 77,015.26(50)	clarifying RevRul 71-47
74-321, 1974-2 CB 16 .... 615.241(17); 1625.347(90)	74-362, 1974-2 CB 170 .... 5015.21(10)
superseding RevRul 69-96	obsoleted by RevRul 81-291
74-322, 1974-2 CB 17 .... 615.165(55); 34,015.11(65)	74-363, 1974-2 CB 290 .... Estate
amplified by RevRul 78-80	74-364, 1974-2 CB 321 .... Estate
74-323, 1974-2 CB 40 .... 1625.386	revoked by RevRul 80-363
74-324, 1974-2 CB 66 .... 1675.114(25)	74-365, 1974-2 CB 324 .... Estate
revoking RevRul 57-510	74-366, 1974-2 CB 345 .... Excise
modifying RevRul 58-420	74-367, 1974-2 CB 375 .... Excise
74-325, 1974-2 CB 127 .... 4015.13(10)	

Notice that "Kickbacks" is just one of the several topics related to Regulation §1.162-18.

The numbers at the top and bottom of the Compilation page reproduced in Exhibit 7–12 each have a specific meaning. The top line of the page includes a centered heading with the Code section and the beginning Compilation paragraph number plus the page number. The page number, 22,207 in this sample, is generally used only for filing the weekly updates in the loose-leaf binders. For updated pages, the page publication date is listed in the upper inside corner. The bottom of the page shows the ending page Compilation paragraph number at the lower outside corner, ¶ 8808.5623 in this example. Just to the inside of the paragraph number is the Code or Regulation section that is the subject of the page, Reg. § 1.162-18(c).

The "Kickbacks" entry in the Annotations by Topic (Exhibit 7–12) list leads to ¶ 8808.564. A condensed portion of the annotations is reproduced in Exhibit 7–13. The actual annotations for "Kickbacks" run almost three pages. From reading these summaries, it appears that the important issues in determining the deductibility of kickbacks are (1) whether the kickbacks are ordinary and necessary business expenses and (2) whether the kickbacks are in violation of any generally enforced state law. A review of the annotations, however, cannot substitute for reading and analyzing the full text of the primary material. The three or four sentences in the summaries cannot present all the relevant facts or decisions in any case or ruling, thus, the researcher should use these summaries to identify relevant materials and then locate and read the actual primary sources.

The RIA Compilations

While the RIA *United States Tax Reporter* is similar to the CCH *Standard Federal Tax Reports* in many aspects, it does have some special features that deserve inves-

EXHIBIT 7–11   CCH *Standard Federal Tax Reports* format

—'86 Code—

Each Code section is reproduced in full and flagged as shown in the left margin. "Historical Notes" indicate whether there has been any amendment since 1954 and cite the location of other pertinent information such as Committee Reports. Code sections are always kept up-to-date. Amendments and changes are published promptly, and new pages are included in current Reports for insertion in the Compilations.

● *Regulations*

This "catch-line" always introduces Regulations. The full texts of all final and temporary Regulations follow the Code sections they construe. The Regulations are printed in larger type across the full width of the page.

> Full text Regulations standing in *proposed* form and *proposed amendments* to existing Regulations are reported in place in the Compilations, following the Code section they are intended to construe. Their unique presentation within boxes alerts readers to their status as proposals and to their relationship to existing Regulations.

Committee reports.—In the absence of Regulations, as in the case of recent legislation, controlling Committee Reports are frequently reproduced to indicate legislative intent. Code Section 195, located in Volume 4, is followed by Committee Reports. Note that Committee Reports are printed in double column format.

● ● *CCH Explanation*

> These editorial comments are set in larger type. They have their own "catch-line" and are enclosed within boxes to distinguish them from official contents. CCH Explanations lead into the digests of decisions and rulings, supply refinements of interpretation, and point out trends or conflicts among authorities.

● ● ● *Annotations by Topic*

Digests of decisions and rulings, called "annotations," are arranged by topic under the Code section and Regulations construed. Each large group of digests is preceded by a table indexing the annotations alphabetically. The "catch-line" is centered. Annotations are arranged in double column format. The case name or ruling number, as well as the citation to the full text, is noted under each digest.

tigation. RIA Compilations have a unique and functional paragraph numbering system. All paragraphs pertaining to a particular Code section incorporate that section number into the paragraph number. A single digit is added to the end of the Code section number, indicating the nature of the material contained in the paragraph. Exhibit 7–14 summarizes the coding system employed by RIA, using IRC § 162 as an example.

Review the Index (Exhibit 7–3b) and the Table of Contents (Exhibit 7–5) for § 162 with the uniqueness of the numbering system in mind. You should be able to ascertain the general content of the RIA paragraph references. For instance, in

EXHIBIT 7–12 CCH explanation and annotations

TRADE OR BUSINESS EXPENSES— § 162 [¶ 8450]   **22,207**

Illegal Bribes, Kickbacks, and Other Payments

● ● *CCH Explanation*

payment was not illegal and the taxpayer was able to show that the payments were ordinary and necessary (*Raymond Bertolini Trucking Co.*, 84-2 USTC ¶ 9591, ¶ 8808.564, below). A claimed deduction was not allowed when the kickbacks were not ordinary and necessary (*Car-Ron Asphalt, Co.*, 85-1 USTC ¶ 9298, ¶ 8808.564, below).

Whether payments are ordinary and necessary is a factual issue determined under the facts and circumstances of the case. Ordinary payments are those payments that are normal, usual or customary under the facts and circumstances. The U.S. Supreme Court has held that kickback payments that are widespread in the industry were ordinary and necessary to maintain business (*T.B. Lilly*, 52-1 USTC ¶ 9231, ¶ 8808.564 below). See also *M. Brizell* (Dec. 45,911, ¶ 8808.564, below), where the Tax Court held that kickback payments were ordinary where they were paid by a number of printers for a number of customers over an extended period of time and were necessary to maintain business.

.40 Foreign kickbacks or bribes.—The deductibility, as a business expense, of payments made to foreign government officials or employees is determined *solely* under the Foreign Corrupt Practices Act of 1977 (FCPA) and not under any other law of the United States (Code Sec. 162(c)(1)). Thus, a payment that is not prohibited by the FCPA, but that is classified as illegal under another provision of federal law, is still deductible as a business expense.—CCH.

● ● ● *Annotations by Topic*

Payments in Violation of Law

.5623 Audit procedures.—In April 1976, the IRS announced that examining officers in its Coordinated Examination Program (CEP) would be required to ask 11 specific questions of corporate officials, key employees and others in an effort to cope with revelations concerning schemes involving bribes, kickbacks and political contributions. CEP cases involve examinations of corporations whose gross assets exceed $250 million and financial institutions and utilities with over $1 billion in gross assets.

The questions were later modified and their number reduced from eleven to five. An explanatory preamble was added.

The use of the questions is discretionary based on reason to believe their use is called for during an examination.

Questionnaire

The following questions are submitted in connection with an examination by the Internal Revenue Service of the corporation's Federal tax liabilities. You may state your position with the corporation and your particular area of responsibility. However, the questions are not limited to knowledge acquired in the course of your official responsibility, but should be answered on the basis of your knowledge, belief, and recollection from whatever source.

You should state under the penalties of perjury that you believe your answers to be true and correct as to every material matter. You may provide explanatory details with your answers. If you are unsure whether a particular transaction comes within the scope of the question, you may discuss the matter with the examining agent. If, after the discussion, you believe that any answer requires qualification, you should state clearly the

EXHIBIT 7–13   CCH annotations

.564 Kickbacks.—Where, pursuant to agreements reflecting an established and widespread practice in the optical business, the taxpayers paid doctors who prescribed the eyeglasses which taxpayer sold one-third of the retail sales price received for the glasses, such payments are deductible by taxpayers as ordinary and necessary business expenses. The expenditures did not violate a federal or state law, and that there were no sharply defined national or state policies, evidenced by governmental declaration, which proscribed the payments in question.

T.B. Lilly, SCt, 52-1 USTC ¶ 9231, 343 U.S. 90.

To the contrary, where rebates or gifts to employees of the taxpayer's three largest customers, engaged in the manufacture and sale of draperies for mobile homes, were not ordinary and necessary because they are not common in the industry and were not excludable from gross income. The taxpayer held the entire amounts received from customers under a claim of right.

United Draperies, Inc., CA-7, 65-1 USTC ¶ 9136, 340 F2d 936. Cert. denied, 382 U.S. 813.

A subcontractor at a large shopping mall construction site was allowed deductions for the lawful kickback payments it made to the supervisor of the primary contractor, where the subcontractor understood that it would not be allowed to continue the subcontract work and would not be timely paid if the kickbacks were not forthcoming. There was obviously a logical relationship between the subcontractor's construction business and the kickback payments that it made in order to retain its construction contracts. Thus, the kickbacks were an ordinary cost of doing business, as well as a necessary one, and because deductions are allowable for such costs so long as the payments are within the bounds of federal and state law, they were deductible.

Raymond Bertolini Trucking Co., CA-6, 84-2 USTC ¶ 9591.

But the Sixth Circuit distinguished *Raymond Bertolini Trucking Co.,* above, in refusing to allow a paving subcontractor who obtained contracts for the construction of a mall by having his company pay for services and materials used in the construction of the personal residence of the general contractor's vice president in charge of awarding subcontracts to deduct the kickback payments. The kickbacks were neither ordinary nor necessary, since the company had obtained nearly all of its contracts, including 20 with the same contractor, without paying kickbacks.

Car-Ron Asphalt Paving Co., CA-6, 85-1 USTC ¶ 9298, 758 F2d 1132.

An amount paid by a corporation in connection with a land purchase was expended for its own behalf and had a business purpose. Accordingly, such amount was not a taxable dividend to its stockholder. However, a second amount paid by the corporation to purchase stock in another corporation was made for the benefit of its stockholder and was dividend income to such stockholder. Kickback payments made by the corporation were deductible where it was not shown that such payments were illegal.

J.P. Byrne, 44 TCM 338, Dec. 39,156(M), TC Memo. 1982-373.

A marine supplier or ship chandler who pays to shipmasters, stewards, chief engineers or other personnel of "tramp steamers" commissions of 5% of the gross invoices for goods and services purchased from the chandler for the ship may properly deduct the commissions as expenses where the commissions paid (1) are paid in a manner and under such circumstances as not to be illegal through the violation of any statutory law, (2) relate to transactions that would not be governed by the Federal Trade Commission Act in respect to constituting unfair methods of competition, (3) are normal, usual and customary in the community, (4) are appropriate and helpful in obtaining business and (5) are paid with the knowledge of the owners of the ships.

Rev. Rul. 58-479, 1958-2 CB 60.

Commissions or sales promotion expenses in the nature of "kickbacks" paid by a meat business to managers, chefs, and other purchasing agents were not deductible since they were in violation and frustration of clearly defined state and federal public policy.

Matter of A. Michaud, DC Pa., 70-2 USTC ¶ 9658, 317 FSupp 1002. Rev'd and rem'd on other issues, CA-3, 72-1 USTC ¶ 9346, 458 F2d 953. Cert. denied, 409 US 876.

Kickbacks of approximately 10 percent of the cost of repair work performed on foreign vessels, paid to the captain and chief engineer of the vessel in order to secure the repair work, were not deductible where the testimony of shipowners that they did not have knowledge that the repair bills were padded to include such kickbacks controverted the taxpayer's contention that such payments were universal, and where the payments were in violation of the state Commercial Bribery Statute and of state public policy as established by court decisions.

Dixie Machine Welding & Metal Works, Inc., CA-5, 63-1 USTC ¶ 9355, 315 F2d 439. Cert. denied, 373 U.S. 950.

EXHIBIT 7–14   RIA's *United States Tax Reporter* Compilation numbering system for § 162

Appending Digit	Type of Material	Comments	Example
0	Text of Code		1620
1	Committee Reports		1621
2	Regulations	Final *and* Temporary	1622
3	Proposed Regulations		1623
4	Explanations	RIA editorial commentary	1624
5	Annotations	Specific cases and rulings	1625
6	Procedural matters	Tax Court procedural material	1626
7	Miscellaneous items		1627
8	Prior law	Only if it is still relevant to some taxpayers	1628
9	Crossovers	Cross-reference materials to other Code sections	1629

Exhibit 7–3b under "Kickbacks, professional people, referral fees," the citation ¶ *1622.18* refers to Regulation 1.162-18. The correspondence between the RIA subparagraph number, .18, and Regulation subsection number, 18, is simply a coincidence. Because both Final and Temporary Regulations are included under the appending digit 2, Regulation and paragraph numbers seldom correspond. Verify in Exhibit 7–5, for instance, that the text of Reg. § 1.162-2, relating to travel expenses, which might be expected to appear at § 1622.02, actually appears at RIA ¶ 1622.01. Also, the RIA editors allow for subsequent additions to the Compilations by leaving unused paragraph numbers in the system. For instance, ¶ 1624.384 is followed by ¶ 1624.388.

Unlike the CCH, RIA does not replace the binders each year. This causes a volume numbering problem when the tax law in one area increases beyond the size of its binder. To rectify this problem, there are four volumes numbered the same as the prior volume but they have an "a" extension. For instance, there is a "Volume 3" and a "Volume 3a" in the Compilations for 1998. Consequently, the volumes are numbered from 1 to 18 but there are actually 22 binders.

Current Information

New primary tax law such as statutes, administrative materials, and judicial interpretations are generated almost daily. Therefore, it is of utmost importance that practitioners are notified of all of the latest changes in the tax law. *Taxes on Parade* by CCH and *Weekly Alert* by RIA are weekly newsletters that include summaries and highlights of the latest court cases, administrative rulings, and other modifications to the primary sources of the tax laws. Where appropriate, the newsletter summaries include paragraph citations to the services.

For the loose-leaf tax services, the weekly newsletter is accompanied by an updating packet containing replacement pages to be integrated into the Compilation volumes. As primary law changes, the publishers generate revised pages that reflect these modifications. These replacement pages include accompanying revisions to indexes, finding lists, and other aids for the researcher. The body of the service can thus react very quickly to reflect changes in the tax law. Instructions sent with the replacement pages indicate where the new pages should be placed in the service volumes and which existing pages should be removed.

If the service is not to become hopelessly disorganized, the updating must be conscientiously performed as soon as the replacement pages arrive. A lag of even one week not only jeopardizes the ability of the researcher to identify current law, but it makes the subsequent updating process much more difficult, due to both the sequential nature of the replacement pages and the amount of the insertion work itself. Also not paying close attention to the filing instructions can decrease the effectiveness of the tax service. A page misfiled is a page lost. To determine when your library last updated its CCH service look in the Advance Sheets volume. Behind the tab "Last Report Letter" will be the latest instructions used by the person who updates the services.

The editorial staffs of the annotated services cannot be expected to produce a set of comprehensive revisions to the Compilations instantaneously. Given that a change in any one aspect of the tax law may require a dozen or more textual revisions to the tax service, the editors need some lag time to construct, print, and distribute the replacement pages. In advance of these updates, the services provide current developments material organized by paragraph number and compose "news release" type announcements, summaries of the most recent primary source revisions to the tax law, and the text of selected administrative pronouncements.

CCH includes its current development collection in Compilation Volume 16, New Matters. The RIA provides their materials in Volume 16, Recent Developments. In both services, indexes to the supplemental material furnish the paragraph and subparagraph numbers of the affected Compilation volume appearing in the left column, in numerical order.

Before you invest time in reading § 162, Regulation §1.162-18, and the court cases or rulings identified by the annotations as germane to our client's tax problem, you should check for recent developments in this area of the tax law. The CCH Cross Reference Tables have a Topical Index section and two sections arranged by Code section, the Cumulative Index and the Latest Additions to Cumulative Index. The portion of the Topical Index shown in Exhibit 7–15a lists one update for Kickbacks, however it does not appear to pertain to our client's situation. Examining the condensed portions of the Cumulative Index (for Reports 1–14, 1998) in Exhibit 7–15b and the Latest Additions to Cumulative Index (for Reports 15–26, 1998) in Exhibit 7–15c, we find no entries with respect to ¶ 8807, the cite for Regulation § 1.162-18, or ¶ 8808 where the CCH explanation and annotations are found. Thus, we can assume for the moment that there are no new developments affecting our research.

Other Features of the Services

The practitioner receives several additional research aids as part of the CCH and RIA tax services. Although all of these features cannot be discussed in this text, an effective researcher should be aware of their existence. For instance, both services include a separate volume of Advance Sheets, which are composed of the full text of the current year's non–Tax Court income tax decisions. CCH also provides advance sheets for current-year Tax Court decisions. The material that is found in these advance sheets will be published later in bound format as the RIA AFTR2d and

EXHIBIT 7–15a CCH New Matters Topical Indexes

75,130

Topical Index to 1998 Developments
References are to Volume 16 and the U.S. Tax Cases Volume.

20 5-14-98

K

Kickbacks
- gross income, inclusion in . . . . .47,764(M)

L

Large gifts from foreign persons, information returns
- reporting requirement 46,086

Last known address
- deficiency notice 38,549.0251
- notification of new address 48,749
- use of computer transcript 38,549.0252

EXHIBIT 7–15b CCH New Matters Cumulative Indexes

14 4-2-98

Cumulative Index to 1998 Developments
(For Reports 1–14)
(See also Cumulative Index at page 75,251.)

75,315

**From Compilation
Paragraph No.**

**To New Development
Paragraph No.**

Code Sec. 162—Trade or business expenses

8470	.0195	Employee education expenses require new strategies—Comment 48,745
	.07	*Scofield*, TCM—Creditors claims deductible as business expenses 47,789
	.1546	*Gallo*, TCM—Paralegal not entitled to business expense deductions relating to former occupation 47,947
	.1546	Independent paralegal could deduct expenses during work hiatus—Comment 48,756
	.35	*Cox* aff'd, CA-8—Couple could deduct only half of rent paid by husband's business 49,806
	.37	Independent paralegal could deduct expenses during work hiatus—Comment 48,756
	.507	*Women of the Motion Picture Industry*, TCM—Exempt organizations denied business deductions for funds transferred between accounts 47,757
	.515	*Phillips*, TCM—Individual not entitled to deduct corporate expenses on personal return 47,897
	.517	*Joseph, Sr.*, TCM—Taxpayer allowed deductions for ordinary and necessary business expenses 47,683
	.517	*LaMont*, FedCl—Losses were deductible as ordinary and necessary business expenses despite single sale 50,047

	.455	*Thorpe*, TCM—Rent in excess of fair market value of shareholder condominium not deductible 47,964
	.5365	*Dharma Enterprises*, TCM—Licensing agreement between related parties not the result of arm's-length bargaining 47,684
	.55	*Williams*, TCM—No evidence presented to substantiate claimed business expenses 47,937
8801	.0354	*Ciaravella*, TCM—Reasonable advertising expenses determined 47,867
	.087	*Midwest Industrial Supply, Inc.* aff'd, CA-6—Horse breeding costs not necessary business expense 50,096H
8803	.01	*Dharma Enterprises*, TCM—Licensing agreement between related parties not the result of arm's-length bargaining 47,684
	.01	Guidance on deductibility of expenses incurred by federal advisory committee members—Rev. Proc. 46,041
8806	.07	Optional standard mileage rates updated; Rev. Proc. 96-63 superseded—Rev. Proc. 46,225
	.07	Per diem rates updated; Rev. Proc. 96-64 superseded—Rev. Proc. 46,226
	.07	Travel costs substantiated by electronic mail, facsimile copies—Letter Ruling 47,401

Code Sec. 163—Interest

9104	.08	*Allen, Sr.*, DC N.C.—Interest on deficiencies deductible as business expense 50,196
	.08	Interest deduction for business-related tax deficiency allowed—Comment 48,739
	.274	*Bowater, Inc.*—Cert. denied taxpayer 1/12/98.
	.288	*Restore, Inc.*, TCM—Accrued but unpaid interest nondeductible; all-events test not satisfied 47,826
	.334	*L&C Springs Assocs.*, TCM—Deduction disallowed following transfer of ownership of property 47,706
	.382	*Acierno*, TCM (¶47,677)—Amounts paid to use EOR technology did not reflect genuine debt. Taxpeayer on

EXHIBIT 7–15c   CCH New Matters Cumulative Indexes

75,256   **Latest Additions to Cumulative Index to 1998 Developments**   26   6-25-98
(For Reports 15–26)
(See also Cumulative Index at page 75,301.)

From Compilation Paragraph No.			To New Development Paragraph No.
	.4251	*Silberman,* FedCl—Issue of business connection to corporate officer's legal expenses precluded summary judgment	.50,474
	.45	*Liberty Vending, Inc.,* TCM—Shareholder's legal fees for recovery of business from estranged spouse were deductible	.48,032
	.45	*Silberman,* FedCl—Issue of business connection to corporate officer's legal expenses precluded summary judgment	.50,474
8520	.03	Divided Ninth Circuit Rejects Travel Expenses While Away from Parents' Home—Comment	.48,792
	.03	*Henderson* aff'd, CA-9—Traveling stage hand's living expenses while on tour were not deductible	.50,375
8540	.0368	*Shepherd,* TCM—Traveling salesperson's substantial automobile expense deductions allowed	.48,029
	.2535	*Mohan Roy, M.D., Inc.,* TCM (¶47,816)—Medical corporation denied business deductions for luxury auto. Taxpayer on appeal to CA-9.	
8560	.015	*Bundridge,* TCM—Business owners entitled to cost of good sold allowance for amount reported as supplies	.48,066
8580	.048	IRS allows deduction of environmental cleanup costs to replace storage tanks—Comment	.48,785
	.048	Waste underground storage tank replacement costs were deductible business expenses—Rev. Rul	.46,392
8586	.069	Commissions paid by cellular phone retailer to distributors were capital expenditures—Letter Ruling	.47,429
	.075	*Huynh,* TCM—Taxpayer denied deduction for commission paid to an intermediary	.48,045
	.265	*Wang,* TCM—Reasonable amount of real estate commissions paid by corporation determined	.47,977
8587	.12	*Wang,* TCM—Reasonable compensation paid to corporate officer for selling land determined	.47,977
	.2829	*Alpha Medical, Inc.,* TCM (¶47,700)—Amounts paid as compensation was unreasonable. Taxpayer on appeal to CA-6.	
	.284	*Alpha Medical, Inc.,* TCM (¶47,700)—Amounts paid as compensation was unreasonable. Taxpayer on appeal to CA-6.	
	.284	*Dexsil Corp.* vac'd and rem'd, CA-2—Tax Court incorrectly determined corporate officer's compensation was unreasonable	.50,471
	.284	*Leonard Pipeline Contractors, Ltd.* rev'd, CA-9—Explanation lacking for amount of reasonable compensation set by court	.50,356
	.284	Ninth Circuit reverses reasonable compensation case, criticizes both IRS and Tax Court—Comment	.48,788
8592	.041	*Wang,* TCM—Bonus not deductible absent proof of reasonableness	.47,977
8704	.118	*Bundridge,* TCM—Unsubstantiated rental expense deduction disallowed	.48,066
	.118	*Schaefer,* TCM—Attorneys' fees incurred in rental property purchase had to be capitalized	.48,017
	.455	*Wysong,* TCM—Rental expenses incurred under lease between related corporations excessive	.47,978
8706	.099	Nursery's purchase of bare-root trees was business expense—Letter Ruling	.47,442

CCH USTC tax case reporters, so the researcher need not wait until the semiannual binding takes place to have access to such opinions.

Besides furnishing current tax developments, Volume 16 of the services provides items such as a glossary of tax terms, a calendar of important tax filing deadlines, checklists of commonly encountered income and deduction items, discussions of tax planning principles and strategies, information about the status of pending legislation, and selected scheduled court cases.

Topical Tax Services

The focus of the remainder of this chapter now switches to the topical tax services. Unlike the annotated tax services, topical tax services organize the tax law by subject matter or transactions, therefore materials are presented together that are found in various nonadjacent Code sections. Consequently, a topical tax service can be efficient in meeting the needs of the researcher in a typical client project.

For example, a client might need help with issues concerning shifting income among related taxpayers. The applicable law might include provisions relating to short-term trusts, low-interest loans, investments in taxable and tax exempt bonds or mutual funds, and life insurance. The annotated services would present this material by Code section number, making it more difficult for a practitioner to assemble an integrated picture of the many effects that the assignment-of-income doctrine might have in the client's situation. The topical tax service, on the other hand, would have a section that includes a discussion of provisions relating to general types of transactions, with analysis, suggested transaction structures, issues to consider, and problems to avoid.

Nature of Topical Tax Services

A topical approach to the tax law functionally integrates related Code sections and other primary and secondary sources of the federal tax law, including court cases, administrative pronouncements, and general editorial commentary. The strength of topical services is their organization of materials into commonly encountered taxable events or types of transactions. However, like the Code, a topical service may incompletely address transactions that don't neatly fit into its organizational pattern. The editors of topical services cannot possibly address all of the tax ramifications of every type of transaction.

The various topical tax services available differ in their organization and the type of analysis they emphasize. If the organization of a given topical service suits a client's fact situation, the use of the service can be very effective. If not, using the service may be quite inefficient. Thus it is important, more than is the case with an annotated service, to choose the right topical service for the specific research project, or to use several services for different aspects of the same project.

Topical tax services typically have variety of indexes and finding lists for their analytical material, including key word (topic), Code section, Regulations, rulings and administrative releases, and court case names. These indexes often parallel those that are available within the annotated services. Also like the annotated services, the topical services print the titles of their major divisions on the spines of the volume binders. The topical services are distinguished from each other chiefly by the structure of their material, not the structure of their indexes.

The following is a selective list of the titles (and our abbreviations) of the more commonly used topical tax services:

Research Institute of America's *Federal Tax Coordinator 2d (Coordinator)*
Research Institute of America's *Analysis of Federal Taxes: Income (Analysis)*
Bureau of National Affairs' *Tax Management Portfolios (Portfolios)*
Warren, Gorham, & Lamont's *Federal Taxation of Income, Estates, and Gifts* (Bittker)
West Group's *Mertens Law of Federal Income Taxation (Mertens)*

Survey the libraries you frequently use for research to determine which of these services are available for your use. Throughout this section, the RIA services will be utilized to illustrate how to conduct research with a topical tax service. As with the annotated services, we will use the kickbacks paid to insurance claim adjusters tax question of Example 7–1 to learn how to conduct research with a topical tax service. Remember that it is important that **you go to the library** and follow the research steps outlined in this section. The illustrations are not substitutes for actually using the services.

RIA *Coordinator and Analysis*

The **RIA** *Federal Tax Coordinator 2d* is among the most comprehensive of the topical tax services. Thus, it frequently is an appropriate tool for commencing a tax research project. One of its strong points, particularly for a researcher who may have a weak background in a particular subject area, is its general background discussions summarizing the major issues. The **RIA** *Analysis of Federal Taxes: Income* is a condensed version of the *Coordinator* and covers only income tax issues. It is a more affordable option for the practitioners with a general tax practice.

Entering the RIA topical services can be accomplished using the three major methods outlined for the annotated services: by key words, Code section, or case name. A spine scan using broad topics printed on the spines of the binders is also an option. Exhibit 7–16 reproduces edited sections of the Topic Index and Finding Lists for the Code and for cases. Notice that for our illustrative research, we can enter the topical service using the same key terms we used earlier, "Kickbacks, deductibility," or by the cases *Bertolini Trucking* or *Car-Ron Asphalt*.

As Exhibit 7–17 demonstrates, the format begins with a general discussion of the treatment of kickbacks, bribes, and other illegal payments. Directly following is a listing of references for subtopics of this section. The subtopics that are germane to our tax inquiry are located at ¶¶ L-2605, L-2606, and L-2608 (Exhibit 7–18). Turning to these paragraph sites we find an editorial explanation and analysis of the tax issues. Notice that the Code, Regulations, cases, and rulings are integrated into the explanation. Throughout the explanation there are numerous footnotes to the primary and secondary law sources plus citations to other paragraphs in the service. You should always confirm the editorial explanations by reviewing the primary sources cited. The portions of the Code and Regulations relevant to the chapter top-

---

EXHIBIT 7–16   RIA Topic Index and Finding Lists

Main Topic Index — Kickbacks

Kickbacks
- audit of slush funds . . . . T-1080 *et seq.*
- business expenses, as L-2600; L-2608
- controlled foreign corporations, illegal payments to government officials by O-2401; O-2529
- deductibility . . . . L-2600 *et seq.*
- government officials and employees, to . L-2601 *et seq.*
- gross income, inclusion in J-1610
- IC DISC shareholders, illegal payments to government officials deemed distributed to O-2125
- illegality J-1610
- income from J-1601; J-1612
- investment-related expenses, as L-1417
- law, in violation of . . . L-2605 *et seq.*; L-2613; L-2616; L-2617
- liability for income from J-1612
- Medicare and Medicaid L-2610
- ordinary and necessary business payment L-2608
- private persons, to . . . . L-2605 *et seq.*
- public policy restrictions L-2609
- restitution of, deductibility L-2614
- specific types of . . . . L-2610 *et seq.*
- state law
  - generally enforced, deductibility L-2605; L-2606
- taxability J-1610; J-1612

1,993

Internal Revenue Code Table — 162(h)(4)

Code Sec.	Discussed at ¶
152(e)(4)(A)(ii)	A-3807
152(e)(4)(B)	A-3808
152(e)(5)	A-3810
161	A-2601, L-1001
162	E-3101, H-3652, 3922, L-1001, 6134, 6604, N-1326, 4202
162(a)	H-3910, L-1200, 1811, 1811.1, 1817, 2014, 2608, 2902, 4116, 5101, 6101
162(a)*	L-1815
162(a)(1)	H-3600
162(a)(2)	L-1701, 1705, 1709, 1712
162(a)(3)	L-3203, 6201, 6601, 6602, 6616, 6701
162(b)	K-3068, 3658, L-4229
162(c)	L-2608, O-2125, P-1122
162(c)(1)	L-2601, 2602
162(c)(2)	L-2605
162(c)(3)	L-2610
162(d)	L-4219

Main Table—Cases and Decisions

Bertolini Trucking Co, Raymond, (1982) TC Memo 1982-643, PH TCM ¶ 82643, 45 CCH TCM 44, revd (1984, CA6) 54 AFTR 2d 84-5413, 736 F2d 1120, 84-2 USTC ¶ 9591 . . . L-2608

Bertolino, Rudolph, (1991, CA9) 67 AFTR 2d 91-905, 930 F2d 759, 91-1 USTC ¶ 50201 . . . U-1271

Bertram, William, (1978) TC Memo 1978-247, PH TCM ¶ 78247, 37 CCH TCM 1058 . . . L-2952

Bertucci, Frank, (1957, Ct Cl) 50 AFTR 1277, 137 Ct Cl 323, 146 F Supp 949, 57-1 USTC ¶ 9325 . . . G-1759

〰〰〰

Car-Ron Asphalt Paving Co Inc, (1983) TC Memo 1983-548, PH TCM ¶ 83548, 46 CCH TCM 1314, affd (1985, CA6) 55 AFTR 2d 85-1258, 758 F2d 1132, 85-1 USTC ¶ 9298 . . . L-2608, T-10161

Carroro, Joseph, (1933) 29 BTA 646 . . . S-1816

Carr Staley Inc, (1973, DC TX) 32 AFTR 2d 73-5566, 73-2 USTC ¶ 9652, affd (1974, CA5) 34 AFTR 2d 74-5362, 496 F2d 1366, 74-2 USTC ¶ 9549, reh den (1974, CA5) 502 F2d 1167, & cert den (1975, S Ct) 420 US 963, 43 L Ed 2d 441 . . . N-4401, 4414

Carruth, Ostella Est, (1957) 28 TC 871, acq 1957-2 CB 4, and acq 1957-2 CB 5 . . . C-2508, 2519

Carruthers, Eban, (1953, DC OR) 44 AFTR 1304, 53-1 USTC ¶ 9316, affd (1955, CA9) 46 AFTR 1626, 219 F2d 21, 55-1 USTC ¶ 9223 . . . I-2001, 2006

Carsendino, Rosin, (1994) TC Memo 1994-79, RIA TC Memo ¶ 94079, 67 CCH TCM 2248 . . . V-8516

Carson, Dick, (1975, CA5) 35 AFTR 2d 75-593, 506 F2d 745, 75-1 USTC ¶ 9203 . . . V-5706, 5709

EXHIBIT 7–17 RIA explanations

Kickbacks, Bribes, Etc. ¶ L-2601

The dispute was settled for a sum exceeding the damages which B could have been awarded had it prevailed in the Securities Act suit.

IRS held that the payments couldn't be split between capital (the amount in the SEC suit) and ordinary business expenses (overpayment) because all claims settled arose from the sale of a capital asset.[19]

The Tax Court held that no part of a payment made in settlement of a stockholder's suit against the taxpayer corporation was deductible by the taxpayer as an ordinary and necessary business expense where the settlement agreement expressly provided that the entire payment was for the stockholder's stock, even though the stockholder also released other claims he had against the corporation.[20]

L-2600. Kickbacks, Bribes and Other Illegal Payments.

No deduction is permitted for illegal bribes, kickbacks, rebates and other payments. Business payments, however, which may violate unenforced laws are deductible if they otherwise qualify as ordinary and necessary business expenses.

For illegal payments to government officials or employees, see ¶ L-2601 et seq.

➤ For bribes, kickbacks and other illegal payments, see ¶ L-2605 et seq.

➤ For ordinary and necessary requirement for otherwise deductible illegal payments, see ¶ L-2608 et seq.

For specific kinds of illegal payments, see ¶ L-2610 et seq.

For treatment of restitution, see ¶ L-2614 et seq.

For expenses of illegal business, see ¶ L-2616 et seq.

For treatment of fines, penalties, treble damage payments under the antitrust laws and similar payments, see ¶ L-2700.

L-2601. Bribes or kickbacks to government officials and employees.

No deduction is allowed for illegal bribes or kickbacks paid directly or indirectly to an official or em-

19. Rev Rul 80-119, 1980-1 CB 40.

20. G.C. Services Corp, (1979) 73 TC 406.

ics are reproduced in an appendix following the chapter. Each Code section is followed by a history of its amendments in reverse chronological order.

The explanation at ¶ L-2605 states that kickbacks and illegal payments under any state law are not deductible. However, the state law must generally be enforced for this treatment to be required. At this point, the explanation references ¶ L-2606, which describes what general enforcement of state law means. Because the state law against kickbacks is rarely enforced in our client's state, it does not appear to fall within the description given in ¶ L-2606.

In the section explaining the ordinary and necessary requirements (¶ L-2608), we find informative synopses of the *Bertolini* and the *Car-Ron* cases. Integrating the cases into the explanation in this manner helps the researcher see the interplay among the various cases and their relationship to the other authoritative tax law. Lastly, the explanation of ordinary and necessary expenses contains an observation by the editors. Such RIA highlights are editorial in nature and are not legal author-

EXHIBIT 7–18   RIA analysis

L-2605. Bribes, kickbacks and other illegal payments to persons other than government officials.

An illegal bribe, illegal kickback or other illegal payment under any law of the U.S. (other than described in ¶ L-2601) or under any law of a state, but only if that state law is generally enforced (¶ L-2606) which subjects the payor to a criminal penalty or the loss of license or privilege to engage in a trade or business isn't deductible as a business expense.[9]

Illustration: Taxpayer burned his building down and obtained a gain to the extent the insurance proceeds he received exceeded his basis in the building. However, taxpayer may not deduct payments made by him to the arsonist since they are illegal payments.[10]

The burden of proof as to whether a payment is an illegal bribe, illegal kickback or other illegal payment is upon IRS to the same extent as it is under Code Sec. 7454 (relating to fraud).[11]

A kickback includes a payment in consideration of the referral of a client, patient or customer.[12]

Business bribes and kickbacks which aren't specially disallowed by the above rules are allowable as business expense deductions if they otherwise qualify as ordinary and necessary expenses.[13]

In one case, a construction company made payments to the chairman of the board of a construction management company in return for which the management company allowed the construction company to get a major subcontract without going through the normal bid process. The payments represented kickbacks, but IRS didn't prove they were illegal kickbacks.[14]

Another taxpayer gave cash gifts to buyers at clothing store chains, department stores, etc., at the end of the year, although the companies the buyers worked for generally prohibited their buyers from accepting gifts from manufacturers' sales representatives. Taxpayer stated that the gifts were a way to maintain relationships with the buyers. The Tax Court held that the fact that employers may have a policy against their buyers' accepting gifts from sales reps doesn't make the payments nondeductible under the rules denying a deduction for an illegal bribe or illegal kickback.[15]

A printing company was allowed business expense deductions for kickbacks paid to purchasing agents of its customers. The kickbacks weren't illegal under then applicable New York law because, although they were within the definition of commercial bribery, the payments were the result of extortion, and then applicable New York made extortion a complete defense to bribery.[16] However, payments made by a taxpayer to stock loan managers to generate business that were illegal under then applicable New York law as bribery weren't deductible where no extortion was involved.[16.1]

The Tenth Circuit held that where a lawyer advanced the litigation expenses of a personal injury case that he took on a contingency fee basis under an agreement that provided the lawyer would receive a portion of the recovery, but wouldn't be reimbursed for the amounts advanced (a gross fee contract), the payment of the litigation expenses wasn't an illegal payment. Although the state bar Rules of Professional Conduct required, at a minimum, that lawyers be reimbursed for expenses they advance from the amount recovered in the litigation, even if the bar rules are treated as a state law under which a lawyer could lose his license to practice law, there was no evidence that this rule was enforced.[17]

L-2606. General enforcement of state law.

A state law is considered to be generally enforced unless it is never enforced or the only persons normally charged with violations are infamous or those whose violations are extraordinarily flagrant. For example, a criminal statute of a state is considered to be generally enforced unless violations of the statute which are brought to the attention of appropriate enforcement authorities do not result in any enforcement action in the absence of unusual circumstances.[18]

---

7. Reg § 1.162-18(a)(2).
8. Farnsworth, A.L., (1973) TC Memo 1973-195, PH TCM ¶ 73195.
9. Code Sec. 162(c)(2).
10. Rev Rul 82-74, 1982-1 CB 110.
11. Code Sec. 162(c)(2).
12. Code Sec. 162(c)(2).
13. S Rept, PL 91-172, 12/30/69, p. 274.
14. Byrne, Joseph, (1982) TC Memo 1982-373, PH TCM ¶ 82373, 44 CCH TCM 338.
15. Bondy, Arthur, (1991) TC Memo 1991-545, TC Memo ¶ 91545, 62 CCH TCM 1126.
16. Brizell, Murray, (1989) 93 TC 151.
16.1. Zecchini, Anthony, (1992) TC Memo 1992-8, TC Memo ¶ 92008, 63 CCH TCM 1717.
17. Boccardo, James v. Com., (1995, CA9) 1995 US App LEXIS 12700.
18. Reg § 1.162-18(b)(3).

(continued)

EXHIBIT 7–18 continued

L-2608. Ordinary and necessary requirement for otherwise deductible illegal payments.

A bribe or kickback not specifically disallowed by the Code,[23] must still satisfy the ordinary and necessary test[24] (¶ L-1200 et seq.).

Expenses were ordinary and necessary in these cases:

~~~~~~~~~

... A subcontractor at a shopping mall construction site made kickback payments of $90,000 to the prime contractor's supervisor. The payments did not violate local (OH) law or any federal statute, and the subcontractor was not subject to any loss of license or business permit as a result of the kickback payments. The Sixth Circuit found that where there is some normal, logical connection between the taxpayer's business and the payment, then it is deductible. The court said a legal kickback is a cost of doing business like any other, and Congress has written the tax laws so as to allow deductions for such costs so long as the payments made are within the bounds of federal and state law.[26]

... Payments were made by an insulation contractor to employees of the general contractor and of other subcontractors involved in a job on which it was working to facilitate the taxpayer's access to the job site and to motivate certain persons—for example, engineers, elevator operators, union officials— whose cooperation the taxpayer needed to perform its tasks properly. The payments were also customary in the taxpayer's business.[27]

Expenses weren't ordinary and necessary in these cases:

... A secret payments to an officer of a savings and loan association for his influence in arranging loans to the taxpayer could not be deducted on the ground that the expense, though necessary, was not ordinary.[28]

~~~~~~~~~

... A taxpayer subcontractor, in order to get paving subcontracts, paid off a general contractor's vice president with services and materials for construction of the vice-president's personal residence. At the time, these kickbacks were not illegal. However, the kickbacks did not qualify as ordinary business expenses because the taxpayer failed to establish that kickbacks were common or ordinary in the construction business generally or in the paving business in particular. The Sixth Circuit distinguished *Bertolini Trucking* (footnote 26) because there the kickbacks were conceded by IRS to be necessary, and the Sixth Circuit held that the payments were ordinary as the term is understood in the context of the tax law. Therefore, *Bertolini* controls only the issue of whether the payments were ordinary. Here, on the other hand, the Tax Court had found the payments were not necessary, based on the fact that almost all of the subcontractor's other contracts had been obtained without the payment of kickbacks.[32]

✔ *observation:* The Supreme Court construes a necessary expense as one appropriate and helpful in the taxpayer's business, see ¶ L-1201.

23. Code Sec. 162(c).
24. Code Sec. 162(a).
25. Brizell, Murray, (1989) 93 TC 151.
26. Bertolini Trucking Co, Raymond v. Com., (1984, CA6) 54 AFTR 2d 84-5413, 736 F2d 1120, 84-2 USTC ¶ 9591, revg (1982) TC Memo 1982-643, PH TCM ¶ 82643.
27. American Insulation Corp, (1985) TC Memo 1985-436, PH TCM ¶ 85436.
28. Rev Rul 58-525, 1958-2 CB 63.
29. Greater Display & Wire Forming Inc, (1988) TC Memo 1988-231, PH TCM ¶ 88231, 55 CCH TCM 922.
30. Diamond, Sol, (1971) 56 TC 530, affd (1974, CA7) 33 AFTR 2d 74-852, 492 F2d 286, 74-1 USTC ¶ 9306.
31. United Draperies Inc v. Com., (1964, CA7) 15 AFTR 2d 50-1, 340 F2d 936, 65-1 USTC ¶ 9136, affg (1963) 41 TC 457, cert den (1965, S Ct) 382 US 813, 15 L Ed 2d 61.
32. Car-Ron Asphalt Paving Co Inc, (1983) TC Memo 1983-548, PH TCM ¶ 83548, affd (1985, CA6) 55 AFTR 2d 85-1258, 758 F2d 1132, 85-1

ity. Observations are indicated with the special check mark symbol. Other editorial comments also are designated with this check mark symbol. Exhibit 7–19 lists the four types of editorial comments found in the RIA services.

The RIA service, the *Federal Tax Coordinator 2d,* divides its discussion of federal income, gift, estate, and excise taxes into twenty-three chapters, designated by capital letters (A through W), contained in its twenty-eight-volume service. These volumes consist of loose-leaf binders that are updated weekly in the same manner as annotated services. The topical (key word) index is in the unnumbered Index Volume. Other finding lists are included in Volumes 1 and 2. All references in the Index and Finding Lists are to paragraph numbers in the chapters.

A particularly valuable RIA feature that helps the researcher quickly find material addressing a specific issue is the hierarchical and distributed table of contents

EXHIBIT 7–19   RIA in-text comments

illustration: To clarify the tax rules and problems discussed, with simple easy-to-follow illustrations.

caution: To warn of dangers which arise in particular tax situations and, where appropriate, to indicate what should be done.

recommendation: To provide specific, carefully studied guides to action which will keep taxes at a legal minimum.

observation: For professional analysis or commentary which is not part of cited authorities.

---

system. The titles for RIA's chapters are found on a table of contents page located at the front of every volume. At the beginning of each RIA chapter, a tab card is followed by a Detailed Table of Topics, which indicates, by paragraph number, the tax provisions that are discussed in that chapter. The Detailed Reference Table, immediately following the Table of Topics, gives greater detail of the chapter's contents. In these tables researchers can scan the outline of topics to identify the paragraph, or series of paragraphs, that may be most useful to their research task. Finally, before the tax law analysis paragraphs are presented, a "Treated Elsewhere" table identifies other chapters and paragraphs of the service where related data can be found.

As with the RIA annotated services, subscribers to the topical services receive the *Weekly Alert.* The articles in the *Weekly Alert* are keyed into the body of the RIA service itself, making it less likely for a researcher to omit an examination of the current status of a pertinent law. The RIA *Weekly Alert* also periodically includes special studies of integrated tax topics.

The weekly *Internal Revenue Bulletins* are reproduced by the *Coordinator* RIA service. This provides the practitioner with a convenient source for current Revenue Rulings, Revenue Procedures, and other IRS announcements. Proposed income, estate, and gift tax Regulations, and certain proposed excise tax Regulations, are also furnished. Lastly, tax treaties that are in effect between the United States and foreign countries are included in one volume.

BNA *Portfolios*

The Bureau of National Affairs (BNA) offers a wide range of services in various areas of the federal law. Its federal tax series, the **BNA *Tax Management Portfolios,*** is a topical tax service published in magazine-size folders, with replaceable pages for updating.

The more than 300 *Portfolios* are divided into three series, each having front covers printed in distinctive colors. The U.S. Income Tax series are printed in red ink; the Estates, Gifts, and Trusts series, in green ink; and the Foreign Income series, in blue ink. The size of the *Portfolio* library varies as topics are added, deleted, or combined. For example, *Portfolios* 446, 447, and 475 were superseded by *Portfolio* 561 due to the changes in the tax treatment of capital assets. While the number of *Portfolio* appears vast, the series is not truly comprehensive. There are no *Portfolios* for many of the issues practitioners may encounter, thus necessitating the use of other reference materials for certain topics. Alternatively, it may be necessary to jump from one *Portfolio* to another to cover a topic completely.

The *Portfolio* Index is a comprehensive guide to the BNA service. The Index is divided by tab cards into five sections. The Code Section Index traces specific Code sections to all of the various *Portfolios*. Three of the other four index sections correspond to the major *Portfolio* series: (1) U.S. Income; (2) Estates, Gifts, & Trusts; and (3) Foreign Income. The tab cards for the tax sections are red, green, and blue, corresponding to the color of the cover lettering of each *Portfolio* series.

Following each series' tab card is a Portfolio Classification Guide, which lists by topic and number all of the *Portfolios* in that series. The topics section is a very broad-based index, whereas the numerical listing is like a table of contents for the series. Immediately following the numerical listing is the Master Index for the series, which is updated at least quarterly. It directs the researcher to a specific page, rather than a paragraph, of the appropriate *Portfolio*.

The last section of the Index, with a white tab, is the IRS Forms and Publications Finding Table. This index identifies, either by form number or alphabetical form title, the *Portfolio* that includes a discussion or reproduction of the form. The *Portfolios* indexes do not, however, include global finding lists for such things as Regulations, Letter Rulings, and Revenue Rulings.

Since our illustrative fact pattern involves illegal kickback payments and their potential deductibility, we might turn first to the Code Section Index, excerpted in Exhibit 7–20. Under §162(c), "Illegal Bribes, Kickbacks, and Other Payments," we find "Deductibility of Legal and Accounting Fees, Bribes and Illegal Payments." The asterisk in front of the entry indicates *Portfolio* 523 contains the primary coverage of this topic. If you were uncertain of the appropriate Code section, the Master Index entry "Kickbacks, Deductibility" (Exhibit 7–20) lists several *Portfolios* on the topic of which *Portfolio* 523 is one.

Portfolio 523, like all of the *Portfolios* in the U.S. Income Series, begins with a Description Sheet summarizing its contents. Next is a Table of Contents, a shortened version of which is shown in Exhibit 7–21. Each page number is preceded by a letter because the *Portfolios* are divided into three sections: (A) Detailed Analysis, (B) Working Papers, and (C) Bibliography and References. From this table, we see that the discussion of kickbacks germane to our illustrative problem begins on page A-54 in the Detailed Analysis section.

The Detailed Analysis is written by one or more tax practitioners who are chosen on the basis of specialized expertise in a given area. These practitioners are thought to be more sensitive to the information requirements of service users than a more isolated editorial board would be. Code sections, Regulations, rulings, and court case opinions are integrated into the analysis as well as pitfalls and probable IRS positions on the transactions. In addition, the authors suggest effective tax planning techniques and alternative means of structuring transactions in a tax-favorable manner. Citations to primary and secondary reference materials are included in the text and in footnote form at the bottom of each page. Part of the Detailed Analysis pertinent to our client's situation is reproduced in Exhibit 7–22.

The Working Papers section of the BNA *Portfolios*, denoted with a "B," is perhaps the service's most unique and useful feature. This portion includes practitioner checklists; reproduced IRS forms, occasionally filled in for an illustrative fact situation; computation worksheets; reproductions of pertinent Code sections, Regulations, and court case opinions; sample draft agreements and contract clauses; sample board or shareholder resolutions and employment contracts; and other practical materials that can assist the professional in implementing tax planning techniques

EXHIBIT 7–20   BNA *Portfolio* Code and Master Index

INTERNAL REVENUE CODE SECTION

§162 - TRADE OR BUSINESS EXPENSES

Allocation and Apportionment of Expenses – Regs. §1.861-8 (F), 906

Amortization of Intangibles (US), 533

Bad Debts (US), 538

Cafeteria Plans (US), 397

Charitable Contributions by Corporations (US), 290

Choice of Entity (US), 700

* Deductibility of Legal and Accounting Fees, Bribes and Illegal Payments (US), 523

Deduction Limitations: General (US), 504

Deductions: Overview and Conceptual Aspects (US), 503

Employee Fringe Benefits (US), 394

Employee Plans – Deductions, Contributions and Funding (US), 371

Employment Status – Employee v. Independent Contractor (US), 391

§162(c) - ILLEGAL BRIBES, KICKBACKS, AND OTHER PAYMENTS

* Deductibility of Legal and Accounting Fees, Bribes and Illegal Payments (US), 523

Deduction Limitations: General (US), 504

Subpart F – General (F), 926

Tax Crimes (US), 636

U.S. INCOME PORTFOLIOS

KICKBACKS

Deductibility, 401:A-81; 504:A-66; 523:A-51, A-52, A-54, A-58

Gross income, 501:A-146

KIDDIE TAX, 507:A-12

See also TAX MANAGEMENT EGT PORTFOLIOS INDEX

Allocable parental tax, 507:A-13

AMT, 288:A-44(1), C&A:A-44(1); 507:C&A:A-41

Assignment of income doctrine, 502:A-72, C&A:A-72

Computation of tax, 507:A-12

Election to include in parent's gross income applicable children's gross income, 507:A-14

Net unearned income, 507:A-12

Taxpayer Relief Act of 1997 changes, 288:C&A:A-44(1); 507:C&A:A-41

---

and procedures. For instance, the Working Papers for *Portfolio* 523 include, among other items, an Internal Revenue Manual Excerpt on Corporate Improper Payments and Related Exhibits.

The Bibliography and References section of a BNA *Portfolio* has a comprehensive listing of the primary and secondary sources of the tax law that the author(s) used in the preparation of the *Portfolio*. Reproductions of relevant Committee Reports, Code sections, Regulations, administrative pronouncements, and similar primary source material also are included. Revenue Rulings and Private Letter Rulings are presented in summary or "headnote" fashion. Finally, this section of the *Portfolio* often includes a brief listing of journal articles and treatises that are relevant to the *Portfolio* topic.

BNA updates its material in response to important tax developments that cause a *Portfolio* to become outdated. Revised pages are sent to replace the existing Detailed Analysis and Working Paper pages. For example, page (v) of the Table of Contents in Exhibit 7–21 was revised on 1/5/98. The *Tax Management Weekly Report* (TMWR), which is part of the BNA tax service, includes an analysis of significant

EXHIBIT 7–21   BNA *Portfolio* Table of Contents

TABLE OF CONTENTS

PAGE

developments. Any law change affecting a particular *Portfolio* contains a cross-reference to the affected pages of that *Portfolio*. The back page of each weekly issue contains a Table of Affected Portfolios. A cumulative Table of Affected Portfolios is printed in each TMWR index. Interim indexes are printed at approximately six-week intervals, and each successive index is accumulated with the previous index.

Depending on when a development occurs during an update cycle, the lag time before its appearance in a *Portfolio* can vary from three to eight weeks. Therefore, a researcher should use the TMWR to update *Portfolio* research. One should note the

EXHIBIT 7–22   BNA *Portfolio* Detailed Analysis

Detailed Analysis

The burden of proving that a payment made to a foreign government official or employee constitutes a bribe or kickback which is unlawful under the FCPA is on the IRS.[717] In order to prevail, the IRS must present clear and convincing evidence of such illegality.[718]

C. *Bribes and Kickbacks Other Than to Government Employees or Officials Under Section 162(c)(2)*

1.   Under the Tax Reform Act of 1969

The Tax Reform Act of 1969 added §162(c)(2) to the Code, which provided guidelines for determining under what circumstances illegal bribes or kickbacks to persons other than government officials or employees would be disallowed. This section provided that, in order for a deduction with regard to a payment to a person other than a government official or employee to be disallowed (a) the taxpayer must have been convicted in a criminal proceeding of making the payment, (b) the taxpayer must have entered a plea of guilty or *nolo contendere* to an indictment or information charging the making of such a payment, or (c) a plea of guilty or *nolo contendere* must have been accepted with regard to such indictment or information.

Because the provisions of §162(c)(2) contain the sole criteria for determining the allowability or nonallowability of a deduction for ordinary and necessary payments made to a person other than a government official or employee constituting bribes, kickbacks, or other payments, payments which are not illegal under any law of the United States or under any law of a State which is generally enforced are deductible under §162(a).

In that regard, in *Raymond Bertolini Trucking Co. v. Comr.*,[730] the Sixth Circuit, reversing the Tax Court, upheld deductions for kickbacks paid by a subcontractor to the site supervisor of a general contractor as being "ordinary" within the meaning of §162(a). The IRS did not dispute the legality of the payments and conceded that they were "necessary" as required by §162(a). Citing the Supreme Court's decision in *Deputy v. DuPont*,[731] the IRS argued that the payments were not "ordinary" because they were not normal or habitual. The Sixth Circuit read *DuPont* to require "some logical connection between a taxpayer's particular business and the expenditure" as a condition to deductibility. The court found the requisite connection in the instant case because the kickbacks were made to retain construction contracts. The court bolstered its decision by noting that §162(c)(2) and Regs. §1.162-1 effectively prevented the IRS from disallowing the deductions on public-policy grounds.

Note: The court noted that allowing deductions for the payments may be wise tax policy because the deductions by the payor may, on audit, reveal the recipient's failure to report the payments as income.

a.   The Requirement that State Statute be "Generally Enforced"

When Congress codified the illegal-payment disallowance provisions in 1969, it intended to bring some uniformity of treatment to an area governed by conflicting views of what constituted public policy. By adding the requirement that a statute be "generally enforced" to §162(c)(2), Congress seemingly reverted to a codification of the pre-1969 case law.

The words "generally enforced," as used in §162(c)(2), have been the subject of limited judicial construction. Thus, the frequency with which statutes will be found to be generally enforced is as yet unknown. It has been suggested that "generally enforced" could reasonably be construed to mean any degree of law enforcement between (but not including) the extremes of dead-letter status and that required by the 1969 version of §162(c)(2). Because the range of permissible interpretations is so wide, it is difficult to predict which statutes will be found to be not "generally enforced" and, therefore, which classes of taxpayers will be allowed to deduct payments constituting bribes, kickbacks, or other payments to persons other than government officials or employees.

b.   The Treasury's Definition of "Generally Enforced"

Regs. §1.162-18(b)(3) provides that a State law:

shall be considered to be generally enforced unless it is never enforced or the only persons normally charged with violations thereof in the State (or the District of

date on the Detailed Analysis pages to determine the date from which to bring the *Portfolio* research forward. The researcher would finish BNA research by checking the most recent six-week index and the subsequent individual issues of TMWR, since information in those issues would not yet be in the index. All of these efforts do not replace the necessity of reading the relevant primary sources of law pertaining to the tax problem under investigation.

The *Tax Management Memorandum* accompanies the *U.S. Income Portfolios*, and it is filed chronologically in a separate three-ring binder. Similarly, the *Estates, Gifts, and Trusts Journal* accompanies the Estates, Gift, and Trusts series of *Portfolios*.

Other Topical Services

Bittker Service

Warren, Gorham & Lamont, a major legal and accounting periodical publisher, distributes Boris I. Bittker's five-volume bound treatise, **Federal Taxation of Income, Estates, and Gifts.** The Bittker service is less comprehensive and more conceptual than many other topical tax services discussed in this chapter. Its stated objective is "provid[ing] guidance and orientation [to income and transfer taxation] by emphasizing the purpose, structure, and principal effects of the *Internal Revenue Code*, without bogging down in the details." Due to its goals, the service sometimes reads like a collection of essays and journal articles rather than a systematic analysis of the workings of the Code.

The publishers issue one revised bound volume each year, so the service is on a five-year cycle. Because the volumes are bound (precluding the use of replacement pages), as each volume nears the end of its five-year update cycle, the update materials can be disproportionately large. The update volume is larger than any of the other five volumes. Thus, a researcher must always check the current material section for every research project. Because the update materials can be voluminous, when the researcher finds material of interest in the Bittker service, it is especially important to check immediately the current materials for the section or paragraph in question to determine the status of the material in the main text. It would be a poor use of time to take extensive notes on a topic, only to learn from the new matters material that Congress or a recent court case has dramatically changed the relevant tax provisions.

The Bittker service may serve as a good starting point for the researcher who needs to obtain an initial grasp of a selected area of the tax law. Its citations can either provide easy access into the other tax services or immediately direct the practitioner to the primary sources of tax law. Currently, it stands somewhere between a one-volume treatise or textbook and a free-standing comprehensive topical tax service.

Mertens Service

The West Group, an important legal publisher, produces **Mertens Law of Federal Income Taxation.** This nineteen-volume tax treatise service is more legally oriented than the RIA *Coordinator* because its designed chiefly by and for attorneys. This legal orientation is evident in that the text material is heavily footnoted. On occasion, there is more footnote material than text material on a *Mertens* page. These footnotes provide more than mere citations to the relevant primary tax law sources. Often they annotate cases, quote freely from the Code, Regulations, and Committee Reports, or review legislative history.

Each volume of the *Mertens* service has a Cumulative Supplement, with a semiannual cumulative updated monthly. When the amount of the cumulative supplement material warrants, the entire volume is rewritten. Therefore, to be certain of the current law, the supplements must be read. The supplements for a volume are found at the front of the volume. The monthly updates are at the very front, printed on yellow stock. The Table of New or Changed Section Titles, which appears at the beginning of the semiannual supplement, provides a listing of sections that have changed since the main volume text was last updated.

The *Mertens* service also includes a Code Commentary, which furnishes contextual explanation of Code provisions. In addition, the service provides loose-leaf collections for both current Regulations and Revenue Rulings. The Code, Regulations, and Rulings volumes each contain Amendment Tables, which allow the researcher to trace the statutory or administrative evolution of any provision.

Finally, the service has "snapshot" versions of previous years' Code, Regulations, and Rulings volumes. This extremely useful feature of the *Mertens* service can facilitate one's analysis of the evolution of a law. For a client whose prior years' tax returns are under audit or at trial, the tax practitioner can use this feature of *Mertens* to reconstruct the details of the primary law sources that applied at the date of the original return.

CFTS

The **CCH *Federal Tax Service*** (CFTS) is organized in a manner similar to the RIA *Federal Tax Coordinator 2d* tax service. As of August 1998, CFTS was no longer offered in published form to new subscribers. Access to the CFTS will be via CD-ROM or through the Internet. Therefore, this service will be discussed in Chapter 8, Computer Tax Services.

Single-Topic Treatises and Loose-Leaf Services

Various publishers have issued one-, two-, or three-volume bound **tax treatises** or loose-leaf services that are devoted to a detailed analysis of a narrow range of tax issues. Such single-topic works can be effective to round out an analysis of open tax issues, but research seldom will be confined to these works. Many of these publications resemble the tax services because they include updates, web sites and CD support, and replacement pages or newsletters. Within the range of analysis that the authors have selected, the researcher may enjoy a detailed discussion of the law including citations to primary or secondary sources. These services may be limited in range but not in quality.

▶_____ Summary

The market supports a variety of annotated and topical tax services, all designed to facilitate the research process of the practitioner. The annotated services are collections of various indexes and summaries of the primary sources of the federal tax law organized around the *Internal Revenue Code*. CCH and RIA both provide thorough and complete reference materials meeting the highest professional standards. The topical services organize their material along the logical threads that connect non-contiguous Code sections. While some services provide different features than others, all have a high degree of professional quality. Topical services are most efficient when the organization of the service matches the issues in a client's tax situation. Research in a topical service, though, involves the extra step of finding the most efficient service with which to find the answer to the research problem.

The tax researcher should employ tax services as gateways to the primary sources and not as a substitute for primary source research. The annotated services can make the research process more efficient and productive but should not replace professional judgment and effort.

▶ Key Words

By the time you complete your work in this chapter, you should be comfortable discussing each of the following terms. If you need additional review of any of these items, return to the appropriate material in the chapter or consult the glossary to this text.

Annotated Tax Service	RIA *Analysis of Federal Taxes: Income*
Annotations	RIA *Federal Tax Coordinator 2d*
Bittker's *Federal Taxation of*	RIA *United States Tax Reporter*
Income, Estates, and Gifts	Spine Scan
BNA *Tax Management Portfolios*	Tax Treatises
CCH *Federal Tax Service*	Topical Tax Service
CCH *Standard Federal Tax Reports*	West Group *Mertens Law of*
Compilation	*Federal Income Taxation*
Finding List	

▶ Discussion Questions

1. Compare and contrast the general format of an annotated tax service with that of a topical tax service.
2. Why are the volumes of the annotated services called Compilation volumes?
3. Describe how the CCH and RIA annotated tax services are arranged.
4. Explain the paragraph numbering system used in the CCH and RIA annotated tax services.
5. What feature does the CCH *Standard Federal Tax Reports* include in its service that RIA's *United States Tax Reporter* does not include but offers as a separate service?
6. In using the annotated compilations effectively, what step number is "find and analyze the relevant update materials and *Citator* materials"? Why is this step done before the "read the all primary materials" step?
7. What are the three major methods of searching for materials in the compilations?
8. What are annotations?
9. What information would a researcher discover by performing a spine scan?
10. How does a researcher enter the RIA annotated service using a case name without using a citator?

11. How could a researcher use a Revenue Ruling to enter an annotated service?

12. Describe how the loose-leaf services are updated. How often does the updating occur?

13. What information is found in the CCH Volume 16, New Matters, and the RIA Volume 16, Recent Developments?

14. Which topical service discussed in this chapter is the most comprehensive in its coverage?

15. How are the Code, Regulations, cases, and rulings presented in a topical tax service?

16. Where are the Code sections relevant to a chapter's topic found in a topical service?

17. How are the BNA *Tax Management Portfolios* different from the RIA *Coordinator*?

18. How is each volume of the BNA *Tax Management Portfolios* arranged?

19. Where are copies of primary sources such as the *Internal Revenue Code* found in the BNA *Tax Management Portfolios*?

20. Describe the manner in which main text material is updated in the BNA *Tax Management Portfolios*? How often is the material updated?

21. What is the scope or objective of Bittker's *Federal Taxation of Income, Estates, and Gifts* service?

22. Describe the manner in which the volumes of Bittker's *Federal Taxation of Income, Estates, and Gifts* are updated. How often are new bound volumes published?

23. Describe the manner in which the main text material is updated in the *Mertens Law of Federal Income Taxation.*

24. Explain when the "snapshot" versions of previous years' Code, Regulations, and Rulings volumes in the *Mertens* service would be useful.

25. Why was the CCH *Federal Tax Service* not discussed in this chapter?

▶ _____ Exercises

26. Indicate the relevant Code section and the nature of the material found in each of the following CCH *Standard Federal Tax Reports* paragraphs:

   a. ¶12622.04
   b. ¶18925
   c. ¶ 26,633.0225
   d. ¶5704.2892

27. Indicate the relevant Code section and the nature of the material found in each of the following RIA *United States Tax Reporter* paragraphs:

   a. ¶ 4712.02
   b. ¶ 6642.01
   c. ¶ 34062.06
   d. ¶ 10165.32(5)

28. Indicate the relevant Code section and the nature of the material found in each of the following RIA *Federal Tax Coordinator 2d* paragraphs:

   a. ¶A-8501
   b. ¶ G-5464

    c. ¶ E-5203

    d. ¶ K-5341

29. Distinguish the attributes and location of the CCH and RIA annotated tax services case finding lists.

30. Locate each of the following topics in the main topical index of CCH's *Standard Federal Tax Reports*. Give the first paragraph number listed for each.

    a. Medical deduction

    b. Foreign tax credit

    c. Wash sales

    d. Golden parachutes

31. Repeat Exercise 30 using RIA's *United States Tax Reporter.*

32. Repeat Exercise 30 using RIA's *Federal Tax Coordinator 2d.*

33. Repeat Exercise 30 using *Mertens Law of Federal Income Taxation.*

34. Locate the material on vacation homes in CCH's *Standard Federal Tax Reports.*

    a. In what volume is the primary discussion?

    b. What is the paragraph number of the first Code section?

    c. What is the paragraph number of the first Regulation?

    d. What is the paragraph number of the first Service discussion?

    e. What is the paragraph number of the first annotation?

35. Repeat Exercise 34 using RIA's *United States Tax Reporter.*

36. Locate the discussion of Rev. Rul. 97–32 in CCH's *Standard Federal Tax Reports.*

    a. What is the number of the volume where you found this discussion?

    b. At what paragraph did you find this discussion?

    c. What is the subject matter of this discussion?

37. Repeat Exercise 36 using RIA's *United States Tax Reporter.*

38. Repeat Exercise 36 using RIA's *Federal Tax Coordinator 2d.*

39. Repeat Exercise 36 using *Mertens Law of Federal Income Taxation.*

40. Identify the paragraphs in the CCH *Standard Federal Tax Reports* that include a discussion of the following cases:

    a. *Morton Zuckerman*

    b. *Shirley McVay Wiseman*

    c. *Sun Micro Systems* (the 1995 decision)

    d. *William H. Roundtree*

41. Repeat Exercise 40 using RIA's *United States Tax Reporter.*

42. Repeat Exercise 40 using RIA's *Federal Tax Coordinator 2d.*

43. Repeat Exercise 40 using *Mertens Law of Federal Income Taxation.*

44. Identify the CCH and RIA service paragraph number at which each of the following finding lists commences.

    a. Revenue Rulings

    b. Private Letter Rulings

    c. Executive Orders

    d. Current listing, Private Letter Rulings

45. Use RIA's *Federal Tax Coordinator 2d* to locate a Proposed Regulation and to answer the following questions.

    a. Where was the regulation located?
    b. State its general content, including the Code section(s) to which it relates.
    c. When was it first published?

46. Repeat Exercise 45 using BNA's *Tax Management Portfolios* and a different Proposed Regulation.

47. Repeat Exercise 45 using Bittker's *Federal Taxation of Income, Estates, and Gifts* and a different Proposed Regulation.

48. Use RIA's *Federal Tax Coordinator 2d* to locate a Final Regulation and to answer the following questions.

    a. Where was the regulation located?
    b. State its general content, including the Code section(s) to which it relates.
    c. When was it first adopted? If amended, date amended? Where is this "historical" information about the Regulation located?

49. Repeat Exercise 48 using BNA's *Tax Management Portfolios* and a different Final Regulation.

50. Repeat Exercise 48 using Bittker's *Federal Taxation of Income, Estates, and Gifts* and a different Final Regulation.

51. Use BNA's *Tax Management Portfolios* to answer the following questions.

    a. In what portfolio is the main discussion of bad debts?
    b. Who is (are) the author(s) of the bad debts portfolio?
    c. What is the topic discussed at Section IX of this portfolio?
    d. How many worksheets are in the Working Papers section of this portfolio?
    e. What are the titles of the first two worksheets in the Working Papers section?

52. Use BNA's *Tax Management Portfolios* to answer the following questions.

    a. Which portfolio(s) discuss(es) the deductibility of gifts to clients? When was the most recent update for the portfolio(s).
    b. In the discussion of the deductibility of fines and penalties, what Ninth Circuit case is cited as concerning a "responsible person" penalty?
    c. Which portfolio(s) address(es) whether chemicals and fertilizers must be capitalized into the cost of the crop for family farmers? What authority is offered to support the treatment suggested?

53. Use BNA's *Tax Management Portfolios* to answer the following questions.

    a. Where do you find a discussion of the gain recognition being accelerated for a seller of nondepreciable property using installment reporting if the buyer was a related party and makes an early "second disposition" of the property? What Code section is cited? What case is suggested as an example?
    b. Where do you find the cutoff rule concerning related party resales? What Code section should be cited in this analysis?

54. Answer these questions concerning Bittker's *Federal Taxation of Income, Estates, and Gifts.*

    a. How many volumes are there in the service?

  b. How is each volume arranged?

  c. Where are copies of primary sources such as the *Internal Revenue Code* found?

55. Use Bittker's *Federal Taxation of Income, Estates, and Gifts* to answer the following questions.

  a. What is the first topic discussed in Volume 3?

  b. What is the first paragraph number of the corporate formation (§ 351) discussion?

  c. What is the nature of the discussion found at ¶ 54.2.1?

  d. How many footnotes are in ¶ 54.2.1?

  e. In the Bittker service, are footnotes short annotations or just citations to primary sources?

56. Use Bittker's *Federal Taxation of Income, Estates, and Gifts* to answer the following questions.

  a. According to the Supreme Court case of *Diedrich v. CIR,* the payment of gift taxes by the donee may result in a taxable gain for the donor. State the circumstances that will cause this to happen.

  b. What is the official citation for *Diedrich v. CIR*?

  c. Give the volume and page number of the *Iowa Law Review* that has a comment on this case.

57. Use Bittker's *Federal Taxation of Income, Estates, and Gifts* to answer the following questions.

  a. What is meant by the statement that no foreign tax credit will be available to the extent that the foreign country's tax is found to be a "soak-up" tax?

  b. What case, Revenue Ruling, or Regulation should be cited in this analysis?

58. Use Mertens *Law of Federal Income Taxation* to answer the following questions.

  a. What is the topic discussed in Chapter 12B?

  b. Who is (are) the author(s) of Chapter 12B?

  c. What are the first two footnotes used in the chapter?

  d. In what volume are the Regulations for § 1033 found?

59. Use Mertens *Law of Federal Income Taxation* to answer the following questions, stating where the discussion of the relevant law is found.

  a. The sale of a patent by the original individual inventor generally is treated as a capital gains transaction. Is this true even for a professional inventor?

  b. According to the footnotes to the paragraph that reviews the historical development of this tax benefit, one house of Congress would have allowed this treatment only if payments were made in full within five years from the date of sale. Which house would have imposed this restriction? Can payments be contingent on profits earned by the buyer from the patent?

  c. In the *Mertens* service, are footnotes short annotations or just citations to primary sources?

60. Use Mertens *Law of Federal Income Taxation* to answer the following questions, stating where the discussion of the relevant law is found.

    a. Can a hospital be a charitable institution even though it charges market rates for its services?

    b. What case, Revenue Ruling, or Regulation is cited for the proposition that a tax-exempt hospital can charge a physician reasonable fees for the use of its facilities?

▶ _____ Research Cases

61. Three friends form a small manufacturing partnership, each owning equal interests. Their contributions to the start-up entity are as follows.

Glen   Cash $10,000; equipment, FMV $5,000, basis $4000

Alex   Land with a small building, FMV $70,000, basis $20,000, recourse mortgage $55,000 (assumed by the partnership)

Debra   Neither cash nor other property, just extensive and valuable business knowledge.

    a. Use both an annotated and a topical service to determine the partners' bases in their respective partnership interests, and the partnership's basis in each of the assets transferred to it. State a general rule for deriving such computations, and cite a primary law source to back up your comments.

    b. Provide the locations of each of the indicated items of information for both of the services, relative to the preparation of your answer to part (a).

    c. With respect to the current-matter sections of both services, did you find any items relevant? If so, identify them. If not, what came closest in subject matter to being related to the tax issue on which you were working?

62. Can a business traveler to your town use the high-cost-city meal allowance for travel away from home overnight? Using the CCH annotated service, in which volume and on which page did you find the answer? What would the meal allowance be for a business trip to Washington, DC? Using an RIA topical service, in which volume and on which page did you find the answer?

63. Using a tax service of your choice, discuss the tax consequences of an NCAA athletic scholarship.

    a. Is any gross income created upon its receipt?

    b. How is the dependency exemption of the parent affected by the scholarship?

    c. Can the athlete claim deductions for any of her or his expenses with respect to clothing, equipment, meals, trainer's fees, or summer conditioning camps?

    d. How does your analysis change with respect to payments received by the athlete outside of NCAA rules?

    e. How does your analysis change with respect to payments received by the athlete in violation of criminal law?

    f. Which tax service did you use and why did you choose that tax service?

64. Repeat Research Case 63 using a different tax service.

    a. What were the advantages, if any, of the service you chose to use first in answering Research Case 63 over the second service chosen for this case?

    b. What were the advantages, if any, of the second service you chose over the first service chosen for case 63?

    c. Which service do you prefer for this type of research and why do you prefer it?

65. Brian's alimony payments to Anne drop from $1,000 per month to $400 per month for the three months each year during which the children visit him. What are the tax effects related to this transaction? List the steps that you went through to reach your conclusion using both an annotated and a topical service.

66. Nancy and Curtis had not spoken to each other since their mother's funeral in 1971. Nancy broke the family discord this year by selling to Curtis a family heirloom, basis to her $10,000, for $1,700. Use an annotated and a topical service to determine whether Nancy can deduct this loss. Reference the paragraph numbers in the service that you used to answer this question.

67. Use BNA's *Tax Management Portfolios* to address the following tax problem. Tillie received a lump-sum distribution from her qualified pension plan in the form of $300,000 cash and IBM stock worth $100,000. Within fifteen days, she contributed $400,000 cash to her IRA. What is Tillie's gross income from the distribution? Indicate which portfolio(s) (name and number) you used in addressing this issue. What pages within the portfolio(s) were most useful?

68. Use BNA's *Tax Management Portfolios* to address the following tax problem. Dolores is a limited partner in the Houston Hopes partnership. This year, she was forced under the terms of the agreement to make a $50,000 contribution to capital because the general partners were unable to meet the operating expenses of the entity. Dolores's basis in the partnership prior to the contribution was $40,000, but her at-risk amount was zero because of her limited partner status and her prior-year pass-through losses. What is her at-risk amount after the $50,000 cash call?

69. Use BNA's *Tax Management Portfolios* to address the following tax problem. Steve is an usher at his local church. May he deduct as a charitable contribution the commuting expenses for the Sundays that he is assigned to usher? Give the portfolio name and page numbers you used in solving this case.

70. Use Mertens *Law of Federal Income Taxation* to address the following tax problem. Phil is a used-car manager. To obtain advanced skills in management and marketing, he enrolls in the weekend MBA program at Montana State University, twenty miles from his home. What items associated with Phil's education are deductible, assuming that he receives no reimbursements for any of them?

71. Jon and Mary have been married for twenty years. Without Mary's knowledge, Jon has been operating as a bookie at his local pub. This year's earnings from the operation were the highest ever. In fact, if Jon had reported any of the net gambling income, their joint federal income tax liability would have increased by $140,000. When Jon finally is nabbed by the FBI, he is taken to jail. Mary is unable to locate any of Jon's earnings in bank or brokerage accounts. Can Mary fend off the IRS's charge that she should pay the $140,000 in tax, plus interest and penalties, from her salary as a physician? Use a service of your choice to answer this case.

72. Maria has an unusually strong constitution and the highest quality blood and plasma available for transfusion. She manages to stay healthy while donating blood at the hospital two or three times a week. For each donation, the Blood Center pays Maria $175 for the blood. Maria drives forty miles round-trip to the hospital to make her donation. Moreover, she spends about $35 every month for vitamins and other pills prescribed by her physician to ensure that her general health and blood quality do not degenerate in light of her frequent donations. Last year, Maria quit all of her part-time jobs and now survives financially solely by these blood donations. Specify the tax consequences of this regular activity. Use a service of your choice to answer this case.

73. Chang, a brain surgeon, pays for the *Journal of Brain Research* under the three-year plan: he paid $3,000 this year for a three-year subscription to the weekly scientific journal, which charges $1,500 for an annual renewal. In what year(s) can Chang deduct this $3,000? Use a service of your choice to answer this case.

74. Handy Corporation assists its relocated executives by buying their homes if an acceptable deal cannot be struck before the move. Purchase is made at appraised value. What is the nature of Handy's gain or loss on subsequent sale? Use a service of your choice to answer this case.

75. Summarize the income tax treatment surrounding the assignment of book, movie, and photo rights concerning the trial of Heidi Fleiss. Use a service of your choice to answer this case.

76. Hugo was burying his (dead) dog when he unearthed 100,000 certificates of ITT bearer bonds, current value $4,000,000. He speculated that they had been placed there by the (also dead) former owner of Hugo's home, at a time when they were worth nearly $400,000. Hugo did not sell the bonds by the end of the year. Must Hugo recognize any gross income with respect to the bonds? Use a service of your choice to answer this case.

77. Using the experience that you developed in completing the exercises and research cases, prepare a brief list comparing the relative advantages and drawbacks of the CCH and RIA annotated services.

78. Using the experience that you developed in completing the exercises and research cases, prepare a brief list comparing the relative advantages and drawbacks of the annotated services and topical services.

Computer Tax Services

LEARNING OBJECTIVES

► Understand the advantages and disadvantages of published and computerized tax services

► Know the major features of computerized tax services

► Use the key word, Code section, and court case methods to find relevant materials in the computerized tax services

► Know which tax services are most appropriate for different research objectives

CHAPTER OUTLINE

Published Versus Computerized
Currency
Accessing Information
Computerized Services
The Research Process
Illustrative Example
Approaching the Research Problem
Assessing Computerized Tax Information

RIA CHECKPOINT
Key Word Search
Case and Code Searches
CCH Tax Research NetWork
WESTLAW
LEXIS
Kleinrock
Other Internet Sites

Chapter 7 explored the published versions of the major tax services and discussed the steps important in developing effective and efficient tax research. This chapter surveys the computerized tax services available to the practitioner. Most of the services examined in detail in Chapter 7 are computer accessible through CD-ROMs, online services, and over the Internet. Each of these computer media could be examined individually, but the similarities in use of the products makes it more productive to discuss their common features.

The tremendous benefit of any computerized tax service is its ability to store immense amounts of information in a small physical space (or even off-site via online and Internet services), and then to find, organize, and display the information very quickly. Further, the computerized tax services can link references to full-text documents making retrieval of the relevant data virtually **seamless.** The methods of accessing this wealth of computerized information are essentially the same for **CD-ROM, online,** and **Internet services.** Based on this notion, access to the computerized tax services will cover all three media but only one media will be illustrated for each service.

Published Versus Computerized

More and more tax information is becoming available through computers. However, more information does not translate to more effective research. This is because more information takes more time to sort, read, and comprehend, which can lead to information overload and inefficiency. For example, using the key words "business expense, illegal payments, and kickbacks" from the example research problem in Chapter 7 produced more than 200 possible documents to examine. This is too many to consider efficiently. Thus, the information obtained needs to be managed; otherwise, using computers for tax research can be less effective than using published tax services.

In addition, with the nationwide increase of computer use, access to computerized information can be delayed as a result of having to wait for terminal use or because Internet connections are overused. The advancements in graphics for web pages have also caused a slowdown in access of information as the user waits for all the images to load. It is sometimes faster, therefore, to look up the answer to a simple question in a desk copy of the CCH *Master Tax Guide* than to log on the computer and search for the solution. With these caveats aside, computers can greatly increase the efficiency and effectiveness of tax research through instant access to an abundance of primary sources and explanations of the tax law.

Currency

One of the great advantages of the Internet is the currency of the information it provides. For published services, changes in the tax law must be processed by editors, printed, shipped, and then, with loose-leaf services, filed by the practitioner or employee. This can result in a substantial time lag, especially if the updates are not filed on a weekly basis. Further, there is the likelihood of human filing errors—and a page misfiled is information lost to the researcher. For services that are not loose-leaf, the practitioner must constantly refer to the supplements to ensure that the information read is up to date.

CD-ROMs overcome the drudgery of filing updates and the possibility of misfiled information. The cost, however, is that CD-ROM services are generally updated only monthly. Alternatively, most Internet services update **in-text** (i.e., no supplements) on a daily or continuous basis. Keep in mind that daily updating does not necessarily mean that what happened yesterday will be accessible today. Processing time is still required. It does mean, however, that as soon as the information is processed it can be entered into the system. There is no waiting to batch information for distribution.

Accessing Information

In defense of published tax services, books offer a level of browsing ability that cannot be attained with computerized services. With a published service, researchers can scan the binders to determine which one is related to their area of interest. They can flip through the pages until they find an entry that looks relevant or interesting. The computerized services are not structured to facilitate this type of browsing. Each document or section of explanation is treated as a separate retrievable document; access of a complete binder of information is not possible. This is a problem when the researcher knows the general area of interest but not the specifics. There is a place for both published and computerized services in many research projects.

The most common entry to a published tax service is through its index. The usefulness of an index is limited by the perspicacity of the indexer. Frequently, a researcher cannot find the specific topic in the index because the terms the indexer uses are not the ones the researcher anticipates. In paper-based research, one must become efficient at using preorganized finding devices developed by third parties.

The key word **full-text search** is the computerized version of the index. This technique can be much more powerful than a traditional index. A full-text search locates every occurrence of a word or phrase in everything from a single document to an entire collection of documents. It can be quick and easy when the appropriate words or phrases for the search are selected. The downside, however, is that *every* occurrence of the word or phrase may not be relevant to the research. The context of the words is not evaluated by the computer. It is, therefore, important for tax professionals to learn to construct searches in an effective manner. If the key words are very selective, the research may be very precisely targeted. However, if the search terms are too narrow, they can miss important materials. This can result in reaching an inappropriate conclusion. If the terms are too broad, the information overload problem will materialize. An effective search saves time by relieving the researcher of reviewing materials that are not on point.

Computerized Services

The number of tax resources offered in computer-compatible media is expanding rapidly. Some tax services simply compile primary source information obtained from the government while others originate the information and include substantial analysis. CD-ROM tax resources have been very popular, in part, due to their ability to replace large primary source tax libraries with just a few CDs. While the amount varies with the nature of the material and how much information the publisher chooses to put on a particular CD-ROM, the standard disk can hold more than 250,000 pages of text, or as much as 100 feet of bookshelf space. An added advantage of a CD-ROM's storage ability is that the information is accessible through the computer without having to be loaded on the computer. Valuable hard disk space is not usurped by the data contained on the CDs.

CD-ROMs are particularly suited to maintaining archival information that a practitioner needs to access fairly frequently. Yet, CD-ROM services are becoming old technology as more commercial publishers are offering their products through the Internet. One strategy of practitioners is to do as much research as possible on CD-ROMs, and then go to an online or Internet service, briefly (due to some services's search-time charges), to procure the most current information. While practitioners can retrieve many primary tax sources through the Internet free (see the exhibits at the end of the chapter), this free access cannot substitute for the comprehensive tax services. Besides checking the validity of primary tax sources, tax services furnish various methods of searching the tax sources, editorial analysis and comments, organization, and an integration of the tax resources.

With CD-ROM services (as well as published services), the practitioner has to be in physical possession of the product. If the practitioner is not at the same location as the CDs, access is unavailable. The Internet, in most situations, provides the practitioner access to information from any locality equipped with a computer and a modem. This means research can be performed at a client's office or late at night at home. Some services, however, such as WESTLAW and LEXIS, do require proprietary software be loaded on the computer before Internet access is available.

The Research Process

As in Chapter 7, we will use an actual research problem to explore the use of each computerized tax service. It is important that **you** attempt the illustrative research project using the computerized tax services available to you. The procedural knowledge necessary for efficient use of computerized tax services can only be required through hands-on practice. The remainder of this chapter is designed to guide you through the basic computer services and is *not* a substitute for you actually using the services.

Illustrative Example

The sample research project concerns the following situation.

> **Example 8–1** Our client, Ms. Sanski, an executive with International Marketing, was a guest professor at a local university for one semester. She found that one of the tenured professors, Dr. Nu, shared her interest in the acquisition and distribution networks for products during the European Renaissance. They decided to write a book on the subject and began working in March of the current year. Most of the documents they needed for the book, however, were located in Europe. In June, Ms. Sanski and Dr. Nu traveled to Italy, France, and Spain to examine documents germane to their book. Returning to the United States, they stopped in Washington, DC, to gather more information at the Library of Congress. By the end of the current year, they expect to have collected most of the materials needed for writing the book. Ms. Sanski has

incurred all of the expenses in obtaining these materials. Actual writing of the book will start next year and should be completed by the end of that year. When they have several chapters of the book written, they will contact a publisher. They hope the book will come out in print within one year of completing the manuscript. Ms. Sanski wants to deduct all of the costs associated with data collection in the current year. Ms. Sanski asks you if it is possible to treat the costs as business expenses in the current year.

Approaching the Research Problem

Regardless of the media used for tax research, the starting point in approaching any tax research problem is to formulate the tax question being asked. Our research question appears to be this: How should the current expenses for a book that may be published in the future be treated for tax purposes? Should they be immediately expensed or capitalized and expensed as the revenues from the book are received? This formulation of questions suggests that the main issue is expensing versus capitalization of the author's business costs. Therefore, the relevant key words appear to be *author, business, expenses,* and *capitalization.* From your basic knowledge of the Code you know that capitalization of costs is governed by § 263A, the uniform capitalization rules. Finally, in your prior research of other topics you have seen references to a case called *Hadley* that was about an author's prepublication expenses. The case is old but it may have some bearing on situation.

Assessing Computerized Tax Information

The research steps presented in Chapter 7, when slightly modified, are applicable to research using computer services. As with published services, the key to effective tax research is finding the pertinent material necessary to formulate an informed conclusion about the optimum treatment of the transaction. How the computer tax services are entered will determine how efficiently the relevant material is found. Some services present the documents found in some order of relevance to the search. Other services list the documents and let the researcher decide which documents should be examined first. Regardless of the order displayed, a researcher unfamiliar with the topic should start with an editorial explanation of the topic. This overview of the topic will help a researcher identify the most pertinent elements of the project and introduce the primary tax law relevant to the topic. It is easy to gain access to the primary sources from the explanation because they are usually directly linked to their citations.

From this initial analysis, a researcher may decide that a new more targeted search is warranted. Once the relevant primary sources are identified, but before they are carefully read, it is necessary to determine which of the sources are still good law by checking them through a citator. The fact that the tax service locates a document and places it high on the relevance list does not mean the researcher can assume it is still valid law. The last step, as Chapter 7 indicated, is to read carefully the selected primary tax law sources that are germane to the tax question. After evaluating these sources, the optimum treatment for the item in question can be ascertained.

Keep in mind that the commercial providers of CD-ROM, online, and Internet tax services offer a plethora of tax products (databases) that can be bundled in a variety of ways. This chapter's description of the tax databases within any of the services may not be what is available to the reader. Each firm (or library) performs a type of cost–benefit analysis and purchases only those resources that it can afford and finds useful in its practice. While all the tax databases may not be available to the reader, the basic methodology described here should apply to the databases to which the reader has access.

RIA CHECKPOINT

Computer services can be entered using the same three major methods utilized with published services: key word, Code section, and case name. How to use each method will be illustrated using **CHECKPOINT,** the RIA Internet tax service. This is one of the most authoritative and well-known Internet tax services available. The general computer research methodology that applies to CHECKPOINT also applies to its CD-ROM version, TAXPOINT. This presentation will be followed by less detailed examples of other Internet, online, and CD tax services.

CHECKPOINT provides the full gambit of federal tax information with several different product packages available. Depending on which services of CHECK-POINT are subscribed to, the costs can range from about $400 to more than $5,500 for one user license with unlimited access. The most inclusive package includes all primary tax sources, the *Federal Tax Coordinator 2d* (topical tax service), the *United States Tax Reporter* (annotated tax service), *Citator 2nd Series* (citations before 1954 are not available), WG&L journals, WG&L textbooks, IRS publications, etc. With so much information available it is important to limit a search to only those databases that are pertinent to the research project; otherwise too many irrelevant documents will be retrieved. Hence, products like pension analysis and benefits analysis will be omitted from our project's search list.

Exhibit 8–1 shows the opening research screen that appears after the CHECK-POINT log-on screen. The choices on this screen allow a practitioner to proceed

EXHIBIT 8–1   RIA CHECKPOINT Main Menu screen

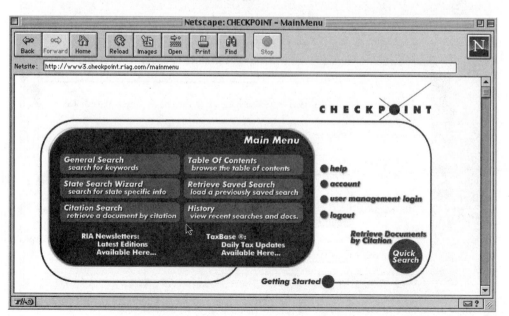

with the research or read the most recent news through *TaxBase®*, *Daily Tax Updates,* or the latest editions of the RIA newsletters, *Federal Taxes Weekly Alert* or *State & Local Taxes Weekly.* Since we are starting a new search, we can either select a general search by keyword or a citation search by case name or code section. Let's start with a key word search.

Key Word Search

At the General Search screen (Exhibit 8–2), the search terms are entered in the Keywords box. If an order to the words is desired, parentheses are used. To indicate that the words constitute a phrase "quotes" are used. For example, if we want *business expenses* to be treated as a phrase, we would type *"business expenses"* in the Keywords box. The spaces between words in phrases imply an *and* connection. For our search we are going to use the words *authors, business,* and *expenses.* CHECK-POINT will search for these exact words. If we want to search for *author* and *authors,* we need to put *author** where the asterisk is a holder for zero or more characters at the end of a word. To have the search include words that are synonymous with the key terms, a *$* is placed immediately after the word and a thesaurus search is performed. In our search, we could enter *expense$* and CHECKPOINT would also search for words like *cost* and *deductions.* Lastly, when a keyword has a irregular conjugation, such as the word *write,* placing a *%* after the word will ensure that *written,* and *wrote* are included in the search. More information on formatting keyword entries can be found by clicking on "Search Tips page" above the Keywords box. The box below the key words retains previous keyword searches. These may be selected to rerun a search perhaps using a different database or search type.

EXHIBIT 8–2 RIA CHECKPOINT General Search screen

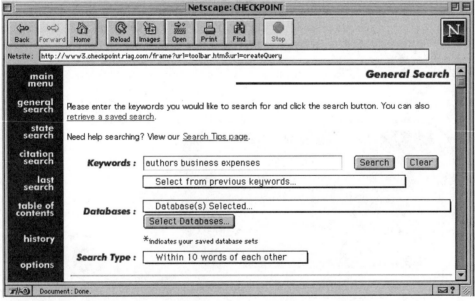

The Databases box has a pull-down file that lists the different databases available in the practitioner's CHECKPOINT package. To limit the databases searched to the particular needs of the research project, choose the button below the Databases box that says "Select Databases. . ." This will bring up a screen that is split in two vertically (Exhibit 8–3). The left half lists the Available Databases and the right half shows the Selected Databases. Below the title on each half of the screen, there is a Clear all Databases line that can be chosen for a fresh start. In addition, the left half of the screen lists the database names, Federal, State, International, Tax News Alert, and Saved, in the heading box. Depending on the background in the heading box, these may be hard to read (see Exhibit 8–3). The second part of the screen presents the actual lists of available (left half) and selected (right half) databases. By selecting a heading, all the databases below the heading are included in the search. If all the databases are not desired, individual databases can be selected. Whatever is selected in the left half of the screen will appear on the right half of the screen. After the selection process is complete, return to the General Search screen by selecting "Search" in the upper left-hand corner of the screen. This is much more efficient than using the Back button on the browser tool bar.

It is important that the databases be limited to those that are relevant to the current research project. For instance, without limiting the databases in our illustrative research problem , 405 documents containing our three key words were located. This is obviously too many documents to examine. Accordingly, our search was limited to only federal income tax databases.

The last selection to be made on the General Search screen is the **Search Type.** The pull-down menu for this box appears in Exhibit 8–4. The choices are Folio/Boolean Syntax, All of these keywords, Any of these words, This exact phrase,

EXHIBIT 8–3   RIA CHECKPOINT Databases screen

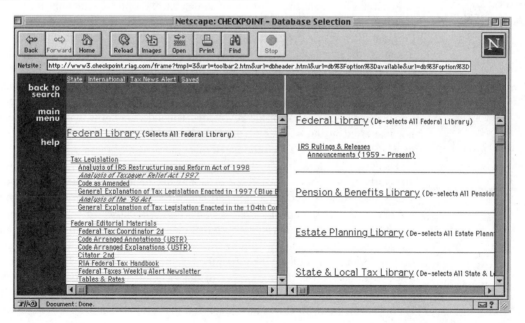

EXHIBIT 8–4 RIA CHECKPOINT Search Types

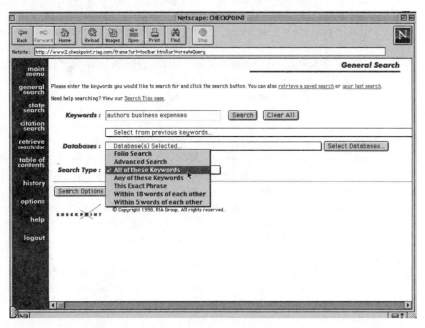

Within 10 words of each other, and Within 5 words of each other. The default is within 10 words of each other. Our search was initially performed with "All of these keywords," which means any document containing all of these words anywhere in their text were selected. This presented a problem. As previously discussed, a full-text search looks for the term *authors* anywhere in the text of the documents. It is not considering our desire that the document be about the taxation of author's expenses. The program literally searches for the term. Thus, every document about business expenses that listed who was the *author* of the document was selected. Regulations, for examples, often have in their last paragraph "the authors of this Regulation are . . . ." If the Regulation discussed business expenses, it was included in the document list. This problem would not occur with a published service because the indexers take into consideration context of the key words. The indexers know that the researcher is not interested in the authors of the Regulations. Therefore, using the "Within 10 words of each" Search Type eliminated most but not all of these selections.

Using only Federal income tax databases and searching for the keywords within 10 words of each other, the search produced six documents. With only six documents, one wonders whether all the pertinent information has been found. Moreover, not one of the six documents was a Code section. Because we were expecting that § 263A might apply, there is a concern that the search was too narrow. Accordingly, the search was expanded by running the search without *business* as a key word. To do this, "Modify Search" at the top of the Database List (Exhibit 8–5) was selected. This selection returns the researcher to the General Search screen (Exhibit 8–2). Using the new key words produced eleven documents (see Exhibit 8–5). These results seems more likely to have captured the relevant sources. Unlike other tax

EXHIBIT 8–5   RIA CHECKPOINT Database List screen

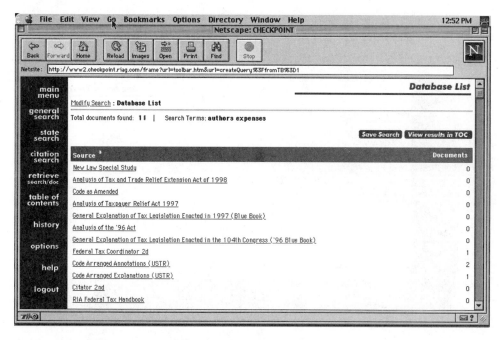

services, CHECKPOINT displays in which databases the documents are found. Hence, for our search, there is one document in the *Federal Tax Coordinator 2d* and there are two documents in Code Arranged Annotations (this is the *United States Tax Reporter*). Normally the Database List screen also lists the terms it searched. However, if the special key word options like *, $, or % are utilized in the search, the program does not list the terms used for the search in the top portion of this screen.

Clicking on *Federal Tax Coordinator 2d* in the Document List produces a screen that summarizes what documents from the search are found in the *Coordinator*. Clicking on any item on this screen displays the full text of the item. For our project, the *Coordinator* section retrieved in the Document View screen concerns "Films, sound recordings, video tapes, books, etc." (Exhibit 8–6). Notice that this screen supplies a record of the location of the particular section being retrieved.

Selecting the First keyword ▶ button displays the first occurrence of any one of the key words. The key words throughout the text are highlighted for easy identification. Also highlighted are any cites in the explanation that are linked to the full-text documents.

While browsing the text in the Document View screen, buttons are available at the bottom of the screen that allow the researcher to move from one document to the next. The "Doc 1 of 11" in our case would allow us to go to any of the documents by clicking on the forward or backward arrows. The other buttons at the bottom of the screen are self-explanatory with the exception of "View Text." This button merely displays the text full screen rather than having the left side bar that appears in each screen.

EXHIBIT 8–6   RIA CHECKPOINT Document View screen

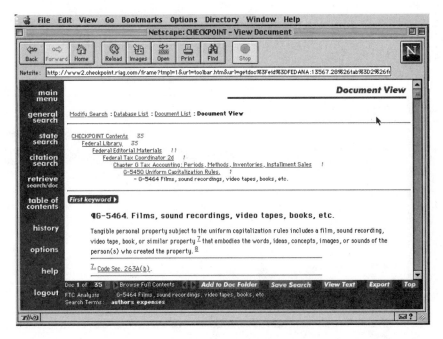

Case and Code Searches

To perform a search by case name or Code section, choose Citation Search on the opening research screen (see Exhibit 8–1). This search type was briefly described in Chapter 6, under the CCH and RIA Citators heading. The following description will provide more details of this search process.

The Citation Search screen requires that a database be selected before the search can commence. Notice that only one of the databases may be selected at a time (Exhibit 8–7). This is one drawback of using the Citator Search. After the database is chosen [American Federal Tax Reports (1860–1997) for our project], clicking on the Display Template button displays the next screen. This screen provides templates for entering the citation of the case to be located. Unlike the other major computer citator services, CHECKPOINT allows the researcher to enter the name of the case or its citation. Key words can also be entered in lieu of the name or citation. As can be seen in Exhibit 8–8, the templates make entering the citation quite simple. The AFTR2d citation for the *Hadley* case has been entered for our illustrative project. The results of the search appear on the next screen. Click on the citation for the case and it appears in full text (Exhibit 8–9). The full citation is given at the top of the screen along with the Code section to which the case applies.

As with the published services, a case can be used as entry into the services. The buttons that appear above the citation for the *Hadley* case allow the researcher to examine the annotation for the case or provide entry into the *Federal Tax Coordi-*

EXHIBIT 8–7   RIA CHECKPOINT Citation Search screen

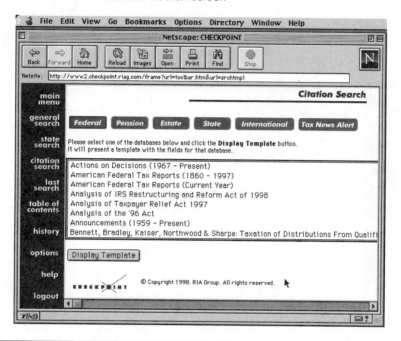

nator (FTC) service. Selecting the FTC button, lists the two paragraphs in the *Federal Tax Coordinator* that reference the *Hadley* case (Exhibit 8–10). The paragraph regarding writers, L-4110, is relevant to our research project. Clicking on this paragraph number retrieves the document view of the paragraph (Exhibit 8–11). This paragraph appears to provide a solution to our research question. Since the solution is based on the *Hadley* case, we should check this case through the citator to make sure that it is still good law.

Going back to the Citation Search, we would now select the *Citator 2nd* database. The search can be designated to yield citations for the cited case, citing cases, or both. Selecting both, the results of the search appear in Exhibit 8–12. Reviewing this screen indicates that several cases were combined with the *Hadley* case upon appeal to the Second Circuit. The *Susan Bryant, Lloyd McKim Garrison,* and *Messina Builders & Contractors Co.* cases all have the same citation, 59 AFTR 2d 87-1078. Since the *Hadley* case involved more than one issue, these cases may not be relevant to the treatment of the prepublication expenses. Clicking on the *Hadley* Second Circuit reference displays the citing cases with the RIA notations regarding the holdings of this and other courts that have cited this case (Exhibit 8–13). Rather than using the symbols discussed in Chapter 6, the notations are written out making it easier to immediately determine the relevances of the cases. In examining the list of cases, we find that *Hadley* has not been overruled on the writing issue but the *Doubleday & Co.* case does distinguish itself from *Hadley*. This case should be examined to determine if its facts more closely resemble those of our client.

To search by Code section, choose the Current Code database at the Citation Search screen (Exhibit 8–7). The template for the Code sections that appears is

EXHIBIT 8–8 RIA CHECKPOINT Citation Input screen

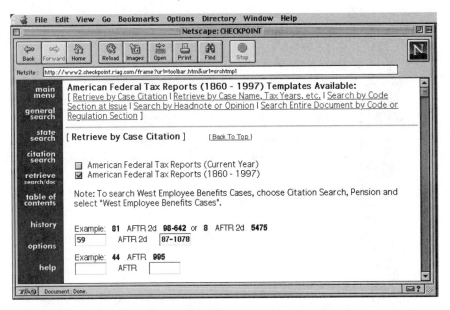

EXHIBIT 8–9 RIA CHECKPOINT Document View screen

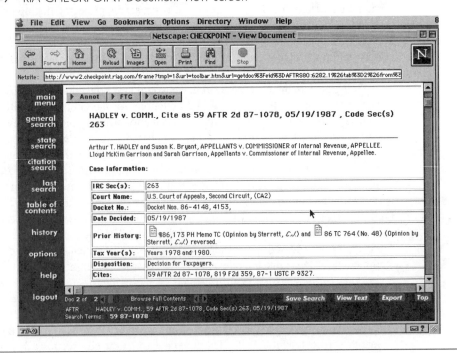

EXHIBIT 8–10   RIA CHECKPOINT Reference FTC paragraphs

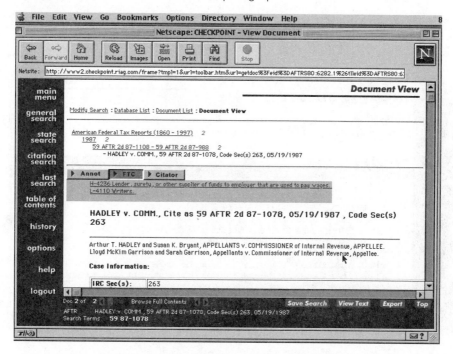

EXHIBIT 8–11   RIA CHECKPOINT *Federal Tax Coordinator* paragraph

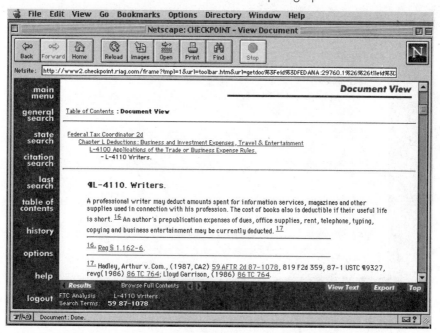

EXHIBIT 8–12   RIA CHECKPOINT Citator 2nd results

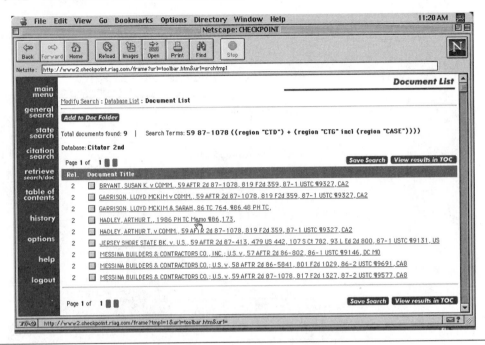

EXHIBIT 8–13   RIA CHECKPOINT *Hadley* citations

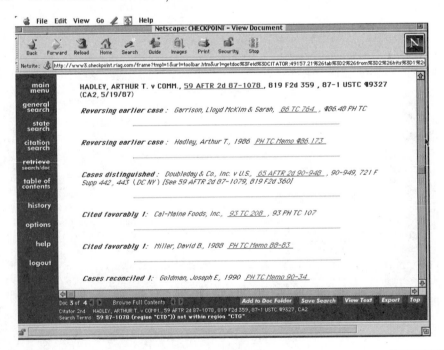

shown in Exhibit 8–14. Note that, as with cases, the researcher may enter key words as well as the Code section number. The result of our search is the full text of § 263A for which the initial screen is reproduced in Exhibit 8–15. The top part of the screen contains the exact location of the Code section within the *Internal Revenue Code,* providing the Subtitle, Chapter, Subchapter, Part, and Section numbers.

With a case or Code section search, the results are the specific case or section. These types of searches do not facilitate the retrieval of other documents that might be relevant to the research project. To use cases or Code sections to locate other documents, a key word search would be employed. It would be important with this type of search to include other key words to ensure that *every* document containing the name of the taxpayer or the Code section number is not retrieved. These latter searches are not demonstrated because they would follow the same steps as any key word search.

CCH Tax Research NetWork

Like RIA, CCH has a CD-ROM and an Internet tax service. Again, we will focus on the Internet service; however, a little background on the CD-ROM services will be provided. The CD-ROM service, called ACCESS, is based on the *Standard Federal Tax Reports* (SFTR), the annotated tax service discussed in detail in Chapter 7. CCH also has a topical service, CCH's *Federal Tax Service* (CFTS), that as of August 1998, is available to new subscribers only on CD-ROM or through the Internet. The CFTS's explanatory text, called the analysis, is divided into sixteen major topic

EXHIBIT 8–14   RIA CHECKPOINT Code Section input screen

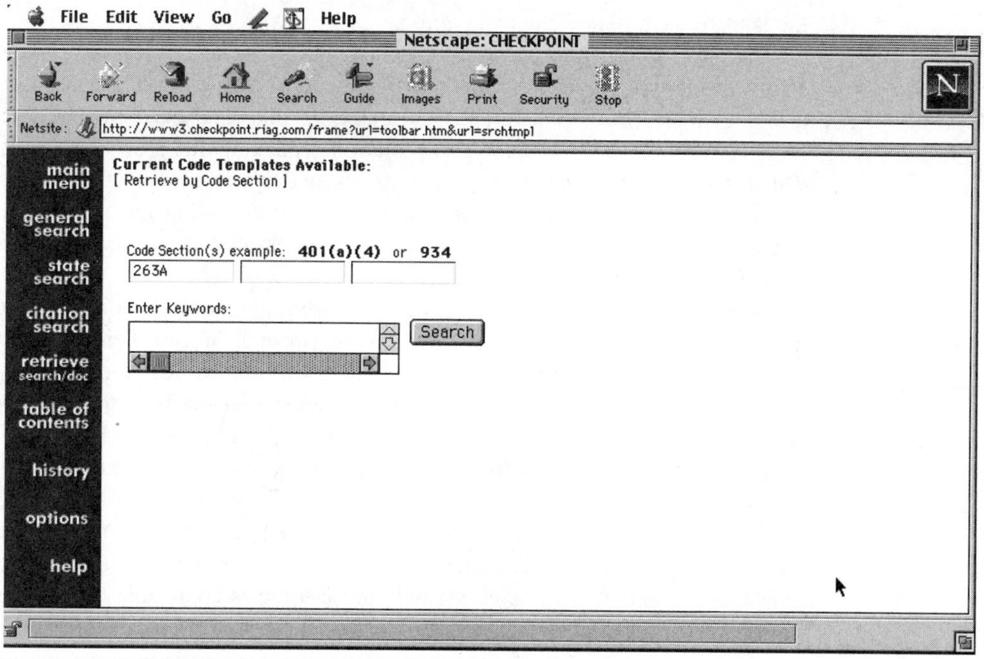

EXHIBIT 8–15   RIA CHECKPOINT Code Section screen

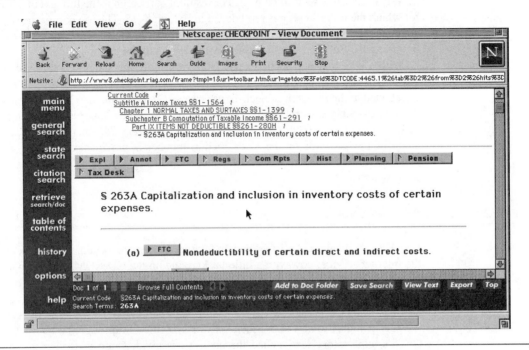

areas, designated A through P. Similar to the RIA *Coordinator,* it utilizes footnotes to direct researchers to primary sources. The editors' comments and evaluations of the law are the basis of the main text.

The CCH Internet tax service is called **Tax Research NetWork** (NetWork). Using the NetWork is fairly similar to using the RIA Internet service. The first screen after logging on provides a variety of search types and database choices. Current tax news is available in the opened news folder by selecting Tax News Direct (Exhibit 8–16). This news can be personalized to focus on only those areas of the tax law that are of particular interest to the practitioner. This time-saving feature alerts practitioners to tax law changes in their area of specialization without making them wade through all news articles for the day.

To begin a search project, one of the database folders must first be selected. The choices are Federal, State, Financial & Estate, Special Entities, Pension & Payroll, or International. The placement of these folders is a little confusing in that they must be selected before the Search Type but they appear in the bottom portion of the screen under the Search Types. For our project, the Federal database is selected (Exhibit 8–17). Within this folder there are a variety of resources from which to choose, including primary sources of tax law, CCH's annotated (SFTR) and topical (CFTS) tax services, the *Master Tax Guide,* IRS publications and manuals, legislative developments, etc. Researchers have the option of selecting all services within a database or individually selecting only those services applicable to their research project. If a researcher decides to change the selection, the Clear Selections button

EXHIBIT 8–16   CCH Tax Research Network opening screen

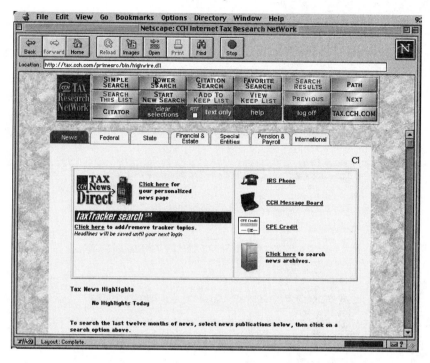

is clicked and the selection process can start over again, or the researcher can just unmark the database boxes not desired.

To locate editorial explanations on our research question, we selected only the SFTR and CFTS in the Federal tax folder. Reading these explanations will help develop an overview of the topic of our research. After locating and reading the explanation we ran the search again but changed our databases to include all primary tax sources as well. This method of searching ensures that in the first retrieval, the editorial explanations are at the top of the documents list. Unlike the RIA service, NetWork automatically sorts the document citations into their defined relevancy order and the editorial explanations are not always listed as highly relevant. The advantage of listing documents by their relevancy is that time is saved when sorting through the documents selected. The disadvantage is that NetWork's idea of relevancy may be different than the researcher's. If the disadvantages outweigh the advantages, this sorting feature can be disabled.

After selecting the database, the type of search desired must be selected. A Simple Search locates documents containing all of the words or phrases entered as key words, whereas a Power Search allows the search to be customized as to document types, dates, and word restrictions. Both of these searches will automatically apply a thesaurus to the key words selected, thus retrieving documents containing terms with similar meanings. This automatic thesaurus is an outstanding feature of NetWork because it simplifies the selection of key words. Another search type is the

EXHIBIT 8–17   CCH Tax Research NetWork Federal file screen

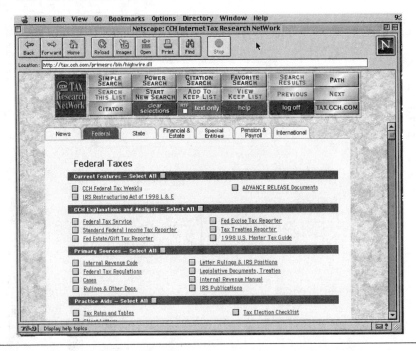

Citation Search, which accesses the CCH citator. This type of search was discussed in Chapter 6.

Having selected Power Search for our illustrative research, our key words are entered on the screen reproduced in Exhibit 8–18. Since the Search Method selected is All Terms, the spaces between the words imply an *and* connector. The other Search Methods available are Any of the Terms, Exact Phrase, the Terms Should Be Near to Each Other, or Boolean. The Power Search screen also allows the researcher to decide how many documents should be retrieved (50 is the default) and how the documents will be sorted. The default is to sort by relevance and apply the thesaurus. Not visible in Exhibit 8–18 are the boxes for restricting the dates of the documents retrieved. The part of the documents searched can also be designated as all parts, headings, topic, case-name, IRC-reference, and date. Lastly, the search can be limited as to the type of documents examined.

When the search is complete, NetWork provides a list of possible sources in relevancy order. The terms searched are furnished at the top of the page (Exhibit 8–19). Notice the extensive list of terms searched based on the three words we provided. Due to the breadth of the search, 1,015 documents were found. Many of these are documents regarding expenses that have the authors of the document listed and are not relevant to this project. This type of document, however, was not listed high on the relevancy list. To examine any of the sources on the document list, merely click on the highlighted name and the full-text document appears. If the listing is an explanation, any references to primary sources within the explanation will also be linked to their full text.

When the current search is completed, the researcher can click on Start New Search and it displays the initial research screen. Another search can be performed or the research can select the Log Off button and end the search program.

EXHIBIT 8–18   CCH Tax Research NetWork Power Search screen

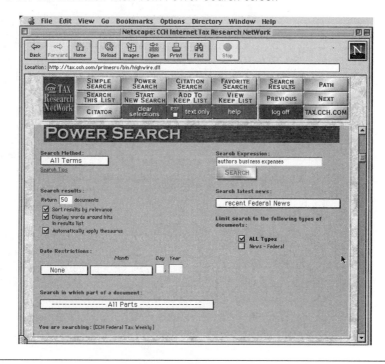

EXHIBIT 8–19   CCH Tax Research NetWork Document screen

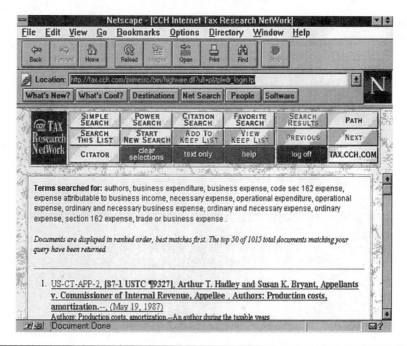

WESTLAW

Besides the citator services discussed in Chapter 6, the West Group, through WESTLAW, offers tax research capabilities. As mentioned in Chapter 7, WESTLAW is more legally oriented than the RIA or CCH because it is designed by and for attorneys. This legal orientation is evident in that the text material in its tax service, *Mertens,* is heavily footnoted and citators are emphasized in the service. (WESTLAW has five types of citators whereas CCH and RIA offer one type.) Because WESTLAW is more attorney oriented, it is less represented in accounting firms than RIA and CCH.

WESTLAW has a large data bank with information provided by numerous sources such as, BNA, CCH, DIALOG, H. W. Wilson Company, Shepard's, Tax Management, and the University of Washington. Access to these sources has traditionally been offered through a dedicated online service. WESTLAW is now available through the Internet but it requires the downloading of the *WESTMATE* software to access it. Depending on the modem speed, this software can take up to 50 minutes to load. *PREMISE* software, available on CD-ROM, may also be used to access WESTLAW online. Since the West Group illustrations in Chapter 6 were of WESTLAW using the WESTMATE software, the PREMISE platform will be utilized in these examples. There are some differences in the appearance of the screens and the order of the tool bar buttons between the two pieces of software, but they generally function in the same manner.

EXHIBIT 8–20 WESTLAW (PREMISE) opening screen

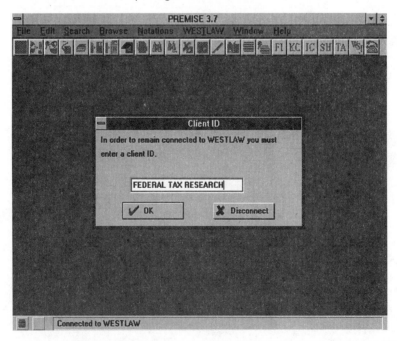

After the online "Welcome to PREMISE" screen, a Client ID screen appears (Exhibit 8–20). A client name must be entered in order to proceed with the research project. This is just another feature that is included for the benefit of attorneys. This allows the attorney to keep track of the research by client, and the program keeps track of the time spent on each search for billing purposes.

After selecting the databases to search and clicking on the search button, the next screen accepts the keywords for the search in the box called Terms and Connectors Query. The West Group products give the researcher the option of searching using either a Term Search or a Natural Language Search. The Natural Language Search allows the researcher to enter standard English (natural language) phrases or sentences. The tax question is entered and the program determines the key terms for searching. This type of search is useful when the researcher is not sure what the most effective key words would be. This natural language option, however, is not available with all databases offered by WESTLAW.

The Term Search is the standard key word search. A thesaurus is conveniently provided to help the researcher select the best words for the search. It is not automatically activated as in the NetWork program, however; the synonyms must be added to the key words by the researcher. The list of connectors and expanders available with a Term Search is expansive. Many of the relationships that can be designated are shown in Exhibit 8–21. For our project, the terms *authors & "business expenses"* were entered. Our method of entering the terms tells WESTLAW to look for *business expenses* as a single term and that both *business expenses* and *authors* must appear in the document. Unlike the other computerized tax services, in WESTLAW a space between two words is treated as *or* not as *and*.

EXHIBIT 8–21   WESTLAW (PREMISE) search screen

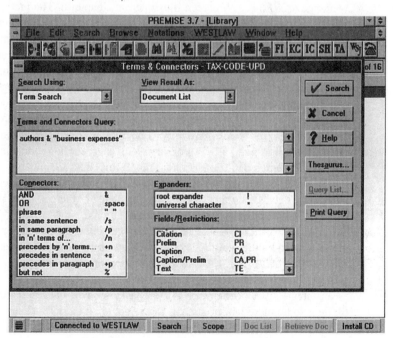

EXHIBIT 8–22   WESTLAW Mertens search screen

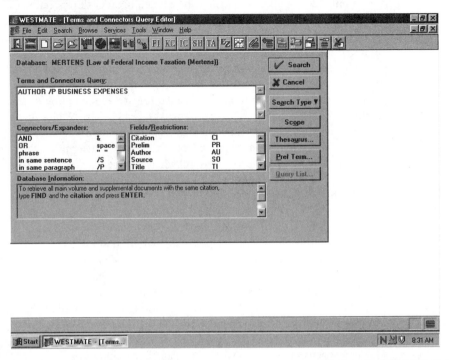

If WESTMATE is used to connect to WESTLAW, the researcher sees the same Welcome to WESTLAW screen illustrated in Chapter 6. The picture buttons on the left of the screen (see Chapter 6, Exhibit 6–18) contain two selections of interest for our current research project. The top picture button displays the databases available for searching and the second button reveals the researcher's customized list of WESTLAW databases. For instance, if the practitioner specializes in estate planning, the customized list might include only databases associated with estate taxes. At the bottom of the screen is a box in which the WESTLAW identifier code for a database (its abbreviation) can be entered. The identifier code for each data base is listed in the WESTLAW Database Directory. Since we are interested in obtaining explanatory information as well as primary sources regarding our illustrative project, *Mertens* is entered in the box. The Terms and Connectors Screen (Query Editor–Mertens) then appears. Exhibit 8–22 illustrates these features of WESTLAW. Notice that between *author* and *"business expenses"* there is *"/p,"* which means that the terms must appear within the same paragraph.

As with the other computerized tax services, the next screen is a list of the documents located by the search. Clicking on any of the document titles will retrieve its full text. *Mertens* is in a separate database category from the primary sources. In this respect, *Mertens* is treated more like a complement to the citator services rather than as an integral part of the WESTLAW package. This causes searches that include Mertens to be more laborious than when including the topical services in CCH and RIA searches.

LEXIS

The amount of information available through LEXIS/NEXIS is staggering. It has more than 13,500 business and news sources and 4,800 legal sources. There are 7,300 databases included in LEXIS/NEXIS, making it possibly the world's largest full-text information source. *LEXIS,* for legal (tax) sources, was started in 1973 and NEXIS, for news, financial, and business information, was started in 1979. The services were initially offered on dedicated terminals because they were available before the universal use of personal computers.

LEXIS is structured like a tree with a trunk and branches. The main libraries are the trunks, and the files within the libraries are the branches. For example, the main library screen shows the major areas in which the libraries are grouped (Exhibit 18–23). In the second section is the library for Federal taxes, FEDTAX (trunk). In choosing this library, the files (branches) within this library appear (Exhibit 18–24). Notice the variety of files within this library. All of the primary sources are available (OMNI) as well as all of the BNA services including the *Tax Management Portfolios, Daily Tax Report,* and *Tax Management Weekly Report.* Both the annotated and topical RIA services are available on LEXIS as is RIA's *Citator 2d Series.* IRS materials and WG&L journals such as *Journal of Taxation* and *Taxation for Accountants* are included in this library. Tax Analysts services such as *Tax Notes Weekly* and *Tax Notes Daily* are available. BNA, RIA, and Tax Analysts have their own library designations as well as having their information listed under FEDTAX. About the only tax information not available on LEXIS is CCH services and WESTLAW.

The actual formation of a search for LEXIS is very similar to constructing a WESTLAW search. It uses the same connectors and limiters as the WESTLAW service. Also, like WESTLAW, LEXIS is offered online and now over the Internet. LEXIS proprietary software must be installed in order to use the service over the Internet. The Internet version has simplified the search process by supplying easy fill-in-the-blank forms. This is a very helpful improvement over the online service.

EXHIBIT 8–23   LEXIS opening library screen

```
NAME     PG NAME    PG NAME    PG NAME    PG NAME    PG NAME    PG NAME    PG

-------General Legal-------- Publisher --Public Records--- Financial --News--
MEGA     1  2NDARY  2 LITGAT  2 BNA      2 ASSETS  4 LEXDOC  5 COMPNY  7 NEWS    22
GENFED   1  ALR     2 LAWREV  3 MATBEN   2 DOCKET  4 LIENS   5 NAARS   7 REGNWS  22
STATES   1  ABA     2 MARHUB  3 PLI      2 INCORP  4 VERDCT  5          TOPNWS  22
CODES    1  CAREER  2 LEXREF  3                               LEGNEW  22
CITES    1  CLE     2 HOTTOP  3                               CMPGN   22
LEGIS    1          FORMS    3                               WORLD   22

-----------------------------------Area of Law---------------------------------- Medical
ACCTG    8  CORP    9 ESTATE  9 HEALTH  11 LABOR   11 PUBCON  12 TAXRIA  13 GENMED  15
ADMRTY   8  CRIME   9 ETHICS 10 HR      10 LEXPAT  12 PUBHW   13 TORTS   14 EMBASE  15
ADR      8  CYBRLW  9 FAMILY 10 IMMIG   11 M&A     12 REALTY  13 TRADE   14 MEDLNE  15
BANKNG   8  ENERGY  9 FEDCOM 10 INSURE  11 MILTRY  12 STSEC   13 TRANS   14  -Helps-
BKRTCY   8  ENVIRN  9 FEDSEC 10 INTLAW  11 PATENT  12 STTAX   13 TRDMRK  14 EASY     C
COPYRT   8          FEDTAX 10 ITRADE  11 PENBEN  12 TAXANA  13 UCC     14 TERMS    6
```

EXHIBIT 8–24   LEXIS tax library screen

NAME	PG	DESCRIP	NAME	PG	DESCRIP
		Combined Files			**Tax Analysis**
MEGA	1	Comb. Federal & State Cases	ALLFED	14	FED+ESGIFT+EXCISE
RELS	1	IRB/CB,PLR/TAM,GCM,AOD,TM	FED	14	RIA U.S. Tax Reporter-Income
CASES	1	Combined Fed. Ct. Tax Cases	RIAFTC	4	RIA Fed. Tax Coordinator 2d
CASREL	1	RELS + CASES	TXNMAG	14	Tax Notes Wkly Mag. frm 1/82
TXLAWS	2	REGS + P-REGS + LEGIS	TMPORT	5	BNA TaxMgmt Ports-US,EGT&FOR
OMNI	2	RELS+CASES+TXLAWS+MANUAL			**Daily Tax News**
CBTR	2	Code-Based Tax Research	TAXTXT	5	TNT + STN + TNI
		Tax Laws & Regulations	TNT	5	Tax Notes Today from 1/9/84
USCS	4	USCS Title 26-Tax Annotated	TNI	9	Worldwide Tax Daily frm 6/84
CODE	3	RIA Int.Rev.Code from '86	STN	5	State Tax Today from 1/84
IRCODE	3	Tax Analysts' Int.Rev.Code'86	BNADTR	5	BNA Daily Tax Report frm 9/86
CFR	3	Code of Fed. Regs. Title 26			**Legislative History**
REGS	3	Final&TempTreasRegs - current	LEGIS	3	H,S,&ConfCommBills&Rpts;PLs
P-REGS	3	Proposed Treas.Regs.- current	RECORD	3	Congress'l Record from 1/85
ALLREG	3	REGS + P-REGS			
TNTREG	3	TNT Regs-FinTempProp&Comments			

Enter file name;.gu for file content & coverage. Example: RELS;.gu

Auto-Cite (R) Citation Service, (c) 1998 LEXIS-NEXIS. All rights reserved.

Kleinrock

Kleinrock, a division of United Communications Group, Ltd., produces an afford-able, easy-to-use tax research library with search capabilities. It also has a separate forms package, Forms Library Plus, which is a complete federal and state tax forms service (more than 30,000 pages of forms and instructions) on one CD-ROM. Forms can be filled out on screen and easily printed.

Kleinrock's Tax Library service contains nearly a gigabyte of tax law sources on a single CD-ROM. Thus, not only is the Tax Library comprehensive, it is very portable. The CD-ROM includes up-to-date versions of the Code and Regulations (proposed, temporary, and final), comprehensive tax case law, IRS Taxpayer Information Publica-tions, complete IRS pronouncements (Revenue Rulings, Letter Rulings, TAMs, GCMs, etc), IRS Audit Guidelines, U.S. tax treaties, and even explanations of recent tax law enactments with full text of the related Congressional Committee Reports—all of this for under $350 for monthly updating and under $300 for quarterly updating.

Upon loading the CD-ROM, the Main Menu database choice screen appears (Exhibit 8–25). The choices are Single Database Search or Multiple Database Search. To get an idea of what is included in each database, scroll through the Sin-gle Database Search list and a description of each database will appear in the Data-base Info box to the right of the list. The box in the lower right-hand corner shows the date of the last CD-ROM update.

The Significant Developments database consists of recent significant changes in the tax law provided in a news brief format. Double clicking on it will display the different methods available for retrieving the data (Exhibit 8–26). Notice that these are the same choices that are listed at the bottom of the screen. Choosing the Browse button provides a list of all of the significant developments available on the disk. Exhibit 8–27 reproduces the first screen of the Significant Developments for May 1998. The developments are categorized into two groups, Public Laws and Regula-

EXHIBIT 8–25   Kleinrock Main Menu screen

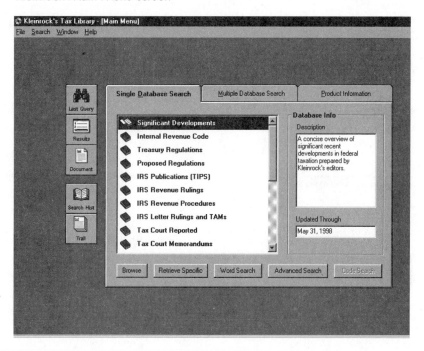

EXHIBIT 8–26   Kleinrock Search Choices screen

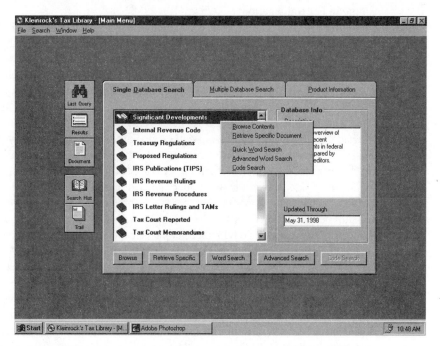

EXHIBIT 8–27   Kleinrock Significant Developments screen

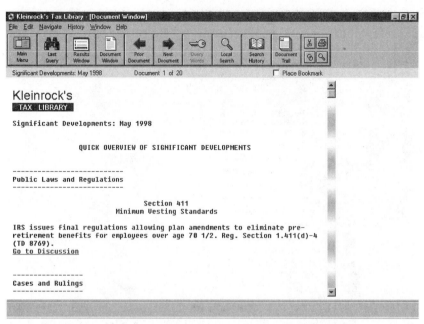

tions and Cases and Rulings. The news briefs are linked to lengthier explanations of the changes through the Go to Discussion line. The explanations, developed by Kleinrock editors, provide the practitioner with a concise overview of what is happening in Federal taxation.

Returning to the main menu, the Multiple Database Search was chosen for our research example. The screen lists all of the possible databases available; the default setting is Select All. To alter the default setting, the boxes can be unchecked or the researcher can use the Clear All button at the bottom of the screen and then check those databases desired (Exhibit 8–28). Once the databases are identified, the type of search is selected. Kleinrock supports a Quick Word Search, Advanced Word Search, and a Code Search. Case name searches can be performed using the Quick Word Search. We selected a Quick Word Search using *authors* and *expenses* as key words with the words required to be within twenty-five words of each other, the default setting (Exhibit 8–29).

The Advanced Word Search allows two sets of research words or phrases to be designated. For each set, the researcher can designate that the words occur within a specified number of words or that the exact phrase be found. The connector relationship between the two sets of words (*or, and,* or *not*) can also be defined. The last type of search, the Code Search, is just for locating documents containing references to a particular Code section. Entering Code section 263A, the search returned the actual section, all of its Regulations and Revenue Rulings, and cases in which the section is mentioned.

Our key word search resulted in a list of twenty documents, one of which is Reg. Sec 1.263A-1. The full text of Reg. Sec. 1.263A-1 is retrieved by clicking on its title. The Document Window button at the top of the screen can also be used to retrieve a document. Exhibit 8–30 shows the Document Window screen. The other buttons at

EXHIBIT 8–28   Kleinrock Multiple Database Search screen

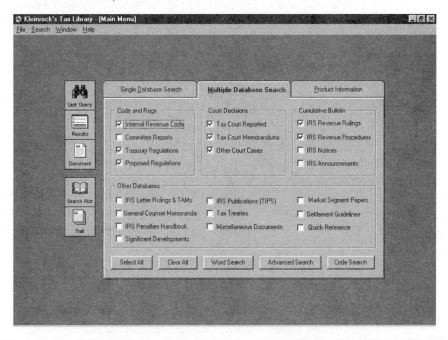

EXHIBIT 8–29   Kleinrock Quick Word Search screen

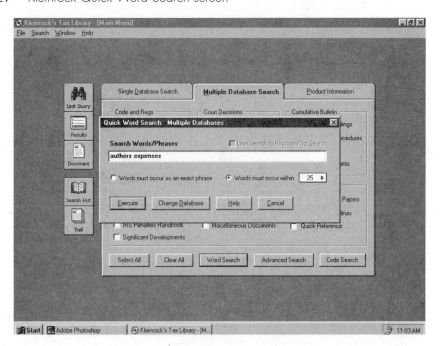

the top of this screen help the researcher move through the document(s) and the Tax Library. For example, the Query Words button will take the researcher to the first occurrence of the key words in the document. The key words are highlighted for easy identification. The Local Search button lets the researcher search for terms other than the key words in the selected document. This is very useful when a Code Search is employed and the researcher wants to search the retrieved documents for specific terms. The Search History button will display the key words that have been used in searches, the database used, and the number of documents found. The Document Trail shows what documents have been examined during this search. Exhibit 8–31 shows a sample search history. The left-hand side of the screen displays the documents viewed, and the right-hand side provides the opening text of the highlighted entry. To retrieve the full text of any document, highlight the document and click on the Retrieve Document button at the bottom of the page.

Although Kleinrock does not provide the editorial explanations of CCH or RIA, it is easy to use, everything is on disk so it is very portable, it requires no special software, and it is very affordable. It would be a good choice in those situations where the practitioner is familiar with the tax topic and is looking for the authoritative sources to back up his or her conclusions.

Other Internet Sites

As mentioned previously in this chapter, most of the primary tax source documents are available free of charge on the Internet. The Federal government has numerous web sites to disseminate its documents to the general public. As will be discussed in

---

EXHIBIT 8–30 Kleinrock Document Window screen

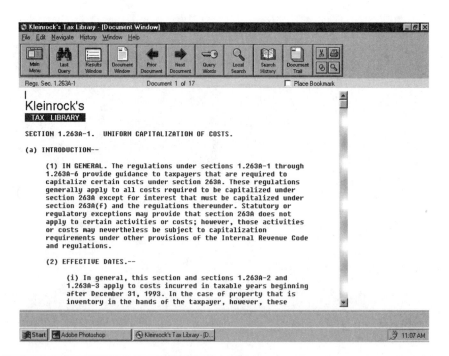

EXHIBIT 8–31   Kleinrock Document Trail screen

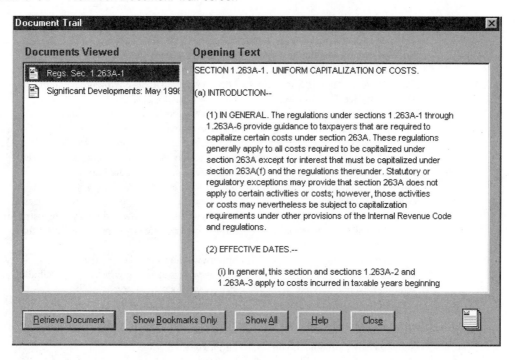

Chapter 9, there are also many web sites maintained by companies, organizations, and individuals that have links to the government sites to facilitate retrieval of primary sources of the tax law. A list of web sites offering government documents is presented in Exhibit 8–32. The web sites for the tax services discussed in this chapter are listed in Exhibit 8–33.

▶ _____ Summary

Tax services are offered in print, on CD-ROM, online, and through the Internet. All have their advantages and disadvantages. No one medium is better than another just as no one tax service is the best. Each medium and tax service has its place in tax research. The problem for practitioners is to determine which media and tax services best serve the needs of their business at a price they can afford. The needs of a business are likely to change over time and practitioners need to evaluate their tax resource choices often, at least once a year when it is time to renew a service.

Some of the choices regarding which medium to select for tax resources are being made for the practitioner by the commercial providers. One service, CCH's *Federal Tax Service,* is no longer going to be offered in print. WESTLAW and LEXIS, which have traditionally been offered only online, are now providing access through the Internet. With technology advances occurring at such a rapid pace, what seemed innovative when this text was written may be passè by the time it's printed.

EXHIBIT 8–32 Web sites for tax services

Information Available	Web Sites
Code of Federal Regulations	http://www.access.gpo.gov/nara/cfr/index.html
Congressional Record	http://www.access.gpo.gov/su_docs/aces/aces150.html
Daily Digital/current IRS tax info	http://www.irs.ustreas.gov/prod/cover.htm
Dept. of Justice Tax Division	http://www.usdoj.gov/tax/
Fedworld FTP site	http://www.fedworld.gov/ftp.htm
Fedworld Info Network	http://www.fedworld.gov/
Federal Register	http://www.access.gpo.gov/su_docs/aces/aces140.html
Federal Register Table of Contents	http://www.access.gpo.gov/su_docs/aces/fr-cont002.shtml
Federal Tax Code	http://www.tns.lcs.mit.edu/uscode/
Financial Accounting Standards Board	http://www.fasb.org
GPO Access Databases	http://www.access.gpo.gov/su_docs/aces/aaces002.html
GPO Access Searching Tips	http://www.ll.georgetown.edu/wtaylor/gposrch.html
Highlights of Tax Provisions	http://www.irs.ustreas.gov/prod/hot/tax-law.html
House Ways and Means Committee Rpts	http://www.house.gov/ways_means/
Internal Revenue Bulletins	http://www.irs.ustreas.gov/prod/bus_info/bullet.html
Internal Revenue Service	http://www.irs.ustreas.gov
Joint Committee on Taxation	http://www.house.gov/jct/
Legislation on Internet	http://thomas.loc.gov/bss/d105/hot-subj.html
Senate Finance Committee	http://www.senate.gov/~finance/
Social Security Administration	http://www.ssa.gov
Tax Forms	http://www.irs.ustreas.gov/prod/forms_pubs/forms.html
Tax Regulations	http://www.irs.ustreas.gov/prod/tax_regs/index.html
U.S. Code, Title 26	http://www.law.cornell.edu/uscode/26/
U.S. House of Representatives	http://www.house.gov
U.S. House of Representatives	http://law.house.gov/usc.htm
U.S. Senate	http://www.senate.gov
U.S. Treasury Department	http://www.ustreas.gov
White House	http://www.whitehouse.gov

EXHIBIT 8–33 Web sites for commercial tax services

Commercial Services	Web Sites
Bureau of National Affairs (BNA)	http://www.bna.com
Commerce Clearing House	http://tax.cch.com
Tax Research NetWork	http://tax.cch.com/network
LEXIS/NEXIS (Reed Elsevier, Inc)	http://www.lexis.come/xchange
Kleinrock	http://www.kleinrock.com
Research Institute of America	http://www.riatax.com
CHECKPOINT	http://checkpoint.riag.com
Tax Analysts	http://www.taxanalysts.com OR
	http://www.taxanalysts.org
	http://www.tax.com OR http://www.tax.prg
Tax Management Resources (BNA)	http://www.taxmanagement.bna.com
West Group	http://www.westgroup.com

▶ _____ Key Words

By the time you complete your work in this chapter, you should be comfortable discussing each of the following terms. If you need additional review of any of these items, return to the appropriate material in the chapter or consult the glossary at the end of this text.

CD-ROM Service	LEXIS
CHECKPOINT	Online Services
Folio/Boolean Syntax Search	PREMISE
Full Text Searches	Seamless
Internet Services	Search Type
In Text	Tax Research NetWork
Kleinrock's Tax Library	WESTMATE

▶ _____ Discussion Questions

1. What are some of the benefits of computerized tax services?
2. What does "making retrieval of the relevant data virtually seamless" mean?
3. Computer services can provide more information and therefore produce better tax research. Comment on this statement.
4. What is one solution to the information overload occurring from computer searches?
5. Give an example of when using published resources could be more efficient than using computerized sources.
6. What are some of the problems with updating published loose-leaf services?
7. What problems do CD-ROMs overcome that are associated with published services?
8. What does updating "in-text" mean?
9. Because the Internet services tend to update on a daily or continuous basis, they are current up to the minute. Comment on this statement.
10. What can you do with published services that is more difficult with computer services? Why?
11. Define an index.
12. What problems can a researcher run into when using a published index?
13. What is the equivalent to an index in a computerized tax service?
14. What are some potential problems with full-text searches?
15. Why is it useful to read editorial explanations of the tax law?
16. What is an advantage of having to replace loose-leaf pages for tax law changes rather than having the service automatically updated electronically?
17. How can a practitioner be sure that the court case identified by a computerized tax service as relevant to the tax project is still valid?
18. To what type of data are CD-ROMs particularly suited?
19. Explain why a practitioner might use tax services on both CD-ROMs and the Internet.
20. Why would a practitioner subscribe to a tax service when most of the primary sources are available for free on the Internet?
21. What is different about accessing WESTLAW and LEXIS than most other Internet tax services?

22. Why is it important for you to actually try research projects on the various computerized tax services?

23. Published services are very different from computerized services, therefore, the steps for computerized tax research are much different than for published tax research. Comment on this statement.

24. The fact that a tax service located a document and placed it high on the relevance list means you can assume it is still valid law. Comment on this statement.

25. What is the difference between CHECKPOINT and TAXPOINT?

26. Which annotative and topical tax services are included in CHECKPOINT?

27. Why is it important to limit the databases searched when using a computerized tax service?

28. What are the new sources offered with RIA's CHECKPOINT?

29. What are the functions of the following special symbols in a keyword search: ( ), " ", *, $, % ?

30. What Search types are available with CHECKPOINT?

31. The Citation Search mode is used for locating what two kinds of cites? What is a drawback of the Citation Search in CHECKPOINT?

32. What is ACCESS?

33. Describe CCH's *Federal Tax Service*.

34. How is the new service on CCH's Tax Research NetWork different from the other new services?

35. What are some of the tax resources offer with Tax Research NetWork?

36. Within the Tax Research NetWork, what is the difference between a Simple Search and a Power Search?

37. What are some of the sources from which WESTLAW receives data?

38. When was LEXIS/NEXIS started? What topic areas are covered by each of them?

39. What tax sources are not included in the LEXIS offerings?

40. What makes Kleinrock's Tax Library different from the computerized tax services discussed in this chapter?

41. What is included in Kleinrock's Significant Developments?

42. Describe the three types of searches available in Kleinrock's Tax Library.

43. Which tax services include WG&L journals in the databases they offer?

44. Which computerized tax service allows the researcher to enter the name of the case instead of requiring a citation?

45. Which computerized tax service automatically applies a thesaurus to the key words?

46. Which two services have traditionally been offered only online?

47. Compare Kleinrock with CCH and RIA computerized tax services.

► _____ Research Cases

48. Candidate Feldman ran for Congress in 1996, raising $1.7 million for the campaign, including $300,000 in Federal matching amounts. Seven months after his opponent had been sworn into office, auditors discovered that he had kept $150,000 of this amount for a personal vacation, taken immediately after the unsuccessful campaign. What are the tax consequences of this unexpected use of election funds?

49. Benito and Julia divorced several years ago. Through her job with a law firm,

Julia provides all of the household expenditures for herself and Delia, her daughter by Benito. Delia lives with Benito, who remains unemployed. This year, Julia married Ralph. What are Benito and Julia's filing statuses for the year?

50. When Max refinanced her mortgage this year, she had the bank "roll" the $2,000 in points into the balance of the new loan. Specifically, Max transformed an 11 percent, $100,000 mortgage into a 7.5 percent, $102,000 loan. In what year(s) can Max deduct the $2,000 interest?

51. Which of the following items qualifies for the child care credit claimed by the Rodriguez family?

   ▶ Salary for nanny
   ▶ Employer's share of FICA tax for nanny, paid by Rodriguez
   ▶ Employee's share of FICA tax for nanny, paid by Rodriguez
   ▶ Health insurance premiums on nanny, paid by Rodriguez
   ▶ One-half of nanny's hotel bill while on her own during a European vacation, paid by Rodriguez
   ▶ Dry cleaning bills for nanny's clothes soiled by youngsters, paid by Rodriguez

52. Kenny has been a waiter at the Burger Pitt for four years. The Pitt treats its employees well, allowing them a 30 percent discount for any food that they buy and consume on the premises. This year, the value of this discount for Kenny amounted to $500 for days on which he was working, and $150 for days when he was not assigned to work but still stopped by during mealtimes. How much gross income must Kenny recognize this year with respect to the discount plan?

53. Ollie died this year in September, after a long illness. His wages prior to death totaled $15,000, and his state taxes thereon came to $600.

   a. Who must file Ollie's last tax return?
   b. How is the return signed?
   c. Who collects Ollie's $440 federal refund?

54. When Fifi, a sheriff's deputy, was injured on the job, she was allowed under her contract with the state to choose between a $1,000 weekly sick-pay distribution and a $700 weekly workers' compensation payment. What must Fifi include in gross income with respect to her $1,000 weekly check?

55. Willie was tired of cleaning up the messes that his wife had made in their house. One morning, he found a crumpled Kleenex on the bathroom vanity, so he disgustedly flushed it down the toilet. Unfortunately, the Kleenex was wrapped around Barbara's engagement ring, which she had removed the previous evening after cutting her finger while shoveling snow. Is the couple allowed a deductible casualty loss for federal income tax purposes under IRC § 165?

56. Louella was born into a poor family that lives in a poor section of town. She recently got a job as wardrobe consultant at High Fashions, Ltd., a retailer of expensive women's clothing at an Elm Grove shopping mall. Can Louella claim a § 162 business expense deduction on her federal income tax return for the cost and upkeep of the expensive Yves St. Laurent outfits that she is required to wear on the job?

57. Harriet purchased a variety of birth control devices during the year. To what

extent, and under what circumstances, do such items qualify under § 213 for a medical expense deduction?

58. Phyllis sued Martin's estate and won a $65,000 settlement. She showed the probate court that she carried out her end of a compensatory arrangement with her companion, whereunder she provided "traditional wifely services" without benefit of matrimony during Martin's life, in exchange for all of his estate. Martin left his entire estate to his faithful dog, via a trust. How much gross income is recognized by Phyllis?

59. How much gross income is recognized by Carol, who received $10,000 damages (two months' salary) for pain and suffering due to the school administration's critical reaction to her negative comments about ineffective recruiting of minority athletes?

60. Carol and Jerry, CPAs, SC, pay the monthly bill at the Good Eats Cafe. The two accountants eat lunch there every day and discuss business. Is there any tax benefit available to the firm under § 119?

61. Lila bought three insurance policies on her life. She borrowed $2,850 and prepaid the first five years' worth of annual payments on a whole life policy. In addition, she borrowed $4,200 and paid one of the two required premiums on a group term policy, through her professional organization. Finally, she borrowed $3,000 and bought into a utilities mutual fund; principal and interest of the fund's assets were to be appropriated in a timely fashion by Lila to make payments on a five-premium endowment contract. Interest charges for the three loans were $3,500, $420, and $310, respectively. How much of this interest can Lila deduct?

62. CPA Joe reimburses a client for a $75,000 tax liability that is traceable to Joe's bad tax advice. For fear of increasing his already steep malpractice insurance premiums, Joe fails to file a claim with the insurer. Can Joe deduct the $75,000 loss?

63. Gardener Toni lent Harry a new $500 lawn mower. Harry ruined the lawn mower, but replaced it with a $425 model. Later in the same year, Toni lent Harry $100 for bail, $800 to start up a fencing operation, and $15 for a meal. According to Harry's parole officer, none of these items ever will be paid back. Can Toni deduct any of these losses?

64. Geraldine bought a Kandinsky for her art collection from a mail-order advertisement for $310,000. The painting, however, was a fake, actually painted by Klenke, which was worth no more than $3,100, according to Geraldine's dealer. What is her deductible loss, upon discovery of the forgery?

65. Roger lent, at gunpoint, $2,000 from the cash register at his hardware store to four large youths who told Roger that they would set up their own store to compete with Roger's. Not having the phone number of any of the sprightly entrepreneurs, Roger could not recover any of the invested funds. Can Roger claim any deduction with respect to this loan? In what tax year?

66. Phyllis, a Virginia resident, owns some property in Florida. Every year, she travels to Florida (coincidentally, during baseball's spring training season) to inspect the property, initiate repairs, and look for new tenants and new properties to invest in. She also attends about twenty ball games. Determine Phyllis's deductible travel expenses.

67. Bruce wanted to be an Olympic skater. His family paid $12,000 in 1995 and $14,000 in 1996 for travel and training expenses related to skating practices and competitions. Bruce made the 1998 U.S. Olympic team. The U.S. Olympic

Committee is an exempt organization. How much of Bruce's expenses are deductible, and when?

68. Harold installed a safe and an alarm system and bought a German shepherd (dog) to protect his vintage movie and video collection. What are his deductible items?

69. Donna's children attend her church's parochial grade school. The school charges $500 annual tuition to children of parents who are not members of the congregation. No tuition is charged for members of the congregation. Donna contributed $600 in the offering plate this year. How much of this amount is deductible?

70. Julie sings in the Seattle Symphony Chorus. The rules of the chorus require that its members wear traditional formal wear (i.e., $400 tuxedos for the men and long black $250 gowns for the women) during performances. In addition, because of her annual $15,000 contribution to the chorus's patron drive, Julie is a member of the symphony's board of directors. The board chooses the works to be performed, sites for the concerts, and the resident conductor. How much of Julie's $15,250 expenditures on behalf of the exempt orchestra this year can she deduct?

▶ _____ Advanced Cases

These items require that you have access to research materials other than the federal tax law and related services. For instance, you might need to refer to an international tax or multistate service to prepare your solution for these cases. Consult with your instructor before beginning your work, so that you are certain to have available to you all of the necessary research resources for the case(s) that you choose.

71. Which of the following receipts are taxable to the state high school athletic association as unrelated business income?

   ▶ Ticket revenues from the basketball tournaments
   ▶ Advertising revenues from the programs sold at the tournaments
   ▶ Subsidy from the state budget for the tournaments
   ▶ Payment from Grand Central Limited to be the official sponsor of the tournaments

72. VanDelay, a citizen of the United States but a resident of Dulcinea, is an important sculptor. This year, he came to the United States to appear at a showing of his work in San Francisco. The United States has no tax treaty with Dulcinea. Does the $250,000 that VanDelay netted from the show qualify for the § 911 earned income exclusion?

73. Which of the following payments by International Partners, Inc., a Montana corporation, qualifies for the foreign tax credit?

   ▶ Income tax paid to Germany, covered by an existing treaty
   ▶ Income tax paid to Adagio, with which the United States has no income tax treaty
   ▶ Value-added tax paid to Largetto, with which the United States has no income tax treaty
   ▶ Oil extraction tax paid to Tedesco, with which the United States has no income tax treaty

▶ Transportation tax paid to Santa Lucia, with which the United States has no income tax treaty, and which is reduced dollar-for-dollar when International provides consulting services in designing Santa Lucia's new bullet train system. This year, International incurred $1 million in the tax, but earned a $600,000 reduction for its services.

74. Heather had named Brenda the executrix of her estate. Brenda had no experience in this domain, but she filed the return, and the estate paid a federal death tax of $2 million. This year, Heather's son Dylan, studying for a master's degree in taxation, discovered that Brenda had not reported any of Heather's realty in the gross estate, and that an additional $250,000 in tax and interest was due. The IRS then assessed various penalties, totaling $30,000. How can the estate, now administered by Dylan, avoid this penalty?

75. Popular Inc. makes a sale to its first out-of-state customer ever. The goods (sale price, $1 million; cost of sales, $300,000), are shipped by a common carrier trucking firm from Popular's Vermont corporate headquarters/plant/warehouse to the purchaser's dock in Indiana. The truck stops for gasoline in New York and Ohio, and its driver spends a night in Ohio. To which states must Popular apportion income from the sale? How much income is taxed in each such state?

Tax Journals and Newsletters

LEARNING OBJECTIVES

► Survey tax periodicals and the role they play in the tax research process

► Use correct citation form for tax periodicals

► Identify the most important tax periodicals

► Examine various indexes to tax periodicals that can facilitate the task of locating pertinent journal articles

► Become familiar with Internet sources of tax information

► Analyze the costs and benefits to be considered in establishing a tax library

CHAPTER OUTLINE

Tax journals and newsletters are secondary sources of the tax law. These periodicals take many forms, ranging from the strictest of law reviews, which accept no advertising of any sort, to newsletters in which the tax articles seem like little more than an excuse for breaking up the advertising copy. Because articles are considered secondary sources, they generally should not be cited as the controlling authority, especially when primary sources supporting the position are available. With that caveat aside, researchers who ignore the tax periodicals might be accused, at best, of reinventing the wheel and, at worst, of professional malpractice. Such periodicals optimize research time by capitalizing on the author's expert judgments and references on a relevant topic, and by bolstering one's own argument during an audit or before a court, via a reference to the work of a noted tax authority.

Nature of Tax and Law Periodicals

Tax periodicals contain a variety of articles and news briefs that are designed to keep readers relatively knowledgeable of developments in specific or general areas of the tax law. These articles might contain, for example, an in-depth review of a recently decided court case, a broad analysis of the factors that should enter into the practitioner's decision on whether to make a certain tax accounting election, a mathematical analysis of the effects of a tax law modification on the overall economy, or a call for reform of a statute by a neutral (or biased) observer. Tax articles can suggest new approaches to tax problems, give guidance for solving complex problems, or just explain a new law in a readable form.

Any given periodical may contain an article that is right "on point" with research a practitioner is conducting. Through its references, the practitioner may be quickly led to pertinent primary sources of the law. In effect, the researcher is using the author of the article as a research associate, thereby saving hours of additional research.

Traditionally, citing articles in professional tax research is limited to two situations: (1) If the researcher is referring to the author's analysis and conclusions as stated in an article concerning, for instance, an interpretation of a Code section or court opinion, the citation is proper; (2) if the researcher cannot find any controlling primary sources of law and a secondary source addresses the issue, then a citation to a secondary source is appropriate.

As discussed in several previous chapters, tax articles are now being cited more frequently in case opinions than in the past. When they are lacking both the appropriate primary law sources and adequate judicial staff, the authors of these opinions may draw on tax articles to support the views of the court. In any event, it is imperative that the researcher understand the practical implications of using secondary law sources.

Citing a Tax Article

A citation to a tax journal article should take the following standard form.

Richard B. Toolson and Ron G. Wright, "TRA '97 Narrows Situations When Variable Annuities Make Sense," 15 *Journal of Taxation of Investments* 4 (Summer 1998) at 316.

Notice the proper placement of capital letters, periods, and commas in the citation. Notice, too, that the volume and page numbers of the journal follow the citation conventions of court cases (i.e., volume number, journal, first page of article). The denotation "at 316" indicates that the researcher is referencing or quoting from a specific portion of the article. If the entire article is being referenced, the citation would merely contain the beginning page number of the article. For the citation above, this would be ". . . (Summer 1998) 315."

Types of Tax Periodicals

Tax periodicals can be categorized according by the depth of the coverage of their articles and the audience for which they are written. From the most extensive coverage to the least, they are as follows.

- ▶ Annual proceedings
- ▶ Scholarly reviews
- ▶ Professional journals
- ▶ Newsletters

Although each publication has its unique characteristics, several general characteristics of each category will be identified. This discussion should provide an initial introduction to the broad market of secondary source tax commentary.

Annual Proceedings

A number of annual conferences for tax practitioners and academics are conducted every year. Usually sponsored by a professional organization, law school, or educational agency, these conferences last from two to five days. The agenda at these conferences may include any of the following: lectures, paper presentations with or without discussion, panel discussions, seminars, demonstrations, and luncheon addresses.

Often, the conference speakers allow the sponsoring agency to publish their presentations as **proceedings** of the meeting. These proceedings are distributed to the participants at the conference, and later to the general public in the form of a collection of articles. Most of these papers exhibit considerable depth of coverage and practical insight by the authors, and they can be a valuable resource for the tax researcher.

A few of the more established tax conferences include the following.

- ▶ New York University Institute on Federal Taxation had its first annual meeting in 1942.
- ▶ University of Chicago Law School's Annual Federal Tax Conference first met in 1947.
- ▶ University of Southern California's Major Tax Planning Institute first met in 1948.
- ▶ Tulane Tax Institute started in 1952.

The proceedings and indexes to these conferences are widely available. For example, CCH publishes the proceedings of the Annual Federal Tax Conference as the December issue of *Taxes—The Tax Magazine*. Exhibit 9–1 provides an excerpt from the table of contents for the December 1997 *Taxes*.

EXHIBIT 9–1   Table of Contents for *Taxes—the Tax Magazine*

CONTENTS

VOL. 75 NO. 12   **DECEMBER 1997**

While some conferences select different areas of tax each year as the theme of the meetings, other annual conferences focus on a specialized area year after year. Examples of specialized tax conferences include the Practicing Law Institute's Conference on International Taxation, which meets annually in New York; the Institute on Oil and Gas Law and Taxation, which meets in Dallas; and the University of Miami Law Center's Heckerling Institute on Estate Planning, held each January in Miami Beach.

Scholarly Reviews

All major law schools and a few business schools produce publications referred to as **law reviews** or **academic journals.** These publications are edited either by faculty members or by graduate students under the guidance of the school's faculty. Most law reviews also use an outside advisory board comprised of practicing attorneys and law professors at other universities to aid in selecting and reviewing articles. The articles appearing in these publications are usually written by tax practitioners, academics, graduate students, or other noted commentators.

Many scholarly tax articles follow an introduction to the authors' chosen topics with a brief history of the law that is the subject of the review. The authors then present an analysis of the prevailing status of the selected area of the law, typically concentrating on a current case or recently issued Regulation to delineate the existing interpretation of the law. In most articles, the authors then discuss their own analysis of the precedents. The researcher may find analyses of this type useful in identifying the development of a point of law or in strengthening the client's similar case against the government. Due to the extensive references included as footnotes, law articles often run from 60 to more than 100 pages in length, prior to their publication in the law review.

Some law schools produce journals that are limited to a specific area of the law, such as constitutional or labor law, in addition to the regular multitopic law review. Most of the general law reviews feature one to three tax articles per year; however, some law reviews are dedicated exclusively to tax matters. Besides law reviews, a few business school graduate programs edit journals concentrating on tax matters. Here are several of the tax law reviews and business school publications.

- ▶ *Tax Law Review* by New York University School of Law
- ▶ *Virginia Tax Review* by University of Virginia School of Law
- ▶ *The American Journal of Tax Policy* by University of Alabama
- ▶ *Akron Tax Journal* by University of Akron
- ▶ *Florida Tax Review* by University of Florida
- ▶ *Boston University Journal of Tax Law* by Boston University
- ▶ *Journal of State Taxation* by University of Wisconsin–Milwaukee

Besides law and business schools, academic organizations such as the National Tax Association–Tax Institute of America (NTA-TIA) and the American Taxation Association (ATA) publish scholarly journals. The NTA-TIA produces tax journals in conjunction with the Sloan School of Management at the Massachusetts Institute of Technology. While NTA-TIA membership is dominated by economists, the organization also includes attorneys, accountants, professors, businesspeople, and government employees with an interest in taxation. The articles appearing quarterly in *National Tax Journal* and the proceedings from the NTA-TIA annual conference, published in *Proceedings of the Annual Conference,* tend to take an analytical or mathematical approach to identifying the broad economic and social implications of taxation on the population.

The ATA, a subdivision of the American Accounting Association, is composed chiefly of business school professors of taxation and tax professionals. It publishes two regular issues of *The Journal of the American Taxation Association* and, like the NTA-TIA, the ATA prints a special conference supplement containing the papers presented at its yearly national conference. This journal is a research publication that offers a combination of taxation articles that employ (1) quantitative or analytical, (2) empirical, (3) theoretical, (4) legal, or (5) tax education methodologies in analyzing issues considered of interest to the tax community. Exhibit 9–2 provides the table of contents for a recent copy of *The Journal of the American Taxation Association.*

Professional Tax Journals

A wide variety of tax journals are published for the purpose of keeping tax practitioners abreast of the current changes and trends in the tax law. This category of journals, commonly referred to as **professional journals** or **practitioner journals,** includes publications by professional organizations as well as commercial companies. Examples of the former are the AICPA's *Tax Adviser,* the ABA Section on Taxation's *Tax Lawyer,* and journals published by state CPA or law societies.

Because the commercial publications are numerous, the tax coverage of these journals can accommodate the needs of the general tax practitioner and those who specialize in a specific area of tax law. For example, journals such as Warren, Gorham & Lamont's *Journal of Taxation* and *Taxation for Accountants,* or Commerce Clearing House's *Taxes,* cover a variety of tax areas, whereas journals such as Tax Management's *The Compensation Planning Journal* or Warren, Gorham & Lamont's *Journal of Partnership Taxation* cover singular topics. Further, the articles appearing in these journals also vary greatly in their coverage from being very complex with an exceedingly narrow focus to being extremely practical "how to" type articles designed for immediate implementation. Exhibits 9–3 and 9–4 provide examples of the table of contents for a multitopic and a specialized journal, respectively.

The editors of most professional journals presume that their readers have access to little, if any, other current tax resource material. Thus, any major change in the tax law, or important Court tax decision, will spawn numerous articles in the various periodicals on the same or similar topics. Accordingly, the Taxpayer Relief Act of 1997 caused a proliferation of journal articles aimed at apprising tax practitioners of various changes contained in the Act as well as offering analyses of the Act's impact on taxpayers and the economy. Many of the articles include hypothetical examples of relevant transactions, using specified dollar amounts, to explain or clarify major points.

To accommodate the tax practitioner's need for timely information, most of the multitopic tax journals are published monthly, whereas the more specialized tax journals tend to be issued on a quarterly basis. The journals ensure the quality of their articles by accepting solicited and unsolicited articles prepared by appropriate tax experts. In each case, an editorial review board assesses the timeliness, accuracy, and readability of each article before it is accepted for publication.

EXHIBIT 9–2   Table of contents for *The Journal of the American Taxation Association*

Spring 1998

The
JOURNAL of the
AMERICAN
TAXATION
ASSOCIATION

A   Publication   of   the   Tax   Section   of   the   American   Accounting   Association

Main Articles
Investments in Tax Planning
    Lillian Mills, Merle M. Erickson and Edward L. Maydew

Wealth Effects of Tax-Related Court Rulings
    Dan S. Dhaliwal and Merle M. Erickson

How Tax Policy Can Thwart Regulatory Reform: The Case of Sulfur Dioxide
Emissions Allowances
    Richard C. Sansing and Todd Strauss

Taxpayer Reaction to Perceived Inequity: An Investigation of Indirect
Effects and the Equity-Control Model
    James I. Maroney, Timothy J. Rupert and Brenda H. Anderson

Tax Accountants' Judgment/Decision-Making Research: A Review and
Synthesis
    Michael L. Roberts

Research Note
Optimal Capital Gains Realization by Individual Taxpayers in the Presence
of Capital Losses
    David S. Hulse

Summaries of Papers in this Issue

Tax Software Review
Book Reviews—Second Tax Course Texts
Doctoral Research in Taxation

EXHIBIT 9–3   Table of contents for *Journal of Taxation*

JOURNAL OF TAXATION

IN FUTURE ISSUES
IRS targets foreign tax credit "abuse"

Sales of remainder interests—still useful?

Warren,
Gorham &
Lamont
RIA GROUP

EXHIBIT 9–4 Table of contents for *Journal of Partnership Taxation*

Journal of Partnership Taxation

Volume 15, Number 2 **Summer 1998**

Warren,
Gorham &
Lamont
RIA GROUP

Tax Newsletters

The major tax services, discussed in Chapters 7 and 8, each include a **tax newsletter** as a part of their service. The Internet and online services tend to have daily newsletters, whereas the published services send the newsletters weekly. These newsletters help the subscriber keep abreast of important tax law developments. They are designed to give the practitioner both a capsule summary of tax law modifications and a reference to the paragraphs in the compilation materials that contain a more detailed analysis. Some of these newsletters also publish information concerning tax seminars and professional meetings, a short review of (or citations for) selected current tax articles, and editorial highlights concerning recent tax developments. *Tax News Direct,* which is received by subscribers to CCH's web tax services, has a special feature that allows subscribers to customize the newsletter's coverage to the tax areas of interest to the subscriber. Several of the most popular tax newsletters are listed in Exhibit 9–5, and examples of the coverage of *Taxes on Parade* and *Tax News Direct* are produced in Exhibit 9–6 and 9–7, respectively.

By far the most important of these newsletters is the BNA *Daily Tax Report.* Showing both breadth of topic and quality of analysis, the *Daily Tax Report* offers the subscriber up-to-date information concerning changes in statutory, administrative, and judicial law that affect state, federal, and international taxation. In addition, the newsletter provides interviews with government officials, articles reviewing the day's events, and the full text of key documents discussed in the newsletter. In some instances these documents are not available from other tax services. Exhibit 9–8 demonstrates the breadth of this newsletter.

The *Daily Tax Report* is available through Lotus Notes, the Internet, e-mail (summaries/table of contents), LEXIS/NEXIS, and by paper subscription. It offers the equivalent of thirty to fifty pages of single-spaced printed copy every weekday. Because this is clearly too much to digest every day, the *Daily Tax Report* is organized to facilitate accessing only the material of most interest to the subscriber.

EXHIBIT 9–5   Selected tax newsletters

Title	Frequency	Publisher
CCH Tax Day	Daily	Commerce Clearing House
Daily Tax Report	Daily	Bureau of National Affairs
Features of the Week	Weekly	Tax Analyst
State Tax Review	Weekly	Commerce Clearing House
Tax Base®	Daily	Tax Analysts
Tax Management Weekly Report	Weekly	Bureau of National Affairs
Tax Management Memorandum	Biweekly	Bureau of National Affairs
Tax News Alert	Daily	Research Institute of America
Tax News Direct	Daily	Commerce Clearing House
Tax Notes	Weekly	Tax Analyst
Taxes on Parade	Weekly	Commerce Clearing House
Today's Tax News	Continuously	Tax Analyst
Weekly Alert	Weekly	Research Institute of America

EXHIBIT 9–6 *Taxes on Parade*

STANDARD FEDERAL TAX REPORTS®

Taxes on Parade

Vol. 85 • Issue No. 26 • Report 25   **June 18, 1998**

Congress Pushes To Finish Tax Legislation Before Recess

◆ *HR 2676; HR 2646; HR 3150; Sen 1415*

Not every piece of tax legislation comes plainly labeled "tax bill." Although the IRS Restructuring and Reform bill presently in conference committee is aptly named, the Bankruptcy Reform Act of 1998, without changing a single provision of the Code, will have a major impact on tax collection and make it much harder to have tax liabilities discharged. And the Senate recently chose to use the tobacco bill as a vehicle to eliminate the marriage penalty. Here's the latest on the important tax legislation now before Congress.

IRS Restructuring and Reform Bill

The House-Senate conference on the IRS Reform Bill began June 10, with the Chairmen of the tax-writing committees expressing the hope that the conference could finish its work before Congress adjourns for the Fourth of July recess on June 27. But Chairman Archer admitted that the conference committee has a lot of work to do to meet that goal. With one exception, Sen. Sam Brownback (R-Kan.), no one mentioned what may be the most contentious issue of all: the composition of the IRS Oversight Board, particularly the question of whether there will be union representation on the board and if so, whether that representative will be subject to the same conflict of interest rules as the other board members. An effort to withdraw the waiver of the conflict of interest provisions extended to the union representative was defeated in the Senate.

That's not the only knotty problem the conferees have to untangle. The House and Senate versions of the bill differ on congressional oversight of the IRS, abatement of interest and

penalties, imposition of proportionate liability for innocent spouse relief, the degree of due process in collection procedures, and increasing eligibility for Roth IRA conversions.

■ *Comment.* The conference has already reached agreement at the staff level on a number of non-controversial "underbrush issues," as they are called in Washington. At press time, members just began to work formally on the high-profile political issues.

However, the so-called "underbrush issues" can create unanticipated problems. House Ways and Means Chairman Bill Archer came out in opposition to an apparently uncontroversial technical correction to TRA '97 that would increase the reach of the 60 percent estate tax rate to include an estimated 300 individuals with estates over $20 million. Since the provision is designed to correct what was widely conceded to be a drafting mistake, this high-level opposition came as a surprise. A spokesman said the Chairman expressed renewed concerned over any provision that does not work toward eliminating the estate tax completely.

Education savings conference

Chairman Archer announced that the House and Senate conferees have reached agreement on the educational savings account measure that the President has threatened to veto. The conference agreement on the Coverdale bill preserves the increase in the annual contribution limit for an education savings account from $500 to $2,000 and the expansion of qualified education expenses from just un-

continued on p. 2

EXHIBIT 9–7   *Tax News Direct*

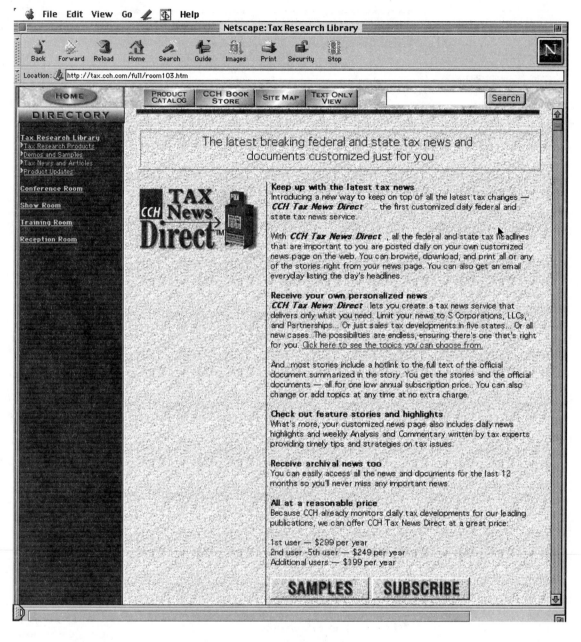

The latest breaking federal and state tax news and documents customized just for you

Keep up with the latest tax news
Introducing a new way to keep on top of all the latest tax changes — *CCH Tax News Direct* ... the first customized daily federal and state tax news service.

With *CCH Tax News Direct*, all the federal and state tax headlines that are important to you are posted daily on your own customized news page on the web. You can browse, download, and print all or any of the stories right from your news page. You can also get an email everyday listing the day's headlines.

Receive your own personalized news
CCH Tax News Direct lets you create a tax news service that delivers only what you need. Limit your news to S Corporations, LLCs, and Partnerships... Or just sales tax developments in five states... Or all new cases. The possibilities are endless, ensuring there's one that's right for you. Click here to see the topics you can choose from.

And...most stories include a hotlink to the full text of the official document summarized in the story. You get the stories and the official documents — all for one low annual subscription price.. You can also change or add topics at any time at no extra charge.

Check out feature stories and highlights
What's more, your customized news page also includes daily news highlights and weekly Analysis and Commentary written by tax experts providing timely tips and strategies on tax issues.

Receive archival news too
You can easily access all the news and documents for the last 12 months so you'll never miss any important news.

All at a reasonable price
Because CCH already monitors daily tax developments for our leading publications, we can offer CCH Tax News Direct at a great price:

1st user — $299 per year
2nd user -5th user — $249 per year
Additional users — $199 per year

SAMPLES | **SUBSCRIBE**

EXHIBIT 9–8 BNA *Daily Tax Report*

Contents
Highlights
Code Section
State Developments
International Taxes
Case Citations
    Alphabetically
    By issue date

TaxCore
  Primary Source Material
    By BNA Issue Date
    By Agency Date
    By Document Type
    By IRC Section
TaxCore IRS Transcripts
Tax Calendar
_____

Publication
Information

Previous Page | Next Page | Search | Collapse

BNA

Daily Tax
REPORT

▼**06/22/98**

▼**HIGHLIGHTS**

▼**In this Issue ...**

▢ Highlights for this Issue

▼**Lead Tax Report**

▼**IRS**

▢ Archer, Roth Announce Near-Final Accord On IRS Reform; Revenue Rais

▼**Tax, Budget & Accounting**

▼**Electronic Commerce**

▢ State, Local Organizations Evaluate Competing Versions of Internet Tax B

▼**Financial Products**

▢ Decision on Retroactivity of Proposed Rules Depends on Reliability of Pas

▼**Subpart F**

▢ Treasury, IRS Withdraw Notice 98-11, Follow-Up Rules, Outline Future P

▼**Tax-Exempt Bonds**

▢ Bill to Provide Tax-Exempt Financing Of Certain Electric Facilities Introd

▼**Tax Administration**

▢ IRS Seeking Public Comment On Various Tax Forms, Three Rules Project

▼**Tax Forms**

→ ▢ IRS Announces Proposed Changes To Forms W-2 and W-3, Seeks Comme

▼**State Taxes**

▼**Minnesota**

▢ State Will Conform to Federal Treatment Of Qualified Subchapter S Subsi

▢ Minnesota Announces It Will Follow 'Check-the-Box' Elections for Eligible

▼**Tax, Budget & Accounting Text**

▼**IRS**

▢ Summary of Tentative Agreement on IRS Restructuring Bill (H.R. 2676)

▼**Subpart F**

▢ IRS Notice 98-35 Announcing Withdrawal of Notice 98-11 and Regulation

▼**Tax Forms**

▢ IRS Announcement 98-15 Seeking Comment on Proposed Changes To 199

EXHIBIT 9–8   *Continued*

No. 119
Monday June 22, 1998

HIGHLIGHTS

Archer, Roth Announce Near-Final Accord on IRS Reform

House and Senate conferees are close to final agreement on legislation to restructure IRS (H.R. 2676), Senate Finance Committee Chairman Roth and House Ways and Means Committee Chairman Archer say after a marathon meeting. Roth and Archer say they have reached a general agreement with the ranking Democrats of the tax-writing committees on "virtually all" of the major substantive issues under the bill. Despite the fact that the sticky issue of revenue raisers remains to be dealt with, "today will go down as a day in history which can well be called Taxpayer Protection Day," Archer says. Staff-level negotiation were to continue over the weekend, and the agreement is still subject to approval by the other conferees. GG-1, Text L-7

Guidance on Hybrid Entities Withdrawn, Future Proposal Outlined

Treasury and IRS issue Notice 98-35 withdrawing Notice 98-11 and proposed and temporary rules that aimed to prevent the use of arrangements involving controlled foreign corporations and hybrid branches under Subpart F. Treasury will issue proposed rules at a later date addressing hybrid transactions. Specifically, the proposal will question whether payments between a CFC and its hybrid branch, or between hybrid branches of a CFC, or between a CFC and the hybrid branch of a related CFC, will give rise to Subpart F income under circumstances described in the notice. G-2, Text L-4

IRS Announces Proposed Changes to Forms W-2 and W-3, Asks Comment

IRS issues Announcement 98-55 proposing changes to Forms W-2 and W-3 for 1999. The proposed changes are based on recommendations from the Information Reporting Program Advisory Committee, the Social Security Administration, and other organizations, IRS says. The revisions are intended to reduce the reporting burden, which will enable the social Security Administration to "more accurately capture the data reported on the forms," according to IRS. The agency is asking for comments on the proposed changes by July 31. G-1, Text L-1

EXHIBIT 9–8   *Continued*

Back to Highlights   Search   Contents

BNA

Daily Tax
REPORT

No. 119
Monday June 22, 1998

Tax, Budget & Accounting

Tax Forms
IRS Announces Proposed Changes
To Forms W-2 and W-3, Seeks Comment

The Internal Revenue Service June 19 issued Announcement 98-55 proposing changes to Forms W-2 and W-3 for 1999.

The proposed changes are based on recommendations from the Information Reporting Program Advisory Committee, the Social Security Administration, and other organizations, IRS said.

The revisions are intended to reduce the reporting burden, which will enable the Social Security Administration to "more accurately capture the data reported on the forms," according to IRS.

The overall size of Form W-2, Wage and Tax Statement, and Form W-3, Transmittal of Wage and Tax Statements, will remain the same, IRS said.

Changes for both forms include adding shading in certain areas, including dollar signs in boxes, and adding special instructions.

IRS is seeking comments by July 31 on the proposed changes from employers, payers, payees, and anyone interested in the forms.

Following the comment period, IRS said it will evaluate the comments and announce the changes to the 1999 Forms W-2 and W-3.

Text of Announcement 98-55 is in Section L.

Back to Highlights   Search   Contents

EXHIBIT 9–8   *Continued*

No. 119
Monday June 22, 1998

Tax, Budget & Accounting Text

Tax Forms
IRS Announcement 98-15 Seeking Comment on Proposed Changes To 1999 Forms W-2 and W-3

Announcement 98-15 is scheduled to appear in Internal Revenue Bulletin 1998-26, dated June 29, 1998.

Items of General Interest

Announcement 98 - 55

Proposed Changes to 1999 Forms W-2 and W-3

Background

Based on recommendations from the Information Reporting Program Advisory Committee (IRPAC), the Social Security Administration (SSA), and others, the Internal Revenue Service (IRS) plans to revise Form W-2, Wage and Tax Statement, and Form W-3, Transmittal of Wage and Tax Statements. Some revisions will reduce reporting burden and some will enable the SSA to more accurately capture the data reported on the forms.

The revisions are proposed for the 1999 Forms W-2 and W-3 to be filed in 2000.

Purpose

The purpose of this announcement is to request comments on the proposed 1999 Forms W-2 and W-3.

Note: Forms W-2 and W-3 as shown are subject to change and OMB approval before final release.

Changes to Form W-2

The overall size of Form W-2 will remain the same, as shown in the draft of Copy A of the 1999 version. A summary of the proposed changes follows:

● The document code "**22222**" is relocated to the upper right corner of the form.

● A shaded box separates box a and the "Void" box, which is enlarged and repositioned.

● The "For Official Use Only" area has no top rule and is reformatted.

● The widths of boxes b through e are narrower and boxes 1 through 17 are wider.

● Box e is expanded into four distinct entry areas for employee information:

While the contents lists only the title of each note by category, the highlights provide brief paragraphs describing the notes. Through the Internet, the listings in the contents and highlights sections are linked to the notes. Further, from the new notes or the highlights, the subscriber can access the actual government document on which the story is based. Using Exhibit 9–8 documents, for example, selection of "IRS Announces Proposed Changes to Forms W-2 and W-3" on the contents page or the "G-1" box after the paragraph describing the same note on the highlights page will take the reader to the note. After reading the note, the full text of Announcement 98-55 can be examined by selecting the "L" box. The text of Announcement 98-55 can also be reached from the highlights page by selecting the "Text L-1" box appearing after the description of the Announcement. This organization and the use of links allow the subscriber to tailor the amount of detail examined on a given tax topic.

The BNA *Daily Tax Report* sells for an annual subscription license price of about $2,500 for one to five authorized users. The publisher offers volume and educational discounts through its representatives, and, as previously mentioned, the *Daily Tax Report* (as well as many newsletters produced by other publishers) is available online to subscribers of various electronic tax research services. Thus, if already subscribing to one of the major tax database systems, the practitioner has access to the daily newsletters at no incremental cost. Further, the documents discussed in the report are available in full-text versions through the online services. To sample the *Daily Tax Report* or other BNA publications, visit the BNA's Internet web site at http://www.bna.com/newsstand.

Other important newsletters are ***Tax Base*** ® and ***Tax Notes,*** published weekly by Tax Analysts. *Tax Base* ® is a daily electronic newsletter that includes several databases. It covers federal, state, and worldwide tax news as well as court petitions and complaints and highlights of the daily tax news. The contents of *Tax Notes* is similar to that of *Tax Base* ® and the *Daily Tax Report* by BNA. In addition, *Tax Notes* often includes in-depth policy-oriented research articles submitted by tax professionals and academics. In Exhibit 9–9 the first item on the cover page, the special report titled "Guidance Improves Treatment of Reorg Exchanges," is such a note. Other new notes are listed by topic headings such as White House, Congress, Courts, and Commentary. The listing of departments, at the bottom of the cover page, and the first page of the summary of contents indicate the breadth of this weekly publication. The first page for the *Internal Revenue Bulletin* Department shows the manner in which the editors summarize current tax news. These summaries are for materials appearing in IRB 1998-21. The notice at the bottom left of the page alerts practitioners that there were no Revenue Rulings or Revenue Procedures issued in IRB 1998-22, dated June 1, 1998.

Tax Analysts also makes full-text documents available to subscribers of *Tax Base* ® and online to subscribers of LEXIS, DIALOG, and WESTLAW. Every document mentioned in *Tax Notes,* whether a case, a Letter Ruling, or a Committee Report, is given a Tax Analysts' document number to facilitate location of the document online. This document number along with the proper tax citation follows each discussion in *Tax Notes*. The length of the document is also provided right after the document number. For instance, in the June 1, 1998, issue, immediately following the summary of the Exempt Organizations Announcement 98-42 is "Full Text Citations: 1998-21 IRB 93; Doc 98-16261 (1 page); H & D, May 26, 1998, p. 2282."

EXHIBIT 9–9   *Tax Notes*

tax notes.sm

Volume 79, Number 9 • Monday, June 1, 1998

EXHIBIT 9–9 *Continued*

Summary of Contents

Tax Notes • June 1, 1998

Quote of the Week: "Let me be clear: I will oppose any budget that fails to set aside the surpluses until we have strengthened social security for the 21st century. Let me also be clear that does not mean that in the future there could never be a tax cut." — President Clinton on using the growing federal budget surplus. (See story on p. 1093.)

News

IRS REFORM. Some congressional Democrats are looking to the REIT/RIC antiabuse bill to replace the Roth IRA provision in the IRS reform bill. *(See p. 1087.)*

RICs & REITs. The chairs of the congressional taxwriting committees introduced legislation that would effectively treat liquidating distributions from closely held real estate investment trusts and regulated investment companies as taxable dividends. *(See p. 1088.)*

MIPS. In a news analysis, contributing editor Lee A. Sheppard discusses the battle between Enron Corp., and the IRS about the classification of monthly income preferred shares. *(See p. 1089.)*

TAX CUTS. With a growing surplus, President Clinton has said he could start talking tax cuts sometime next year. *(See p. 1093.)*

CONTINUITY RULES. Witnesses at an IRS hearing on the proposed continuity of interest rules complained that the rules have been expanded beyond their proper focus. *(See p. 1094.)*

INTUIT DEAL. Intuit corporation's recent announcement that it will buy Lacerte Software means that Intuit will control about half of the professional tax preparation software market. *(See p. 1096.)*

ACCOUNTANT-CLIENT PRIVILEGE. The controversial tax adviser privilege in the Senate-passed IRS restructuring bill was debated at several panels during the recent meeting of the ABA Tax Section. *(See p. 1097.)*

JOINT VENTURE RULING. In a speech at the National Press Club, the IRS's Marcus Owens said that charities other than hospitals can find value in the Service's recently released whole hospital joint venture revenue ruling. *(See p. 1102.)*

EXEMPTION APPLICATION PROCESSING. The IRS's processing of applications for tax-exempt status at one central site is going well despite a few problems, according to the agency's Thomas Miller, who spoke to the D.C. Bar Tax Section. *(See p. 1103.)*

IRS and Treasury

Estate & Gift

Charitable Remainder Trusts. The Service ruled that a trust can be a donor for purposes of the charitable remainder unitrust rules, and that the recipient trust qualifies as a CRUT because it meets the requirements of Rev. Rul. 72-395, 1972-2 C.B. 340. *(See p. 1133.)*

Charitable Deduction. The Service ruled that a trust reformation is qualified, that the reformed trust is a

charitable remainder unitrust, and that the interest passing to charities is deductible under section 2055. *(See p. 1134.)*

Gifts. The Service ruled that a donor's *inter vivos* gifts to a charitable foundation will be deductible for gift tax purposes, and that her estate will be allowed to deduct the value of an irrevocable trust transferred to the foundation on her death. *(See p. 1135.)*

Family-Owned Business Exclusion. Robert M. Bellatti of Bellatti & Barton suggested further amendments to the new estate tax exclusion for family-owned businesses. *(See p. 1108.)*

Exempt Bonds

Arbitrage. Mark Schwartz of the National League of Cities applauded Treasury's efforts to work jointly with the Securities and Exchange Commission and the Justice Department to reach a settlement in the Corestates yield burning case. *(See p. 1107.)*

Exempt Organizations

Publications. The Service announced that Publication No. 3079, "Gaming Publication for Tax-Exempt Organizations," is now available. *(See p. 1119.)*

Charities. The Service ruled that the sale of medical literature by an organization exempt under section 501(c)(3) will not affect the organization's exempt status and will not generate unrelated business taxable income. *(See p. 1132.)*

UBTI. The Service ruled that income from contestant entry fees, rental of lodgings to contestants, and licensing and sale of merchandise by an exempt organization that hosts national amateur competitions is not unrelated business taxable income. *(See p. 1132.)*

Financial Institutions

MSAs. The Service ruled on several aspects of a banking association's proposal to create a new type of medical savings account product. *(See p. 1130.)*

Property Distributions. The Service ruled that the distribution of excess cash generated in a public offering by the acquirer of a recently converted federally chartered stock bank will be a section 301 distribution. *(See p. 1130.)*

International

Foreign Tax Credit. The Service ruled in technical advice that a domestic corporation is entitled to foreign tax credits for a portion of the taxes a 50-percent-owned

EXHIBIT 9–9   *Continued*

internal revenue
bulletin

IRB No. 1998-21

Doc 98-16259 (102 pages)

(Page Numbers Refer to IRB Pages)

Income Tax

REV. RUL. 98-26, page 4. MARCH BLS PRICE INDEXES ACCEPTED. The Service has accepted the Bureau of Labor Statistics price indexes for March 1998. The indexes are for use by department stores using the retail inventory and last-in, first-out methods for valuing inventories for tax years ended on, or with reference to, March 31, 1998.

Full Text Citations: *1998-21 IRB 4; Doc 98-16260 (2 pages);* H&D, May 26, 1998, p. 2281

Exempt Organizations

ANNOUNCEMENT 98-42, page 93. IRS ANNOUNCES AVAILABILITY OF GAMING PUB FOR EXEMPT ORGANIZATIONS. The Service has announced that Publication No. 3079, "Gaming Publication for Tax-Exempt Organizations," is now available.

According to the Service, Pub 3079 provides general information on tax exemption, unrelated business tax, recordkeeping, filing requirements (income tax, withholding tax, excise, and employment tax), and provides examples of the type of records that exempt organizations should maintain if they are conducting bingo, pull-tabs, and other games of chance. Pub. 3079 also provides information on related publications containing additional information on the same topics.

Interested individuals may obtain copies of Pub 3079 by calling 1-800-TAX-FORM (1-800-829-3676). Alternatively, copies may be obtained through the IRS's Web site at www.irs.ustreas.gov/bus_info/eo.

Full Text Citations: *1998-21 IRB 93; Doc 98-16261 (1 page);* H&D, May 26, 1998, p. 2282

NO FORTHCOMING REVENUE RULINGS OR REVENUE PROCEDURES THIS WEEK

The Service did not publish any new revenue rulings or revenue procedures in Internal Revenue Bulletin No. 1998-22, dated June 1, 1998.

ANNOUNCEMENT 98-43, page 93. IRS LISTS WOULD-BE CHARITIES NOW CLASSIFIED AS PRIVATE FOUNDATIONS. The Service has published a list of organizations that have failed to establish, or have been unable to maintain, their status as public charities or as operating foundations. The organizations are now classified as private foundations.

Full Text Citations: *1998-21 IRB 93; Doc 98-16262 (3 pages);* H&D, May 26, 1998, p. 2282

Administrative

REV. PROC. 98-35, page 6. IRS RELEASES ELECTRONIC AND MAGNETIC MEDIA FILING REQUIREMENTS. The Service has published requirements for filing Forms 1098, 1099 series, 5498, 5498-IRA, 5498-MSA, and W-2G electronically or on magnetic media. Rev. Proc. 98-35 applies to current and prior year information returns filed between January 1, 1999, and December 15, 1999.

According to the Service, legislative changes for tax year 1998 necessitated major changes in the record format for information returns filed magnetically or electronically. Some of the changes include the addition of Form 1098-E, "Student Loan Interest Statement," and Form 1098-T, "Tuition Payments Statement"; adding more fields to some of the existing records; redesigning the record layouts; expanding the record lengths from 420 positions to 750 positions for some records; and adding a transmitter "T" record to the first record on the file.

The Service notes that it will discontinue processing 5-1/4 inch diskettes as an acceptable form of media within the next few years. Accordingly, it says, filers should explore optional types of media or methods for submitting information returns.

The Service also notes that Rev. Proc. 98-35 includes format changes for tax year 1998 and calendar year 1999 to accommodate Year 2000 changes. Also, it notes, the current bisynchronous electronic filing communications package will be changed next year to comply with Year 2000 changes.

Rev. Proc. 98-35 supersedes Rev. Proc. 97-34, 1997-30 IRB 14, which was published as Publication 1220 (Rev. 7-97), "Specifications for Filing Forms 1098, 1099 series, 5498, and W-2G Magnetically or Electronically."

Full Text Citations: *1998-21 IRB 6; Doc 98-16263 (87 pages)*

Locating Relevant Tax Articles

Several published and computerized indexes are available that facilitate locating the tax, business, and law journal articles most pertinent to one's research. However, the CCH *Federal Tax Articles* and the WG&L *Index to Federal Tax Articles* are the two indexes specifically designed for locating tax articles.

CCH *Federal Tax Articles*

The ***Federal Tax Articles*** index, published by Commerce Clearing House, has many outstanding features that make it one of the best tax indexes available. However, its most valuable feature is the concise abstracts furnished for each article cited in the index. Reading these abstracts helps the practitioner reduce the false starts that commonly occur when trying to find pertinent articles based solely on their titles. The framework for organizing these abstracts is the *Internal Revenue Code.* This organization also facilitates finding articles addressing the Code section under investigation by the researcher. Lastly, CCH updates this index monthly so the citations are timely. Because the *Federal Tax Articles* current volume is a loose-leaf service, the updates either replace existing pages or are added to the binder. A Report Letter is also provided each month and is cumulated twice a year. This letter is the first page of each monthly issue and highlights new developments.

The more than 250 journals, law reviews, papers, and proceedings included in the index encompass federal income, excise, estate, gift, and employment taxation. In the division called "Publishers and Publications," CCH provides the following information for each of the 250 periodicals: the publisher's name and address, frequency of publication, and the subscription cost. The cost of a single copy of each journal is also provided for those instances when the only source of a particular article is the publisher.

The main division of the index, called "Articles by Code Section," is where the full citation for each article and its abstract is located. This cumulative index uses each Code section with a brief description of the section as its headings. In the bound volumes, the cited articles with their abstracts are arranged alphabetically by title under each Code section heading. The article citations are preceded by a paragraph number (see Exhibit 9–10).

Articles can also be located by using the topic and author indexes. Each of these indexes refers the researcher to the "Article by Code Section" division, through a system of section/paragraph numbering. The index's main cite numbers (i.e., to the left of the decimal point) correspond to the appropriate Code section. The numbers to the right of the decimal point refer to the specific paragraph number of the article abstract. Using Exhibit 9–11 indexes, the article "The Identification Theory of Basis" is referenced in the Index by Topic under "Basis–identification theory" as 1012.016 and in the Index by Author under "Kohl, Glen Arlen" by the same number. This article citation and abstract are found in Exhibit 9–10 under "Code Sec. 1012: Basis of Property–Cost at paragraph .016."

The *Federal Tax Articles* index does have one important drawback. As the loose-leaf volume accumulates a number of monthly updates, called reports, it becomes more difficult to use this service. Twice a year the reports are consolidated and new paragraph numbers are assigned. These consolidated reports are maintained as sep-

EXHIBIT 9–10   Code section index of the *Federal Tax Articles*

838   **Articles by Code Section**

Explores various tax aspects of going-concern value, focusing on the treatment of the buyer and the seller. Reviews cases which decide issues affecting going-concern value, and suggests application of tax theories to determine issues in certain cases. Analyzes factors which cause a difference in value of the assets of a business and its purchase price, and illustrates how those

factors affect tax treatment of the parties to a sale of the business, categorizing purchase price as attributable to asset-specific or non-asset-specific value. Addresses negative value of the going-concern and bargain sales, and suggests an approach to problems surrounding tax treatment of the buyer and the seller.

CODE SEC. 1012: BASIS OF PROPERTY-COST

.01   **"Determining Basis in Mutual Fund Shares Sold."** Jacob R. Brandzel. 20 Tax Adviser, October 1989, p. 674.

Examines the problem of the determination of basis in shares that are sold when a taxpayer buys stock or shares in a mutual fund on different dates and with different costs and subsequently sells a part of the stock, and notes that the problem can be exacerbated if the shares are purchased over a period of many years if dividends are reinvested and if ownership is evidenced by noncertificate shares.

.012   **"How to Control the Interest and Basis Problems Created by the New Types of Mortgages."** Marshall R. Pasternack and Andrew H. Weinstein. 33 Taxation for Accountants, December 1984, pp. 358-362.

Describes the variations to the traditional fixed-rate mortgage, and analyzes the tax consequences generated by those involving principal adjustments, interest rate adjustments, and the ability of the lender to share in the increase in value of the subject property. Suggests that, to put the interest and basis problems caused by these variations within manageable levels, particular attention must be accorded the following considerations: the taxpayer's basis in the property and the deductibility of interest payments. Cites the relevant statutory authority, the Service's position in this area, the case law that has evolved, and the planning opportunities that may be utilized.

.014   **''How to Minimize the Problems in Basis Determinations."** Irving Weintraub and Robert M. Braun. 19 Practical Accountant, March 1986, pp. 47-54.

Explains various rules for determining basis of property acquired in different types of transactions, and considers rules governing special situations. Outlines basis rules for property acquired in the following types of transactions: transactions prior to May 1, 1913; gifts; inheritances; like-kind

exchanges; transfers to controlled corporations; and exchanges or distributions in connection with a reorganization. Also sets forth provisions governing allocation of basis in certain situations, such as purchases of a portion of a large property, lump-sum purchases of a number of assets, contributions of property to a partnership, and property transferred incident to a divorce.

.016   **"The Identification Theory of Basis."** Glen Arlen Kohl. 40 Tax Law Review, Spring 1985, pp. 623-651.   ←

Questions the traditional premise of basis as cost, and suggests that a more appropriate means of measuring basis is the fair market value of assets acquired. Explains the purpose of determining basis as the need to identify wealth which will not be subject to income tax in the future, and examines the role of Sec. 1012 of the Internal Revenue Code in the current system of basis determination. Reclassifies transactions into categories for purpose of basis determination, indicating that transactions in which calculation of realized gain or loss is deferred should be treated differently than other transactions. Considers various types of transactions under the Code, including installment sales, open transactions, loans, and certain nonrecognition transactions in view of the position that the unadjusted basis of property is a means of identifying the value of the property at the time of receipt. Reviews cases addressing the issue of basis in certain transactions, and concludes that although the traditional determination of basis as cost usually leads to the correct result, difficulties arise in situations where no clear exception exists to the general basis rule.

.018   **"Recent Changes Make Basis Determination More Than Just a Mechanical Process."** Steven C. Thompson and William H. Hoffman, Jr. 35 Taxation for Accountants, September 1985, pp. 178-183.

1012.01

EXHIBIT 9–11 Topic and author indexes of the *Federal Tax Articles*

3008

Index by Topic
References are to Articles by Code Section

BASIS—continued
. basis adjustments, consolidated return
. . parent's basis in stock of subsidiary . . .
  1502.01
. corporate acquisitions
. . carryover basis election . . . 338.038
. . determination . . . 1012.014; 1012.018
. . assets in nontaxable estates . . . 1014.01
→ . identification theory . . . 1012.016
. mortgages
. . controlling interest and basis problems . . .
  1012.012
. partners and partnerships
. . adjustments subsequent to liquidation and
  recontribution . . . 708.022
. . allocation of debt . . . 752.048
. property acquired from a decedent . . .
  1014.012
. real property
. . repossession by seller . . . 1038.012
. recovery of
. . nonannuity distributions . . . 72.018
. redemption treated as dividend
. . recovery of basis . . . 302.048
. social security taxes of self-employment
  income . . . 1402.01
. stock purchase treated as asset acquisition
. . basis to acquiring corporation . . . 338.014;
  338.034
. valuation of annuities, life estates, and
  remainder and reversionary interests . . .
  2031.102

BENEFICIARIES
. lapsed powers of withdrawal
. . income taxation . . . 678.012
. trust beneficiaries
. . WPT credit or refund . . . 6430.01

BONDS

BUSINESS—continued
. business assets
. . acquisition and disposition . . . 168.04
. business equipment
. . disposition of . . . 11.032
. business purpose doctrine . . . 355.012
. closely held business
. . choice of entity . . . 11.042; 11.054
. . inter vivos trust, interest placed in . . .
  672.01
. . special use valuation . . . 2032A.022
. . valuation . . . 2031.094; 2031.142
. deductions
. . business rentals . . . 162.014
. depreciation methods . . . 168.072
. . modified accelerated cost recovery
  system . . . 11.064
. entity
. . choice of . . . 11.078
. . corporation v. partnership . . . 11.028; 11.116
. . partnership classification . . . 701.03
. expansion and relocation
. . expenses . . . 162.05
. expansion or contraction
. . checklist . . . 368.122
. family owned business
. . employment of children . . . 73.01
. . estate freeze, effect . . . 2036.024
. . tax planning techniques for the retiring
  owner of family business . . . 302.04
. . transfer of . . . 302.06; 2036.07; 2036.088; 2036.09
. financing
. . R&D limited partnerships . . . 174.03
. form, change of
. . checklists . . . 351.024
. form of entity . . . 11.028
. . Tax Reform Act of 1986, effect . . . 11.04
. investment tax credit

4016

Index by Author
References are to Articles by Code Section

Kirkpatrick, Thomas L. 7453.018	Kreiser, Larry 72.012; 403.034
Kirkpatrick, Thomas Lee 1254.012	Kretschman, Stephen R. 48.016; 162.044
Kirkwood, Peter 7805.034	Kretschmar, Paula W. 280A.022
Kirschbaum, Thomas A. 4980A.04	Kretschmar, Paula Wiehrs 302.044
Kissire, James L. 1502.012	Kreuze, Jerry G. 446.028
Kladder, Ronald A. 4980.01	Krevolin, Douglas P. 11.068
Klane, Murray R. 1.508	Krisel, William E. 871.024
Klassen, Joel D. 817.01	Kroll, Arthur H. 401.182; 401.588
Klebanow, Anatole 301.01; 1031.054; 1031.056;	Kronenberg, James M. 7805.078
1361.022; 1362.048	Krueger, Herbert W., Jr. 280G.03
Klein, Allen J. 2503.026	Kruger, Daniel F. 263.028
Klein, James P. 401.612; 401.614; 3121.024	Krumwiede, Timothy 263A.026
Klein, Paul E. 385.024	Krzystofik, Anthony T. 401.202
Klein, Stanley 482.042	Kubasiak, Gerald E. 4688.012
Klein, Stanley J. 401.05	Kuchinos, David M. 1296.01
Klein, Susan F. 881.016	Kuckelman, Claire H. 6001.016
Klein, Thomas D. 56.014	Kuckuck, Randy L. 61.014; 104.016
Kleinbard, Edward D. 1256.01	Kuenster, Karen A. 921.022
Kleinhans, Evelyn A. 704.012	Kuhn, Gregory B. 165.046
Kliegman, Michael J. 337.014; 368.126; 382.034;	Kuller, Mark A. 704.124
1042.016	Kulsrud, William N. 333.014
Kline, Scot L. 7602.06	Kulunas, Joseph J. 2056.048
Klinger, Max E. 444.012	Kung, Felicia H. 871.016
Klingstedt, John P. 291.012; 469.014; 469.088	Kunze, Carol A. 884.024
Klosterman, Karen L. 280A.05	Kupferberg, Alan 101.016
Kniceley, Robert 457.01	Kurinsky, Deborah Macktez 2040.014
Knight, Lee G. 162.084; 265.01; 280A.012; 338.04;	Kurnick, Robert H., Jr. 165.038
351.036; 385.028; 448.02; 451.014; 461.018; 521.014;	Kurtz, Jerome 163.02
1034.016; 1388.01; 7430.016	Kurtzman, Melissa B. 170.116
Knight, Ray A. 162.084; 265.01; 280A.012; 338.04;	Kurzer, Martin J. 501.138
351.036; 385.028; 448.02; 451.014; 461.018; 521.014;	Kurzman, Stephen A. 2031.212
1034.016; 1388.01; 7430.016	Kutz, Karen S. 1.052; 401.294; 461.01
Kniskern, Douglas 1.618	Kuznicki, Joseph M. 170.162
Knott, Hiram 163.064	Kwall, Jeffrey J. 532.012
Knotts, Melton E., Jr. 354.012	Kwall, Jeffrey L. 1001.014
Knowles, Linda L. 401.01	Kyser, Nickolas J. 356.014
Knox, Peter L. 125.02; 401.212; 401.296; 414.032;	
416.016	**L**
Knox, Ruth A. 142.01; 144.01	
Knox, William T., IV 416.01; 416.012	La Conte, Robert J. 280F.04
Koehler, Reginald S., III 642.012	Laarman, Linda M. 401.378
Koenig, Rodney C. 170.158	Lacock, Linda J. 280A.026
Kogan, Bruce 2031.15	Lacy, Bud 469.078
Kogan, Bruce I. 74.02	Lacy, Bud, Jr. 6702.01
→ Kohl, Glen Arlen 1012.016	Lacy, Paul 922.012
Kohn, Alan 46.026	Lager, Richard H. 163.092; 1222.022
Kohn, Jerrold H. 7805.042	LaGree, Bryan R. 170.044; 170.046; 2036.07
Kokot, Eugene V. 673.024	Lai, Richard T. 1368.01; 1372.01
Kolasa, Robert J. 189.014	Lajoie, David E. 1201.012
Kolb, Jeffrey B. 2032A.04	Lammert, Thomas B. 263A.106
Kolk, J. Michael 1362.028	Lamon, Harry V., Jr. 401.23
Kolling, John F. 403.02	Lancaster, William J. 174.014; 7701.038
Konides Smith, Amy 336.056	

arate sections in the loose-leaf binder. Thus, a researcher may have to examine up to ten separate consolidated reports indexes (Code section, topic, or author) when examining a five-year period of publications. Exhibit 9–12, demonstrates that paragraph numbers, in this case ¶ 3176, in the loose-leaf binder, are not numerically tied to Code section, here §7701. When articles related to Section 7701, from all the reports in the present loose-leaf binder, are placed in the next bound volume, they will be placed together and 7701 will become their main cite number.

EXHIBIT 9–12   Article summaries in loose-leaf *Federal Tax Articles*

404 4-96	1996 Article Summaries—Report 404	2465

¶ 3176   Definitions (Code Sec. 7701)

.198 Estate Planning Using Limited Liability Companies. Brian Reeves. 60 Kentucky Bench & Bar, Winter 1996, pp. 44-48.

Explores the use of the limited liability company (LLC) as an estate planning technique that allows the transfer of wealth to children without losing control over the business interests transferred. Highlights the unified credit and annual exclusion estate and gift tax provisions. Illustrates with an example some gift-giving techniques that utilize these provisions. Discusses the valuation of LLC interests and the impact of minority and lack of marketability discounts. Demonstrates with examples how discounts can reduce the estate and gift tax value of the LLC interests transferred. Discusses appreciation and ways in which to freeze the values for estate tax purposes. Touches upon the gift tax return filing requirements. Compares the LLC with other estate planning tools, including S corporations, family limited partnerships and trusts.

.20 The Costs of Converting a Partnership to an LLC: Look Before You Leap. Carol Mayo Cochran, Michele M. Blazek and Patricia C. Elliott. 26 Tax Adviser, August 1995, pp. 455-464.

Provides a practical analysis of issues to consider in electing to convert an existing partnership to a limited liability company (LLC). Observes that, although many rulings and cases have addressed the classification of an LLC as partnership for tax purposes under IRS Regs. § 301.7701-2, few have examined the conversion issue. Summarizes the general rule that no gain or loss is recognized, unless a partner is relieved of liabilities. States that if the partnership business continues, the partnership does not terminate. Discusses the transfer of partnership interests to a new or an existing LLC and merging a partnership with an LLC. Demonstrates how to compute the basis of property contributed to an LLC and provides the rules for allocating liabilities. Addresses unrealized receivables and substantially appreciated inventory and the disguised sales rules. Details the substantial economic effect provisions. Discusses optional basis adjustments. Highlights the self-employment tax implications, provides the requirements for requesting an IRS ruling, and mentions IRS Notice 95-14, IRB 1995-14, 7, which would allow election of entity classification. Concludes that the conversion of a partnership into an LLC triggers two events—the liquidation of the partnership and the formation of the LLC—and that the tax cost of converting is not always as clear as often believed.

.202 Taxation of Kentucky Limited Liability Companies. Charles J. Lavelle and Charles Fassler. 60 Kentucky Bench & Bar, Winter 1996, pp. 41-43.

Overviews the classification of a limited liability company (LLC) as a partnership for tax purposes, setting forth the corporate characteristics and noting that an LLC will almost always possess the limited liability characteristic. Discusses the taxability of contributions to an LLC, and provides the rules for determining basis in the LLC interest. Addresses allocations of income, gain, loss, deduction and credit, in accordance with substantial economic effect, and highlights the passive loss rules. Summarizes the tax consequences of LLC distributions and payments upon withdrawal. Touches upon self-employment tax implications.

.204 New Business Options in Pennsylvania: A Critical Analysis of

Every four to six years, the CCH monthly and consolidated reports sufficiently fill the loose-leaf volume to require the publication of a bound volume. At this time the article abstracts are reorganized and the various indexes are consolidated for the entire period. Subsequently, a new loose-leaf volume is issued relative to the articles that are published after the issuance of the bound volume. CCH bound volumes cover the periods of 1968–1972, 1973–1978, 1979–1984, and 1985–1989. A transfer binder is provided for 1990–1996. Thus, the current loose-leaf volume includes articles published in late 1996 and thereafter.

WG&L Index to Federal Tax Articles

Warren, Gorham & Lamont's *Index to Federal Tax Articles* provides citations and occasionally summaries for articles covering federal income, gift, and estate taxation or tax policy that appear in more than 350 periodicals. The index surveys not only traditional tax journals, but also law reviews, major annual tax symposia, and certain economics, accounting, and finance journals. The *Index to Federal Tax Articles* is issued in paper-bound volumes and includes permanent cumulations of references for the periods 1913–1974, 1974–1981, 1982–1983, 1984–1987, 1988–1992, and 1993–1996. A quarterly paperback cumulative supplement augments the main index volumes. Because the supplements are cumulative, the researcher need only consult one supplement for articles appearing in journals from 1996 to the present.

Unlike the CCH index, both the topic and the author indexes contain full article citations (see Exhibit 9–13). Using the full citations in the author index, the researcher can identify other current articles by the same author pertaining to a specific topic. Authors with several articles on the same topic are more likely to have an expertise in that field and, thus, their analysis may be more effectual. Further, the custom of listing citations for each author and topic heading in reverse chronological order (rather than in alphabetical order) expedites finding the most recent publications.

The *Index to Federal Articles* contains a users guide that explains how to use the index, lists the topical index subject headings, supplies a key to abbreviations of periodical titles, and lists the periodicals included in the first three volumes. Further, each cumulation volume and the current supplement lists not only the periodical titles but also the volumes and issues numbers searched for that volume. This information is useful, for example, when the practitioner is preparing an audit defense for a tax return of a prior year.

Whereas every citation in the CCH index is accompanied by an abstract, only articles judged by the compilers and Editorial Advisory Board to be of special interest are furnished a brief summary in the *Index to Federal Tax Articles*. Few articles receive this distinction.

Shepard's *Citators*

Shepard's publishes two additional citators that include tax articles appearing legal documents and law reviews. *Shepard's Law Review Citations* indicates where the selected articles have been cited in court case opinions and *Federal Law Citations in Selected Law Reviews* indicates where federal cases and Code sections have been cited in law review articles.

Shepard's Law Review Citations provides a method of finding articles that have been cited in U.S. Supreme Court cases; lower federal courts opinions included in

EXHIBIT 9–13   Topical and author indexes for *Index to Federal Tax Articles*

SPRING 1998 CUMULATIVE SUPPLEMENT

INDEX TO FEDERAL TAX ARTICLES: *Author Index*

Tax-exempt Organizations—*Cont'd*

Prohibited Transactions—*Cont'd*

Private Inurement and the Intermediate Sanctions Regime, Anthony P. Polito, 77 Tax Notes No. 5, 599 (1997)

A New Look at Campaign Finance Reform: Regulation of Nonprofit Organizations Through the Tax Code, Brent Coverdale, 46 University of Kansas Law Review No. 1, 155 (1997)

A Nonprofit Director's Road Map for Survival: How To Be a Road Warrior and Not an Accident Victim, Roy M. Adams, 31 University of Miami Philip E. Heckerling Institute on Estate Planning, 18 (1997)

Protecting "Donor Intent" in Charitable Foundations: Wayward Trusteeship and the Barnes Foundation, Chris Abbinante, 145 University of Pennsylvania Law Review No. 3, 665 (1997)

Subversive Organizations

Unrelated Business and Debt Financed Income

Tax Considerations of Pooled Investment Financing from Tax-Exempt Investors [See Special Edition 1998-1 in Vol. 39 No. 2.], Peter J. Lanza, 39 Tax Management Memorandum No. 2, 17 (1998)

Treasury Proposes Regulations on Exempt Organizations and the Repeal of *General Utilities*, Philip G. Royalty and David S. Colton, 9 Journal of Taxation of Exempt Organizations No. 2, 51 (1997)

TRA '97 Has Both Good News and Bad News on UBIT, Amy R. Segal and Michael C. Fondo, 9 Journal of Taxation of Exempt Organizations No. 3, 132 (1997)

Tax-Exempt Investors in Real Estate: Tax Opportunity or Tax Trap? Michael Hirschfeld, 11 Probate and Property No. 6, 39 (1997)

Self-Dealing and Unrelated Business Income Tax Implications of Charitable Remainder Trust Investments—Recent Developments, Deborah M. Beers, 38 Tax Management Memorandum No. 14, 195 (1997)

Wrong Plan Investments Can Create Unrelated Business Income Tax, Gerald E. Whittenburg and William A. Raabe and James E. Williamson, 58 Taxation for Accountants No. 6, 350 (1997)

When is a Business Not a Business? Exploiting Business Opportunities and Enhancing Economic Returns by Capitalizing on the Income Tax Exemption of Tax-Exempt Organizations, Thomas J. Gallagher, 75 Taxes No. 12, 928 (1997)

Sierra Club v. Commissioner and the Royalty Exemption to the Unrelated Business Income Tax: How Much Activity is Too Much? Katherine A. VanYe, 72 Washington Law Review No. 4, 1171 (1997)

Foundation's Ownership of Professional Baseball Team is Fair Play Under I.R.C. Section 501(c)(3), Stephanie Newkirk, 65 University of Missouri at Kansas City Law Review No. 2, 263 (1996)

Corporate Sponsorship in Transactional Perspective: General Priciples and Special Cases in the Law of Tax-

Gore, Richard

Accounting Methods Determine Timing of Income and Deduction, 56 Taxation for Accountants No. 1, 32 (1996) (With Hugh Pforsich)

Quandary for S Corp. COD Income Pass-Throughs, 56 Taxation for Accountants No. 3, 157 (1996)

Quandary for S Corp. COD Income Pass-Throughs, 24 Taxation for Lawyers No. 6, 339 (1996)

Realty Corps. Benefit By Tax-Free REIT Conversion, 54 Taxation for Accountants No. 2, 97 (1995) (With Robert J. Lauer)

Accountable Plans Can Cut the Tax on Reimbursements, 55 Taxation for Accountants No. 3, 132 (1995) (With Jack R. Petralia Jr)

Using REITs to Overcome the Capital Crunch in Real Estate, 11 Journal of Taxation of Investments No. 4, 279 (1994) (With Robert J. Lauer)

Character of Boot Depends on Overall Transaction, 52 Taxation for Accountants No. 2, 76 (1994) (With Robert J. Lauer)

S Corp. Final Regs. Add Flexibility in Basis and Distributions, 52 Taxation for Accountants No. 3, 138 (1994) (With Debra Sanders)

S Corp. Final Regs. Add Flexibility in Basis and Distributions, 22 Taxation for Lawyers No. 5, 276 (1994) (With Debra Sanders)

Practitioner Comment: Troubled "S" Corporation That Recognizes COD Income May Yield Substantial Tax Benefits, 9 Tax Management Real Estate Journal No. 4, 80 (1993)

Shareholder's Return Starts S Corporation Assessment Period, 50 Taxation for Accountants No. 4, 203 (1993) (With Robert J. Lauer)

Shareholder's Return Starts S Corporation Assessment Period, 21 Taxation for Lawyers No. 6, 332 (1993) (With Robert J. Lauer)

New Regs. on S Corporation Adjustments Adopt Separate Basis Rules, 49 Taxation for Accountants No. 2, 72 (1992)

Gorgy, Sonia Elias

The Effect of the Revenue Reconciliation ACt of 1993 on Real Estate Owners, 25 Tax Adviser No. 8, 491 (1994) (With Judith A. Sage and Lloyd G. Sage)

Gorrin, Eugene

New Substantiation and Disclosure Rules Increase Burden on Charities and Donors, 81 Journal of Taxation No. 5, 310 (1994) (With Marc J. Honigfeld)

Gould, Arnold J.

Supreme Court Will Clarify Nonfiler Refund Period, 56 Taxation for Accountants No. 2, 76 (1996) (With Akshay K. Talwar)

the *Federal Reporter* (Second Series), the *Federal Supplement,* or the *Federal Rules Decisions;* and the state court decisions recorded in the state reports or the national reporter system. To a limited extent, the service also indicates where other law reviews have cited the selected articles. One can check the current supplement of *Shepard's Law Review Citations* to determine whether there are any very recent citations of an article under examination.

The *Federal Law Citations in Selected Law Reviews* service lists where Supreme Court decisions from the *United States Supreme Court Reports* and lower federal court decisions that are reported in the *Federal Reporter,* the *Federal Supplement,* and *Federal Rules Decisions* are cited in selected law reviews. In addition, the service gives citations for the U.S. Constitution, the U.S. Code, and the Federal Court Rules. Consequently, citations for the *Internal Revenue Code* are included in the section for Title 26 of the U.S. Code. Unfortunately, the list of selected law reviews is quite short when compared to other indexes' coverage. Fewer than 20 reviews are represented.

Other Law and Accounting Indexes

Because it is not possible to review all the commercial indexes a practitioner might have access to, a few indexes have been selected to illustrate the variety of services available. Most of these services are available in print, CD-ROM, or online format, thus, they can accommodate the preference of any user. The print and CD-ROM versions tend to be updated monthly, whereas the online version is generally updated weekly. Many of the online services are accessible through DIALOG, LEXIS, or WESTLAW. Additionally, some indexes can be found on the publisher's own online service such as WILSONLINE for the H. W. Wilson Company products.

The *Current Law Index* is published in print format by the Information Access Company in cooperation with the American Association of Law Libraries. It catalogs more than 700 law journals published in the United States and other English-speaking nations. Thus, it includes nearly all the periodicals referenced in the CCH or WG&L indexes plus numerous other law publications that explore a variety of tax and nontax topics. This service provides five separate methods of locating pertinent tax articles—by topic, author, article title, case name, and statute. Article citations tend to appear much more quickly in the *Current Law Index* than in the CCH and WG&L services. On the other hand, it furnishes only article citations, lacking the article abstracts of CCH and to a lesser extent of WG&L. The current supplements are bound yearly into two volumes; one for the subject indexing and the other for the author, title, case, and statute indexing. Information Access Company has similar indexes on CD-ROM, called *LegalTrac,* and on online, called *Legal Resource Index*™. These services cover more journals than *Current Law Index* and does provide selected article abstracts.

The *Index to Legal Periodicals* is similar to the *Current Law Index* in the number and type of journals cataloged, methods of indexing article citations, and timely updates of the service. It too provides only citations for articles with no abstracts. However, unlike *Current Law Index,* it is accessible in print, CD-ROM, and online.

The advantage of these legal indexes is that the scope of periodicals coverage is much larger than that of the dedicated tax indexes. However, both the *Current Law Index* and the *Index to Legal Periodicals* omit some of the accounting and other specialty-oriented journals. For instance, some of the most important tax journals, including *Taxation for Accountants* and *The Estates, Gifts, and Trusts Journal,* are not currently indexed.

Glandville Publications, Inc., issues the *Index to Periodical Articles Related to Law* only in print format. It indexes selected periodicals publishing law-related articles, but only in those publications that are not referenced in the major law indexes—that is, ones not covered by the *Current Law Index* or the *Index to Legal Periodicals.* The Glandville *Index* canvasses a very broad spectrum of journals, including such publications as the *American Economic Review, The Tax Adviser,* and *Rolling Stone.* The special utility of this legal index lies in its ability to locate tax-related articles in nontraditional tax publications.

On the other hand, the *Accounting and Tax Index (Database),* published by University Microfilms Inc. (UMI) in all formats, catalogs tax, accounting, and related articles from worldwide professional journals, general business and news magazines, newsletters, and new papers. This index includes abstracts along with its citations. The contents is based in part on the *Accountants' Index* published by the AICPA.

Other Indexes

Sometimes practitioners want to start their research by obtaining an overall appreciation of a tax topic before confronting a detailed tax journal explanation. How does a practitioner locate tax-related articles written for the general public's consumption? An index practitioners can turn to is the H. W. Wilson *Business Periodicals Index.* It covers a large number of business periodicals, including a few professional tax journals, and is available in all three formats. Another general business index is *Business Source Plus* of EBSCO Publishing. It supplies both citations and abstracts to more than a million articles in 650 worldwide journals. About one-third of the journals are full-text searchable. Lastly, many public and university libraries will have a product like *ABI/FORM*® or a web database such as *ProQuest* published by UMI. Both of these catalog more than 1,000 periodicals (3,000 for *ProQuest*) with full text for a substantial portion of the journals. All citations are accompanied by an abstract. However, use of these products at university libraries may be limited to individuals affiliated with the school.

This review of the possible indexes for locating tax and tax-related articles is just a sampling of what is available. Furthermore, the CD-ROM and online service industry is growing and changing so rapidly that by the time this book is in print there will be many more worthwhile index databases for the interested practitioner to consider. An exceptional guide to online and CD-ROM databases is the *Gale Directory of Databases,* edited by Eric E. Holmberg. The *Gale Directory of Databases* was formed by the merger of Gale's *Computer-Readable Databases,* Cuadra/Gale's *Directory of Online Databases,* and *Directory of Portable Databases.* It is published by Gale Research in two volumes; one covers online databases and the other includes CD-ROM, diskette, magnetic tape, handheld, and batch access database products. The directory is available in print, CD-ROM, and online through GaleNet and DIALOG, and is also accessible through the Web.

The *Gale Directory of Databases* provides a descriptive summary for more than 13,000 databases that cover numerous and diverse disciplines, including that of tax law. Some of these databases consist merely of online versions of the printed indexes, but others provide additional services and others are only available online.

For instance, the LEXIS and WESTLAW databases provide, as a part of their general service, access to finding lists of articles that are published in selected periodicals and law reviews. To call up the LEXIS/NEXIS online index, for example, the researcher would select NEWS from the library lists of the first screen and MAGS on the second screen, as shown in Exhibit 9–14.

Other Resources

The BNA *Tax Management* portfolios, discussed in detail in Chapter 8, also provide a source for locating pertinent tax articles. The bibliography located in Section C of most portfolios typically lists titles and citations of numerous articles that pertain to the subject of the portfolio. The citations are provided by year of publication, alphabetically by author. The new-material sheets for Section C update the bibliography listing. However, researchers should not rely on this feature of the BNA portfolios as their primary source for identifying relevant tax articles because the portfolios are uneven as to the magnitude, timeliness, and comprehensiveness of their bibliographies.

EXHIBIT 9–14   Library screens for LEXIS/NEXIS

```
 -------General Legal-------- Publisher --Public Records--- Financial --News--
MEGA     1 2NDARY  2 LITGAT  2 BNA     2 ASSETS  4 LEXDOC   5 COMPNY➔7 NEWS    22
GENFED   1 ALR     2 LAWREV  3 MATBEN  2 DOCKET  4 LIENS    5 NAARS   7 REGNWS  22
STATES   1 ABA     2 MARHUB  3 PLI     2 INCORP  4 VERDCT   5          TOPNWS  22
CODES    1 CAREER  2 LEXREF  3                                        LEGNEW  22
CITES    1 CLE     2 HOTTOP  3                                        CMPGN   22
LEGIS    1           FORMS   3                                        WORLD   22


 --------------------------------Area of Law-------------------------------- Medical
ACCTG    8 CORP    9 ESTATE  9 HEALTH 11 LABOR   11 PUBCON 12 TAXRIA 13 GENMED 15
ADMRTY   8 CRIME   9 ETHICS 10 HR     10 LEXPAT  12 PUBHW  13 TORTS  14 EMBASE 15
ADR      8 CYBRLW  9 FAMILY 10 IMMIG  11 M&A     12 REALTY 13 TRADE  14. MEDLNE 15
BANKNG   8 ENERGY  9 FEDCOM 10 INSURE 11 MILTRY  12 STSEC  13 TRANS  14   -Helps-
BKRTCY   8 ENVIRN  9 FEDSEC 10 INTLAW 11 PATENT  12 STTAX  13 TRDMRK 14 EASY    6
COPYRT   8           FEDTAX 10 ITRADE 11 PENBEN  12 TAXANA 13 UCC    14 TERMS   6
```

```
        ------   T H E   N E W S   L I B R A R Y   ------
-- Full-Text Group Files -- --- Full-Text By Type --- - Full Text By Region -
TODAY    1 Today's News   ➔  MAGS    3 Magazines        -- Papers & Wires --
CURNWS   1 Last 2 years      MAJPAP  3 Major Papers    NON-US  1 English Non-US
90DAYS   1 Last 90 days      NWLTRS  3 Newsletters     US      1 US News
ARCNWS   1 Beyond 2 years    PAPERS  3 Newspapers        -- US Sources --
                             SCRIPT  3 Transcripts     MWEST   3 Midwest
-- Group File Exclusions --  WIRES   3 Wires           NEAST   3 Northeast
ALLABS   4 All Abstracts     ------- Hot Files -------  SEAST   3 Southeast
NONENG   1 Non-English News  HOTTOP  2 Hot Topics *    WEST    3 West
TXTNWS   1 Textline News *   Y2KNWS  2 Year 2000 Nws*  ------- Assists -------
ALLBBN   1 Bloomberg News *                            GUIDE   2 Descriptions*
                                                       LNTHS   2 L-N Index Ths*

Files marked * may not be combined.
```

In addition, tax journals themselves can provide references to tax articles that can be of interest to the researcher. Nearly every journal provides an annual index (usually by topic, author, case name, and Code section) for its own articles. Occasionally, this index appears in each issue of the journal, in a cumulative twelve-month, rather than a more arbitrary volume or calendar year, format. Moreover, several of the journals regularly provide citations or summaries of articles that appear in some of their sister journals and even in their competitors' journals, presumably to facilitate the reader's efficient use of the entire tax literature.

A number of other sources provide a listing of current tax articles, but most of these would be better classified as tax update material, rather than as a comprehensive research resource. Most of these finding lists are included as part of a weekly or monthly information newsletter that accompanies a general tax service or treatise, and they are intended merely as a "tickler" to make the practitioner aware of recent publications that might be of interest. Generally, they provide no article abstracts, they are not indexed by any attribute other than journal and title, and they are not accumulated or reorganized after a specified period. For instance, once a month, the RIA *Weekly Alert* includes a listing of selected current tax articles, and the Callaghan service provides a similar listing in its monthly *Law of Federal Income Taxation—Current Tax Highlights*.

Internet Sites

A growing source of tax materials that literally changes daily is the Internet. Organizations, commercial enterprises, and individuals have web sites with links to valuable tax information. There are even online magazines for accountants that feature tax articles. Exhibit 1–15 contains a list of tax articles that have appeared in *The Accountant's Ledger*. There is so much information available on the Internet that it can be almost overwhelming. A list of tax-related web sites is given in Exhibit 9–16. The web addresses in this list were accurate as of the date of publication and by no means should be considered a comprehensive list. It is merely a selected list of useful sites found by this author.

Establishing a Tax Research Library

Eventually, every tax practitioner is faced with the problem of what to include in a tax research library. As we have seen in the preceding three chapters of this text, a large amount of material is available to include in one's tax research collection. Most practitioners cannot afford (nor would they need) all the material that could be included in such a tax library.

In deciding what to purchase for a tax library, the practitioner must answer several questions. First, she or he must evaluate the level of the affected tax practice. The more sophisticated and complex one's clients' tax problems are, the more items one usually needs for the tax library. Second, one must evaluate the extent to which the practice is concentrated in a narrow area of taxation. Specialists generally require tax libraries to match, combining a great deal of depth in the relevant field with a few broad-based tax publications to keep current on general tax matters. Third, one must identify the availability of public (or otherwise easily accessible) tax research materials. For example, if the tax practitioner's office is across the street from a

EXHIBIT 9–15   The Accountant's Ledger

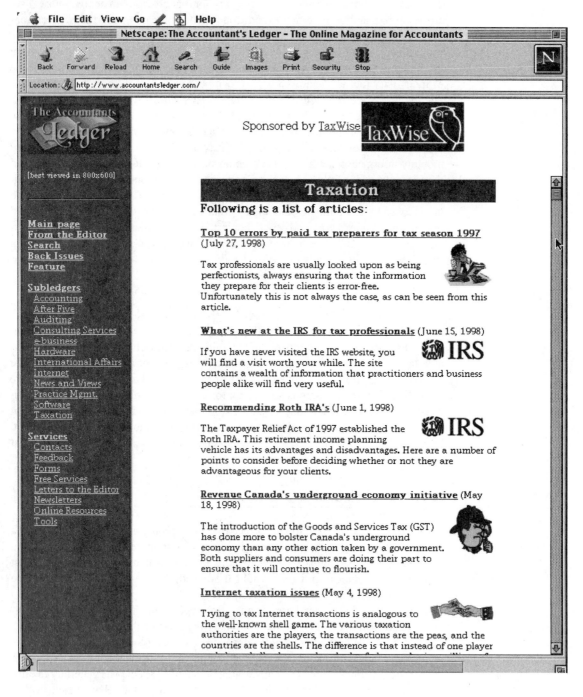

File   Edit   View   Go   Help

Netscape: The Accountant's Ledger – The Online Magazine for Accountants

Back   Forward   Reload   Home   Search   Guide   Images   Print   Security   Stop

Location: http://www.accountantsledger.com/

The Accountants Ledger

[best viewed in 800x600]

Main page
From the Editor
Search
Back Issues
Feature

Subledgers
  Accounting
  After Five
  Auditing
  Consulting Services
  e-business
  Hardware
  International Affairs
  Internet
  News and Views
  Practice Mgmt.
  Software
  Taxation

Services
  Contacts
  Feedback
  Forms
  Free Services
  Letters to the Editor
  Newsletters
  Online Resources
  Tools

Sponsored by TaxWise

Taxation
Following is a list of articles:

Top 10 errors by paid tax preparers for tax season 1997
(July 27, 1998)

Tax professionals are usually looked upon as being
perfectionists, always ensuring that the information
they prepare for their clients is error-free.
Unfortunately this is not always the case, as can be seen from this
article.

What's new at the IRS for tax professionals (June 15, 1998)

If you have never visited the IRS website, you
will find a visit worth your while. The site
contains a wealth of information that practitioners and business
people alike will find very useful.

Recommending Roth IRA's (June 1, 1998)

The Taxpayer Relief Act of 1997 established the
Roth IRA. This retirement income planning
vehicle has its advantages and disadvantages. Here are a number of
points to consider before deciding whether or not they are
advantageous for your clients.

Revenue Canada's underground economy initiative (May
18, 1998)

The introduction of the Goods and Services Tax (GST)
has done more to bolster Canada's underground
economy than any other action taken by a government.
Both suppliers and consumers are doing their part to
ensure that it will continue to flourish.

Internet taxation issues (May 4, 1998)

Trying to tax Internet transactions is analogous to
the well-known shell game. The various taxation
authorities are the players, the transactions are the peas, and the
countries are the shells. The difference is that instead of one player

EXHIBIT 9–16   Web sites

American Bar Association	http://www.abanet.org/tax/sites.html
The Accountant's Ledger	http://www.accountantsledger.com
Accounting Net	http://www.accountingnet.com
Bricker & Eckler LLP	http://benet-np1.bricker.com/practice/taxation/links.htm
Tax Gateways	http://www.best.com/~ftmexpat/html/taxsites/ gateways.html
Essential Links	http://www.el.com/elinks/taxes
Internet Law Library (Damon Key Leong Kupchak Hastert)	http://www.hawaiilawyer.com/interlaw.html
Tax World (Thomas Omer)	http://omer.actg.uic.edu
Alan G. Kalman home page	http://pages.prodigy.net/agkalman
Practitioners Publishing Company	http://www.ppcinfo.com/links.htm
Smeal College	http://www.smeal.psu.edu/acctg/links.html
Tax Analysts	http://www.taxanalysts.com
Tax Prophet	http://www.taxprophet.com
Tax Resources (Frank McNeil)	http://www.taxresources.com
Tax and Accounting Sites (Dennis Schmidt)	http://www.taxsites.com
Tax Web	http://taxweb.com
Tax Analysts	http://www.tax.org
American Taxation Association	http://www.uni.edu/ata/taxlinks.html
Will Yancey home page	http://www.willyancey.com

major law library, or if he or she is enrolled in a graduate taxation program that provides hardcopy or computerized access to numerous reference materials, it may not be necessary to acquire a large number of little-used or specialized items. Finally, the tax practitioner must determine how much should be spent on tax research materials. The materials in the following list represent the major elements and the range or approximate annual cost of items to be considered for a tax research library.

1. *Code and Regulations.* Either a paperback, not updated ($100 per set), or a loose-leaf volume(s) that is updated periodically ($200 to $400 per year).
2. *Tax Guide. Abridged one- or two-volume tax service, updated, but limited coverage on many topics ($250 to $400 per year).*
3. *Complete Tax Service.* Ten to twenty volumes of full service, should include updated Code and Regulations ($1,000 to $2,000 per year). Online or CD-ROM versions of these services are available for about the same annual charge.
4. *Professional Tax Journals.* Monthly or quarterly publication(s) needed in the tax researcher's practice ($150 to $275 each journal per year).
5. *Newsletters.* Daily or weekly updates on current tax matters ($200 for a weekly to $2,500 for a daily). Recall that most tax guides and tax services include a newsletter as part of the service.
6. *Court Reporters and the Cumulative Bulletin.* T.C., USTC, AFTR2d, and other court reporters, and the bound *Internal Revenue Bulletins* (several thousand dollars each to establish, and up to $500 per year to update several reporters).
7. *Online Tax Service.* LEXIS, WESTLAW, or another such service (charges rendered by the hour with various monthly minimums, which can average up to $125 per hour of usage).

▶ _____ Summary

Tax journals and other periodicals not only help researchers locate primary sources of the tax law, but also enlighten them as to other ways of analyzing a tax issue. Tax articles can synthesize information from the Code, Regulations, and pertinent court cases into a more logical presentation, which may be useful as the practitioner identifies relevant tax issues or precedents during the research process or prepares for litigation on behalf of a client. Finally, such publications are an integral part of the means by which the tax professional remains current with respect to the evolution of the federal tax law.

▶ _____ Key Words

By the time you complete your work relative to this chapter, you should be comfortable discussing each of the following terms. If you need additional review of any of these items, return to the appropriate material in the chapter or consult the glossary to this text.

Academic Journals	Professional Journals
Daily Tax Report	*Tax Base*
Federal Tax Articles	Tax Journal
Law Reviews	Tax Newsletter
Practitioner Journals	*Tax Notes*
Proceedings	

▶ _____ Discussion Questions

1. Why are tax journals and newsletters generally not cited as authority in professional tax research? However, when is it appropriate to cite tax journals or newsletters as authority in professional tax research?
2. What does the denotation "at 407" indicate in the citation of a journal?
3. Briefly describe each of the following.

   a. Annual proceedings
   b. Scholarly reviews
   c. Professional journals
   d. Newsletters

4. Name four major tax conferences and when they originated.
5. What are some of the distinctive characteristics of law reviews and academic journals?
6. Name four universities that publish tax-oriented journals or law reviews. Give the name of the journal or law review they publish.
7. What type of articles would a reader find in the *National Tax Journal* and *The Journal of the American Tax Association*? What academic organizations publish these journals?
8. What type of articles would a reader expect to find in *Taxes* versus the type you would expect to find in *Journal of Limited Liability Companies*? Which one of these would you expect to be published monthly and which quarterly?
9. Many tax services offer tax newsletters. How often are the Internet, online, and published newsletters made available to their subscribers?

10. Why is the *Daily Tax Report* one of the most important newsletters? What are the different sources available for accessing this newsletter?

11. Who publishes *Daily Tax Report, Tax Base*® and *Weekly Alert*? How are the *Daily Tax Report* and *Tax Base*® similar? How are the *Daily Tax Report* and *Tax Base*® different than *Weekly Alert*?

12. Why is every document mentioned in *Tax Notes* given a Tax Analysts' document number?

13. What is one of the most outstanding features of the CCH *Federal Tax Articles* that is not available in most other journal indexes?

14. How does the organizational framework of the CCH *Federal Tax Articles* differ from the WG&L *Index to Federal Tax Articles*?

15. What are three methods that can be used to locate articles in the CCH *Federal Tax Articles*? Can these same three methods of locating an article be used with the WG&L *Index to Federal Tax Articles*? Explain your answer.

16. Where are full article citations found in the *Federal Tax Articles* and the WG&L *Index to Federal Tax Articles*?

17. What is the function of the asterisk that appears next to an entry in the original volumes? How is this function treated in the current editions?

18. How frequently are the journal indexes, *Federal Tax Articles* and *Index to Federal Tax Articles,* updated?

19. What is included in *Shepard's Law Review Citations*?

20. What is included in *Federal Law Citations in Selected Law Reviews*? How many law reviews are "selected" for this index?

21. How often do CD-ROM and online indexes tend to be updated?

22. Name three indexes that contain references to tax articles but are not dedicated to taxation. Indicate whether they provide abstracts of articles or just citations. Indicate the formats in which they are available.

23. What type of information is available in the *Gale Directory of Databases*?

24. What is *The Accountant's Ledger*?

25. In deciding what to purchase for the tax library, the practitioner must answer several questions. Give a list of pertinent questions the practitioner should consider.

▶ _____ Exercises

26. Who is the publisher of each of the following tax journals or newsletters?

   a. *Taxation for Accountants*
   b. *The Tax Adviser*
   c. *Tax Notes*
   d. *Tax Management Memorandum*

27. For each of the following annual proceedings, give the dates on which the most recent meeting took place; list the name of the chair or editor of the session; indicate whether, in the preface or introduction to the proceedings, there is a central theme or concentration for that annual meeting; and give the title of the third article in the published proceedings.

   a. Institute on Federal Taxation (New York University)
   b. Annual Federal Tax Conference (University of Chicago Law School)
   c. Major Tax Planning Institute (University of Southern California)
   d. Institute on Oil and Gas Law and Taxation (Southwestern Legal Foundation)

28. Use CCH's *Federal Tax Articles* index to answer the following questions.

   a. Give the title and author(s) of the first article listed that discusses § 3121.
   b. Use the topic index to find the paragraph number and title of the most recent article about Limited Liability Companies (LLCs).
   c. Give the title of the most recent article listed by James H. Boyd.
   d. What is the date on the last update filed in your library's current binder of *Federal Tax Articles*? (Check behind the tab "Last Report Letter" to find the answer.)

29. Use CCH's *Federal Tax Articles* index to determine the publication schedule for the following journals.

   a. *Appraisal Journal*
   b. *Florida Certified Public Accountants*
   c. *New Mexico Law Review*
   d. *The Tax Adviser*

30. Use the WG&L *Index to Federal Tax Articles* to perform the following tasks. Include in your response the supplement and page number where each answer is located.

   a. Use the author index to determine the kind of "reclassification" mentioned in the title of a 1996 article by Jane O. Burns.
   b. Use the topic index to locate a 1998 article with four authors that discusses the Federal Insurance Contribution Act taxes application to ministers as employees or independent contractors.
   c. Who is the co-author with Zebulon R. Law of a 1998 article discussing the exclusion of gross income of the tenant allowances?
   d. In what year and by whom was an article in the *National Tax Journal* written on deducting education costs as medical expenses?

31. Find two current articles on short sales of stocks (§ 1233) using CCH's *Federal Tax Articles* index . Find the two different articles using the WG&L *Index to Federal Tax Articles*. List the articles in standard citation format and provide the index name, volume, and page number on which each citation was found. Compare the search strategies in using each index. Which one provides easier access?

32. Find an article on related party transactions that was presented at the Heckerling Institute of Estate Planning in 1997 using the CCH's *Federal Tax Articles* index. Find the same article using the WG&L *Index to Federal Tax Articles*. List the article in standard citation format and provide the index name, volume, and page number on which the citation was found. Compare the search strategies in using each index. Which one provides easier access?

33. Find current articles written by Richard B. Toolson using CCH's *Federal Tax Articles* index. Find the same articles using the WG&L *Index to Federal Tax Articles*. List the articles in standard citation format and provide the index name, volume, and page number on which each citation was found. What is the area of taxation covered by most of these articles? Compare the search strategies in using each index. Which one provides easier access?

34. Using the information collected in Exercises 31, 32, and 33, discuss the compatibility of CCH's *Federal Tax Articles* and the WG&L *Index to Federal Tax*

Articles with the three methods of locating an article (by Code section, by author, and by topic).

35. Use *Shepard's Federal Tax Citations in Selected Law Reviews* to find law review citations for each of the following. List the most recent citation if more than one appears. Indicate in which volume it occurs.

   a. 296 U.S. 1
   b. 114 S.Ct. 1473
   c. IRC § 401
   d. IRC §1276

36. Find a recent article in the following journals on the topics described. Give the full citation of the articles.

   a. *Journal of Corporate Taxation,* which discusses corporate organizations and reorganizations
   b. *The Journal of Real Estate Taxation,* which discusses final regulations under § 469(c)(7)
   c. *The Tax Adviser,* which discusses single-member LLCs and §357(c)
   d. *The Tax Lawyer,* which discusses a proposal to make credit shelter trusts obsolete

37. Locate the following articles and give the title and author(s) of the article.

   a. *Taxation for Accountants,* volume 60, number 2, p. 96
   b. *International Tax Journal,* volume 23, number 4, p. 76
   c. *National Public Accountant,* volume 41 number 3, p. 21
   d. *Taxes—The Tax Magazine,* volume 76, number 2, p. 25

38. Use an online service that is available to you to perform the following tasks.

   a. Start with the subject guide, enter "tax," and then "deferred tax (accounting)" to determine how articles are arranged. Is it by author, title, chronological, or reverse chronological order?
   b. Enter "estate tax" to address the following items.

   (i) How many subdivisions are under the general listing "estate tax"?
   (ii) Within the subdivisions, which has the most entries?
   (iii) Are there abstracts for every article or just selected ones?

39. Use the author index to one of the tax article services or an electronic periodical index to perform the following task. Select four authors and determine what tax area seems to be his or her main focus. Give the name of the index that you used and the type of information you found when you entered the author's name.

40. Use the most recent issue of the published newsletters to answer the following questions.

   a. What is the topic of the lead brief in "Policy Briefs" in *Tax Notes*?
   b. What is the topic of the first brief listed under "Highlight" in *Tax Management Weekly Report*?
   c. What is the topic of the first brief listed under "Tax Briefs" in *Taxes on Parade*?
   d. What is the lead article in *Weekly Alert*?

41. Select the most recent issue of an Internet newsletter such as *Daily Tax Report* (sample copy at http://subscript.bna.com/samples) to answer the following questions.

   a. What newsletter did you choose and what is the date of the newsletter?
   b. What is the lead article in the newsletter?
   c. What are the "departments" of the newsletter?
   d. Are there links to documents from the newsletter?

42. Use a computer journal index at your library that provides full-text access. Find a recent article on taxpayer noncompliance. Summarize the article and copy of the first page of the article.

43. Using the *Gale Directory of Databases,* identify a tax library database that is offered on CD-ROM. List the name of the CD-ROM, vender, and cost of the database.

44. Select one of the individual's home pages given in Exhibit 9–16 and list the major categories of links provided.

45. Select one of the organization's web pages given in Exhibit 9–16 and list the major categories of links provided.

46. Using the data collected in Exercises 44 and 45, compare the two sites. Which one provided more useful links? Which one was easier to use?

▶ _____ Research Cases

47. Using the CCH *Federal Tax Articles* index, list, in standard citation format, all of the articles that have been published since 1985 on § 1311, Correction of an Error.

48. In the 1985–1989 CCH *Federal Tax Articles* index, under § 1221, Capital Assets Defined, is the article "TAXES—A Safe Harbor for Authors and Artists" 70 *Management Accounting* (August 1988) 12 by Israel Blumenfrucht. From reading the abstract, it appears that this article addresses the tax issues of your research project. However, it's a 1988 article and you wonder if it's still relevant. Read the article and summarize what a taxpayer must do to elect the safe-harbor method. Determine whether this safe harbor is still available to authors and artists.

49. Using the WG&L *Index to Federal Tax Articles,* find an article that examines moral suasion and vertical equity issues with respect to taxpayer noncompliance. Write a brief summary of the article. Select two cites from this article to locate. Provide summaries of these two articles.

50. It is 3 a.m. and your dog just ate your only copy of the Code. (Some dogs will eat anything!) Find a text version of the Code on the Internet and print § 61. Where did you find the Code and who maintains the site? Send the site manager an e-mail message, expressing your appreciation for the manager's hard work in keeping the site up to date. Print your e-mail and if you get an answer, print it also. Does the version of the Code you found use text hyperlinks? What happens when you click on a hyperlink? Download and print a copy of a page with hyperlinks then click on several hyperlinks and print the page to which it links.

51. Through surfing on the Internet, you have seen some information about proposed regulations that would let partnerships and corporations change their entity status through what is called "check-the-box" provisions. You would like to know more about this. Find three articles from *Tax Notes* and two other journals on this topic. Write an integrative summary of the articles using standard citation format for the articles. Indicate which service you used to find the articles.

52. The Zuba S corporation is considering a reorganization involving Yabba S corporation. Their big concern is with the continuity of interest and continuity of business enterprise requirements. Two of the Zuba S shareholders are friends of yours and they ask for your opinion on the matter. You hedge and say that this is a complicated area and you'll get back them. You have a vague recollection of these requirements and remember for your corporate class that some final Regulations were recently issued in this area. An article on this would be helpful to refresh your memory. Find an article on the topic and briefly describe the changes the final regulations made on the continuity of interest and continuity of business enterprise requirements.

53. Using the Internet, find a copy of the final Regulations mentioned in Research Case 52. Print the first page of the Regulations. Indicate where you found the Regulations and who maintains the site. Send the site manager an e-mail message, expressing your appreciation for the manager's hard work in keeping the site up to date. Print your e-mail and if you get an answer, print it also. Does the version of the final Regulations you found use text hyperlinks? What happens when you click on a hyperlink? Download and print a copy of a page with hyperlinks then click on several hyperlinks and print the page to which it links.

54. Use the Internet to locate the Committee Reports for the most recent tax act passed by Congress. Print the first page of the House, Senate, and Joint Conference reports. Indicate where you found the Committee Reports and who maintains the site.

55. Select eight of the sites listed in Exhibit 9–16. Make a table showing the links each site provides. How much overlap is there? Determine the minimum number of sites you need to use to get the maximum amount of coverage. Out of your list, which site is the most essential?

56. Find five noncommercial web sites not listed in Exhibit 9–16 that provide useful tax information. List each site's address and what links to tax materials they provide.

Implementing the Research Tools

Communicating Research Results

▶ Produce a standard format for the construction of a file memorandum to contain the results of one's research efforts and professional judgment

▶ Develop other forms of communicating research results, including oral presentations and client letters

Communications and the Tax Professional
The Heart of Tax Research Communication:
  The File Memo
Evaluating the Sources of Law

Client Letters
Comprehensive Illustration of Client File
Oral Presentations of Research Results

Once the practitioner has begun to develop effective tax research skills, he or she must hone them with practice—whether by working through tax research cases presented as a class exercise in a university course, or immediately beginning work for professional clients. Accordingly, the overriding purpose of this chapter is to provide the reader with guidance and opportunities to apply the research skills, and examine the tax research resources, that have been discussed in previous chapters.

In addition, this chapter will discuss the means by which the tax professional conveys the results of a tax research project—in other words, applying some of the judgment and communications skills required. Direction as to the proper format and content of memorandums to the file, of client letters, and of oral presentations is addressed, with development of professional skills the overriding goal.

Communications and the Tax Professional

As we suggested in our initial discussions of the tax research process, illustrated in Exhibit 2–1, a tax research assignment often concludes with some form of communication by the tax professional. The audience for this communication often is the practitioner's supervisor or client, but tax-related communications can take many forms.

▶ A telephone call
▶ An informal discussion in person, or via e-mail
▶ A letter prepared for reading by someone at least as familiar with the tax law as the writer
▶ A letter prepared for reading by someone less familiar with the tax law than is the writer
▶ A letter prepared for reading by someone who is essentially untrained in the tax law
▶ An article for publication in a newspaper or magazine directed at the general public
▶ An article for publication in a professional journal read by tax generalists
▶ An article for publication in a professional journal read by tax specialists
▶ A speech to a general audience
▶ A speech at a conference of tax professionals
▶ A memorandum to be read in the future by the writer or by a peer with similar training
▶ An appearance on a news broadcast or program with a serious tone
▶ An appearance on a broadcast with a less serious tone
▶ A posting on an Internet bulletin board or news group

For the most part, the tax professional's preparation for these communications is similar. For the purposes of this chapter, we assume that all of the pertinent tax research techniques developed in earlier parts of this text have been planned and conscientiously applied, so the practitioner is qualified and current enough with respect to prevailing tax law to address the audience in terms of the content of the communication. The challenge then becomes how to deliver this information in a manner that will be accepted and understood by the audience.

Actually, though, one's preparation for the delivery of tax communication must go far beyond obtaining control over the technical tax knowledge required for the assignment. As illustrated in Exhibit 10–1, communication truly occurs only when the message desired to be sent by the speaker or writer is received by the intended audience. Distractions of all sorts can make this process difficult to accomplish. Thorough research into the nature and expectations of the audience, factors that may interfere with the delivery of the message, and feedback and corrective measures must make up a critical part of the communicator's preparation.

Examples of "noise" that can disrupt the communications process include a mismatching of expectations as to message, the chosen delivery method, the identity and nature of the sender and receiver of the message, other events competing for the attention of those involved, logistical difficulties, and technological problems. Feedback and corrective devices that can aid in accomplishing the delivery of the desired message include formal and informal evaluation processes, "real-time" opportunities such as question-and-answer periods and written comments received during the drafting of the document, and the sending and receiving of intended and unintended body language or other communicative signals.

Tax professionals generally are virtually untrained as to the application of communication methods in conveying tax messages, but this shortcoming can be remedied. The chief ingredients necessary to become an effective tax-content communicator are the desire to learn and improve as a communicator in general, and the use of every opportunity possible to obtain and develop skills in the delivery of tax information. Given the nature of today's competitive tax profession, plenty of such opportunities for practice exist, and pressures from others who are competing for clients and promotions provides most professionals with more than enough motivation to make improvements in their communication skills a lifelong process.

EXHIBIT 10–1 The communication process

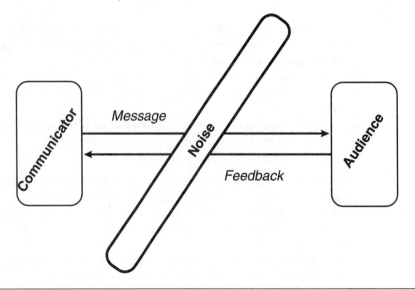

EXHIBIT 10–2   The structure of technical tax communications

Element of the Message	Purposes	Comments
Introduction	Provide a roadmap for what is to come. Place the message in context. Generate audience interest, if necessary. Set the tone for the message.	10% of allotted time/space. Could include a story/anecdote, current news development, or "object lesson."
Body	Generally, the technical tax 80% of allotted material is presented here. Usually follows an order suggested by the hierarchy of the sources of the tax law. Alternative ordering methods: historical, strengths/weaknesses, cost/benefit.	Must be brief, to the point, hard-hitting; not trite or condescending. time/space. Identify three to six key points that all readers/ listeners must take away from the message.
Conclusion	Tie back to the introduction. Reinforce key elements of the message. Bring the presentation to a climax. Indicate next steps and follow-up action.	10% of allotted time/space. Tip off the reader/listener that the conclusion is starting, with "In closing," "To sum up," or "I'll conclude with. . . ."

We begin a more detailed review of the communication process with an examination of the most commonly encountered written communications demanded in the tax practice. The chapter concludes with a discussion of skills needed in delivering spoken communications. In either case, the structure of the communication follows the basic format delineated in Exhibit 10–2.

The Heart of Tax Research Communication: The File Memo

The tax researcher spends most of his or her time reviewing primary and secondary sources of the federal tax law, redefining pertinent issues, and attempting to discover additional facts concerning the client's situation. On completion of this review, the researcher must integrate the disparate results of the research process into a more usable form. Thorough practitioners generate a memorandum to the client's file for this purpose. This **file memorandum** is designed to:

▶ organize the facts, issues, and conclusions of the project,
▶ facilitate a review of the research activities by the practitioner's supervisors or colleagues, and

▶ allow for a subsequent examination of the research issue, by the original researcher or by his or her successor, with respect to the same or another client's identical or related fact situation.

Accordingly, the file memo should be constructed in a general, usable format that lends itself to a quick perusal of the pertinent tax facts and issues. Many accounting and law firms impose a standardized format. If the reader's employer has enacted no such requirement, he or she should consider adopting the format illustrated in Exhibit 10–3.

A file memo should include a brief introductory summary of the facts and issues that face the client. In all but the most complex instances, this statement should require no more than two paragraphs. Similarly, the rare file-memo footnote should be restricted to current developments, for example, with respect to an appeal relative to one of the critical cases that is cited in the memo or a statutory amendment.

The file memo then includes a listing of the tax issues that are in dispute, and a matching conclusion for each identified issue. This format allows the subsequent reader to determine quickly whether each issue is "pro" or "con" for the taxpayer, and limits the time required to sort through a number of such memos. In the analysis section, a detailed review and evaluation of controlling laws is derived, with full citations presented in the standard forms. The "meat" of the memo is presented here, and the strengths and weaknesses of both sides of the tax argument are developed and discussed. In the summary material, conclusions are repeated, recommendations for subsequent actions with the client may be enumerated, and other strategies as to tax return or audit positions are identified.

Often, the gathering of the pertinent facts is the most challenging of the tax professional's tasks. Tax engagements typically begin with client contact in the form of a phone call or meeting, followed by an exchange of copies of pertinent documents such as letters, spreadsheets, trusts or wills, contracts, life insurance or annuity agreements, employer handbooks, and diaries or logbooks belonging to the client. In reality, though, the initial determination of the facts is likely to be incomplete.

▶ Taxpayers tend to see the dispute only from "their side," so that facts and circumstances that may cast doubt on the ability to determine or document the pro-taxpayer position may be hidden or "forgotten."

▶ Taxpayers are not trained in the details of the technical tax law, so they may be unable to determine which documents or other evidence of the facts is important in determining the controlling tax law.

▶ For tax research that requires the full professional judgment and experience of the practitioner, there may be no clearly controlling tax statute or precedent, facts may be truly incomplete, or they may unfold as the evaluation of tax law occurs. The researcher may discover that issues of taxpayer motive, knowledge, or other circumstances turn on facts that were not immediately known to be critical.

Moreover, fact gathering often turns on such intangible factors as the reliability of the memories of the taxpayers and key witnesses, the ability of witnesses to withstand scrutiny in the deposition and testimony phases of the case, the unanticipated death or disappearance of key parties, destruction of records due to casualty or computer mismanagement, and the tendency of some taxpayers to "fix the truth" after the fact. Recalling our language of Chapters 2 and 3, more research engagements

EXHIBIT 10–3   File memorandum for tax research

September 15, 19x9

To: File
From: Johnson
Re: Client Brown's Interest Deductions

Facts

The Browns live in Minnesota. They own their home and hold investments in the debt of several domestic corporations. The interest that they received on this debt was gross income to them. To diversify their portfolio, the Browns took out a sizable second mortgage on their home and applied a portion of the proceeds to some City of Chandler School Bonds. The remainder of the proceeds was used to expand the facilities of Mrs. Brown's dental clinic.

Issue

How much of the mortgage interest paid can be claimed as an itemized deduction by the Browns?

Conclusion

That portion of the mortgage proceeds applied to the dental clinic generates an interest deduction, to be claimed against clinic income on Schedule C. No other deduction is allowed.

Analysis

The Code disallows the deduction of interest on indebtedness that is incurred or continued to purchase or carry obligations, the interest on which is exempt from the federal income tax. IRC § 265(a)(2). This provision denies the double benefit that would be enjoyed by the taxpayer who would receive tax-exempt income while simultaneously claiming an investment interest deduction for the interest expense paid; e.g., by incurring a bank loan and using the proceeds to purchase municipal bonds.

The IRS examines evidence to infer the intent of the taxpayer who is incurring the indebtedness. Under Rev. Proc. 72–18, 1972–1 C.B. 740, a taxpayer who purchases exempt bonds can claim an interest deduction if the debt in question has been incurred (1) for personal reasons (e.g., via a mortgage to finance the purchase of residential property) or (2) for valid business reasons, as long as the borrowing does not exceed legitimate business needs.

Several court decisions have emphasized that the existence of such business motives must be documented clearly, as to both presence and amount. *Wisconsin Cheeseman v. U.S.,* 388 F.2d 420 (CA–7, 1968), *Bradford,* 60 T.C. 253 (1973), *Israelson v. U.S.,* 367 F.Supp. 1104 (D.Md., 1973). However, if the taxpayer's holdings of tax-exempt securities are deemed to be immaterial in amount, the § 265(a)(2) disallowance will not be invoked. *Indian Trail Trading Post Inc. v. Comm.,* 503 F.2d 102 (CA–6, 1974). Typically, if the average adjusted basis of the exempt bonds does not exceed 2 percent of the average adjusted basis of the entire investment portfolio, the entire interest deduction is allowed. *Batten v. U.S.,* 322 F.Supp. 629 (E.D.Va., 1971), *Ball v. Comm.,* 54 T.C. 1200 (1970).

Mortgage indebtedness is a classic illustration of an investment that will generate deductible interest expenses for the taxpayer who holds exempt bonds. However, the timing of such a mortgage transaction must be monitored, to exhibit the proper motives for the benefit of the IRS. In one case, the taxpayer paid for his home with cash. Only later was an investment program (that included municipal bonds) initiated and a residential mortgage secured. The IRS inferred that the mortgage proceeds were in indirect support of the exempt indebtedness, and the deduction for the mortgage interest was disallowed. *Mariorenzi v. Comm.,* 490 F.2d 92 (CA–8, 1974), 32 TCM 681 (1973). Had the taxpayer secured a mortgage before the home was completed, purchasing the exempt bonds out of savings, it appears that the deduction could have been preserved. The IRS has applied this doctrine outside of the Eighth Circuit, in PLR 80041291.

Summary

Only the interest payments that are traceable to the family business are deductible, probably on Schedule C as a business expense, not as a Schedule A itemized deduction.

Because the Browns live in the Eighth Circuit, the *Mariorenzi* doctrine prevails, and no itemized deduction is allowed at all, i.e., for that portion of the loan that is applied to the school bonds. Rev. Proc. 72–18 is insensitive to portfolio diversification motives, and no personal motive appears to exist that supports any other possible deduction. According to the logic of these precedents, the Browns should have sold the exempt bonds and then used the proceeds to finance their portfolio acquisitions.

entail closed-fact settings than open-fact situations by far, but those facts may be fairly difficult to determine and support in a manner that will satisfy the IRS or the courts. Such fact-gathering travails make for interesting anecdotes at conferences of tax practitioners, and they seldom are apparent from the clean, "black-and-white" statements of facts that accompany file memos and case briefs.

The tone and nature of the file memo should recognize that its readers will be restricted to fellow tax practitioners who are well versed in the federal tax law. Thus, references to primary and secondary sources of the tax law should be frequent and complete, but usually limited to the tax case reporters that are available in the office of the researcher's firm. One must presume that the ultimate reader of the memo's comments will need no introduction to the hierarchy of the federal tax system, nor to statutory citation practices. In addition, it often is helpful to include pertinent references to one or more of the commercial tax services to which the researcher's firm subscribes, perhaps on a "sticky note" or other attachment to the memo, providing a clear paper trail to facilitate subsequent review and commentary concerning the tax issue.

Seldom will the researcher's efforts result in merely the preparation of a research memorandum to the file. In general, the memo will be accompanied in the file by briefs of one or more pertinent court cases or administrative pronouncements. (Review Exhibit 5–6 and your related class exercises concerning the format and content of a well-constructed court case brief.) In addition, many practitioners append to the file memo photocopies of or hyperlinks to critical court case opinions, regulations or rulings, and journal articles, much of which features "highlighting" (markup with a pastel marker). The authors recommend that practitioners restrict such appended material to only those resources that are of utmost importance, to reduce both the associated client costs and the volume of the typical memo. In this regard, we believe that an effective statement of facts and issues, followed by a concise synthesis of the controlling law, is far more valuable than a mass of duplicated, small-print tax reference materials.

Evaluating the Sources of Law

The tax researcher will have made a number of judgments and creative applications concerning the client's fact situation before preparing the file memo. For instance, the researcher may select and eliminate competing issues and direct the research process onto one or more pathways to the exclusion of others. Nonetheless, in deriving an analysis of the various elements of the controlling sources of the tax law, the practitioner must choose from among a number of varied interpretations of the statute and of its (interpretive) regulations and court case opinions.

Often the researcher will be guided in this regard by the opinions of the most recent of the court cases discovered. Well-written case opinions typically provide a summary of the evolution of the pertinent tax law and a discussion of the competing interpretations thereof by the parties to the lawsuit. In this manner, the researcher regularly can obtain an indication of both the critical facts and issues that the court has identified in the present case, and its interpretation as to the distinguishing features of seemingly relevant precedents. (In reality, most of these sections of the opinion are written by law clerks or law school students, who obtain and retain their positions by preparing thorough and insightful file memos of their own!) Moreover, an increasing number of case opinions include lengthy dissenting or concurring opinions, from which the researcher can further identify the pertinent facts and issues relative to the opinion.

Lacking (or in lieu of) such judicial direction, the researcher's evaluation of the efficacy of a precedent or pronouncement often is guided by no more than a review of the hierarchy of the sources of the federal tax law. (For a review of these sources, see Chapters 3 through 5.)

In addition, we offer the following points to be considered in the evaluation of a series of apparently conflicting tax laws.

▶ Regulations seldom are held to be invalid by a court. In the typical year, fewer than a dozen such holdings are issued. Thus, challenges to the provisions of a Regulation should be based on more than a simple challenge to the Treasury's authority or a self-serving competing interpretation of the statute offered by the taxpayer.

▶ Revenue Rulings and Revenue Procedures, however, are frequently modified or otherwise held to be invalid by a court. Accordingly, the taxpayer's attempted restructuring of the pertinent law in his or her favor with respect to such an administrative pronouncement is more likely to be heard openly by the court and, therefore, to be based on the weight of the competing arguments rather than simply on the Treasury's preemptive interpretive rights.

▶ The decisions of courts that are higher in the judicial hierarchy should receive additional precedential weight. Given an adequate degree of similarity in fact situations, district and circuit court opinions have direct bearing on the taxpayer only if they were issued in the corresponding jurisdiction. On the other hand, opinions of the Court of Federal Claims and Tax Court are binding on the taxpayer, even though they were issued with respect to a taxpayer who works or resides in another jurisdiction, unless they are overturned in a pertinent appeal.

▶ Thus, a taxpayer who works in Wyoming is not bound by decisions of, say, the Seventh Circuit or Alaska District courts. The practitioner should not feel restricted in a trial or appeal hearing by the doctrine of *stare decisis*. Conversely, an Alaska taxpayer's Court of Federal Claims decision is binding on the Wyoming citizen's Court of Federal Claims case. If this Court of Federal Claims decision was held in a manner that is detrimental to the Wyoming taxpayer, another trial court should be pursued.

▶ Other factors being equal, decisions of the Second, Ninth, and Federal Circuits should be assigned additional precedential value. Among other reasons, this additional weight can be attributed to the inclusion of the cities of New York and Washington, and the state of California, in these circuits. Typically, the Ninth Circuit is the first to introduce an innovative or otherwise unusual interpretation of the law, and the Second and Federal Circuits are authoritative in a more traditional vein.

▶ Older court decisions should be assigned a geometrically declining degree of importance, unless (1) they are Supreme Court cases, (2) they are Second, Ninth, or Federal Circuit cases, or (3) they are the only precedents available. The roster and philosophical makeup of a court change over time and often reflect the changing societal culture and philosophies. Thus, recent case opinions are more likely to identify issues that are held to be critical by the sitting judges that the taxpayer will face, and they are likely to be better predictors of the outcome relative to the current taxpayer's issues.

▶ Tax journal articles are a useful source by which to identify current, critical tax issues. They also can be utilized in the formation of the practitioner's research schedule, because they often include both a comprehensive summary of the evolution of the controlling law and a thorough list of citations concerning prior interpretive court decisions.

▶ IRS agents are bound only by the Code, administrative pronouncements, and Supreme Court decisions. Some of the most difficult decisions a tax practitioner must face include those in which one must determine whether the time, effort, and expense of litigation will generate a reward that is sufficient to justify, in essence, the construction of new (judicial) tax law, that is, to overcome this narrow scope of the agent's concern.

▶ Court decisions are never completely predictable. Thus, even if absolutely all of the judicial precedent that is available supports the taxpayer's position, the court still may hold against him or her. Negative decisions may be the result of a poor performance by the attorney, other tax adviser, or witnesses that are heard by the court; changes in the makeup or philosophy of the members of the court; changes in societal mores, as reflected by the court; or an incorrect interpretation of the law by the court that hears the present case. The practitioner, however, can do little more than conduct a thorough tax research analysis concerning the case, identify convincing witnesses, and trust that justice will prevail.

Client Letters

Our discussion to this point in the chapter has concentrated on the communication of tax research by the practitioner to him- or herself, or to other tax professionals, in a fairly sophisticated document—a memorandum to the file. We now shift the focus for the communication to a different audience, namely, the client, and to a different setting, the written or oral presentation.

By far the most common form of communication between the tax professional and his or her client is the telephone call. We must stress the danger inherent in placing too great a dependence on the phone call to convey the results of tax research, given the intricacies of both the fact situation and the (tax adviser's interpretation of) controlling law, in most professional situations. If the telephone must be used (perhaps because of time pressures or convenience) to convey tax research results, the practitioner should always send a fairly detailed follow-up **client letter,** confirming his or her understanding as to the information that was conveyed and the actions that are to be taken as a result of the call.

Foremost among the attributes of the client letter is its brevity. Except in the most unusual circumstances, it should not exceed two pages. This rule should only be violated when the subject of the research is especially complex or grave, perhaps in anticipation of extended litigation, or with respect to a more sophisticated client, where, for instance, one might be tempted to attach a copy (or a "client version") of the research file memo.

The brevity of the client letter is, most often, in response to the desire of the client for "the answer" that has been found concerning the extant tax issues. Clients do tend to see tax issues as black-and-white ones, and they want to know whether they will "win or lose" with the IRS. Of course, tax practitioners are aware of the colorful world that tax practice presents, and the various shades of emphasis and interpretation sometimes make the view quite murky. Thus, to accommodate the desire of the client, one typically must convey no more than the absolute highlights of the research process.

Another factor that leads to brief client letters is the tax practitioner's professional responsibilities. Responding to client questions is generally easier in a face-to-face meeting. Thus, most practitioners use the client letter to deliver the general conclusions of the research project and to request a follow-up meeting in which questions, comments, and the need for more detail can be addressed.

Exhibits 10–4 and 10–5 illustrate the format and content of typical client letters. The sole difference between these two letters is the degree of sophistication that is possessed by the receiving party.

In general, the client letter should be structured as follows, perhaps allowing one paragraph for each of the noted topics.

- ▶ Salutation/social graces/general conclusion
- ▶ Summary of the research project results
- ▶ Objective of the report
- ▶ Statement of facts and disclaimer as to the scope of the tax professional's knowledge base
- ▶ Summary of critical sources of law that lead to result
- ▶ Implications of the results
- ▶ Assumptions/limitations
- ▶ Closing/reference to follow-up meeting/social graces
- ▶ Attachments, if any (e.g., engagement letter, file memo, illustrative charts, bibliography), on a separate page

Effective written business communication often makes use of the following guidelines. Notice that most of these elements are present in each of the two sample client letters that we have included in this chapter.

- ▶ Make your main point(s) in the first paragraph of the communication.
- ▶ State a well-defined purpose for the document, and stick to it.
- ▶ Avoid "filler" language, e.g., "at the present time," "the fact that," "as you know," and "enclosed please find."
- ▶ Avoid cliches and trendy jargon; e.g., "interface," "input," "parameter," "hands-on," "state-of-the- art," and any number of sports analogies.
- ▶ Don't be afraid to revise the letter several times to improve its format or to expand or narrow (as needed) its content. In this regard, allow enough time for the preparation of the document in a professional manner.
- ▶ Use the social amenities to your advantage by spelling names correctly, keeping current on the recipient's promotions and current title, and adding handwritten messages at the beginning or end of the document.
- ▶ *Practice writing* until it becomes easier and more enjoyable for you to do. Word processing programs, with the editing and proofreading capabilities that they provide, will aid you in this task.

Comprehensive Illustration of Client File

Exhibit 10–6 provides a comprehensive illustration of the two major elements of a client file: a client letter and a file memo. Notice the degree of correspondence

EXHIBIT 10–4 Sample client letter—sophisticated client

November 19, 19x9

M/M Dale Brown
2472 North Mayfair Road
Fillingham, SD 59990

Dear Dale and Rae,

Thanks again for requesting my advice concerning the tax treatment of your interest expenses. I am sorry to report that only a portion of your expenses can be deducted this year.

I have uncovered a series of court cases in which the IRS has prevailed over the taxpayer's requests for a deduction that is similar to yours. Unfortunately, the Tax Court's position is that interest such as yours is nondeductible, and additional litigation would be necessary to bring about a more favorable result for you.

My efforts have concentrated on the treatment of interest expenses that are incurred by taxpayers who hold exempt bonds while maintaining a bank loan that requires interest payments.

Over the last twenty-five years or so, a number of Circuit Court decisions have held that a taxpayer effectively must divest him- or herself of investments in such municipal bonds, regardless of portfolio diversification objectives, before a deduction for the interest payments to the bank is allowed. Fortunately, however, an exception exists relative to business-related loans, so that interest that is related to Rae's clinic will be allowed as a deduction. Conversely, that portion of the loan that relates to your school bond investment is nondeductible, even though it is secured by your residence.

You may wish to reconsider your use of the mortgage for this purpose, as your tax advantages therefrom are somewhat limited. This appears to be more palatable for you than would be the alternative of expensive further (and, probably, fruitless) litigation of the issue.

My conclusion is based upon the facts that you have provided me, and upon the efficacy of these somewhat dated court decisions. As you've requested, I've attached a copy of my research memo for you to read and from which you might develop subsequent inquiries.

I'm sorry that the news from me wasn't more favorable. I look forward to seeing you, though, at the firm's holiday reception!

Sincerely,
Tax Researcher

---

between the two documents in that some portions of the client letter are no more than quotations or paraphrases of the file memo.

The remainder of the internal file for this hypothetical client would include, among many other possibilities, (1) an engagement letter, (2) a billing and collection history, (3) case, regulation, and ruling briefs that are pertinent to the file memo, and (4) reproductions of important analyses of the client's prevailing tax issues from treatises, journal articles, and other resources.

Each consulting firm or tax department has its own formatting requirements with respect to client files. As tax research becomes conducted almost exclusively using

EXHIBIT 10–5   Sample client letter—less sophisticated client

November 19, 19x9

M/M Dale Brown
2472 North Mayfair Road
Fillingham, SD 59990

Dear Dale and Rae,

Thanks again for requesting my advice concerning the tax treatment of your interest expenses. I am sorry to report that only a portion of your expenses can be deducted this year.

My research has uncovered a series of successes by the IRS in convincing several important courts that interest such as yours should not be allowed as a deduction to reduce your taxes. Unfortunately, the court whose decision initially would prevail upon us would hold against you, and a series of court hearings, over two or three years or so, would be necessary for you to win the case.

This research has been restricted to situations that are similar to yours, that is, in which the taxpayer both owns a municipal bond and owes money to the bank from an interest-bearing loan.

It seems that the IRS would rather have you purchase the municipal bonds with your own money, rather than with the bank's. It maintains that you get a double benefit from the nontaxability of the School Bond interest income and the deductibility of the interest expense that is paid to the bank. Thus, that portion of the interest that relates to the bond investment is not allowed. A business purpose for the loan salvages the deduction, however, so you can deduct the interest from the loan that relates to Dr. Rae's clinic.

You may just have to live with this situation, as the IRS has been winning cases like these for about twenty-five years. Yours is not likely to be the one that changes their mind, so you might reconsider your investment in the municipals in the near future.

My conclusion is based upon the facts that you have provided me, and upon the reliability of the court cases that I found.

I'm sorry that the news from me wasn't more favorable. I look forward to seeing you, though, at the firm's holiday reception!

Sincerely,
Tax Researcher

---

computer and telephone equipment, the temptation will be for the tax researcher to reduce the thickness of the client file, as duplications of controlling law and other precedent are deemed unnecessary. This paper reduction movement constitutes a laudable goal, yet one must not shortchange the importance of the client file as a roadmap by which to retrace the researcher's line of thinking that leads to the conclusions and recommendations evidenced in the file memo and client letter. Electronic equivalents of the mind-map of the researcher, and of underlining or pastel highlighting of portions of lengthy legal documents, must be developed.

Accordingly, every tax researcher must develop or work with a scheme by which to cross-reference the steps of the professional critical thinking model undertaken on

EXHIBIT 10-6 Client file illustration

December 10, 19x9

Harold and Frieda van Briske
2000 Fox Point Heights
Whitefish Bay, RI 02899

Dear Harold and Frieda,

Congratulations on your recent marriage! I hope that you found your honeymoon at Club Med to be an enjoyable and memorable experience.

Thank you again for requesting my advice concerning the tax treatment of your antenuptial agreement. I am happy to report that the transaction will not result in the imposition of any federal tax for either of you.

My research has uncovered a series of successes by the IRS in convincing several important courts, including the Supreme Court, that an agreement such as yours is not supported by "full and adequate consideration," and, therefore, that it is to be treated as a gift. Although you did not intend for your property transfer to be a gift, the intent of the parties in such agreements does not control for federal tax purposes.

Fortunately, however, the treatment of your transaction as a gift will result in the imposition of neither federal income tax nor federal gift tax upon you. Federal income tax is not imposed upon the transfer because gross income is not recognized by either the donor or donee in the context of a gift. Although a gift has occurred, no gift tax is due, because the unlimited gift tax marital deduction neutralizes the transfer.

This research has been restricted to fact situations that are similar to yours, that is, in which, pursuant to an antenuptial agreement, a married taxpayer surrendered his or her other marital rights in exchange for a sum of money or other property.

My conclusion is based upon the facts that you have provided to me, and upon the reliability of the court cases that I found.

I look forward to seeing you at the Christmas Charity Ball!

Sincerely,
Karen J. Boucher, CPA, JD, MST

December 10, 19x9
To: File
From: Boucher
Re: van Briske Antenuptial Agreement

Facts   On the morning of their wedding, Frieda gave to Harold $400,000 of appreciated stock, pursuant to a prenuptial agreement. Frieda's basis in the stock was $150,000. In exchange for these securities, Harold surrendered all other marital rights and claims to Frieda's assets, under the terms of the agreement. Harold and Frieda both are residents of Arizona.

Issues   (1) What are the gift tax consequences of this exchange?
                 (2) What are the income tax consequences of this exchange?

Conclusions (1) Frieda incurs no gift tax liability as the agreement is executed and implemented.
                 (2) Asset basis carries over to Harold, the new owner of the securities. Neither Frieda nor Harold recognize gross income as a result of the exchange.

EXHIBIT 10–6   *Continued*

Analysis   *Issue One*

Donative intent on the part of the donor is not an essential element in the application of the gift tax. Reg. § 25.2511–1(g)(1)

The Supreme Court has held that antenuptial transfers in relinquishment of marital rights are not adequate and full consideration in money or money's worth for the transfer of property, within the meaning of IRC § 2512(b). *Merrill v. Fahs,* 324 U.S. 308, 65 S.Ct. 655 (1945); *Comm. v. Wemyss,* 324 U.S. 303, 65 S.Ct. 652 (1945); Reg. § 25.2512–8. However, the Second Circuit has held that an antenuptial agreement was acquired for valuable consideration and did not constitute a gift, for income tax (basis computation) purposes. *Farid-Es-Sultaneh v. Comm.,* 160 F.2d 812 (CA–2, 1947). This decision is not critical to the present analysis, though, because the van Briskes do not live in the Second Circuit, and because the somewhat dated decision may be aberrational.

Although the van Briske transaction resulted in a gift, no gift tax is imposed, due to the application of the annual exclusion and the unlimited gift tax marital deduction. IRC §§ 2503(b) and 2523; Reg. § 25.2511–2(a); Rev. Rul. 69–347, 1969–2 C.B. 227.

IRC § 2501 imposes a tax on the transfer of property by gift; the gift tax is not imposed, though, upon the receipt of property by the donee. Rather, it is the transfer itself that triggers the tax. Since the prenuptial agreement here is enforceable by state law only when consummated by marriage, the transfer has not taken place until after the marriage occurred. Thus, the transfer appears to be eligible for the gift tax marital deduction, regardless of the timing of the transfer relative to the marriage ceremony on the wedding day. Even if the securities had been physically transferred to Harold prior to the completion of the ceremonies, the agreement was only enforceable after the couple was married. The IRS likely would not need or attempt to establish the exact moments of both (1) the transfer of the securities, and (2) the consummation of the marriage. *C.I.R. v. Bristol,* 121 F.2d 129 (CA–1, 1960); *Bradford,* 34 T.C. 1059 (1960, A); *Archbold,* 42 B.T.A. 453 (1940, A in result only); *Harris v. Comm.,* 178 F.2d 861 (1949).

Issue Two

Neither Harold nor Frieda recognize any gross income upon Harold's release of his marital rights. Gross income does not include the value of property that is acquired by gift. IRC §102(a); Reg. §1.102–1(a); Rev. Rul. 79–312; Rev. Rul. 67–221; *Howard v. C.I.R.,* 447 F.2d 152 (CA–5, 1971).

The transfer of securities is not deductible in any way by Frieda, but under the *Farid* decision, Harold's basis may be stepped up to fair market value. Recall our earlier comments, though, concerning the reliability of this precedent. *Illinois National Bank v. U.S.,* 273 F.2d 231 (CA–7, 1959), cert. den. 363 U.S. 803, 80 S.Ct. 1237 (1960); *C.I.R. v. Marshman,* 279 F.2d 27, cert. den. 364 U.S. 918, 81 S.Ct. 282 (1960); Rev. Rul. 79–312. In the typical gift situation, the donee takes the donor's income tax basis in the transferred property. IRC §§ 1015(a), 1041(a)(1).

Summary   The van Briske prenuptial agreement prompts a gift from Frieda to Harold. However, no gift tax liability results, as the unlimited gift tax marital deduction neutralizes the transfer. Neither Harold nor Frieda recognizes gross income from the transfer, and Frieda can claim no income tax deduction therefor. Most likely, Frieda's $150,000 basis in the assets carries over to Harold.

the client's behalf. This might entail a listing of legal citations and computer files that would bear upon a reconstruction of the researcher's analysis, perhaps in the form of a decision tree or project management summary. Various software applications will be useful in this regard, not the least of which is the "footsteps" feature of many electronic tax research products, which records the detailed sequencing of commands and decisions made during the online or CD-based project. Regardless of the form this project diary takes, its importance for professional quality control cannot be overstated.

Oral Presentations of Research Results

Psychologists tell us that most people's greatest fear is speaking before groups of other people. Indeed, the thought of being the only one in the room who is standing, of having your listeners whispering their evaluations of you to each other, of having members of the audience taking notes on (or tape recording) your comments (certainly so that your errors of omission and commission can be parroted back at a later date), and of fielding extemporaneous questions, is enough to bring many people to tears.

Yet, public speaking is an important part of the tax practitioner's professional life. In many ways, it is the most accurate predictor of success. As politicians have long known, when one is delivering an oral presentation in an effective and professional manner, the audience becomes convinced that all of the other professional qualities that they desire from the speaker are also present. Conversely, an ill-prepared or ill-delivered message can do much to erode the audience's confidence in the speaker, not just with respect to the topic of the presentation, but in general.

Thus, it behooves the tax professional to develop skill in public speaking. In contexts that range from the presentation of an award to a colleague or the conduct of a staff meeting, to the presentation of a keynote address at the annual tax conference of your peers, such skills can mean the difference between enhancing and damaging your reputation.

What is advised here is not a series of "tricks" to fool the audience into believing that you are more knowledgeable than you really are. Rather, we convey here some time-tested techniques leading to an effective communication of ideas—from one who has developed a secure base of knowledge in a subject, to an audience with a specified background that has a desire to learn more about that subject. Whether making a presentation of one's results to a supervisor in one's own firm, or elaborating on a research project with the client's board of directors, the communication of tax research results poses special problems that make a review of oral communications procedures all the more valuable. Specifically, we can make the following suggestions concerning **oral presentations** of tax research.

► General preparation for the talk should include a thorough, frank examination of the following set of questions by the presenter. Nearly all of these observations can be characterized as knowledge of the makeup of the audience.

Why me? Why was I asked to speak? What knowledge or celebrity do I bring to the event?

What do they want? What does the audience hope to take away from the presentation? Technical knowledge? Relief from stress? Inspiration? Skill development? Amusement or entertainment? Should I present an overview or a detailed technical update or analysis?

What is their attitude? Is the audience coming to the event curious or anxious to hear from me, or must they be persuaded of the relevance or importance of my topics?

From what should I stay away? Are there topics that are taboo for this audience, due to their age, experiences, or existing attitudes? One must not alienate the audience, wittingly or unwittingly, in any way if the message is to get across.

What do they already know? What is the knowledge base of the audience? It would be ideal to speak to a homogeneous audience, especially in the level of knowledge that it brings into the event, but this seldom is the case. One must decide, then, whether to aim at the median knowledge base, above, or below. The stakes are high in exercising this judgment, though, and either repeating what is common knowledge to the group, or presenting information at a high level that is accessible to only a few in the audience, can make communication impossible.

Who is the audience? Details as to the audience's demographic characteristics such as age, education and income level, political leanings, and so forth can be vital for tailoring one's style, presentation speed and media, references to literature and popular culture, and use of humor in an effective manner. Remember to play to as many members of the audience as possible, not just the majority of those in attendance or those who were involved directly in hiring or retaining your services.

▶ Be prepared in the technical aspects of your discussion, particularly the basic research. Spend most of your preparation time on your main points and conclusions rather than on the fine points. If you are caught without a piece of technical information, it is clearly better for you if that information is specific (so that you can refer the questioner to a more detailed reference, or to a later, private conversation with you), rather than basic in nature.

▶ Resist the temptation to tell the audience all that you know about the subject. You almost certainly have neither the time nor the organizational abilities that are necessary to command the attention of the audience for that long a time. Direct your remarks to the highlights and general results of the research, and allow a questions-and-comments period in which more detailed subjects can be addressed. In this manner, you will provide the greatest amount of information to the greatest number of listeners in the audience.

▶ Use visual aids effectively. Handouts, overhead transparencies, or videotapes can serve to clarify or emphasize your key points (and, not incidentally, to transfer the "spotlight" of the presentation away from you). Most advisers recommend that you not repeatedly look at the screen, or read the text of the visual aid word for word along with the audience, but, rather, that you use the visual aid as a means of keeping the audience focused on the discussion points by the use of a pointer or other highlighter. Avoid a sequence that allows a "blank screen" for more than a second or two. Inexpensive computer software will assist you in preparing electronic presentations, slides, or transparencies, and in delivering your talk and staying on schedule. If you are a regular on the lecture circuit, consider the purchase of an ink-jet or color laser printer with which to prepare your visual aids.

Many speakers are tempted to overuse visual aids, especially because they are so easy to create, even at professional-quality levels, given today's software packages. Visual aids, though, generally should be used only for the following purposes.

▶ To illustrate things that are difficult to convey strictly with words by using a photograph, videotape, map, blueprint, or flowchart.

▶ To save time by consolidating ideas, committing to a time frame or strategy, or listing conflicting viewpoints or tactics.

▶ To create interest in a subject, perhaps by presenting the concept in a manner with which the audience is unfamiliar (e.g., an extra-large view, a view from "the other side of the issue," or an evolutionary time or growth line).

▶ To emphasize a point or concept by highlighting a graphic, picture, mnemonic, or list of key words or concepts.

▶ To organize the introduction, body, or conclusion of the presentation.

▶ To introduce humor to the event with a tasteful quotation or cartoon.

▶ To place ideas in the audience's memories, through a visual "take away" item.

Overhead transparencies, electronic presentations, or slides should be designed with care and diligence. When using this technology, as opposed to the hand-drawn flipchart or on-the-fly whiteboard drawing, one essentially is competing with professional graphic and television artists, and the audience will hold your efforts to these high standards. Most visual and graphic artists offer guidelines for presentation layouts including the following.

▶ Use the slide to emphasize pictures, not text or numbers. Except to be able to point to a specific position on the page and keep the members of the audience in the same spot throughout the presentation, do not use transparencies to duplicate pages of text or spreadsheets with voluminous numbers. Employ graphs, charts, arrows, and other pictorial devices instead.

▶ When text is involved, use the "six and six" rule: No more than six lines of type, and no more than six words on a line. This directive will help to dictate the font chosen and the corresponding size of print.

▶ Keep the font style simple. Use sans serif or newspaper-type fonts, not script or modern fonts, unless corporate logos or other protected styles are used. Most designers recommend that no more than two colors of text be used on a slide, and that the color scheme of the graphics blend well with that of the text. Be conservative—stick to the primary colors, colors of local sports teams, and multiple shades of gray, so as not to frustrate the duplication process for related handout materials.

▶ Similarly, try to use some background music if your available technology will support it at a professional-quality level. In this regard, select audio clips that do not draw attention to themselves, but are memorable in a more subtle way. Music can signal the start or end of a presentation or its subunits, a change in direction, or a specific idea (e.g., a Frank Sinatra clip sends a different message than does one by Jimi Hendrix or a New Age group).

▶ On the average, allow at least three minutes of spoken presentation for each slide. In this way, you will not overproduce your number of slides. If you want to provide your audience with a content outline, use some other medium, not the slides.

▶ Prepare for the worst: Number your slides and have hardcopy backups in case of emergency.

Without exception, determine ahead of the presentation how long your talk is supposed to be and be absolutely certain not to exceed it. You need to be fair to the other speakers, if any, who follow your presentation. Moreover, with very few exceptions, the audience also is aware of the schedule for the session, and if the speaker exceeds the allotted time, the audience, at best, will stop paying attention and, at worst, will become restless or angry. Because of their technical nature, most tax presentations should not exceed forty-five minutes, and one-half of that time might be ideal for both speaker and audience.

Have an outline for your discussion that includes miniature versions of slides and transparencies, and your business address, phone and fax numbers, and Internet addresses. Use the visual aids to convince the audience that you are following the outline. This will (1) ensure that you will cover the material that you desire, (2) build confidence among the audience as to your speaking abilities, and (3) convince yourself that you are doing a good job in leading the discussion of the assigned topic.

Rehearse your presentation, word for word, at least once. The most effective means of preparing yourself in this manner probably is with a video recorder, because your distracting mannerisms (e.g., clearing the throat repeatedly, saying the words "ah" or "you know" too often, or pounding on the lectern) quickly will become apparent. Lacking such a device, use an (audio) tape recorder. Family members or colleagues should not be used for this rehearsal.

Be kind to yourself in evaluating your video performance, but be observant for the following "I didn't know I did that" items.

▶ In all but the very largest presentation venues, get as physically close to the audience as you can, ideally removing the lectern, stepping down from the stage or platform, and moving to a series of different spots in the room throughout your speaking time.

▶ Eliminate nervous and visual distractions, such as jingling coins, playing with pen and marker tops, and adjusting clothing. Minimize the use of crossing your arms, pounding the table, and finger-pointing, reserving them as means of emphasizing key points or declaring victory over competing viewpoints.

▶ Vary the pitch of your voice, avoiding both a dry monotone and a "classic actor" dramatic approach. Many speakers talk too fast or too loud; check yourself throughout the talk on these matters. Test the microphone system before the audience arrives, so that you don't need to ask, "Can you hear me in the back?"

▶ Don't be afraid of silence. Pauses invariably seem longer to the speaker than they do to the audience, so don't let natural breaks in the talk add to your anxiety. In fact, well-paced pauses can relieve tension (both yours and the audience's), signal changes of pace, and allow you to emphasize the importance of certain ideas.

▶ Don't read directly from your outline, except for a selected quote of three lines or so from the material once or twice in the presentation. Try not to have a separate set of note cards, because the tendency again is to break your contact with the audience and hide behind the scripting device. Disguise your notes in the form of comments on hardcopies of transparencies and flip charts, and notes in the margin of your copy of the outline. Keep your eyes up and on the audience.

Avoid references to administrative or "housekeeping" aspects of the event—leave these to be conveyed by the host of the event. Be enthusiastic and positive about your comments—don't apologize for a lack of discussion on a tangential point, a logistical snafu, or a misstatement of fact or law. The audience generally wants you to succeed, so don't undermine this trust with self-destructive comments. Don't refer to the schedule for the event or other timing issues, because they can distract the audience or otherwise detract from conveying your message (e.g., "Only ten minutes to go," "We may be out of here early," "The previous speakers ran over into my time slot," or "I'll try to get through this quickly, so we can finish on time").

Rehearse the logistical aspects of the presentation, such as the lighting, projectors, or computer presentation software and terminals, before you begin to speak, ideally both the night before and one hour before your presentation. Have adequate numbers and varieties of markers, pointers, flip chart pads, and remote control devices. You don't want to encounter any surprises after it is too late to do anything about them! On your script, note cards, or transparency masters, make notes to yourself as to when, for instance, to pass out the handout material, turn on or turn off the projector, or refer to a flip chart.

Avoid cliches, such as opening with a joke, or saying, "It's a pleasure to be here." Don't take the risk of boring or offending the audience with a joke that (1) they may have heard already or (2) you may not tell effectively under pressure. This is not to suggest that you avoid humor altogether, however. Audiences, and speakers' reputations, thrive on it. If you are sure of your skill in this area, you might venture a joke, but it would probably be wiser to open with a "punch line" summary of some of the most interesting of your results or fact situations.

Have a "Plan B" ready to go—flexibility is the watchword of the effective speaker. If the time actually allowed for your talk is shorter than you had thought, due to a misunderstanding or unanticipated events, have a list of topics, videos, or slides that can be eliminated without changing the nature of the talk. Practice your question-and-answer-session skills, especially for occasions where there is more time available than you had anticipated. Do not mention any of these on-the-fly adjustments to the audience—make the changes, don't talk about them.

Observe audience body language, and use signals conveying interest, enthusiasm, boredom, or restlessness to your advantage. Make consistent eye contact with the audience, smile when appropriate, and take a few seconds at the completion of the presentation to accept the audience's show of thanks and savor your job well done.

▶ ## Summary

The tax professional must become proficient in communicating his or her research results. Recipients of these communications might include oneself or one's peers, via the file memorandum; the client, via a brief letter; or a number of other listeners, via an oral presentation. In each case, the practitioner must be sensitive to the needs, background, and interests of the recipients of the messages, without sacrificing professional demeanor or responsibilities.

▶ ## Key Words

By the time you complete your work relative to this chapter, you should be comfortable discussing each of the following terms. If you need additional review of any of these items, return to the appropriate material in the chapter or consult the glossary to this text.

Client Letter   Oral Presentation
File Memorandum

▶＿＿＿＿＿＿＿＿＿   Tax Research Assignments

As we have discussed them in this chapter, develop solutions and appropriate documentation for one or more of the problems that you have worked on in previous chapters or for following fact situations. In this context, proper format and professional content are of equal importance, so that the development of the reader's tax research communication skills will be facilitated.

Specifically, as assigned by your instructor, prepare one or more of the following means of communicating your research results for your chosen problem or case.

- ▶ File memorandum
- ▶ Letter to tax-sophisticated client
- ▶ Letter to unsophisticated client
- ▶ Article for local business news weekly
- ▶ Speech to local chamber of commerce
- ▶ Article for *Taxation for Accountants*
- ▶ Speech to State Bar Association conference
- ▶ Presentation to client's board of directors
- ▶ Presentation to client's senior counsel
- ▶ Posting to the Internet Tax Forum for Practitioners
- ▶ Posting to the Internet Tax Help group for taxpayers

▶＿＿＿＿＿＿＿＿＿   Problems

1. Professor White operates a popular bar review course as a sole proprietorship. He charges $1,000 tuition of each student, and he guarantees a full refund of the tuition if the student passes an in-course exam but does not pass the actual bar exam on the first try. White is bold enough to do this because the first-time-pass rate is more than 80 percent for the bar exam (as opposed to less than 15 percent for the CPA exam). He collected $50,000 tuition for his Fall 1999 review section, but he reported the gross receipts on his 2000 Form 1040, because the grades for those taking the fall review are not released until February 2000. Thus, White asserted that he had no constructive receipt of the tuition until February 2000. Is this treatment correct?

2. Lisa, usually a stay-at-home mother, went to the hospital one day for some outpatient surgery. She hired a babysitter for $35 to watch her four-year-old son while she was gone. What tax benefits are available to Lisa for this cash payment?

3. Same as 2, except that Lisa paid the sitter while she worked as a scout leader for the Girl Scouts.

4. Joan, a traveling sales representative, kept no formal books and records to summarize her gross receipts for the year, but she retained copies of all customer invoices and reported her gross income for the year from these totals. Is she liable for a negligence penalty under § 6662 for failing to keep any books and records?

5. Tex's credit union has provided him with financing to acquire his $200,000 home. The loan is set up as a three-year note with a balloon payment, but the credit union always renews the loan for another three years at the current interest rate. This year, the credit union renewed Tex's loan for the third time, charging $3,000 in points. In what year(s) can Tex deduct this $3,000?

6. Barb and Bob were one-fourth shareholders of a C corporation. When the entity had negative E&P, Barb and Bob secretly withdrew $200,000 in cash, hiding this fact from the other owners. How much gross income do Barb and Bob report?

7. Detail the tax effects to the Prasads of making the election to include their seven-year-old daughter's $10,000 unearned income on their current-year joint return.

8. Eighty percent of the Willigs' AGI comes from their submarine sandwich proprietorship. In 2000, the Willigs lost an IRS audit and owed $12,000 in 1998 federal income taxes, all attributable to inventory computations in their business. Interest on this amount totaled $3,200. All amounts due were paid by the end of 2000. How much of the interest can the Willigs deduct on their 2000 Schedule C?

9. Al and Amy are divorced. In which of the following cases can legal fees be deducted?

   a. Al pays $5,000 to get the court to reduce his alimony obligation.

   b. Amy pays $5,000 to get the court to increase her alimony receipts.

   c. Al pays Amy's attorney fees in B., as required by the original divorce decree.

10. Katie is a one-third owner of an S corporation. After a falling-out with the other shareholders, Katie signed an agreement early in January 1999. Under the terms of the agreement, Katie took $200,000 of her capital from the corporation and had eight months to negotiate a purchase of the stock of the other shareholders. She did not complete this task by the end of August 1999. Thus, contrary negotiations began and on March 1, 2000, Katie sold all of her shares to the remaining shareholders for a $2.5 million gain. For how many of these months does Katie report flow-through income from the S corporation?

11. Can an individual make a contribution to an IRA based on unemployment compensation proceeds received?

12. Duane paid his 1995 federal income taxes in January 1998 in the amount of $10,000, and then paid $4,000 interest and penalties on this amount in May 1999. In April 2001, Duane filed a claim for refund of the $14,000, due to a sizable operating loss from his business in tax year 2000. Can he recover the 1995-related amounts?

13. After an audit was completed, IRS agent van Court informed Harris of the latter's $10,000 federal income tax deficiency, by leaving a summary memo on Harris's e-mail account. Harris shared this account with his mother, who read the mail first and in a panic confronted Harris with a two-hour "What's this all about?" interrogation. Did van Court violate Harris's right to privacy by using e-mail in this manner?

14. SlimeCo spent $250,000 to build storage tanks for its waste by-products. This is a recurring expenditure for SlimeCo, because once the tanks are filled, new ones must be built. When can SlimeCo deduct the $250,000?

15. Prudence was named a shareholder in her law firm, which operates as an S corporation. Her payments into the capital of the firm were to start in about nine months, after an audit would determine the full value of the firm and a new corporate year would commence. Paperwork with the pertinent state offices was completed, naming Prudence as a shareholder and director, and adding her

name to that of the firm. But Prudence left the firm eight months after the announcement, that is, before she paid any money for shares. Is Prudence liable for tax on her share of the entity's earnings for the eight months?

16. Laura deducted $8,100 in state income taxes on her 1998 federal income tax return. Her refund, received in 1999, after all credits and the minimum tax, was $7,800 for these taxes.

   a. How much 1999 gross income must Laura recognize?
   b. How does your answer change if Laura's 1998 deduction was limited to $7,200, due to the application of IRC § 68?

17. Cal's son has been labeled a "can't miss" NBA prospect since junior high school. This year, while the son is a college freshman and classified as an amateur under NCAA rules, Cal spent $14,000 for special clothing, equipment, camps, and personal trainers to keep improving his son's skills. Can Cal deduct these items?

18. CPA Myrna forgot to tell her client Freddie to accelerate the payment of state income and property taxes in a year when Freddie was in an unusually high tax bracket. Upon discovering the error, the parties negotiated a $15,000 payment from Myrna (and her insurance company) to Freddie to compensate Freddie for Myrna's inadequate professional advice. Is this payment gross income to Freddie?

19. How much of the $100,000 interest that is paid on a loan from Everett National Bank can Ben deduct if he invests the loan proceeds in the following? Consider each item independently.

   a. South Chicago School District bonds
   b. AT&T bonds, paying $125,000 interest income this year
   c. Computer Futures, Inc., shares, a growth stock that pays no dividend this year
   d. A life insurance policy on Betty

20. Lilly leases a car that she uses solely for business purposes. The car would be worth $40,050 on the market, and Lilly paid $7,400 in lease payments for 1998. How are these items treated on her tax return?

▶ _____   Research Cases

21. Dave took a $100,000 cash withdrawal from his IRA. He bought $100,000 of Microcraft stock and, within the rollover period, transferred the stock to another IRA. Does Dave report any gross income?

22. Gold Partners wanted to complete a like-kind exchange just before it liquidated. Accordingly, it sold the real estate it meant to transfer to the other party, and a qualified intermediary held the resulting cash. When the intermediary found acceptable replacement realty, the intermediary transferred cash and the like-kind property directly to the partners, thereby liquidating Gold. Does § 1031 apply?

23. HelpCo pays Hank two $100,000 salaries per year, one through its WestCo subsidiary, and one through its EastCo subsidiary. How do Hank and HelpCo treat his Social Security tax obligations?

24. Jack died three years after winning the lottery grand prize. He had elected to take the prize as a series of $500,000 payments for the rest of his life. Once the payment method was chosen, the annuity was not transferable to any other

party, except for Jack's estate. According to IRS annuity tables, the present value of the remaining payments, to be received by the estate, was $8 million. How much should be included in Jack's federal gross estate?

25. Karen files jointly in a year when she incurs $2,000 of job-related education expenses. No one else in her family incurred tax-favored education expenses this year. AGI is $80,000, and Karen's miscellaneous itemized deductions for employee business expenses total $400. How should Karen treat her education costs so as to maximize her federal tax benefits for the year?

26. On December 6, Ed Grimely appeared on the game show, "The Wheel of Fate." As a result of his appearance, Grimely won the following prizes.

	Manufacturer's Suggested List Price	Fair Market Value	Actual Cost to the Show
All-expenses-paid trip to Hawaii	$8,432	$6,000	$5,200
One case of Twinkies	16	12	-0-
Seven music lessons for the calliope	105	35	-0-
One year of free haircuts	120	60	15

   a. Assuming that Grimely received all of these prizes by the end of the year, compute his gross income from these prizes.

   b. Will this amount change if Grimely refuses to accept the calliope lessons, immediately after the program's taping session is completed?

27. Josh bought $120,000 worth of furnishings on his MasterCard in 1999, paying off the entire principal and interest in 2000. Interest charges of $7,800 relate to 1999 for the furnishings. How much can Josh deduct for interest relative to this transaction for 1999?

28. Rita's family had a history of heart disease. To reduce Rita's risk of future heart problems, and to enable her to lose about ten pounds, her physician recommended a rigid running program. Accordingly, Rita joined the Vic Tanny Health Club. One-fourth of her time at the club was spent on a supervised running program. How much of her $450 annual fee is deductible as a medical expense?

29. Ellie owned five apartment buildings, each worth $200,000. For three of the buildings, she worked with employees to keep the property in good repair. This entailed maintaining electrical and plumbing fixtures, common areas, walls and roofs, and providing janitorial services such as garbage removal, vacuum, and rest room supplies. For the other two buildings, Ellie's lease required the tenants to perform this work. Can her estate claim a § 6166 estate tax deferral for any of the buildings?

30. HardCo spent $4 million this year on a new graphic design for its product, a yo-yo. Under the prior design, HardCo's name and logo only appeared on the box and wrapping paper, which were discarded by most customers once they started using the product. The new design displayed HardCo's name and newer, flashier logo on both sides of the yo-yo, with a paint that also made it glow in the dark. When can HardCo deduct the $4 million?

▶ _____ ## Advanced Cases

These items require that you have access to research materials other than the federal tax law and related services. For instance, you might need to refer to an international tax or multistate service, or to access Internet sources, to prepare your solution for these cases. Consult with your instructor before beginning your work, so that you are certain to have available to you all of the necessary research resources for the case(s) that you choose.

31. Summarize the economic process requirements that apply to an electing Foreign Sales Corporation.

32. According to the Tax Foundation, what was Tax Freedom Day in 1998? How much of this time was spent with respect to tax liabilities, and how much in meeting tax compliance costs? Which states bear the heaviest tax burden? The lightest? Per capita, how much annual total income and total tax does the U.S. citizen generate? What is the average U.S. citizen's average tax rate?

33. Chan's only transaction in the United States this year was to sell the biggest office building in Denver at a $100 million gain. Chan has no assets, offices, or employees in the United States. Can he be taxed on the gain? Why or why not?

34. As the result of a federal audit, your 1997 federal taxable income increased by $27,000. By when must you report this adjustment to your state's revenue department? What form is used for this purpose, where do you obtain it, and where is it to be filed?

35. Does your state provide a form with which to file for a manufacturer's exemption from sales/use tax? Which form is used for this purpose, where do you obtain it, and where is it to be filed?

36. For the current period, What is the short-term, quarterly compounded federal AFR? Mid-term? Long-term exempt interest rate for computing loss carryforwards under §382?

37. SalesCo sold Tom a prepaid phone card for $100 in 1999. Tom used the phone card for communications services in 2000. When can your state collect sales/use tax from SalesCo for the sale to Tom?

38. GoodCo donated $40,000 of goods from its inventory to the Red Cross. Does your state require GoodCo to collect or pay sales/use tax on these donated goods?

Tax Planning

In this chapter, we return to that element of the tax practice consisting of tax planning, as it was introduced in Chapter 1. A working knowledge of tax planning concepts is imperative for the researcher, because tax avoidance constitutes both (1) an important part of tax practice and (2) a prime motivation in the "open-fact" research context.

For most practitioners, tax research and planning represent the "glamor" end of the business. Properly accomplished tax planning (1) forces the client to identify financial goals and general means by which to achieve them, (2) allows the tax professional to exercise a higher degree of creativity than in any other part of the practice, and (3) affords the practitioner the greatest possible degree of control over the prescribed transactions and then tax consequences.

The tax planning process finds the tax professional in the roles of technical expert, friend, seer, and confessor priest for the client. It offers an opportunity for the most psychologically and financially rewarding work possible, in the context of a tax practice.

Economics of Tax Planning, Avoidance, and Evasion

From both the Treasury and the taxpayer viewpoint, taxes can modify individual decisions. Taxes represent an additional cost of doing business or of accumulating wealth. Assuming that economists are correct in speaking about the ways in which a rational citizen makes day-to-day decisions, taxpayers employ tax planning techniques to accomplish the overall goal of wealth maximization.[1] Because taxes deplete the wealth of the taxpayer, planning behavior is designed to reduce the net present value of the tax liability. This is not the same as a simple reduction of taxes in nominal dollar terms, an objective that is so often assumed by laypeople, the media, and others, including too many tax advisors.

> **Example 11–1** Sharon can choose between two business plans. One will cost her enterprise $1,000 in taxes today. The other will cost the business $2,000 in taxes ten years from now. The plans are identical in all other ways. Prevailing interest rates average 10 percent. Because the present value of the taxes levied with respect to the second alternative are about $800, Sharon should choose the latter plan, that is, the one with the higher nominal dollar tax cost.

In one important sense, the federal income tax is its own worst enemy. Taxpayers are rewarded more for finding ways to save taxes than for earning an equal amount in the marketplace. This incentive for tax planning is the result of two rules of tax law.

The first such rule is that the federal income tax itself is not allowed as a deduction in determining taxable income. Consequently, reducing the amount of income taxes that are paid does not decrease one's allowable deductions and, hence, does not trigger any further increase in taxable income. Instead, the full amount of any tax that is saved increases after-tax income; that is, the tax savings themselves do not

---

[1]We use "wealth" in its broadest sense here; that is, an individual may choose increased leisure time or other forms of so-called psychic income over traditional forms of wealth. Wealth, the accumulation of which constitutes the overall goal for the specified time period, thus can include measures of happiness, satisfaction, investment, and control over time and other resources.

constitute taxable income. Unlike most profit-seeking activities, tax planning produces benefits that are completely exempt from income taxation.

The second such rule allows a deduction for any business-related expenses that are incurred in connection with the determination of a tax. Most tax planning costs are deductible by business owners and sole proprietors, but only a few employee-individuals qualify for such a deduction. The net cost of a tax planning project, then, is its gross cost minus the amount of the reduction in the tax liability that is generated by the attendant deduction. In concise terms, the after-tax cost of tax planning can be expressed as follows.

ATC = BTC × (1 − MTR)
where
ATC = after-tax cost
BTC = before-tax cost
MTR = marginal tax rate

In relating both rules to tax planning projects, one can see that such endeavors enjoy an economic advantage over most other profit-seeking activities. In evaluating most other investment projects, the decision maker must compare after-tax benefits with after-tax costs. Yet, for tax planning projects, the payoffs are tax free, while the costs usually remain tax-deductible. Thus, for tax planning activities, one effectively compares pretax benefits with after-tax costs.

Example 11–2 A corporate taxpayer, subject to a marginal state and federal income tax rate of 40 percent, is considering two mutually exclusive alternatives. Alternative A is to hire a university accounting major for the summer at a cost of $2,000; his task would be to undertake research on a tax avoidance plan. If it is successful, the plan would save the corporation $1,600 in federal income taxes. The probability of success for the plan is estimated at 80 percent. Alternative M is to hire a university marketing major for the summer at a cost of $1,800; her task would be to undertake research on a marketing plan. If it is successful, this plan would generate new revenues of $2,000. The probability of such success is estimated to be 85 percent. Which, if either, alternative should the corporation pursue?

	Alternative A	**Alternative M**
Before-tax cost	$2,000	$1,800
Tax reduction (40%)	− 800	− 720
After-tax cost	$1,200	$1,080
Possible pre-tax payoff	$1,600	$2,000
Probability of success	× .80	× .85
Expected pre-tax payoff	$1,280	$1,700
Tax on expected payoff (40%)	− 0	− 680
Expected after-tax payoff	$1,280	$1,020
Excess of after-tax payoff over after-tax cost	$ 80	$ (60)

Decision: Even though Alternative M offers a higher pretax payoff, a lower before-tax cost, and a higher probability of success, Alternative A should be accepted.

The facts of this example illustrate the apparent built-in economic bias of current tax law for tax planning projects, relative to other, seemingly more productive activities.

The analysis of Example 11–2, like most of the illustrations in this book, is based on a "marginal" viewpoint. Its purpose is to determine the effect of the transactions at issue, assuming that all other characteristics of the situation do not change. When it is viewed from this perspective, the after-tax cost of any deductible expenditure decreases if the marginal tax rate is increased. This fact may explain why lower income taxpayers, who are subject to lower marginal tax rates, engage in tax planning activities less often than do higher income taxpayers.

Example 11–3 Assume the same situation and opportunities as in Example 11–2, except that the corporation's marginal tax rate is 20 percent.

	Alternative A	**Alternative M**
Before-tax cost	$2,000	$1,800
Tax reduction (20%)	− 400	− 360
After-tax cost	$1,600	$1,440
Possible pre-tax payoff	$1,600	$2,000
Probability of success	× .80	× .85
Expected pre-tax payoff	$1,280	$1,700
Tax on expected payoff (20%)	− 0	− 340
Expected after-tax payoff	$1,280	$1,360
Excess of after-tax payoff over after-tax cost	$ (320)	$ (80)

Decision: Accept Alternative M, because it generates the lesser after-tax loss, or undertake neither (seemingly profitable) project.

Tax Rate Terminology

The basic formula for computing a taxpayer's liability is

Tax Liability = Tax Base × Rate

Thus, in many respects, the function of a legislative body is to define adequately the appropriate tax base and construct a schedule of tax rates, so that the ensuing liabilities will be in accordance with the prevailing revenue and nonrevenue objectives of the tax system. Once a tax has been included in a society's tax structure, legislative efforts seem to focus on slight modifications of the existing tax base and rates; major overhauls, additions, or deletions to the structure rarely are considered. Tax reform legislation thus usually takes the form of "fine-tuning" the system rather than "changing channels" altogether.

Tax Base

The income tax is the most modern of the taxes that are commonly found in contemporary industrialized societies. Allowing for the difficulties in constructing a definition for a virtually imaginary concept, most policymakers believe that a tax that is based on "ordinary taxable income," allowing deductions for the costs of earning such income and for certain personal expenditures, best reflects the capacity of the taxpayer to support government finance.

Previous efforts to base taxation on ability to pay have included taxes on individual consumption and wealth. Consumption taxes are supported by the rationale that the taxpayer receives personal benefit from society in accordance with the amount of goods and services that he or she exhausts during the period; thus, the government should appropriate its share of finances from what people take out of society's "kitty" for personal reasons, not from what they put into it, as is the case under income taxation.

Wealth, or property, taxes also have been structured to base levies on one's capacity to support the government. Most often, wealth taxes take the form of levies against the net holdings of tangible assets that are controlled by the taxpayer at a given time. In accounting terminology, the tax on the net tangible assets is assessed on what appears on the taxpayer's balance sheet at the end of the taxable year.

Tax Rates

Most tax scholars identify three distinct tax rate structures: proportional, progressive, and regressive, as illustrated in Exhibit 11–1. The classification of a rate structure depends on the trend of the tax rate as the tax base increases. Under a **proportional tax rate** system, the tax rate is constant; for example, it might stand at 29 percent of net wealth, over all possible values of the tax base. Most American sales and property taxes employ a proportional rate structure. Under a tax system with **progressive tax rates,** the applicable tax rate increases as the tax base grows larger. American income, estate, and gift taxes typically use nominally progressive rates. Finally, the tax rate decreases as the tax base grows larger under a system of

---

EXHIBIT 11–1   Alternative tax rate structures: graphic illustrations and applicable schedules

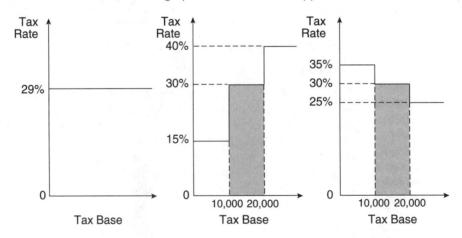

Proportional Rates		Progressive Rates		Regressive Rates	
Tax Base	**Rate**	**Tax Base**	**Rate**	**Tax Base**	**Rate**
All amounts	29%	1st $10,000	15%	1st $10,000	35%
		2nd 10,000	30	2nd 10,000	30
		3rd 10,000	40	3rd 10,000	25

regressive tax rates. Using the present scheme of classification, no American tax to date has employed a system of nominally regressive tax rates.

> **Example 11–4** In the typical year, Social Security taxes are imposed on employees at a flat rate (before credits), say, of 8 percent on all wages up to $75,000. For wages in excess of $75,000, there is no additional tax. Technically, this tax is proportional, because all covered wages (the tax base) are subject to the same rate of tax. However, many people regard Social Security taxes as being regressive, presumably because they tend to relate their analysis to all of one's income and not just to the statutory tax base. Under this view, because the marginal tax rate is zero on wages in excess of $75,000 for the year, the tax is both effectively and nominally regressive.

Many taxpayers confuse the appropriate meaning of their **marginal tax rate.** Typically, they assume that if a taxpayer is subject to a 36 percent marginal tax rate (i.e., 36 cents is payable in tax on the next dollar of taxable income), he or she owes 36 percent of the *entire* taxable income. One often hears people fall victim to this fallacy, when they state, "I wish I hadn't gotten that raise, because it threw me into a higher tax bracket!" The truth is that even under a system of progressive tax rates, one is never left worse off by earning more money. The higher marginal rates that apply to additional income affect only those increments; the tax liability on the original income layers does not change.

Such comments reflect a confusion on the part of the taxpayer concerning marginal tax rate and average tax rate. The **average tax rate** is a simple division of the total tax liability by the corresponding tax base.

> **Example 11–5** Lydia earned $30,000 this year. After applying various deductions, exclusions, and exemptions, though, Lydia's statutory taxable income is $21,000; further, the middle tax rate system of Exhibit 11–1 is in effect. Lydia's tax is computed as follows.
>
> | | | |
> |---|---|---|
> | 15% × | $10,000 = | $1,500 |
> | 30% × | 10,000 = | 3,000 |
> | 40% × | 1,000 = | 400 |
> | Tax Liability | | $4,900 |
>
> Lydia's marginal tax rate is 40 percent, but her average rate is only 23.33 percent ($4,900 tax due / $21,000 taxable income).

The reader should make sure that he or she understands this distinction between marginal and average tax rates, because all tax planning analyses should be based on the marginal tax that the individual will pay or save by adopting a particular course of action. The average tax rate is an interesting statistic, but it is solely the marginal rate that affects the change in tax liability and any corresponding changes in taxpayer behavior.

Of course, this definition of statutory taxable income allows for certain deductions, exemptions, and exclusions from total receipts in determining the tax base for the year. Often, because one has received tax-exempt income during the period, and because of the tax base's exemptions and standard deduction, an individual controls more receipts than he or she legally must report as taxable income. In this case, the distinction between the nominal and effective average tax rates becomes important.

The **nominal average tax rate** can be computed in Example 11–5 as the division of total tax liability by taxable income (i.e., 23.33 percent). However, before considering Lydia's exclusions, exemptions, and deductions effectively she had command over $30,000 of income during the year, even though only $21,000 of this amount was defined technically as taxable income. Thus, Lydia's **effective average tax rate** of tax for the year can be found by dividing the total tax liability by "total," or economic, income. Here, the effective average rate of tax is only $4,900 / $30,000 = 16.33 percent. Exhibit 11–2 summarizes the various tax rate computations that have been introduced in this section.

Tax Planning in Perspective

The entrepreneurial tax professional should not see tax planning as an end in itself. Rather, especially when dealing with individual clients, tax planning must be seen as part of two sets of major services provided by the practitioner, as illustrated in Exhibits 11–3 and 11–4. As we discussed in Chapter 1, tax planning is part of the entire menu of tax services that the tax professional makes available. Although the compliance and litigation aspects of the profession increasingly are shared with paraprofessionals (who prepare the bulk of tax returns for many professional firms) or attorneys (when a seemingly irresolvable conflict arises, usually between the client and the IRS), tax planning rightly is initiated by the well-educated and experienced tax practitioner.

EXHIBIT 11–2 Various tax rate computations illustrated

Lydia files a tax return for $30,000 of economic income and $9,000 of exemptions, exclusions, and deductions. Taxable income is $21,000. Tax liability is $4,900 under the prevailing rate system.

Marginal tax rate	40% (from tax rate schedule, middle system, Exhibit 11–1)
Average tax rates	Nominal average rate: $4,900 / $21,000 = 23.33%
	Effective average rate: $4,900 / $30,000 = 16.33%

EXHIBIT 11–3 Tax planning in the typical tax practice

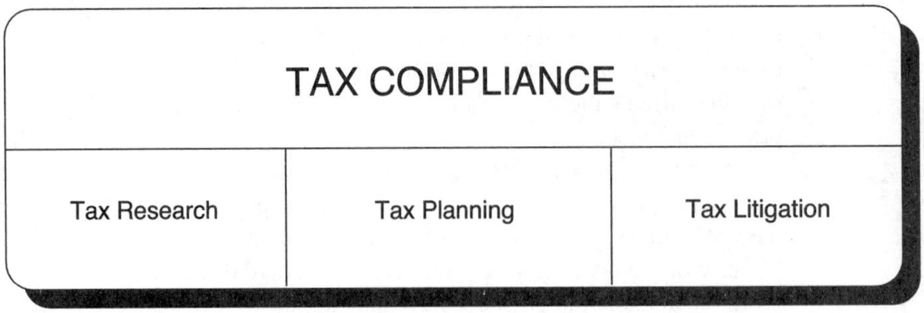

TAX COMPLIANCE

Tax Research	Tax Planning	Tax Litigation

EXHIBIT 11–4   Tax planning in the client's wealth planning process

EDUCATION PLANNING Trusts for Minors Special Investments	**ESTATE PLANNING** Asset Management Distributions and Control

RETIREMENT PLANNING	INCOME TAX PLANNING	INVESTMENT PLANNING
RETIREMENT PLANNING Qualified Plans Nonqualified Plans Distributions Plans and Vehicles	**INCOME TAX PLANNING** Timing Tax Entity Exclusions and Deductions Income Classification Special Taxes Withholding Interest and Penalties	**INVESTMENT PLANNING** Risks Rewards Control Purchases/Sales Asset Allocation Regulations

CASH PLANNING Budgeting Finance	**RISK PLANNING** Insurance Security

Similarly, tax planning is but one of the various types of planning services that a tax professional offers to clients. As the U.S. population collectively ages, the importance of portfolio, estate, and retirement planning will increase. As the "baby boom echo" materializes in the early part of the twenty-first century, education planning again will take center stage. Planning for cash and risk contingencies is mandatory for business clients, but even the most modestly endowed of individual clients can benefit from an introduction to such planning.

Thus, to the extent that the tax professional offers tax planning and counseling services, he or she must be facile with the rudiments of the planning process, and with the dynamic nature of the evolution of the tax law as it affects planning engagements.

Fundamentals of Tax Planning

As we noted in Chapter 1, tax planning is a completely legal means for saving taxes.[2] The basic objective of such planning is to arrange one's financial activities in a way that will reduce the present value of tax costs, such that maximum wealth accumulation can occur in the time period specified.

Opportunities for effective tax planning almost always are greater when tax effects are given consideration before transactions are finalized, rather than after they are completed. Decision makers should constantly be alert for tax-optimizing alternatives in the everyday conduct of their affairs. In other words, the first require-

[2]Portions of this section are adapted from Raabe and Parker, *Tax Concepts for Decision Making* (St. Paul, MN: West Publishing Co., 1985).

ment for effective tax planning is **tax awareness** on the part of decision makers, rather than tax expertise by tax professionals.

Example 11–6 Russell and Phyllis Cohen, a married couple subject to a 30 percent marginal tax rate, currently are negotiating the purchase of their first home, with the Hacienda Heights Construction Company, a land developer. The company has offered to sell the Cohens a selected house and lot at a price of $60,000, with a 20 percent down payment and 10 percent interest on annual payments over a five-year period. Under these terms, payments would be as follows.

Year	Beginning Balance	Interest	Principal	Total
0	$60,000	$ —	$12,000	$12,000
1	48,000	4,800	7,862	12,662
2	40,138	4,014	8,648	12,662
3	31,490	3,149	9,513	12,662
4	21,977	2,198	10,464	12,662
5	11,513	1,151	11,513	12,664
Totals		$15,312	$60,000	$75,312

The Cohens are aware that mortgage interest payments are tax-deductible, and that the purchase price of a home is not. Thus, they make a counteroffer to purchase the home at a price of $54,445, with $12,000 down and 15 percent interest on annual payments over a five-year period. Under these new terms, Hacienda Heights receives the same cash payments (and gross income) as it did under the original terms. However, the amount of allowable deductions to the Cohens would be increased, with no change in total cash payments.

Year	Beginning Balance	Interest	Principal	Total
0	$54,445	$ —	$12,000	$12,000
1	42,445	6,367	6,295	12,662
2	36,150	5,423	7,239	12,662
3	28,911	4,337	8,325	12,662
4	20,586	3,088	9,574	12,662
5	11,012	1,652	11,012	12,664
Totals		$20,867	$54,445	$75,312

These results are not uncommon in a robust tax planning context. Often, decision makers can benefit by recognizing how the rearrangement of a planned transaction can produce tax savings, even if the economic substance of the transaction is left unaltered (or altered very little). The key, of course, is to pay close attention to the structural and transactional categories that have been established by Congress and the courts. In Example 11–6, by reclassifying a portion of their housing expenditures as (deductible) interest, rather than (nondeductible) principal, the Cohens were able to increase their allowable deductions and save taxes. Stated differently, the taxpayer's ability to conceptualize actions or events within stated legal definitions is of utmost importance.

Tax planning behavior can be characterized as falling into one or more of the general categories enumerated in Exhibit 11–5. Virtually every tax planning technique employed by the tax professional fits one or more of these overriding planning objectives.

Avoiding Income Recognition

Taxpayers often can reduce their exposure to taxation by avoiding the accumulation of gross income that must be recognized. This is not to suggest that a taxpayer should avoid accumulating real economic income. As long as marginal tax rates remain less than 100 percent, few people would be willing to go to that extreme. Rather, one usually should strive to obtain economic wealth in some manner that does not create recognized income under the tax law.

> **Example 11–7** Julie earned $3,500 when she sold the crop of fruits and vegetables that she grew, and she was subject to income tax on the full amount. Warren also grew a crop of produce of the same size, but he and his family ate the food. Thus, Warren recognized no gross income and paid no income tax relative to his gardening activities, but his family enjoyed $3,500 worth of fruits and vegetables.

Another method by which one can avoid obtaining recognized income is through the use of debt. Since neither the borrowing of money nor the receipt of funds that previously were lent generates gross income, taxpayers sometimes can use loans to avoid the recognition of taxable income on appreciated investments and enjoy the temporary use of the cash.

> **Example 11–8** Doug owns a tract of land that he acquired many years ago for $10,000. Currently, the land is worth $100,000. Doug needs $50,000 cash for a business venture. He is considering two alternatives: one is to sell half of the land, and the other is to borrow the $50,000 by giving a mortgage on the land.

If Doug sells one-half of the land, he will recognize a $45,000 ($50,000 − ½ of $10,000) taxable gain. However, Doug recognizes no taxable income if he borrows the money, even though the amount that he borrows will be in excess of the basis of the land.

> **Example 11–9** Barbara Ward formed a new corporation by investing $100,000 cash. Following the advice of her tax consultant, Barbara designated $60,000 to be used for the purchase of corporate stock and $40,000 as a loan to the corporation. In this way, if Barbara wants to receive large amounts of cash back from the corporation in the future, the entity simply will repay part or all of the loan principal to her, tax free, rather than making a large (taxable and nondeductible) dividend payment. Barbara also can direct the corporation to pay interest on the loan; such payments are deductible by the

---

EXHIBIT 11–5   Goals of tax planning behavior

- ► Avoiding statutory income
- ► Postponing income recognition
- ► Changing tax jurisdictions
- ► Controlling the classification of income
- ► Spreading income among related taxpayers

---

corporation. Of course, both interest and dividends are taxable to Barbara when she receives them.

Still another, and perhaps more obvious, way in which one can avoid the recognition of income for tax purposes is to take advantage of the many exclusions that the law permits. For example, an employee might arrange to receive certain nontaxable fringe benefits (such as health insurance) from the employer, in lieu of an equivalent value in (taxable) cash salary. This relationship should affect all negotiations as to compensation arrangements: The employer is indifferent between the two choices because both salary and fringe benefit payments are fully deductible against gross income, but the employee's after-tax wealth increases more where tax-free benefits are received.

Example 11–10 Lee Schrader, who is subject to a 40 percent overall marginal tax rate, is better off if she receives a tax-free fringe benefit than if she receives an equivalent raise in her salary.

	If Salary Increases	If Fringe Benefit Is Chosen
Value of compensation received	$2,000	$2,000
Tax on employee's compensation	− 800	
After-tax increase in employee's wealth	$1,200	$2,000

Postponing Income Recognition

By delaying the recognition of income, one also delays the payment of the tax and, hence, can continue to enjoy the use of that tax money. Given the relatively higher interest rates that are anticipated in coming years, this delay takes on increased importance. At 12 percent annual interest, the present value of a $1,000 tax that is postponed for ten years is only $322. For longer periods and/or higher interest rates, the economic significance of the delay would be even greater. Appendix F includes a series of tables computing factors to reflect the time value of money.

Example 11–11 Agatha Fraser paid $1,000 for 4,800 Swiss francs in 19X1. At the same time, her sister, Betty, put $1,000 into a U.S. bank savings account. By the current year, the value of Agatha's francs had increased to $1,800, and Betty's bank account had increased, due to interest accumulations, to the same amount. Since the increase in the value of the Swiss francs was unrealized, Agatha had not been taxed yet on her $800 increase in economic wealth. On the other hand, Betty's increase was realized from interest that was credited annually to her account. Under the tax doctrine of *constructive receipt,* Betty had recognized gross income, accumulated over the nine-year planning period, of $800.

Example 11–12 Janie Heller owns land adjacent to her home that appreciated in value by $5,000 this year. However, because she did not sell the land, the appreciation in market value was not realized in a market transaction or recognized for income tax purposes. Janie has no recognized income from the land for that year.

Example 11–13 Janie Heller, of Example 11–12, paid interest of $4,000 on a mortgage that was used to finance her home and land investment. Janie can deduct the interest amount to offset the income that she derived from other investment sources in computing her taxable income. In effect, Janie is able to achieve a deliberate mismatching of current-year costs and unrealized revenues.

Example 11–14 Janie Heller, of Example 11–12, constructed an apartment building on her land, at a cost of $500,000, of which $475,000 was borrowed. By electing accelerated depreciation, which is based on the total $500,000 cost of the building, rather than on Janie's $25,000 equity therein, Janie is able to take a depreciation deduction of about $24,000 in the construction year alone, nearly equal to her entire cash outlay for the current year.

Changing Tax Jurisdictions

Tax systems are not universal in breadth, nature, or application. Taxes are adopted by governmental jurisdictions, to be collected from those who live and do business within their boundaries. Often, by moving assets or income out of one tax jurisdiction and into another, tax reductions can be effected. Over time, governments tend to modify their tax systems to prevent the "leakage" of tax revenues through such cross-border transactions. Yet, in an effort to attract businesses and resulting jobs into their jurisdictions, governments often retain or create border incentives in the form of tax reductions that are limited in time or scope.

Example 11–15 The island country of Ricardo meets its revenue needs with tariffs on the fishing industry. Ricardo never has adopted an income tax system. Harris, a U.S. corporation, could build its new assembly plant through a wholly owned subsidiary incorporated and doing business only in Ricardo, thereby reducing its costs of conducting business because there is no income tax on executive salaries or annual profits. Perhaps by design, Ricardo has attracted new business, profits, jobs, and other benefits through its tax policies.

Example 11–16 State A includes in its statutory definition of taxable business income the interest paid on U.S. Treasury obligations. OneBank holds billions of dollars in Treasury notes, bills, and bonds, so, in an effort to reduce its tax costs, it creates a wholly owned subsidiary incorporated and doing business only in State B, which does not tax interest income. The subsidiary "repatriates" the interest to OneBank through quarterly dividend distributions, not taxed under the laws of State A. The economy of State A has been depleted because of its tax policy, but the taxpayer has responded with rational behavior in accord with its overall financial goals, through judicious tax planning techniques.

Controlling Classification of Income

For federal income tax purposes, several distinct categories of income, deductions, and credits are recognized. The most important of these are (1) ordinary income, which is fully taxable, and ordinary deductions, which decrease the tax base dollar for dollar; (2) investment or "portfolio" income, which usually is fully taxable, except for tax-exempt state and local bond interest, and related expenses of which typically can be subtracted only against investment income; and (3) income from passive activities, such as the ownership of rental or "tax shelter" assets, which usually is fully taxable, and related expenses of which can be subtracted only against passive income.

In addition, a fourth classification of income and expenses should be identified. If the taxpayer is subject to the alternative minimum tax, preference and adjustment items such as accelerated depreciation deductions may be included, and other expenditures may not be available as deductions.

Effective tax planning often includes the proper identification or reclassification of income or expenditure items, using these statutory definitions.

Example 11–17 Phil Jankowski is the sole shareholder of a management consulting corporation. In addition, he has invested in tax shelter entities that are generating $40,000 per year in passive losses for him. According to the Code, such losses from passive activities cannot be applied as deductions to offset fully taxable income, for example, from Phil's salary or capital gain transactions. Accordingly, Phil cannot reduce current taxable income by the $40,000 passive loss from his tax shelter.

As the dominant shareholder of his corporation, however, Phil may be in a position to salvage the $40,000 deduction. If he reduces his salary from the corporation by $40,000, and takes instead from the corporation a $40,000 properly structured lease payment for the use of specified personal or real property that he owns but the corporation uses, like office equipment or automobiles, he may be able to create $40,000 in passive income from rental activities, against which the tax shelter loss can be offset.

Example 11–18 Matt Young Eagle is subject to the alternative minimum tax for the first time ever this year, because of his deductions for accelerated depreciation from his sole proprietorship. Nonbusiness taxes paid and miscellaneous itemized deductions, among other familiar items, are not allowed as deductions when computing alternative minimum taxable income. Accordingly, Young Eagle should defer the payments of his fourth-quarter state income tax estimates and of the real estate tax on his home until next year, when the usual definitions of taxable income will apply to him again.

Spreading Income among Related Taxpayers

Because different types of legal entities are taxed separately and at different rates, an individual often can produce an overall tax savings by conducting various business and investment activities within separate taxpaying entities. The progressive nature of the various tax rate schedules further tends to increase the advantage of income splitting. This benefit might result from shifting income, either among different economic entities that are owned by the same individual, or among the individual's family members. Accordingly, tax considerations often play an important role both in the selection of organizational forms for a business enterprise and in family financial arrangements.

Example 11–19 Bob and Lorraine Whitehead are currently providing for Lorraine's parents' retirement out of after-tax income. Given the Whiteheads' marginal income tax rate of 30 percent, $1,000 of pretax income is needed to produce $700 of savings [$1,000 − (.30 of $1,000) = $700]. Assuming that the parents have a marginal income tax rate of only 18 percent, a transfer to them of $1,000 of pretax income, say, by the placement of income-producing assets into an appropriate trust, would raise the after-tax contribution to the parents' retirement to $820 [$1,000 − (18% of $1,000)].

Example 11–20 Sally Campbell is the sole shareholder and only employee of the Newark Corporation. The corporation's operating income this year is expected to be

$125,000. Sally is subject to an overall marginal income tax rate of 30 percent. Sally wishes to know, considering only the federal income tax, what amount of salary payments to her would produce the smallest combined tax for both herself and the corporation. Sally's income from other sources is sufficient to meet her living expenses and it precisely equals her total income tax deductions, so her taxable income is exactly equal to any salary that she receives from the corporation.

Currently, marginal corporate income tax rates do not exceed the 30 percent marginal individual tax bracket until corporate taxable income exceeds $75,000. Accordingly, the tax advisor should be certain to plan the corporation's compensation policy so that a corporate taxable income of at least $75,000 exists every year.

Departing from the Fundamentals

The general principles of tax planning that have been presented usually produce an optimal tax liability for the taxpayer. However, unusual circumstances may dictate that such principles should be violated purposely, to produce a desired effect. Again, however, the tax awareness of the parties is utmost in proper planning activities.

Example 11–21 Gretchen's manufacturing business is unincorporated. It has generated an operating loss of $265,000, which Gretchen can deduct on her tax return. Although there may be other tax uses for this loss, Gretchen may want to accelerate the recognition of other gross income into the current year, for example, by selling appreciated investments, exercising more sophisticated tax accounting elections, or simply sending out bills to customers in a more timely fashion. Economically, such income has been earned gradually by Gretchen, but it has had no tax effect yet because it has not been realized. Realization this year, however, will result in no tax liability for Gretchen because of the loss, so income acceleration should be considered.

Example 11–22 Brian's gross income is lower than he expected because of an unanticipated decrease in the sale of his homemade sandals. From a tax standpoint, it may be better to delay deductible expenditures of a discretionary or personal nature (e.g., advertising, medical expenses, and charitable contributions) until business picks up again. In this manner, the value of such deductions will increase, as will the marginal income tax rate to which he is subject.

Example 11–23 Dolores is subject to the alternative minimum tax this year, so her marginal tax rate is 24 percent, not the usual 36 percent. She might consider accelerating some gross income into the current year, to take advantage of this structural decrease in her marginal tax rate. The tax advisor must be certain, though, to compare the present values of the resulting taxes, not just the nominal dollar amounts (i.e., the proper tax planning comparison is between the $32,400 and the $24,000), and Dolores should accelerate the gross income in this setting.

	If Regular Tax Applies, taxed next year	If AMT Applies, taxed this year
Nominal tax liability	$36,000	$24,000
Present value of tax liability	$32,400	$24,000

Exploiting Inconsistencies in the Statute

Inconsistencies between Transactions

Most forms of self-provided in-kind income go unrecognized for tax purposes. Often, the same items are not deductible, however, when they are purchased in market transactions. Thus, providing for one's own needs can be an important technique in managing the recognition of taxable income.

> **Example 11–24** Jerry has $50,000 in savings. If the money were invested in securities, the yield on his investment would be taxable, although no deduction would be allowed for his "personal" expense of renting a home. If the $50,000 were invested in a home for his own use, however, the net rental value of the home would escape taxation, since such in-kind value is not recognized as gross income under the law.

Inconsistencies between Taxpayers

Inconsistencies often exist between Code sections that control the recognition of income and those that control the allowance of deductions for the same items. When a transaction is between related taxpayers, such inconsistent treatments sometimes can be used to the taxpayers' advantage. The objective in such a situation usually is to structure the terms of the transaction so as to decrease taxable income to the taxpayer group as a whole.

> **Example 11–25** Marilyn is the sole owner-employee of a corporation. To the extent that the corporation pays dividends to Marilyn, she will recognize gross income, but the corporation will receive no deduction. To the extent that Marilyn is paid a reasonable salary, she will recognize gross income and the corporation will receive a deduction. To the extent that she receives certain employee fringe benefits, such as medical insurance, Marilyn is not required to recognize taxable income, and the corporation is allowed an ordinary business expense deduction. In summary, the payment of dividends increases combined taxable income of a shareholder and the corporation, the payment of salary does not change combined taxable income, and providing qualified fringe benefits reduces combined taxable income.

> **Example 11–26** Don and Ann Evans operate a farm, producing a net taxable income of about $30,000 per year. Their nondeductible expenses for housing average $12,000 per year.
>
> The Evanses should consider forming a corporation and making a tax-free transfer of all of the farm property to the corporation, including their personal living quarters. As shareholders of the corporation, they could hire themselves as employees, with a requirement that they live on the business premises. The value of the lodging would not be taxable to the Evanses as individuals, under § 119 of the Code, but it would be deductible as a business expense of the corporation, thus reducing the corporation's taxable income before salaries to $18,000 ($30,000 − $12,000).
>
> The Evanses then should have the corporation pay them reasonable salaries totaling $18,000. In this manner, taxable income of $18,000 would be taxed directly to them as individuals, and the corporation's taxable income would be reduced to zero, thus avoiding any double taxation. By using this combination of income splitting and an employee fringe benefit, the Evanses could effectively reduce their taxable income (i.e., from $30,000 to $18,000) by the amount of their lodging costs ($12,000), even

though such costs are generally nondeductible by both self-employed persons and employees.

This result is based on the assumptions that $18,000 is a reasonable salary for the work that they perform, and that the requirement for living on the farm is for a bona fide business purpose (other than merely for tax avoidance).

Inconsistencies between Years

Another form of inconsistency concerns timing differences in the recognition of income and deductions. Such inconsistencies may relate to the transactions of one taxpayer, or they may concern two taxpayers engaging in a single transaction. In both cases, careful planning to take advantage of tax law inconsistencies can result in a considerable delay in the payment of taxes.

Example 11–27 Sarah Carter uses borrowed funds to acquire nondividend-paying corporate stocks. Appreciation on the stocks is not taxed until it is realized on the sale of the shares; yet, Carter might be able to claim investment-interest deductions for the interest that she pays on the borrowed funds.

Example 11–28 Harry Fischer is 40 percent shareholder and junior executive of the Able Corporation. Harry's performance incentive bonus is set at 30 percent of the corporation's pre-tax earnings for the year. It is payable on January 31 of the following year.

Because the corporation is an accrual-basis taxpayer, the bonus is deductible in the year in which it is earned. As a cash-basis minority shareholder, however, Harry need not recognize the income until the following taxable year, (i.e., when he receives it). To the extent of Harry's bonus, the recognition of combined corporate and shareholder income thus is delayed for one year.

Example 11–29 Jane Summer is an employee of the Orange Corporation and is covered by the company's qualified pension plan. The corporation makes a contribution to the plan for Jane's retirement, which will occur in thirty years. Although Jane will not receive any gross income from the pension benefits until her retirement in thirty years, the corporation is entitled to a current-year business expense deduction.

Avoiding Tax Traps

Ever since the enactment of the first income tax law, taxpayers have been trying to find ways to avoid such taxes. Likewise, Congress, the IRS, and the courts have enacted rules and doctrines to prevent, or at least restrict, various avoidance schemes. As a result, current tax law includes a maze of tax traps for the unwary.

Statutory Tax Traps

Many of the statutory provisions encountered in a tax planning context can best be understood when they are viewed as preventive provisions, that is, as rules designed by Congress to prevent certain techniques of tax avoidance. However, remember that any transaction that falls within the scope of a given provision, whether or not it is intended as part of a tax avoidance scheme, is subject to that provision. Thus, a basic knowledge of the tax system is necessary for the tax planner if certain disastrous pitfalls are to be avoided.

As we noted earlier in this chapter, income splitting between related taxpayers often can generate significant tax savings. To be effective for tax purposes, though, the income actually must be earned by the separate entities and not merely assigned by means of artificial transactions between them. Section 482 gives the IRS the power to reallocate both income and deductions among certain related taxpayers so as to reflect "true taxable income."

In applying § 482, the regulations indicate that the IRS's right to determine true taxable income is not limited to fraudulent or sham transactions, but also situations where income inadvertently has been shifted between controlled parties. The courts have held, however, that there truly must be a "shifting" of income before the IRS's power comes into play. Bona fide business transactions that bring tax advantages in their wake should not subject the related parties to reallocation. In concept, at least, § 482 can be applied by the IRS only where there has been some manipulation of income or deductions by the taxpayers.

Thus, while its boundaries are, in practice, both broad and sometimes hazy, § 482 does not prohibit the use of multiple entities for the purpose of earning income. It does, however, give the IRS a potent weapon with which to combat the artificial shifting of income between those entities.

> **Example 11–30** X and Y are two corporations that are fully owned by the same individual. X operates an international airline, and Y owns several hotels that are located in cities served by X. In conjunction with the advertising of its airlines, X often pictures Y's hotels. Although the primary benefit of the advertising is to X's airline operations, Y's hotels also obtain patronage by travelers who respond to the ads. X does not charge Y for the advertising. Because an unrelated hotel operator presumably would have been charged for such advertising, the IRS may make an allocation of income from X to Y to reflect the fair market value of the advertising services that were provided.

The Code restricts the amount of passive income that can be taxed at the (lower) marginal rates of one's dependent child who has not yet attained age 14, to less than $1,500 per year, an amount indexed for inflation. Any unearned income of the child that exceeds this amount is taxed to the child, but at the (higher) marginal rates of his or her parents. The purpose of this portion of the *Internal Revenue Code* is not to discriminate against children (who cannot vote in congressional elections), nor to place a higher tax burden on interest and dividend income, nor even to make the family the chief taxable unit in this country. Rather, the provision was enacted simply to discourage the shifting of taxable income from the higher tax brackets of the parent, through a temporary trust or some other accepted income-shifting vehicle, to the more favorable rates of the child, without any permanent loss by the parent of control over the use of the asset. Such tax planning techniques had been undertaken for many years, as a means (similar to that of Example 11–19) of accumulating after-tax contributions to an educational fund, by transferring income to the lowest marginal tax rates that were available within the family.

Whereas the objective of this part of the statute may be defensible by some, the broad provision that was enacted to implement it may create undue hardships in some circumstances, because it affects all taxpayers, not only those with the now-forbidden income-shifting motivation.

> **Example 11–31** Jimmy, age 7, received an inheritance from his grandmother's estate last year. Grandmother wanted Jimmy to attend a good graduate program in taxation

someday, so she invested in high-income securities that produce about $12,000 in interest income annually. Jimmy's parents are to see that he accumulates this income for his education. The interest will be taxed at the parents' 40 percent marginal rate, however, and not at Jimmy's (zero and) 15 percent rate, so a smaller after-tax amount of this income will be available for this laudable educational purpose.

Judicial Tax Traps

In the final analysis, the words of the tax law mean only what the courts say that they mean. Often, judicial decisions must be consulted to determine the allowable limits of various Code provisions.

Example 11–32 An employee-shareholder of a 50 percent family-owned corporation received an annual salary in excess of $1 million, an amount greater than that then paid to the heads of such corporations as General Motors and Sears.[3] Yet, despite IRS arguments to the contrary, the Tax Court upheld the entire amount paid as "reasonable" under the circumstances of the case, because of the special talents and abilities that the employee brought to the corporation.

Example 11–33 A widow changed her will to disinherit her relatives and leave her assets to her attorney and his wife.[4] When the widow died, her relatives brought suit against the attorney, alleging that he had influenced the widow improperly, through a personal relationship with her. The attorney paid them $121,000 to withdraw their litigation and deducted the payment as a business expense. The Tax Court upheld the deduction, on the grounds that the payment was made for the purpose of maintaining the professional reputation of the lawyer.

On appeal, the Tax Court's decision was overturned. According to the appeals court, a taxpayer's reasons for paying do not determine whether the payment is deductible. Because the lawsuit arose from the attorney's personal relationship with the widow, the $121,000 settlement was deemed to be a personal, nondeductible cost.

Example 11–34 Housing is expensive in Japan. A unit of Mobil Oil owned the house that was used by its president, at his discretion, when he stayed in Japan.[5] The house would have rented for $4,400 a year in the United States, but in Tokyo its annual rental value was $20,000. The executive included it in income and paid tax on $4,400, the U.S. rental value. However, the IRS asserted that the full $20,000 should have been included in his gross income.

The U.S. Court of Claims agreed with the taxpayer, holding that the excess rental value was primarily of benefit to the company, rather than to the individual. The home's prestige value was held to be important to the employer because of social values that were peculiar to Japan, where, in the words of the court, "'face' is an almost tangible reality."

Two pervasive judicial doctrines that often limit the taxpayer's ability to employ effective planning techniques are the concepts of *business purpose* and *substance over form*. To be upheld for tax purposes, transactions must possess some nontax, or "business," purpose in addition to that of tax avoidance. Moreover, there is always

[3]*Home Interiors and Gifts, Inc.,* 73 T.C. 92 (1980).
[4]*William J. McDonald, Jr.,* 592 F.2d 635, 78—2 USTC ¶ 9631, 42 AFTR2d 78—5797 (CA-2).
[5]*Faneuil Adams,* 585 F.2d 106, 77—2 USTC ¶ 9613, 40 AFTR2d 77—5607.

the possibility that the court may ignore the form of a transaction if it perceives that such structural false colors cloud the actual substance of the arrangement.

Whenever a series of transactions results in significant tax savings, the IRS may attempt to apply the concept of substance over form by "telescoping" or "collapsing" several transactions into one. If it is upheld by a court, this *step-transaction doctrine* sometimes can negate what had been a good tax plan (where the steps were viewed as separate transactions). To guard against this possibility, the taxpayer should have a bona fide business purpose for each individual step in the transaction. Of course, documenting nontax purposes is usually much easier if the various transactions are separated by reasonable time spans, since they are then less likely to be viewed as component parts of an overall plan.

Example 11–35 Sandra is the sole shareholder of a real estate development corporation. On January 15, she purchased ten additional shares of stock from her corporation for $100,000. On the same day, she sold a tract of undeveloped land to the corporation for its fair market value of $100,000. To the corporation, the land will be inventory. For Sandra, it had been a capital asset, having been held for investment purposes since its purchase ten years previously for $20,000. If these events are viewed as two separate transactions, Sandra will have increased the basis of her investment in the corporation by $100,000 and realized a fully taxable capital gain of $80,000 ($100,000 − $20,000). The corporation's basis in the land will be $100,000. Thus, if the corporation were to sell the land for, say, $110,000, its income therefrom would be only $10,000 ($110,000 − $100,000).

Alternatively, if these events are collapsed into a single transaction, Sandra's payment and receipt of cash would be ignored. Instead, she would be viewed as having given a tract of land in exchange for ten shares of stock of a corporation that she already controls. Under this single-transaction view, Sandra would recognize no taxable capital gain, and the corporation's basis in the stock would be the same as her prior basis, $20,000. Thus, if the corporation were to sell the land for $110,000, its ordinary income would be $90,000 ($110,000 − $20,000).

Taxpayers are restricted to the actual legal forms of the transactions in which they engage, but the IRS has the option of employing the step-transaction doctrine. Thus, the lack of any time lapse between the two transactions effectively gives the IRS its choice as to which interpretation it wishes to follow.

A Special Technique: Loans among Taxpayers

One particularly powerful tax planning technique that has seen some popularity in recent years is the **interest-free loan**. This type of loan sometimes can be used to spread income among related taxpayers so as to minimize the tax liability of the entire group.

Example 11–36 Albert is subject to a 36 percent marginal income tax rate. Betty is subject to a 15 percent marginal income tax rate. Albert has $10,000 cash, which he could invest in corporate bonds that pay 10 percent interest. However, if Albert makes an interest-free loan of the $10,000 to Betty, then Betty could invest the funds, and Betty, rather than Albert, would realize interest income of $1,000 per year. In effect, Albert has shifted $1,000 of taxable income to Betty.

We undertake a full discussion of the interest-free loan (1) to illustrate how various law sources are subject to taxpayer use and administrative and judicial interpretation, as discussed throughout this text, and (2) to demonstrate the dynamic evolution of tax planning techniques in the practice.

Income Tax Considerations

Incredible as it may seem, the issue of taxable benefits from interest-free loans was not litigated during the first forty-seven years of modern income tax law. In the 1961 *Dean* decision, the Tax Court ruled that a shareholder realized no taxable income from the interest-free use of more than $2 million from his controlled corporation's funds.[6] The issue lay dormant for the next twelve years, until the Commissioner announced his refusal in 1973 to follow the *Dean* decision. After 1973, the IRS continued to litigate in this area, but with only limited success. Finally, effective in 1984, Congress passed legislation that severely limited the opportunities for taxpayers who wish to shift income by means of an interest-free loan.

In the authors' opinion, the IRS made a serious error in the first case that was brought before the courts concerning interest-free loans. In *Dean,* a shareholder enjoyed the interest-free use of more than $2 million from his controlled corporation, thereby shifting income from the corporation to the shareholder. Rather than arguing that the corporation should be required to recognize income, the IRS alleged that an implicit income value should be imputed to the shareholder. This position was at odds with economic reality. The shareholder presumably already had recognized income as a result of using the $2 million. To impute additional income to the shareholder would have been to engage in double counting. If implicit income were to be imputed, it should have been a matter of reassigning income from the shareholder back to the corporation, thus increasing taxes at the corporate level rather than at the shareholder level.

Although presented with the wrong question in *Dean,* the court answered it correctly. The shareholder was not required to recognize additional income for several reasons. First, most interest payments are deductible in determining taxable income. Thus, if the shareholder had been paid taxable dividends instead of being given an interest-free loan, he could have borrowed on a normal interest-bearing note, made a cash payment for interest, and still have had a net taxable income of zero. This "offsetting deduction" viewpoint of *Dean* is the basic precedent by which the receipts of interest-free loans are justified as not resulting in taxable income.

The judicial doctrine of offsetting deductions was incomplete, though. The court's attention was on the borrower, while the lender was ignored in what is essentially a two-sided matter of income shifting. A borrower might use the funds that he or she acquired from an interest-free loan to generate exempt income and hence be ineligible for the usual deduction for interest paid. However, it is also possible that the lender might grant such a loan for the acquisition of nondeductible goods or services. Under this approach, lenders are not held to the same standards as borrowers. Consequently, inequitable results can occur. Such results should be of considerable interest to tax planners who are considering the use of interest-free loans.

[6]*J. Simpson Dean,* 35 T.C. 1083 (1961).

Example 11–37 Phil has access to $100,000 in discretionary cash. He is considering an investment in a tax-exempt state bond that pays 6 percent. Instead, he makes an interest-free loan to his daughter Greta. Greta then makes the same investment with the loan proceeds. Following the Tax Court's reasoning, Greta is required to recognize taxable income as a result of the interest-free loan, because she would not have been entitled to an offsetting deduction had actual cash interest been paid. Thus, while taxable income can be shifted effectively under current law, tax-exempt income cannot.

Code-Imputed Transactions

The IRS scored a significant victory relative to the gift tax aspects of interest-free loans early in 1984.[7] In *Dickman,* the Supreme Court held that the creation of an interest-free demand loan did indeed constitute a gift from the lender to the borrower. This case overturned a previous decision that had asserted that the creation of an interest-free demand loan was not subject to a federal gift tax, because the (indeterminate) term of such a demand loan made difficult the calculation of the value of the attributable taxable gift.[8]

Although it assigned the computational aspects of this situation to the IRS, the Court suggested that family members could make such loans in a *de minimis* amount (say, $100,000) without incurring any taxable gift. Moreover, because of the annual gift tax exclusion and the unified transfer tax credit, the mere presence of such a gift does not guarantee that the donor will incur any actual, immediate tax liability from such a loan.

Given the IRS's recent interest in interest-free loans, it is likely that this matter soon will be challenged in court. In the authors' opinion, such an attack most likely will be based on a substance-over-form argument, with interest-free loans to family members being compared to trust arrangements, and a § 482-type reallocation being made. If such a view is accepted by the courts, any resulting investment income would be taxed directly to the grantor-lender. Moreover, the creation of a term loan could be subject to the gift tax.

In addition, demand loans now are subject to a direct statutory income attribution procedure. Loans that are subject to a below-market interest rate generate gross income to the *borrower,* of a nature that is appropriate to the source of the loan, and a deduction to the lender, if such a deduction would have resulted had a direct cash payment been made. The amount of this income and deduction is a function of the excess of the short-term Treasury interest rate over that charged in the loan agreement. The borrower then is deemed to transfer the amount of the "interest discount" back to the lender as interest.

In general, then, below-market-rate loans receive arm's-length income tax treatment, and the income-shifting possibilities of a *Dean-* or *Crown*-like loan are curtailed. Moreover, this procedure can result in severe liquidity problems for the lender. Section 7872's income attribution procedure does not apply, however, if the amount of the outstanding loan does not exceed $10,000, unless the only purpose for the loan is found to be tax avoidance. This *de minimis* amount is $100,000 if the use

[7]*Dickman v. C.I.R.,* 465 U.S. 330, 104 S.Ct. 1086, 84—1 USTC ¶ 9240, aff'g 690 F.2d 812 (CA-11, 1982), rev'g 41 T.C.M. 620.

[8]*Lester Crown v. C.I.R.,* 585 F.2d 234, 78—2 USTC ¶ 13,260, 42 AFTR2d 78—6503 (CA-7), aff'g 67 T.C. 1060 (1977).

of the loan funds constitutes a gift, unless such funds are invested in income-producing assets.

Example 11–38 Mary Jane made a $1,000,000 demand loan to her nephew, Bud, charging 2 percent interest, when the prevailing Treasury short-term interest rate was 10 percent. Bud invested the loan proceeds in his stock portfolio. Under § 7872, this loan is treated as an arm's-length transaction between the relatives.

Accordingly, Mary Jane is deemed to have made an $80,000 gift to Bud (8 percent "interest discount" × $1,000,000 loan). This amount may be subject annually to a federal gift tax, after Mary Jane applies any available gift tax exemptions and credits.

Bud can deduct the $20,000 interest payment that he makes to Mary Jane (2 percent × $1,000,000) if he has sufficient investment income from the portfolio dealings, and Mary Jane must include this amount in her gross income. In addition, she must include the $80,000 deemed interest in her gross income, and Bud can deduct this additional amount, even though no corresponding cash changed hands.

Example 11–39 Assume the same facts as in Example 11–38, except that the amount of the loan is $100,000, and that Bud invests the proceeds in a new home. No income attribution is required. Bud's interest deduction includes only the $2,000 that he actually paid (2 percent × $100,000), and Mary Jane's gross income is limited to that amount.

Example 11–40 Quaintly Inn Corporation makes a $600,000 interest-free demand loan to Lynn Foreman, its majority stockholder. The loan is designed to provide Foreman with a valuable fringe benefit that will allow her to acquire a residence in a desirable suburb. The prevailing Treasury short-term interest rate is 12 percent.

Quaintly Inn is deemed to have made a $72,000 dividend payment to Foreman ($600,000 × 12%). The corporation cannot deduct this amount, but it does reduce its earnings and profits accordingly. Foreman's dividend income is $72,000. In addition, though, the corporation includes interest income, and Foreman secures an interest deduction for the $72,000.

Example 11–41 The American Soccer League has imposed a $3,000,000 per-team salary maximum on its members. One of the teams, the Lincoln Lions, has reached the salary maximum, but it wishes to give a $200,000 raise to its star forward, Carlheinz von Rahmig. It manages to avoid the league's sanction by making a $2,000,000 interest-free loan to von Rahmig, when the prevailing Treasury short-term interest rate is 10 percent.

The use of this loan is ineffective for tax purposes, however. Von Rahmig's compensation income includes both his direct salary and his $200,000 imputed wages, and the Lions can deduct this total amount. In addition, though, the Lions incur interest income, and von Rahmig secures an interest deduction, for the $200,000.

Using High-Interest Loans to Shift Income

Interest-free loans sometimes are useful in shifting income between family members, as discussed in the preceding segment of this chapter. At the opposite extreme, intrafamily loans carrying abnormally high interest rates also might be used to achieve the same end.

Example 11–42 Ralph Jones, Sr., who is subject to a marginal tax rate of 20 percent, recently moved into a retirement community and sold his longtime family home for

$50,000 in cash. Ralph Jones, Jr., who is subject to a marginal tax rate of 30 percent, wishes to provide support for his father by shifting some of his own income to the family patriarch.

Market investments currently generate a 10 percent pretax rate of return. If Ralph, Jr., borrowed $50,000 from his father at a 40 percent interest rate, annual income of $15,000 effectively could be shifted from him to his father [$50,000 × (40% − 10%) = $15,000].

In response to the suggestion that extraordinarily high interest rates be used on loans between related taxpayers, the reader might question whether such a plan would meet the general requirement that business expenses be reasonable in amount. If only reasonable amounts of interest paid could be deducted, while all interest that is received must be included in gross income, such loans would be a tax disaster: There would be an increase in total taxable income to the family as a whole.

However, the Third Circuit has held that interest paid need not be ordinary, necessary, or even reasonable in amount to be deductible. The authority for interest deductions is not §162, concerning general business expenses, but rather §163, which allows deductions "for all interest paid." In the words of the court:

> Throughout the ages lenders have extracted all they could from borrowers for the use of money. How much has been extracted has depended upon the desperation of the borrower and the exigency of the moment. Hence the phrase 'all interest paid' contained in the section must be taken in its plain and literal meaning to include whatever sums the taxpayer has actually had to pay for the use of money which he had borrowed.[9]

Following this doctrine, the U.S. Tax Court held in 1979 that interest payments at a rate of 60 percent between a taxpayer and his or her in-laws were fully deductible.[10] This case and others (*Dorzback, Kena, Inc.,*[11] and *Berger*[12]) seem to indicate that there is no statutory limit on the amount of interest that can be deducted if actually paid, even when the debtor and the creditor are related taxpayers.

Unlimited "rates" of interest do not necessarily guarantee that all intrafamily transactions seeking such treatment will be successful. The IRS may assert that these exchanges are, in reality, gifts and not loans. Loans are unconditional obligations that are enforceable by law. To defend cash exchanges as loans or repayments of interest and principal, as opposed to reciprocal gifts, legally enforceable written loan agreements are necessary. Details regarding interest rates and payment dates should be included. Otherwise, family relationships are apt to predispose the courts to view these transactions as gifts and thus void any allegedly deductible interest payments.

►_____ ## Summary

The study of taxes can be viewed as an examination of various ways to optimize one's tax liability. Tax rules that otherwise might seem as dry as a mouthful of sawdust have a way of becoming interesting, stimulating, and challenging, when one realizes their economic significance and the resulting implications on human behav-

[9]*Karl D. Dorzback v. Collison,* 195 F.2d 69, 52—1 USTC ¶ 9263, 41 AFTR 878 (CA-3).
[10]*Raymond S. Barton,* 38 T.C.M. 933, P-H T.C. Memo ¶ 79,234 (1979).
[11]*Kena, Inc.,* 44 B.T.A. 217 (1941).
[12]*Samuel & Lillian Berger,* 13 T.C.M. 177, P-H TC Memo ¶ 54,063 (1954).

ior. Tax optimization, therefore, can be viewed both as the heart of professional tax work and as the most important aspect of taxation for nontax specialists.

▶ _____   Key Words

By the time you complete your work relative to this chapter you should be comfortable discussing each of the following terms. If you need additional review of any of these items, return to the appropriate material in the chapter or consult the glossary to this text.

Average Tax Rate   Progressive Tax Rate
Effective Average Tax Rate   Proportional Tax Rate
Interest-Free Loan   Regressive Tax Rate
Marginal Tax Rate   Tax Awareness
Nominal Average Tax Rate

▶ _____   Exercises

1. Using the following codes, identify the basic approach(es) to tax avoidance that are used in each of the cases described below.

   Av   = Avoiding income recognition
   Cl   = Controlling the classification of income or expenditure
   Ju   = Changing tax jurisdictions
   Po   = Postponing income recognition
   Sp   = Spreading income among related taxpayers
   None = None of the above

   a. Albert invests his savings in tax-exempt state bonds.
   b. Betty invests in nondividend-paying corporate stocks by using borrowed funds.
   c. Chuck lent $100,000 to his daughter on an interest-free demand note.
   d. Doris lent $10,000 to her son on a five-year note, bearing interest at the annual rate of 65 percent.
   e. Ed invests $100,000 of his savings in a home for his own use.
   f. Frankie invested in a mutual fund that purchases only the indebtedness of the state in which he lives.
   g. Grace invested in a mutual fund that purchases only the shares of U.S. corporations that pay no dividends, but whose share prices increase in value over a five-year time period.

2. Using the codes from Exercise 1, identify the basic approach(es) to tax avoidance that are used in each of the cases described below.

   a. Annie invested in a mutual fund that purchases only the shares of Colonnia corporations, a country that has no tax treaty with the United States.
   b. Burt moves his manufacturing plant to Mexico. Mexico has a tax treaty with the United States, but its labor and utility rates are much lower than is the case where Burt's Ohio plant now operates.
   c. Cheryl moves her manufacturing plant to Allegro. Allegro has no tax treaty with the United States, and its labor and utility rates are much lower than is the case where Cheryl's Ohio plant now operates.

    d. Donna failed to report on her tax return the interest earned on her savings account.

    e. Evelyn had her controlled corporation pay her a salary instead of a dividend during the current year.

    f. Flip operates his business as a regular corporation because of his high marginal tax rate. He plans to sell the corporation in five years.

    g. Georgia grows most of her own food, instead of taking a second job.

3. With respect to the system of coding used in Exercises 1 and 2, create one new illustration in each tax planning category.

4. How do taxes fit into the general economic goals of most taxpayers?

5. How might a tax advisor ignoring the present value approach to tax planning arrive at an improper conclusion? Illustrate.

6. Give some examples of U.S. taxes that employ proportional, progressive, and regressive rate structures.

7. Give an example of a transaction between two taxpayers in which an inconsistent treatment is afforded the two taxpayers. Explain how related taxpayers might structure a transaction to take advantage of this inconsistency.

8. Give an example to show when a taxpayer might consider shifting income from the ordinary classification to capital.

9. Name two types of tax traps and give an example of each.

10. How does the typical tax practitioner divide his or her time among planning, compliance, research, and litigation?

11. What planning engagements can the tax professional offer? Why is he or she in an ideal position to offer these services?

12. What is the maximum rate of interest that can be deducted when it is paid to a related taxpayer? Explain.

13. Why does tax planning analysis focus on the marginal tax rate?

14. When might a taxpayer undertake transactions seemingly opposite to the usual tax planning principles?

15. Higher income taxpayers tend to engage in tax planning more than do lower income taxpayers. Why?

16. Is the objective of tax planning always to minimize taxes? Explain.

► Problems

17. Examples 11–2 and 11–3 in the text concern a decision between the same two mutually exclusive alternatives under identical conditions, except for the corporation's marginal tax rate. In Example 11–2, where the marginal tax rate was 40 percent, the conclusion was to accept Alternative A. In Example 11–3, where the marginal tax rate was 20 percent, the conclusion was to accept Alternative M.

    Determine the marginal tax rate at which the two alternatives would be economic equivalents, that is, they would generate the same excess after-tax payoff over after-tax cost. Your answer should be based on all of the conditions and assumptions as stated in Examples 11–2 and 11–3.

18. On creating a new 100 percent owned corporation, Ben was advised by his tax consultant to treat 50 percent of the total amount that was invested as a loan and 50 percent as a purchase of corporate stock. What tax advantage does this arrangement have over structuring the entire investment as a purchase of stock? Explain.

19. Julia currently is considering the purchase of some land to be held as an investment. She and the seller have agreed on a contract under which Julia would pay $1,000 per month for 60 months or $60,000 total. The seller, not in the real estate business, acquired the land several years ago by paying cash of $10,000. Two alternative interpretations of this transaction are (a) a price of $51,726 with 6 percent interest and (b) a price of $39,380 with 18 percent interest. Which interpretation would you expect each party to prefer? Why?

20. George, a high-bracket taxpayer, wishes to shift some of his own taxable income to his fifteen-year-old daughter, Debra, and is considering two alternative methods of doing so. One is to make a gift of the interest on some corporate bonds that he owns. The other is to make an interest-free demand loan to Debra, so that she can invest in corporate bonds. Evaluate the pros and cons of each alternative.

21. Betty Smith has two sons, Bob and Jack. Bob made an interest-free loan to Jack. Betty owns two corporations, Alt and Bip. Alt made an interest-free loan to Bip. In which situation is imputed income most likely to be reallocated between the borrower and the lender? Explain.

22. Should Ferris Corporation elect to forgo the carryback of its $60,000 year 2000 net operating loss? Ferris is subject to a 15 percent cost of capital. Corporate tax rates are as in IRC § 11.

a.

Tax Year	Actual or Projected Taxable Income
1999	$700,000
2001	$700,000

b.

Tax Year	Actual or Projected Taxable Income
1999	$70,000
2001	$700,000

c.

Tax Year	Actual or Projected Taxable Income
1999	$70,000
2001	($70,000)
2002	($70,000)
2003	($70,000)
2004	$700,000

23. Should Harris Corporation accelerate gross income into 2000, its first year subject to the alternative minimum tax? Harris is subject to a 15 percent cost of capital. The corporate AMT rate is a flat 20 percent, and Harris exceeds the annual AMT exemption phase-out.

a.

Tax Year	Actual or Projected Taxable Income
2001	Regular Tax $700,000
2002	Regular Tax $700,000

b.

Tax Year	Actual or Projected Taxable Income
2001	AMT $700,000
2002	Regular Tax $700,000

c.

Tax Year	Actual or Projected Taxable Income
2001	AMT $700,000
2002	AMT $700,000
2003	AMT $700,000
2004	AMT $700,000
2005	Regular Tax $700,000

24. Paris Corporation holds a $100,000 unrealized net capital gain. Should Paris accelerate the recognition of this gain, given a net capital loss carryforward in each of the following amounts? Paris is subject to a fifteen percent cost of capital. Its marginal tax rate is 40 percent.

    a. $40,000
    b. $120,000

25. Maris Corporation put into service in 1999 $100,000 of equipment that qualifies for its state's 10 percent research credit. To the extent that the credit is claimed, no cost recovery deductions are allowed. Maris is subject to a 15 percent cost of capital. If the credit were not claimed, the property would qualify for cost recovery deductions using a three-year life, straight line with no salvage value, and a half-year convention. The state's flat income tax rate is as follows.

    a. 2 percent
    b. 4 percent
    c. 8 percent

Tax Practice and Administration: Working with the IRS

We have discussed various aspects of tax practice throughout this text, including both the principles of tax research and the structure of the judicial decision-making process. In this chapter, we will examine in more detail the workings of the **Internal Revenue Service** (IRS) and the **Treasury Department,** with an eye toward an overview of the elections and other opportunities and pitfalls that face the practitioner in working with these administrative bodies.

After all, when the researcher has decided that his or her client should prevail with respect to a specified tax issue, a challenge to the IRS must be issued and implemented. In this chapter, we present some of the procedural aspects of this course of action.

Organization of the Internal Revenue Service

The Department of the Treasury is responsible for administering and enforcing the internal revenue laws of the United States. However, most revenue functions and authority have been delegated by the Secretary of the Treasury to the **Commissioner of Internal Revenue.** The commissioner is the chief executive officer of the Internal Revenue Service and is appointed by the President of the United States. The Commissioner holds the responsibility for overall planning and for directing, coordinating, and controlling the policies and programs of the IRS.

The Internal Revenue Service is one of about a dozen bureaus within the Department of the Treasury. It was established by Congress on July 1, 1862, to meet the fiscal needs of the Civil War. At that time, the name of the agency was the Bureau of Internal Revenue. In 1953 the name was changed to the Internal Revenue Service.

Since 1962 the agency has undergone a period of steady growth as the means for financing government operations shifted from the levying of import duties on outsiders to one of internal taxation on U.S. citizens and businesses. This expansion increased substantially after 1913 with the ratification of the Sixteenth Amendment, which authorized the modern income tax on noncorporate entities.

Until 1951 the agency was organized on a type-of-tax basis (i.e., with income, alcohol and tobacco, etc., divisions), with jurisdictionally separate departments that were responsible for administering these different revenue sources. Since 1952 the agency has undergone five major reorganizations, including one in 1994 aimed at downsizing the organization. The most important aspects of these reengineering exercises have been the reorganization of the IRS along functional lines (i.e., into administration, operations, technical, planning, and inspection divisions), and the abandonment of the system of political appointments to positions other than that of the Commissioner and the Chief Counsel.

Another major restructuring effort was initiated in 1998, as a response to perceived abuses by the agency. Recognizing that most Commissioners serve only a short tenure, and that the Treasury Department carries a myriad of duties, Congress believed that the addition of an IRS-oversight board would improve the chances for the development of consistent long-term strategies and priorities. Private sector input is provided through the IRS Oversight Board, which functions as part of the Treasury Department. The Board has no authority to affect tax policy, to intervene in IRS personnel or procurement matters, or to affect the processing of individual tax cases. Its major duties include the following.

▶ Review and approve IRS mission, strategic plans, and annual planning documents.

▶ Review IRS operational functions, including modernization, outsourcing, and training efforts.

▶ Recommend to the President candidates for Commissioner.

▶ Review the process of selecting, evaluating, and compensating senior IRS executives.

▶ Review and approve the IRS annual budget request.

▶ Ensure the proper treatment of taxpayers.

The Board is designed to function like a corporate board of directors. It is made up of six members of the private sector, appointed to five-year terms by the President, and of the Treasury Secretary, the IRS Commissioner, and a representative of IRS employees.

Today, the IRS is an organization of more than 100,000 employees. With the exception of the Department of Defense, it is the largest agency of the federal government. It consists of a national office in Washington, DC, and a large decentralized field organization that is composed of a handful of regions and about thirty districts. Exhibit 12–1 illustrates the IRS regions, districts, and service centers that are assigned to the geographic areas of the country.

The Service is under a congressional mandate to restructure its operations somewhat dramatically. It is likely that this will entail some movement away from a geographically based organization into one solely reflecting functional areas. The restructuring effort had no timetable or deadline as this text went to press, but it is one of the duties of the IRS Oversight Board, which is likely to become fully functional in early 1999. The descriptions that follow were still valid at press time.

IRS National Office

The IRS's national office is located in the District of Columbia. It is staffed by the office of the Commissioner of Internal Revenue, which includes a Deputy Commissioner, and various chief officers and assistants to the Commissioner. Functional Assistant Commissioners and the Chief Counsel of the service number about a dozen, and an Associate Commissioner for Modernization reports directly to the Commissioner.

The IRS Commissioner is appointed by the President to a renewable five-year term. He or she is the chief executive officer of the agency and is charged under § 7803(a) to administer, manage, conduct, direct, and supervise the execution of the federal tax laws. The Commissioner's nomination is reviewed by the Senate. He or she must demonstrate some level of experience in the management of organizations. The Commissioner is the agency's final authority as to the interpretation of tax law.

The Chief Counsel is the agency's highest ranking legal adviser, and he or she reports to the Commissioner, relative to the administration and enforcement of the tax laws. In effect, the Chief Counsel is the IRS's attorney. Rulings and other written determinations are prepared by the Chief Counsel's office. The Chief Counsel represents the agency in Tax Court cases and often assists in preparing proposed legislation, treaties, regulations, and executive orders. Associate Chief Counsels are

EXHIBIT 12–1   IRS regions, districts, and service centers

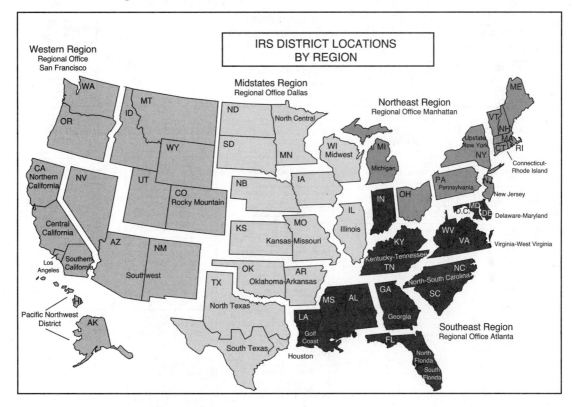

assigned duties relative to litigation, technical matters, international transactions, and finance and management. To promote uniformity between the settlement and litigation divisions of the IRS, though, the agency's Appeals Division is under the Commissioner's supervision.

The independent Inspector General for Tax Administration reports to the Treasury Secretary. He or she audits, investigates, and evaluates IRS programs, to improve the quality and credibility of the agency. The Inspector General makes semiannual reports to congressional committees.

The national office is responsible for developing broad nationwide policies and programs for the administration of the tax laws. In addition, it directs, guides, coordinates, and controls the activities of its field personnel. Exhibits 12–2 and 12–3 illustrate the organization of the Commissioner's and Chief Counsel's offices.

IRS Regional Offices

The IRS maintains regional offices in four locations, namely, New York City, Atlanta, Dallas, and San Francisco. Each regional office is headed by a Regional Commissioner, whose staff includes Assistant Commissioners for functional areas such as collection, data processing, resource management, examination, and criminal investigation. The regional offices are responsible for executing the broad

EXHIBIT 12–2 Office of the IRS Commissioner

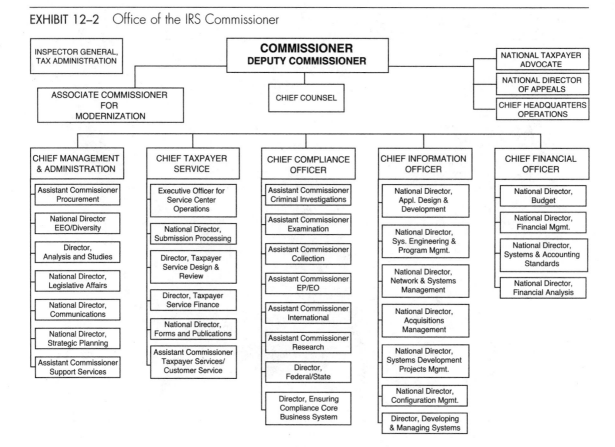

nationwide policies and programs for the administration of the internal revenue laws. In addition, they direct and coordinate the functions and activities of the district offices and service centers that are located within the jurisdiction. Exhibit 12–4 illustrates the organization of a typical regional office.

IRS Service Centers

The first **Internal Revenue Service Center** was established in 1955 in Kansas City, on a pilot basis. Later that same year, a second center was activated in Lawrence, Massachusetts. Additional service centers were established during the 1960s to meet the processing needs of the various geographic regions of the country. Today, ten service centers serve the IRS regions. They are located at Andover, Massachusetts; Austin, Texas; Brookhaven, New York; Chamblee, Georgia; Covington, Kentucky; Fresno, California; Kansas City, Missouri; Memphis, Tennessee; Ogden, Utah; and Philadelphia, Pennsylvania.

The primary function of the service centers is to process and perform mathematical verifications of the massive volume of federal tax returns. The centers are also responsible for performing miscellaneous special projects or programs as assigned by an appropriate Regional Commissioner.

EXHIBIT 12-3 Office of the Chief Counsel

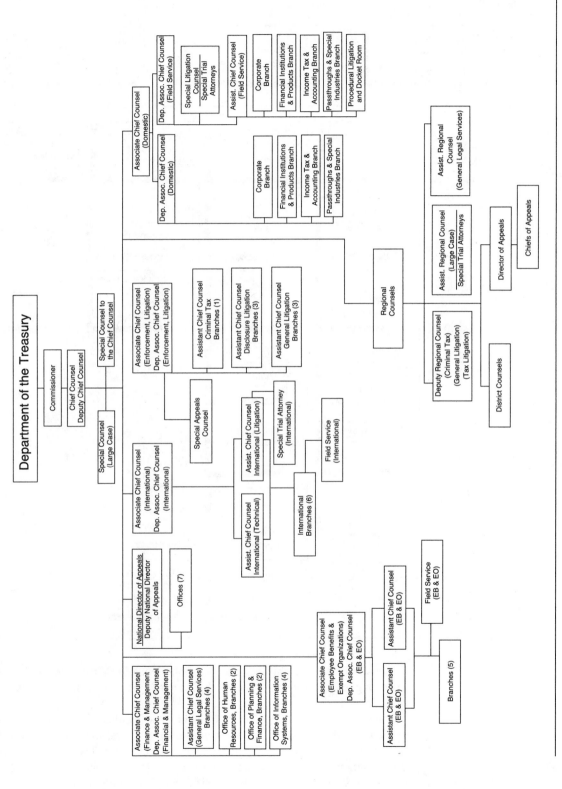

EXHIBIT 12–4 IRS regional office organization

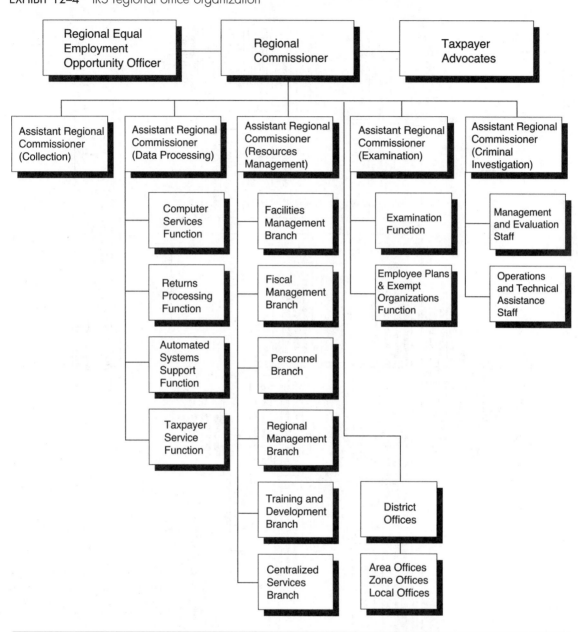

Statistical data are compiled at the IRS Data Center in Detroit, and special return-processing functions are performed at the National Computer Center in Martinsburg, West Virginia.

Functions of the existing Service Centers are scheduled to be reassigned by the year 2000 in the following manner. **Computing Centers,** located in Detroit, Martinsburg, and Memphis, will manipulate data collected from tax returns at **Processing Centers** in Austin, Cincinnati, Kansas City, Memphis, and Ogden. In addition, about twenty-five **Customer Service Sites** will deal with telephone and electronic contacts from taxpayers, in working with electronic filing of returns, and in answering telephone and online taxpayer inquiries.

Exhibit 12–5 illustrates the internal organization of the typical Internal Revenue Service Center.

IRS District Offices

The service operations of the IRS have been decentralized into more than thirty district offices. A typical district office is organized along functional lines, with separate divisions for resource management, examination, collection, employee benefit plans and exempt organizations, criminal investigation, and taxpayer service. Each district office is led by a **District Director,** who reports to the Regional Commissioner. Exhibit 12–6 diagrams the organization of a typical IRS district office.

Taxpayer Assistance Orders

The **National Taxpayer Advocate** administers a taxpayer-intervention system, which is designed to resolve a wide range of tax administration problems that are

EXHIBIT 12–5   IRS Service Center organization

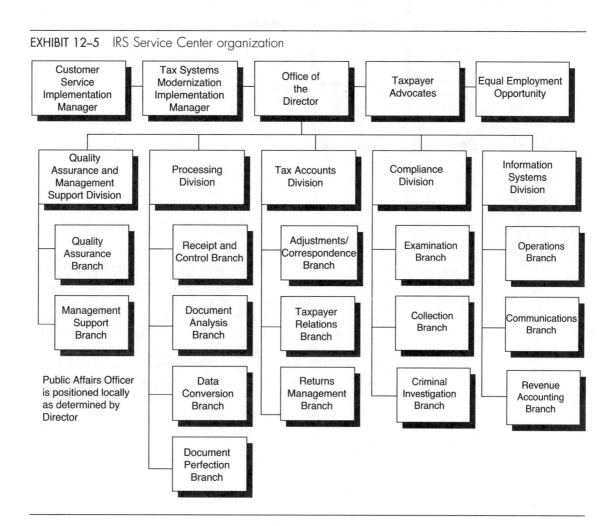

EXHIBIT 12–6   IRS district office organization

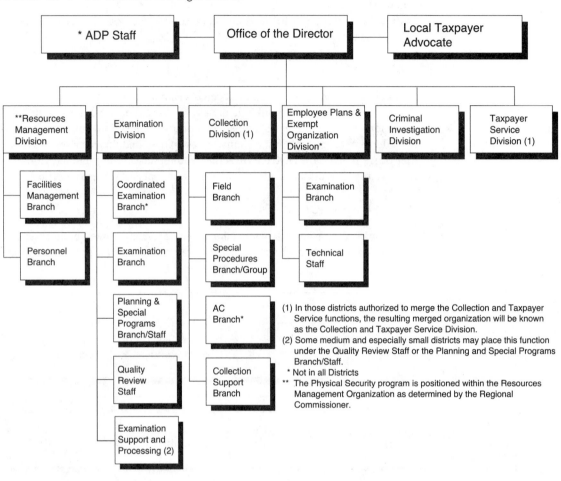

(1) In those districts authorized to merge the Collection and Taxpayer Service functions, the resulting merged organization will be known as the Collection and Taxpayer Service Division.

(2) Some medium and especially small districts may place this function under the Quality Review Staff or the Planning and Special Programs Branch/Staff.

  * Not in all Districts

 ** The Physical Security program is positioned within the Resources Management Organization as determined by the Regional Commissioner.

not remedied through the agency's normal operating procedures or administrative channels. The Advocate reports directly to the Commissioner and works through a system of local Taxpayer Advocates, one of which is located in each state. The National Taxpayer Advocate has statutory authority to issue a **Taxpayer Assistance Order** (TAO) to suspend, delay, or stop actions where, in the determination of the Advocate, the taxpayer is suffering or about to suffer a significant hardship as a result of the manner in which the IRS is administering the revenue laws.[1]

"Hardships" refer to any circumstance that includes an immediate threat of adverse action for the taxpayer, his or her irreparable injury, a delay of more than thirty days in settling the taxpayer's account, or the incurring of significant costs (such as professional advisory fees) to handle the dispute. The IRS's action that is the subject of a TAO must be such that it would offend one's sense of fairness, given all the related facts.

[1]§ 7811.

Typically, the TAO requires remedial actions, such as a release from the IRS's levy of specific property or the cessation of a collection activity, or it gives the IRS a deadline for action. A TAO is binding on the IRS, short of its rescission by the Advocate, the Commissioner, or a Deputy Commissioner.

A taxpayer applies for a TAO by filing Form 911, Application for Taxpayer Assistance Order (Taxpayer's Application for Relief from Hardship), reproduced as Exhibit 12–7.

EXHIBIT 12–7   Application for hardship relief

Form **911** (Rev. January 1994)	Department of the Treasury – Internal Revenue Service **Application for Taxpayer Assistance Order (ATAO)** (Taxpayer's Application for Relief from Hardship)	If sending Form 911 with another form or letter, put Form 911 on top.

Note: If you have not tried to obtain relief from the IRS office that contacted you, use of this form may not be necessary. Use this form only after reading the instructions for When To Use This Form. Filing this application may affect the statutory period of limitations. (See instructions for line 14.)

Section I. Taxpayer Information

1. Name(s) as shown on tax return	2. Your Social Security Number	4. Tax form
	3. Social Security of Spouse Shown in 1.	5. Tax period ended
6. Current mailing address (number & street). For P.O. Box, see instructions Apt. No.	8. Employer identification number, if applicable.	
7. City, town or post office, state and ZIP Code	9. Person to contact	
If the above address is different from that shown on latest filed tax return and you want us to update our records with this new address, check here......... ☐	10. Daytime telephone number ( )	11. Best time to call

12. Description of significant hardship *(If more space is needed, attach additional sheets.)*

A
T
A
O

13. Description of relief requested *(If more space is needed, attach additional sheets.)*

14. Signature of taxpayer or Corporate Officer *(See instructions.)*	15. Date	16. Signature of spouse shown in block 1	17. Date

Section II. Representative Information *(If applicable)*

18. Name of authorized representative (Must be same as on Form 2848 or 8821)	22. Firm name
19. Centralized Authorization File (CAF) number	23. Mailing address
20. Daytime telephone number ( )	21. Best time to call	

24. Representative Signature	25. Date

Section III. (For Internal Revenue Service only)

26. Name of initiating employee	27. ☐ IRS Identified ☐ Taxpayer request	28. Telephone ( )	29. Function	30. Office	31. Date

Cat. No. 16965S

Form **911** (Rev. 1-94)

Local Taxpayer Advocates

The IRS uses local Taxpayer Advocates in a system designed to help resolve taxpayer problems or complaints that are not being satisfied through regular agency channels. The primary objective of the Advocate system is to provide taxpayers with a local advocate within the IRS who has access to the pertinent regional, district, or service center official. In addition, the program enables the IRS to identify its own organizational, procedural, and systematic problems, and to take corrective action as needed.

The system is not intended to circumvent the existing IRS channels of managerial authority or established administrative procedures and formal avenues of appeal. Rather, it is designed to ensure that taxpayer problems or complaints that have not been resolved adequately through such normal procedures are referred and controlled within the program. When a case is referred to a member of the National Taxpayer Advocate team, he or she will ensure that the problem will not be lost or overlooked, and that it will be resolved as promptly and efficiently as is possible. If a case cannot be resolved within five working days after receipt of the statement of the problem or complaint, the taxpayer will be contacted by telephone, advised of the status of the case, and given the name and telephone number of the IRS employee who is responsible for the resolution of the problem. Typically, the Advocate system is used to resolve billing, procedural, computer-generated, and other problems that taxpayers cannot correct after one or more contacts with the IRS office that is handling the matter.

The National Taxpayer Advocate works through local team members, who are responsible for the work that is conducted within his or her jurisdiction. Local advocates are independent from IRS examination, collection, and appeals functions. They are responsible only to the National Taxpayer Advocate.

Taxpayer Rights

Under three incarnations of the so-called *Taxpayer Bill of Rights,* taxpayers are guaranteed various rights to representation before the IRS, a recording of any proceedings, and an IRS explanation of its position relative to the pertinent disagreement. Specifically, the taxpayer has a right to know why the IRS is requesting information, exactly how the IRS will use the information it receives, and what might happen if the taxpayer does not submit the requested information. Accordingly, prior to an initial audit or collection interview, an IRS employee or officer must explain, orally or in written form, the pertinent aspects of the procedures to come.[2]

A taxpayer may be represented by an attorney, CPA, or other person who is permitted to represent a taxpayer before the IRS and who has obtained a properly executed power of attorney. Absent an administrative summons, a taxpayer cannot be required to accompany the representative to an interview. Moreover, if a taxpayer

---

[2] § 7521(b)(1).

clearly states during an interview that he or she wishes to consult with such a representative, the interview is suspended until such counsel is secured.[3]

After meeting a ten-day notice requirement, the taxpayer is allowed to make a tape recording of the IRS interview, using the taxpayer's own equipment. Similarly, if the IRS intends to record an interview with a taxpayer or his or her representative, it must give a ten-day notice to the taxpayer. In addition, upon receiving a request from the taxpayer and a reimbursement for duplication costs, the IRS must make available to the taxpayer a transcript of the interview or a copy of its tape recording.[4]

To protect the rights of so-called innocent spouses on joint returns, the IRS must inform spouses of their joint and several liability for tax deficiencies, and both spouses must receive separately mailed notices as to audit, appeals, and Tax Court proceedings. This may be especially important where the spouses have divorced or separated subsequent to filing the original joint return.

The Service must inform taxpayers of their rights to representation in carrying out a dispute with the agency, and of rights to suspend at any time an interview with IRS personnel so as to include their representatives.

With respect to noncriminal tax matters before the IRS or a federal court, the common law privilege of confidentiality exists between a taxpayer and his or her tax practitioner, that is, one who is authorized to practice before the IRS. The privilege exists with respect to tax advice the practitioner has rendered. These provisions extend existing privilege protection previously only applicable between a taxpayer and his or her attorney. The privilege does not exist with respect to dealings with tax shelters.

The Audit Process

The U.S. federal income tax system is based primarily on an assumption of self-assessment. All persons with taxable incomes that exceed a specific amount are required to prepare an accurate statement of annual income (i.e., an income tax return) and to remit in a timely fashion any amount of tax that is due. In a somewhat paternalistic sense, the IRS uses the examination of returns as an enforcement device to promote such voluntary compliance with the internal revenue laws. In a manner that is somewhat similar to the treatment by a parent of a child who is considering some forbidden behavior, the threat of an IRS audit encourages many taxpayers to report accurately their taxable incomes and to pay any tax liability that remains outstanding.

Because only a small number of tax returns can be audited each year, the IRS attempts to select for examination only those returns that will generate additional revenues for the Treasury. It primarily relies on sophisticated statistical models and computer technology to identify those returns that possess the greatest revenue return for the agency's investment of audit resources. However, in addition to this scientific selection process, a number of returns are manually selected for examination at an examiner's discretion.

[3]§§ 7521(b)(2) and (c).
[4]§ 7521(a).

Preliminary Review of Returns

All business and individual tax returns are reviewed routinely by IRS personnel for simple and obvious errors, such as the omission of required signatures and Social Security numbers, at one of the service centers. After this initial (often computer-based) review, income tax returns are processed through the IRS Automatic Data Processing (ADP) program.

One of the most important functions performed by the ADP program is the matching of the information recorded on a return with corresponding data received from third parties, for example, from an employer on Form W-2. This procedure, which is referred to as the Information Document Matching Program (IDMP), has uncovered millions of cases of discrepancies between the amount, say, of income that recipients have reported on tax returns and corresponding deductions or other information that has been transmitted by payors. In addition, the IDMP provides the IRS with a means by which to detect taxpayers who fail to file any return at all. In the typical year, about 5 million taxpayers are sent such failure-to-file inquiries as a result of the matching program.

ADP is also used to conduct the Service's Mathematical/Clerical Error Program. This process is designed to uncover relatively simple and readily identifiable problems that can be resolved easily through the mail.

Mathematical/Clerical Error Program   The Mathematical/Clerical Error Program is one of a number of special programs that are conducted at the service centers. This program checks every return for mathematical errors, recomputes the tax due after properly applying the numbers that are included in the return, and summarily assesses any additional tax that is due, or allows refunds or credits based on (previously) miscomputed deductions or credits. A summary assessment may be made concerning any deficiency that results from a mathematical or clerical error.[5] Consequently, the IRS need not send the taxpayer a formal notice of deficiency (i.e., a ninety-day letter, as discussed subsequently in this chapter) before the additional tax is assessed.

When a mathematical or clerical error is identified by the service center, the IRS mails the taxpayer a corrected tax computation and requests that he or she pay the additional tax within ten days of the date of the notice, or twenty-one days if the tax underpayment is less than $100,000. If the deficiency is paid within this period, no interest is charged on the underpayment. However, if the deficiency is not paid in a timely fashion, interest is imposed on the unpaid amount for a period that begins on the date of the notice and demand, and ends on the date of payment.

A taxpayer may not petition the U.S. Tax Court with respect to a deficiency that results from a mathematical or clerical error. However, other administrative procedures will allow the taxpayer to contest the summary assessment without first paying the tax.

An explanation of the asserted error must be given to the taxpayer by the IRS. After receiving this explanation, the taxpayer has sixty days within which to request that the additional tax be abated. If a request for abatement is made, the assessment will be canceled automatically. However, the return is then identified for further examination if the taxpayer cannot justify satisfactorily or substantiate the figures that were included on the original return.

---

[5] § 6213(b)(1).

When an error results in a taxpayer overpayment of the tax, the IRS usually sends a corrected computation of the tax, together with a brief explanation of the error and a refund of the excess amount that was paid.

The IRS does not consider such a contact that it makes with the taxpayer to be an examination. Therefore, a taxpayer who is contacted under Mathematical/Clerical Error Program is not entitled to the administrative remedies that are available to taxpayers who are involved in a formal examination.

In addition to this testing of mathematical computations, the ADP program is useful for verifying one's compliance with estimated tax payment requirements. As a result of utilizing this system, the IRS has discovered that thousands of taxpayers have not been complying with the statutory estimated tax requirements, and that others collectively have been claiming millions of dollars in payments that actually never were made.

Unallowable Items Program   The IRS conducts another program at each service center that is similar to the Mathematical/Clerical Error Program called the Unallowable Items Program. Under this program IRS personnel at each service center question items that have been included on individual income tax returns that appear to be unallowable by law. These items may be identified manually or on their face by computer, and include such return elements as an overstatement of the standard deduction, the claiming of an incorrect filing status, the deduction of federal income taxes, or the deduction of lost (but not stolen) assets as a casualty loss.

If a return is identified as including an unallowable item, the IRS computes the seemingly necessary adjustment in taxes, and the taxpayer is notified by mail. Again, the IRS does not consider the contact that it makes with a taxpayer under the Unallowable Items Program to be an examination. Consequently, it treats an adjustment in this circumstance as a correction of a mathematical or clerical error, and the taxpayer is not sent a formal notice of deficiency.

If the taxpayer is able to explain the questioned item adequately, the assessment is abated. However, the case will be continued as a correspondence or office audit if the taxpayer's response is deemed unsatisfactory.

Selection of Returns for Examination

Each year the IRS determines the approximate number and types of returns that it intends to audit. The national office then prepares an audit plan to allocate its personnel to achieve the desired audit coverage. The primary goal of the IRS in selecting a return for examination is to review only those returns that will result in a satisfactory increase in the tax liability.

Computer and manual methods are used to select returns for examination. Computer programs select certain returns for examination, based on the potential that exists for changes in the tax treatment of certain items on the return. Generally, this is done through the use of mathematical models, including correlations and discriminant functions. IRS personnel also manually select returns that they believe warrant special attention. The Service describes in nontechnical terms its selection procedures in its annual Publication 1.

Although an increasing amount of the initial IRS screening of the returns for audit is performed by computers, a most detailed selection procedure is employed manually in the Examination Division of the District Director's office, where the classification staff ultimately selects those specific cases that will be examined. The number of returns that finally is selected by the staff is based on the examination resource (and other) capabilities of the respective district offices.

Discriminant Function System

Once a return has been processed through the Service's ADP program, a magnetic tape that contains the information from each return, as prepared at the service center, is sent to the National Computer Center in Martinsburg, West Virginia. There, each return is rated by computer for its audit potential by means of a mathematical model, the **discriminant function formula** (DIF). This formula assigns numeric weights to certain (undisclosed by the IRS) return items, generating a composite score for the return. In this regard, the higher the DIF score, the greater the potential for a favorable-to-the-Treasury change to the return upon audit. Statistics provided by the Commissioner show a high correlation between DIF scores and such tax modifications.

When the computer selects a return that has a high probability for an adjustment, as indicated by a high DIF score, an employee at the service center manually inspects the return to confirm its audit potential. If an acceptable explanation for the DIF score cannot be found after this manual examination of the return and its attachments, including explanatory data that the computer did not consider, the return is forwarded to the Examination Division at the appropriate district office.

Taxpayer Compliance Measurement Program

The Taxpayer Compliance Measurement Program (TCMP) is a research program that is designed to furnish the IRS with statistics concerning the type and number of errors that are made on a representative sample of individual income tax returns. These statistics then are used to develop and update the DIF formulas. Under the TCMP procedures, 50,000 to 100,000 individual income tax returns are selected randomly for an extremely thorough examination, based on the ending digits of the taxpayer's Social Security number. These returns then are examined comprehensively to determine the degree of their accuracy as filed.

Unlike the treatment that is given returns that are selected for general audit, the TCMP examiner may not exercise any judgment in dealing with an item on the return. Every item must be substantiated, and all errors must be noted and corrected, regardless of their amount. This procedure is necessary to a determination of the actual error patterns that individual income tax returns exhibit, so that the statistics that underlie the DIF procedure are free from any major bias. TCMP audits last took place more than a decade ago, and they now are out of political favor. Thus, data underlying the assumption of the DIF procedure are quite dated and likely are significantly inaccurate in today's economy.

Other Selection Methods

In addition to the previously discussed computerized methods for identification of returns for IRS examination, returns may be selected manually, for a variety of different reasons. An examination may be initiated, for instance, because of information that is provided by an informant, or because the selected return is linked to another return that is currently under examination (e.g., a partner's return may be selected as a result of a partnership audit).

Moreover, some returns automatically are reviewed by IRS personnel because the reported taxable income, gross receipts, or total assets exceed a predetermined materiality amount. For instance, individual returns with total positive income of $50,000 or more, or partnership returns with gross receipts or gross income of $500,000 or more, can be selected in this manner. Finally, a return may be selected for examination because the taxpayer has filed a claim for refund or otherwise has indicated that an adjustment in the original amount of tax liability is necessary.

"Economic reality" factors can be considered by the IRS in selection of returns for audit, but only where the agency has some other evidence that the taxpayer has underreported taxable income for the year. For instance, manual selection of a return and an economic-reality review might occur when an IRS employee, reviewing data in three-filing-year periods, finds indications that income might be underreported or deductions might be overstated or misclassified. Some of the factors believed to be perused in an economic reality audit include the following.

▶ Significant increases in interest, dividend, and other investment income
▶ Significant decreases in mortgage and other reportable interest paid
▶ Significant variance in self-employment or farming income during the period, relative to industry norms
▶ Business and other expenditures not seemingly justified by income levels

Chances of Audit   Taxpayers often want to know what their overall probability of selection for an audit might be for a given year. In general, barely 1 percent of all returns are selected for examination by the IRS, and this figure includes the results of the mathematical error program. The chances for selection increase, though, if the taxpayer:

▶ claims tax shelter losses;
▶ claims office-in-the-home deductions;
▶ operates a cash-oriented business, such as a restaurant (both as an owner, selling food and drink for cash, and as a waiter, collecting tips) or repair/construction trade;
▶ claims business deductions that are excessive for the income level;
▶ has had prior-year returns that were audited and found incorrect; or
▶ claims itemized deductions that are excessive for the income level.

Relative to the last point, one should not hesitate to claim all legitimate deductions, but it is useful to know what raises the IRS's "red flag" for itemized deduction amounts. The data in Exhibit 12–8 were current for calendar-year 1996 returns. They vary quite a bit from state to state, given differing income levels, types and deductibility of state and local taxes, and spending patterns. Note also in Exhibit 12–8 the varying degrees to which taxpayers itemize deductions, approaching (but not attaining) 100 percent at upper income levels. Non-itemizers at upper income levels usually indicate the lack of a state income tax, a paid-up residence, or the presence of comprehensive health insurance coverage.

The probabilities of selection for audit in 1995 were as shown in Exhibit 12–9. In general, office audits were up by about 10 percent from the prior year, while field audits were down by about 30 percent.

Examinations

After a return is selected for audit, it is scheduled for a review by an IRS agent in either a correspondence, office interview, or field examination. The type of exami-

EXHIBIT 12–8 Average itemized deductions

AGI ($000)	0–15	15–30	30–50	50–100	100–200	200+
Medical	$5,637	$4,498	$3,791	$5,697	$13,105	$37,191
Taxes	1,884	2,189	3,056	5,001	9,544	35,386
Contributions	1,224	1,389	1,536	2,025	3,367	17,973
Interest	5,088	5,427	5,873	7,220	11,023	22,258
Total	9,837	10,131	11,052	14,627	23,301	63,058
Percent Itemizing	3.64	15.63	39.77	73.03	91.79	93.20

nation to which the taxpayer is subject generally is determined by the audit potential of the return, the nature of the asserted error, and the type of taxpayer.

Correspondence Examinations

Many times, IRS personnel at a service center or a district office will question only one or two items on a selected return. In these cases, an examination is typically conducted by telephone or mail. The IRS examiner will request that the taxpayer verify the questioned item of income, deduction, or credit, by mailing copies of receipts, canceled checks, or other documentation to the district office or service center. If the taxpayer requests an interview, or the issues become too complex, or the taxpayer is unable to communicate effectively in writing, the case is referred to the appropriate district office for resolution as an office or field examination.

Correspondence examinations are usually conducted by district office personnel. However, service center staff will conduct such a review if the questioned item is an itemized deduction on an individual taxpayer's income tax return.

A taxpayer who is subject to a correspondence examination is entitled to the same administrative and judicial appeal rights that are allowed to persons who are involved in office or field audits.

Issues that typically are addressed in the correspondence audit setting include itemized deductions for interest, taxes, charitable contributions, medical expenses, and simple miscellaneous deductions such as union dues.

Office Examinations

When a return that has been selected for examination involves one or more issues that will require some analysis and the exercise of the IRS personnel's judgment, rather than a mere verification of record-keeping requirements, the audit is usually conducted at the pertinent IRS district office. An office interview also will be scheduled if the examiner believes that an office examination is necessary to guarantee that the taxpayer's legal rights will be respected.

If the IRS decides to conduct an office examination, the taxpayer is asked to come to the district office for an interview, and to bring any records and documents that will support the questioned items. Generally, the auditor is given very little time in which to prepare for the session, and the scope of the examination is limited to the items that are listed in the audit notification letter.

Office audits are usually confined to individuals' income tax returns that include no business income. However, in recent years, the IRS has increased the scope of

EXHIBIT 12–9   Various audit statistics

Types of Audit Conducted

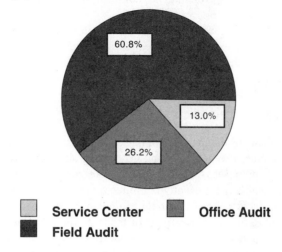

60.8%

13.0%

26.2%

▢ **Service Center**	▨ **Office Audit**	
■ **Field Audit**		

Individuals' returns filed	116,059,700	
Individuals' returns audited	1,941,546	1.67% of filed returns
Office audits	509,420	
Field audits	252,430	1.33% of Schedule Cs
		2.2% of corporate returns

Chances of audit

Individual's Total Positive Income ($000)	Nonbusiness Returns	With Schedule C
0–25	1.82 %	4.21 %
25–50	0.95	2.85
50–100	1.16	2.85
100+	2.85	4.09
S Corporations		0.92
Partnership		0.49
Gift Tax		0.89
Estate Tax, Gross Estate ($000,000)		
0–1		7.85
1–5		21.42
5+		49.33

Average proposed tax and penalty assessment, individuals' returns

Office audit	$3,051
Field audit	15,942
Service Center (math/clerical)	1,714

"No change" audit report

Office audit, individuals' return	14%
Field audit, individuals' return	8
Service Center correspondence	35
Office audit, corporate return	24
Field audit, corporate return	47

some office audits to include a limited number of small business returns. Issues that typically are examined in an office audit setting include dependency exemptions; income from tips, rents, and royalties; income from partnerships, estates, and trusts; deductions for travel and entertainment; deductions for bad debts; and casualty and theft losses.

A field examination may be conducted in lieu of an office audit if it is difficult for the taxpayer to bring the requested records to the district office, or if the taxpayer for some other valid reason requests that the audit be conducted on his or her premises.

Field Examinations

Examinations that present complex issues that require more advanced knowledge of the internal revenue laws and accounting skills usually are conducted on the taxpayer's premises. A **field audit** is more comprehensive than a correspondence or office audit, and it usually is limited to an examination of corporation and individual business returns. In a field examination, the revenue agent reviews completely the entire financial operations of the taxpayer, including the business history of the taxpayer; the nature, amount, and location of taxpayer assets; the nature of the business operations; the extant accounting methods and system of internal control; and other financial attributes of the entity.

While an office audit ordinarily is limited to the items that are specified in the audit notification letter, a field examination may be open-ended. The agent is free to pursue any unusual items that are recorded in the tax return(s) or the records of the taxpayer (i.e., journals, ledgers, and worksheets), and to investigate other areas of which he or she may be suspicious.

The IRS prefers to conduct the field audit on the taxpayer's premises, because the taxpayer's books and records may be more accessible, and because the agent will be better able to observe the taxpayer's business facilities and the scope of its operations. However, it is sometimes possible to have the audit conducted at the office of the taxpayer's representative instead. Only one such inspection of taxpayer books and records may be made for a tax year.[6] The Code includes a broad set of restrictions as to access to the taxpayer's physical office by the IRS.[7] Taxpayers refusing to admit IRS personnel are subject to a $500-per-refusal fine.[8]

The IRS uses a team approach in its field audits, known as the Coordinated Examination Program, when it examines the returns of large corporate taxpayers. During this type of examination, a large group of IRS agents will be used to investigate the operations of the taxpayer. Normally, such an investigation will span more than one IRS district as well.

Dealing with an Auditor

Most practitioners develop over time a list of "dos and don'ts" in negotiating with a government auditor. In the very best case, one will have dealt with the same auditor many times and will have become familiar with the nuances of that particular audi-

[6]§ 7605(b).
[7]§ 7606.
[8]§ 7342.

tor's mode of operation. Whether this is the case or not, the following guidelines, dictated as much by common courtesy and decorum as by ethics and hardcore negotiating techniques, are likely to be useful.[9]

- ▶ Do conduct yourself courteously and professionally, showing that you have prepared yourself for the audit.
- ▶ Do review the strengths and weaknesses of your position before the agent arrives.
- ▶ Do cooperate with the auditor and promptly respond to all requests.
- ▶ Do establish internal timetables and responsibilities for completing the audit.
- ▶ Do provide the auditor with adequate work accommodations.
- ▶ Don't impede the audit process.
- ▶ Don't allow the auditor free access to and through the taxpayer's building.
- ▶ Don't let the agent browse through taxpayer information.
- ▶ Don't volunteer comments or information not requested by the agent.
- ▶ Don't attempt to bully or intimidate the auditor.
- ▶ Do assign one person to be the primary on-premises contact with the auditor—he or she cannot interview taxpayer employees on a random basis.
- ▶ Do verify the auditor's credentials before providing any information.
- ▶ Do request that all communications be in writing.
- ▶ Do keep track of time spent (by taxpayer, practitioner, and auditor) on the audit.
- ▶ Do meet at least daily with the auditor to review issues.
- ▶ Do agree to disagree on major irreconcilable issues.
- ▶ Do conduct a concluding conference to discuss audit recommendations.
- ▶ Do obtain copies of all government workpapers affecting the potential assessment.
- ▶ Do request clarification of the rest of the appeals process.

Conclusion of Examination

Upon the conclusion of the examination, the IRS auditor or agent must explain to the taxpayer any proposed adjustments to the tax liability. A written **Revenue Agent's Report** (RAR) is prepared by the agent and is given to the taxpayer. The RAR contains a brief explanation of the proposed adjustments and lists the balance due or the overpayment.

The RAR also includes a waiver of the restrictions on assessment, which the taxpayer is asked to sign if he or she agrees with the proposed modifications. This waiver will permit the IRS to assess any deficiency in tax immediately, without sending the taxpayer a formal notice of deficiency.

Even though the taxpayer may agree with the proposed adjustments to his or her return, and sign the form, thereby indicating acceptance of the proposal, the case technically is not closed until the agent's report is reviewed and accepted by the district office review staff. Therefore, it is possible that an agreement that is worked out with the agent may not be accepted by the IRS.

After the taxpayer agrees to any increase in tax, he or she may either make an advance payment of the deficiency and accrued interest, to eliminate additional interest charges, or wait for a formal request for payment from the service center.

[9]Some of the material is adapted from Robert E. Dallman, "The Audit Process," Wisconsin State and Local Tax Club, February 10, 1993.

If the taxpayer disagrees with the agent's proposals, the IRS will make an immediate attempt to resolve the disagreement. The taxpayer normally will be given an opportunity to discuss the proposed adjustments with the agent's group supervisor, or with an appeals officer. If an immediate interview is not possible, or if the issues remain unresolved after such an interview, the taxpayer will receive a preliminary notice of deficiency, which is also referred to as a "thirty-day letter."

Thirty-Day Letter

When the taxpayer does not agree with the agent's proposed adjustments, the taxpayer will receive a **thirty-day letter.** This correspondence from the IRS District formally notifies the taxpayer of the examiner's findings, requests that the taxpayer agree to the proposed adjustments, and informs the taxpayer of his or her appeal rights. If the taxpayer does not respond to the notice within thirty days, he or she will receive a statutory notice of deficiency, also known as a "ninety-day letter," discussed later in this chapter.

The taxpayer has thirty days from the date of the thirty-day letter to request a conference with an appeals officer. This request may be made orally with respect to an office examination, or if the total proposed additional tax and penalties total $2,500 or less. The taxpayer's appeal must be in written form if the total proposed additional tax and penalties exceed $2,500,[10] and a formal protest, setting forth the specific facts and applicable law or other authority in support of the taxpayer's position, is required if the proposed tax and penalties exceeds $10,000.[11]

File a Protest or Go Straight to Court?

In deciding whether to file a protest and request a hearing in the appeals office, or to allow a ninety-day letter to be issued and skip directly to the courts for satisfaction, the taxpayer and his or her advisor must consider a number of factors.[12]

Factors in Favor of the Protest/Appeals Process

▶ An appeals officer can consider the hazards of litigation. This allows for the possibility of a settlement without the costs of litigation.
▶ The litigation path remains a possibility even if an appeal is pursued.
▶ The appeals process allows a further delay in the payment of the disputed tax. This can be an important criterion if (1) funds are not available with which to pay the tax, and (2) the taxpayer can earn more on the funds during the administrative period than is assessed in the form of interest.
▶ During the appeals process, the taxpayer will discover more of the elements of the government's position. In addition, the taxpayer will gain additional time in which to formulate or polish his or her own position.
▶ Recovery of some court costs and attorney fees is available if the court finds that the government's case was largely unjustified *and* all administrative remedies were attempted. Thus, working through the appeals process is required if any costs are to be recovered.

---

[10]Reg. §§ 601.105(c)(2)(iii) and (d)(2)(iv).
[11]Reg. §§ 601.105(d)(2) and 601.106(a)(1)(ii).
[12]Saltzman, *IRS Practice and Procedure,* Warren, Gorham & Lamont, 1992, ¶9.04(1).

Factors in Favor of Bypassing Appeals

▶ The likelihood of the government finding and raising new issues during the appeal is eliminated.

▶ The government receives a psychological message that the taxpayer is firmly convinced of his or her position, and negotiating advantages for the taxpayer may result.

▶ The conclusion of the dispute, whether for or against the taxpayer, is expedited.

The Appeals Process

To minimize the costs of litigation in both time and money, the IRS encourages the resolution of tax disputes through an administrative appeals process. If a case cannot be resolved at the examination level, the taxpayer is allowed to appeal to a separate division of the IRS, known as the **Appeals Division.**

The Appeals Division has the exclusive and final authority to settle cases that originate in a district that is located within its jurisdiction. This division is under the supervision of the Commissioner of the IRS, with input from the Chief Counsel. The appeals function provides the taxpayer with a final opportunity to resolve tax disputes with the IRS without incurring litigation. Its objective is to resolve tax controversies without litigation on a basis which is fair and impartial to both the government and the taxpayer.

Appeals Conference

The conference with the appeals officer is an informal proceeding. Although the appeals office may require allegations to be submitted in the form of affidavits or declarations under the penalty of perjury, testimony typically is not taken under oath.[13] The taxpayer, or his or her representative, meets with the appeals officer and discusses the dispute informally. According to the IRS's conference and practice rules, the appeals officer is to maintain a standard of strict impartiality toward the taxpayer and the government.

The appeals officer has the authority to settle all factual and legal questions that are raised in the examiner's report. He or she also can settle a tax dispute on the basis of the hazards of litigation. However, no settlement can be made that is based on the nuisance value of the case to the government.

The appeals officer may use a considerable amount of personal judgment in deciding how to handle the disputed issues of a case. He or she can split or trade issues where substantial uncertainties exist as to the law or the facts. On the other hand, the appeals officer may defer action on, or refuse to settle, a case or an issue to achieve greater uniformity concerning the application of the revenue laws, and to improve the overall voluntary compliance with the tax laws.

Ninety-Day Letter

If the taxpayer and the IRS cannot agree on the proposed adjustments after an appeals conference, the regional director of appeals will issue a **statutory notice of**

[13]Reg. § 601.106(c).

deficiency. The statutory notice is issued by the District Director if the taxpayer does not request an appeals conference.[14]

A statutory notice of deficiency, commonly referred to as a **ninety-day letter,** must be sent to the taxpayer's last known address by certified or registered mail before the IRS can assess the additional taxes that it believes are due.[15] Once a formal assessment has been made, the IRS is entitled to collect and retain the tax. However, a statutory notice is not required relative to deficiencies that result from mathematical errors, or from the overstatement of taxes that were withheld or paid as estimated taxes.

After the statutory notice of deficiency is mailed, the taxpayer has ninety days (150 days if the letter is addressed to a taxpayer who is outside the United States) to file a petition with the U.S. Tax Court for a redetermination of the deficiency. If such a petition is not filed in a timely fashion, the deficiency is assessed and the taxpayer receives a notice and demand for payment of the tax.[16] Once this ninety-day period expires, the taxpayer cannot contest the assessment without first paying the tax, filing a claim for refund, and, if the claim is denied by the IRS, instituting a refund suit in a district court or the U.S. Court of Federal Claims.

Generally, no assessment or collection effort may be made during the ninety-day period, or, if a Tax Court petition is filed, until after the decision becomes final.

A mailing of the statutory notice to the taxpayer's last known address is sufficient to commence the running of the ninety-day period, unless the commissioner has been notified formally of a change of address.[17] The statute does not require actual notice; therefore, a notice that is sent by certified or registered mail to the proper address is effective, even though it is never received by the taxpayer him- or herself.[18]

After a case has been scheduled *(docketed)* for review in the Tax Court, the taxpayer is invited to attend a pretrial settlement conference with an appeals officer and an IRS attorney. However, this conference typically is offered only if the case was not considered previously by the appeals office, and if no related criminal prosecution is pending. If the taxpayer and the IRS agree to settle the dispute at this stage, they will enter into a written agreement stipulating the amount of any deficiency or overpayment. This stipulation is filed with the Tax Court, which will enter a decision in accordance with the agreement. The Tax Court can levy a penalty of up to $5,000 if it determines that the taxpayer did not pursue the available administrative remedies prior to approaching the court.

Entering the Judicial System

If a taxpayer cannot resolve his or her dispute with the IRS administratively, he or she may seek judicial relief. As we have discussed throughout this text, the taxpayer can choose from among the U.S. Tax Court, the pertinent District Court, and the U.S. Court of Federal Claims to initiate the lawsuit against the government.

The Tax Court will review the taxpayer's case, provided that he or she files a petition with the court within ninety days of the date of his or her statutory notice of deficiency. The District Courts and the Court of Federal Claims cannot hear the tax-

---

[14]A short-form notice often is issued relative to office audit disputes of no more than $5,000 per tax year.
[15]§§ 6212(a), 6212(b)(1).
[16]§ 6213(c).
[17]See, for example, *Brown,* 78 T.C. 215 (1989), and *Weinroth,* 74 T.C. 430 (1980).
[18]See, for example, *Lifter,* 59 T.C. 818 (1973), and *U.S. v. Ahrens,* 530 F.2d 781 (CA–8, 1976).

EXHIBIT 12–10   Income tax appeal procedure

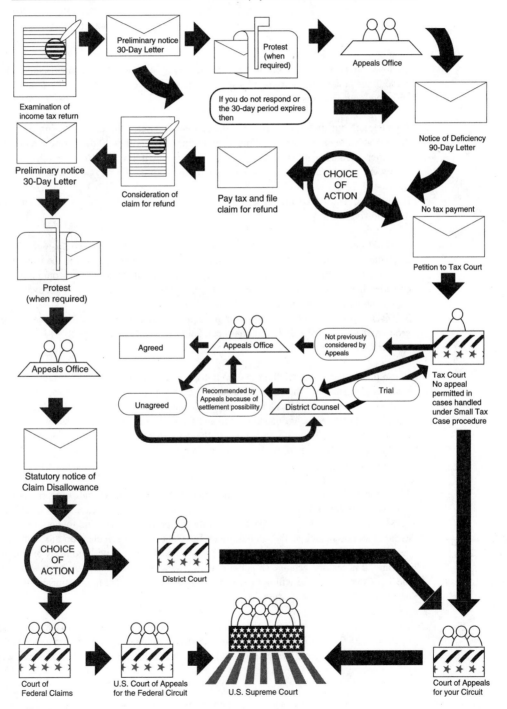

Income Tax Appeal Procedure

Internal Revenue Service

At any stage of procedure:
- You can agree and arrange to pay.
- You can ask the Service to issue you a notice of deficiency so you can file a petition with the Tax Court.
- You can pay the tax and file a claim for a refund.

Examination of income tax return

Preliminary notice 30-Day Letter

Protest (when required)

Appeals Office

If you do not respond or the 30-day period expires then

Notice of Deficiency 90-Day Letter

Preliminary notice 30-Day Letter

Consideration of claim for refund

Pay tax and file claim for refund

CHOICE OF ACTION

No tax payment

Protest (when required)

Petition to Tax Court

Appeals Office

Agreed

Not previously considered by Appeals

Recommended by Appeals because of settlement possibility

Unagreed

District Counsel

Trial

Tax Court No appeal permitted in cases handled under Small Tax Case procedure

Statutory notice of Claim Disallowance

CHOICE OF ACTION

District Court

Court of Federal Claims

U.S. Court of Appeals for the Federal Circuit

U.S. Supreme Court

Court of Appeals for your Circuit

EXHIBIT 12–11   Sample thirty- and ninety-day letters

Notice of Adjustment—Thirty-Day Letter

Internal Revenue Service   Department of the Treasury
Date: Tax Year Ended:
                                Person to Contact:
                                Contact Telephone Number:
                                Contact Address:

Dear

Enclosed are two copies of our report explaining why we believe adjustments should be made in the amount of your tax. Please look this report over and let us know whether you agree with our findings.

If you accept our findings, please sign the consent to assessment and collection portion at the bottom of the report and mail one copy to this office within 30 days from the date of this letter. If additional tax is due, you may want to pay it now and limit the interest charge; otherwise, we will bill you. (See the enclosed Publication 5 for payment details.)

If you do not accept our findings, you have 30 days from the date of this letter to do one of the following:

1. Mail us any additional evidence or information you would like us to consider.
2. Request a discussion of our findings with the examiner who conducted the examination. At that time you may submit any additional evidence or information you would like us to consider. If you plan to come in for a discussion, please phone or write us in advance so that we can arrange a convenient time and place.
3. Discuss your position with the group manager or a senior examiner (designated by the group manager), if an examination has been held and you have been unable to reach an agreement with the examiner.

If you do not accept our findings and do not want to take any of the above actions, you may write us at the address shown above or call us at the telephone number shown above within 30 days from the date of this letter to request a conference with an Appeals Officer. You must provide all pertinent documentation and facts concerning disputed issues to the examiner before your case is forwarded to the Appeals Office. If your examination was conducted entirely by mail, we would appreciate your first discussing our findings with one of our examiners.

The Appeals Office is independent of the District Director. The Appeals Officer, who had not examined your return previously, will take a fresh look at your case. Most disputes considered by Appeals are resolved informally and promptly. By going to Appeals, you may avoid court costs (such as the United States Tax Court filing fee), clear up this matter sooner, and prevent interest from mounting. An Appeals Officer will promptly telephone you and, if necessary, arrange an appointment. If you decide to bypass Appeals and petition the Tax Court, your case will normally be assigned for settlement to an Appeals Office before the Tax Court hears the case.

Under Internal Revenue Code Section 6673, the Tax Court is authorized to award damages of up to $5,000 to the United States when a taxpayer unreasonably fails to pursue available administrative remedies. Damages could be awarded under this provision, for example, if

EXHIBIT 12–11   *Continued*

the Court concludes that it was unreasonable for a taxpayer to bypass Appeals and then file a petition in the Tax Court. The Tax Court will make that determination based upon the facts and circumstances of each case. Generally, the Service will not ask the Court to award damages under this provision if you make a good faith effort to meet with Appeals and to settle your case before petitioning the Tax Court.

The enclosed Publication 5 explains your appeal rights.

If we do not hear from you within 30 days, we will have to process your case on the basis of the adjustments shown in the examination report. If you write us about your case, please write to the person whose name and address are shown in the heading of this letter and refer to the symbols in the upper right corner of the enclosed report. An envelope is enclosed for your convenience. Please include your telephone number, area code, and the most convenient time for us to call, in case we find it necessary to contact you for further information.

If you prefer, you may call the person at the telephone number shown in the heading of this letter. This person will be able to answer any questions you may have. Thank you for your cooperation.

Sincerely yours,

District Director

Enclosures:
Examination Report (2)
Publication 5
Envelope

Notice of Deficiency—Ninety-Day Letter

Internal Revenue Service   Department of the Treasury
District Director
Date: Social Security or Employer Identification Number:
Tax Year Ended and Deficiency:
Person to Contact:
Contact Telephone Number:

We have determined that there is a deficiency (increase) in your income tax as shown above. This letter is a NOTICE OF DEFICIENCY sent to you as required by law. The enclosed statement shows how we figured the deficiency.

If you want to contest this deficiency in court before making any payment, you have 90 days from the above mailing date of this letter (150 days if addressed to you outside of the United States) to file a petition with the United States Tax Court for a redetermination of the deficiency. To secure the petition form, write to United States Tax Court, 400 Second Street, NW., Washington, D.C. 20217. The completed petition form, together with a copy of this letter must be returned to the same address and received within 90 days from the above mailing date (150 days if addressed to you outside of the United States).

The time in which you must file a petition with the Court (90 or 150 days as the case may be) is fixed by law and the Court cannot consider your case if your petition is filed late. If

(continued)

EXHIBIT 12–11 *Continued*

this letter is addressed to both a husband and wife, and both want to petition the Tax Court, both must sign the petition or each must file a separate, signed petition.

If you dispute not more than $50,000 for any one tax year, a simplified procedure is provided by the Tax Court for small tax cases. You can get information about this procedure, as well as a petition form you can use, by writing to the Clerk of the United States Tax Court at 400 Second Street, NW., Washington, D.C. 20217. You should do this promptly if you intend to file a petition with the Tax Court.

You may represent yourself before the Tax Court, or you may be represented by anyone admitted to practice before the Court. If you decide not to file a petition with the Tax Court, we would appreciate it if you would sign and return the enclosed waiver form. This will permit us to assess the deficiency quickly and will limit the accumulation of interest. The enclosed envelope is for your convenience. If you decide not to sign and return the statement and you do not timely petition the Tax Court, the law requires us to assess and bill you for the deficiency after 90 days from the above mailing date of this letter (150 days if this letter is addressed to you outside the United States).

If you have questions about this letter, please write to the person whose name and address are shown on this letter. If you write, please attach this letter to help identify your account. Keep the copy for your records. Also, please include your telephone number and the most convenient time for us to call, so we can contact you if we need additional information.

If you prefer, you may call the IRS contact person at the telephone number shown above. If this number is outside your local calling area, there will be a long distance charge to you.

You may call the IRS telephone number listed in your local directory. An IRS employee there may be able to help you, but the contact person at the address shown on this letter is most familiar with your case.

Thank you for your cooperation.

                                        Sincerely yours,

                                        Commissioner
                                        By

Enclosures:
Copy of this letter
Statement
Envelope

                                        District Director

---

payer's case unless he or she is suing for a refund. Consequently, the taxpayer first must pay the disputed tax, and then file an (unsuccessful) claim for refund to obtain a judicial review in either of these latter two forums.

Possibilities for appeal after completing the trial-level suit have been discussed in Chapters 2, 3, and 5. Exhibit 12–10 illustrates the appeals procedures, from the ini-

EXHIBIT 12–12   Taxpayer and government victories in tax litigation

Forum	Percent of Partial Taxpayer Victories	Percent of Total Taxpayer Victories	Percent of Total Government Victories
U.S. Tax Court, Small Cases Division	49.0	5.0	46.0
U.S. Tax Court, all other	64.0	3.0	33.0
U.S. District Court	11.6	23.2	65.2
U.S. Court of Federal Claims	12.2	14.3	73.5

tial IRS examination to the final hearing before the Supreme Court. Exhibit 12–11 offers sample thirty- and ninety-day letters for the reader's perusal.

One should not consider tax litigation lightly, however. The additional costs to the taxpayer for attorney and accountant fees, in addition to filing and processing fees and the cost and time involved in gathering supporting documentation for the taxpayer's position, finding and coaching expert and other witnesses, and providing for one's own travel to the site of the hearing, make litigation a costly prospect. Given the right combination of facts and law, though, a suit might be the taxpayer's only chance to achieve an equitable solution.

Remember, nonetheless, that the IRS tends to litigate only cases that (1) it expects to win and (2) it expects will make good precedent to discourage other taxpayers. Moreover, because many taxpayers represent themselves before the Tax Court, procedural errors occur, usually to the detriment of the taxpayer. Thus, it is not surprising that the deck appears to be stacked against the taxpayer once he or she enters the judicial system, especially outside the Tax Court. The information in Exhibit 12–12 relates to calendar year 1990.

▶ _____ Summary

In counseling clients, the tax professional must be aware of the organization and inner workings of the Internal Revenue Service. Strategic and tactical decisions as to how and when to appeal within the administrative system of the Service, assessing the strengths and weaknesses of the client's case, and determining available remedies can be made only with a thorough understanding of the agency and its operating style. Some of the most valuable advice that a client receives can be in the context of an audit selection letter, or the handling of settlement alternatives thereafter.

▶ _____ Key Words

By the time you complete your work relative to this chapter, you should be comfortable discussing each of the following terms. If you need additional review of any of these items, return to the appropriate material in the chapter or consult the glossary to this text.

Appeals Division	National Taxpayer Advocate
Commissioner of Internal Revenue	Ninety-Day Letter
Computing Center	Office Audit
Correspondence Examination	Problem Resolution Program
Customer Service Site	Processing Center
Discriminant Function Formula	Revenue Agent's Report
District Director	Statutory Notice of Deficiency
Field Audit	Taxpayer Assistance Order
Internal Revenue Service	Thirty-Day Letter
Internal Revenue Service Center	Treasury Department

► _____ Discussion Questions

1. Why must the tax professional be cognizant of how tax law administration works?
2. What are the major functions of the national office of the IRS?
3. What are the chances of having a tax return audited this year?
4. What techniques other than the random selection of returns for audit does the IRS use in its enforcement function?
5. Why might it be desirable to settle with an agent, rather than to continue by appealing to a higher level within the IRS?
6. Relate some of the "audit etiquette" tactics that you have heard taxpayers or tax professionals discuss.
7. Which of the following methods is used to select tax returns for audit? More than one answer may be correct.

   a. DIF procedures
   b. Random samples
   c. Amount of gross income
   d. Type of income, for example, business or wages

8. Which type of audit is used most often for individuals who have only wages, to substantiate the reported items of income or deduction?

   a. Field
   b. Office
   c. Correspondence
   d. Home

9. A revenue agent may do which of the following in an attempt to negotiate a settlement after the completion of an audit? More than one answer may be correct.

   a. Attempt to settle an unresolved issue based on the hazards of litigation.
   b. Settle a question of fact.
   c. Reach an agreement that will be accepted unconditionally by the District Director.
   d. Turn the case over to the Appeals Division.

10. When an agreement cannot be reached with a Revenue Agent, a letter is transmitted stating that the taxpayer has thirty days to do which of the following?

    a. File a suit in the U.S. Tax Court.
    b. Request an administrative appeal.
    c. Pay the tax.
    d. Find additional facts to support his or her position.

11. A statutory notice of deficiency gives the taxpayer ninety days to do which of the following?

    a. Pay the tax.
    b. Request an administrative appeal.
    c. File a suit in the U.S. Tax Court.
    d. File a protest.

12. Consider the IRS's Problem Resolution Program.

    a. When might a tax adviser request a hearing with the appropriate PRP officer?
    b. What are the risks to the taxpayer of such a request?
    c. Suggest an operational or functional improvement that should be implemented in the PRP.

13. Distinguish among the various means by which the IRS selects a tax return for examination. For this purpose, examine the criteria of (a) scope of review, (b) probability of selection, and (c) preservation of taxpayer constitutional rights.

14. Add two items to the "Dos and Don'ts" list included in the discussion of audit etiquette.

15. Suggest other information documents that the IRS computers could add to the IDMP.

16. Identify several items that you believe are included in the prevailing DIF model.

▶   Exercises

17. Distinguish among the various types of examinations that the IRS conducts relative to individual income tax returns, namely, office, correspondence, field, and TCMP audits. For this purpose, examine the criteria of (a) scope of review, (b) type of documentation that typically is required of the taxpayer, (c) use of IRS personnel time and other resources, and (d) opportunity for agent to use professional judgment in resolving issues.

18. Respond to a client's comment: "We have a better than even chance of winning in the Tax Court, according to an article I read. Let's sue the government!"

19. With respect to the Small Cases Division of the U.S. Tax Court, which statement is true?

    a. The taxpayer (but not the IRS) can appeal a contrary judgment.
    b. The IRS (but not the taxpayer) can appeal a contrary judgment.
    c. Either the IRS or the taxpayer can appeal a contrary judgment.
    d. Neither the IRS nor the taxpayer can appeal a contrary judgment.

20. How should the tax professional advise a client whose charitable contributions are double that of the U.S. norm for his or her income level?

▶   Problem

21. The President of the United States has hired you to assist in a trim-the-fat program with respect to the federal government. He has asked you to recommend specific steps to downsize the bureaucracy of the IRS, from the national office through the district headquarters, by 15 percent. Draft a memo to the President summarizing your recommendations. Augment your memo with diagrams supporting your proposals.

Tax Practice and Administration: Sanctions, Agreements, and Disclosures

LEARNING OBJECTIVES

► Identify various penalties that may be applied to tax practitioners who fail to perform as directed by the Internal Revenue Service, and related computations of interest charges

► Identify various penalties that may be applied to taxpayers whose returns reflect improper amounts, and related computations of interest charges

► Understand the application of the statutes of limitations, and taxpayer–government agreements that may be made with respect thereto

CHAPTER OUTLINE

The adversarial nature of the federal tax system has become apparent throughout this text, especially in Chapter 12. The revenue system is based on the notion of self-assessment, but the failure of the taxpayer to comply in detail with the requirements of the structure can lead to painful negotiations with the Internal Revenue Service and prolonged litigation.

Yet, the Treasury need not wait for a resolution of the disputed tax issues alone to collect revenues. Penalties and interest play an ever-increasing role in the makeup of the federal tax system—in many cases, the accumulated penalties and interest assessed by the IRS equal 50 percent of the disputed tax or more.

Interest charges are made by the Treasury so that the taxpayer gains no advantage or disadvantage with respect to the time value of money in deciding how to handle a tax dispute—to the extent that interest rates are developed to parallel those of the rest of the financial market, both parties are indifferent as to cash flow issues, and the negotiations can center on the tax issues alone. In Chapter 11, we discussed the role of present values in assisting taxpayers to make these decisions in an economically prudent manner.

Penalties have become more prominent in the federal tax system for several reasons. In this chapter, we will discuss the workings of tax penalties as they have developed since the 1980s.

▶ In an environment where nominal tax increases are politically unpopular, penalty increases can supplement revenues in a manner that is acceptable to the public.

▶ Politics aside, penalties increase the tax cost of negotiating with the Treasury and may discourage challenges to tax precedents that are not founded in sound tax law.

▶ Penalties can bolster the self-assessment process by discouraging taxpayers from behaviors that the Treasury wishes to repress, such as working with tax shelters and ignoring filing deadlines and requirements.

▶ As professional tax preparers and advisors play a more important role in the development of tax return positions, the behavior of such third parties also must be controlled, both in keeping a free flow of information between the government and the taxpayer, and in interpreting the tax law in an objective manner.

We conclude this chapter with a review of alternatives and strategies available to taxpayers in making various compromises and other agreements with the IRS as a result of the examination process. In today's tax practice, the professional must have a full working knowledge of the details of the tax administration process, so as best to serve clients and the fisc.

Taxpayer Penalties

To promote and enforce taxpayer compliance with the U.S. voluntary self-assessment system of taxation, Congress has enacted a comprehensive array of penalties. Tax penalties may involve both criminal and civil offenses. Criminal tax penalties are imposed only after the usual criminal process, in which the taxpayer is entitled to the same constitutional guarantees that are given to nontax criminal defendants. Normally, a criminal penalty provides for imprisonment. Civil tax penalties are collected in the same manner as other taxes, and they usually only provide for monetary fines. Criminal and civil penalties are not mutually exclusive; therefore, a taxpayer may be liable under both types of sanctions.

Civil Penalties

The Code imposes two types of **civil penalties.** *Ad valorem penalties* are additions to tax that are based on a percentage of the delinquent tax. Unlike assessable penalties, ad valorem penalties are subject to the same deficiency procedures that apply to the underlying taxes. *Assessable penalties* typically are expressed as a flat dollar amount. Because of the lack of jurisdiction by the Tax Court or a specific statutory exemption, assessable penalties are not subject to review by the Tax Court. Note that the Code characterizes tax penalties as additions to tax; thus, they cannot subsequently be deducted by the taxpayer.

Civil penalties are imposed when the tax statutes are violated (1) without **reasonable cause,** (2) as the result of **negligence** or intentional disregard of pertinent rules, or (3) through a willful disobedience or outright **fraud.** The most important civil penalties include the following.

- ▶ Failure to file a tax return
- ▶ Failure to pay tax
- ▶ Failure to pay estimated income taxes
- ▶ Negligence, fraud, or substantial understatement of income tax
- ▶ Substantial understatement of the tax liability
- ▶ Failure to make deposits of taxes or overstatement of such deposits
- ▶ Giving false information with respect to withholding
- ▶ Filing a frivolous return

Failure to File a Tax Return   When a taxpayer fails to file a required tax return, a penalty is imposed unless it is shown that the failure is due to some reasonable cause, and not to the taxpayer's willful neglect. The penalty is 5 percent of the amount of the tax, less any prior payments and credits, for each month (or fraction thereof) that the return is not filed. The maximum penalty that may be imposed is 25 percent (or five months' cumulative penalty).[1] A fraudulent failure to file is subject to a 15 percent monthly penalty, to a 75 percent maximum.[2]

If the taxpayer's failure to file is due to willful neglect, there is a minimum penalty for a failure to file an income tax return within sixty days of the due date, including extensions. This minimum penalty is the lesser of $100 or the full amount of taxes that are required to be shown on the return. The penalty does not apply if the failure is due to reasonable cause.[3] This penalty is applied in lieu of rather than in addition to some other penalty.

No statutory or administrative definition exists for the term "reasonable cause." However, some courts define it to include such action as would prompt an ordinary,

---

[1] § 6651(a)(1).
[2] § 6651(f).
[3] § 6651(a)(3).

intelligent person to act in the same manner as did the taxpayer, under similar circumstances. One of the most commonly encountered examples of reasonable cause is the reliance on the advice of competent tax counsel. Other examples of reasonable cause that the *Internal Revenue Manual* describes include the following.[4]

- ▶ A timely mailed return that is returned for insufficient postage.
- ▶ Death or serious illness of the taxpayer or his or her immediate family.
- ▶ Destruction of the taxpayer's residence, place of business, or records by fire or other casualty.
- ▶ Proper forms were not furnished by the IRS.
- ▶ Erroneous information was obtained from IRS personnel.
- ▶ A timely mailed return was sent to the wrong district.
- ▶ An unavoidable absence by the taxpayer.
- ▶ An unavoidable inability to obtain records necessary to compute the tax.
- ▶ Some other inability to obtain assistance from IRS personnel.

However, the penalty will not be excused for any of the following reasons.

- ▶ The taxpayer lacks the necessary funds with which to pay the tax.[5]
- ▶ The taxpayer was hospitalized and suffered from an illness that was not incapacitating.[6]
- ▶ Lost or destroyed records were not necessary to the completion of the return.[7]
- ▶ The taxpayer was incarcerated.[8]
- ▶ The taxpayer allegedly was ignorant of the laws.[9]

To avoid the penalty, the taxpayer must meet the burden of proof that the failure to file (or to pay) was due to reasonable cause. In these situations, the IRS's determination of the penalty is presumed to be correct.

Failure to Pay Tax   If a taxpayer fails to pay either a tax that is shown on his or her return or an assessed deficiency within ten days of an IRS notice and demand, a penalty is imposed. The ten-day period becomes twenty-one days when the tax due is less than $100,000. The penalty is 0.5 percent of the required liability, after adjusting for any prior payments and credits, for each month (or fraction thereof) that the tax is not paid—but it increases to 1 percent of the underpaid tax per month after notice from the IRS.[10] The maximum penalty that may be imposed is 25 percent of the outstanding tax. This penalty does not apply if the failure to pay is attributable to a reasonable cause, or to the failure to pay an estimated tax for which there is a different penalty.

For this purpose, reasonable cause is defined in a manner that is identical to that discussed in conjunction with the failure-to-file penalty, except that, if an individual is granted an automatic filing extension, reasonable cause is presumed to exist, provided that the balance due does not exceed 10 percent of the total tax.[11]

---

[4]IRM Audit, § 4562.2(a).
[5]*Langston,* 36 T.C.M. 1703 (1977).
[6]*Hernandez,* 72 T.C. 1234 (1979).
[7]*Long,* 37 T.C.M. 733 (1978).
[8]*Jones,* 55 T.C.M. 1556 (1988).
[9]*Lammerts Estate v. Comm.,* 456 F.2d 681 (CA—2, 1972).
[10]§ 6651(a)(2). After 1999, the monthly penalty rate is cut in half for taxpayers paying delinquent taxes under an installllment agreement.
[11]§ 6654(a)(1)(B)(i).

The failure-to-file penalty is reduced by the 0.5 percent failure-to-pay penalty for any month in which both apply. Thus, no more than a 5 percent total (nonfraud) penalty typically can be assessed against a taxpayer for any month. Nonetheless, after rendering sufficient notice to the taxpayer, the IRS can assess both the failure-to-pay and the failure-to-file penalties.

A taxpayer can avoid the failure-to-file penalty if an extension of the return's due date is granted by the IRS. However, with the two exceptions that we just discussed, the failure-to-pay penalty is imposed when the total amount of the tax is not paid by the unextended due date of the return.

Example 13–1 John Gray, a calendar-year taxpayer, filed his 1999 income tax return on October 10, 2000, paying an amount due of $1,000. On April 1, 1999, John had obtained a four-month extension of time in which to file his return. However, he could not assert a reasonable cause for failing to file the return by August 15, 2000 (the extended due date), nor did he show any reasonable cause for failing to pay the tax that was due on April 15, 2000. Gray's failure to file was not fraudulent. As a result, Gray is subject to a $35 failure-to-pay penalty and a $135 failure-to-file penalty, determined as follows.

Failure to pay

Underpayment	$1,000
Penalty percentage	× .005
Penalty per month outstanding	$ 5
Months (or fractions thereof) for which required payment was not made	× 7
Failure-to-pay penalty	$ 35

Failure to file

Underpayment	$1,000
Penalty percentage	× .05
Penalty per month outstanding (before reduction)	$ 50
Months (or fractions thereof) for which return was not filed	× 3
Unreduced penalty	$ 150
Less: concomitant failure-to-pay penalty (i.e., for August–October) [3 months × (.005 × $1,000)]	− 15
Failure-to-file penalty	$ 135

Accuracy-Related Penalty   Major penalties relating to the accuracy of the return data, including the existing negligence penalty and the penalty for substantial understatement of income tax liability, are combined in a single Code section. This consolidation of related penalties into a single levy eliminates the possibility of the stacking of multiple penalties when more than one type of penalty applies to a single understatement of tax.

The **accuracy-related penalty** amounts to 20 percent of the portion of the tax underpayment that is attributable to one or more of the following.

▶ Negligence or disregard of applicable federal tax rules and Regulations
▶ Substantial understatement of income tax
▶ Substantial valuation overstatement
▶ Substantial overstatement of pension liabilities
▶ Substantial understatement of estate and gift tax valuation

The penalty applies only where the taxpayer fails to show either a reasonable cause for the underpayment or a good-faith effort to comply with the tax law.[12] When the

---

[12]§ 6662.

accuracy-related penalty applies, interest on the penalty accrues from the due date of the return, rather than merely from the date on which the penalty was imposed.

Occasionally, a valuation overstatement penalty is encountered. This 20 percent penalty applies when an asset value has been overstated on a return, for example, to substantiate a charitable contribution deduction. It is assessed when the valuation used is 200 percent or more of the actual value, resulting in an underpayment of over $5,000 ($10,000 for C corporations).

Similarly, a 20 percent transfer valuation understatement penalty is assessed where the claimed value is 50 percent or less than the asset's actual value, resulting in an underpayment of over $5,000. The rate of both penalties is 40 percent if a gross valuation misstatement is made, that is, the income tax valuation was at least 400 percent of actual value, or the transfer tax value was 25 percent or less of actual.[13]

The practitioner is likely to encounter two of the elements of this penalty most frequently: (1) negligence or disregard of rules and (2) substantial understatement of tax. In the first penalty, "negligence" includes any failure to make a reasonable attempt to comply with the provisions of the Code.[14] This might occur when the taxpayer fails to report gross income, overstates deductions, or fails to keep adequate records with which to comply with the law. "Disregard" includes any careless, reckless, or intentional disregard of the elements of the tax law.[15]

The negligence component of the penalty is waived where the taxpayer has made a good-faith attempt to comply with the law, as indicated by a full disclosure of the non-frivolous position that may be contrary to that of the IRS. Such disclosure is made by completing Form 8275, reproduced as Exhibit 13–1, and attaching it to the return. If the return position is contrary to the language of a Regulation, Form 8275-R is used.

The second commonly encountered penalty, substantial understatement of income tax, occurs if the determined understatement exceeds the greater of (1) 10 percent of the proper tax liability or (2) $5,000 ($10,000 for a corporation other than an S corporation or a personal holding company).[16] The amount that is subject to this penalty is reduced if the taxpayer either has substantial authority for the position that was taken in the return, or makes a full disclosure of the position taken in the return, on Form 8275 or 8275-R. More specifically, the taxpayer is not subject to this penalty where the weight of **substantial authority** for his or her position exceeds that supporting contrary positions.[17]

For this purpose, "substantial authority" includes the Code, Regulations (proposed and temporary), court decisions, administrative pronouncements, tax treaties, IRS information and press releases, IRS Notices and Announcements, Letter Rulings, Technical Advice Memoranda, General Counsel Memoranda, Committee Reports, and "Blue Book" explanations of tax legislation. Substantial authority does not include conclusions reached in tax treatises, legal periodicals, and opinions rendered by tax professionals.[18]

Clearly, greater weight will be placed on the Code and temporary Regulations than will be assigned to Letter Rulings and IRS Notices, but the derivation of a weighted average among all of the competing positions with respect to a given tax question is not likely to be easily obtained.

[13]§ 6662(h).
[14]§ 6662(c).
[15]§ 6662(c).
[16]§ 6662(d)(1).
[17]§ 6662(d)(2)(A) and (B).
[18]Reg. § 1.6661–3(b)(2).

EXHIBIT 13–1 Disclosure statement

Form **8275** (Rev. April 1995) Department of the Treasury Internal Revenue Service	**Disclosure Statement** Do not use this form to disclose items or positions that are contrary to Treasury regulations. Instead, use Form 8275-R, Regulation Disclosure Statement. See separate instructions. ► Attach to your tax return.	OMB No. 1545-0889 Attachment Sequence No. **92**
Name(s) shown on return		Identifying number shown on return

Part I General Information (See instructions.)

	(a) Rev. Rul., Rev. Proc., etc.	**(b)** Item or Group of Items	**(c)** Detailed Description of Items	**(d)** Form or Schedule	**(e)** Line No.	**(f)** Amount
1						
2						
3						

Part II Detailed Explanation (See instructions.)

1

2

3

Part III Information About Pass-Through Entity. To be completed by partners, shareholders, beneficiaries, or residual interest holders.

Complete this part only if you are making adequate disclosure with respect to a pass-through item.

Note: *A pass-through entity is a partnership, S corporation, estate, trust, regulated investment company, real estate investment trust, or real estate mortgage investment conduit (REMIC).*

1 Name, address, and ZIP code of pass-through entity	**2** Identifying number of pass-through entity
	3 Tax year of pass-through entity / / to / /
	4 Internal Revenue Service Center where the pass-through entity filed its return

For Paperwork Reduction Act Notice, see separate instructions.   Cat. No. 61935M   Form **8275** (Rev. 4-95)

Civil Fraud   If any part of an underpayment of tax is attributable to fraud, a substantial civil penalty is imposed. In addition, the taxpayer may be liable for a criminal penalty, which we will discuss later in this chapter. The civil fraud penalty is 75 percent of the underpayment that is attributable to the fraud.[19]

---

[19]§§ 6663(a) and (b).

If any part of an underpayment is attributable to fraud, only the fraud penalty may be imposed with respect to that amount.[20] Neither the failure-to-file nor the failure-to-pay penalty, nor the civil accuracy-related penalty, is assessed in these circumstances. However, the penalty for underpayment of estimated tax (discussed here) may still be assessed, and interest is assessed from the (extended) due date of the return.

Fraud is not defined in either the Code or the Regulations. One long-standing judicial definition of fraud describes it as "... actual, intentional wrongdoing ... the intent required is the specific purpose to evade a tax believed to be owing."[21] This definition has been expanded to include acts that are done without a "bad or evil purpose." In *U.S. v. Pomponio,* the Supreme Court held that "willfulness," which is a crucial element of fraud, is present when the taxpayer's actions constitute "... a voluntary, intentional violation of a known legal duty."[22] Consequently, the taxpayer's deceptive or misleading conduct distinguishes fraud from mere negligence, or from other actions that are taken to avoid taxation, and not the presence of some (inherent or documented) evil purpose.

If a taxpayer is convicted of criminal fraud, he or she cannot contest a civil fraud determination. However, a charge that the taxpayer is guilty of criminal fraud may be contested when a civil fraud determination has been upheld. In a criminal fraud case, the IRS must prove "beyond a shadow of any reasonable doubt" that the taxpayer's actions were fraudulent. In a civil fraud case, there must be "clear and convincing evidence" that the taxpayer committed fraud.

Under an all-or-nothing rule, if the IRS establishes that any portion of an underpayment is attributable to fraud, the entire underpayment is treated as attributable to fraud, and the penalty applies to the entire amount due.[23] Ordinarily, the evidence that indicates that a taxpayer's conduct was fraudulent is circumstantial. Thus, the court must infer the taxpayer's state of mind from the evidence. Examples of fraud include the following.

▶ Keeping two sets of books, one in English and one in Japanese.[24]
▶ Making false accounting entries.[25]
▶ Destroying books or records.[26]
▶ Concealing assets or sources of income.[27]
▶ Consistently understating income or overstating deductions.[28]
▶ Purposely avoiding the making of business records and receipts.[29]

Failure to Make Estimated Payments   A penalty is imposed on both individuals and corporations who fail to pay quarterly estimated income taxes. This penalty is based on the amount and duration of the underpayment, and the rate of interest that currently is established by the Code. This rate, for instance, was 9 percent late in

[20]§ 6663(b).
[21]*Mitchell v. Comm.,* 118 F.2d 308, 310 (CA–5, 1941).
[22]97 429 U.S. 10, S.Ct. 22 (1976).
[23]§ 6663(b).
[24]*Noro v U.S.,* 148 F.2d 696 (CA–5, 1945).
[25]*U.S. v Lange,* 161 F.2d 699 (CA–7, 1947).
[26]*U.S. v Ragen,* 314 U.S. 513, 62 S.Ct. 374 (1942).
[27]*Gendelman v U.S.,* 191 F.2d 993 (CA–9, 1952).
[28]*Holland v. U.S.,* 348 U.S. 121, 75 S.Ct. 127 (1954) and *Ragen,* op.cit.
[29]*Garispy v U.S.,* 220 F.2d 252 (CA–6, 1955).

1998. Unlike the similar interest computation, however, this penalty is computed without any daily compounding and is not deductible.

The penalty is calculated separately for each quarterly installment. Each penalty period begins on the date on which the installment was required, and it runs through the earlier of either the date that the amount is paid or the due date for filing the return. Any overpayment is first applied to prior underpayments, and the excess is credited to later installments.[30]

Individuals An individual's underpayment of estimated tax is computed as the difference between the amounts that were paid by the quarterly due dates, and the least of (1) 90 percent of the tax that is shown on the current year's return; (2) 100 percent of the prior year's tax; and (3) 90 percent of the tax that would be figured by annualizing the income that was earned during the year, up to the month in which the quarterly payment is due.[31] For this purpose, unless the taxpayer can prove otherwise, taxes that are withheld are considered to have been remitted to the IRS in equal quarterly installments.[32]

The underpayment penalty will not apply if less than $1,000 in underwithheld tax is due, or if the total payments that are made by the applicable installment date are equal to an amount that would have been required on that date if the estimated tax (1) was based on the tax that is shown on the previous year's return (i.e., using 100 or 110 percent), or (2) equaled 90 percent of the tax, computed on the basis of the annualized income for the period that ends on the installment date.[33] In addition, an individual can avoid the estimated tax underpayment penalty if (1) the preceding taxable year included twelve months, (2) the individual did not have any tax liability for the preceding year, and (3) he or she was a citizen or resident of the United States throughout the preceding taxable year.

The IRS can waive the estimated tax underpayment penalty (but not the penalty that is based on the outstanding interest attributable thereto) (1) if the failure to make the payment was due to a casualty, disaster, or other unusual circumstance where it would be inequitable to impose the penalty, or (2) if the failure was due to reasonable cause rather than willful neglect during the first two years after the taxpayer retires, attains age 62 or becomes disabled.[34] The fourth installment penalty is waived if the corresponding tax return is filed with full tax payment by the end of the first month after the tax year-end (January 31 for calendar-year taxpayers).

Corporations An underpayment on the part of a corporation is defined as the difference between the amount of the installment that would be required to be paid if the estimated tax was equal to 100 percent of the tax that is shown on the return (or, if no return was filed, 100 percent of the actual tax that is due), and the amount that was actually paid on or before the prescribed payment date.[35]

The underpayment penalty will not apply if less than $1,000 in tax is due, or if the total payments that are made by the applicable installment date are equal to the least of

---

[30]§§ 6654(b) and 6655(b).

[31]§ 6654(d). The rule is 110 percent of the prior-year tax if that year's AGI > $150,000. This percentage varies after 1998.

[32]§ 6654(g).

[33]§§ 6654(e)(1) and (2).

[34]§ 6654(e)(3).

[35]§ 6655(b)(1).

1. 100 percent of the nonzero amount of tax that is shown on the corporation's tax return for the preceding year, provided that the preceding year contained twelve months;
2. 100 percent of the current-year tax liability; or
3. 100 percent of the tax that is due using a seasonal installment method, or annualizing the current year's income received for (a) the first two or three months, relative to the installment that is due in the fourth month of the tax year, (b) the first three, four, or five months, for the installment that is due in the sixth month, (c) the first six, seven, or eight months, for the installment that is due in the ninth month, or (d) the first nine, ten, or eleven months, for the installment that is due in the twelfth month as elected.[36]

Exception 1 does not apply to a "large corporation," that is, one that had a taxable income of $1 million or more in any of its three immediately preceding taxable years. To avoid an underpayment penalty, a large corporation must remit quarterly estimated tax payments that are equal to its current year's tax liability, or it must meet Exception 3, as discussed.[37]

Failure to Make Deposits of Taxes or Overstatements of Deposits   The Code requires employers to collect and withhold income and Social Security taxes from their employees. Amounts that are withheld are considered to be held in a special trust fund for the United States, and they must be deposited in a government depository on or before certain dates prescribed by the statute and Regulations. An employer who does not have either the inclination or sufficient funds with which to meet its deposit obligations may be tempted to postpone the making of these deposits, that is, to "borrow" from the government the cash provided by employees. Consequently, the Code imposes heavy civil and criminal penalties on those who are responsible for the failure to make a timely deposit of the withheld funds.[38] A responsible party may be an officer or board member of a corporation rather than the corporation itself, even for charities and other exempt entities.

If an employer fails to deposit on a timely basis taxes that were withheld from employees, a penalty equal to a percentage of the underpayment is imposed. This rate varies from 2 to 15 percent, depending on when the failure is corrected.[39] The penalty may be avoided where the taxpayer can show that his or her actions were due to reasonable cause, and not to willful neglect.

If any person who is required to collect, truthfully account for, and remit employment taxes willfully fails to do so, a penalty equal to 100 percent of the tax is imposed.[40] Therefore, when a corporate employer does not pay to the government employment taxes that it withheld from an employee, the IRS effectively may collect the tax from those who are responsible for the corporate actions, such as the corporate directors, president, or treasurer.[41]

---

[36]§§ 6655(d), (e), and (f).
[37]§§ 6654(d)(2) and (g)(2). The prior-year exception can be used in making the first-quarter installment, however. § 6654(d)(2)(B).
[38]§ 6656.
[39]§ 6656(b)(1).
[40]§ 6672(a).
[41]§ 7809(a).

In addition to the civil penalties that have been discussed, criminal penalties may be imposed in an aggravated case of nonpayment.

Giving False Information with Respect to Withholding All employees are required to give their employer a completed Form W-4, Employee Withholding Allowance Certificate. This form notifies the employer of the number of withholding exemptions that the employee is entitled to claim. The employer then calculates the amount of tax that must be withheld from each employee. A civil penalty of $500 is imposed on any person who gives to his or her employer false information with respect to withholding status or the number of exemptions to which he or she is entitled. This penalty is not imposed where there was a reasonable basis for the taxpayer's statement. Moreover, the IRS may waive all or a part of the penalty if the actual income taxes that are imposed are not greater than the sum of the allowable credits and estimated tax payments.[42]

The Regulations require that employers who receive a Form W-4 from an employee, on which he or she claims more than ten exemptions, must submit a copy of the form to the IRS.[43]

Filing a Frivolous Return A separate $500 civil penalty is assessed when the taxpayer is found to have filed a frivolous return.[44] Returns of this sort have been used to assert that the taxpayer's Fifth Amendment rights are violated by tax return disclosures,[45] that the taxpayer objects to the use of his or her tax receipts for defense or other uses,[46] that the government can collect taxes only in gold-based coins and certificates (which no longer circulate freely in the United States), or some other argument. Specifically, the penalty applies when the return:

▶ does not contain information by which to judge the completeness of the taxpayer's self-assessment (e.g., if the return is blank);
▶ contains information or statements that on their face indicate that the self-assessment requirement has not been met (e.g., a "tax protestor" statement is attached); or
▶ otherwise takes positions that are frivolous or are meant to impede the administration of the tax law, for example, it takes a return position contrary to a decision of the U.S. Supreme Court, or it is not presented in a readable format.

Other Civil Penalties A variety of other civil penalties may be imposed on taxpayers who fail to comply with the Code. Most of these penalties involve a specialized area of the tax law and ordinarily are not encountered by taxpayers. Consequently, one should be aware of the existence of such sanctions and refer to the Code and Regulations when working in such a specialized field to identify the events that might trigger such penalties.

Reliance on Written Advice of the IRS The Secretary of the Treasury must abate any civil penalty or addition to tax that is attributable to the taxpayer's reliance on

---

[42]§ 6682.
[43]Reg. § 31.3402(f)(2)–1(g).
[44]§ 6702.
[45]*Welch v. U.S.*, 750 F.2d 1101 (CA–1, 1985).
[46]*Fuller v. U.S.*, 786 F.2d 1437 (CA–9, 1986).

erroneous written advice furnished by an IRS officer or employee. This abatement is available only with respect to advice given in response to a specific request by the taxpayer, and it is negated if the IRS error was made due to a lack of information provided by the taxpayer.[47]

Criminal Penalties

In addition to the civil penalties that we have discussed so far, the Code prescribes a number of **criminal penalties** for certain acts of taxpayer noncompliance. The criminal penalties are intended "to prohibit and punish fraud occurring in the assessment and collection of taxes."[48] They are imposed only after the implementation of the constitutional criminal process, under which the taxpayer is entitled to the same rights and privileges as other criminal defendants.

Nature of Criminal Penalties   Criminal and civil penalties are not mutually exclusive. Consequently, a taxpayer may be acquitted of a criminal tax offense, but still be liable for a corresponding civil tax penalty.

The IRS bears a greater burden of proof with respect to a criminal case. Moreover, the taxpayer holds the right to refuse to answer inquiries that are made by the IRS in a criminal setting if he or she would suffer a loss of some constitutional right by answering.

Ordinarily, criminal prosecutions are limited to flagrant offenses for which the IRS believes it is virtually certain to obtain a conviction. As a result, the IRS usually limits its charges to the civil penalty provisions. In the typical context, according to Section 100 of the *IRS Law Enforcement Manual IX*, criminal prosecutions are limited to cases in which (1) the additional tax that will be generated from a successful prosecution is substantial, (2) the crime appears to have been committed in three consecutive years, or (3) the taxpayer's flagrant or repetitive conduct was so egregious that the IRS believes that it is virtually certain to obtain a conviction. As a result, the IRS usually will not engage in a criminal prosecution when the taxpayer's noncompliance can be corrected by imposing civil penalties.

Criminal Tax Offenses   The principal criminal offenses that are addressed by the Code include the following.

▶ Willful attempt to evade or defeat a tax (i.e., tax evasion)—a felony offense that is punishable by a fine that is not to exceed $100,000 ($500,000 for corporations) and/or imprisonment for a period that is not to exceed five years.[49]

▶ Willful failure to collect, account for, and remit any tax, by any person who is required to do so—a felony offense that is punishable by a fine that is not to exceed $10,000 and/or imprisonment for a period that is not to exceed five years.[50]

▶ Willful failure to file a return, supply information, or pay tax or estimated tax—a misdemeanor offense that is punishable by a fine that is not to exceed $25,000 ($100,000 for corporations) and/or imprisonment for a period that is

---

[47]IR–88–75 (4/88) and § 6404(f).
[48]*U.S. v. White,* 417 F.2d 89, 93 (CA–2).
[49]§ 7201.
[50]§ 7202.

not to exceed one year (five years and felony status for returns relative to cash received by a business).[51]

► Willful making, subscribing, or aiding or assisting in the making of a return or other document that is verified by a declaration under the penalties of perjury, and that the person does not believe to be true and correct as to every material matter—a felony offense that is punishable by a fine not to exceed $100,000 ($500,000 for corporations) and/or imprisonment for a period that is not to exceed three years.[52]

► Willful filing of any known-to-be-false or fraudulent document—a misdemeanor offense that is punishable by a fine that is not to exceed $10,000 ($50,000 for corporations) and/or imprisonment for a period not to exceed one year.[53]

► Disclosure or use of any information that is furnished to a person who is engaged in the business of preparing tax returns, or providing services in connection with the preparation of tax returns, for purposes other than the preparation of the return—a misdemeanor offense that is punishable by a fine not to exceed $1,000 and/or imprisonment for a period not to exceed one year.[54]

In addition to the penalties that we have just described, the Code prescribes a number of other criminal penalties that ordinarily are not encountered on a regular basis. Most of these penalties involve a specialized area of the tax law. Consequently, one should be aware of the existence of such sanctions and refer to the Code and Regulations when working in such a specialized field to identify them.

Defenses to Criminal Penalties   The standard for conviction in a criminal case is establishment of guilt beyond a reasonable doubt. With respect to criminal tax cases, taxpayers have had some success in presenting one or more of the following defenses—that is, to establish some doubt in the minds of the court or the jury.

► Unreported income was offset fully by unreported deductions.[55]

► Unreported income was in reality a gift or some other excludible receipt.[56]

► The taxpayer was confused or ignorant as to the applicable law—one cannot intend to violate the tax law if he or she does not know what that law is.[57]

► The taxpayer relied on the erroneous advice of a competent tax advisor.[58]

► The taxpayer has a mental disease or defect, so could not have acted willfully to violate the tax law.[59]

► The statute of limitations (discussed later in this chapter) has expired.

► The taxpayer enters a plea bargain and accepts conviction on a lesser offense.

Penalties on Return Preparers

Individuals who prepare income tax returns or refund claims for compensation are subject to a number of disclosure requirements and penalties for improper conduct

[51]§§ 7203 and 6050I.
[52]§ 7206.
[53]§ 7207.
[54]§ 7216.
[55]*Koontz v. U.S.*, 277 F.2d 53 (CA–5, 1960).
[56]*DiZenzo v. Comm.*, 348 F.2d 122 (CA–2, 1965).
[57]*U.S. v. Critzer*, 498 F.2d 1160 (CA–4, 1974).
[58]*U.S. v. Phillips*, 217 F.2d 435 (CA–7, 1954).
[59]*U.S. v. Erickson*, 676 F.2d 408 (CA–10, 1982).

in the preparation of those documents. These provisions were added to the Code after Congress found that about one-half of all taxpayers utilized some form of professional assistance in preparing their income tax returns. Moreover, a significant percentage of returns that were prepared by return preparers indicated some fraud potential.

The return preparer penalties apply only to income tax returns. Most of them are mild, ranging from $50 for the failure to furnish an identification number to $1,000 for the aiding and abetting of an understatement of a tax liability. However, as these sanctions may be applied cumulatively, their magnitude can become more substantial. In addition, the criminal penalties that may be imposed on the return preparer provide for substantial monetary fines and jail terms.

Definition of Return Preparer

An income tax **return preparer** (ITRP) is any person who prepares for compensation, or employs one or more persons to prepare for compensation, all or a substantial portion of a tax return or claim for income tax refund.[60] An ITRP can be an employer, employee, or a self-employed person. This distinction is important because certain penalties are imposed only on a selected type of preparer. For instance, only an employee preparer is subject to a negligence or fraud penalty, unless the employer participated in the wrongdoing. To determine whether the employer or employee return preparer (or both) is liable for a certain penalty, the Regulations that relate to that penalty must be consulted.

A person must prepare an income tax return for compensation if he or she is to be subject to the return preparer sanctions. If a return is prepared gratuitously, the preparer is not an ITRP. The preparer also must prepare all or a substantial portion of a return if the ITRP sanctions are to apply. In determining whether the work that has been performed by the party is substantial, a comparison must be made between the length and complexity of the prepared schedule, entry, or other item, and the total liability or refund claim.

The Regulations adopt two objective safe harbors in determining the constitution of a substantial portion of a return or claim. If a schedule, entry, or other item involves amounts that are (1) less than $2,000 or (2) less than $100,000 and also less than 20 percent of the gross income (or adjusted gross income, where the taxpayer is an individual) that is shown on the return, then the item is not substantial.[61]

Definition of Return Preparation

In constructing a definition of the ITRP, one first must define the domain of *return preparation*. Return preparation includes activities other than the mere physical completion of a return. The IRS asserts that tax advisors, planners, software designers, and consultants are all tax preparers, even though they may only review the return or give the taxpayer instructions on its completion. According to the Regulations, one who furnishes a taxpayer or other preparer with "sufficient information and advice so that completion of the return or claim for refund is largely a mechanical matter" is an ITRP.[62] However, an advisor is not an ITRP when the

---

[60]§ 7701(a)(36).
[61]Reg. § 301.7701–15(b)(2).
[62]Reg. § 301.7701–15(a)(1).

advice is given with respect to completed transactions or for other than tax return filing purposes.

A person is not an ITRP merely because he or she:[63]

▶ furnishes typing, reproducing, or other clerical assistance;
▶ prepares a return or refund claim of his or her regular employer or of an officer or employee of the employer;
▶ prepares as a fiduciary a return or claim for refund; or
▶ prepares a claim for refund during the course of an audit or appeal.

Preparer Disclosure Penalties

Five different **preparer penalties** may be imposed on those who do not comply with certain disclosure requirements.[64]

▶ A penalty of $50 for each return may be imposed on an (employer of an) ITRP if the taxpayer is not given a complete copy of the return when it is presented to him or her for signature.
▶ A penalty of $50 for each return may be imposed on an employee ITRP if he or she fails to sign the return.
▶ A penalty of $50 for each return will be imposed on an (employer of an) ITRP if the preparer's identification number, or that of his or her employer, or both, is not listed on each completed return.
▶ A penalty of $50 for each failure will be imposed on an (employer of an) ITRP if he or she does not retain a copy of all returns that he or she prepared. Alternatively, he or she may retain a list of all of the taxpayers, and their identification numbers, for whom returns were prepared for the previous three years.
▶ A penalty of $50 for each failure to retain, and $50 for each item that is omitted, is imposed on an (employer of an) ITRP who does not retain records that indicate the name, identification number, and place of work of each preparer who is employed during the twelve-month period that begins on July 1 of each year.

In each instance, the maximum penalty for any calendar year is $25,000.

Preparer Conduct Penalties

The Code contains a number of civil and criminal penalties that may be imposed on return preparers relative to their misconduct. The civil penalties were added to the Code because Congress found that a significant number of return preparers were engaging in improper practices, such as guaranteeing refunds or having taxpayers sign blank returns. However, except for the criminal penalty of aiding and assisting in the preparation of a false return, there were no lesser sanctions that could be applied to return preparers who were guilty of misconduct.

Civil penalties that may be imposed on preparers relate to:

▶ endorsing or negotiating a refund check;
▶ negligent understatement or intentional disregard of rules and Regulations;

---

[63]§ 7701(a)(36)(B).
[64]§ 6695.

- ▶ willful understatement of tax liability;
- ▶ organizing, or assisting in organizing, or promoting and making or furnishing statements with respect to an abusive tax shelter;
- ▶ aiding and abetting the understatement of a tax liability; and
- ▶ disclosure or use of return information for other than return preparation.

Return preparers have always been subject to criminal prosecution for willful misconduct. The two principal criminal preparer penalties involve those who:

- ▶ aid or assist in the preparation or presentation of a false return, affidavit, claim, or other document,[65] or
- ▶ disclose or use information for other than return preparation purposes.[66]

Endorsing or Negotiating a Refund Check   An income tax return preparer may not endorse or otherwise negotiate an income tax refund check that is issued to another person. A preparer who violates this rule is subject to a $500 penalty.[67]

Understatements Due to Unrealistic Positions   A tax preparer incurs a $250 penalty for each occurrence of an understatement of tax due to the taking of an unrealistic position in the return. This criterion is not subject to a materiality threshold. Rather, where there is no **realistic possibility** that the preparer's position will be maintained on its merits, the penalty simply applies.[68] The levy will be waived if the return includes a disclosure of the preparer's nonfrivolous position, or if the preparer has acted in good faith in preparing the return.

For this purpose, a realistic possibility exists where a reasonable and well-informed analysis by a person knowledgeable in the tax law would result in the conclusion that there was at least about a one-in-three likelihood that the position would be upheld on its merits. Thus, this criterion does not require certainty nor, indeed, even a preponderance of the evidence. Most likely, the party whose likelihood of sustaining the position is being measured is an appropriate judicial forum.

This penalty also is applied where the preparer fails to make adequate inquiries of the taxpayer relative to information that appears to be incomplete or incorrect.[69] The penalty is assessed only on the preparer who is required to sign the return.

Willful Understatement   A preparer is subject to a $1,000 penalty if any part of an understatement of a taxpayer's liability is attributable to the preparer's willful attempt in any manner to understate the liability, or to the reckless or intentional disregard of IRS rules or Regulations.[70] A preparer is considered to have willfully attempted to understate the tax in this manner if he or she disregards information that has been supplied by the taxpayer, or by any other person, in an attempt wrongfully to reduce the taxpayer's levy.

The willful understatement penalty is not imputed to the employer of the return preparer unless the employer also participated in the wrongdoing. The penalty focuses only on the conduct of the actual ITRP.

[65] § 7206(2).
[66] § 7213(a)(3).
[67] § 6695(f).
[68] § 6694(a).
[69] § 6694(a)(2).
[70] § 6694(b).

It is possible that both the willful and unrealistic position understatement penalties will apply to the same return. A penalty for willful understatement of liability may be based on an intentional disregard of the pertinent rules and Regulations. If a penalty is collected under the unrealistic-position penalty rule, the amount that may be collected under the willful-understatement penalty rule is reduced by a corresponding amount.

Organizing Abusive Tax Shelters   A civil penalty may be imposed on any person who organizes or assists in organizing, or (even indirectly) participates in the sale of any interest in, a tax shelter, and who makes or furnishes a statement regarding an expected tax benefit that the person knows or has reason to know is either false or fraudulent, or a gross valuation understatement.[71]

For this purpose, a gross valuation understatement is a statement of the value of any property or service that exceeds 200 percent of the amount that is determined to be its correct value, if the value of the property or service is directly related to the amount of any allowable deduction or credit.[72] Accordingly, there does not need to be an understatement of tax before this penalty can be applied. The penalty can be triggered without an IRS audit, and it can be based only on the shelter's offering materials.

The amount of the penalty is the greater of $1,000 or 100 percent of the gross income that is derived, or is to be derived, by the taxpayer from the project. The IRS may waive all or a portion of the penalty that is attributable to a gross valuation understatement if there was a reasonable basis for the valuation, and it was made in good faith.[73]

Although the penalty is not aimed specifically at tax preparers, but rather at the tax shelter industry itself, professional tax advisors may be subject to the penalty, because they often assist in organizing tax shelter projects.

Aiding and Abetting Understatement   The Code imposes a civil penalty on any person who aids or assists, or procures or advises, in the preparation or presentation of any portion of a return or other tax-related document, if he or she knows or has reason to believe that the return or other document will be used in connection with any material tax matter, and that this use will result in the understatement of another person's tax liability.[74] This penalty may also be imposed on a person who acts in violation of the statute through a subordinate (e.g., an employee or agent) by either ordering or causing the subordinate to act, or knowing of and not attempting to prevent the subordinate from acting, wrongfully.[75]

The amount of the penalty is $1,000 ($10,000 for corporations) for each understating taxpayer. This penalty may be imposed only once per year for each understating taxpayer who is serviced by the ITRP. However, it may be imposed in addition to other penalties. Thus, the preparer may also be prosecuted under the criminal statutes.[76]

[71] § 6700.
[72] § 6700(b)(1).
[73] §§ 6700(a)(2) and (b)(2).
[74] § 6701(a).
[75] § 6701(c).
[76] § 6701(b).

Aiding or Assisting in the Preparation of a False Return   A criminal penalty may be imposed on any person who willfully aids or assists in the preparation of a return or other document that is false as to any material matter. This penalty is the criminal equivalent to the civil penalty for aiding and abetting the understatement of any tax liability.

A person who is convicted of violating this statute is guilty of a felony, and is subject to imprisonment for up to three years and/or may be fined an amount that cannot exceed $100,000 ($500,000 for corporations). This is one of the most severe tax preparer penalties under the Code.[77]

The persons who are prosecuted under this statute usually are accountants or other return preparers. However, a person who supplies false information that is used in the preparation of a return may also be subject to this penalty.

Disclosure or Use of Information by Return Preparers   The Code imposes a civil penalty on any return preparer who discloses or uses any tax return information for other than the purpose of preparing a tax return. This penalty amounts to $250 per improper use; a preparer's maximum penalty for any calendar year is $10,000. The Code also imposes a criminal penalty on any return preparer who knowingly or recklessly discloses or uses any tax return information for other than the specific purpose of preparing a tax return. One who is convicted of violating this statute is guilty of a misdemeanor and is subject to imprisonment for not more than one year and/or may be fined an amount that cannot exceed $1,000.[78]

The definition of a tax return preparer for purposes of this criminal penalty is broader than that under the civil preparer statutes. For instance, a clerical assistant who types or otherwise works on returns that are completed by the preparer is a "tax return preparer" for purposes of this provision; however, he or she would not be considered to be an ITRP for purposes of the civil preparer penalty statutes.

The preparer, as here defined, may disclose information that is obtained from the taxpayer without being subject to the civil or criminal penalty if such disclosure is pursuant to any other provisions of the Code, or to a court order.

See Exhibit 13–2 for a summary of the most important of the civil and criminal penalties that may apply to taxpayers, preparers, and shelter distributors.

Conflict among Taxpayer and Preparer Penalty Provisions   Exhibit 13–3 illustrates the possibility for conflict between a taxpayer and his or her preparer, with respect to the taking and disclosure of a position on a return. No taxpayer substantial-understatement penalty is incurred if the substantial-authority criterion is met; that is, the taxpayer's position has the highest probability for success in a hypothetical court proceeding with respect to the disputed issue. With respect to nonfrivolous positions, no penalty is incurred if the substantial-authority test is failed but a Form 8275 disclosure is made on the return. At first glance, this criterion comes close to a "more likely than not" or greater-than-50-percent standard. Yet, where there are more than two defensible positions with respect to the disputed issue, this is not the case.

[77]§ 7206(2).
[78]§§ 6713 and 7216(a).

EXHIBIT 13-2 Summary of tax-related penalties

Criminal and civil penalties are not mutually exclusive, so a taxpayer or a preparer may be liable for both. Unlike civil penalties, which are collected in the same manner as would be true for the regular tax, criminal penalties are imposed only after the completion of the normal criminal process, in which the defendant is entitled to a number of constitutional guarantees and other rights, i.e., he or she is deemed to be innocent until proven guilty.

IRC Section	Type of Infraction	Penalty
Civil Penalties		
6694(a)	Understatement due to unrealistic position	$250 per return
6694(b)	Willful understatement of liability	$1,000 per return
6695(a)	Failure to furnish copy to taxpayer	$50 per failure
6695(b)	Failure to inform taxpayer of certain record-keeping requirements or to sign return	$50 per failure
6695(c)	Failure to furnish identifying number	$50 per failure*
6695(d)	Failure to retain copy or list	$50 per failure*
6695(e)	Failure to file correct information return	$50 per failure to file; $50 per omitted item*
6695(f)	Negotiation or endorsement of refund checks	$500 per check
6700	Organizing (or assisting in doing so) or promoting and making or furnishing statements with respect to abusive tax shelters	Greater of $1,000 or 100% of gross income derived by preparer from the project
6701	Aiding and abetting an understatement of tax liability	$1,000 per return; $10,000 per return if taxpayer is a corporation
6713	Improper disclosure or use of return data	$250 per improper use; annual maximum $10,000
Criminal Penalties		
7201	Attempt to evade or defeat tax	Felony; fine of not more than $100,000 ($500,000 if a corporation) and/or imprisonment for not more than five years
7202	Willful failure to collect or pay over a tax	Felony; fine of not more than $10,000 and/or imprisonment for not more than five years
7203	Willful failure to file return, supply information, or pay tax	Misdemeanor; fine of not more than $25,000 ($100,000 if a corporation) and/or imprisonment for not more than one year (five years relative to cash received by a business)
7204	Fraudulent statement or failure to make statement to employees	Fine of not more than $1,000 and/or imprisonment for not more than one year
7205	Fraudulent withholding exemption certificate or failure to supply information	Fine of not more than $1,000 and/or imprisonment for not more than one year
7206	Fraud and false statements	Felony; fine of not more than $100,000 ($500,000 if a corporation) and/or imprisonment for not more than three years
7206(2)	Aid or assistance in the preparation or presentation of a false return, claim, or other document	Felony; fine of not more than $100,000 ($500,000 if a corporation) and/or imprisonment for not more than three years
7207	Fraudulent returns, statements, or other documents	Fine of not more than $10,000 ($50,000 if a corporation) and/or imprisonment for not more than one year
7210	Failure to obey summons	Fine of not more than $1,000 and/or imprisonment for not more than one year
7212	Attempts to interfere with administration of internal revenue laws	Fine of not more than $5,000 and/or imprisonment for not more than three years
7216	Disclosure or use of information by preparer	Misdemeanor; fine of not more than $1,000 and/or imprisonment for not more than one year

*Annual maximum penalty = $25,000.

EXHIBIT 13–3   Comparing taxpayer and preparer penalties, non-tax-shelter disputes

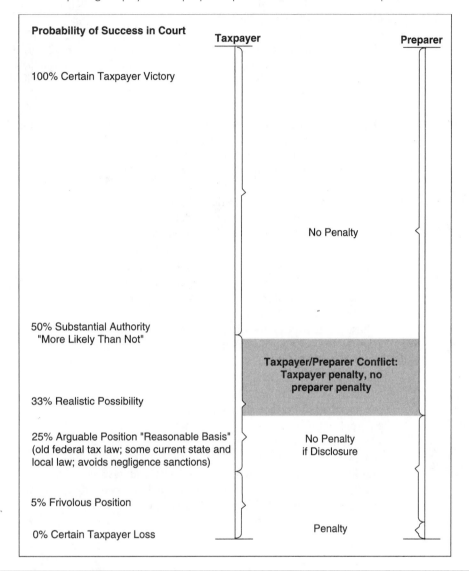

Example 13–2 Josie's return includes the claiming of a deduction that is contrary to an extant Revenue Ruling. Because of a new court decision in another circuit that is favorable to the deduction, Josie believes that there is a 70 percent chance that she would prevail in a suit relative to the deduction. No substantial-understatement penalty will apply to Josie, whether she wins or loses in court, and she need not disclose in any way her variance from the government position on her return.

Example 13–3 Continue with the facts of Example 13–2, except assume that Josie believes the following probabilities exist with respect to a court's treatment of her deduction, as supported by substantial authority.

Full support for her position 40%
Partial deduction allowed 35%
No deduction allowed 25%

No substantial-understatement penalty will apply to Josie, whether she wins or loses in court, and she need not disclose in any way her variance from the government position on her return. The weight of substantial authority for her position exceeds that supporting any other contrary position.

Example 13–4 Return to the facts of Example 13–2, except assume that Josie believes that she has a 40 percent probability of success in a court hearing. To avoid any substantial-understatement penalty, Josie must attach a Form 8275 to the return, revealing where and how she has deviated from the government's position relative to the deduction.

This discussion begs the question of how the typical lay taxpayer would arrive at the table of probabilities necessary to determine whether an additional Form 8275 disclosure would be necessary. It is clear that the substantial-authority criterion needs refinement to make it applicable to all but the most educated of taxpayers.

To avoid the preparer penalty for understatement-due-to-an-unrealistic-position, a one-in-three *realistic possibility* must exist that the return position will prevail on its merits. Lacking that level of likely success, a nonfrivolous position must be supported by a Form 8275 disclosure thereof.

Thus, the two penalties discussed here apply different disclosure criteria, and therein lies the possibility for preparer–taxpayer conflict. In many cases, the preparer will be likely to overstate the probability of success with respect to the disputed issue, because the no-disclosure-necessary level of certainty is lower for avoiding the preparer penalty than is the case for avoiding the taxpayer penalty. Again, one must conclude that further refinement of the penalty provisions is necessary, because the purpose of the tax law certainly is not to place at odds the taxpayer with his or her professional representative.

Under previous law, any *arguable position* taken in good faith on a return would be sufficient to avoid a taxpayer penalty. Thus, with respect to prior-year audits, and concerning applications of state laws that may have retained the previous standards, the picture in Exhibit 13–3 can get even more complex.

Injunctions

The IRS is empowered to seek **injunctions** against two classes of persons of interest to our discussion: (1) income tax return preparers and (2) promoters of abusive tax shelters. An injunction is a judicial order that prohibits the named person from engaging in certain specified activities. The courts have broad authority to structure any injunctive relief that is granted to fit the circumstances of the case as appropriate.

Action to Enjoin Income Tax Return Preparers

The IRS may seek an injunction against an ITRP who is guilty of certain misconduct, to prohibit him or her from engaging in such misconduct, or from practicing as a return preparer.

Before such an injunction can be issued, however, the preparer must have (1) violated a preparer penalty or a criminal provision of the Code, (2) misrepresented his or her eligibility to practice before the IRS, (3) guaranteed the payment of any tax refund or the allowance of a credit, or (4) engaged in other fraudulent or deceptive conduct that substantially interferes with the administration of the tax laws.

In addition, it must be shown that the injunctive relief is appropriate to prevent the conduct from recurring. An injunction to prohibit the preparer from acting as an income tax return preparer may be obtained if the court finds that the preparer continually or repeatedly has engaged in misconduct, and that an injunction prohibiting such specific misconduct would be effective.[79]

Action to Enjoin Promoters of Abusive Tax Shelters

The IRS may obtain an injunction against a person who is guilty of promoting abusive tax shelters, or of aiding and abetting an understatement of the tax liability, to prohibit him or her from engaging in such conduct or activities. Before such an injunction is issued, a court must find that injunctive relief is appropriate to prevent this conduct from recurring.[80]

Interest

The Code provides for the payment of interest on underpayments and overpayments of tax, at an adjustable rate, compounded daily. The objective of these provisions is to compensate offended parties for the use of their funds. Moreover, the interest charge eliminates the benefits that taxpayers (or the government) could obtain by adopting aggressive positions in the creation or processing of tax returns in order to postpone or avoid the payment of their taxes.

Interest–Computation Conventions

Interest on underpayments is payable at a federally specified rate, from the last date that is prescribed for the payment of the tax to the date on which the tax is actually paid. The last date that is prescribed for payment of the tax is usually the unextended due date of the return that reports the amount of tax that is due.[81]

Interest is compounded on a daily basis.[82] Thus, given an interest rate that equals or exceeds about 15 percent, the obligation of the taxpayer or government could double in five years. The IRS has published interest-factor tables in Revenue Procedure 83-7, which automatically calculate the daily compounding for various rates of interest.[83]

The rate of interest that is used for underpayments and overpayments is adjusted quarterly to reflect the federal short-term interest rate for the first day of the quarter.[84] The new prevailing rate is published in a timely fashion, typically in a Revenue Ruling.

The interest rate on underpayments is set at one percentage point higher than that for overpayments. Thus, the taxpayer is subject to an interest rate that is higher than

---

[79]§ 7407.
[80]§ 7408.
[81]§§ 6601(a) and (b).
[82]§ 6622(a).
[83]1983–1 CB 583.
[84]§ 6621.

that which applies to the government. Large corporations add two more percentage points to the underpayment rate. Corporate overpayments in excess of $10,000 earn interest at only a discounted rate. Exhibit 13–4 documents the various IRS rates of interest that applied to over- and underpayments occurring through 1998.

Where the taxpayer is subject to both underpayment and overpayment computations for the same time period, whether the prior disputes involve income, transfer,

---

EXHIBIT 13–4   IRS overpayment and underpayment interest rates

Period			Rate
Prior to July 1975			6%
July 1, 1975	–	January 31, 1976	9
February 1, 1976	–	January 31, 1978	7
February 1, 1978	–	January 31, 1980	6
February 1, 1980	–	January 31, 1982	12
February 1, 1982	–	December 31, 1982	20
January 1, 1983	–	June 30, 1983	16*
July 1, 1983	–	December 31, 1984	11*
January 1, 1985	–	June 30, 1985	13*
July 1, 1985	–	December 31, 1985	11*
January 1, 1986	–	June 30, 1986	10*
July 1, 1986	–	December 31, 1986	9*

Period			Overpayment Rate*†	Underpayment Rate*†	Large Corporation Underpayment Rate*	Rate for Corporation Overpayments >$10,000*
January 1, 1987	–	September 30, 1987	8%	9%		
October 1, 1987	–	December 31, 1987	9	10		
January 1, 1988	–	March 31, 1988	10	11		
April 1, 1988	–	September 30, 1988	9	10		
October 1, 1988	–	March 31, 1989	10	11		
April 1, 1989	–	September 30, 1989	11	12		
October 1, 1989	–	March 31, 1991	10	11		
April 1, 1991	–	December 31, 1991	9	10	12%	
January 1, 1992	–	March 31, 1992	8	9	11	
April 1, 1992	–	September 30, 1992	7	8	10	
October 1, 1992	–	June 30, 1994	6	7	9	
July 1, 1994	–	September 30, 1994	7	8	10	
October 1, 1994	–	December 31, 1994	8	9	11	
January 1, 1995	–	March 31, 1995	8	9	11	6.5
April 1, 1995	–	June 30, 1995	9	10	12	7.5
July 1, 1995	–	March 31, 1996	8	9	11	6.5
April 1, 1996	–	June 30, 1996	7	8	10	5.5
July 1, 1996	–	March 31, 1998	8	9	11	6.5
April 1, 1998	–	September 30, 1998	7	8	10	5.5

*Daily compounding required.
†After 1998, noncorporate taxpayers use the second column for both under- and overpayments. Corporations still receive one percentage point less with respect to their overpayments; i.e., the first column still applies.

or employment taxes, the amounts due and payable to the government are netted and a zero interest rate applies to those amounts.

> **Example 13–5** Mary Brown, a calendar-year taxpayer, filed her 1988 tax return and showed a balance due of $1,000. The return was filed on June 30, 1989, pursuant to a properly executed extension of time to file, and the tax was paid in full with the return. The prevailing IRS interest rate that applies to Brown's underpayment was 12 percent. (Verify this statement.) She must pay about $25 of interest with her return, determined as follows.
>
> | | |
> |---|---:|
> | Total tax outstanding | $ 1,000 |
> | Factor from Rev. Proc. 83–7, for 12% interest and 74 days' late payment | × .024622982 |
> | Interest assessed | $ 24.62 |
>
> April 15 was a Saturday, so Brown's return was due on April 17. If Brown does not remit the interest that she owes when she files the return, interest will accrue, on both the tax and the $24 of interest itself, until the obligation is paid in full. If this amount is paid within ten days of the receipt of an IRS notice and demand for payment, however, no further interest accrues.

Interest accrues on the full amount of the tax liability that is appropriate under the Code, regardless of the amount of tax that is entered on the return. Moreover, interest is imposed on an assessable penalty, additional amount, or addition to the tax if these amounts are not paid within ten days of the date on which the IRS requests its payment. Interest on penalties generally is imposed only from the date of this IRS notice and demand, and not from the due date of the return. However, the fraud, accuracy-related, and failure-to-file penalties run from the (extended) due date of the return.[85]

No interest is charged on criminal penalties or delinquent estimated tax payments. However, recall that a nondeductible penalty is imposed in lieu of interest with respect to delinquent estimated tax payments. This penalty is computed in the same manner as would be the required interest, except that daily compounding of the penalty is not required.

In general, the IRS has no authority to forgive the payment of interest. Consequently, a taxpayer will be required to pay the total amount of interest assessed on any underpayment, even though the delinquency was attributable to a reasonable cause, including an IRS loss of records and the illness, transfer, or leave of a pertinent IRS employee. However, the IRS can abate such interest where it is attributable to an error or delay caused by an employee or officer of the IRS, in response to the taxpayer's filing a claim on Form 843. Such a delay cannot be traceable to an interpretation of the tax law, but rather must relate to nondiscretionary, administrative, or managerial duties of procedure or return processing, including an IRS loss of records and the illness, transfer, or leave of a pertinent IRS employee.[86]

The government is required to pay interest at the applicable federal rate to any taxpayer who has made an overpayment of tax. Interest on an overpayment runs from the date of the overpayment to the date on which the overpayment is credited against another tax liability, or, in the case of a refund, to a date that is not more than thirty days before the date of the refund check.

[85] § 6601(e)(2).
[86] § 6404(e) and Rev. Proc. 87–42, 1987–2 CB 589.

However, the IRS is allowed a specific period in which it may refund an over-payment without incurring interest. This interest-free period runs for forty-five days after the unextended due date of the return or, if the return is filed after its due date, for forty-five days after it is actually filed. If the refund is not made within this forty-five day period, interest begins to accrue from the later of (1) the due date of the return or (2) the date on which the return was actually filed.[87]

> **Example 13–6** Joan Jeffries, a calendar-year taxpayer, filed her 1998 federal income tax return on October 1, 1999. Her return showed an overpayment of $2,500, for which Jeffries requested a full refund. If the IRS refunds the $2,500 overpayment on or before November 14, 1999, no interest will be due from the government. However, if the refund is paid after November 14, 1999, interest will accrue from October 1, 1999, through a date that is not more than thirty days before the date of the refund check.

The date that is stated on the government's refund check determines whether the overpayment is refunded within the forty-five-day interest-free period. The date on which the refund is actually received does not control for this purpose. Thus, an interest-free refund may be paid, even though it is not received by the taxpayer until the forty-five-day period has expired.

Applicable Interest Rate

Different rates are used with respect to IRS overpayments and underpayments after 1986, as is evident in Exhibit 13–4. The overpayment rate (paid by the IRS) is two percentage points greater than the federal short-term interest rate, compounded daily, and the underpayment rate (paid to the IRS) is three percentage points greater than the same federal rate.

Large corporations pay interest at two percentage points higher than the usual underpayment rate. These rates are determined at the beginning of each calendar quarter, using the federal rates in effect for the first month of that quarter.

Statutes of Limitations

The Code establishes a specific period of time, commonly referred to as a **statute of limitation,** within which all taxes must be assessed and collected, and all refund claims must be made. After the pertinent statute of limitations expires, certain actions may not be taken, because the expiration establishes an absolute defense for the party against whom legal action is brought. In other words, a taxpayer cannot be required to pay taxes that he or she rightfully owes if these taxes are not assessed and collected within the time periods that the Code has established.

Nature of Statutes of Limitations

Although the statute of limitations appears to be a legal loophole that rewards delin-quent taxpayers who avoid detection, Congress believes that, at some point, the right to be free of stale claims must prevail over the government's right to pursue them. If the statutes permitted the lapse of an extended period of time between the initiation

[87]§ 6611(c).

of a claim and its pursuit, the defense could be jeopardized because witnesses might have died or disappeared, memories might have faded, and records or other evidence might have been lost. Moreover, some statutes of limitations are designed solely to protect the government (e.g., the statute of limitations on credits or refunds). A number of such statutes limit the time period within which assessment, collection, and claim for refund or credit activities must be conducted.[88]

Assessment

Assessment of an internal revenue tax generally must be made within three years of the later of the date that the return was actually filed or the unextended due date of the return. A return that is filed prior to its due date, for this purpose, is deemed to be filed on its due date. The assessment period for a return that is filed after the due date starts on the day that follows the actual filing date, regardless of whether the return is delinquent or the due date was extended properly.

The period in which a tax may be assessed is extended to six years if the taxpayer omits from his or her reported gross income an amount that is greater than 25 percent of the reported gross income.[89] For this purpose, § 61 gross income is used in the 25 percent computation, with two exceptions. First, the gross income of a business is *not* reduced by cost of sales. Second, income that is omitted from the return is ignored for purposes of constructing the base for the 25 percent test, if the omission is disclosed in the return or in an attached document.[90]

Although the limitations period will be extended for a substantial omission of income, it (surprisingly) is not extended where the taxpayer has overstated the amount of his or her deductions, regardless of the amount of the overstatement.

Irregular Returns

A tax may be assessed at any time when a taxpayer files a false or fraudulent return with the intent to evade tax liability.[91] Once the fraudulent return is filed, the limitations period remains open indefinitely. A later filing of a nonfraudulent amended return will not start the running of the three- (or six)-year limitation period.[92]

When a taxpayer fails to file a return, the tax may be assessed at any time. For this purpose, one's failure to file need not be willful. A taxpayer who innocently or negligently fails to file is still subject to an unlimited period of assessment for the tax.[93]

Acceleration, Extension, and Carryback Effects   Generally, the filing of an amended return does not affect the length of the limitations period. However, the limitations period is extended by sixty days if the IRS receives, within sixty days of the expiration of the applicable statute of limitations, an amended return that shows the taxpayer owes an additional tax.[94] This provision was enacted to discourage taxpayers from waiting until the limitations period on an assessment was about to

---

[88]§ 6501.
[89]§ 6501(e)(1)(A).
[90]§§ 6501(e)(1)(A)(i) and (ii).
[91]§ 6501(c)(1).
[92]*Badaracco v. Comm.*, 464 U.S. 386, 104 S.Ct. 756 (1984).
[93]§ 6501(c)(3).
[94]§ 6501(c)(7).

expire before submitting an erroneous amended return. Prior to the enactment of this provision, it was beneficial for the taxpayer to wait to file an amended return this way, because the IRS would not have enough time to assess more tax if an examination of the original return uncovered additional unreported errors or omissions.

The usual three-year assessment period can be reduced to eighteen months if a request for a prompt assessment is filed with the IRS.[95] This request usually is made for an income tax return of a decedent or an estate, or for a corporation that is in the midst of a dissolution. Generally, a prompt assessment is requested when all of the involved parties wish to accelerate the final determination of the tax liability.

A deficiency for a carryback year that is attributable to the carryback of a net operating loss, capital loss, or unused research or general business credit can be assessed at any time before the expiration of the limitations period for the year in which the loss occurred or the credit originated. This extension in the period of assessment for the carryback year is necessary to ensure that there is adequate time to process the refund claim, and to allow the IRS to examine the return that gave rise to the carryback item.[96]

The period for assessment is not extended when a net operating loss, capital loss, or unused credit is carried forward.

IRS-Requested Extensions   An extension of the period of limitations typically will be requested by the IRS when an audit or an appellate review cannot be completed until after the statute of limitations expires. The taxpayer is not bound to agree with such a request, but such a refusal may prompt the IRS to stop negotiations prematurely and assess a deficiency against the taxpayer. Although the issuance of a statutory notice of deficiency does not preclude the taxpayer from obtaining a negotiated settlement with the IRS, he or she will be required to undertake a more costly procedure and file a petition with the U.S. Tax Court or pay the assessment and file a claim for refund. Consequently, a taxpayer normally should not refuse to sign a waiver of the statute of limitations, as requested by the IRS, unless the agent has completed the examination and there exist one or more unagreed-upon issues that the taxpayer is ready to litigate.

Collection

All taxes must be collected within ten years after a timely assessment has been made.[97] **Collection** can be made either by IRS levy or by the agency's commencement of an action in court. If the tax is not collected administratively by levy within the ten-year period, the IRS must commence an action in court to reduce the assessment to a judgment before the statute of limitation expires. Once a judgment for the assessed tax is awarded, the tax may be collected at any time after the normal period of collections has expired. Thus, collection is not barred after the ten-year period expires, provided that the IRS has obtained a timely judgment against the taxpayer.

The taxpayer and the IRS may agree to an extension of the normal collection period. The IRS will request such an extension whenever the taxpayer has agreed to extend the period of limitations for assessment of the tax. In addition, the taxpayer

[95]§ 6501(d).
[96]§§ 6501(h) through (k).
[97]§ 6502(a)(1).

may request an extension to allow additional time in which to (raise and) submit any delinquent taxes. If the taxpayer agrees to extend the period of limitation on collections, the IRS may agree not to seize and sell the taxpayer's property to satisfy the tax liability.

The ten-year period of limitations begins only after an assessment is made. If an assessment can be made at any time, for example, because the taxpayer failed to file a return or filed a fraudulent return, the tax may be collected within ten years of the date of assessment, regardless of when it eventually is made.

Claim for Refund or Credit

A taxpayer must file a timely and valid claim at the service center for the district in which the tax was paid to receive a refund or credit of an overpayment of tax. The claim should be made by individuals on Form 1040X, Individual Amended Income Tax Return, and by corporations on Form 1120X, Corporate Amended Income Tax Return.

Generally, an overpayment can be refunded or credited only to the person who was subject to the original tax. However, the IRS can apply overpayments to delinquent support obligations and certain certified nontax debts that are owed to the federal government. Refunds in excess of $1,000,000 may not be made until they have been reviewed by the Joint Committee on Taxation.[98]

A taxpayer who reports a net operating loss, capital loss, or credit carryback can accelerate the processing of the refund by filing an Application for Tentative Carryback Adjustment on Form 1045 (for individuals) or Form 1139 (for corporations). The IRS has ninety days from the later of the date on which the application was filed or the last day of the month in which the return for the loss is due to examine the application and accept or deny the claim.[99] However, if the application is denied, the taxpayer cannot bring a suit for recovery of the overpayment, because the IRS's determination is only tentative. Instead, the taxpayer must file a refund claim on the appropriate form and wait for six months from the date on which the claim was filed, or until the IRS denies the refund claim, before legal action can be started.

Before a refund or credit can be issued, the IRS must review the taxpayer's claim. Even if the Commissioner agrees that the taxpayer has overpaid a tax, he or she has no authority to refund or credit the overpayment unless the taxpayer files the claim within the allowable period. Any refund of an overpayment that is made after the period for filing a timely claim is considered erroneous, and a credit is considered void.

Limitations Period   A taxpayer who has filed a return must file a claim for credit or refund within three years of the date on which the return was filed, or two years of the date on which the tax was paid, whichever is later. If the taxpayer did not file a return (e.g., because taxes were withheld from the taxpayer's wages, but the taxpayer did not file a return because his or her taxable income did not exceed the applicable exemptions and standard deduction), the claim for credit or refund must be made within two years of the date on which the tax was paid.[100]

The period within which a claim for credit or refund may be filed is extended when the taxpayer and the IRS agree to extend the statute of limitations on assess-

[98]§ 6405(a).
[99]§ 6411(b) and Reg. § 1.6411–1(b).
[100]§ 6511(a).

ments. A claim can be filed within six months after the expiration of the extended assessment period.[101]

Other Extensions

The limitations period also can be extended where an overpayment results from a business bad debt or from a discovery of worthless securities.[102] A claim for refund or credit that is attributable to losses sustained from worthless securities or business bad debts may be filed within seven years from the date that the return was due, without regard to any extension for filing the return. This period is extended further if the debt or loss increases a net operating loss carryback, since the taxpayer will be entitled to three additional years for the filing of a claim that is based on the carryback.[103]

This provision was enacted because the determination of the date on which a debt or share of stock becomes worthless is a question of fact that may not be determined until after the year in which the loss actually occurred. If taxpayers were not allowed additional time in which to file refund claims for these items, they could incur substantial losses without the receipt of any tax benefits, because the deductions must be taken in the taxable year of the loss, not in a later year.

The period for filing a claim for refund is extended when the claimed overpayment results from the carryback of a net operating loss, capital loss, or certain credits. If a claim for credit or refund is attributable to the carryback of a net operating loss, net capital loss, or business credit, it can be filed within three years of the extended due date of the return for the year in which the losses occurred or the credits originated, rather than within three years of the due date of the return for the carryback year. Again, this provision was enacted because the existence and amount of these items might not be known until after the expiration of the usual three-year period for filing the claim.

Amount of the Credit or Refund

If a claim for refund or credit is filed in a timely fashion, the amount of the taxpayer's refund or credit is limited to the portion of the tax that was paid during the three immediately preceding years, plus the period of any extension for filing the return.[104] The amount of tax that is subject to the claim may include amounts that were withheld, and estimated payments that were made more than three years before the date on which the claim was filed, because these amounts are all deemed to have been paid on the due date of the return.

If a claim is filed after the three-year period, the amount of any refund or credit is limited to the portion of the tax that was paid during the two years that immediately precede the filing of the claim. This two-year period also is effective if a claim is filed for a year in which a return was not filed. Because this claim relates only to a two-year period, it may not protect payments that were made with the original return.

Suspension of Period of Assessment and Collection

Usually, a tax must be assessed within three years after the filing of a tax return, and it must be collected within six years of the assessment. However, under certain cir-

[101]§ 6511(c)(2).
[102]§ 6511(d).
[103]§ 6511(d)(2)(A).
[104]§ 6511(b)(2)(A).

cumstances, the running of the statutes of limitations on assessment or collection is suspended.

When the IRS mails a statutory notice of deficiency (i.e., a 90-day letter) to the taxpayer, the assessment and collection period is suspended for 150 days (210 days if the letter is addressed to a person who is outside the United States).[105] The statutes of limitations on assessment and collection also are suspended when a case is pending before the U.S. Tax Court. This suspension period begins when the taxpayer files a petition in the Tax Court, contesting the deficiency, and it continues until 60 days after the decision of the Tax Court becomes final.

When a taxpayer submits an offer in compromise for consideration by the IRS, the statute of limitations on assessment is suspended. This suspension period begins when the offer is submitted, and it continues until one year after the offer is terminated, withdrawn, or formally rejected.[106]

In addition to the circumstances just discussed, the statute of limitations also can be suspended when:[107]

▶ the taxpayer's assets are in the custody of the court;
▶ the taxpayer is outside the United States for six or more consecutive months;
▶ the taxpayer's assets are wrongfully seized;
▶ a fiduciary or receiver is appointed in a bankruptcy case;
▶ the IRS is prohibited under bankruptcy law from any assessment or collection of a tax; or
▶ the collection of excise or termination taxes on certain retirement plans or private foundations are suspended.

Mitigation of Statute of Limitations

Generally, the IRS cannot make an assessment, and a taxpayer cannot obtain a refund, after the statute of limitations has expired. However, §§1311 through 1314 of the Code include a complex set of rules designed to prevent the taxpayer or the IRS from taking advantage of an oncoming expiration of the period of limitations on assessment, collection, or refunds.

When an error has been made in the inclusion of an item of income, allowance, or disallowance of a deduction, or other tax treatment of a transaction that affects the basis of property, the mitigation provisions will allow a submission of the error to be corrected, even though the normal period of limitations has expired for that year.

Statutory Agreements

The Code provides for two types of agreements that may be used to resolve tax disputes, namely, closing agreements and offers in compromise.

Closing Agreements

A **closing agreement** is a formal, written agreement that is made between a taxpayer and the IRS. It is the only agreement that the Code recognizes as being binding.

---

[105]§ 6503(a)(1).
[106]Reg. § 301.7122-1(f).
[107]§§ 6503(b) through (f). That section also contains other, less frequently encountered suspension possibilities.

Once it is approved, a closing agreement is final and conclusive on the part of both the government and the taxpayer, unless there is a showing of fraud, malfeasance, or a misrepresentation of a material fact, by either party.[108]

The purpose of a closing agreement is either (1) to enable the taxpayer and the IRS to resolve, finally and completely, a tax controversy for any period prior to the date of the agreement, and to protect the taxpayer against the reopening of the matter at a later date; or (2) to determine a matter in a tax year that arises after the date of the agreement.

The IRS is authorized to enter into a closing agreement in any case where there appears to be a benefit to the government in closing the case permanently and conclusively, or if the taxpayer demonstrates a need to close the case and the government's interests are not harmed. Typically, a closing agreement is used in cases where the IRS and the taxpayer have made mutual concessions relative to the case, and it is necessary or desirable to bar further actions by either party. Such an agreement also may be used when a corporation is winding up its business affairs, or when a taxpayer needs some authentic evidence of his or her tax liability, say, to satisfy creditors.

As a matter of practice, the IRS discourages the use of closing agreements because of their finality. Moreover, the IRS would have a difficult time processing a large number of requests for these agreements. Consequently, it prefers to use a number of informal agreements that may not resolve conclusively the tax dispute that is under examination, or that may not provide for the same degree of finality as would a closing agreement. Examples of such informal agreements include (1) Form 870, Waiver of Restrictions on Assessment and Collection of Deficiency in Tax and Acceptance of Overassessment; and (2) Form 870-AD, Offer of Waiver of Restrictions on Assessment and Collection of Deficiency in Tax and of Acceptance of Overassessment. Form 870 is reproduced in Exhibit 13–5.

Offers in Compromise

The Commissioner can make an **offer in compromise** for any civil or criminal case that does not involve sales of illegal drugs, prior to the time that the case is referred to the Justice Department for prosecution or defense. Once the case is referred to the Justice Department, however, the U.S. Attorney General has the final authority to compromise the case.[109] Compromise proposals entailing more than $50,000 in tax also must be supported by an opinion of the Chief Counsel.

In this context, the government will compromise a case only if there is doubt as to the liability or collectibility of the assessed tax. The IRS will not enter into a compromise with the taxpayer if the liability has been established by a valid judgment, and if there is no doubt as to the ability of the IRS to collect the amounts that are due.

A compromise agreement may cover the principal amount of tax, plus any corresponding interest or penalties. Ordinarily, the IRS will not compromise a criminal tax case unless it involves a violation of a regulatory provision of the Code or of a related statute that was not deliberately violated with an intent to defraud.

Although the IRS has complete authority to compromise most civil and criminal cases, there are certain cases that, as a matter of policy, it will not settle. These cases

[108] § 7121(b).
[109] § 7122(a).

involve tax questions referred to as **prime issues.** If a case involves a prime issue, the IRS will not compromise its position. The taxpayer's only alternatives for resolving the issue in such a situation are (1) to concede the matter fully or (2) to proceed to litigate the matter.

Generally, the IRS designates a topic as a prime issue when the matter may be subject to taxpayer abuse and clearly threatens the IRS's ability to guard the currency. A list of prime issues is published in Volume 4 of the *Internal Revenue Manual.* However, this portion of the manual is not released to the general public, so its exact contents are not known. One issue that is known to be on the list of prime

---

EXHIBIT 13–5   Sample form for closing agreement

[¶ 174] 251 11-86	[Form 870]	1133

Form 870 (Rev. February 1986)	Department of the Treasury — Internal Revenue Service **Waiver of Restrictions on Assessment and Collection of Deficiency in Tax and Acceptance of Overassessment**	Date received by Internal Revenue Service

Names and address of taxpayers *(Number, street, city or town, State, ZIP code)*	Social security or employer identification number

Increase (Decrease) in Tax and Penalties

Tax year ended	Tax	Penalties		
	$	$	$	$	$
	$	$	$	$	$
	$	$	$	$	$
	$	$	$	$	$
	$	$	$	$	$
	$	$	$	$	$
	$	$	$	$	$

(For instructions, see back of form)

Consent to Assessment and Collection

I consent to the immediate assessment and collection of any deficiencies *(increase in tax and penalties)* and accept any overassessment *(decrease in tax and penalties)* shown above, plus any interest provided by law. I understand that by signing this waiver, I will not be able to contest these years in the United States Tax Court, unless additional deficiencies are determined for these years.

Signatures		Date
		Date
	By	Title	Date

Form 870 (Rev. 2-86)

EXHIBIT 13-5 *Continued*

Instructions

General Information

If you consent to the assessment of the deficiencies shown in this waiver, please sign and return the form in order to limit any interest charge and expedite the adjustment to your account. Your consent will not prevent you from filing a claim for refund *(after you have paid the tax)* if you later believe you are so entitled. It will not prevent us from later determining, if necessary, that you owe additional tax; nor extend the time provided by law for either action.

We have agreements with State tax agencies under which information about Federal tax, including increases or decreases, is exchanged with the States. If this change affects the amount of your State income tax, you should file the required State form.

If you later file a claim and the Service disallows it, you may file suit for refund in a district court or in the United States Claims Court, but you may not file a petition with the United States Tax Court.

We will consider this waiver a valid claim for refund or credit of any overpayment due you resulting from any decrease in tax and penalties shown above, provided you sign and file it within the period established by law for making such a claim.

Who Must Sign

If you filed jointly, both you and your spouse must sign. If this waiver is for a corporation, it should be signed with the corporation name, followed by the signatures and titles of the corporate officers authorized to sign. An attorney or agent may sign this waiver provided such action is specifically authorized by a power of attorney which, if not previously filed, must accompany this form.

If this waiver is signed by a person acting in a fiduciary capacity *(for example, an executor, administrator, or a trustee)* Form 56, Notice Concerning Fiduciary Relationship, should, unless previously filed, accompany this form.

issues, though, concerns the deductibility of rent payments for a gift-leaseback arrangement when the payments are made to a reversionary short-term trust.

A compromise agreement relates to the entire liability of the taxpayer, and it conclusively settles all of the issues for which an agreement is to be made. It is a legally enforceable promise that cannot be rescinded unless there has been a misrepresentation of the assets of the taxpayer by falsification or concealment, or a mutual mistake relative to a material fact. Consequently, a taxpayer cannot decide later to bring a suit for refund with respect to any item that is so compromised. Moreover, if a taxpayer defaults on a compromise agreement, the IRS may collect the original tax liability, less any payments that were actually made, or sue to enforce the agreement.

An offer in compromise is typically made via Form 656, Offer in Compromise, and it must be accompanied by a comprehensive set of the taxpayer's financial statements. The offer may be revoked or withdrawn at any time prior to its acceptance.

▶ Summary

In dealing with tax underpayments, the stakes include more than just the disputed tax. Interest charges accrue and both the taxpayer and tax advisor can be subjected to significant amounts of civil and criminal penalties. Restrictions on the actions of the taxpayer and practitioner are expressed using such ambiguously defined terms as *reasonable cause* and *substantial authority,* such that the lay taxpayer is expected to project accurately the final holding of a judicial forum. Such is the condition of a tax system under which tax rates virtually cannot be raised, yet revenue needs continue to escalate.

▶ Key Words

By the time you complete your work relative to this chapter, you should be comfortable discussing each of the following terms. If you need additional review of any of these items, return to the appropriate material in the chapter or consult the glossary to this text.

Accuracy-Related Penalty	Negligence Offer in Compromise
Assessment	Preparer Penalties
Civil Penalty	Prime Issues
Closing Agreement	Realistic Possibility
Collection	Reasonable Cause
Criminal Penalty	Return Preparer
Fraud	Statute of Limitations
Injunction	Substantial Authority

▶ _____ Discussion Questions

1. When should prevailing interest rates bear on tax decision making?

   a. The taxpayer is contemplating litigation in either the Tax Court or the Court of Federal Claims.
   b. An understatement of estimated tax payments is discovered late in the tax year.

2. What is the role of the statute of limitations in the federal income tax system?

3. Indicate whether each of the following statements is true or false.

   a. The government never pays a taxpayer interest on an overpayment of tax.
   b. Penalties may be included as an itemized deduction on an individual's tax return.
   c. An extension of time for filing a return results in an automatic extension of the time in which the tax may be paid.
   d. The IRS can compromise on the amount of tax liability if there is doubt as to the taxpayer's ability to pay.
   e. The statute of limitations for assessment of taxes never extends beyond three years from the filing of a return.
   f. There is no statute of limitations relative to a taxpayer's claim for a refund.

4. Indicate whether, after both parties sign a Form 870, the following result(s) occur. More than one answer may be correct.

   a. The taxpayer still may appeal to a higher level of the IRS.
   b. The interest on the assessment stops accruing immediately.
   c. The agreement is binding on both the taxpayer and the IRS.
   d. The tax must be paid, but a suit for refund can be filed in the District Court or U.S. Court of Federal Claims.

5. Ace filed her 1998 income tax return on January 25, 1999. There was no material understatement of income on her return, and the return was properly signed and filed. The statute of limitations for Ace's 1998 return expires on:

   a. January 25, 2002
   b. April 15, 2002
   c. January 25, 2005
   d. April 15, 2005

6. Blanche filed her 1993 income tax return on April 4, 1999. On December 14, 1999, she learned that 100 shares of stock that she owned had become worthless in 1998. Since she did not deduct this loss on the 1998 return, Blanche

intends to file a claim for refund. This claim must be filed by no later than April 15,

   a. 2000

   b. 2003

   c. 2005

   d. 2006

   e. There is no expiration date for the statute of limitations in this context.

7. Carl purposely omitted from his 1998 tax return $40,000 of the gross receipts that he collected as the owner of a saloon. His 1998 return indicated collective gross receipts of $25,000. The IRS no longer can pursue Carl with the threat of a collection of the related tax, interest, and penalties, as of April 15,

   a. 2000

   b. 2003

   c. 2005

   d. 2006

   e. There is no expiration date for the statute of limitations in this context.

8. Diane accidentally omitted from her 1998 tax return $40,000 of the gross receipts that she collected as the owner of a saloon. Her 1998 return indicated collective gross receipts of $25,000. The IRS no longer can pursue Diane with the threat of a collection of the related tax, interest, and penalties, as of April 15,

   a. 2000

   b. 2003

   c. 2005

   d. 2006

   e. There is no expiration date for the statute of limitations in this context.

9. List some of the liabilities and penalties that the Code imposes on tax preparers.

10. How has Congress used tax penalties to discourage the development of certain tax shelters?

11. Distinguish between or among the following.

   a. Offer in compromise and closing agreement

   b. Failure to file and failure to pay

   c. I.R.S. Service Center, district, and region

   d. PRP, TCMP, RAR, ITRP, DIF, and ADP

   e. Ninety-day letter and thirty-day letter

   f. Office, field, and correspondence reviews

   g. Negligence and fraud

   h. Criminal and civil penalties

   i. Injunction, suspension, and mitigation

   j. Assessment, collection, and claim

►   Exercises

12. Construct a scenario in which the tax advisor should recommend that the client terminate the challenge of the IRS with the following.

   a. Lawsuit

   b. Offer in compromise

    c. Closing agreement

    d. Appeals conference

    e. Office audit

    f. Correspondence audit

13. The client's return is found to include fraudulent data. Which of the following could the IRS charge with a preparer penalty?

    a. Taxpayer

    b. Partner of the accounting firm that prepared the return

    c. Employee of the client, who provided the accounting firm with the fraudulent data

    d. Staff member of the accounting firm, who used the fraudulent data to prepare the return and did not verify its accuracy

    e. Secretary of the accounting firm, who made copies of the fraudulent return

14. The client's return is found by the U.S. Tax Court to have included improper business deductions. The court agreed that the taxpayer's position had some statutory and judicial merit, but it held for the government nonetheless. Which of the following could the IRS charge with a preparer penalty?

    a. Taxpayer

    b. Partner of the accounting firm that prepared the return

    c. Employee of the client, who provided the accounting firm with the deduction data

    d. Staff member of the accounting firm, who used the deduction data to prepare the return

    e. Secretary of the accounting firm, who made copies of the return

15. Discuss the role of the hazards of litigation in the conduct of a client's tax case.

16. Define and illustrate the following terms or concepts.

    a. Fraud

    b. Negligence

    c. Reasonable cause

    d. Lack of reasonable cause

    e. Civil penalty conviction

    f. Criminal penalty conviction

17. Discuss which penalties, if any, the tax advisor might be charged with in each of the following independent circumstances. In this regard, assume that the tax advisor

    a. provided information about the taxpayer's federal income tax returns to the pertinent state income tax agency.

    b. provided information about the taxpayer's federal income tax returns to the pertinent county's property tax agency.

    c. provided information about the taxpayer's federal income tax returns to the FBI, which was interested in gathering evidence concerning the client's alleged drug dealing activities.

    d. suggested to the client various means by which to acquire excludible income.

    e. suggested to the client various means by which to conceal cash receipts from gross income.

f. suggested to the client means by which to improve her cash flow by delaying for six months or more the deposit of the employees' share of federal employment taxes.

g. suggested to the client means by which to improve her cash flow by delaying for six months or more the deposit of the employer's share of federal employment taxes.

h. kept in his safe deposit box the concealed income of item (e).

i. suggested that the client invest in a real estate tax shelter.

j. provided a statement of assurance as to the accuracy of the financial data that is included in the prospectus of a real estate tax shelter.

k. suggested to the promoters of a real estate tax shelter that a specific accounting technique, not recognized by generally accepted accounting principles, should be used to construct the prospectus.

l. failed, because of pressing time conflicts, to conduct the usual review of the client's tax return. The IRS discovered that the return included fraudulent data.

m. failed, because of pressing time conflicts, to conduct the usual review of the client's tax return. The IRS discovered a mathematical error in the computation of the taxpayer's standard deduction.

18. What is a prime issue, and why is it designated as such?

19. For the completion and filing of his 1998 federal income tax return, Ron retains the services of a tax preparer. Because of a particularly hectic tax preparation season, the preparer does not complete and file the return until June 1999. Is Ron excused from the failure to file and pay penalties under the reasonable cause exception?

► _____ Problems

20. Lefty, a calendar-year taxpayer subject to a 34 percent marginal tax rate, claimed a charitable contribution deduction of $15,000 for a sculpture that the IRS later valued at $10,000. The applicable overvaluation penalty is:

a. $0
b. $100 (minimum penalty)
c. $340
d. $1,700
e. Some other amount

21. Righty, a calendar-year taxpayer subject to a 34 percent marginal tax rate, claimed a charitable contribution deduction of $170,000 for a sculpture that the IRS later valued at $100,000. The applicable overvaluation penalty is:

a. $0
b. $100 (minimum penalty)
c. $4,760
d. $5,950
e. Some other amount

22. Shorty, a calendar-year taxpayer subject to a 34 percent marginal tax rate, claimed a charitable contribution deduction of $400,000 for a sculpture that the IRS later valued at $150,000. The applicable overvaluation penalty is:

a. $0
b. $17,000
c. $21,250
d. $10,000 (maximum penalty)
e. Some other amount

23. Baldy, a calendar-year taxpayer subject to a 34 percent marginal tax rate, claimed a charitable contribution deduction of $600,000 for a sculpture that the IRS later valued at $100,000. The applicable overvaluation penalty is:

a. $0
b. $34,000
c. $68,000
d. $10,000 (maximum penalty)
e. Some other amount

24. Slim, who is subject to a 50 percent marginal gift tax rate, made a gift of a sculpture to Red, valuing the property at $7,000. The IRS later valued the gift at $15,000. The applicable undervaluation penalty is:

a. $1,000
b. $800
c. $100 (minimum penalty)
d. $0
e. Some other amount

25. Tiny, who is subject to a 50 percent marginal gift tax rate, made a gift of a sculpture to Blondie, valuing the property at $80,000. The IRS later valued the gift at $150,000. The applicable undervaluation penalty is:

a. $8,750
b. $7,000
c. $1000 (minimum penalty)
d. $0
e. Some other amount

26. Fuzzy, who is subject to a 50 percent marginal gift tax rate, made a gift of a sculpture to Pinky, valuing the property at $100,000. The IRS later valued the gift at $250,000. The applicable undervaluation penalty is:

a. $10,000 (maximum penalty)
b. $18,750
c. $15,000
d. $0
e. Some other amount

27. Jumbo, who is subject to a 50 percent marginal gift tax rate, made a gift of a sculpture to Curly, valuing the property at $100,000. The IRS later valued the gift at $500,000. The applicable undervaluation penalty is:

a. $10,000 (maximum penalty)
b. $80,000
c. $40,000
d. $0
e. Some other amount

28. Kim underpaid her taxes by $15,000. Of this amount, $7,500 was due to negligence on her part, because her record-keeping system is highly inadequate. Determine the amount of any negligence penalty.

29. Compute Dana's total penalties. She underpaid her tax by $50,000 due to negligence, and by $150,000 due to civil fraud.

30. Trudy's AGI last year was $50,000. Her federal income tax came to $16,000, which she paid through a combination of withholding and estimated payments. This year, her AGI will be $170,000, with a projected tax liability of $46,000, all to be paid through estimates. Ignore the annualized income method. Compute Trudy's quarterly estimated payment schedule for the year, assuming that she wants to make the minimum necessary payments to avoid any underpayment penalties.

31. When Maggie accepted employment with Martin Corporation, she completed a Form W-4, listing fourteen exemptions. Since Maggie was single and had no exemptions, she misrepresented her tax situation in an attempt to increase her cash flow. What penalties is Maggie exposed to?

32. What is the applicable filing period under the statute of limitations in each of the following independent situations?

    a. No return was filed by the taxpayer.
    b. The taxpayer incurred a bad debt loss that she failed to claim.
    c. A taxpayer inadvertently omitted a large amount of gross income.
    d. Same as part (c), except that the omission was deliberate.
    e. A taxpayer inadvertently overstated her deductions by a large amount.

33. Kold Corporation estimates that its 1998 taxable income will be $900,000. Thus, it is subject to a flat 34 percent income tax rate and incurs a $306,000 liability. For each of the following independent cases, compute the minimum quarterly estimated tax payments that will be required from Kold to avoid an underpayment penalty.

    a. Taxable income for 1997 was ($100,000). Kold carried back all of its loss to prior years and exhausted the entire net operating loss in creating a zero 1997 liability.
    b. For 1997, taxable income was $200,000, and tax liability was $68,000.
    c. For 1996, taxable income was $2 million, and tax liability was $680,000. For 1997, taxable income was $200,000, and tax liability was $68,000.

34. Mimi had $40,000 in federal income taxes withheld in 1998. Due to a sizable amount of itemized deductions, she figured that she had no further tax to pay for the year. For this reason and because of personal problems, and without securing an extension, she did not file her 1998 return until July 1, 1999. Actually, the return showed a refund of $2,400, which Mimi ultimately received. On May 10, 2002, Mimi filed a $16,000 claim for refund of her 1998 taxes.

    a. How much of the $16,000 will Mimi rightfully recover?
    b. How would your analysis differ if Mimi had secured from the IRS an automatic four-month extension of time for filing her 1998 return?

▶ _____   Research Cases

35. The Church of Freedom encourages its members to file "tax protestor" returns with the IRS, objecting to both (a) the government's failure to use a gold standard in payment of tax liabilities, and (b) its sizable expenditures for social welfare programs. These returns routinely are overturned by the tax court as frivolous, with delinquent taxes, penalties, and interest due, and the church has engaged in a long-standing, sometimes ugly battle with the IRS over various constitutional rights. Meanwhile, church members continue to file returns in this manner.

Ellen overheard church members talking about "roughing up" the IRS agents who were scheduled to conduct an audit of various members' returns. She went to the IRS and informed them of the danger that they might encounter. At the IRS's direction, Ellen then took a key clerical job at church headquarters. In this context, she had access to useful documentation and over a period of a few months gave to the IRS copies of church mailing lists and computer disks. She also helped tape record key conversations among church leaders and search the church's trash for other documents. In other words, Ellen helped the IRS build a case of civil and criminal tax fraud against the church and various of its members.

All of these materials were given voluntarily to Ellen by church leaders in her context as an employee. Church members never suspected that she was working with the IRS. After delivering the various materials to the IRS, Ellen quit her job with the church and severed all communications with the IRS.

After the parties were charged with fraud, the government's case was found to be insufficiently supported by the evidence, and no penalties were assessed. Afterward, church leaders sued Ellen in her role as IRS informant, charging that she had violated their First Amendment rights of free association, and their Fourth Amendment rights against illegal search and seizure. Government employees are immune from such charges, but Ellen was only an informant to the IRS and not its employee. Can the church collect damages from Ellen for informing on them?

36. Butcher attended meetings of tax protestors for many years in which the constitutionality of the federal income tax, and its means of collection, were routinely challenged. Members of various protestor groups were provided with materials to assist them in preparing returns such that little or no tax would be due on the basis that, for instance, only gold- or silver-backed currency need be submitted to pay the tax or that a tax bill had originated in the Senate rather than the House of Representatives. Some of the groups maintained that no returns need be filed by individuals at all on the grounds that the current law supporting a federal income tax violates various elements of the U.S. Constitution.

The U.S. Tax Court routinely overturned such means of avoiding the tax, charging that such protestor returns were frivolously filed, and charging the protestors with delinquent taxes, interest, and a variety of negligence and other accuracy-related penalties, especially where taxpayers failed to file altogether. The results of these cases never were discussed in the meetings that Butcher attended, though. Thus, although he never joined any of the groups, Butcher felt comfortable with the arguments of the protestor groups and never filed a federal income tax return for himself or his profitable sole-proprietorship carpentry business.

When the IRS discovered his failure to file and charged him with tax, interest, and penalties, Butcher went to the tax library and found that judicial precedent and administrative authority were stacked against him. He asked the court for relief from the civil fraud penalties related to his failure to file and failure to pay tax on the basis of his good-faith belief that the tax protestor information he had received was an acceptable interpretation of the law. Under this argument, a taxpayer cannot be found to willfully have failed to file and pay if he or she had a good-faith belief that no such requirement was supported by the Constitution. Should Butcher be required to pay civil fraud penalties?

37. Compute the overvaluation penalty for each of the following independent cases involving the taxpayer's reporting of the fair market value of charitable contribution property. In each case, assume a marginal income tax rate of 30 percent.

	Taxpayer	Corrected IRS Value	Reported Valuation
a.	Individual	$ 10,000	$ 20,000
b.	C Corporation	10,000	30,000
c.	S Corporation	10,000	30,000
d.	Individual	100,000	150,000
e.	Individual	100,000	300,000
f.	C Corporation	100,000	500,000

38. Compute the undervaluation penalty for each of the following independent cases involving the executor's reporting of the value of a closely held business in the decedent's gross estate. In each case, assume a marginal estate tax rate of 50 percent.

	Reported Value	Corrected IRS Valuation
a.	$12,000	$ 15,000
b.	50,000	90,000
c.	50,000	150,000
d.	50,000	200,000

39. Chang wants to claim a cost recovery deduction for the acquisition of masterwork paintings to be hung in the reception area of her dental office. The paintings were specially chosen because of their tendency to relax the patients who would be viewing them, thereby facilitating the conduct of Chang's business. Chang lives and works in the Fifth Circuit. A recent Eleventh Circuit case seems to support such a deduction, in limited circumstances. Complete the following chart, indicating for each independent assumption the actions that Chang can take without incurring the civil penalty for substantial understatement of taxes, but still maximizing her legitimate deductions for the year.

Probability of Success in Court	Claim the Deduction?	File a Form 8275 Disclosure?
80%		
40		
20		
2		

40. Continue with the facts of Research Case 39. Now assume that you are Chang's tax advisor. You wish to eliminate any chance of incurring a preparer civil unrealistic-position penalty. Indicate the actions that you would recommend that Chang take.

Probability of Success in Court	Claim the Deduction?	File a Form 8275 Disclosure?
80%		
40		
20		
2		

41. Your client, Lee Ann Harkness, has been accused of criminal tax fraud. A high school dropout, she received hundreds of thousands of dollars over the years from Bentley, an elderly gentleman, in exchange for love and companionship. When Bentley died and Harkness was left out of the will, she sued the estate for compensatory payments earned throughout her years of attending to Bentley. The government now accuses Harkness of fraud in failing to file income and self-employment tax returns for the open tax years. Construct a defense on Harkness's behalf.

42. The Scooter Company, owned equally by Julie (chair of the board of directors) and Jeff (company president), is in very difficult financial straits. Last month, Jeff used the $100,000 withheld from employee paychecks for federal payroll and income taxes to pay off a creditor who threatened to cut off all supplies. To keep the company afloat, Jeff used these government funds willfully for the operations of the business, but even that effort was not enough. The company missed the next two payrolls, and today other creditors took action to shut down Scooter altogether. How much will the IRS assess in taxes and penalties in the matter and from whom?

Appendixes

IRS Circular 230

Treasury
Department
Circular No. 230
(Rev. 7-94)

**Regulations Governing the
Practice of Attorneys,
Certified Public Accountants,
Enrolled Agents,
Enrolled Actuaries, and
Appraisers before the
Internal Revenue Service**

Department
of the
Treasury
**Internal
Revenue
Service**

**Title 31 Code of Federal Regulations,
Subtitle A, Part 10, revised as of
July 1, 1994**

Regulations Governing
the Practice of Attorneys,
Certified Public Accountants,
Enrolled Agents, Enrolled
Actuaries, and Appraisers
before the Internal
Revenue Service

Treasury
Department
Circular
No. 230
(Rev. 7-94)

This publication contains the revision of Treasury Department Circular No. 230 appearing in 31 F.R. 10773, dated August 13, 1966, and includes the following amendments:

Amendment appearing in 31 F.R. 12638, dated September 27, 1966, which adds omitted section heading § 10.58.

Amendments appearing in 31 F.R. 13992, dated November 2, 1966, which add subparagraphs (b) and (c) to § 10.57 and add a sentence at the end, and as a continuation, of paragraph (c) of § 10.51.

Amendments appearing in 31 F.R. 13205, dated August 19, 1970, which are intended primarily to clarify the language of certain provisions of the regulations, strengthen certain conflict of interest and disciplinary provisions, and update statutory references.

Amendment appearing in 36 F.R. 8671, dated May 11, 1971, which corrects error in the August 19, 1970, amendments, which incorrectly added a new sentence to subparagraph 10.3(c) rather than subparagraph 10.3 (e).

Amendments appearing in 42 F.R. 38350, dated July 28, 1977, which eliminate outdated terms and provisions, and which increase the restrictions on practice by former Government employees.

Amendments appearing in 44 F.R. 4940, dated January 24, 1979, which prescribe rules

permitting the expansion of advertising and solicitation provisions of the regulations governing practice by attorneys, certified public accounts, enrolled agents and others who represent clients before the Internal Revenue Service.

Amendments appearing in 44 F.R. 4944, dated January 24, 1979, which prescribe rules to permit enrolled actuaries to engage in practice before the Internal Revenue Service in connection with the provisions of the Internal Revenue Code involving pension plans under the Employee Retirement Income Security Act of 1974 (ERISA).

Amendments appearing in 49 F.R. 6719, dated February 23, 1984, which clarify who may prepare a tax return and furnish information to the Internal Revenue Service, and set standards for providing opinions used in the promotion of tax shelter offerings.

Amendments appearing in 50 F.R. 42014, dated October 17, 1985, which implement section 156 of the Deficit Reduction Act of 1984, 98 Stat. 695, to provide for the disqualification of appraisals and appraisers' testimony in connection with Treasury Department or Internal Revenue Service proceedings with respect to any appraiser who has been assessed an aiding and abetting penalty under 26 U.S.C. 6701(a) after July 18, 1984.

Amendments appearing in 51 F.R. 2875, dated January 22, 1986, which require that those who are enrolled to practice before the Internal Revenue Service renew their enrollment on a periodic basis. A condition of eligibility for renewal of enrollment will be the satisfaction of continuing professional education requirements. In addition, the amendments modify the regulations reflecting the transfer to the Office of Director of Practice of certain functions formerly performed by the Commissioner of Internal Revenue relative to the enrollment of individuals who wish to practice before the Internal Revenue Service.

Amendments appearing in 57 F.R. 41093, dated September 9, 1992, which relate to the provisions of the regulations addressing advertising and solicitation by those eligible to practice before the IRS, which were occa-sioned by judicial determinations impacting on the subject.

Amendments appearing in 59 F.R. 31523, dated June 20, 1994, which establish tax return preparation standards and prescribe the circumstances under which a practitioner may be disciplined for violating those standards, limit the use of contingent fees for preparing tax returns, clarify that certain existing restrictions governing limited practice before the IRS apply to all individuals who are eligible to engage in limited practice before the IRS, establish expedited proceedings to suspend individuals from practice before the IRS in cases in which certain determinations have been made by independent bodies, and permit attorneys and certified public accountants in good standing to obtain or retain enrolled agent status.

PART 10—PRACTICE BEFORE THE INTERNAL REVENUE SERVICE

Authority: Sec. 3, 23 Stat. 258, secs. 2-12, 60 Stat. 237 *et seq.;* 5 U.S.C. 301, 500, 551-559, 31 U.S.C. 1026; Reorg. Plan No. 26 of 1950, 15 FR 4935, 64 Stat. 1280, 3 CFR, 1949-1953 Comp., p. 1017.

Source: Treasury Department Circular 230, Revised, 31 FR 10773, Aug. 13, 1966, unless otherwise noted.

Editorial Note: Nomenclature changes affecting this part appear at 57 FR 41095, Sept. 9, 1992.

§10.0 Scope of part.

This part contains rules governing the recognition of attorneys, certified public accountants, enrolled agents, and other persons representing clients before the Internal Revenue Service. Subpart A of this part sets forth rules relating to authority to practice before the Internal Revenue Service; subpart B of this part prescribes the duties and restrictions relating to such practice; subpart C of this part contains rules relating to disciplinary proceedings; subpart D of this part contains rules applicable to disqualification of appraisers; and Subpart E of this part contains general provisions, including provisions relating to the availability of official records.

[59 FR 31526, June 20, 1994]

Subpart A — Rules Governing Authority To Practice

§10.1   Director of Practice.

(a) *Establishment of office*. There is established in the Office of the Secretary of the Treasury the office of Director of Practice. The Director of Practice shall be appointed by the Secretary of the Treasury.

(b) *Duties*. The Director of Practice shall act upon applications for enrollment to practice before the Internal Revenue Service; institute and provide for the conduct of disciplinary proceedings relating to attorneys, certified public accountants, enrolled agents, enrolled actuaries and appraisers; make inquiries with respect to matters under his jurisdiction; and perform such other duties as are necessary or appropriate to carry out his functions under this part or as are prescribed by the Secretary of the Treasury.

(c) *Acting Director*. The Secretary of the Treasury will designate an officer or employee of the Treasury Department to act as Director of Practice in the event of the absence of the director or of a vacancy in that office.

[31 FR 10773, Aug. 13, 1966, as amended at 51 FR 2878, Jan. 22, 1986]

§10.2   Definitions.

As used in this part, except where the context clearly indicates otherwise:

(a) *Attorney* means any person who is a member in good standing of the bar of the highest court of any State, possession, territory, Commonwealth, or the District of Columbia.

(b) *Certified Public Accountant* means any person who is duly qualified to practice as a certified public accountant in any State, possession, territory, Commonwealth, or the District of Columbia.

(c) *Commissioner* refers to the Commissioner of Internal Revenue.

(d) *Director* refers to the Director of Practice.

(e) *Practice before the Internal Revenue Service* comprehends all matters connected with a presentation to the Internal Revenue Service or any of its officers or employees relating to a client's rights, privileges, or liabilities under laws or regulations administered by the Internal Revenue Service. Such presentations include preparing and filing necessary documents, corresponding and communicating with the Internal Revenue Service, and representing a client at conferences, hearings, and meetings.

(f) *Practitioner* means any individual described in §10.3 (a), (b), (c), or (d) of this part.

(g) A *return* includes an amended return and a claim for refund.

(h) *Service* means the Internal Revenue Service.

[59 FR 31526, June 20, 1994]

§10.3   Who may practice.

(a) *Attorneys*. Any attorney who is not currently under suspension or disbarment from practice before the Internal Revenue Service may practice before the Service upon filing with the Service a written declaration that he or she is currently qualified as an attorney and is authorized to represent the particular party on whose behalf he or she acts.

(b) *Certified public accountants*. Any certified public accountant who is not currently under suspension or disbarment from practice before the Internal Revenue Service may practice before the Service upon filing with the Service a written declaration that he or she is currently qualified as a certified public accountant and is authorized to represent the particular party on whose behalf he or she acts.

(c) *Enrolled agents.* Any person enrolled as an agent pursuant to this part may practice before the Internal Revenue Service.

(d) *Enrolled Actuaries.* (1) Any individual who is enrolled as an actuary by the Joint Board for the Enrollment of Actuaries pursuant to 29 U.S.C. 1242 may practice before the Internal Revenue Service upon filing with the Service a written declaration that he/she is currently qualified as an enrolled actuary and is authorized to represent the particular party on whose behalf he/she acts. Practice as an enrolled actuary is limited to representation with respect to issues involving the following statutory provisions.

Internal Revenue Code (Title 26 U.S.C.) sections: 401 (qualification of employee plans), 403(a) (relating to whether an annuity plan meets the requirements of section 404(a)(2)), 404 (deductibility of employer contributions), 405 (qualification of bond purchase plans), 412 (funding requirements for certain employee plans), 413 (application of qualification requirements to collectively bargained plans and to plans maintained by more than one employer), 414 (containing definitions and special rules relating to the employee plan area), 4971 (relating to excise taxes payable as a result of an accumulated funding deficiency under section 412), 6057 (annual registration of plans), 6058 (information required in connection with certain plans of deferred compensation), 6059 (periodic report of actuary), 6652(e) (failure to file annual registration and other notifications by pension plan), 6652(f) (failure to file information required in connection with certain plans of deferred compensation), 6692 (failure to file actuarial report), 7805(b) (relating to

the extent, if any, to which an Internal Revenue Service ruling or determination letter coming under the herein listed statutory provisions shall be applied without retroactive effect), and 29 U.S.C. 1083 (relating to waiver of funding for nonqualified plans).

(2) An individual who practices before the Internal Revenue Service pursuant to this subsection shall be subject to the provisions of this part in the same manner as attorneys, certified public accountants and enrolled agents.

(e) *Others.* Any individual qualifying under §10.5(c) or §10.7 is eligible to practice before the Internal Revenue Service to the extent provided in those sections.

(f) *Government officers and employees, and others.* An individual, including an officer or employee of the executive, legislative, or judicial branch of the United States Government; officer or employee of the District of Columbia; Member of Congress; or Resident Commissioner, may not practice before the Service if such practice would violate 18 U.S.C. 203 or 205.

(g) *State officers and employees.* No officer or employee of any State, or subdivision thereof, whose duties require him to pass upon, investigate, or deal with tax matters of such State or subdivision, may practice before the Service, if such State employment may disclose facts or information applicable to Federal tax matters.

[31 FR 10773, Aug. 13, 1966, as amended at 35 FR 13205, Aug. 19, 1970; 36 FR 8671, May 11, 1971; 44 FR 4946, Jan. 24, 1979; 59 FR 31526, June 20, 1994]

§10.4 Eligibility for enrollment.

(a) *Enrollment upon examination.* The Director of Practice may grant enrollment to an applicant who demonstrates special competence in tax matters by written examination administered by the Internal Revenue Service and who has not engaged in any conduct which would justify the suspension or disbarment of any attorney, certified public accountant, or enrolled agent under the provisions of this part.

(b) *Enrollment of former Internal Revenue Service employees.* The Director of Practice may grant enrollment to an applicant who has not engaged in any conduct which would justify the suspension or disbarment of any attorney, certified public accountant, or enrolled agent under the provisions of this part and who, by virtue of his past service and technical experience in the Internal Revenue Service has qualified for such enrollment, as follows:

(1) Application for enrollment on account of former employment in the Internal Revenue Service shall be made to the Director of Practice. Each applicant will be supplied a form by the Director of Practice, which shall indicate the information required respecting the applicant's qualifications. In addition to the applicant's name, address, educational experience, etc., such information shall specifically include a detailed account of the applicant's employment in the Internal Revenue Service, which account shall show (i) positions held, (ii) date of each appointment and termination thereof, (iii) nature of services rendered in each position, with particular reference to the degree of technical experience involved, and (iv) name of supervisor in such positions, together with such other information regarding the experience and training of the applicant as may be relevant.

(2) Upon receipt of each such application, it shall be transmitted to the appropriate officer of the Internal Revenue Service with the request that a detailed report of the nature and rating of the applicant's services in the Internal Revenue Service, accompanied by the recommendation of the superior officer in the particular unit or division of the Internal Revenue Service that such employment does or does not qualify the applicant technically or otherwise for the desired authorization, be furnished to the Director of Practice.

(3) In examining the qualification of an applicant for enrollment on account of employment in the Internal Revenue Service, the Director of Practice will be governed by the following policies:

(i) Enrollment on account of such employment may be of unlimited scope or may be limited to permit the presentation of matters only of the particular class or only before the particular unit or division of the Internal Revenue Service for which his former employment in the Internal Revenue Service has qualified the applicant.

(ii) Application for enrollment on account of employment in the Internal Revenue Service must be made within 3 years from the date of separation from such employment.

(iii) It shall be requisite for enrollment on account of such employment that the applicant shall have had a minimum of 5 years continuous employment in the Service during which he shall have been regularly engaged in applying and interpreting the provisions of the Internal Revenue Code and the regulations thereunder relating to income, estate, gift, employment, or excise taxes.

(iv) For the purposes of paragraph (b)(3)(iii) of this section an aggregate of 10 or more years of employment, at least 3 of which occurred within the 5 years preceding the date of application, shall be deemed the equivalent of 5 years continuous employment.

(c) *Natural persons.* Enrollment to practice may be granted only to natural persons.

[31 FR 10773, Aug. 13, 1966, as amended at 35 FR 13205, Aug. 19, 1970; 42 FR 38352, July 28, 1977; 51 FR 2878, Jan. 22, 1986; 59 FR 31526, June 20, 1994]

§10.5   Application for enrollment.

(a) *Form; fee.* An applicant for enrollment shall file with the Director of Practice an application on Form 23, properly executed under oath or affirmation. Such application shall be accompanied by a check or money order in the amount set forth on Form 23, payable to the Internal Revenue Service, which amount shall constitute a fee which shall be charged to each applicant for enrollment. The fee shall be retained by the United States whether or not the applicant is granted enrollment.

(b) *Additional information; examination.* The Director of Practice, as a condition to consideration of an application for enrollment, may require the applicant to file additional information and to submit to any written or oral examination under oath or otherwise. The Director of Practice shall, upon written request, afford an applicant the opportunity to be heard with respect to his application for enrollment.

(c) *Temporary recognition.* Upon receipt of a properly executed application, the Director of Practice may grant the applicant temporary recognition to practice pending a determination as to whether enrollment to practice should be granted. Such temporary recognition shall not be granted if the application is not regular on its face; if the information stated therein, if true, is not sufficient to warrant enrollment to practice; if there is any information before the Director of Practice which indicates that the statements in the application are untrue; or which indicates that the applicant would not otherwise qualify for enrollment. Issuance of temporary recognition shall not constitute enrollment to practice or a finding of eligibility for enrollment, and the temporary recognition may be withdrawn at any time by the Director of Practice.

(d) *Appeal from denial of application.* The Director of Practice, in denying an application for enrollment, shall inform the applicant as to the reason(s) therefor. The applicant may, within 30 days after receipt of the notice of denial, file a written appeal therefrom, together with his/her reasons in support thereof, to the Secretary of the Treasury. A decision on the appeal will be rendered by the Secretary of the Treasury as soon as practicable.

(Sec. 501, Pub. L. 82-137, 65 Stat. 290; 31 U.S.C. 483a)

[31 FR 10773, Aug. 13, 1966, as amended at 42 FR 38352, July 28, 1977; 51 FR 2878, Jan. 22, 1986]

§10.6 Enrollment.

(a) *Roster.* The Director of Practice shall maintain rosters of all individuals:

(1) Who have been granted active enrollment to practice before the Internal Revenue Service;

(2) Whose enrollment has been placed in an inactive status for failure to meet the requirements for renewal of enrollment;

(3) Whose enrollment has been placed in an inactive retirement status;

(4) Who have been disbarred or suspended from practice before the Internal Revenue Service;

(5) Whose offer of consent to resignation from enrollment to practice before the Internal Revenue Service has been accepted by the Director of Practice under §10.55 of this part; and

(6) Whose application for enrollment has been denied.

(b) *Enrollment card.* The Director of Practice will issue an enrollment card to each individual whose application for enrollment to practice before the Internal Revenue Service is approved after the effective date of this regulation. Each such enrollment card will be valid for the period stated thereon. Enrollment cards issued individuals before February 1, 1987 shall become invalid after March 31, 1987. An individual having an invalid enrollment card is not eligible to practice before the Internal Revenue Service.

(c) *Term of enrollment.* Active enrollment to practice before the Internal Revenue Service is accorded each individual enrolled, so long as renewal of enrollment is effected as provided in this part.

(d) *Renewal of enrollment*. To maintain active enrollment to practice before the Internal Revenue Service, each individual enrolled is required to have his/her enrollment renewed as set forth herein. Failure by an individual to receive notification from the Director of Practice of the renewal requirement will not be justification for circumvention of such requirement.

(1) All individuals enrolled to practice before the Internal Revenue Service before November 1, 1986 shall apply for renewal of enrollment during the period between November 1, 1986 and January 31, 1987. Those who receive initial enrollment between November 1, 1986 and January 31, 1987 shall apply for renewal of enrollment by March 1, 1987. The first effective date of renewal will be April 1, 1987.

(2) Thereafter, applications for renewal will be required between November 1, 1989 and January 31, 1990, and between November 1 and January 31 of every third year subsequent thereto. Those who receive initial enrollment during the renewal application period shall apply for renewal of enrollment by March 1 of the renewal year. The effective date of renewed enrollment will be April 1, 1990, and April 1 of every third year subsequent thereto.

(3) The Director of Practice will notify the individual of renewal of enrollment and will issue a card evidencing such renewal.

(4) A reasonable nonrefundable fee may be charged for each application for renewal of enrollment filed with the Director of Practice.

(5) Forms required for renewal may be obtained from the Director of Practice, Internal Revenue Service, Washington, DC 20224.

(e) *Condition for renewal: Continuing Professional Education*. In order to qualify for renewal of enrollment, an individual enrolled to practice before the Internal Revenue Service must certify, on the application for renewal form prescribed by the Director of Practice, that he/she has satisfied the following continuing professional education requirements.

(1) *For renewed enrollment effective April 1, 1987*. (i) A minimum of 24 hours of continuing education credit must be completed between January 1, 1986 and January 31, 1987.

(ii) An individual who receives initial enrollment between January 1, 1986 and January 31, 1987 is exempt from the continuing education requirement for the renewal of enrollment effective April 1, 1987, but is required to file a timely application for renewal of enrollment.

(2) For renewed enrollment effective April 1, 1990 and every third year thereafter. (i) A minimum of 72 hours of continuing education credit must be completed between February 1, 1987 and January 31, 1990, and during each three year period subsequent thereto. Each such three year period is known as an enrollment cycle.

(ii) A minimum of 16 hours of continuing education credit must be completed in each year of an enrollment cycle.

(iii) An individual who receives initial enrollment during an enrollment cycle must complete two (2) hours of qualifying continuing education credit for each month enrolled during such enrollment cycle. Enrollment for any part of a month is considered enrollment for the entire month.

(f) *Qualifying continuing education — (1) In General*. To qualify for continuing education credit, a course of learning must:

(i) Be a qualifying program designed to enhance the professional knowledge of an individual in Federal taxation or Federal tax related matters, i.e. programs comprised of current subject matter in Federal taxation or Federal tax related matters to include accounting, financial management, business computer science and taxation; and

(ii) Be conducted by a qualifying sponsor.

(2) *Qualifying programs. (i) Formal programs*. Formal programs qualify as continuing education programs if they:

(A) Require attendance;

(B) Require that the program be conducted by a qualified instructor, discussion leader or speaker, i.e. a person whose background, training, education and/or experience is appropriate for instructing or leading a discussion on the subject matter of the particular program; and

(C) Require a written outline and/or textbook and certificate of attendance provided by the sponsor, all of which must be retained by the attendee for a three year period following renewal of enrollment.

(ii) *Correspondence or individual study programs (including taped programs).* Qualifying continuing education programs include correspondence or individual study programs completed on an individual basis by the enrolled individual and conducted by qualifying sponsors. The allowable credit hours for such programs will be measured on a basis comparable to the measurement of a seminar or course for credit in an accredited educational institution. Such programs qualify as continuing education programs if they:

(A) Require registration of the participants by the sponsor;

(B) Provide a means for measuring completion by the participants (e.g., written examination); and

(C) Require a written outline and/or textbook and certificate of completion provided by the sponsor which must be retained by the participant for a three year period following renewal of enrollment.

(iii) *Serving as an instructor, discussion leader or speaker.*

(A) One hour of continuing education credit will be awarded for each contact hour completed as an instructor, discussion leader or speaker at an educational program which meets the continuing education requirements of this part.

(B) Two hours of continuing education credit will be awarded for actual subject preparation time for each contact hour completed as an instructor, discussion leader

or speaker at such programs. It will be the responsibility of the individual claiming such credit to maintain records to verify preparation time.

(C) The maximum credit for instruction and preparation may not exceed 50% of the continuing education requirement for an enrollment cycle.

(D) Presentation of the same subject matter in an instructor, discussion leader or speaker capacity more than one time during an enrollment cycle will not qualify for continuing education credit.

(iv) *Credit for published articles, books, etc.*

(A) Continuing education credit will be awarded for publications on Federal taxation or Federal tax related matters to include accounting, financial management, business computer science, and taxation, provided the content of such publications is current and designed for the enhancement of the professional knowledge of an individual enrolled to practice before the Internal Revenue Service.

(B) The credit allowed will be on the basis of one hour credit for each hour of preparation time for the material. It will be the responsibility of the person claiming the credit to maintain records to verify preparation time.

(C) The maximum credit for publications may not exceed 25% of the continuing education requirement of any enrollment cycle.

(3) *Periodic examination.* Individuals may establish eligibility for renewal of enrollment for any enrollment cycle by:

(i) Achieving a passing score on each part of the Special Enrollment Examination administered under this part during the three year period prior to renewal; and

(ii) Completing a minimum of 16 hours of qualifying continuing education during the last year of an enrollment cycle.

(g) *Sponsors.* (1) Sponsors are those responsible for presenting programs.

(2) To qualify as a sponsor, a program presenter must:

(i) Be an accredited educational institution;

(ii) Be recognized for continuing education purposes by the licensing body of any State, possession, territory, Commonwealth, or the District of Columbia responsible for the issuance of a license in the field of accounting or law;

(iii) Be recognized by the Director of Practice as a professional organization or society whose programs include offering continuing professional education opportunities in subject matter within the scope of this part; or

(iv) File a sponsor agreement with the Director of Practice to obtain approval of the program as a qualified continuing education program.

(3) A qualifying sponsor must ensure the program complies with the following requirements:

(i) Programs must be developed by individual(s) qualified in the subject matter;

(ii) Program subject matter must be current;

(iii) Instructors, discussion leaders, and speakers must be qualified with respect to program content;

(iv) Programs must include some means for evaluation of technical content and presentation;

(v) Certificates of completion must be provided those who have successfully completed the program; and

(vi) Records must be maintained by the sponsor to verify completion of the program and attendance by each participant. Such records must be retained for a period of three years following completion of the program. In the case of continuous conferences, conventions, and the like, records must be maintained to verify completion of the program and attendance by each participant at each segment of the program.

(4) Professional organizations or societies wishing to be considered as qualified sponsors shall request such status of the Director of Practice and furnish information in support of the request together with any further information deemed necessary by the Director of Practice.

(5) Sponsor agreements and qualified professional organization or society sponsors approved by the Director of Practice shall remain in effect for one enrollment cycle. The names of such sponsors will be published on a periodic basis.

(h) *Measurement of continuing education coursework.* (1) All continuing education programs will be measured in terms of contact hours. The shortest recognized program will be one contact hour.

(2) A contact hour is 50 minutes of continuous participation in a program. Credit is granted only for a full contact hour, i.e. 50 minutes or multiples thereof. For example, a program lasting more than 50 minutes but less than 100 minutes will count as one contact hour.

(3) Individual segments at continuous conferences, conventions and the like will be considered one total program. For example, two 90-minute segments (180 minutes) at a continuous conference will count as three contact hours.

(4) For university or college courses, each semester hour credit will equal 15 contact hours and a quarter hour credit will equal 10 contact hours.

(i) *Recordkeeping requirements.* (1) Each individual applying for renewal shall retain for a period of three years following the date of renewal of enrollment the information required with regard to qualifying continuing professional education credit hours. Such information shall include:

(i) The name of the sponsoring organization;

(ii) The location of the program;

(iii) The title of the program and description of its content, e.g., course syllibi and/or textbook;

(iv) The dates attended;

(v) The credit hours claimed;

(vi) The name(s) of the instructor(s), discussion leader(s), or speaker(s), if appropriate; and

(vii) The certificate of completion and/or signed statement of the hours of attendance obtained from the sponsor.

(2) To receive continuing education credit for service completed as an instructor, discussion leader, or speaker, the following information must be maintained for a period of three years following the date of renewal of enrollment:

(i) The name of the sponsoring organization;

(ii) The location of the program;

(iii) The title of the program and description of its content;

(iv) The dates of the program; and

(v) The credit hours claimed.

(3) To receive continuing education credit for publications, the following information must be maintained for a period of three years following the date of renewal of enrollment:

(i) The publisher;

(ii) The title of the publication;

(iii) A copy of the publication; and

(iv) The date of publication.

(j) *Waivers.* (1) Waiver from the continuing education requirements for a given period may be granted by the Director of Practice for the following reasons:

(i) Health, which prevented compliance with the continuing education requirements;

(ii) Extended active military duty;

(iii) Absence from the United States for an extended period of time due to employ-ment or other reasons, provided the individual does not practice before the Internal Revenue Service during such absence; and

(iv) Other compelling reasons, which will be considered on a case-by-case basis.

(2) A request for waiver must be accompa-nied by appropriate documentation. The individual will be required to furnish any additional documentation or explanation deemed necessary by the Director of Practice. Examples of appropriate documentation could be a medical certificate, military orders, etc.

(3) A request for waiver must be filed no later than the last day of the renewal application period.

(4) If a request for waiver is not approved, the individual will be so notified by the Director of Practice and placed on a roster of inactive enrolled individuals.

(5) If a request for waiver is approved, the individual will be so notified and issued a card evidencing such renewal.

(6) Those who are granted waivers are required to file timely applications for renewal of enrollment.

(k) *Failure to comply.* (1) Compliance by an individual with the requirements of this part shall be determined by the Director of Practice. An individual who fails to meet the requirements of eligibility for renewal of enrollment will be notified by the Director of Practice at his/her last known address by first class mail. The notice will state the basis for the non-compliance and will provide the individual an opportunity to furnish in writing information relating to the matter within 60 days of the date of the notice. Such information will be considered by the Director of Practice in making a final determination as to eligibility for renewal of enrollment.

(2) The Director of Practice may require any individual, by first class mail to his/her last known mailing address, to provide copies of any records required to be maintained under this part. The Director of Practice may disallow any continuing professional education hours claimed if the individual concerned fails to comply with such requirement.

(3) An individual who has not filed a timely application for renewal of enrollment, who has not made a timely response to the notice of non-compliance with the renewal requirements, or who has not satisfied the requirements of eligibility for renewal will be placed on a roster of inactive enrolled individuals for a period of three years. During this time, the individual will be ineligible to practice before the Internal Revenue Service.

(4) During inactive enrollment status or at any other time an individual is ineligible to practice before the Internal Revenue

Service, such individual shall not in any manner, directly or indirectly, indicate he or she is enrolled to practice before the Internal Revenue Service, or use the term "enrolled agent," the designation "E. A.," or other form of reference to eligibility to practice before the Internal Revenue Service.

(5) An individual placed in an inactive status may satisfy the requirements for renewal of enrollment during his/her period of inactive enrollment. If such satisfaction includes completing the continuing education requirement, a minimum of 16 hours of qualifying continuing education hours must be completed in the 12 month period preceding the date on which the renewal application is filed. Continuing education credit under this subsection may not be used to satisfy the requirements of the enrollment cycle in which the individual has been placed back on the active roster.

(6) An individual placed in an inactive status must file an application for renewal of enrollment and satisfy the requirements for renewal as set forth in this section within three years of being placed in an inactive status. The name of such individual otherwise will be removed from the inactive enrollment roster and his/her enrollment will terminate. Eligibility for enrollment must then be reestablished by the individual as provided in this part.

(7) Inactive enrollment status is not available to an individual who is the subject of a discipline matter in the Office of Director of Practice.

(l) *Inactive retirement status.* An individual who no longer practices before the Internal Revenue Service may request being placed in an inactive status at any time and such individual will be placed in an inactive retirement status. The individual will be ineligible to practice before the Internal Revenue Service. Such individual must file a timely application for renewal of enrollment at each applicable renewal or enrollment as provided in this part. An individual who is placed in an inactive re-

tirement status may be reinstated to an active enrollment status upon filing an application for renewal of enrollment and providing evidence of the completion of the required continuing professional education hours for the enrollment cycle. Inactive retirement status is not available to an individual who is the subject to a discipline matter in the Office of Director of Practice.

(m) *Renewal while under suspension or disbarment.* An individual who is ineligible to practice before the Internal Revenue Service by virtue of disciplinary action is required to meet the requirements for renewal of enrollment during the period of ineligibility.

(n) *Verification.* The Director of Practice may review the continuing education records of an enrolled individual and/or qualified sponsor in a manner deemed appropriate to determine compliance with the requirements and standards for renewal of enrollment as provided in this part.

(Approved by the Office of Management and Budget under control number 1545-0946)

[51 FR 2878, Jan. 22, 1986]

§10.7   **Representing oneself; participating in rulemaking; limited practice; special appearances; and return preparation.**

(a) *Representing oneself.* Individuals may appear on their own behalf before the Internal Revenue Service provided they present satisfactory identification.

(b) *Participating in rulemaking.* Individuals may participate in rulemaking as provided by the Administrative Procedure Act. See 5 U.S.C. 553.

(c) *Limited practice* — (1) *In general.* Subject to the limitations in paragraph (c)(2) of this section, an individual who is not a practitioner may represent a taxpayer before the Internal Revenue Service in the circumstances described in this paragraph (c)(1), even if the taxpayer is not present, provided the individual presents satisfactory identification and proof of his or her authority to represent the taxpayer. The circumstances described in this paragraph (c)(1) are as follows:

(i) An individual may represent a member of his or her immediate family.

(ii) A regular full-time employee of an individual employer may represent the employer.

(iii) A general partner or a regular full-time employee of a partnership may represent the partnership.

(iv) A bona fide officer or a regular full-time employee of a corporation (including a parent, subsidiary, or other affiliated corporation), association, or organized group may represent the corporation, association, or organized group.

(v) A trustee, receiver, guardian, personal representative, administrator, executor, or regular full-time employee of a trust, receivership, guardianship, or estate may represent the trust, receivership, guardianship, or estate.

(vi) An officer or a regular employee of a governmental unit, agency, or authority may represent the governmental unit, agency, or authority in the course of his or her official duties.

(vii) An individual may represent any individual or entity before personnel of the Internal Revenue Service who are outside of the United States.

(viii) An individual who prepares and signs a taxpayer's return as the preparer, or who prepares a return but is not required (by the instructions to the return or regulations) to sign the return, may represent the taxpayer before officers and employees of the Examination Division of the Internal Revenue Service with respect to the tax liability of the taxpayer for the taxable year or period covered by that return.

(2) *Limitations.*

(i) An individual who is under suspension or disbarment from practice before the Internal Revenue Service may not engage in limited practice before the Service under §10.7(c)(1).

(ii) The Director, after notice and opportunity for a conference, may deny eligibility to engage in limited practice before the Internal Revenue Service under §10.7(c)(1) to any individual who has engaged in conduct that would justify suspending or disbarring a practitioner from practice before the Service.

(iii) An individual who represents a taxpayer under the authority of §10.7(c)(1)(viii) is subject to such rules of general applicability regarding standards of conduct, the extent of his or her authority, and other matters as the Director prescribes.

(d) *Special appearances.* The Director, subject to such conditions as he or she deems appropriate, may authorize an individual who is not otherwise eligible to practice before the Service to represent another person in a particular matter.

(e) *Preparing tax returns and furnishing information.* Any individual may prepare a tax return, appear as a witness for the taxpayer before the Internal Revenue Service, or furnish information at the request of the Service or any of its officers or employees.

[59 FR 31526, June 20, 1994]

§10.8 Customhouse brokers.

Nothing contained in the regulations in this part shall be deemed to affect or limit the right of a customhouse broker, licensed as such by the Commissioner of Customs in accordance with the regulations prescribed therefor, in any customs district in which he is so licensed, at the office of the District Director of Internal Revenue or before the National Office of the Internal Revenue Service, to act as a representative in respect to any matters relating specifically to the importation or exportation of merchandise under the customs or internal revenue laws, for any person for whom he has acted as a customhouse broker.

Subpart B — Duties and Restrictions Relating to Practice Before the Internal Revenue Service

§10.20   Information to be furnished.

(a) *To the Internal Revenue Service.* No attorney, certified public accountant, enrolled agent, or enrolled actuary shall neglect or refuse promptly to submit records or information in any matter before the Internal Revenue Service, upon proper and lawful request by a duly authorized officer or employee of the Internal Revenue Service, or shall interfere, or attempt to interfere, with any proper and lawful effort by the Internal Revenue Service or its officers or employees to obtain any such record or information, unless he believes in good faith and on reasonable grounds that such record or information is privileged or that the request for, or effort to obtain, such record or information is of doubtful legality.

(b) *To the Director of Practice.* It shall be the duty of an attorney or certified public accountant, who practices before the Internal Revenue Service, or enrolled agent, when requested by the Director of Practice, to provide the Director with any information he may have concerning violation of the regulations in this part by any person, and to testify thereto in any proceeding instituted under this part for the disbarment or suspension of an attorney, certified public accountant, enrolled agent, or enrolled actuary, unless he believes in good faith and on reasonable grounds that such information is privileged or that the request therefor is of doubtful legality.

[31 FR 10773, Aug. 13, 1966, as amended at 57 FR 41095, Sept. 9, 1992]

§10.21   Knowledge of client's omission.

Each attorney, certified public accountant, enrolled agent, or enrolled actuary who, having been retained by a client with respect to a matter administered by the Internal Revenue Service, knows that the client has not complied with the revenue laws of the United States or has made an error in or omission from any return, document, affidavit, or other paper which the client is required by the revenue laws of the United States to execute, shall advise the client promptly of the fact of such noncompliance, error, or omission.

[42 FR 38352, July 28, 1977, as amended at 57 FR 41095, Sept. 9, 1992]

§10.22   Diligence as to accuracy.

Each attorney, certified public accountant, enrolled agent, or enrolled actuary shall exercise due diligence:

(a) In preparing or assisting in the preparation of, approving, and filing returns, documents, affidavits, and other papers relating to Internal Revenue Service matters;

(b) In determining the correctness of oral or written representations made by him to the Department of the Treasury; and

(c) In determining the correctness of oral or written representations made by him to clients with reference to any matter administered by the Internal Revenue Service.

[35 FR 13205, Aug. 19, 1970, as amended at 42 FR 38352, July 28, 1977; 57 FR 41095, Sept. 9, 1992]

§10.23   Prompt disposition of pending matters.

No attorney, certified public accountant, enrolled agent, or enrolled actuary shall unreasonably delay the prompt disposition of any matter before the Internal Revenue Service.

§10.24   Assistance from disbarred or suspended persons and former Internal Revenue Service employees.

No attorney, certified public accountant, enrolled agent, or enrolled actuary shall, in practice before the Internal Revenue Service, knowingly and directly or indirectly:

(a) Employ or accept assistance from any person who is under disbarment or suspension from practice before the Internal Revenue Service.

(b) Accept employment as associate, correspondent, or subagent from, or share fees with, any such person.

(c) Accept assistance from any former government employee where the provisions of §10.26 of these regulations or any Federal law would be violated.

[44 FR 4943, Jan. 24, 1979, as amended at 57 FR 41095, Sept. 9, 1992]

§10.25 Practice by partners of Government employees.

No partner of an officer or employee of the executive branch of the U.S. Government, of any independent agency of the United States, or of the District of Columbia, shall represent anyone in any matter administered by the Internal Revenue Service in which such officer or employee of the Government participates or has participated personally and substantially as a Government employee or which is the subject of his official responsibility.

[31 FR 10773, Aug. 13, 1966, as amended at 35 FR 13205, Aug. 19, 1970]

§10.26 Practice by former Government employees, their partners and their associates.

(a) *Definitions.* For purposes of §10.26: (1) *Assist* means to act in such a way as to advise, furnish information to, or otherwise aid another person, directly of indirectly.

(2) *Government employee* is an officer or employee of the United States or any agency of the United States, including a *special government employee* as defined in 18 U.S.C. 202(a), or of the District of Columbia, or of any State, or a member of Congress or of any State legislature.

(3) *Member of a firm* is a sole practitioner or an employee or associate thereof, or a partner, stockholder, associate, affiliate or employee of a partnership, joint venture, corporation, professional association or other affiliation of two or more practitioners who represent non-Government parties.

(4) *Practitioner* includes any individual described in §10.3(e).

(5) *Official responsibility* means the direct administrative or operating authority, whether intermediate or final, and either exercisable alone or with others, and either personally or through subordinates, to approve, disapprove, or otherwise direct Government action, with or without knowledge of the action.

(6) *Participate* or *participation* means substantial involvement as a Government employee by making decisions, or preparing or reviewing documents with or without the right to exercise a judgment of approval or disapproval, or participating in conferences or investigations, or rendering advice of a substantial nature.

(7) *Rule* includes Treasury Regulations, whether issued or under preparation for issuance as Notices of Proposed Rule Making or as Treasury Decisions, and revenue rulings and revenue procedures published in the Internal Revenue bulletin. *Rule* shall not include a *transaction* as defined in paragraph (a)(9) of this section.

(8) *Transaction* means any decision, determination, finding, letter ruling, technical advice, contract or approval or disapproval thereof, relating to a particular factual situation or situations involving a specific party or parties whose rights, privileges, or liabilities under laws or regulations administered by the Internal Revenue Service, or other legal rights, are determined or immediately affected therein and to which the United States is a party or in which it has a direct and substantial interest, whether or not the same taxable periods are involved. *Transaction* does not include *rule* as defined in paragraph (a)(7) of this section.

(b) *General rules.* (1) No former Government employee shall, subsequent to his Government employment, represent anyone in any matter administered by the Internal Revenue Service if the representation would violate 18 U.S.C. 207 (a) or (b) or any other laws of the United States.

(2) No former Government employee who participated in a transaction shall, subsequent to his Government employment, represent or knowingly assist, in that transaction, any person who is or was a specific party to that transaction.

(3) No former Government employee who within a period of one year prior to the termination of his Government employment had official responsibility for a transaction shall, within one year after his Government employment is ended, represent or knowingly assist in that transaction any person who is or was a specific party to that transaction.

(4) No former Government employee shall, within one year after his Government employment is ended, appear before any employee of the Treasury Department in connection with the publication, withdrawal, amendment, modification, or interpretation of a rule in the development of which the former Government employee participated or for which, within a period of one year prior to the termination of his Government employment, he had official responsibility. However, this subparagraph does not preclude such former employee for appearing on his own behalf or from representing a taxpayer before the Internal Revenue Service in connection with a transaction involving the application or interpretation of such a rule with respect to that transaction: *Provided,* That such former employee shall not utilize or disclose any confidential information acquired by the former employee in the development of the rule, and shall not contend that the rule is invalid or illegal. In addition, this subparagraph does not preclude such former employee from otherwise advising or acting for any person.

(c) *Firm representation.* (1) No member of a firm of which a former Government employee is a member may represent or knowingly assist a person who was or is a specific party in any transaction with respect to which the restrictions of paragraph (b)(1) (other than 18 U.S.C. 207 (b)) or (b)(2) of this section apply to the former Government employee, in that transaction, unless:

(i) No member of the firm who had knowledge of the participation by the Government employee in the transaction initiated discussions with the Government employee concerning his becoming a member of the firm until his Government employment is ended or six months after the termination of his participation in the transaction, whichever is earlier;

(ii) The former Government employee did not initiate any discussions concerning becoming a member of the firm while participating in the transaction or, if such discussions were initiated, they conformed with the requirements of 18 U.S.C. 208(b); and

(iii) The firm isolates the former Government employee in such a way that he does not assist in the representation.

(2) No member of a firm of which a former Government employee is a member may represent or knowingly assist a person who was or is a specific party in any transaction with respect to which the restrictions of paragraph (b)(3) of this section apply to the former employee, in that transaction, unless the firm isolates the former Government employee in such a way that he does not assist in the representation.

(3) When isolation of the former Government employee is required under paragraphs (c)(1) or (c)(2) of this section, a statement affirming the fact of such isolation shall be executed under oath by the former Government employee and by a member of the firm acting on behalf of the firm, and shall be filed with the Director of Practice and in such other place and in the manner prescribed by regulation. This statement shall clearly identify the firm, the former Government employee, and the transaction or transactions requiring such isolation.

(d) *Pending representation.* Practice by former Government employees, their partners and associates with respect to representation in specific matters where actual representation commenced before publication of this regulation is governed by the regulations set forth in the June 1972 amendments to the regulations of this part (published at 37 FR 11676): *Provided,* That the burden of showing that representation commenced before publication is with the former Government employees, their partners and associates.

[42 FR 38352, July 28, 1977, as amended at 57 FR 41095, Sept. 9, 1992; 59 FR 31527, June 20, 1994]

§10.27   Notaries.

No attorney, certified public accountant, enrolled agent, or enrolled actuary as notary public shall with respect to any matter administered by the Internal Revenue Service take acknowledgments, administer oaths, certify papers, or perform any official act in connection with matters in which he is employed as counsel, attorney, or agent, or in which he may be in any way interested before the Internal Revenue Service (26 Op. Atty. Gen. 236).

[31 FR 10773, Aug. 13, 1966, as amended at 57 FR 41095, Sept. 9, 1992]

§10.28   Fees.

(a) *Generally.* A practitioner may not charge an unconscionable fee for representing a client in a matter before the Internal Revenue Service.

(b) *Contingent fees for return preparation.* A practitioner may not charge a contingent fee for preparing an original return. A practitioner may charge a contingent fee for preparing an amended return or a claim for refund (other than a claim for refund made on an original return) if the practitioner reasonably anticipates at the time the fee arrangement is entered into that the amended return or claim will receive substantive review by the Service. A contingent fee includes a fee that is based on a percentage of the refund shown on a return or a percentage of the taxes saved, or that otherwise depends on the specific result attained.

[59 FR 31527, June 20, 1994]

§10.29   Conflicting interests.

No attorney, certified public accountant, enrolled agent, or enrolled actuary shall represent conflicting interests in his practice before the Internal Revenue Service, except by express consent of all directly interested parties after full disclosure has been made.

[31 FR 10773, Aug. 13, 1966, as amended at 57 FR 41095, Sept. 9, 1992]

§10.30   Solicitation.

(a) *Advertising and solicitation restrictions.* (1) No attorney, certified public accountant, enrolled agent, enrolled actuary, or other individual eligible to practice before the Internal Revenue Service shall, with respect to any Internal Revenue Service matter, in any way use or participate in the use of any form of public communication containing (i) A false, fraudulent, unduly influencing, coercive, or unfair statement or claim; or (ii) a misleading or deceptive statement or claim.

Enrolled agents, in describing their professional designation, may not utilize the term of art "certified" or indicate an employer/employee relationship with the Internal Revenue Service. Examples of acceptable descriptions are "enrolled to represent taxpayers before the Internal Revenue Service," "enrolled to practice before the Internal Revenue Service," and "admitted to practice before the Internal

Revenue Service." Enrolled agents and enrolled actuaries may abbreviate such designation to either EA or E.A.

(2) No attorney, certified public accountant, enrolled agent, enrolled actuary, or other individual eligible to practice before the Internal Revenue Service shall make, directly or indirectly, an uninvited solicitation of employment in matters related to the Internal Revenue Service. Solicitation includes, but is not limited to, in-person contacts and telephone communications. This restriction does not apply to (i) Seeking new business from an existing or former client in a related matter; (ii) communications with family members; (iii) making the availability of professional services known to other practitioners, so long as the person or firm contacted is not a potential client; (iv) solicitation by mailings; or (v) non-coercive in-person solicitation by those eligible to practice before the Internal Revenue Service while acting as an employee, member, or officer of an exempt organization listed in sections 501(c)(3) or (4) of the Internal Revenue Code of 1954 (26 U.S.C.).

Any targeted direct mail solicitation, i.e. a mailing to those whose unique circumstances are the basis for the solicitation, distributed by or on behalf of an attorney, certified public accountant, enrolled agent, enrolled actuary, or other individual eligible to practice before the Internal Revenue Service shall be clearly marked as such in capital letters on the envelope and at the top of the first page of such mailing. In addition, all such solicitations must clearly identify the source of the information used in choosing the recipient.

(b) *Fee information.* (1) Attorneys, certified public accountants, enrolled agents, or enrolled actuaries and other individuals eligible to practice before the Internal Revenue Service may disseminate the following fee information:

(i) Fixed fees for specific routine services.

(ii) Hourly rates.

(iii) Range of fees for particular services.

(iv) Fee charged for an initial consultation.

Any statement of fee information concerning matters in which costs may be incurred shall include a statement disclosing whether clients will be responsible for such costs.

(2) Attorneys, certified public accountants, enrolled agents, or enrolled actuaries and other individuals eligible to practice before the Internal Revenue Service may also publish the availability of a written schedule of fees.

(3) Attorneys, certified public accountants, enrolled agents, or enrolled actuaries and other individuals eligible to practice before the Internal Revenue Service shall be bound to charge the hourly rate, the fixed fee for specific routine services, the range of fees for particular services, or the fee for an initial consultation published for a reasonable period of time, but no less than thirty days from the last publication of such hourly rate or fees.

(c) *Communications.* Communication, including fee information, may include professional lists, telephone directories, print media, mailings, radio and television, and any other method: *Provided,* that the method chosen does not cause the communication to become untruthful, deceptive, unduly influencing or otherwise in violation of these regulations. It shall be construed as a violation of these regulations for a practitioner to persist in attempting to contact a prospective client, if such client has made known to the practitioner a desire not to be solicited. In the case of radio and television broadcasting, the broadcast shall be pre-recorded and the practitioner shall retain a recording of the actual audio transmission. In the case of direct mail communications, the practitioner shall retain a copy of the actual mailing, along with a list or other description of persons to whom the communication was mailed or otherwise distributed. Such copy shall be retained by the practitioner for a period of at least 36 months from the date of the last transmission or use.

(d) *Improper associations.* An attorney, certified public accountant, enrolled agent, or enrolled actuary may, in matters related to the Internal Revenue Service, employ or accept employment or assistance as an associate, correspondent, or subagent from, or share fees with, any person or entity who, to the knowledge of the practitioner, obtains clients or otherwise practices in a manner forbidden under this section: *Provided,* That a practitioner does not, directly or indirectly, act or hold himself out as an Internal Revenue Service practitioner in connection with that relationship. Nothing herein shall prohibit an attorney, certified public accountant, or enrolled agent from practice before the Internal Revenue Service in a capacity other than that described above.

[44 FR 4943, Jan. 24, 1979, as amended at 57 FR 41095, Sept. 9, 1992]

§10.31 Negotiation of taxpayer refund checks.

No attorney, certified public accountant, enrolled agent, or enrolled actuary who is an income tax return preparer shall endorse or otherwise negotiate any check made in respect of income taxes which is issued to a taxpayer other than the attorney, certified public accountant or enrolled agent.

[42 FR 38353, July 28, 1977, as amended at 57 FR 41095, Sept. 9, 1992]

§10.32 Practice of law.

Nothing in the regulations in this part shall be construed as authorizing persons not members of the bar to practice law.

[31 FR 10773, Aug. 13, 1966. Redesignated at 42 FR 38353, July 28, 1977]

§10.33 Tax shelter opinions.

(a) *Tax shelter opinions and offering materials.* A practitioner who provides a tax shelter opinion analyzing the Federal tax effects of a tax shelter investment shall comply with each of the following requirements:

(1) *Factual matters.* (i) The practitioner must make inquiry as to all relevant facts, be satisfied that the material facts are accurately and completely described in the offering materials, and assure that any representations as to future activities are clearly identified, reasonable and complete.

(ii) A practitioner may not accept as true asserted facts pertaining to the tax shelter which he/she should not, based on his/her background and knowledge, reasonably believe to be true. However, a practitioner need not conduct an audit or independent verification of the asserted facts, or assume that a client's statement of the facts cannot be relied upon, unless he/she has reason to believe that any relevant facts asserted to him/her are untrue.

(iii) If the fair market value of property or the expected financial performance of an investment is relevant to the tax shelter, a practitioner may not accept an appraisal or financial projection as support for the matters claimed therein unless:

(A) The appraisal or financial projection makes sense on its face;

(B) The practitioner reasonably believes that the person making the appraisal or financial projection is competent to do so and is not of dubious reputation; and

(C) The appraisal is based on the definition of fair market value prescribed under the relevant Federal tax provisions.

(iv) If the fair market value of purchased property is to be established by reference to its stated purchase price, the practitioner must examine the terms and conditions upon which the property was (or is to be) purchased to determine whether the stated purchase price reasonably may be considered to be its fair market value.

(2) *Relate law to facts.* The practitioner must relate the law to the actual facts and, when addressing issues based on future activities, clearly identify what facts are assumed.

(3) *Identification of material issues.* The practitioner must ascertain that all material Federal tax issues have been considered, and that all of those issues which involve the reasonable possibility of a challenge by the Internal Revenue Service have been fully and fairly addressed in the offering materials.

(4) *Opinion on each material issue.* Where possible, the practitioner must provide an opinion whether it is more likely than not that an investor will prevail on the merits of each material tax issue presented by the offering which involves a reasonable possibility of a challenge by the Internal Revenue Service. Where such an opinion cannot be given with respect to any material tax issue, the opinion should fully describe the reasons for the practitioner's inability to opine as to the likely outcome.

(5) *Overall evaluation.* (i) Where possible, the practitioner must provide an overall evaluation whether the material tax benefits in the aggregate more likely than not will be realized. Where such an overall evaluation cannot be given, the opinion should fully describe the reasons for the practitioner's inability to make an overall evaluation. Opinions concluding that an overall evaluation cannot be provided will be given special scrutiny to determine if the stated reasons are adequate.

(ii) A favorable overall evaluation may not be rendered unless it is based on a conclusion that substantially more than half of the material tax benefits, in terms of their financial impact on a typical investor, more likely than not will be realized if challenged by the Internal Revenue Service.

(iii) If it is not possible to give an overall evaluation, or if the overall evaluation is that the material tax benefits in the aggregate will not be realized, the fact that the practitioner's opinion does not constitute a favorable overall evaluation, or that it is an unfavorable overall evaluation, must be clearly and prominently disclosed in the offering materials.

(iv) The following examples illustrate the principles of this paragraph:

Example (1). A limited partnership acquires real property in a sale-leaseback transaction. The principal tax benefits offered to investing partners consist of depreciation and interest deductions. Lesser tax benefits are offered to investors by reason of several deductions under Internal Revenue Code section 162 (ordinary and necessary business expenses). If a practitioner concludes that it is more likely than not that the partnership will not be treated as the owner of the property for tax purposes (which is required to allow the interest and depreciation deductions), then he/she may not opine to the effect that it is more likely than not that the material tax benefits in the aggregate will be realized, regardless of whether favorable opinions may be given with respect to the deductions claimed under Code section 162.

Example (2). A corporation electing under subchapter S of the Internal Revenue Code is formed to engage in research and development activities. The offering materials forecast that deductions for research and experimental expenditures equal to 75% of the total investment in the corporation will be available during the first two years of the corporation's operations, other expenses will account for another 15% of the total investment, and that little or no gross income will be received by the corporation during this period. The practitioner concludes that it is more likely than not that deductions for research and experimental expenditures will be allowable. The practitioner may render an opinion to the effect that based on this conclusion, it is more likely than not that the material tax benefits in the aggregate will be realized, regardless of whether he/she can opine that it is more likely than not that any of the other tax benefits will be achieved.

Example (3). An investment program is established to acquire offsetting positions in commodities contracts. The objective of the program is to close the loss positions in year one and to close the profit positions in year two. The principal tax benefit offered by the program is a loss in the first year, coupled with the deferral of offsetting gain until the following year. The practitioner concludes that the losses will not be deductible in year one. Accordingly, he/she may not render an opinion to the effect that it is more likely than not that the material tax benefits in the aggregate will be realized, regardless of the fact that he/she is of the opinion that losses not allowable in year one will be allowable in year two, because the principal tax benefit offered is a one-year deferral of income.

Example (4). A limited partnership is formed to acquire, own and operate residential rental real estate. The offering material forecasts gross income of $2,000,000 and total deductions of $10,000,000, resulting in net losses of $8,000,000 over the first six taxable years. Of the total deductions, depreciation and interest are projected to be $7,000,000, and other deductions $3,000,000. The practitioner concludes that it is more likely than not that all of the depreciation and interest deductions will be allowable, and that it is more likely than not that the other deductions will not be allowed. The practitioner may render an opinion to the effect that it is more likely than not that the material tax benefits in the aggregate will be realized.

(6) *Description of opinion*. The practitioner must assure that the offering materials correctly and fairly represent the nature and extent of the tax shelter opinion.

(b) *Reliance on other opinions* — (1) In general. A practitioner may provide an opinion on less than all of the material tax issues only if:

(i) At least one other competent practitioner provides an opinion on the likely outcome with respect to all of the other material tax issues which involve a reasonable possibility of challenge by the Internal Revenue Service, and an overall evaluation whether the material tax benefits in the aggregate more likely than not will be realized, which is disseminated in the same manner as the practitioner's opinion; and

(ii) The practitioner, upon reviewing such other opinions and any offering materials, has no reason to believe that the standards of paragraph (a) of this section have not been complied with.

Notwithstanding the foregoing, a practitioner who has not been retained to provide an overall evaluation whether the material tax benefits in the aggregate more likely than not will be realized may issue an opinion on less than all the material tax issues only if he/she has no reason to believe, based on his/her knowledge and experience, that the overall evaluation given by the practitioner who furnishes the overall evaluation is incorrect on its face.

(2) *Forecasts and projections*. A practitioner who is associated with forecasts or projections relating to or based upon the tax consequences of the tax shelter offering that are included in the offering materials, or are disseminated to potential investors other than the practitioner's clients, may rely on the opinion of another practitioner as to any or all material tax issues, provided that the practitioner who desires to rely on the other opinion has no reason to believe that the standards of paragraph (a) of this section have not been complied with by the practitioner rendering such other opinion, and the requirements of paragraph (b)(1) of this section are satisfied. The practitioner's report shall disclose any material tax issue not covered by, or incorrectly opined upon, by the other opinion, and shall set forth his/her opinion with respect to each such issue in a manner that satisfies the requirements of paragraph (a) of this section.

(c) *Definitions*. For purposes of this section:

(1) *Practitioner* includes any individual described in §10.3(e).

(2) A *tax shelter,* as the term is used in this section, is an investment which has as a significant and intended feature for Federal income or excise tax purposes either of the following attributes:

(i) Deductions in excess of income from the investment being available in any year to reduce income from other sources in that year, or

(ii) Credits in excess of the tax attributable to the income from the investment being available in any year to offset taxes on income from other sources in that year. Excluded from the term are municipal bonds; annuities; family trusts (but not including schemes or arrangements that are marketed to the public other than in a direct practitioner-client relationship); qualified retirement plans; individual retirement accounts; stock option plans; securities issued in a corporate reorganization; mineral development ventures, if the only tax benefit would be percentage depletion; and real estate where it is anticipated that in no year is it likely that deductions will exceed the tax attributable to the income from the investment in that year. Whether an investment is intended to have tax shelter features depends on the objective facts and circumstances of each case. Significant weight will be given to the features described in the offering materials to determine whether the investment is a tax shelter.

(3) A *tax shelter opinion,* as the term is used in this section, is advice by a practitioner concerning the Federal tax aspects of a tax shelter either appearing or referred to in the offering materials, or used or referred to in connection with sales promotion efforts, and directed to persons other than the client who engaged the practitioner to give the advice. The term includes the tax aspects or tax risks portion of the offering materials prepared by or at the direction of a practitioner, whether or not a separate opinion letter is issued or whether or not the practitioner's name is referred to in the offering materials or in connection with the sales promotion efforts. In addition, a fi-

nancial forecast or projection prepared by a practitioner is a tax shelter opinion if it is predicated on assumptions regarding Federal tax aspects of the investment, and it meets the other requirements of the first sentence of this paragraph. The term does not, however, include rendering advice solely to the offeror or reviewing parts of the offering materials, so long as neither the name of the practitioner, nor the fact that a practitioner has rendered advice concerning the tax aspects, is referred to in the offering materials or in connection with the sales promotion efforts.

(4) A *material* tax issue as the term is used in this section is

(i) Any Federal income or excise tax issue relating to a tax shelter that would make a significant contribution toward sheltering from Federal taxes income from other sources by providing deductions in excess of the income from the tax shelter investment in any year, or tax credits available to offset tax liabilities in excess of the tax attributable to the tax shelter investment in any year;

(ii) Any other Federal income or excise tax issue relating to a tax shelter that could have a significant impact (either beneficial or adverse) on a tax shelter investor under any reasonably foreseeable circumstances (e.g., depreciation or investment tax credit recapture, availability of long-term capital gain treatment, or realization of taxable income in excess of cash flow, upon sale or other disposition of the tax shelter investment); and

(iii) The potential applicability of penalties, additions to tax, or interest charges that reasonably could be asserted against a tax shelter investor by the Internal Revenue Service with respect to the tax shelter. The determination of what is material is to be made in good faith by the practitioner, based on information available at the time the offering materials are circulated.

(d) For purposes of advising the Director of Practice whether an individual may have violated §10.33, the Director of Practice is authorized to establish an Advisory Committee, composed of at least five individuals authorized to practice before the Internal Revenue Service. Under procedures established by the Director of Practice, such Advisory Committee shall, at the request of the Director of Practice, review and make recommendations with regard to alleged violations of §10.33.

(Sec. 3, 23 Stat. 258, secs. 2-12, 60 Stat. 237 *et seq.;* 5 U.S.C. 301; 31 U.S.C. 330; 31 U.S.C. 321 (Reorg. Plan No. 26 of 1950, 15 FR 4935, 64 Stat. 1280, 3 CFR, 1949-53 Comp., p. 1017))

[49 FR 6722, Feb. 23, 1984; 49 FR 7116, Feb. 27, 1984; 59 FR 31527, 31528, June 20, 1994]

§10.34 Standards for advising with respect to tax return positions and for preparing or signing returns.

(a) *Standards of conduct* — (1) *Realistic possibility standard.* A practitioner may not sign a return as a preparer if the practitioner determines that the return contains a position that does not have a realistic possibility of being sustained on its merits (the realistic possibility standard) unless the position is not frivolous and is adequately disclosed to the Service. A practitioner may not advise a client to take a position on a return, or prepare the portion of a return on which a position is taken, unless —

(i) The practitioner determines that the position satisfies the realistic possibility standard; or

(ii) The position is not frivolous and the practitioner advises the client of any opportunity to avoid the accuracy-related penalty in section 6662 of the Internal Revenue Code of 1986 by adequately disclosing the position and of the requirements for adequate disclosure.

(2) *Advising clients on potential penalties.* A practitioner advising a client to take a position on a return, or preparing or signing a return as a preparer, must inform the client of the penalties reasonably likely to apply to the client with respect to the position advised, prepared, or reported. The practitioner also must inform the client of any opportunity to avoid any such penalty by disclosure, if relevant, and of the requirements for adequate disclosure. This paragraph (a)(2) applies even if the practitioner is not subject to a penalty with respect to the position.

(3) *Relying on information furnished by clients.* A practitioner advising a client to take a position on a return, or preparing or signing a return as a preparer, generally may rely in good faith without verification upon information furnished by the client. However, the practitioner may not ignore the implications of information furnished to, or actually known by, the practitioner, and must make reasonable inquiries if the information as furnished appears to be incorrect, inconsistent, or incomplete.

(4) *Definitions.* For purposes of this section:

(i) *Realistic possibility.* A position is considered to have a realistic possibility of being sustained on its merits if a reasonable and well-informed analysis by a person knowledgeable in the tax law would lead such a person to conclude that the position has approximately a one in three, or greater, likelihood of being sustained on its merits. The authorities described in 26 CFR 1.6662 - 4(d)(3)(iii), or any successor provision, of the substantial understatement penalty regulations may be taken into account for purposes of this analysis. The possibility that a position will not be challenged by the Service (e.g., because the taxpayer's return may not be audited or because the issue may not be raised on audit) may not be taken into account.

(ii) *Frivolous.* A position is frivolous if it is patently improper.

(b) *Standard of discipline.* As provided in §10.52, only violations of this section that are willful, reckless, or a result of gross incompetence will subject a practitioner to suspension or disbarment from practice before the Service.

[59 FR 31527, June 20, 1994]

Subpart C — Rules Applicable to Disciplinary Proceedings

§10.50   Authority to disbar or suspend.

Pursuant to 31 U.S.C. 330(b), the Secretary of the Treasury after notice and an opportunity for a proceeding, may suspend or disbar any practitioner from practice before the Internal Revenue Service. The Secretary may take such action against any practitioner who is shown to be incompetent or disreputable, who refuses to comply with any regulation in this part, or who, with intent to defraud, willfully and knowingly misleads or threatens a client or prospective client.

[59 FR 31528, June 20, 1994]

§10.51   Disreputable conduct.

Disreputable conduct for which an attorney, certified public accountant, enrolled agent, or enrolled actuary may be disbarred or suspended from practice before the Internal Revenue Service includes, but is not limited to:

(a) Conviction of any criminal offense under the revenue laws of the United States, or of any offense involving dishonesty, or breach of trust.

(b) Giving false or misleading information, or participating in any way in the giving of false or misleading information to the Department of the Treasury or any officer or employee thereof, or to any tribunal authorized to pass upon Federal tax matters, in connection with any matter pending or likely to be pending before them, knowing such information to be false or misleading. Facts or other matters contained in testimony, Federal tax returns, financial statements, applications for enrollment, affidavits, declarations, or any other document or statement, written or oral, are included in the term "information."

(c) Solicitation of employment as prohibited under §10.30 of this part, the use of false or misleading representations with intent to deceive a client or prospective client in order to procure employment, or intimating that the practitioner is able improperly to obtain special consideration or action from the Internal Revenue Service or officer or employee thereof.

(d) Willfully failing to make a Federal tax return in violation of the revenue laws of the United States, or evading, attempting to evade, or participating in any way in evading or attempting to evade any Federal tax or payment thereof, knowingly counseling or suggesting to a client or prospective client an illegal plan to evade Federal taxes or payment thereof, or concealing assets of himself or another to evade Federal taxes or payment thereof.

(e) Misappropriation of, or failure properly and promptly to remit funds received from a client for the purpose of payment of taxes or other obligations due the United States.

(f) Directly or indirectly attempting to influence, or offering or agreeing to attempt to influence, the official action of any officer or employee of the Internal Revenue Service by the use of threats, false accusations, duress or coercion, by the offer of any special inducement or promise of advantage or by the bestowing of any gift, favor or thing of value.

(g) Disbarment or suspension from practice as an attorney, certified public accountant, public accountant, or actuary by any duly constituted authority of any State, possession, territory, Commonwealth, the District of Columbia, any Federal court of record or any Federal agency, body or board.

(h) Knowingly aiding and abetting another person to practice before the Internal Revenue Service during a period of suspension, disbarment, or ineligibility of such other person. Maintaining a partnership for the practice of law, accountancy, or other related professional service with a person who is under disbarment from practice before the Service shall be presumed to be a violation of this provision.

(i) Contemptuous conduct in connection with practice before the Internal Revenue Service, including the use of abusive language, making false accusations and statements knowing them to be false, or circulating or publishing malicious or libelous matter.

(j) Giving a false opinion, knowingly, recklessly, or through gross incompetence, including an opinion which is intentionally or recklessly misleading, or a pattern of providing incompetent opinions on questions arising under the Federal tax laws. False opinions described in this paragraph include those which reflect or result from a knowing misstatement of fact or law; from an assertion of a position known to be unwarranted under existing law; from counseling or assisting in conduct known to be illegal or fraudulent; from concealment of matters required by law to be revealed; or from conscious disregard of information indicating that material facts expressed in the tax opinion or offering material are false or misleading. For purposes of this paragraph, reckless conduct is a highly unreasonable omission or misrepresentation involving an extreme departure from the standards of ordinary care that a practitioner should observe under the circumstances. A pattern of conduct is a factor that will be taken into account in determining whether a practitioner acted knowingly, recklessly, or through gross incompetence. Gross incompetence includes conduct that reflects gross indifference, preparation which is grossly inadequate under the circumstances, and a consistent failure to perform obligations to the client.

(Sec. 3, 23 Stat. 258, secs. 2-12, 60 Stat. 237 *et seq.;* 5 U.S.C. 301; 31 U.S.C. 330; 31 U.S.C. 321 (Reorg. Plan No. 26 of 1950, 15 FR 4935, 64 Stat. 1280, 3 CFR, 1949-53 Comp., p. 1017))

[31 FR 10773, Aug. 13, 1966, as amended at 35 FR 13205, Aug. 19, 1970; 42 FR 38353, July 28, 1977; 44 FR 4946, Jan. 24, 1979; 49 FR 6723, Feb. 23, 1984; 57 FR 41095, Sept. 9, 1992; 59 FR 31528, June 20, 1994]

§10.52   Violation of regulations.

A practitioner may be disbarred or suspended from practice before the Internal Revenue Service for any of the following:

(a) Willfully violating any of the regulations contained in this part.

(b) Recklessly or through gross incompetence (within the meaning of §10.51(j)) violating §10.33 or §10.34 of this part.

[59 FR 31528, June 20, 1994]

§10.53   Receipt of information concerning attorneys, certified public accountants, enrolled agents, or enrolled actuaries.

If an officer or employee of the Internal Revenue Service has reason to believe that an attorney, certified public accountant, enrolled agent, or enrolled actuary has violated any provision of this part, or if any such officer or employee receives information to that effect, he shall promptly make a written report thereof, which report or a copy thereof shall be forwarded to the Director of Practice. If any other person has information of such violations, he may make a report thereof to the Director of Practice or to any officer or employee of the Internal Revenue Service.

[31 FR 10773, Aug. 13, 1966, as amended at 57 FR 41095, Sept. 9, 1992]

§10.54   Institution of proceeding.

Whenever the Director of Practice has reason to believe that any attorney, certified public accountant, enrolled agent, or enrolled actuary has violated any provision of the laws or regulations governing practice before the Internal Revenue Service, he may reprimand such person or institute a proceeding for disbarment or suspension of such person. The proceeding shall be instituted by a complaint which names the respondent and is signed by the Director of Practice and filed in his office. Except in cases of willfulness, or where time, the nature of the proceeding, or the public interest does not permit, a proceeding will not be instituted under this section until facts or conduct which may warrant such action have been called to the attention of the proposed respondent in writing and he has been accorded opportunity to demonstrate or achieve compliance with all lawful requirements.

[31 FR 10773, Aug. 13, 1966, as amended at 57 FR 41095, Sept. 9, 1992]

§10.55   Conferences.

(a) *In general.* The Director of Practice may confer with an attorney, certified public accountant, enrolled agent, or enrolled actuary concerning allegations of misconduct irrespective of whether a proceeding for disbarment or suspension has been instituted against him. If such conference results in a stipulation in connection with a proceeding in which such person is the respondent, the stipulation may be entered in the record at the instance of either party to the proceeding.

(b) *Resignation or voluntary suspension.* An attorney, certified public accountant, enrolled agent, or enrolled actuary, in order to avoid the institution or conclusion of a disbarment or suspension proceeding, may offer his consent to suspension from practice before the Internal Revenue Service. An enrolled agent may also offer his resignation. The Director of Practice, in his discretion, may accept the offered resignation of an enrolled agent and may suspend an attorney, certified public accountant, or enrolled agent in accordance with the consent offered.

[31 FR 10773, Aug. 13, 1966, as amended at 35 FR 13206, Aug. 19, 1970; 57 FR 41095, Sept. 9, 1992]

§10.56   Contents of complaint.

(a) *Charges.* A complaint shall give a plain and concise description of the allegations which constitute the basis for the proceeding. A complaint shall be deemed sufficient if it fairly informs the respondent of the charges against him so that he is able to prepare his defense.

(b) *Demand for answer.* In the complaint, or in a separate paper attached to the complaint, notification shall be given of the place and time within which the respondent shall file his answer, which time shall not be less than 15 days from the date of service of the complaint, and notice shall be given that a decision by default may be rendered against the respondent in the event he fails to file his answer as required.

[31 FR 10773, Aug. 13, 1966, as amended at 42 FR 38353, July 28, 1977]

§10.57   Service of complaint and other papers.

(a) *Complaint.* The complaint or a copy thereof may be served upon the respondent by certified mail, or first-class mail as hereinafter provided; by delivering it to the respondent or his attorney or agent of record either in person or by leaving it at the office or place of business of the respondent, attorney or agent; or in any other manner which has been agreed to by the respondent. Where the service is by certified mail, the return post office receipt duly signed by or on behalf of the respondent shall be proof of service. If the certified matter is not claimed or accepted by the respondent and is returned undelivered, complete service may be made upon the respondent by mailing the complaint to him by first-class mail, addressed to him at the address under which he is enrolled or at the last address known to the Director of Practice. If service is made upon the respondent or his attorney or agent of record in person or by leaving the complaint at the office or place of business of the respondent, attorney or agent, the verified return by the person making service, setting forth the manner of service, shall be proof of such service.

(b) *Service of papers other than complaint*. Any paper other than the complaint may be served upon an attorney, certified public accountant, or enrolled agent as provided in paragraph (a) of this section or by mailing the paper by first-class mail to the respondent at the last address known to the Director of Practice, or by mailing the paper by first-class mail to the respondent's attorney or agent of record. Such mailing shall constitute complete service. Notices may be served upon the respondent or his attorney or agent of record by telegraph.

(c) *Filing of papers*. Whenever the filing of a paper is required or permitted in connection with a disbarment or suspension proceeding, and the place of filing is not specified by this subpart or by rule or order of the Administrative Law Judge, the paper shall be filed with the Director of Practice, Treasury Department, Washington, D.C. 20220. All papers shall be filed in duplicate.

[31 FR 10773, Aug. 13, 1966, as amended at 31 FR 13992, Nov. 2, 1966; 42 FR 38354, July 28, 1977]

§10.58 Answer.

(a) *Filing*. The respondent's answer shall be filed in writing within the time specified in the complaint or notice of institution of the proceeding, unless on application the time is extended by the Director of Practice or the Administrative Law Judge. The answer shall be filed in duplicate with the Director of Practice.

(b) *Contents*. The answer shall contain a statement of facts which constitute the grounds of defense, and it shall specifically admit or deny each allegation set forth in the complaint, except that the respondent shall not deny a material allegation in the complaint which he knows to be true, or state that he is without sufficient information to form a belief when in fact he possesses such information. The respondent may also state affirmatively special matters of defense.

(c) *Failure to deny or answer allegations in the complaint*. Every allegation in the complaint which is not denied in the answer shall be deemed to be admitted and may be considered as proved, and no further evidence in respect of such allegation need be adduced at a hearing. Failure to file an answer within the time prescribed in the notice to the respondent, except as the time for answer is extended by the Director of Practice or the Administrative Law Judge, shall constitute an admission of the allegations of the complaint and a waiver of hearing, and the Administrative Law Judge may make his decision by default without a hearing or further procedure.

[31 FR 10773, Aug. 13, 1966, as amended at 42 FR 38354, July 28, 1977]

§10.59 Supplemental charges.

If it appears that the respondent in his answer, falsely and in bad faith, denies a material allegation of fact in the complaint or states that the respondent has no knowledge sufficient to form a belief, when he in fact possesses such information, or if it appears that the respondent has knowingly introduced false testimony during proceedings for his disbarment or suspension, the Director of Practice may thereupon file supplemental charges against the respondent. Such supplemental charges may be tried with other charges in the case, provided the respondent is given due notice thereof and is afforded an opportunity to prepare a defense thereto.

§10.60 Reply to answer.

No reply to the respondent's answer shall be required, and new matter in the answer shall be deemed to be denied, but the Director of Practice may file a reply in his discretion or at the request of the Administrative Law Judge.

[31 FR 10773, Aug. 13, 1966 as amended at 42 FR 38354, July 28, 1977]

§10.61   Proof; variance; amendment of pleadings.

In the case of a variance between the allegations in a pleading and the evidence adduced in support of the pleading, the Administrative Law Judge may order or authorize amendment of the pleading to conform to the evidence: *Provided,* That the party who would otherwise be prejudiced by the amendment is given reasonable opportunity to meet the allegations of the pleading as amended; and the Administrative Law Judge shall make findings on any issue presented by the pleadings as so amended.

[31 FR 10773, Aug. 13, 1966, as amended at 42 FR 38354, July 28, 1977]

§10.62   Motions and requests.

Motions and requests may be filed with the Director of Practice or with the Administrative Law Judge.

[31 FR 10773, Aug. 13, 1966, as amended at 42 FR 38354, July 28, 1977]

§10.63   Representation.

A respondent or proposed respondent may appear in person or he may be represented by counsel or other representative who need not be enrolled to practice before the Internal Revenue Service. The Director may be represented by an attorney or other employee of the Internal Revenue Service.

§10.64   Administrative Law Judge.

(a) *Appointment.* An Administrative Law Judge appointed as provided by 5 U.S.C. 3105 (1966), shall conduct proceedings upon complaints for the disbarment or suspension of attorneys, certified public accountants, or enrolled agents.

(b) *Powers of Administrative Law Judge.* Among other powers, the Administrative Law Judge shall have authority, in connection with any disbarment or suspension proceeding assigned or referred to him, to do the following:

(1) Administer oaths and affirmations;

(2) Make rulings upon motions and requests, which rulings may not be appealed from prior to the close of a hearing except, at the discretion of the Administrative Law Judge, in extraordinary circumstances;

(3) Determine the time and place of hearing and regulate its course and conduct;

(4) Adopt rules of procedure and modify the same from time to time as occasion requires for the orderly disposition of proceedings;

(5) Rule upon offers of proof, receive relevant evidence, and examine witnesses;

(6) Take or authorize the taking of depositions;

(7) Receive and consider oral or written argument on facts or law;

(8) Hold or provide for the holding of conferences for the settlement or simplification of the issues by consent of the parties;

(9) Perform such acts and take such measures as are necessary or appropriate to the efficient conduct of any proceeding; and

(10) Make initial decisions.

[31 FR 10773, Aug. 13, 1966, as amended at 42 FR 38353, 38354, July 28, 1977]

§10.65   Hearings.

(a) *In general.* An Administrative Law Judge will preside at the hearing on a complaint furnished under §10.54 for the disbarment or suspension of a practitioner. Hearings will be stenographically recorded and transcribed and the testimony of witnesses will be taken under oath or affirmation. Hearings will be conducted pursuant to 5 U.S.C. 556. A hearing in a proceeding requested under §10.76(g) will be conducted *de novo.*

(b) *Failure to appear.* If either party to the proceeding fails to appear at the hearing, after due notice thereof has been sent to him, he shall be deemed to have waived the right to a hearing and the Administrative Law Judge may make his decision against the absent party by default.

[31 FR 10773, Aug. 13, 1966, as amended at 42 FR 38354, July 28, 1977; 59 FR 31528, June 20, 1994]

§10.66 Evidence.

(a) *In general.* The rules of evidence prevailing in courts of law and equity are not controlling in hearings on complaints for the disbarment or suspension of attorneys, certified public accountants, and enrolled agents. However, the Administrative Law Judge shall exclude evidence which is irrelevant, immaterial, or unduly repetitious.

(b) *Depositions.* The deposition of any witness taken pursuant to §10.67 may be admitted.

(c) *Proof of documents.* Official documents, records, and papers of the Internal Revenue Service and the Office of Director of Practice shall be admissible in evidence without the production of an officer or employee to authenticate them. Any such documents, records, and papers may be evidenced by a copy attested or identified by an officer or employee of the Internal Revenue Service or the Treasury Department, as the case may be.

(d) *Exhibits.* If any document, record, or other paper is introduced in evidence as an exhibit, the Administrative Law Judge may authorize the withdrawal of the exhibit subject to any conditions which he deems proper.

(e) *Objections.* Objections to evidence shall be in short form, stating the grounds of objection relied upon, and the record shall not include argument thereon, except as ordered by the Administrative Law Judge. Rulings on such objections shall be a part of the record. No exception to the ruling is necessary to preserve the rights of the parties.

[31 FR 10773, Aug. 13, 1966, as amended at 35 FR 13206, Aug. 19, 1970; 42 FR 38354, July 28, 1977]

§10.67 Depositions.

Depositions for use at a hearing may, with the written approval of the Administrative Law Judge be taken by either the Director of Practice or the respondent or their duly authorized representatives. Depositions may be taken upon oral or written interrogatories, upon not less than 10 days' written notice to the other party before any officer duly authorized to administer an oath for general purposes or before an officer or employee of the Internal Revenue Service who is authorized to administer an oath in internal revenue matters. Such notice shall state the names of the witnesses and the time and place where the depositions are to be taken. The requirement of 10 days' notice may be waived by the parties in writing, and depositions may then be taken from the persons and at the times and places mutually agreed to by the parties. When a deposition is taken upon written interrogatories, any cross-examination shall be upon written interrogatories. Copies of such written interrogatories shall be served upon the other party with the notice, and copies of any written cross-interrogatories shall be mailed or delivered to the opposing party at least 5 days before the date of taking the depositions, unless the parties mutually agree otherwise. A party upon whose behalf a deposition is taken must file it with the Administrative Law Judge and serve one copy upon the opposing party. Expenses in the reporting of depositions shall be borne by the party at whose instance the deposition is taken.

[31 FR 10773, Aug. 13, 1966, as amended at 42 FR 38354, July 28, 1977]

§10.68 Transcript.

In cases where the hearing is stenographically reported by a Government contract reporter, copies of the transcript may be obtained from the reporter at rates not to exceed the maximum rates fixed by contract between the Government and the reporter. Where the hearing is stenographically reported by a regular employee of the Internal Revenue Service, a copy thereof will be supplied to the respondent either without charge or upon the payment of a reasonable fee. Copies of exhibits introduced at the hearing or at the taking or depositions will be supplied to the parties upon the payment of a reasonable fee (Sec. 501, Pub. L. 82 - 137, 65 Stat. 290 (31 U.S.C. 483a)).

[31 FR 10773, Aug. 13, 1966, as amended at 42 FR 38354, July 28, 1977]

§10.69 Proposed findings and conclusions.

Except in cases where the respondent has failed to answer the complaint or where a party has failed to appear at the hearing, the Administrative Law Judge prior to making his decision, shall afford the parties a reasonable opportunity to submit proposed findings and conclusions and supporting reasons therefor.

[31 FR 10773, Aug. 13, 1966, as amended at 42 FR 38354, July 28, 1977]

§10.70 Decision of the Administrative Law Judge.

As soon as practicable after the conclusion of a hearing and the receipt of any proposed findings and conclusions timely submitted by the parties, the Administrative Law Judge shall make the initial decision in the case. The decision shall include (a) a statement of findings and conclusions, as well as the reasons or bases therefor, upon all the material issues of fact, law, or discretion presented on the record, and (b) an order of disbarment, suspension, or reprimand or an order of dismissal of the complaint. The Administrative Law Judge shall file the decision with the Director of Practice and shall transmit a copy thereof to the respondent or his attorney of record. In the absence of an appeal to the Secretary of the Treasury, or review of the decision upon motion of the Secretary, the decision of the Administrative Law Judge shall without further proceedings become the decisions of the Secretary of the Treasury 30 days from the date of the Administrative Law Judge's decision.

[31 FR 10773, Aug. 13, 1966, as amended at 42 FR 38354, July 28, 1977]

§10.71 Appeal to the Secretary.

Within 30 days from the date of the Administrative Law Judge's decision, either party may appeal to the Secretary of the Treasury. The appeal shall be filed with the Director of Practice in duplicate and shall include exceptions to the decision of the Administrative Law Judge and supporting reasons for such exceptions. If an appeal is filed by the Director of Practice, he shall transmit a copy thereof to the respondent. Within 30 days after receipt of an appeal or copy thereof, the other party may file a reply brief in duplicate with the Director of Practice. If the reply brief is filed by the Director, he shall transmit a copy of it to the respondent. Upon the filing of an appeal and a reply brief, if any, the Director of Practice shall transmit the entire record to the Secretary of the Treasury.

[31 FR 10773, Aug. 13, 1966, as amended at 42 FR 38354, July 28, 1977]

§10.72 Decision of the Secretary.

On appeal from or review of the initial decision of the Administrative Law Judge, the Secretary of the Treasury will make the agency decision. In making his decision the Secretary of the Treasury will review the record or such portions thereof as may be cited by the parties to permit limiting of the issues. A copy of the Secretary's decision shall be transmitted to the respondent by the Director of Practice.

[31 FR 10773, Aug. 13, 1966, as amended at 42 FR 38354, July 28, 1977]

§10.73 Effect of disbarment or suspension; surrender of card.

In case the final order against the respondent is for disbarment, the respondent shall not thereafter be permitted to practice before the Internal Revenue Service unless and until authorized to do so by the Director of Practice pursuant to §10.75. In case the final order against the respondent is for suspension, the respondent shall not thereafter be permitted to practice before the Internal Revenue Service during the period of suspension. If an enrolled agent is disbarred or suspended, he shall surrender his enrollment card to the Director of Practice for cancellation, in the case of disbarment, or for retention during the period of suspension.

§10.74 Notice of disbarment or suspension.

Upon the issuance of a final order disbarring or suspending an attorney, certified public accountant, or enrolled agent, the Director of Practice shall give notice thereof to appropriate officers and employees of the Internal Revenue Service and to interested departments and agencies of the Federal Government. Notice in such manner as the Director of Practice may determine may be given to the proper authorities of the State by which the disbarred or suspended person was licensed to practice as an attorney or accountant.

§10.75 Petition for reinstatement.

The Director of Practice may entertain a petition for reinstatement from any person disbarred from practice before the Internal Revenue Service after the expiration of 5 years following such disbarment. Reinstatement may not be granted unless the Director of Practice is satisfied that the petitioner, thereafter, is not likely to conduct himself contrary to the regulations in this part, and that granting such reinstatement would not be contrary to the public interest.

[31 FR 10773, Aug. 13, 1966, as amended at 35 FR 13206, Aug. 19, 1970]

§10.76 Expedited suspension upon criminal conviction or loss of license for cause.

(a) *When applicable.* Whenever the Director has reason to believe that a practitioner is described in paragraph (b) of this section, the Director may institute a proceeding under this section to suspend the practitioner from practice before the Service.

(b) *To whom applicable.* This section applies to any practitioner who, within 5 years of the date a complaint instituting a proceeding under this section is served —

(1) Has had his or her license to practice as an attorney, certified public accountant, or actuary suspended or revoked for cause (not including a failure to pay a professional licensing fee) by any authority or court, agency, body, or board described in §10.51(g); or

(2) Has been convicted of any crime under title 26 of the United States Code, or a felony under title 18 of the United States Code involving dishonesty or breach of trust.

(c) *Instituting a proceeding.* A proceeding under this section will be instituted by a complaint that names the respondent, is signed by the Director, is filed in the Director's office, and is served according to the rules set forth in §10.57(a). The complaint must give a plain and concise description of the allegations that constitute the basis for the proceeding. The complaint, or a separate paper attached to the complaint, must notify the respondent —

(1) Of the place and due date for filing an answer;

(2) That a decision by default may be rendered if the respondent fails to file an answer as required;

(3) That the respondent may request a conference with the Director to address the merits of the complaint and that any such request must be made in the answer; and

(4) That the respondent may be suspended either immediately following the expiration

of the period by which an answer must be filed or, if a conference is requested, immediately following the conference.

(d) *Answer.* The answer to a complaint described in this section must be filed no later than 30 calendar days following the date the complaint is served, unless the Director extends the time for filing. The answer must be filed in accordance with the rules set forth in §10.58, except as otherwise provided in this section. A respondent is entitled to a conference with the Director only if the conference is requested in a timely filed answer. If a request for a conference is not made in the answer or the answer is not timely filed, the respondent will be deemed to have waived his or her right to a conference and the Director may suspend such respondent at any time following the date on which the answer was due.

(e) *Conference.* The Director or his or her designee will preside at a conference described in this section. The conference will be held at a place and time selected by the Director, but no sooner than 14 calendar days after the date by which the answer must be filed with the Director, unless the respondent agrees to an earlier date. An authorized representative may represent the respondent at the conference. Following the conference, upon a finding that the respondent is described in paragraph (b) of this section, or upon the respondent's failure to appear at the conference either personally or through an authorized representative, the Director may immediately suspend the respondent from practice before the Service.

(f) *Duration of suspension.* A suspension under this section will commence on the date that written notice of the suspension is issued. A practitioner's suspension will remain effective until the earlier of the following —

(1) The Director lifts the suspension after determining that the practitioner is no longer described in paragraph (b) of this section or for any other reason; or

(2) The suspension is lifted by an Administrative Law Judge or the Secretary of the Treasury in a proceeding referred to in paragraph (g) of this section and instituted under §10.54.

(g) *Proceeding instituted under §10.54.* If the Director suspends a practitioner under this §10.76, the practitioner may ask the Director to issue a complaint under §10.54. The request must be made in writing within 2 years from the date on which the practitioner's suspension commences. The Director must issue a complaint requested under this paragraph within 30 calendar days of receiving the request.

[59 FR 31528, June 20, 1994]

Subpart D — Rules Applicable to Disqualification of Appraisers

Source: 50 FR 42016, Oct. 17, 1985, unless otherwise noted.

§10.77   Authority to disqualify; effect of disqualification.

(a) *Authority to disqualify.* Pursuant to section 156 of the Deficit Reduction Act of 1984, 98 Stat. 695, amending 31 U.S.C. 330, the Secretary of the Treasury, after due notice and opportunity for hearing may disqualify any appraiser with respect to whom a penalty has been assessed after July 18, 1984, under section 6701(a) of the Internal Revenue Code of 1954, as amended (26 U.S.C. 6701(a)).

(b) *Effect of disqualification.* If any appraiser is disqualified pursuant to 31 U.S.C. 330 and this subpart:

(1) Appraisals by such appraiser shall not have any probative effect in any administrative proceeding before the Department of the Treasury or the Internal Revenue Service; and

(2) Such appraiser shall be barred from presenting evidence or testimony in any such administrative proceeding. Paragraph (b)(1) of this section shall apply to appraisals made by such appraiser after the effective date of disqualification, but shall not

apply to appraisals made by the appraiser on or before such date. Notwithstanding the foregoing sentence, an appraisal otherwise barred from admission into evidence pursuant to paragraph (b)(1) of this section may be admitted into evidence solely for the purpose of determining the taxpayer's reliance in good faith on such appraisal. Paragraph (b)(2) of this section shall apply to the presentation of testimony or evidence in any administrative proceeding after the date of such disqualification, regardless of whether such testimony or evidence would pertain to any appraisal made prior to such date.

§10.78   Institution of proceeding.

(a) *In general*. Whenever the Director of Practice is advised or becomes aware that a penalty has been assessed against an appraiser under 26 U.S.C. 6701(a), he/she may reprimand such person or institute a proceeding for disqualification of such appraiser through the filing of a complaint. Irrespective of whether a proceeding for disqualification has been instituted against an appraiser, the Director of Practice may confer with an appraiser against whom such a penalty has been assessed concerning such penalty.

(b) *Voluntary disqualification*. In order to avoid the initiation or conclusion of a disqualification proceeding, an appraiser may offer his/her consent to disqualification. The Director of Practice, in his/her discretion, may disqualify an appraiser in accordance with the consent offered.

§10.79   Contents of complaint.

(a) *Charges*. A proceeding for disqualification of an appraiser shall be instituted through the filing of a complaint, which shall give a plain and concise description of the allegations that constitute the basis for the proceeding. A complaint shall be deemed sufficient if it refers to the penalty previously imposed on the respondent un-der section 6701(a) of the Internal Revenue Code of 1954, as amended (26 U.S.C. 6701(a)), and advises him/her of the institution of the proceeding.

(b) *Demand for answer*. In the complaint, or in a separate paper attached to the complaint, notification shall be given of the place and time within which the respondent shall file his/her answer, which time shall not be less than 15 days from the date of service of the complaint, and notice shall be given that a decision by default may be rendered against the respondent in the event there is failure to file an answer.

§10.80   Service of complaint and other papers.

(a) *Complaint*. The complaint or a copy thereof may be served upon the respondent by certified mail, or first-class mail as hereinafter provided, by delivering it to the respondent or his/her attorney or agent of record either in person or by leaving it at the office or place of business of the respondent, attorney or agent, or in any other manner that has been agreed to by the respondent. Where the service is by certified mail, the return post office receipt duly signed by or on behalf of the respondent shall be proof of service. If the certified mail is not claimed or accepted by the respondent and is returned undelivered, complete service may be made by mailing the complaint to the respondent by first-class mail, addressed to the respondent at the last address known to the Director of Practice. If service is made upon the respondent in person or by leaving the complaint at the office or place of business of the respondent, the verified return by the person making service, setting forth the manner of service, shall be proof of such service.

(b) *Service of papers other than complaint*. Any paper other than the complaint may be served as provided in paragraph (a) of this section or by mailing the paper by first-class mail to the respondent at the last address known to the Director of Practice, or by mailing the paper by first-class mail to the respondent's attorney or agent of record. Such mailing shall constitute complete service. Notices may be served upon the respondent or his/her attorney or agent of record by telegraph.

(c) *Filing of papers.* Whenever the filing of a paper is required or permitted in connection with a disqualification proceeding under this subpart or by rule or order of the Administrative Law Judge, the paper shall be filed with the Director of Practice, Treasury Department, Internal Revenue Service, Washington, D.C. 20224. All papers shall be filed in duplicate.

§10.81   Answer.

(a) *Filing.* The respondent's answer shall be filed in writing within the time specified in the complaint or notice of institution of the proceeding, unless on application the time is extended by the Director of Practice or the Administrative Law Judge. The answer shall be filed in duplicate with the Director of Practice.

(b) *Contents.* The answer shall contain a statement of facts that constitute the grounds of defense, and it shall specifically admit or deny each allegation set forth in the complaint, except that the respondent shall not deny a material allegation in the complaint that he/she knows to be true, or state that he/she is without sufficient information to form a belief when in fact he/she possesses such information.

(c) *Failure to deny or answer allegations in the complaint.* Every allegation in the complaint which is not denied in the answer shall be deemed to be admitted and may be considered as proved, and no further evidence in respect of such allegation need be adduced at a hearing. Failure to file an answer within the time prescribed in the notice to the respondent, except as the time for answer is extended by the Director of Practice or the Administrative Law Judge, shall constitute an admission of the allega-

tions of the complaint and a waiver of hearing, and the Administrative Law Judge may make his/her decision by default without a hearing or further procedure.

§10.82   Supplemental charges.

If it appears that the respondent in his/her answer, falsely and in bad faith, denies a material allegation of fact in the complaint or states that the respondent has no knowledge sufficient to form a belief, when he/she in fact possesses such information, or if it appears that the respondent has knowingly introduced false testimony during proceedings for his/her disqualification, the Director of Practice may thereupon file supplemental charges against the respondent. Such supplemental charges may be tried with other charges in the case, provided the respondent is given due notice thereof and is afforded an opportunity to prepare a defense thereto.

§10.83   Reply to answer.

No reply to the respondent's answer shall be required, and any new matter in the answer shall be deemed to be denied, but the Director of Practice may file a reply in his/her discretion or at the request of the Administrative Law Judge.

§10.84   Proof, variance, amendment of pleadings.

In the case of a variance between the allegations in a pleading and the evidence adduced in support of the pleading, the Administrative Law Judge may order or authorize amendment of the pleading to conform to the evidence; provided, that the party who would otherwise be prejudiced by the amendment is given reasonable opportunity to meet the allegations of the pleading as amended, and the Administrative Law Judge shall make findings on any issue presented by the pleadings as so amended.

§10.85 Motions and requests.

Motions and requests may be filed with the Director of Practice or with the Administrative Law Judge.

§10.86 Representation.

A respondent may appear in person or may be represented by counsel or other representative. The Director of Practice may be represented by an attorney or other employee of the Department of the Treasury.

§10.87 Administrative Law Judge.

(a) *Appointment.* An Administrative Law Judge appointed as provided by 5 U.S.C. 3105, shall conduct proceedings upon complaints for the disqualification of appraisers.

(b) *Powers of Administrative Law Judge.* Among other powers, the Administrative Law Judge shall have authority, in connection with any disqualification proceeding assigned or referred to him/her, to do the following:

(1) Administer oaths and affirmations;

(2) Make rulings upon motions and requests, which rulings may not be appealed from prior to the close of a hearing except at the discretion of the Administrative Law Judge, in extraordinary circumstances;

(3) Determine the time and place of hearing and regulate its course and conduct;

(4) Adopt rules of procedure and modify the same from time to time as occasion requires for the orderly disposition of proceedings;

(5) Rule upon offers of proof, receive relevant evidence, and examine witnesses;

(6) Take or authorize the taking of depositions;

(7) Receive and consider oral or written argument on facts or law;

(8) Hold or provide for the holding of conferences for the settlement or simplification of the issues by consent of the parties;

(9) Perform such acts and take such measures as are necessary or appropriate to the efficient conduct of any proceeding; and

(10) Make initial decisions.

§10.88 Hearings.

(a) *In general.* The Administrative Law Judge shall preside at the hearing on a complaint for the disqualification of an appraiser. Hearings shall be stenographically recorded and transcribed and the testimony of witnesses shall be taken under oath or affirmation. Hearings will be conducted pursuant to 5 U.S.C. 556.

(b) *Failure to appear.* If either party to the proceeding fails to appear at the hearing after due notice thereof has been sent to him/her, the right to a hearing shall be deemed to have been waived and the Administrative Law Judge may make a decision by default against the absent party.

§10.89 Evidence.

(a) *In general.* The rules of evidence prevailing in courts of law and equity are not controlling in hearings on complaints for the disqualification of appraisers. However, the Administrative Law Judge shall exclude evidence which is irrelevant, immaterial, or unduly repetitious.

(b) *Depositions.* The deposition of any witness taken pursuant to §10.90 may be admitted.

(c) *Proof of documents.* Official documents, records, and papers of the Internal Revenue Service or the Department of the Treasury shall be admissible in evidence without the production of an officer or employee to authenticate them. Any such documents, records, and papers may be evidenced by a copy attested or identified by an officer or employee of the Internal Revenue Service or the Department of the Treasury, as the case may be.

(d) *Exhibits.* If any document, record, or other paper is introduced in evidence as an exhibit, the Administrative Law Judge may authorize the withdrawal of the exhibit subject to any conditions which he/she deems proper.

(e) *Objections*. Objections to evidence shall be in short form, stating the grounds of objection relied upon, and the record shall not include argument thereon, except as ordered by the Administrative Law Judge. Rulings on such objections shall be a part of the record. No exception to the ruling is necessary to preserve the rights of the parties.

§10.90   Depositions.

Depositions for use at a hearing may, with the written approval of the Administrative Law Judge, be taken either by the Director of Practice or the respondent or their duly authorized representatives. Depositions may be taken upon oral or written interrogatories, upon not less than 10 days' written notice to the other party before any officer duly authorized to administer an oath for general purposes or before an officer or employee of the Internal Revenue Service who is authorized to administer an oath in internal revenue matters. Such notice shall state the names of the witnesses and the time and place where the depositions are to be taken. The requirement of 10 days' notice may be waived by the parties in writing, and depositions may then be taken from the persons and at the times and places mutually agreed to by the parties. When a deposition is taken upon written interrogatories, any cross-examination shall be upon written interrogatories. Copies of such written interrogatories shall be served upon the other party with the notice, and copies of any written cross-interrogatories shall be mailed or delivered to the opposing party at least 5 days before the date of taking the depositions, unless the parties mutually agree otherwise. A party upon whose behalf a deposition is taken must file it with the Administrative Law Judge and serve one copy upon the opposing party. Expenses in the reporting of depositions shall be borne by the party at whose instance the deposition is taken.

§10.91   Transcript.

In cases where the hearing is stenographically reported by a Government contract reporter, copies of the transcript may be obtained from the reporter at rates not to exceed the maximum rates fixed by contract between the Government and the reporter. Where a hearing is stenographically reported by a regular employee of the Internal Revenue Service, a copy thereof will be supplied to the respondent either without charge or upon the payment of a reasonable fee. Copies of exhibits introduced at the hearing or at the taking of depositions will be supplied to the parties upon the payment of a reasonable fee (Sec. 501, Pub. L. 82 - 137, 65 Stat. 290 (31 U.S.C. 483a)).

§10.92   Proposed findings and conclusions.

Except in cases where the respondent has failed to answer the complaint or where a party has failed to appear at the hearing, the Administrative Law Judge, prior to making a decision, shall afford the parties a reasonable opportunity to submit proposed findings and conclusions and supporting reasons therefor.

§10.93   Decision of the Administrative Law Judge.

As soon as practicable after the conclusion of a hearing and the receipt of any proposed findings and conclusions timely submitted by the parties, the Administrative Law Judge shall make the initial decision in the case. The decision shall include (a) a statement of findings and conclusions, as well as the reasons or bases therefor, upon all the material issues of fact, law, or discretion presented on the record, and (b) an order of disqualification or an order of dismissal of the complaint. The Administrative Law Judge shall file the decision with the Director of Practice and shall transmit a copy thereof to the respondent or his attorney of record. In the absence of an appeal to the Secretary of the Treasury, or review of the decision upon motion of the Secretary, the decision of the Administrative Law Judge shall without further proceedings become the decision of the Secretary of the Treasury 30 days from the date of the Administrative Law Judge's decision.

§10.94 Appeal to the Secretary.

Within 30 days from the date of the Administrative Law Judge's decision, either party may appeal such decision to the Secretary of the Treasury. If an appeal is by the respondent, the appeal shall be filed with the Director of Practice in duplicate and shall include exceptions to the decision of the Administrative Law Judge and supporting reasons for such exceptions. If an appeal is filed by the Director of Practice, a copy thereof shall be transmitted to the respondent. Within 30 days after receipt of an appeal or copy thereof, the other party may file a reply brief in duplicate with the Director of Practice. If the reply brief is filed by the Director, a copy shall be transmitted to the respondent. Upon the filing of an appeal and a reply brief, if any, the Director of Practice shall transmit the entire record to the Secretary of the Treasury.

§10.95 Decision of the Secretary.

On appeal from or review of the initial decision of the Administrative Law Judge, the Secretary of the Treasury shall make the agency decision. In making such decision, the Secretary of the Treasury will review the record or such portions thereof as may be cited by the parties. A copy of the Secretary's decision shall be transmitted to the respondent by the Director of Practice.

§10.96 Final order.

Upon the issuance of a final order disqualifying an appraiser, the Director of Practice shall give notice thereof to appropriate officers and employees of the Internal Revenue Service and to interested departments and agencies of the Federal Government.

§10.97 Petition for reinstatement.

The Director of Practice may entertain a petition for reinstatement from any disqualified appraiser after the expiration of 5 years following such disqualification. Reinstatement may not be granted unless the Director of Practice is satisfied that the petitioner, thereafter, is not likely to conduct himself/herself contrary to 26 U.S.C. 6701(a), and that granting such reinstatement would not be contrary to the public interest.

Subpart E — General Provisions

§10.98 Records.

(a) *Availability.* There are made available to public inspection at the Office of Director of Practice the roster of all persons enrolled to practice, the roster of all persons disbarred or suspended from practice, and the roster of all disqualified appraisers. Other records may be disclosed upon specific request, in accordance with the disclosure regulations of the Internal Revenue Service and the Treasury Department.

(b) *Disciplinary procedures.* A request by a practitioner that a hearing in a disciplinary proceeding concerning him be public, and that the record thereof be made available for inspection by interested persons, may be granted if agreement is reached by stipulation in advance to protect from disclosure tax information which is confidential, in accordance with the applicable statutes and regulations.

[31 FR 10773, Aug. 13, 1966. Redesignated at 50 FR 42016, Oct. 17, 1985, and amended at 50 FR 42018, Oct. 17, 1985]

§10.100   Saving clause.

Any proceeding for the disbarment or suspension of an attorney, certified public accountant, or enrolled agent, instituted but not closed prior to the effective date of these revised regulations, shall not be affected by such regulations. Any proceeding under this part based on conduct engaged in prior to the effective date of these regulations may be instituted subsequent to such effective date.

[50 FR 42019, Oct. 17, 1985]

§10.101   Special orders.

The Secretary of the Treasury reserves the power to issue such special orders as he may deem proper in any cases within the purview of this part.

[31 FR 10773, Aug. 13, 1966. Redesignated at 50 FR 42016, Oct. 17, 1985]

AICPA Code of Professional Conduct

Code of Professional Conduct

Principles
Rules

and Implementing Resolutions of Council

as amended October 28, 1997

The Principles and Rules as set forth herein are further amplified by interpretations and rulings contained in AICPA Professional Standards (volume 2)

Code of Professional Conduct

Composition, Applicability, and Compliance

The Code of Professional Conduct of the American Institute of Certified Public Accountants consists of two sections — (1) the Principles and (2) the Rules. The Principles provide the framework for the Rules, which govern the performance of professional services by members. The Council of the American Institute of Certified Public Accountants is authorized to designate bodies to promulgate technical standards under the Rules, and the bylaws require adherence to those Rules and standards.

The Code of Professional Conduct was adopted by the membership to provide guidance and rules to all members — those in public practice, in industry, in government, and in education — in the performance of their professional responsibilities.

Compliance with the Code of Professional Conduct, as with all standards in an open society, depends primarily on members' understanding and voluntary actions, secondarily on reinforcement by peers and public opinion, and ultimately on disciplinary proceedings, when necessary, against members who fail to comply with the Rules.

Other Guidance

The Principles and Rules as set forth herein are further amplified by interpretations and rulings contained in *AICPA Professional Standards* (volume 2).

Interpretations of Rules of Conduct consist of interpretations which have been adopted, after exposure to state societies, state boards, practice units and other interested parties, by the professional ethics division's executive committee to provide guidelines as to the scope and application of the Rules but are not intended to limit such scope or application. A member who departs from such guidelines shall have the burden of justifying such departure in any disciplinary hearing.

Ethics Rulings consist of formal rulings made by the professional ethics division's executive committee after exposure to state societies, state boards, practice units and other interested parties. These rulings summarize the application of Rules of Conduct and interpretations to a particular set of factual circumstances. Members who depart from such rulings in similar circumstances will be requested to justify such departures.

Publication of an interpretation or ethics ruling in the *Journal of Accountancy* constitutes notice to members. Hence, the effective date of the pronouncement is the last day of the month in which the pronouncement is published in the *Journal of Accountancy*. The professional ethics division will take into consideration the time that would have been reasonable for the member to comply with the pronouncement.

A member should also consult, if applicable, the ethical standards of his state CPA society, state board of accountancy, the Securities and Exchange Commission, and any other governmental agency which may regulate his client's business or use his report to evaluate the client's compliance with applicable laws and related regulations.

Section I — Principles

Preamble

Membership in the American Institute of Certified Public Accountants is voluntary. By accepting membership, a certified public accountant assumes an obligation of self-discipline above and beyond the requirements of laws and regulations.

These Principles of the Code of Professional Conduct of the American Institute of Certified Public Accountants express the profession's recognition of its responsibilities to the public, to clients, and to colleagues. They guide members in the performance of their professional responsibilities and express the basic tenets of ethical and professional conduct. The Principles call for an unswerving commitment to honorable behavior, even at the sacrifice of personal advantage.

Article I

Responsibilities

In carrying out their responsibilities as professionals, members should exercise sensitive professional and moral judgments in all their activities.

As professionals, certified public accountants perform an essential role in society. Consistent with that role, members of the American Institute of Certified Public Accountants have responsibilities to all those who use their professional services. Members also have a continuing responsibility to cooperate with each other to improve the art of accounting, maintain the public's confidence, and carry out the profession's special responsibilities for self-governance. The collective efforts of all members are required to maintain and enhance the traditions of the profession.

Article II

The Public Interest

Members should accept the obligation to act in a way that will serve the public interest, honor the public trust, and demonstrate commitment to professionalism.

A distinguishing mark of a profession is acceptance of its responsibility to the public. The accounting profession's public consists of clients, credit grantors, governments, employers, investors, the business and financial community, and others who rely on the objectivity and integrity of certified public accountants to maintain the orderly functioning of commerce. This reliance imposes a public interest responsibility on certified public accountants. The public interest is defined as the collective well-being of the community of people and institutions the profession serves.

In discharging their professional responsibilities, members may encounter conflicting pressures from among each of those groups. In resolving those conflicts, members should act with integrity, guided by the precept that when members fulfill their responsibility to the public, clients' and employers' interests are best served.

Those who rely on certified public accountants expect them to discharge their responsibilities with integrity, objectivity, due professional care, and a genuine interest in serving the public. They are expected to provide quality services, enter into fee arrangements, and offer a range of services — all in a manner that demonstrates a level of professionalism consistent with these Principles of the Code of Professional Conduct.

All who accept membership in the American Institute of Certified Public Accountants commit themselves to honor the public trust. In return for the faith that the public reposes in them, members should seek continually to demonstrate their dedication to professional excellence.

Article III

Integrity

To maintain and broaden public confidence, members should perform all professional responsibilities with the highest sense of integrity.

Integrity is an element of character fundamental to professional recognition. It is the quality from which the public trust derives and the benchmark against which a member must ultimately test all decisions.

Integrity requires a member to be, among other things, honest and candid within the constraints of client confidentiality. Service and the public trust should not be subordinated to personal gain and advantage. Integrity can accommodate the inadvertent error and the honest difference of opinion; it cannot accommodate deceit or subordination of principle.

Integrity is measured in terms of what is right and just. In the absence of specific rules, standards, or guidance, or in the face of conflicting opinions, a member should test decisions and deeds by asking: "Am I doing what a person of integrity would do? Have I retained my integrity?" Integrity requires a member to observe both the form and the spirit of technical and ethical standards; circumvention of those standards constitutes subordination of judgment.

Integrity also requires a member to observe the principles of objectivity and independence and of due care.

Article IV

Objectivity and Independence

A member should maintain objectivity and be free of conflicts of interest in discharging professional responsibilities. A member in public practice should be independent in fact and appearance when providing auditing and other attestation services.

Objectivity is a state of mind, a quality that lends value to a member's services. It is a distinguishing feature of the profession. The principle of objectivity imposes the obligation to be impartial, intellectually honest, and free of conflicts of interest. Independence precludes relationships that may appear to impair a member's objectivity in rendering attestation services.

Members often serve multiple interests in many different capacities and must demonstrate their objectivity in varying circumstances. Members in public practice render attest, tax, and management advisory services. Other members prepare financial statements in the employment of others, perform internal auditing services, and serve in financial and management capacities in industry, education, and government. They also educate and train those who aspire to admission into the profession. Regardless of service or capacity, members should protect the integrity of their work, maintain objectivity, and avoid any subordination of their judgment.

For a member in public practice, the maintenance of objectivity and independence requires a continuing assessment of client relationships and public responsibility. Such a member who provides auditing and other attestation services should be independent in fact and appearance. In providing all other services, a member should maintain objectivity and avoid conflicts of interest.

Although members not in public practice cannot maintain the appearance of independence, they nevertheless have the responsibility to maintain objectivity in rendering professional services. Members employed by others to prepare financial statements or to perform auditing, tax, or consulting services are charged with the same responsibility for objectivity as members in public practice and must be scrupulous in their application of generally accepted accounting principles and candid in all their dealings with members in public practice.

Article V

Due Care

A member should observe the profession's technical and ethical standards, strive continually to improve competence and the quality of services, and discharge professional responsibility to the best of the member's ability.

The quest for excellence is the essence of due care. Due care requires a member to discharge professional responsibilities with competence and diligence. It imposes the obligation to perform professional services to the best of a member's ability with concern for the best interest of those for whom the services are performed and consistent with the profession's responsibility to the public.

Competence is derived from a synthesis of education and experience. It begins with a mastery of the common body of knowledge required for designation as a certified public accountant. The maintenance of competence requires a commitment to learning and professional improvement that must continue throughout a member's professional life. It is a member's individual responsibility. In all engagements and in all responsibilities, each member should undertake to achieve a level of competence that will assure that the quality of the member's services meets the high level of professionalism required by these Principles.

Competence represents the attainment and maintenance of a level of understanding and knowledge that enables a member to render services with facility and acumen. It also establishes the limitations of a member's capabilities by dictating that consultation or referral may be required when a professional engagement exceeds the personal competence of a member or a member's firm. Each member is responsible for assessing his or her own competence — of evaluating whether education, experience, and judgment are adequate for the responsibility to be assumed.

Members should be diligent in discharging responsibilities to clients, employers, and the public. Diligence imposes the responsibility to render services promptly and carefully, to be thorough, and to observe applicable technical and ethical standards.

Due care requires a member to plan and supervise adequately any professional activity for which he or she is responsible.

Article VI

Scope and Nature of Services

A member in public practice should observe the Principles of the Code of Professional Conduct in determining the scope and nature of services to be provided.

The public interest aspect of certified public accountants' services requires that such services be consistent with acceptable professional behavior for certified public accountants. Integrity requires that service and the public trust not be subordinated to personal gain and advantage. Objectivity and independence require that members be free from conflicts of interest in discharging professional responsibilities. Due care requires that services be provided with competence and diligence.

Each of these Principles should be considered by members in determining whether or not to provide specific services in individual circumstances. In some instances, they may represent an overall constraint on the nonaudit services that might be offered to a specific client. No hard-and-fast rules can be developed to help members reach these judgments, but they must be satisfied that they are meeting the spirit of the Principles in this regard.

In order to accomplish this, members should

- Practice in firms that have in place internal quality-control procedures to ensure that services are competently delivered and adequately supervised.

- Determine, in their individual judgments, whether the scope and nature of other services provided to an audit client would create a conflict of interest in the performance of the audit function for that client.

- Assess, in their individual judgments, whether an activity is consistent with their role as professionals (for example, Is such activity a reasonable extension or variation of existing services offered by the member or others in the profession?).

Section II — Rules

Applicability

The bylaws of the American Institute of Certified Public Accountants require that members adhere to the Rules of the Code of Professional Conduct. Members must be prepared to justify departures from these Rules.

INTERPRETATION OF APPLICABILITY SECTION

[*The professional ethics executive committee has issued the following interpretation of the applicability section of the Code, effective November 30, 1989.*]

For purposes of the applicability section of the Code, a "member" is a member or international associate of the American Institute of CPAs.

1. The Rules of Conduct that follow apply to all professional services performed except (a) where the wording of the rule indicates otherwise and (b) that a member who is practicing outside the United States will not be subject to discipline for departing from any of the rules stated herein as long as the member's conduct is in accord with the rules of the organized accounting profession in the country in which he or she is practicing. However, where a member's name is associated with financial statements under circumstances that would entitle the reader to assume that U.S. practices were followed, the member must comply with the requirements of rules 202 and 203.

2. A member may be held responsible for compliance with the rules by all persons associated with him or her in the practice of public accounting who are either under the member's supervision or are the member's partners or shareholders in the practice.

3. A member shall not permit others to carry out on his or her behalf, either with or without compensation, acts which, if carried out by the member, would place the member in violation of the rules.

Definitions*

Client. A client is any person or entity, other than the member's employer, that engages a member or a member's firm to perform professional services or a person or entity with respect to which professional services are performed. The term "employer" for these purposes does not include those entities engaged in the practice of public accounting.

Council. The Council of the American Institute of Certified Public Accountants.

Enterprise. For purposes of the Code, the term "enterprise" is synonymous with the term "client."

Financial statements. A presentation of financial data, including accompanying notes, if any, intended to communicate an entity's economic resources and/or obligations at a point in time or the changes therein for a period of time, in accordance with generally accepted accounting principles or a comprehensive basis of accounting other than generally accepted accounting principles.

Incidental financial data to support recommendations to a client or in documents for which the reporting is governed by Statements on Standards for Attestation Engagements and tax returns and supporting

---

*Pursuant to its authority under the bylaws (section 3.6.2.2) to interpret the Code of Professional Conduct, the professional ethics executive committee has issued these definitions of terms appearing in the Code effective November 30, 1989 (revised April 1992 and May 1996).

schedules do not, for this purpose, constitute financial statements. The statement, affidavit, or signature of preparers required on tax returns neither constitutes an opinion on financial statements nor requires a disclaimer of such opinion.

Firm. A form of organization permitted by state law or regulation whose characteristics conform to resolutions of Council that is engaged in the practice of public accounting, including the individual owners thereof.

Holding out. In general, any action initiated by a member that informs others of his or her status as a CPA or AICPA-accredited specialist constitutes holding out as a CPA. This would include, for example, any oral or written representation to another regarding CPA status, use of the CPA designation on business cards or letterhead, the display of a certificate evidencing a member's CPA designation, or listing as a CPA in local telephone directories.

Institute. The American Institute of Certified Public Accountants.

Interpretations of Rules of Conduct. Pronouncements issued by the division of professional ethics to provide guidelines concerning the scope and application of the Rules of Conduct.

Member. A member, associate member, or international associate of the American Institute of Certified Public Accountants.

Practice of public accounting. The practice of public accounting consists of the performance for a client, by a member or a member's firm, while holding out as CPA(s), of the professional services of accounting, tax, personal financial planning, litigation support services, and those professional services for which standards are promulgated by bodies designated by Council, such as Statements of Financial Accounting Standards, Statements on Auditing Standards, Statements on Standards for Accounting and Review Services, Statement on Standards for Consulting Services, Statements of Governmental Accounting Standards, Statements on Standards for Attestation Engagements, and Statement on Standards for Accountants' Services on Prospective Financial Information.

However, a member or a member's firm, while holding out as CPA(s), is not considered to be in the practice of public accounting if the member or the member's firm does not perform, for any client, any of the professional services described in the preceding paragraph.

Professional services. Professional services include all services performed by a member while holding out as a CPA.

Rules

Rule 101 Independence

A member in public practice shall be independent in the performance of professional services as required by standards promulgated by bodies designated by Council.

Rule 102   Integrity and Objectivity

In the performance of any professional service, a member shall maintain objectivity and integrity, shall be free of conflicts of interest, and shall not knowingly misrepresent facts or subordinate his or her judgment to others.

Rule 201   General Standards

A member shall comply with the following standards and with any interpretations thereof by bodies designated by Council.

A. *Professional Competence.* Undertake only those professional services that the member or the member's firm can reasonably expect to be completed with professional competence.

B. *Due Professional Care.* Exercise due professional care in the performance of professional services.

C. *Planning and Supervision.* Adequately plan and supervise the performance of professional services.

D. *Sufficient Relevant Data.* Obtain sufficient relevant data to afford a reasonable basis for conclusions or recommendations in relation to any professional services performed.

   (See implementing resolutions, pages 15–17.)

Rule 202   Compliance With Standards

A member who performs auditing, review, compilation, management consulting, tax, or other professional services shall comply with standards promulgated by bodies designated by Council.

   (See implementing resolutions, pages 15–17.)

Rule 203   Accounting Principles

A member shall not (1) express an opinion or state affirmatively that the financial statements or other financial data of any entity are presented in conformity with generally accepted accounting principles or (2) state that he or she is not aware of any material modifications that should be made to such statements or data in order for them to be in conformity with generally accepted accounting principles, if such statements or data contain any departure from an accounting principle promulgated by bodies designated by Council to establish such principles that has a material effect on the statements or data taken as a whole. If, however, the statements or data contain such a departure and the member can demonstrate that due to unusual circumstances the financial statements or data would otherwise have been misleading, the member can comply with the rule by describing the departure, its approximate effects, if practicable, and the reasons why compliance with the principle would result in a misleading statement.

(See implementing resolutions, pages 15–17.)

Rule 301 Confidential Client Information

A member in public practice shall not disclose any confidential client information without the specific consent of the client.

This rule shall not be construed (1) to relieve a member of his or her professional obligations under rules 202 and 203, (2) to affect in any way the member's obligation to comply with a validly issued and enforceable subpoena or summons, or to prohibit a member's compliance with applicable laws and government regulations, (3) to prohibit review of a member's professional practice under AICPA or state CPA society or Board of Accountancy authorization, or (4) to preclude a member from initiating a complaint with, or responding to any inquiry made by, the professional ethics division or trial board of the Institute or a duly constituted investigative or disciplinary body of a state CPA society or Board of Accountancy.

Members of any of the bodies identified in (4) above and members involved with professional practice reviews identified in (3) above shall not use to their own advantage or disclose any member's confidential client information that comes to their attention in carrying out those activities. This prohibition shall not restrict members' exchange of information in connection with the investigative or disciplinary proceedings described in (4) above or the professional practice reviews described in (3) above.

Rule 302 Contingent Fees

A member in public practice shall not

(1) Perform for a contingent fee any professional services for, or receive such a fee from, a client for whom the member or the member's firm performs

(*a*) an audit or review of a financial statement; or

(*b*) a compilation of a financial statement when the member expects, or reasonably might expect, that a third party will use the financial statement and the member's compilation report does not disclose a lack of independence; or

(*c*) an examination of prospective financial information;
or

(2) Prepare an original or amended tax return or claim for a tax refund for a contingent fee for any client.

The prohibition in (1) above applies during the period in which the member or the member's firm is engaged to perform any of the services listed above and the period covered by any historical financial statements involved in any such listed services.

Except as stated in the next sentence, a contingent fee is a fee established for the performance of any service pursuant to an arrangement in which no fee will be charged unless a specified finding or result is attained, or in which the amount of the fee is otherwise dependent upon the finding or result of such service. Solely for purposes of this rule, fees are not regarded as being contingent if fixed by courts or other public authorities, or, in tax matters, if determined based on the results of judicial proceedings or the findings of governmental agencies.

A member's fees may vary depending, for example, on the complexity of services rendered.

Rule 401   [*There are currently no rules in the 400 series.*]

Rule 501   Acts Discreditable

A member shall not commit an act discreditable to the profession.

Rule 502   Advertising and Other Forms of Solicitation

A member in public practice shall not seek to obtain clients by advertising or other forms of solicitation in a manner that is false, misleading, or deceptive. Solicitation by the use of coercion, over-reaching, or harassing conduct is prohibited.

Rule 503   Commissions and Referral Fees

A. *Prohibited Commissions*

A member in public practice shall not for a commission recommend or refer to a client any product or service, or for a commission recommend or refer any product or service to be supplied by a client, or receive a commission, when the member or the member's firm also performs for that client

(*a*) an audit or review of a financial statement; or

(*b*) a compilation of a financial statement when the member expects, or reasonably might expect, that a third party will use the financial statement and the member's compilation report does not disclose a lack of independence; or

(*c*) an examination of prospective financial information.

This prohibition applies during the period in which the member is engaged to perform any of the services listed above and the period covered by any historical financial statements involved in such listed services.

B. *Disclosure of Permitted Commissions*

A member in public practice who is not prohibited by this rule from performing services for or receiving a commission and who is paid or expects to be paid a commission shall disclose that fact to any person or entity to whom the member recommends or refers a product or service to which the commission relates.

C. *Referral Fees*

Any member who accepts a referral fee for recommending or referring any service of a CPA to any person or entity or who pays a referral fee to obtain a client shall disclose such acceptance or payment to the client.

Rule 504   [*There is currently no rule 504.*]

Rule 505   Form of Organization and Name

A member may practice public accounting only in a form of organization permitted by state law or regulation whose characteristics conform to resolutions of Council.

A member shall not practice public accounting under a firm name that is misleading. Names of one or more past owners may be included in the firm name of a successor organization.

A firm may not designate itself as "Members of the American Institute of Certified Public Accountants" unless all of its owners are members of the Institute.

(See implementing resolution, pages 17–18.)

Council Resolutions to Implement Code of Professional Conduct

Under Rules 201, 202, and 203   Designating Bodies to Promulgate Technical Standards

Financial Accounting Standards Board

WHEREAS: In 1959 the Council designated the Accounting Principles Board to establish accounting principles, and

WHEREAS: The Council is advised that the Financial Accounting Standards Board (FASB) has become operational, it is

RESOLVED: That as of the date hereof the FASB, in respect of statements of financial accounting standards finally adopted by such board in accordance with its rules of procedure and the bylaws of the Financial Accounting Foundation, be, and hereby is, designated by this Council as the body to establish accounting principles pursuant to rule 203 and standards on disclosure of financial information for such entities outside financial statements in published financial reports containing financial statements under rule 202 of the Rules of the Code of Professional Conduct of the American Institute of Certified Public Accountants provided, however, any accounting research bulletins, or opinions of the accounting principles board issued or approved for exposure by the accounting principles board prior to April 1, 1973, and finally adopted by such board on or before June 30, 1973, shall constitute statements of accounting principles promulgated by a body designated by Council as contemplated in rule 203 of the Rules of the Code of Professional Conduct unless and until such time as they are expressly superseded by action of the FASB.

Governmental Accounting Standards Board

WHEREAS: The Governmental Accounting Standards Board (GASB) has been established by the board of trustees of the Financial Accounting Foundation (FAF) to issue standards of financial accounting and reporting with respect to activities and transactions of state and local governmental entities, and

WHEREAS: The American Institute of Certified Public Accountants is a signatory to the agreement creating the GASB as an arm of the FAF and has supported the GASB professionally and financially, it is

RESOLVED: That as of the date hereof, the GASB, with respect to statements of governmental accounting standards adopted and issued in July 1984 and subsequently in accordance with its rules of procedure and the bylaws of the FAF, be, and hereby is, designated by the Council of the American Institute of Certified Public Accountants as the body to establish financial accounting principles for state and local governmental entities pursuant to rule 203, and standards on disclosure of financial information for such entities outside financial statements in published financial reports containing financial statements under rule 202.

AICPA COMMITTEES AND BOARDS

WHEREAS: The membership of the Institute has adopted rules 201 and 202 of the Rules of the Code of Professional Conduct, which authorizes the Council to designate bodies to promulgate technical standards with which members must comply, and therefore it is

Accounting and Review Services Committee

RESOLVED: That the AICPA accounting and review services committee is hereby designated to promulgate standards under rules 201 and 202 with respect to unaudited financial statements or other unaudited financial information of an entity that is not required to file financial statements with a regulatory agency in connection with the sale or trading of its securities in a public market.

Auditing Standards Board

RESOLVED: That the AICPA auditing standards board is hereby designated as the body authorized under rules 201 and 202 to promulgate auditing and attest standards and procedures.

RESOLVED: That the auditing standards board shall establish under statements on auditing standards the responsibilities of members with respect to standards for disclosure of financial information outside financial statements in published financial reports containing financial statements.

Management Consulting Services Executive Committee

RESOLVED: That the AICPA management consulting services executive committee is hereby designated to promulgate standards under rules 201 and 202 with respect to the offering of management consulting services, provided, however, that such standards do not deal with the broad question of what, if any, services should be proscribed.

AND FURTHER RESOLVED: That any Institute committee or board now or in the future authorized by the Council to issue enforceable standards under rules 201 and 202 must observe an exposure process seeking comment from other affected committees and boards, as well as the general membership.

Attestation Standards

RESOLVED: That the AICPA accounting and review services committee, auditing standards board, and management consulting services executive committee are hereby designated as bodies authorized under rules 201 and 202 to promulgate attestation standards in their respective areas of responsibility.

Under Rule 505   Form of Organization and Name

RESOLVED: That with respect to a firm or organization which performs (1) any audit or other engagement performed in accordance with the Statements on Auditing Standards, (2) any review of a financial statement or compilation of a financial statement performed in accordance with the Statements on Standards for Accounting and Review Services, or (3) any examination of prospective financial information performed in accordance with the Statements on Standards for Attestation Engagements, or which holds itself out as a firm of certified public accountants or uses the term "certified public accountant(s)" or the designation "CPA" in connection with its name, the characteristics of such a firm or organization under rule 505 are as set forth below. The characteristics of all other firms or organizations are deemed to be whatever is legally permissible under applicable law or regulation.

1. A majority of the ownership of the firm in terms of financial interests and voting rights must belong to CPAs. The non-CPA owner would have to be actively engaged as a firm member in providing services to the firm's clients as his or her principal occupation. Ownership by investors or commerical enterprises not actively engaged as firm members in providing services to the firm's clients as their principal occupation is against the public interest and continues to be prohibited.

2. There must be a CPA who has ultimate responsibility for all the services provided by the firm and by each business unit[1] performing financial statement attest and compilation services and other engagements governed by Statements on Auditing Standards or Statements on Standards for Accounting and Review Services.

---

[1] "Business unit" is meant to indicate geographic (such as offices) and functional arrangements (such as tax and management consulting services).

3. Non-CPA owners could not assume ultimate responsibility for any financial statement attest or compilation engagement.

4. Non-CPAs becoming owners after adoption of Council's resolution would have to possess a baccalaureate degree and, beginning in the year 2010, have obtained 150 semester hours of education at an accredited college or university.

5. Non-CPA owners would be permitted to use the title "principal," "owner," "officer," "member" or "shareholder," or any other title permitted by state law, but not hold themselves out to be CPAs.

6. Non-CPA owners would have to abide by the AICPA Code of Professional Conduct. AICPA members may be held responsible under the Code for acts of co-owners.

7. Non-CPA owners would have to complete the same work-related CPE requirements as set forth under AICPA bylaw section 2.3 for AICPA members.

8. Owners shall at all times own their equity in their own right and shall be the beneficial owners of the equity capital ascribed to them. Provision would have to be made for the ownership to be transferred to the firm or to other qualified owners if the non-CPA ceases to be actively engaged in the firm.

9. Non-CPA owners would not be eligible for membership in the AICPA.

Statements on Responsibilities in Tax Practice

1991 Revision Statements 1–8 and Interpretation 1–1

Issued by the Tax Executive Committee of the
American Institute of Certified Public Accountants

CONTENTS

Statements on Responsibilities in Tax Practice are published for the guidance of members of the Institute and do not constitute enforceable standards. The statements have been approved by at least two-thirds of the members of the Responsibilities in Tax Practice Committee and the Tax Executive Committee.

Statements containing recommended standards of responsibilities that are more restrictive than those established by the Internal Revenue Code, the Treasury Department, or the Institute's Code of Professional Conduct depend for their authority on the general acceptability of the opinions expressed. These statements are not intended to be retroactive.

FOREWORD

This booklet contains the current version of the Statements on Responsibilities in Tax Practice (SRTPs) plus Interpretation 1-1, "Realistic Possibility Standard." The original Statements on Responsibilities in Tax Practice were issued between 1964 and 1977 to provide a body of advisory opinions on good standards of tax practice, delineating the CPA's responsibilities to the client, the public, the government, and the profession. Statement Nos. 1 through 9 and the Introduction were codified in 1976 as *Statements on Responsibilities in Tax Practice*. Statement No. 10 was issued in 1977.

The original statements concerning the CPA's responsibility to sign the return (Statement Nos. 1 and 2, "Signature of Preparers" and "Signature of Reviewer: Assumption of Preparer's Responsibility") were withdrawn in 1982 after Treasury Department regulations were issued adopting substantially the same standards for all tax return preparers. Statement Nos. 6 and 7, concerning the responsibility of a CPA who becomes aware of an error, were revised in 1991. The first interpretation of the Statements on Responsibilities in Tax Practice, Interpretation 1-1, was approved in December 1990. The previously issued statements have been renumbered as indicated in the Appendix, and the current statements should be cited as "SRTP No. 1," "SRTP No. 2," etc.

This publication is intended to be part of an ongoing process that will require changes to and interpretations of current statements and additions of new statements in recognition of the accelerating rate of change in tax laws and the increasing importance of tax practice to CPAs.

Statements on Responsibilities in Tax Practice are developed by the Responsibilities in Tax Practice Committee and approved by the Tax Executive Committee. This revision was approved by the 1990–91 Responsibilities in Tax Practice Committee and the 1990–1991 Tax Executive Committee, but acknowledgement is also due to the many members whose efforts over the years went into the development of these statements.

Donald H. Skadden
Vice President—Taxation

INTRODUCTION

The Program

.01   The program contemplates publication and dissemination of a numbered series of Statements on Responsibilities in Tax Practice by the Institute's Tax Executive Committee.

The Significance of the Statements

.02   The statements constitute a body of advisory opinion on what are appropriate standards of tax practice, outlining the extent of a CPA's responsibility to clients, the public, the government, and the profession. Each statement covers a particular aspect of tax practice. The statements, which are educational and advisory, take into account applicable legal requirements of tax practice as well as the Tax Division's opinions as to appropriate standards of responsibilities in tax practice.

The Objectives

.03   The principal objectives of the program are—

a.   To recommend appropriate standards of responsibilities in tax practice and to promote their uniform application by CPAs.

b.   To encourage the development of increased understanding of the responsibilities of CPAs by the Treasury Department and Internal Revenue Service and to urge their officials to promote the application of commensurate standards of responsibilities by their personnel.

c.   To foster increased public understanding of, compliance with, and confidence in our tax system through awareness of the recommended standards of responsibilities of CPAs in tax practice.

The Program in Perspective

.04   There are numerous guides to help determine practice responsibilities. The CPA is required to follow the statutes, regulations, and rules governing practice before the Internal Revenue Service (for example, Treasury Department Circular 230). The Institute's Code of Professional Conduct requires the observance of high ethical standards. These statements are published to clarify the CPA's dual responsibilities to the tax system and clients.

.05   Although the CPA has no separate enforceable statement of standards of conduct relating solely to tax practice, the Institute's Code of Professional Conduct requires attitudes and habits of truthfulness and integrity in all of a CPA's practice, including tax practice. Rule 102 of the Code of Professional Conduct states:

> In the performance of any professional service, a member shall maintain objectivity and integrity, shall be free of conflicts of interest, and shall not knowingly misrepresent facts or subordinate his or her judgment to others.

.06   The statements are not intended to establish a code of conduct in tax practice that is separate and apart from the general ethical precepts of the Institute's Code of Professional Conduct. That Code imposes upon individual members obligations to maintain high standards of technical competence and integrity in dealing with clients and the public in all phases of the professional activities of members, including tax practice.

.07   In this environment, the Tax Executive Committee concludes that while the Code of Professional Conduct is a major factor in molding the CPA's professional behavior, it is in the public interest and in the self-interest of the CPA to develop separate statements of recommended standards of responsibilities of CPAs in tax practice for the guidance of taxpayers and CPAs alike.

The Scope and Purpose of the Statements

.08   The statements generally are confined to discussions of the considerations relating to *federal income tax* practice, including the preparation of tax returns, tax planning, and representation before the Internal Revenue Service. The Tax Executive Committee will consider development of statements of responsibilities in other areas of tax practice in the future as part of its ongoing program to review, revise, and add statements as necessary or appropriate.

.09   The primary purpose of the program is educational. The statements do not have the force of authority, in contrast, for example, to the regulations contained in Treasury Department Circular 230, the Internal Revenue Code or its regulations, or the AICPA Code of Professional Conduct. Statements containing recommended standards of responsibilities that are more restrictive than those established by the Internal Revenue Code, the Treasury Department, or the AICPA Code of Professional Conduct are advisory opinions and CPAs should use them as guides.

Authority of the Tax Executive Committee

.10   By resolution of the Institute's Council, the Tax Executive Committee is authorized to express opinions on matters of broad policy related to taxation including the issuance of Statements on Responsibilities in Tax Practice.

The Procedures

.11   The statements present the opinion of at least two-thirds of the members of the Responsibilities in Tax Practice Committee and two-thirds of the Tax Executive Committee.

.12   Drafts of a proposed statement are given appropriate exposure before the Tax Executive Committee issues a statement.

.13   Details of the procedural aspects of issuing the statements can be found in the AICPA *Tax Division Administrative Manual.*

Statement on Responsibilities in Tax Practice No. 1
Issued August 1988

TAX RETURN POSITIONS

Introduction

.01   This statement sets forth the standards a CPA should follow in recommending tax return positions and in preparing or signing tax returns including claims for refunds. For this purpose, a "tax return position" is (1) a position reflected on the tax return as to which the client has been specifically advised by the CPA or (2) a position as to which the CPA has knowledge of all material facts and, on the basis of those facts, has concluded that the position is appropriate.

Statement

.02   With respect to tax return positions, a CPA should comply with the following standards:

a.   A CPA should not recommend to a client that a position be taken with respect to the tax treatment of any item on a return unless the CPA has a good faith belief that the position has a realistic possibility of being sustained administratively or judicially on its merits if challenged.

b.   A CPA should not prepare or sign a return as an income tax return preparer if the CPA knows that the return takes a position that the CPA could not recommend under the standard expressed in paragraph .02*a*.

c.   Notwithstanding paragraphs .02*a* and .02*b*, a CPA may recommend a position that the CPA concludes is not frivolous so long as the position is adequately disclosed on the return or claim for refund.

d.   In recommending certain tax return positions and in signing a return on which a tax return position is taken, a CPA should, where relevant, advise the client as to the potential penalty consequences of the recommended tax return position and the opportunity, if any, to avoid such penalties through disclosure.

.03   The CPA should not recommend a tax return position that—

a.   Exploits the Internal Revenue Service audit selection process; or

b.   Serves as a mere "arguing" position advanced solely to obtain leverage in the bargaining process of settlement negotiation with the Internal Revenue Service.

.04   A CPA has both the right and responsibility to be an advocate for the client with respect to any positions satisfying the aforementioned standards.

Explanation

.05   Our self-assessment tax system can only function effectively if taxpayers report their income on a tax return that is true, correct, and complete. A tax return is primarily a taxpayer's representation of facts, and the taxpayer has the final responsibility for positions taken on the return.

.06   CPAs have a duty to the tax system as well as to their clients. However, it is well-established that the taxpayer has no obligation to pay more taxes than are legally owed, and the CPA has a duty to the client to assist in achieving the result. The aforementioned standards will guide the CPA in meeting responsibilities to the tax system and to clients.

.07   The standards suggested herein require that a CPA in good faith believe that the position is warranted in existing law or can be supported by a good faith argument for an extension, modification, or reversal of existing law. For example, the CPA may reach such a conclusion on the basis of well-reasoned articles, treatises, IRS General Counsel Memoranda, a General Explanation of a Revenue Act prepared by the staff of the Joint Committee on Taxation and Internal Revenue Service written determinations (for example, private letter rulings), whether or not such sources are treated as "authority" under section 6661. A position would meet these standards even though, for example, it is later abandoned due to practical or procedural aspects of an IRS administrative hearing or in the litigation process.

.08   Where the CPA has a good faith belief that more than one position meets the standards suggested herein, the CPA's advice concerning alternative acceptable positions may include a discussion of the likelihood that each such position might or might not cause the client's tax return to be examined and whether the position would be challenged in an examination.

.09   In some cases, a CPA may conclude that a position is not warranted under the standard set forth in the preceding paragraph, .02a. A client may, however, still wish to take such a tax return position. Under such circumstances, the client should have the opportunity to make such an assertion, and the CPA should be able to prepare and sign the return provided the position is adequately disclosed on the return or claim for refund and the position is not frivolous. A "frivolous" position is one which is knowingly advanced in bad faith and is patently improper.

.10   The CPA's determination of whether information is adequately disclosed by the client is based on the facts and circumstances of the particular case. No detailed rules have been formulated, for purposes of this statement, to prescribe the manner in which information should be disclosed.

.11   Where particular facts and circumstances lead the CPA to believe that a taxpayer penalty might be asserted, the CPA should so advise the client and should discuss with the client issues related to disclosure on the tax return. Although disclosure is not required if the position meets the standard in paragraph .02a, the CPA may nevertheless recommend that a client disclose a position. Disclosure should be considered when the CPA believes it would mitigate the likelihood of claims of taxpayer penalties under the Internal Revenue Code or would avoid the possible application of the six-year statutory period for assessment under section 6501(e). Although the CPA should advise the client with respect to disclosure, it is the client's responsibility to decide whether and how to disclose.

Statement on Responsibilities in Tax Practice Interpretation No. 1-1
Issued December 1990

REALISTIC POSSIBILITY STANDARD

Background

.01 The AICPA Tax Division issues Statements on Responsibilities in Tax Practice (SRTPs). The primary purpose of these advisory statements on appropriate standards of tax practice is educational. This interpretation does not have the force of authority, in contrast, for example, to the regulations contained in Treasury Department Circular 230 or the preparer penalty provisions of the Internal Revenue Code.

.02 SRTP No. 1, "Tax Return Positions," contains the standards a CPA should follow in recommending tax return positions and in preparing or signing tax returns and claims for refunds. In general, a CPA should have "a good-faith belief that the [tax return] position [being recommended] has a realistic possibility of being sustained administratively or judicially on its merits if challenged" (see SRTP No. 1, paragraph .02a). This is referred to here as the "realistic possibility standard." If a CPA concludes that a tax return position does not meet the realistic possibility standard, the CPA may still recommend the position to the client or, if the position is not frivolous and is adequately disclosed on the tax return or claim for refund, the CPA may prepare and sign a return containing the position.

.03 A "frivolous" position is one which is knowingly advanced in bad faith and is patently improper (see SRTP No. 1, paragraph .09). The CPA's determination of whether information is adequately disclosed on the client's tax return or claim for refund is based on the facts and circumstances of the particular case (see SRTP No. 1, paragraph .10).

.04 If the CPA believes there is a possibility that a tax return position might result in penalties being asserted against the client, the CPA should so advise the client and should discuss with the client the opportunity, if any, of avoiding such penalties through disclosure (see SRTP No. 1, paragraph .11).

General Interpretation

.05 To meet the realistic possibility standard, a CPA should have a good-faith belief that the position is warranted by existing law or can be supported by a good-faith argument for an extension, modification, or reversal of existing law through the administrative or judicial process. The CPA should have an honest belief that the position meets the realistic possibility standard. Such a belief must be based on sound interpretations of the tax law. A CPA should not take into account the likelihood of audit or detection when determining whether this standard has been met (see SRTP No. 1, paragraph .03a).

.06 The realistic possibility standard cannot be expressed in terms of percentage odds. The realistic possibility standard is less stringent than the "substantial authority" and the "more likely than not" standards that apply under the Internal Revenue Code to substantial understatements of liability by taxpayers. It is more strict than the "reasonable basis" standard under regulations issued prior to the Revenue Reconciliation Act of 1989.

.07   In determining whether a tax return position meets the realistic possibility standard, a CPA may rely on authorities in addition to those evaluated when determining whether substantial authority exists. Accordingly, CPAs may rely on well-reasoned treatises, articles in recognized professional tax publications, and other reference tools and sources of tax analyses commonly used by tax advisors and preparers of returns.

.08   In determining whether a realistic possibility exists, the CPA should do all of the following:[1]

a.   Establish relevant background facts.

b.   Distill the appropriate questions from these facts.

c.   Search for authoritative answers to those questions.

d.   Resolve the questions by weighing the authorities uncovered by that search.

e.   Arrive at a conclusion supported by the authorities.

.09   The CPA should consider the weight of each authority in order to conclude whether a position meets the realistic possibility standard. In determining the weight of an authority, the CPA should consider its persuasiveness, relevance, and source. Thus, the type of authority is a significant factor. Other important factors include whether the facts stated by the authority are distinguishable from those of the client and whether the authority contains an analysis of the issue or merely states a conclusion.

.10   The realistic possibility standard may be met despite the absence of certain types of authority. For example, a CPA may conclude that the realistic possibility standard has been met when the position is supported only by a well-reasoned construction of the applicable statutory provision.

.11   In determining whether the realistic possibility standard has been met, the extent of research required is left to the judgment of the CPA with respect to all the facts and circumstances known to the CPA. The CPA may conclude that more than one position meets the realistic possibility standard.

Specific Illustrations

.12   The following illustrations deal with general fact patterns. Accordingly, the application of the guidance discussed above to variances in such general facts or to particular facts or circumstances may lead to different conclusions. In each illustration there is no authority other than that indicated.

> *Illustration 1.*   The CPA's client has engaged in a transaction that is adversely affected by a new statutory provision. Prior law supports a position favorable to the client. The client believes, and the CPA concurs, that the new statute is inequitable as applied to the client's situation. The statute is clearly drafted and unambiguous. The committee reports discussing the new statute contain general comments that do not specifically address the client's situation.

---

[1]See Ray M. Sommerfeld, et al., *Tax Research Techniques,* 3rd rev. ed. (New York: AICPA, 1989), for a discussion of this process.

The CPA should recommend the return position supported by the new statute. A position contrary to a clear, unambiguous statute would ordinarily be considered a frivolous position.

> *Illustration 2.* The facts are the same as in illustration 1 except that the committee reports discussing the new statute specifically address the client's situation and take a position favorable to the client.

In a case where the statute is clearly and unambiguously against the taxpayer's position but a contrary position exists based on committee reports specifically addressing the client's situation, a return position based on either the statutory language or the legislative history satisfies the realistic possibility standard.

> *Illustration 3.* The facts are the same as in illustration 1 except that the committee reports can be interpreted to provide some evidence or authority in support of the taxpayer's position; however, the legislative history does not specifically address the situation.

In a case where the statute is clear and unambiguous, a contrary position based on an interpretation of committee reports that do not explicitly address the client's situation does not meet the realistic possibility standard. However, since the committee reports provide some support or evidence for the taxpayer's position, such a return position is not frivolous. The CPA may recommend the position to the client if it is adequately disclosed on the tax return.

> *Illustration 4.* A client is faced with an issue involving the interpretation of a new statute. Following its passage, the statute was widely recognized to contain a drafting error, and a technical correction proposal has been introduced. The IRS issues an announcement indicating how it will administer the provision. The IRS pronouncement interprets the statute in accordance with the proposed technical correction.

Return positions based on either the existing statutory language or the IRS pronouncement satisfy the realistic possibility standard.

> *Illustration 5.* The facts are the same as in illustration 4 except that no IRS pronouncement has been issued.

In the absence of an IRS pronouncement interpreting the statute in accordance with the technical correction, only a return position based on the existing statutory language will meet the realistic possibility standard. A return position based on the proposed technical correction may be recommended if it is adequately disclosed, since it is not frivolous.

> *Illustration 6.* A client is seeking advice from a CPA regarding a recently amended Internal Revenue Code section. The CPA has reviewed the Code section, committee reports that specifically address the issue, and a recently published IRS Notice. The CPA has concluded in good faith that, based on the Code section and the committee reports, the IRS's position as stated in the Notice does not reflect congressional intent.

The CPA may recommend the position supported by the Internal Revenue Code section and the committee reports since it meets the realistic possibility standard.

> *Illustration 7.* The facts are the same as in illustration 6 except that the IRS pronouncement is a temporary regulation.

In determining whether the position meets the realistic possibility standard, the CPA should determine the weight to be given the regulation by analyzing factors such as whether the regulation is legislative, interpretative, or inconsistent with the statute. If the CPA concludes that the position does not meet the realistic possibility standard, the position may nevertheless be recommended if it is adequately disclosed, since it is not frivolous.

> *Illustration 8.* A tax form published by the IRS is incorrect, but completion of the form as published provides a benefit to the client. The CPA knows that the IRS has published an announcement acknowledging the error.

In these circumstances, a return position in accordance with the published form is a frivolous position.

> *Illustration 9.* The client wants to take a position that the CPA has concluded is frivolous. The client maintains that even if the return is examined by the IRS, the issue will not be raised.

The CPA should not consider the likelihood of audit or detection when determining whether the realistic possibility standard has been met. The CPA should not prepare or sign a return that contains a frivolous position even if it is disclosed.

> *Illustration 10.* Congress passes a statute requiring the capitalization of certain expenditures. The client believes, and the CPA concurs, that in order to comply fully, the client will need to acquire new computer hardware and software and implement a number of new accounting procedures. The client and the CPA agree that the costs of full compliance will be significantly greater than the resulting increase in tax due under the new provision. Because of these cost considerations, the client makes no effort to comply. The client wants the CPA to prepare and sign a return on which the new requirement is simply ignored.

The return position desired by the client is frivolous, and the CPA should neither prepare nor sign the return.

> *Illustration 11.* The facts are the same as in illustration 10 except that the client has made a good-faith effort to comply with the law by calculating an estimate of expenditures to be capitalized under the new provision.

In this situation, the realistic possibility standard has been met. When using estimates in the preparation of a return, the CPA should refer to SRTP No. 4, "Use of Estimates."

> *Illustration 12.* On a given issue, the CPA has located and weighed two authorities. The IRS has published its clearly enunciated position in a Revenue Ruling. A court opinion is favorable to the client. The CPA has considered the source of both authorities and has concluded that both are persuasive and relevant.

The realistic possibility standard is met by either position.

> *Illustration 13.* A tax statute is silent on the treatment of an item under the statute. However, the committee reports explaining the statute direct the IRS to issue regulations that will require a specified treatment of the item. No regulations have been issued at the time the CPA must recommend a position on the tax treatment of the item.

The CPA may recommend the position supported by the committee reports, since it meets the realistic possibility standard.

> *Illustration 14.* The client wants to take a position that the CPA concludes meets the realistic possibility standard based on an assumption regarding an underlying nontax legal issue. The CPA recommends that the client seek advice from its legal counsel, and the client's attorney gives an opinion on the nontax legal issue.

A legal opinion on a nontax legal issue may, in general, be relied upon by a CPA. The CPA must, however, use professional judgment when relying on a legal opinion. If, on its face, the opinion of the client's attorney appears to be unreasonable, unsubstantiated, or unwarranted, the CPA should consult his or her attorney before relying on the opinion.

> *Illustration 15.* The client has obtained from its attorney an opinion on the tax treatment of an item and requests that the CPA rely on the opinion.

The authorities on which a CPA may rely include well-reasoned sources of tax analysis. If the CPA is satisfied as to the source, relevance, and persuasiveness of the legal opinion, the CPA may rely on that opinion when determining whether the realistic possibility standard has been met.

Statement on Responsibilities in Tax Practice No. 2
Issued August 1988

ANSWERS TO QUESTIONS ON RETURNS

Introduction

.01   This statement considers whether a CPA may sign the preparer's declaration on a tax return where one or more questions on the return have not been answered. The term "questions" includes requests for information on the return, in the instructions, or in the regulations, whether or not stated in the form of a question.

Statement

.02   A CPA should make a reasonable effort to obtain from the client, and provide, appropriate answers to all questions on a tax return before signing as preparer.

Explanation

.03   It is recognized that the questions on tax returns are not of uniform importance, and often they are not applicable to the particular taxpayer. Nevertheless, aside from administrative convenience to the Internal Revenue Service, there are at least two considerations which dictate that a CPA should be satisfied that a reasonable effort has been made to provide appropriate answers to the questions on the return which are applicable to the taxpayer:

a.   A question may be of importance in determining taxable income or loss, or the tax liability shown on the return, in which circumstance the omission tends to detract from the quality of the return.

b.   The CPA must sign the preparer's declaration stating that the return is true, correct, and complete.

.04   While an effort should be made to provide an answer to each question on the return that is applicable to the taxpayer, reasonable grounds may exist for omitting an answer. For example, reasonable grounds may include the following:

a.   The information is not readily available and the answer is not significant in terms of taxable income or loss, or the tax liability shown on the return.

b.   Genuine uncertainty exists regarding the meaning of the question in relation to the particular return.

c.   The answer to the question is voluminous; in such cases, assurance should be given on the return that the data will be supplied upon examination.

.05   The fact that an answer to a question might prove disadvantageous to the client does not justify omitting an answer.

.06 Where reasonable grounds exist for omission of an answer to an applicable question, a CPA is not required to provide on the return an explanation of the reason for the omission. In this connection, the CPA should consider whether the omission of an answer to a question may cause the return to be deemed incomplete.

Statement on Responsibilities in Tax Practice No. 3
Issued August 1988

CERTAIN PROCEDURAL ASPECTS OF PREPARING RETURNS

Introduction

.01   This statement considers the responsibility of the CPA to examine or verify certain supporting data or to consider information related to another client when preparing a client's tax return.

Statement

.02   In preparing or signing a return, the CPA may in good faith rely without verification upon information furnished by the client or by third parties. However, the CPA should not ignore the implications of information furnished and should make reasonable inquiries if the information furnished appears to be incorrect, incomplete, or inconsistent either on its face or on the basis of other facts known to the CPA. In this connection, the CPA should refer to the client's returns for prior years whenever feasible.

.03   Where the Internal Revenue Code or income tax regulations impose a condition to deductibility or other tax treatment of an item (such as taxpayer maintenance of books and records or substantiating documentation to support the reported deduction or tax treatment), the CPA should make appropriate inquiries to determine to his or her satisfaction whether such condition has been met.

.04   The individual CPA who is required to sign the return should consider information actually known to that CPA from the tax return of another client when preparing a tax return if the information is relevant to that tax return, its consideration is necessary to properly prepare that tax return, and use of such information does not violate any law or rule relating to confidentiality.

Explanation

.05   The preparer's declaration on the income tax return states that the information contained therein is true, correct, and complete to the best of the preparer's knowledge and belief "based on all information of which preparer has any knowledge." This reference should be understood to relate to information furnished by the client or by third parties to the CPA in connection with the preparation of the return.

.06   The preparer's declaration does not require the CPA to examine or verify supporting data. However, a distinction should be made between (1) the need to either determine by inquiry that a specifically required condition (such as maintaining books and records or substantiating documentation) has been satisfied, or to obtain information when the material furnished appears to be incorrect or incomplete, and

(2) the need for the CPA to examine underlying information. In fulfilling his or her obligation to exercise due diligence in preparing a return, the CPA ordinarily may rely on information furnished by the client unless it appears to be incorrect, incomplete, or inconsistent. Although the CPA has certain responsibilities in exercising due diligence in preparing a return, the client has ultimate responsibility for the contents of the return. Thus, where the client presents unsupported data in the form of lists of tax information, such as dividends and interest received, charitable contributions, and medical expenses, such information may be used in the preparation of a tax return without verification unless it appears to be incorrect, incomplete, or inconsistent either on its face or on the basis of other facts known to the CPA.

.07   Even though there is no requirement to examine underlying documentation, the CPA should encourage the client to provide supporting data where appropriate. For example, the CPA should encourage the client to submit underlying documents for use in tax return preparation to permit full consideration of income and deductions arising from security transactions and from pass-through entities such as estates, trusts, partnerships, and S corporations. This should reduce the possibility of misunderstanding, inadvertent errors, and administrative problems in the examination of returns by the Internal Revenue Service.

.08   The source of information provided to the CPA by a client for use in preparing the return is often a pass-through entity, such as a limited partnership, in which the client has an interest but is not involved in management. In some instances, it may be appropriate for the CPA to advise the client to ascertain the nature and amount of possible exposures to tax deficiencies, interest, and penalties, by contact with management of the pass-through entity. However, the CPA need not require the client to do so and may accept the information provided by the pass-through entity without further inquiry, unless there is reason to believe it is incorrect, incomplete, or inconsistent either on its face or on the basis of other facts known to the CPA.

.09   The CPA should make use of the client's prior years' returns in preparing the current return whenever feasible. Reference to prior returns and discussion with the client of prior year tax determinations should provide information as to the client's general tax status, avoid the omission or duplication of items, and afford a basis for the treatment of similar or related transactions. As with the examination of information supplied for the current year's return, the extent of comparison of the details of income and deduction between years depends upon the particular circumstances.

Statement on Responsibilities in Tax Practice No. 4
Issued August 1988

USE OF ESTIMATES

Introduction

.01   This statement considers the CPA's responsibility in connection with the CPA's use of the taxpayer's estimates in the preparation of a tax return. The CPA may advise on estimates used in the preparation of a tax return, but responsibility for estimated data is that of the client, who should provide the estimated data. Appraisals or valuations are not considered estimates for purposes of this statement.

Statement

.02   A CPA may prepare tax returns involving the use of the taxpayer's estimates if it is impracticable to obtain exact data and the estimated amounts are reasonable under the facts and circumstances known to the CPA. When the taxpayer's estimates are used, they should be presented in such a manner as to avoid the implication of greater accuracy than exists.

Explanation

.03   Accounting requires the exercise of judgment and in many instances the use of approximations based on judgment. The application of such accounting judgments, as long as not in conflict with methods set forth in the Internal Revenue Code, is acceptable and expected. These judgments are not estimates within the purview of this statement. For example, the income tax regulations provide that if all other conditions for accrual are met, the exact amount of income or expense need not be known or ascertained at year end if the amount can be determined with reasonable accuracy.

.04   In the case of transactions involving small expenditures, accuracy in recording some data may be difficult to achieve. Therefore, the use of estimates by the taxpayer in determining the amount to be deducted for such items may be appropriate.

.05   In other cases where all of the facts relating to a transaction are not accurately known, either because records are missing or because precise information is not available at the time the return must be filed, estimates of the missing data may be made by the taxpayer.

.06   Estimated amounts should not be presented in a manner which provides a misleading impression as to the degree of factual accuracy.

.07   Although specific disclosure that an estimate is used for an item in the return is not required in most instances, there are unusual circumstances where such disclosure is needed to avoid misleading the Internal Revenue Service regarding the degree of accuracy of the return. Some examples of unusual circumstances include the following:

a. The taxpayer has died or is ill at the time the return must be filed.

b. The taxpayer has not received a K-1 for a flow-through entity at the time the tax return is to be filed.

c. There is litigation pending (for example, a bankruptcy proceeding) which bears on the return.

d. Fire or computer failure destroyed the relevant records.

Statement on Responsibilities in Tax Practice No. 5
Issued August 1988

DEPARTURE FROM A POSITION PREVIOUSLY CONCLUDED IN AN ADMINISTRATIVE PROCEEDING OR COURT DECISION

Introduction

.01   This statement discusses whether a CPA may recommend a tax return position that departs from the treatment of an item as concluded in an administrative proceeding or a court decision with respect to a prior return of the taxpayer. For this purpose, a "tax return position" is (1) a position reflected on the tax return as to which the client has been specifically advised by the CPA, or (2) a position about which the CPA has knowledge of all material facts and, on the basis of those facts, has concluded that the position is appropriate.

.02   For purposes of this statement, "administrative proceeding" includes an examination by the Internal Revenue Service or an appeals conference relating to a return or a claim for refund.

.03   For purposes of this statement, "court decision" means a decision by any federal court having jurisdiction over tax matters.

Statement

.04   The recommendation of a position to be taken concerning the tax treatment of an item in the preparation or signing of a tax return should be based upon the facts and the law as they are evaluated at the time the return is prepared or signed by the CPA. Unless the taxpayer is bound to a specified treatment in the later year, such as by a formal closing agreement, the treatment of an item as part of concluding an administrative proceeding or as part of a court decision does not restrict the CPA from recommending a different tax treatment in a later year's return. Therefore, if the CPA follows the standards in SRTP No. 1, the CPA may recommend a tax return position, prepare, or sign a tax return that departs from the treatment of an item as concluded in an administrative proceeding or a court decision with respect to a prior return of the taxpayer.

Explanation

.05   A CPA usually will recommend a position with respect to the tax treatment of an item that is the same as was consented to by the taxpayer for a similar item as a result of an administrative proceeding or that was subject to a court decision concerning a prior year's return of the taxpayer. The question is whether the CPA is required to do so. Considerations include the following:

a. The Internal Revenue Service tends to act consistently with the manner in which an item was disposed of in a prior administrative proceeding, but is not bound to do so. Similarly, a taxpayer is not bound to follow the tax treatment of an item as consented to in an earlier administrative proceeding.

b. An unfavorable court decision does not prevent a taxpayer from taking a position contrary to the earlier court decision in a subsequent year.

c. The consent in an earlier administrative proceeding and the existence of an unfavorable court decision are factors that the CPA should consider in evaluating whether the standards in SRTP No. 1 are met.

d. The taxpayer's consent to the treatment in the administrative proceeding or the court's decision may have been caused by a lack of documentation, whereas supporting data for the later year is adequate.

e. The taxpayer may have yielded in the administrative proceeding for settlement purposes or not appealed the court decision even though the position met the standards in SRTP No. 1.

f. Court decisions, rulings, or other authorities that are more favorable to the taxpayer's current position may have developed since the prior administrative proceeding was concluded or the prior court decision was rendered.

Statement on Responsibilities in Tax Practice No. 6
Issued May 1991

KNOWLEDGE OF ERROR: RETURN PREPARATION

Introduction

.01   This statement considers the responsibility of a CPA who becomes aware of an error in a client's previously filed tax return or of the client's failure to file a required tax return. As used herein, the term "error" includes any position, omission, or method of accounting that, at the time the return is filed, fails to meet the standards set out in SRTP No. 1. The term "error" also includes a position taken on a prior year's return that no longer meets these standards due to legislation, judicial decisions, or administrative pronouncements having retroactive effect. However, an error does not include an item that has an insignificant effect on the client's tax liability.

.02   This statement applies whether or not the CPA prepared or signed the return that contains the error.

Statement

.03   The CPA should inform the client promptly upon becoming aware of an error in a previously filed return or upon becoming aware of a client's failure to file a required return. The CPA should recommend the measures to be taken. Such recommendation may be given orally. The CPA is not obligated to inform the Internal Revenue Service, and the CPA may not do so without the client's permission, except where required by law.

.04   If the CPA is requested to prepare the current year's return and the client has not taken appropriate action to correct an error in a prior year's return, the CPA should consider whether to withdraw from preparing the return and whether to continue a professional relationship with the client. If the CPA does prepare such current year's return, the CPA should take reasonable steps to ensure that the error is not repeated.

Explanation

.05   While performing services for a client, a CPA may become aware of an error in a previously filed return or may become aware that the client failed to file a required return. The CPA should advise the client of the error (as required by Treasury Department Circular 230) and the measures to be taken. It is the client's responsibility to decide whether to correct the error. In appropriate cases, particularly where it appears that the Internal Revenue Service might assert the charge of fraud or other criminal misconduct, the client should be advised to consult legal counsel before taking any action. In the event that the client does not correct an error, or agree to take the necessary steps to change from an erroneous method of accounting, the CPA should consider whether to continue a professional relationship with the client.[1]

.06   If the CPA decides to continue a professional relationship with the client and is requested to prepare a tax return for a year subsequent to that in which the error occurred, then the CPA should take reasonable steps to ensure that the error is not repeated. If a CPA learns the client is using an erroneous method of accounting, when it is past the due date to request IRS permission to change to a method meeting the standards of SRTP No. 1, the CPA may sign a return for the current year, providing the return includes appropriate disclosure of the use of the erroneous method.

.07   Whether an error has no more than an insignificant effect on the client's tax liability is left to the judgment of the individual CPA based on all the facts and circumstances known to the CPA. In judging whether an erroneous method of accounting has more than an insignificant effect, the CPA should consider the method's cumulative effect and its effect on the current year's return.

.08   Where the CPA becomes aware of the error during an engagement which does not involve tax return preparation, the responsibility of the CPA is to advise the client of the existence of the error and to recommend that the error be discussed with the client's tax return preparer.

---

[1]The CPA should consider consulting his or her own legal counsel before deciding upon recommendations to the client and whether to continue a professional relationship with the client. The potential of violating Rule of Conduct 301 (relating to the CPA's confidential client relationship), the Internal Revenue Code and income tax regulations, or state laws on privileged communications and other considerations may create a conflict between the CPA's interests and those of the client.

Statement on Responsibilities in Tax Practice No. 7
Issued May 1991

KNOWLEDGE OF ERROR: ADMINISTRATIVE PROCEEDINGS

Introduction

.01   This statement considers the responsibility of a CPA who becomes aware of an error in a return that is the subject of an administrative proceeding, such as an examination by the IRS or an appeals conference relating to a return or a claim for refund. As used herein, the term "error" includes any position, omission, or method of accounting, which, at the time the return is filed, fails to meet the standards set out in SRTP No. 1. The term "error" also includes a position taken on a prior year's return that no longer meets these standards due to legislation, judicial decisions, or administrative pronouncements having retroactive effect. However, an error does not include an item that has an insignificant effect on the client's tax liability.

.02   This statement applies whether or not the CPA prepared or signed the return that contains the error; it does not apply where a CPA has been engaged by legal counsel to provide assistance in a matter relating to the counsel's client.

Statement

.03   When the CPA is representing a client in an administrative proceeding with respect to a return which contains an error of which the CPA is aware, the CPA should inform the client promptly upon becoming aware of the error. The CPA should recommend the measures to be taken. Such recommendation may be given orally. The CPA is neither obligated to inform the Internal Revenue Service nor may the CPA do so without the client's permission, except where required by law.

.04   The CPA should request the client's agreement to disclose the error to the Internal Revenue Service. Lacking such agreement, the CPA should consider whether to withdraw from representing the client in the administrative proceeding and whether to continue a professional relationship with the client.

Explanation

.05   When the CPA is engaged to represent the client before the Internal Revenue Service in an administrative proceeding with respect to a return containing an error of which the CPA is aware, the CPA should advise the client to disclose the error to the Internal Revenue Service. It is the client's responsibility to decide whether to disclose the error. In appropriate cases, particularly where it appears that the Internal Revenue Service might assert the charge of fraud or other criminal misconduct, the client should be advised to consult legal counsel before taking any action. If the client refuses to disclose or permit disclosure of an error, the CPA should consider whether to withdraw from representing the client in the administrative proceeding and whether to continue a professional relationship with the client.[1]

.06 Once disclosure is agreed upon, it should not be delayed to such a degree that the client or CPA might be considered to have failed to act in good faith or to have, in effect, provided misleading information. In any event, disclosure should be made before the conclusion of the administrative proceeding.

.07 Whether an error has an insignificant effect on the client's tax liability should be left to the judgment of the individual CPA based on all the facts and circumstances known to the CPA. In judging whether an erroneous method of accounting has more than an insignificant effect, the CPA should consider the method's cumulative effect and its effect on the return which is the subject of the administrative proceeding.

---

[1]The CPA should consider consulting his or her own legal counsel before deciding upon recommendations to the client and whether to continue a professional relationship with the client. The potential of violating Rule of Conduct 301 (relating to the CPA's confidential client relationship), the Internal Revenue Code and income tax regulations, or state laws on privileged communications and other considerations may create a conflict between the CPA's interests and those of the client.

Statement on Responsibilities in Tax Practice No. 8
Issued August 1988

FORM AND CONTENT OF ADVICE TO CLIENTS

Introduction

.01   This statement discusses certain aspects of providing tax advice to a client and considers the circumstances in which the CPA has a responsibility to communicate with the client when subsequent developments affect advice previously provided. The statement does not, however, cover the CPA's responsibilities when it is expected that the advice rendered is likely to be relied upon by parties other than the CPA's client.[1]

Statement

.02   In providing tax advice to a client, the CPA should use judgment to ensure that the advice given reflects professional competence and appropriately serves the client's needs. The CPA is not required to follow a standard format or guidelines in communicating written or oral advice to a client.

.03   In advising or consulting with a client on tax matters, the CPA should assume that the advice will affect the manner in which the matters or transactions considered ultimately will be reported on the client's tax returns. Thus, for all tax advice the CPA gives to a client, the CPA should follow the standards in SRTP No. 1 relating to tax return positions.

.04   The CPA may choose to communicate with a client when subsequent developments affect advice previously provided with respect to significant matters. However, the CPA cannot be expected to have assumed responsibility for initiating such communication except while assisting a client in implementing procedures or plans associated with the advice provided or when the CPA undertakes this obligation by specific agreement with the client.

Explanation

.05   Tax advice is recognized as a valuable service provided by CPAs. The form of advice may be oral or written and the subject matter may range from routine to complex. Because the range of advice is so extensive and because advice should meet specific needs of a client, neither standard format nor guidelines for communicating advice to the client can be established to cover all situations.

.06   Although oral advice may serve a client's needs appropriately in routine matters or in well-defined areas, written communications are recommended in important, unusual, or complicated transactions. In the judgment of the CPA, oral advice may be followed by a written communication to the client.

---

[1]The CPA's responsibilities when providing advice that will be relied upon by third parties will be addressed in a future statement.

.07   In deciding on the form of advice provided to a client, the CPA should exercise professional judgment and should consider such factors as the following:

a. The importance of the transaction and amounts involved

b. The specific or general nature of the client's inquiry

c. The time available for development and submission of the advice

d. The technical complications presented

e. The existence of authorities and precedents

f. The tax sophistication of the client and the client's staff

g. The need to seek legal advice

.08   The CPA may assist a client in implementing procedures or plans associated with the advice offered. During this active participation, the CPA continues to advise and should review and revise such advise as warranted by new developments and factors affecting the transaction.

.09   Sometimes the CPA is requested to provide tax advice but does not assist in implementing the plans adopted. While developments such as legislative or administrative changes or further judicial interpretations may affect the advice previously provided, the CPA cannot be expected to communicate later developments that affect such advice unless the CPA undertakes this obligation by specific agreement with the client. Thus, the communication of significant developments affecting previous advice should be considered an additional service rather than an implied obligation in the normal CPA-client relationship.

.10   The client should be informed that advice reflects professional judgment based on an existing situation and that subsequent developments could affect previous professional advice. CPAs should use precautionary language to the effect that their advice is based on facts as stated and authorities that are subject to change.

U.S. Constitution

Preamble

We the People of the United States, in Order to form a more perfect Union, establish Justice, insure domestic Tranquility, provide for the common defence, promote the general Welfare, and secure the Blessings of Liberty to ourselves and our Posterity, do ordain and establish this Constitution for the United States of America.

Article I

Section 1. All legislative Powers herein granted shall be vested in a Congress of the United States, which shall consist of a Senate and House of Representatives.

Section 2. The House of Representatives shall be composed of Members chosen every second Year by the People of the several States, and the Electors in each State shall have the Qualifications requisite for Electors of the most numerous Branch of the State Legislature.

No Person shall be a Representative who shall not have attained to the Age of twenty five Years, and been seven Years a Citizen of the United States, and who shall not, when elected, be an Inhabitant of that State in which he shall be chosen.

Representatives and direct Taxes shall be apportioned among the several States which may be included within this Union, according to their respective Numbers, which shall be determined by adding to the whole Number of free Persons, including those bound to Service for a Term of Years, and excluding Indians not taxed, three fifths of all other Persons. The actual Enumeration shall be made within three Years after the first Meeting of the Congress of the United States, and within every subsequent Term of ten Years, in such Manner as they shall by Law direct. The Number of Representatives shall not exceed one for every thirty Thousand, but each State shall have at Least one Representative; and until such enumeration shall be made, the State of New Hampshire shall be entitled to chuse three, Massachusetts eight, Rhode-Island and Providence Plantations one, Connecticut five, New-York six, New Jersey four, Pennsylvania eight, Delaware one, Maryland six, Virginia ten, North Carolina five, South Carolina five, and Georgia three.

When vacancies happen in the Representation from any State, the Executive Authority thereof shall issue Writs of Election to fill such Vacancies.

The House of Representatives shall chuse their Speaker and other Officers; and shall have the sole Power of Impeachment.

Section 3. The Senate of the United States shall be composed of two Senators from each State, chosen by the Legislature thereof, for six Years; and each Senator shall have one Vote.

Immediately after they shall be assembled in Consequence of the first Election, they shall be divided as equally as may be into three Classes. The Seats of the Senators of the first Class shall be vacated at the Expiration of the second Year, of the second Class at the Expiration of the fourth Year, and of the third Class at the Expiration of the sixth Year, so that one third may be chosen every second Year; and if Vacancies happen by Resignation, or otherwise, during the Recess of the Legislature of any State, the Executive thereof may make temporary Appointments until the next Meeting of the Legislature, which shall then fill such Vacancies.

No Person shall be a Senator who shall not have attained to the Age of thirty Years, and been nine Years a Citizen of the United States, and who shall not, when elected, be an Inhabitant of that State for which he shall be chosen.

The Vice President of the United States shall be President of the Senate, but shall have no Vote, unless they be equally divided.

The Senate shall chuse their other Officers, and also a President pro tempore, in the Absence of the Vice President, or when he shall exercise the Office of President of the United States.

The Senate shall have the sole Power to try all Impeachments. When sitting for that Purpose, they shall be on Oath or Affirmation. When the President of the United States is tried the Chief Justice shall preside: And no Person shall be convicted without the Concurrence of two thirds of the Members present.

Judgment in Cases of Impeachment shall not extend further than to removal from Office, and disqualification to hold and enjoy any Office of honor, Trust or Profit under the United States: but the Party convicted shall nevertheless be liable and subject to Indictment, Trial, Judgment and Punishment, according to Law.

Section 4. The Times, Places and Manner of holding Elections for Senators and Representatives, shall be prescribed in each State by the Legislature thereof; but the Congress may at any time by Law make or alter such Regulations, except as to the Places of chusing Senators.

The Congress shall assemble at least once in every Year, and such Meeting shall be on the first Monday in December, unless they shall by Law appoint a different Day.

Section 5. Each House shall be the Judge of the Elections, Returns and Qualifications of its own Members, and a Majority of each shall constitute a Quorum to do Business; but a smaller Number may adjourn from day to day, and may be authorized to compel the Attendance of absent Members, in such Manner, and under such Penalties as each House may provide.

Each House may determine the Rules of its Proceedings, punish its Members for disorderly Behaviour, and, with the Concurrence of two thirds, expel a Member.

Each House shall keep a Journal of its Proceedings, and from time to time publish the same, excepting such Parts as may in their Judgment require Secrecy; and the Yeas and Nays of the Members of either House on any question shall, at the Desire of one fifth of those Present, be entered on the Journal.

Neither House, during the Session of Congress, shall, without the Consent of the other, adjourn for more than three days, nor to any other Place than that in which the two Houses shall be sitting.

Section 6. The Senators and Representatives shall receive a Compensation for their Services, to be ascertained by Law, and paid out of the Treasury of the United States. They shall in all Cases, except Treason, Felony and Breach of the Peace, be privileged from Arrest during their Attendance at the Session of their respective Houses, and in going to and returning from the same; and for any Speech or Debate in either House, they shall not be questioned in any other Place.

No Senator or Representative shall, during the Time for which he was elected, be appointed to any civil Office under the Authority of the United States, which shall have been created, or the Emoluments whereof shall have been encreased during such time; and no Person holding any Office under the United States, shall be a Member of either House during his Continuance in Office.

Section 7. All Bills for raising Revenue shall originate in the House of Representatives; but the Senate may propose or concur with Amendments as on other Bills.

Every Bill which shall have passed the House of Representatives and the Senate, shall, before it become a Law, be presented to the President of the United States; If he approve he shall sign it, but if not he shall return it, with his Objections to that House in which it shall have originated, who shall enter the Objections at large on their Journal, and proceed to reconsider it. If after such Reconsideration two thirds of that House shall agree to pass the Bill, it shall be sent, together with the Objections, to the other House, by which it shall likewise be reconsidered, and if approved by two thirds of that House, it shall become a Law. But in all such Cases the Votes of both Houses shall be determined by yeas and Nays, and the Names of the Persons voting for and against the Bill shall be entered on the Journal of each House respectively. If any Bill shall not be returned by the President within ten Days (Sundays excepted) after it shall have been presented to him, the Same shall be a Law, in like Manner as if he had signed it, unless the Congress by their Adjournment prevent its Return, in which Case it shall not be a Law.

Every Order, Resolution, or Vote to which the Concurrence of the Senate and House of Representatives may be necessary (except on a question of Adjournment) shall be presented to the President of the United States; and before the Same shall take Effect, shall be approved by him, or being disapproved by him, shall be repassed by two thirds of the Senate and House of Representatives, according to the Rules and Limitations prescribed in the Case of a Bill.

Section 8. The Congress shall have Power To lay and collect Taxes, Duties, Imposts and Excises, to pay the Debts and provide for the common Defence and general Welfare of the United States; but all Duties, Imposts and Excises shall be uniform throughout the United States;

To borrow Money on the credit of the United States;

To regulate Commerce with foreign Nations, and among the several States, and with the Indian Tribes;

To establish an uniform Rule of Naturalization, and uniform Laws on the subject of Bankruptcies throughout the United States;

To coin Money, regulate the Value thereof, and of foreign Coin, and fix the Standard of Weights and Measures;

To provide for the Punishment of counterfeiting the Securities and current Coin of the United States;

To establish Post Offices and post Roads;

To promote the Progress of Science and useful Arts, by securing for limited Times to Authors and Inventors the exclusive Right to their respective Writings and Discoveries;

To constitute Tribunals inferior to the supreme Court;

To define and punish Piracies and Felonies committed on the high Seas, and Offences against the Law of Nations;

To declare War, grant Letters of Marque and Reprisal, and make Rules concerning Captures on Land and Water;

To raise and support Armies, but no Appropriation of Money to that Use shall be for a longer Term than two Years;

To provide and maintain a Navy;

To make Rules for the Government and Regulation of the land and naval Forces;

To provide for calling forth the Militia to execute the Laws of the Union, suppress Insurrections and repel Invasions;

To provide for organizing, arming, and disciplining, the Militia, and for governing such Part of them as may be employed in the Service of the United States, reserving to the States respectively, the Appointment of the Officers, and the Authority of training the Militia according to the discipline prescribed by Congress;

To exercise exclusive Legislation in all Cases whatsoever, over such District (not exceeding ten Miles square) as may, by Cession of particular States, and the Acceptance of Congress, become the Seat of the Government of the United States, and to exercise like Authority over all Places purchased by the Consent of the Legislature of the State in which the Same shall be, for the Erection of Forts, Magazines, Arsenals, dock-Yards, and other needful Buildings; And

To make all Laws which shall be necessary and proper for carrying into Execution the foregoing Powers, and all other Powers vested by this Constitution in the Government of the United States, or in any Department or Officer thereof.

Section 9. The Migration or Importation of such Persons as any of the States now existing shall think proper to admit, shall not be prohibited by the Congress prior to the Year one thousand eight hundred and eight, but a Tax or duty may be imposed on such Importation, not exceeding ten dollars for each Person.

The Privilege of the Writ of Habeas Corpus shall not be suspended, unless when in Cases of Rebellion or Invasion the public Safety may require it.

No Bill of Attainder or ex post facto Law shall be passed.

No Capitation, or other direct, Tax shall be laid, unless in Proportion to the Census or Enumeration herein before directed to be taken.

No Tax or Duty shall be laid on Articles exported from any State.

No Preference shall be given by any Regulation of Commerce or Revenue to the Ports of one State over those of another: nor shall Vessels bound to, or from, one State, be obliged to enter, clear, or pay Duties in another.

No Money shall be drawn from the Treasury, but in Consequence of Appropriations made by Law; and a regular Statement and Account of the Receipts and Expenditures of all public Money shall be published from time to time.

No Title of Nobility shall be granted by the United States: And no Person holding any Office of Profit or Trust under them, shall, without the Consent of the Congress, accept of any present, Emolument, Office, or Title, of any kind whatever, from any King, Prince, or foreign State.

Section 10. No State shall enter into any Treaty, Alliance, or Confederation; grant Letters of Marque and Reprisal; coin Money; emit Bills of Credit; make any Thing but gold and silver Coin a Tender in Payment of Debts; pass any Bill of Attainder, ex post facto Law, or Law impairing the Obligation of Contracts, or grant any Title of Nobility.

No State shall, without the Consent of the Congress, lay any Imposts or Duties on Imports or Exports, except what may be absolutely necessary for executing it's inspection Laws: and the net Produce of all Duties and Imposts, laid by any State on Imports or Exports, shall be for the Use of the Treasury of the United States; and all such Laws shall be subject to the Revision and Controul of the Congress.

No State shall, without the Consent of Congress, lay any Duty of Tonnage, keep Troops, or Ships of War in time of Peace, enter into any Agreement or Compact with another State, or with a foreign Power, or engage in War, unless actually invaded, or in such imminent Danger as will not admit of delay.

Article II

Section 1. The executive Power shall be vested in a President of the United States of America. He shall hold his Office during the Term of four Years, and, together with the Vice President, chosen for the same Term, be elected, as follows

Each State shall appoint, in such Manner as the Legislature thereof may direct, a Number of Electors, equal to the whole Number of Senators and Representatives to which the State may be entitled in the Congress: but no Senator or Representative, or Person holding an Office of Trust or Profit under the United States, shall be appointed an Elector.

The Electors shall meet in their respective States, and vote by Ballot for two Persons, of whom one at least shall not be an Inhabitant of the same State with themselves. And they shall make a List of all the Persons voted for, and of the Number of Votes for each; which List they shall sign and certify, and transmit sealed to the Seat of Government of the United States, directed to the President of the Senate. The President of the Senate shall, in the Presence of the Senate and House of Representatives, open all the Certificates, and the Votes shall then be counted. The Person having the greatest Number of Votes shall be the President, if such Number be a Majority of the whole Number of Electors appointed; and if there be more than one who have such Majority, and have an equal Number of Votes, then the House of Representatives shall immediately chuse by Ballot one of them for President; and if no Person have a Majority, then from the five highest on the List the said House shall in like Manner chuse the President. But in chusing the President, the Votes shall be taken by States, the Representation from each State having one Vote; A quorum for this Purpose shall consist of a Member or Members from two thirds of the States, and a Majority of all the States shall be necessary to a Choice. In every Case, after the Choice of the President, the Person having the greatest Number of Votes of the Electors shall be the Vice President. But if there should remain two or more who have equal Votes, the Senate shall chuse from them by Ballot the Vice President.

The Congress may determine the Time of chusing the Electors, and the Day on which they shall give their Votes; which Day shall be the same throughout the United States.

No Person except a natural born Citizen, or a Citizen of the United States, at the time of the Adoption of this Constitution, shall be eligible to the Office of President; neither shall any Person be eligible to that Office who shall not have attained to the Age of thirty five Years, and been fourteen Years a Resident within the United States.

In Case of the Removal of the President from Office, or of his Death, Resignation, or Inability to discharge the Powers and Duties of the said Office, the Same shall devolve on the Vice President, and the Congress may by Law provide for the Case of Removal, Death, Resignation or Inability, both of the President and Vice President declaring what Officer shall then act as President, and such Officer shall act accordingly, until the Disability be removed, or a President shall be elected.

The President shall, at stated Times, receive for his Services, a Compensation, which shall neither be encreased nor diminished during the Period for which he shall have been elected, and he shall not receive within that Period any other Emolument from the United States, or any of them.

Before he enter on the Execution of his Office, he shall take the following Oath or Affirmation: do solemnly swear (or affirm) that I will faithfully execute the Office of President of the United States, and will to the best of my Ability, preserve, protect and defend the Constitution of the United States.

Section 2. The President shall be Commander in Chief of the Army and Navy of the United States, and of the Militia of the several States, when called into the actual Service of the United States; he may require the Opinion, in writing, of the principal Officer in each of the executive Departments, upon any Subject relating to the Duties of their respective Offices, and he shall have Power to grant Reprieves and Pardons for Offences against the United States, except in Cases of Impeachment.

He shall have Power, by and with the Advice and Consent of the Senate, to make Treaties, provided two thirds of the Senators present concur; and he shall nominate, and by and with the Advice and Consent of the Senate, shall appoint Ambassadors, other public Ministers and Consuls, Judges of the supreme Court, and all other Officers of the United States, whose Appointments are not herein otherwise provided for, and which shall be established by Law: but the Congress may by Law vest the Appointment of such inferior Officers, as they think proper, in the President alone, in the Courts of Law, or in the Heads of Departments.

The President shall have Power to fill up all Vacancies that may happen during the Recess of the Senate, by granting Commissions which shall expire at the End of their next Session.

Section 3. He shall from time to time give to the Congress Information of the State of the Union, and recommend to their Consideration such Measures as he shall judge necessary and expedient; he may, on extraordinary Occasions, convene both Houses, or either of them, and in Case of Disagreement between them, with Respect to the Time of Adjournment, he may adjourn them to such Time as he shall think proper; he shall receive Ambassadors and other public Ministers; he shall take Care that the Laws be faithfully executed, and shall Commission all the Officers of the United States.

Section 4. The President, Vice President and all civil Officers of the United States, shall be removed from Office on Impeachment for, and Conviction of, Treason, Bribery, or other high Crimes and Misdemeanors.

Article III

Section 1. The judicial Power of the United States, shall be vested in one supreme Court, and in such inferior Courts as the Congress may from time to time ordain and establish. The Judges, both of the supreme and inferior Courts, shall hold their Offices during good Behaviour, and shall, at stated Times, receive for their Services, a Compensation which shall not be diminished during their Continuance in Office.

Section 2. The judicial Power shall extend to all Cases, in Law and Equity, arising under this Constitution, the Laws of the United States, and Treaties made, or which shall be made, under their Authority; to all Cases affecting Ambassadors, other public Ministers and Consuls; to all Cases of admiralty and maritime Jurisdiction; to Controversies to which the United States shall be a Party; to Controversies between two or more States; between a State and Citizens of another State; between Citizens of different States, between Citizens of the same State claiming Lands under Grants of different States, and between a State, or the Citizens thereof, and foreign States, Citizens or Subjects.

In all Cases affecting Ambassadors, other public Ministers and Consuls, and those in which a State shall be Party, the supreme Court shall have original Jurisdiction. In all the other Cases before mentioned, the supreme Court shall have appellate Jurisdiction, both as to Law and Fact, with such Exceptions, and under such Regulations as the Congress shall make.

The Trial of all Crimes, except in Cases of Impeachment, shall be by Jury; and such Trial shall be held in the State where the said Crimes shall have been committed; but when not committed within any State, the Trial shall be at such Place or Places as the Congress may by Law have directed.

Section 3. Treason against the United States, shall consist only in levying War against them, or in adhering to their Enemies, giving them Aid and Comfort. No Person shall be convicted of Treason unless on the Testimony of two Witnesses to the same overt Act, or on Confession in open Court.

The Congress shall have Power to declare the Punishment of Treason, but no Attainder of Treason shall work Corruption of Blood, or Forfeiture except during the Life of the Person attainted.

Article IV

Section 1. Full Faith and Credit shall be given in each State to the public Acts, Records, and judicial Proceedings of every other State. And the Congress may by general Laws prescribe the Manner in which such Acts, Records and Proceedings shall be proved, and the Effect thereof.

Section 2. The Citizens of each State shall be entitled to all Privileges and Immunities of Citizens in the several States.

A Person charged in any State with Treason, Felony, or other Crime, who shall flee from Justice, and be found in another State, shall on Demand of the executive Authority of the State from which he fled, be delivered up, to be removed to the State having Jurisdiction of the Crime.

No Person held to Service or Labour in one State, under the Laws thereof, escaping into another, shall, in Consequence of any Law or Regulation therein, be discharged from such Service or Labour, but shall be delivered up on Claim of the Party to whom such Service or Labour may be due.

Section 3. New States may be admitted by the Congress into this Union; but no new State shall be formed or erected within the Jurisdiction of any other State; nor any State be formed by the Junction of two or more States, or Parts of States, without the Consent of the Legislatures of the States concerned as well as of the Congress.

The Congress shall have Power to dispose of and make all needful Rules and Regulations respecting the Territory or other Property belonging to the United States; and nothing in this Constitution shall be so construed as to Prejudice any Claims of the United States, or of any particular State.

Section 4. The United States shall guarantee to every State in this Union a Republican Form of Government, and shall protect each of them against Invasion; and on Application of the Legislature, or of the Executive (when the Legislature cannot be convened) against domestic Violence.

Article V

The Congress, whenever two thirds of both Houses shall deem it necessary, shall propose Amendments to this Constitution, or, on the Application of the Legislatures of two thirds of the several States, shall call a Convention for proposing Amendments, which, in either Case, shall be valid to all Intents and Purposes, as Part of this Constitution, when ratified by the Legislatures of three fourths of the several States, or by Conventions in three fourths thereof, as the one or the other Mode of Ratification may be proposed by the Congress; Provided that no Amendment which may be made prior to the Year One thousand eight hundred and eight shall in any Manner affect the first and fourth Clauses in the Ninth Section of the first Article; and that no State, without its Consent, shall be deprived of its equal Suffrage in the Senate.

Article VI

All Debts contracted and Engagements entered into, before the Adoption of this Constitution, shall be as valid against the United States under this Constitution, as under the Confederation.

This Constitution, and the Laws of the United States which shall be made in Pursuance thereof; and all Treaties made or which shall be made, under the Authority of the United States, shall be the supreme Law of the Land; and the Judges in every State shall be bound thereby, any Thing in the Constitution or Laws of any State to the Contrary notwithstanding.

The Senators and Representatives before mentioned, and the Members of the several State Legislatures, and all executive and judicial Officers, both of the United States and of the several States, shall be bound by Oath or Affirmation, to support this Constitution; but no religious Test shall ever be required as a Qualification to any Office or public Trust under the United States.

Article VII

The Ratification of the Conventions of nine States, shall be sufficient for the Establishment of this Constitution between the States so ratifying the Same.

Done in Convention by the Unanimous Consent of the States present the Seventeenth Day of September in the Year of our Lord one thousand seven hundred and Eighty seven and of the Independence of the United States of America the Twelfth.

Amendments to the Constitution

Amendment 1

Congress shall make no law respecting an establishment of religion, or prohibiting the free exercise thereof; or abridging the freedom of speech, or of the press; or the right of the people peaceably to assemble, and to petition the Government for a redress of grievances.

Amendment 2

A well regulated Militia, being necessary to the security of a free State, the right of the people to keep and bear Arms, shall not be infringed.

Amendment 3

No Soldier shall, in time of peace be quartered in any house, without the consent of the Owner, nor in time of war, but in a manner to be prescribed by law.

Amendment 4

The right of the people to be secure in their persons, houses, papers, and effects, against unreasonable searches and seizures, shall not be violated, and no Warrants shall issue, but upon probable cause, supported by Oath or affirmation, and particularly describing the place to be searched, and the persons or things to be seized.

Amendment 5

No person shall be held to answer for a capital, or otherwise infamous crime, unless on a presentment or indictment of a Grand Jury, except in cases arising in the land or naval forces, or in the Militia, when in actual service in time of War or public danger; nor shall any person be subject for the same offence to be twice put in jeopardy of life or limb; nor shall be compelled in any criminal case to be a witness against himself, nor be deprived of life, liberty, or property, without due process of law; nor shall private property be taken for public use, without just compensation.

Amendment 6

In all criminal prosecutions, the accused shall enjoy the right to a speedy and public trial, by an impartial jury of the State and district wherein the crime shall have been committed, which district shall have been previously ascertained by law, and to be informed of the nature and cause of the accusation; to be confronted with the witnesses against him; to have compulsory process for obtaining witnesses in his favor, and to have the Assistance of Counsel for his defence.

Amendment 7

In Suits at common law, where the value in controversy shall exceed twenty dollars, the right of trial by jury shall be preserved, and no fact tried by a jury, shall be otherwise re-examined in any Court of the United States, than according to the rules of the common law.

Amendment 8

Excessive bail shall not be required, nor excessive fines imposed, nor cruel and unusual punishments inflicted.

Amendment 9

The enumeration in the Constitution, of certain rights, shall not be construed to deny or disparage others retained by the people.

Amendment 10

The powers not delegated to the United States by the Constitution, nor prohibited by it to the States, are reserved to the States respectively, or to the people.

Amendment 11 (Jan. 8, 1798)

The Judicial power of the United States shall not be construed to extend to any suit in law or equity, commenced or prosecuted against one of the United States by Citizens of another State, or by Citizens or Subjects of any Foreign State.

Amendment 12 (Sept. 25, 1804)

The Electors shall meet in their respective states, and vote by ballot for President and Vice-President, one of whom, at least, shall not be an inhabitant of the same state with themselves; they shall name in their ballots the person voted for as President, and in distinct ballots the person voted for as Vice-President, and they shall make distinct lists of all persons voted for as President, and of all persons voted for as Vice-President, and of the number of votes for each, which list they shall sign and certify, and transmit sealed to the seat of the government of the United States, directed to the President of the Senate; The President of the Senate shall, in the presence of the Senate and House of Representatives, open all the certificates and the votes shall then be counted; The person having the greatest number of votes for President, shall be the President, if such number be a majority of the whole number of Electors appointed; and if no person have such majority, then from the persons having the highest numbers not exceeding three on the list of those voted for as President, the House of Representatives shall choose immediately, by ballot, the President. But in choosing the President, the votes shall be taken by states, the representation from each state having one vote; a quorum for this purpose shall consist of a member or members from two thirds of the states, and a majority of all the states shall be necessary to a choice. And if the House of Representatives shall not choose a President whenever the right of choice shall devolve upon them, before the fourth day of March next following, then the Vice-President shall act as President, as in the case of the death or other constitutional disability of the President. The person having the greatest number of votes as Vice-President, shall be the Vice-President, if such number be a majority of the whole number of Electors appointed, and if no person have a majority, then from the two highest numbers on the list, the Senate shall choose the Vice-President; a quorum for the purpose shall consist of two thirds of the whole number of Senators, and a majority of the whole number shall be necessary to a choice. But no person constitutionally ineligible to the office of President shall be eligible to that of Vice-President of the United States.

Amendment 13 (Dec. 18, 1865)

Section 1. Neither slavery nor involuntary servitude, except as a punishment for crime whereof the party shall have been duly convicted, shall exist within the United States, or any place subject to their jurisdiction.

Section 2. Congress shall have power to enforce this article by appropriate legislation.

Amendment 14 (July 28, 1868)

Section 1. All persons born or naturalized in the United States, and subject to the jurisdiction thereof, are citizens of the United States and of the State wherein they reside. No State shall make or enforce any law which shall abridge the privileges or immunities of citizens of the United States; nor shall any State deprive any person of life, liberty, or property, without due process of law; nor deny to any person within its jurisdiction the equal protection of the laws.

Section 2. Representatives shall be apportioned among the several States according to their respective numbers, counting the whole number of persons in each State, excluding Indians not taxed. But when the right to vote at any election for the choice of electors for President and Vice-President of the United States, Representatives in Congress, the Executive and Judicial officers of a State, or the members of the Legislature thereof, is denied to any of the male inhabitants of such State, being twenty-one years of age, and citizens of the United States, or in any way abridged, except for participation in rebellion, or other crime, the basis of representation therein shall be reduced in the proportion which the number of such male citizens shall bear to the whole number of male citizens twenty-one years of age in such State.

Section 3. No person shall be a Senator or Representative in Congress, or elector of President and Vice-President, or hold any office, civil or military, under the United States, or under any State, who, having previously taken an oath, as a member of Congress, or as an officer of the United States, or as a member of any State legislature, or as an executive or judicial officer of any State, to support the Constitution of the United States, shall have engaged in insurrection or rebellion against the same, or given aid or comfort to the enemies thereof. But Congress may by a vote of two thirds of each House, remove such disability.

Section 4. The validity of the public debt of the United States, authorized by law, including debts incurred for payment of pensions and bounties for services in suppressing insurrection or rebellion, shall not be questioned. But neither the United States nor any State shall assume or pay any debt or obligation incurred in aid of insurrection or rebellion against the United States, or any claim for the loss or emancipation of any slave; but all such debts, obligations and claims shall be held illegal and void.

Section 5. The Congress shall have power to enforce, by appropriate legislation, the provisions of this article.

Amendment 15 (March 30, 1870)

Section 1. The right of citizens of the United States to vote shall not be denied or abridged by the United States or by any State on account of race, color, or previous condition of servitude

Section 2. The Congress shall have power to enforce this article by appropriate legislation.

Amendment 16 (Feb. 25, 1913)

The Congress shall have power to lay and collect taxes on incomes, from whatever source derived, without apportionment among the several States, and without regard to any census or enumeration.

Amendment 17 (May 31, 1913)

The Senate of the United States shall be composed of two Senators from each State, elected by the people thereof, for six years; and each Senator shall have one vote. The electors in each State shall have the qualifications requisite for electors of the most numerous branch of the State legislatures.

When vacancies happen in the representation of any State in the Senate, the executive authority of such State shall issue writs of election to fill such vacancies: Provided, That the legislature of any State may empower the executive thereof to make temporary appointments until the people fill the vacancies by election as the legislature may direct.

This amendment shall not be so construed as to affect the election or term of any Senator chosen before it becomes valid as part of the Constitution.

Amendment 18 (Jan. 29, 1919; repealed Dec. 5, 1933)

Section 1. After one year from the ratification of this article the manufacture, sale, or transportation of intoxicating liquors within, the importation thereof into, or the exportation thereof from the United States and all territory subject to the jurisdiction thereof for beverage purposes is hereby prohibited.

Section 2. The Congress and the several States shall have concurrent power to enforce this article by appropriate legislation.

Section 3. This article shall be inoperative unless it shall have been ratified as an amendment to the Constitution by the legislatures of the several States, as provided in the Constitution, within seven years from the date of the submission hereof to the States by the Congress.

Amendment 19 (Aug. 26, 1920)

The right of citizens of the United States to vote shall not be denied or abridged by the United States or by any State on account of sex.

Congress shall have power to enforce this article by appropriate legislation.

Amendment 20 (Feb. 6, 1933)

Section 1. The terms of the President and Vice-President shall end at noon on the 20th day of January, and the terms of Senators and Representatives at noon on the third day of January, of the years in which such terms would have ended if this article had not been ratified; and the terms of their successors shall then begin.

Section 2. The Congress shall assemble at least once in every year, and such meeting shall begin at noon on the third day of January, unless they shall by law appoint a different day.

Section 3. If, at the time fixed for the beginning of the term of the President, the President elect shall have died, the Vice-President elect shall become President. If a President shall not have been chosen before the time fixed for the beginning of his term, or if the President elect shall have failed to qualify, then the Vice-President elect shall act as President until a President shall have qualified; and the Congress may by law provide for the case wherein neither a President elect nor a Vice-President elect shall have qualified, declaring who shall then act as President, or the manner in which one who is to act shall be selected, and such person shall act accordingly until a President or Vice-President shall have qualified.

Section 4. The Congress may by law provide for the case of the death of any of the persons from whom the House of Representatives may choose a President whenever the right of choice shall have devolved upon them, and for the case of the death of any of the persons from whom the Senate may choose a Vice- President whenever the right of choice shall have devolved upon them.

Section 5. Sections 1 and 2 shall take effect on the 15th day of October following the ratification of this article.

Section 6. This article shall be inoperative unless it shall have been ratified as an amendment to the Constitution by the legislatures of three fourths of the several States within seven years from the date of its submission.

Amendment 21 (Dec. 5, 1933)

Section 1. The eighteenth article of amendment to the Constitution of the United States is hereby repealed.

Section 2. The transportation or importation into any State, Territory, or possession of the United States for delivery or use therein of intoxicating liquors, in violation of the laws thereof, is hereby prohibited.

Section 3. This article shall be inoperative unless it shall have been ratified as an amendment to the Constitution by conventions in the several States, as provided in the Constitution, within seven years from the date of the submission hereof to the States by the Congress.

Amendment 22 (March 1, 1951)

Section 1. No person shall be elected to the office of the President more than twice, and no person who has held the office of President, or acted as President, for more than two years of a term to which some other person was elected President shall be elected to the office of the President more than once. But this Article shall not apply to any person holding the office of President when this Article was proposed by the Congress, and shall not prevent any person who may be holding the office of President, or acting as President, during the term within which this Article becomes operative from holding the office of President or acting as President during the remainder of such term.

Section 2. This article shall be inoperative unless it shall have been ratified as an amendment to the Constitution by the legislatures of three fourths of the several States within seven years from the date of its submission to the States by the Congress.

Amendment 23 (April 3, 1961)

Section 1. The District constituting the seat of Government of the United States shall appoint in such manner as the Congress may direct:

A number of electors of President and Vice-President equal to the whole number of Senators and Representatives in Congress to which the District would be entitled if it were a State, but in no event more than the least populous State; they shall be in addition to those appointed by the States, but they shall be considered, for the purposes of the election of President and Vice-President, to be electors appointed by a State; and they shall meet in the District and perform such duties as provided by the twelfth article of amendment.

Section 2. The Congress shall have power to enforce this article by appropriate legislation.

Amendment 24 (Feb. 4, 1964)

Section 1. The right of citizens of the United States to vote in any primary or other election for President or Vice-President, for electors for President or Vice-President, or for Senator or Representative in Congress, shall not be denied or abridged by the United States or any State by reason of failure to pay any poll tax or other tax.

Section 2. The Congress shall have power to enforce this article by appropriate legislation.

Amendment 25 (Feb. 10, 1967)

Section 1. In case of the removal of the President from office or his death or resignation, the Vice-President shall become President.

Section 2. Whenever there is a vacancy in the office of the Vice-President, the President shall nominate a Vice-President who shall take the office upon confirmation by a majority vote of both houses of Congress.

Section 3. Whenever the President transmits to the President pro tempore of the Senate and the Speaker of the House of Representatives his written declaration that he is unable to discharge the powers and duties of his office, and until he transmits to them a written declaration to the contrary, such powers and duties shall be discharged by the Vice-President as Acting President.

Section 4. Whenever the Vice-President and a majority of either the principal officers of the executive departments, or of such other body as Congress may by law provide, transmit to the President pro tempore of the Senate and the Speaker of the House of Representatives their written declaration that the President is unable to discharge the powers and duties of his office, the Vice-President shall immediately assume the powers and duties of the office as Acting President.

Thereafter, when the President transmits to the President pro tempore of the Senate and the Speaker of the House of Representatives his written declaration that no inability exists, he shall resume the powers and duties of his office unless the Vice-President and a majority of either the principal officers of the executive department, or of such other body as Congress may by law provide, transmit within four days to the President pro tempore of the Senate and the Speaker of the House of Representatives their written declaration that the President is unable to discharge the powers and duties of his office. Thereupon Congress shall decide the issue, assembling within 48 hours for that purpose if not in session. If the Congress, within 21 days after receipt of the latter written declaration, or, if Congress is not in session, within 21 days after Congress is required to assemble, determines by two-thirds vote of both houses that the President is unable to discharge the powers and duties of his office, the Vice-President shall continue to discharge the same as Acting President; otherwise, the President shall resume the powers and duties of his office.

Amendment 26 (June 30, 1971)

Section 1. The right of citizens of the United States, who are eighteen years of age or older, to vote shall not be denied or abridged by the United States or any state on account of age.

Section 2. The Congress shall have power to enforce this article by appropriate legislation.

Amendment 27 (May 7, 1992)

No law, varying the compensation for the services of Senators and Representatives, shall take effect until an election of Representatives shall have intervened.

Standard Tax Citations

Statutory

Constitution	U.S. Const. art. I, § 8, cl. 2.
	U.S. Const. amend, XIV, § 2.
Code	§ 101(b)(2)(B)(ii).
Public Laws	P.L. 99-514 Act § 1563.

Administrative

Regulation	Reg. § 1.162-5(a)(1).
Treasury Decision	T.D. 8175, 1988-1 C.B. 191.
Temporary Regulation	Reg. § 1.469-4T(c)(2).
Proposed Regulation	Prop. Reg. § 1.1176(b)(2).
Revenue Ruling	Rev. Rul. 93-4, 1993-1 C.B. 295.
Revenue Ruling (temporary)	Rev. Rul. 95-38, 1995-17 I.R.B. 9.
Revenue Procedure	Rev. Proc. 94-27, 1994-1 C.B. 613.
Revenue Procedure (temporary)	Rev. Proc. 94-73, 1994-52 I.R.B. 23.
Letter Ruling	Ltr. Rul. 9550056.
Technical Advice Memo	TAM 9046004.
Notice	Notice 94-102, 1994-2 C.B. 569.
Notice (temporary)	Notice 94-102, 1995-50 I.R.B. 14.
Announcement	Announcement 94-139, 1994-50 I.R.B. 21.

Judicial

Board of Tax Appeals:	
GPO reporter	*Estate of D. R. Daly,* 3 B.T.A. 1042 (1926).
Tax Court Regular:	
(temporary citation)	*Arnes, John,* 102 T.C. ___ , No. 5 (1994).
Tax Court Regular:	
GPO reporter	*Arnes, John,* 102 T.C. 553 (1994).
Tax Court Memo:	
General (unpublished)	*Epping, Lawrence,* T.C. Memo. 1992-279.
CCH reporter	*Epping, Lawrence,* 63 TCM 3012 (1992).
RIA reporter[1]	*Epping, Lawrence,* RIA T.C. Memo. ¶ 92,279.
Infotax CD-ROM	*Epping, Lawrence,* 92 TNT 103-13 (TC Memo, 1992).
Kleinrock's CD-ROM	*Epping, Lawrence,* T.C. Memo. 1992-279.
District Court:	
West reporter	*Ruhland, Kenneth,* 839 F.Supp. 993 (N.D.N.Y., 1993).
CCH reporter	*Ruhland, Kenneth,* 94-1 USTC ¶ 50,047 (N.D.N.Y., 1993).
RIA reporter[1]	*Ruhland, Kenneth,* 73 AFTR2d 94-872 (N.D.N.Y., 1993).
Infotax CD-ROM	*Ruhland, Kenneth,* 94 TNT 20-66 (N.D.N.Y., 1993)
Kleinrock's CD-ROM	*Ruhland, Kenneth,* KTC 1993-256 (N.D.N.Y., 1993)

Court of Federal Claims:

West reporter	*Bennett, Courtney,* 30 Fed. Cl. 396 (1994).
CCH reporter	*Bennett, Courtney,* 94-1 USTC ¶ 50,044 (Fed.Cl., 1994).
RIA reporter[1]	*Bennett, Courtney,* 73 AFTR2d 94-534 (Fed.Cl., 1994).
Infotax CD-ROM	*Bennett, Courtney,* 95 TNT 30-9 (Fed.Cl., 1994)
Kleinrock's CD-ROM	*Bennett, Courtney,* KTC 1994-647 (Fed.Cl., 1994).

Court of Appeal:

West reporter	*Home of Faith,* 39 F.3d. 263 (CA-10, 1994).
CCH reporter	*Home of Faith,* 94-2 USTC ¶ 50,570 (CA-10, 1994).
RIA reporter[1]	*Home of Faith,* 74 AFTR2d 94-5608 (CA-10, 1994).
Infotax CD-ROM	*Home of Faith,* 94 TNT 225-18 (CA-10, 1994).
Kleinrock's CD-ROM	*Home of Faith,* KTC 1994-564 (CA-10, 1994).

Supreme Court:

GPO reporter	*Indianapolis Power & Light,* 493 U.S. 203 (1990).
West reporter	*Indianapolis Power & Light,* 110 S.Ct. 589 (1981).
CCH reporter	*Indianapolis Power & Light,* 90-1 USTC ¶ 50,007 (USSC, 1990).
RIA reporter[1]	*Indianapolis Power & Light,* 65 AFTR2d 90-394 (USSC, 1990).
Infotax CD-ROM	*Indianapolis Power & Light,* 90 TNT 8-4 (USSC, 1990).
Kleinrock's CD-ROM	*Indianapolis Power & Light,* KTC 1990-53 (USSC, 1990).

Books

W. Raabe, G. Whittenburg, and J. Bost, *West's Federal Tax Research,* 5th ed. (Cincinnati: South-Western College Publishing Co., 1999).

Journals

G. Whittenburg and M. Altus-Buller, "Level Payments Avoid Penalty on Pre-59½ IRA Distributions," *Taxation for Accountants* (December 1994), p. 333.

Capitalization

Proper nouns and words derived from them are capitalized while common nouns are not. The names of specific persons, places, or things are proper nouns. All other nouns are common nouns. Examples of proper nouns include:

the Congress
the Code
Section 172(a)
the Regulations
Regulations Section 1.102-1
the President
the Fifth Circuit
the Tax Court
a Revenue Ruling
a Private Letter Ruling

Italics

In handwritten or typed papers underlining represents italics. The titles of books, magazines, newspapers, pamphlets, court cases, and tax services are shown in italics. Examples of items that are italicized include:

The Wealth of Nations
Journal of Taxation

[1]Before 1992 this reporter was published by Prentice-Hall (P-H).

New York Times
AICPA Code of Conduct
Circular 230
Statements on Responsibility in Tax Practice
Gregory v. Helvering
Cumulative Bulletin
Standard Federal Tax Reports
Federal Tax Coordinator 2d

Note: Do not italicize the titles of legal documents such as the U.S. Constitution, the U.S. Code, or the *Internal Revenue Code*.

Lists

A list is an independent clause followed by a colon with each item in the list separated by a comma. The College of Business Administration has five departments: Accounting, Finance, Information Systems, Management, and Marketing.

Displayed Lists

Displayed lists are used to make items easy to scan by the reader. Such lists should be introduced with an independent clause, or by a complete sentence ending with a period.

Examples of items that it would be appropriate to display in list form would include

▶ steps to solve a problem,
▶ rules,
▶ proposals to be discussed,
▶ checklists,
▶ recommendations, and
▶ procedures.

Periods are not used in lists unless the items in the list are complete sentences. The items in a list should be in the same form (i.e., nouns, phrases, clauses, or sentences). If the items in a list are to be numbered, use an arabic number followed by a period for each item. If the items are not numbered, say, because the list is not prioritized or sequential, consider using a bullet to draw the reader's attention to the items in the list (as shown above).

Other Systems

Many professions and academic disciplines have developed unique systems of citing published material. Examples of other style manuals include:

General Reference:

D. Hacker, *A Pocket Style Manual* (Boston: Bedford Books of St. Martin's Press, 1993).

U.S. Government Printing Office Style Manual (Washington: Government Printing Office, 1984).

Literature and the Humanities:

The Chicago Manual of Style, 13th ed. (Chicago: University of Chicago, 1982).

J. Gibaldi and W. Achtert, *MLA Handbook for Writers of Research Papers,* 3rd ed. (New York: Modern Language Association of America, 1988).

Law:

The Bluebook, A Uniform System of Citation, 15th ed. (Cambridge: Harvard Law Review, 1991).

Social Sciences:

Publication Manual of the American Psychological Association, 3rd ed. (Washington: American Psychological Association, 1983).

In addition to the manuals listed above, there are style manuals published for accounting, biology, chemistry, geology, linguistics, mathematics, medicine, and physics.

Time Value of Money Tables

Future Value of $1

Periods	4%	6%	8%	10%	12%	14%	20%
1	1.040	1.060	1.080	1.100	1.120	1.140	1.200
2	1.082	1.124	1.166	1.210	1.254	1.300	1.440
3	1.125	1.191	1.260	1.331	1.405	1.482	1.728
4	1.170	1.263	1.361	1.464	1.574	1.689	2.074
5	1.217	1.338	1.469	1.611	1.762	1.925	2.488
6	1.265	1.419	1.587	1.772	1.974	2.195	2.986
7	1.316	1.504	1.714	1.949	2.211	2.502	3.583
8	1.369	1.594	1.851	2.144	2.476	2.853	4.300
9	1.423	1.690	1.999	2.359	2.773	3.252	5.160
10	1.480	1.791	2.159	2.594	3.106	3.707	6.192
11	1.540	1.898	2.332	2.853	3.479	4.226	7.430
12	1.601	2.012	2.518	3.139	3.896	4.818	8.916
13	1.665	2.133	2.720	3.452	4.364	5.492	10.699
14	1.732	2.261	2.937	3.798	4.887	6.261	12.839
15	1.801	2.397	3.172	4.177	5.474	7.138	15.407
20	2.191	3.207	4.661	6.728	9.646	13.743	38.338
30	3.243	5.744	10.063	17.450	29.960	50.950	237.380
40	4.801	10.286	21.725	45.260	93.051	188.880	1469.800

Future Value of an Annuity of $1 in Arrears

Periods	4%	6%	8%	10%	12%	14%	20%
1	1.000	1.000	1.000	1.000	1.000	1.000	1.000
2	2.040	2.060	2.080	2.100	2.120	2.140	2.220
3	3.122	3.184	3.246	3.310	3.374	3.440	3.640
4	4.247	4.375	4.506	4.641	4.779	4.921	5.368
5	5.416	5.637	5.867	6.105	6.353	6.610	7.442
6	6.633	6.975	7.336	7.716	8.115	8.536	9.930
7	7.898	8.394	8.923	9.487	10.089	10.730	12.916
8	9.214	9.898	10.637	11.436	12.300	13.233	16.499
9	10.583	11.491	12.488	13.580	14.776	16.085	20.799
10	12.006	13.181	14.487	15.938	17.549	19.337	25.959
11	13.486	14.972	16.646	18.531	20.655	23.045	32.150
12	15.026	16.870	18.977	21.385	24.133	27.271	39.580
13	16.627	18.882	21.495	24.523	28.029	32.089	48.497
14	18.292	21.015	24.215	27.976	32.393	37.581	59.196
15	20.024	23.276	27.152	31.773	37.280	43.842	72.035
20	29.778	36.778	45.762	57.276	75.052	91.025	186.690
30	56.085	79.058	113.283	164.496	241.330	356.790	1181.900
40	95.026	154.762	259.057	442.597	767.090	1342.000	7343.900

Present Value of $1

Periods	4%	5%	6%	8%	10%	12%	14%	16%	18%	20%	22%	24%	26%	28%	30%	40%
1	0.962	0.952	0.943	0.926	0.909	0.893	0.877	0.862	0.847	0.833	0.820	0.806	0.794	0.781	0.769	0.714
2	0.925	0.907	0.890	0.857	0.826	0.797	0.769	0.743	0.718	0.694	0.672	0.650	0.630	0.610	0.592	0.510
3	0.889	0.864	0.840	0.794	0.751	0.712	0.675	0.641	0.609	0.579	0.551	0.524	0.500	0.477	0.455	0.364
4	0.855	0.823	0.792	0.735	0.683	0.636	0.592	0.552	0.516	0.482	0.451	0.423	0.397	0.373	0.350	0.260
5	0.822	0.784	0.747	0.681	0.621	0.567	0.519	0.476	0.436	0.402	0.370	0.341	0.315	0.291	0.269	0.186
6	0.790	0.746	0.705	0.630	0.564	0.507	0.456	0.410	0.370	0.335	0.303	0.275	0.250	0.227	0.207	0.133
7	0.760	0.711	0.665	0.583	0.513	0.452	0.400	0.354	0.314	0.279	0.249	0.222	0.198	0.178	0.159	0.095
8	0.731	0.677	0.627	0.540	0.467	0.404	0.351	0.305	0.266	0.233	0.204	0.179	0.157	0.139	0.123	0.068
9	0.703	0.645	0.592	0.500	0.424	0.361	0.308	0.263	0.225	0.194	0.167	0.144	0.125	0.108	0.094	0.048
10	0.676	0.614	0.558	0.463	0.386	0.322	0.270	0.227	0.191	0.162	0.137	0.116	0.099	0.085	0.073	0.035
11	0.650	0.585	0.527	0.429	0.350	0.287	0.237	0.195	0.162	0.135	0.112	0.094	0.079	0.066	0.056	0.025
12	0.625	0.557	0.497	0.397	0.319	0.257	0.208	0.168	0.137	0.112	0.092	0.076	0.062	0.052	0.043	0.018
13	0.601	0.530	0.469	0.368	0.290	0.229	0.182	0.145	0.116	0.093	0.075	0.061	0.050	0.040	0.033	0.013
14	0.577	0.505	0.442	0.340	0.263	0.205	0.160	0.125	0.099	0.078	0.062	0.049	0.039	0.032	0.025	0.009
15	0.555	0.481	0.417	0.315	0.239	0.183	0.140	0.108	0.084	0.065	0.051	0.040	0.031	0.025	0.020	0.006
16	0.534	0.458	0.394	0.292	0.218	0.163	0.123	0.093	0.071	0.054	0.042	0.032	0.025	0.019	0.015	0.005
17	0.513	0.436	0.371	0.270	0.198	0.146	0.108	0.080	0.060	0.045	0.034	0.026	0.020	0.015	0.012	0.003
18	0.494	0.416	0.350	0.250	0.180	0.130	0.095	0.069	0.051	0.038	0.028	0.021	0.016	0.012	0.009	0.002
19	0.475	0.396	0.331	0.232	0.164	0.116	0.083	0.060	0.043	0.031	0.023	0.017	0.012`	0.009	0.007	0.002
20	0.456	0.377	0.312	0.215	0.149	0.104	0.073	0.051	0.037	0.026	0.019	0.014	0.010	0.007	0.005	0.001
21	0.439	0.359	0.294	0.199	0.135	0.093	0.064	0.044	0.031	0.022	0.015	0.011	0.008	0.006	0.004	0.001
22	0.422	0.342	0.278	0.184	0.123	0.083	0.056	0.038	0.026	0.018	0.013	0.009	0.006	0.004	0.003	0.001
23	0.406	0.326	0.262	0.170	0.112	0.074	0.049	0.033	0.022	0.015	0.010	0.007	0.005	0.003	0.002	
24	0.390	0.310	0.247	0.158	0.102	0.066	0.043	0.028	0.019	0.013	0.008	0.006	0.004	0.003	0.002	
25	0.375	0.295	0.233	0.146	0.092	0.059	0.038	0.024	0.016	0.010	0.007	0.005	0.003	0.002	0.001	
26	0.361	0.281	0.220	0.135	0.084	0.053	0.033	0.021	0.014	0.009	0.006	0.004	0.002	0.002	0.001	
27	0.347	0.268	0.207	0.125	0.076	0.047	0.029	0.018	0.011	0.007	0.005	0.003	0.002	0.001	0.001	
28	0.333	0.255	0.196	0.116	0.069	0.042	0.026	0.016	0.010	0.006	0.004	0.002	0.002	0.001	0.001	
29	0.321	0.243	0.185	0.107	0.063	0.037	0.022	0.014	0.008	0.005	0.003	0.002	0.001	0.001	0.001	
30	0.308	0.231	0.174	0.099	0.057	0.033	0.020	0.012	0.007	0.004	0.003	0.002	0.001	0.001		
40	0.208	0.142	0.097	0.046	0.022	0.011	0.005	0.003	0.001	0.001						

Present Value of an Annuity of $1 in Arrears

Periods	4%	5%	6%	8%	10%	12%	14%	16%	18%	20%	22%	24%	26%	28%	30%	40%
1	0.962	0.952	0.943	0.926	0.909	0.893	0.877	0.862	0.847	0.833	0.820	0.806	0.794	0.781	0.769	0.714
2	1.886	1.859	1.833	1.783	1.736	1.690	1.647	1.605	1.566	1.528	1.492	1.457	1.424	1.392	1.361	1.224
3	2.775	2.723	2.673	2.577	2.487	2.402	2.322	2.246	2.174	2.106	2.042	1.981	1.923	1.868	1.816	1.589
4	3.630	3.546	3.465	3.312	3.170	3.037	2.914	2.798	2.690	2.589	2.494	2.404	2.320	2.241	2.166	1.879
5	4.452	4.330	4.212	3.993	3.791	3.605	3.433	3.274	3.127	2.991	2.864	2.745	2.635	2.532	2.436	2.035
6	5.242	5.076	4.917	4.623	4.355	4.111	3.889	3.685	3.498	3.326	3.167	3.020	2.885	2.759	2.643	2.168
7	6.002	5.786	5.582	5.206	4.868	4.564	4.288	4.039	3.812	3.605	3.416	3.242	3.083	2.937	2.802	2.263
8	6.733	6.463	6.210	5.747	5.335	4.968	4.639	4.344	4.078	3.837	3.619	3.421	3.241	3.076	2.925	2.331
9	7.435	7.108	6.802	6.247	5.759	5.328	4.946	4.607	4.303	4.031	3.786	3.566	3.366	3.184	3.019	2.379
10	8.111	7.722	7.360	6.710	6.145	5.650	5.216	4.833	4.494	4.192	3.923	3.682	3.465	3.269	3.092	2.414
11	8.760	8.306	7.887	7.139	6.495	5.988	5.453	5.029	4.656	4.327	4.035	3.776	3.544	3.335	3.147	2.438
12	9.385	8.863	8.384	7.536	6.814	6.194	5.660	5.197	4.793	4.439	4.127	3.851	3.606	3.387	3.190	2.456
13	9.986	9.394	8.853	7.904	7.103	6.424	5.842	5.342	4.910	4.533	4.203	3.912	3.656	3.427	3.223	2.468
14	10.563	9.899	9.295	8.244	7.367	6.628	6.002	5.468	5.008	4.611	4.265	3.962	3.695	3.459	3.249	2.477
15	11.118	10.380	9.712	8.559	7.606	6.811	6.142	5.575	5.092	4.675	4.315	4.001	3.726	3.483	3.268	2.484
16	11.652	10.838	10.106	8.851	7.824	6.974	6.265	5.669	5.162	4.730	4.357	4.033	3.751	3.503	3.283	2.489
17	12.166	11.274	10.477	9.122	8.022	7.120	6.373	5.749	5.222	4.775	4.391	4.059	3.771	3.518	3.295	2.492
18	12.659	11.690	10.828	9.372	8.201	7.250	6.467	5.818	5.273	4.812	4.419	4.080	3.786	3.529	3.304	2.494
19	13.134	12.085	11.158	9.604	8.365	7.366	6.550	5.877	5.316	4.844	4.442	4.097	3.799	3.539	3.311	2.496
20	13.590	12.462	11.470	9.818	8.514	7.469	6.623	5.929	5.353	4.870	4.460	4.110	3.808	3.546	3.316	2.497
21	14.029	12.821	11.764	10.017	8.649	7.562	6.687	5.973	5.384	4.891	4.476	4.121	3.816	3.551	3.320	2.498
22	14.451	13.163	12.042	10.201	8.772	7.645	6.743	6.011	5.410	4.909	4.488	4.130	3.822	3.556	3.323	2.498
23	14.857	13.489	12.303	10.371	8.883	7.718	6.792	6.044	5.432	4.925	4.499	4.137	3.827	3.559	3.325	2.499
24	15.247	13.799	12.550	10.529	8.985	7.784	6.835	6.073	5.451	4.937	4.507	4.143	3.831	3.562	3.327	2.499
25	15.622	14.094	12.783	10.675	9.077	7.843	6.873	6.097	5.467	4.948	4.514	4.147	3.834	3.564	3.329	2.499
26	15.983	14.375	13.003	10.810	9.161	7.896	6.906	6.118	5.480	4.956	4.520	4.151	3.837	3.566	3.330	2.500
27	16.330	14.643	13.211	10.935	9.237	7.943	6.935	6.136	5.492	4.964	4.525	4.154	3.839	3.567	3.331	2.500
28	16.663	14.898	13.406	11.051	9.307	7.984	6.961	6.152	5.502	4.970	4.528	4.157	3.840	3.568	3.331	2.500
29	16.984	15.141	13.591	11.158	9.370	8.022	6.983	6.166	5.510	4.975	4.531	4.159	3.841	3.569	3.332	2.500
30	17.292	15.373	13.765	11.258	9.427	8.055	7.003	6.177	5.517	4.979	4.534	4.160	3.842	3.569	3.332	2.500
40	19.793	17.159	15.046	11.925	9.779	8.244	7.105	6.234	5.548	4.997	4.544	4.166	3.846	3.571	3.333	2.500

GLOSSARY

The following definitions pertain specifically to the manner in which the identified terms are used in a tax research context. Other uses for such terms are not examined.

ABA   The professional organization for practicing attorneys in the United States, namely, the American Bar Association.

Academic journals   Scholarly publications of law schools, business schools, and academic organizations. These publications are edited either by faculty members or by graduate students under the guidance of the school's faculty. The articles appearing in these publications are usually written by tax practitioners, academics, graduate students, or other noted commentators.

ACCESS   An on-line database resource provided by Commerce Clearing House (CCH). Allows the researcher to access a database consisting of the text of court cases, administrative rulings, and CCH editorial material, and to search these files for tax law sources and interpretations that may be relevant to the research problem.

Accuracy-related penalty   Civil tax penalty assessed where the taxpayer has been negligent in completing the return or is found to have acted with a disregard of IRS rules and regulations, a substantial understatement of the income tax, a substantial valuation or pension liability overstatement, or a substantial transfer tax valuation understatement. A 20 percent penalty usually applies to the pertinent understatement, and related interest accrues from the due date of the return, rather than the date on which the penalty was assessed.

Acquiescence   A pronouncement by the IRS that it will follow the decision of a regular Tax Court case to the extent that it was held for the taxpayer. Announced in the *Internal Revenue Bulletin*. Modifies the citation for the identified case.

Administrative proceeding   A hearing between the taxpayer and an administrative agency of the government, typically the Internal Revenue Service, in an audit or appeal setting.

Administrative sources   Federal tax law that is created by the appropriate use of power that is granted to the Treasury Department by Congress. These sources of the law have a presumption of the authority of the statute, but they are subject to taxpayer challenge. Such sources include regulations, rulings, revenue procedures, and other opinions that are used by the Treasury Department or the Internal Revenue Service.

AFTR   The citation abbreviation for the tax case reporter, *American Federal Tax Reports*. The first series of the reporter includes cases concerning pre-1954 Code litigation, and the second and third series includes cases that address issues relative to the 1954 and 1986 Codes, respectively. Includes most tax case opinions issued by federal courts other than the Tax Court.

AICPA   The professional organization of practicing Certified Public Accountants in the United States, namely, the American Institute of CPAs.

Annotated tax service   A commercial tax research reference collection, i.e., a secondary source of federal tax law. Includes Code, Regulation and ruling analysis, judicial case notes, and other indexes and finding lists, organized by Code section number. The two most important annotated services are published by Commerce Clearing House and Research Institute of America.

Annotation An entry in (especially) an annotated tax service, indicating a summary of a primary source of the federal tax law that is pertinent to one's research, e.g., a court case opinion digest or a reference to a controlling regulation.

Appeals Division The internal group of the Internal Revenue Service that has the greatest authority to come to a compromise solution with a taxpayer concerning a disputed tax liability. Can consider the "hazards of litigation" in its deliberations. Failure to reach an agreement at this level of the IRS's organization means that the only subsequent appeal by either party to the dispute must be before a court of law.

Assessment The process of the IRS fixing the amount of one's tax liability. Although the US tax system exhibits some degree of self-assessment, the IRS has the ultimate authority to assess the liability of every taxpayer.

Auto-Cite A citator in LEXIS. The primary objective of Auto-Cite is to provide accurate of citations as soon as possible, within 24 hours of receipt of each case. Auto-Cite can also be used to determine whether cases, Revenue Rulings, and Revenue Procedures are still good law.

Average tax rate The percentage of a taxpayer's income that is paid in taxes (i.e., computed by dividing the current-year tax liability by the taxpayer's income). The average can be computed as a percentage of total taxable income (this generates the taxpayer's average nominal tax rate) or as a percentage of the taxpayer's total economic income (this generates the taxpayer's average effective tax rate).

Bittker's *Federal Taxation of Income, Estates, and Gifts* A topical tax service published by Warren, Gorham, & Lamont in five volumes, dedicated to federal income and transfer taxation. Supple-

mented annually, the service includes a topical index, and Code section, Regulation, case name, and Revenue Ruling finding lists.

BNA *Daily Tax Report* A daily collection of the latest regulations, rulings, case opinions, and other tax law revisions, as well as news reports, press releases, congressional studies and schedules, interviews, and other items of interest to the tax practitioner. Available through the mail and on various electronic tax services.

BNA Tax Management Portfolios A topical tax service published by the Bureau of National Affairs in a collection of more than three hundred magazine-size portfolios, dedicated to US income, foreign income, and estate and gift taxation. Prepared by an identified expert in the field, each portfolio includes a detailed analysis of the topic, working papers with which to implement planning suggestions, and a bibliography of related literature. Supplemented by a biweekly newsletter, the portfolio series includes a topical index, and case name and Code section finding lists.

Board of Tax Appeals An earlier name for the US Tax Court, which did not have full judicial status. Opinions are recorded in the Board of Tax Appeals reporter, the citation abbreviation for which is BTA.

Case brief A concise summary of the facts, issues, holdings, and analyses of a court case. Used in a tax research context to allow subsequent review of the case by its author or another party. Includes complete citations of the briefed case, and other items addressed in the brief, to facilitate additional review when necessary.

CCH *Citator* A citator published by Commerce Clearing House that is part of the CCH *Standard Federal Tax Reports*. The volumes of this looseleaf service are labeled A to L and M to Z with a Finding List for Rulings in the back of the M to Z volume. This service covers the federal income tax decisions that have been issued since 1913.

CCH *Federal Tax Service* The topical tax service of Commerce Clearing House. As of August

1998 this service was offered to new subscribers only on CD ROMs or through the Internet. Explanatory text, called the analysis, is divided into sixteen major topic areas, designated A through P. The editors' comments and evaluations of the law are the basis of the main text, with footnotes used to direct researchers to primary sources.

CCH *Standard Federal Tax Reports* The annotated service of Commerce Clearing House dedicated to federal income, estate, and gift taxation. Includes a weekly newsletter, topical index, tax calendar, rate tables and schedules, practitioner checklists, and case name, Code section, Regulation, and Revenue Ruling finding lists. In addition, it provides a two volume *Internal Revenue Code* volumes and a two volume *Citator.*

CCH *Federal Tax Articles* A loose-leaf and bound index to federal tax articles published by Commerce Clearing House. This index provides concise abstracts for each article cited in the index. The framework for organizing these abstracts is the Internal Revenue Code. More than 250 journals, law reviews, papers, and proceedings are included in the index.

CCH Tax Research NetWork The Internet tax service provided by Commerce Clearing House. It can include all of the tax services available from CCH if the practitioner is willing to purchase these services.

CD-ROM service West, CCH, RIA, and several other vendors have made available a collection of tax statutes, Regulations, rulings, cases, and other primary-source materials readable by a computer in a CD-ROM format. The related software allows the researcher to conduct an electronic search of the pertinent materials without incurring on-line charges: subscribers receive a series of compact disks containing the source materials, and the software instructs the user which disks to insert into the CD-ROM reader at appropriate times.

Circular 230 An Internal Revenue Service publication detailing the requirements and responsibilities of those who prepare federal tax returns for compensation. Includes educational, ethical, and procedural guidelines.

Citation A means of conveying the location of a document. Appendix E of this text offers a standard format for citations used by tax researchers.

Citing case With respect to a citator, the subsequent case, which includes a reference to the original (cited) case.

Citator A research resource that presents the judicial history of a court case and traces the subsequent references to the case. When these references include the citing case's evaluations of the cited case's precedents, the research can obtain some measure of the efficacy and reliability of the original holding.

Citator 2nd Series Published by Research Institute of America (RIA). The *Citator 2nd Series* is composed of three bound volumes plus paperback supplements which cover from 1954 to the present. This citator series includes the history of cases that have been decided since 1954 and updates for cited cases appearing in the previous series. Within each volume, the cases are arranged in alphabetical order.

Cited case With respect to a citator, the original case, whose facts or holding are referred to in the opinion of the citing case.

Cites When one case refers to another case, it cites the latter case.

Civil penalty In a tax practice context, a fine or other judgment that is brought against a taxpayer or preparer for a failure to comply with one or more of the elements of the federal tax law. Examples include penalties for failure to file a return or pay a tax in a timely fashion.

Client letter A primary means by which to communicate one's research results to the client. Includes, among other features, a summary of the controlling fact situation and attendant assumptions, a summary of the critical sources of the tax law that led to the researcher's conclusions, specific implications of the results of the project, and recommendations for client action.

Closed transaction A tax research situation is closed when all of the pertinent transactions have been completed by the taxpayer and other parties, such that the research issues may be limited to the proper nature and amount of disclosure to the government on the tax return or other document, and to preparation activities relative to subsequent government review.

Closing agreement A form upon which the taxpayer and the IRS finalize their computations of a disputed tax liability.

Collateral estoppel The legal principle that limits one's judicial exposure relative to a disputed item to one series of court hearings. In a tax environment, the principle can present hardships for the taxpayer who wishes to raise additional issues during the course of a judicial proceeding.

Collection The process by which the IRS extracts an assessed tax liability from a taxpayer. Usually takes the form of the receipt of a check or other draft from the taxpayer, but can include liens or other garnishments of taxpayer assets.

Commissioner of Internal Revenue The chief operating and chief executive officer of the Internal Revenue Service. Holds the ultimate responsibility for overall planning, and for directing, coordinating, and controlling the policies and programs of the IRS.

Committee Report A summary of the issues that were considered by the House Ways and Means Committee, Senate Finance Committee, or Joint Conference Committee, here relative to proposed or adopted changes in the language of the Internal Revenue Code. Useful in tax research as an aid to understanding unclear statutory language and legislative history or intent. Published in the Internal Revenue Bulletin.

Compilation Broadly, a collection of annotations in an annotated tax service, i.e., its collection of volumes.

Connectors In using an on-line database or CD-ROM service, connectors are employed to link various parts of a search command using Boolean logic. For instance, or, and, and within are used as connectors in various research services.

Contingent fee The practice under which a professional bases his or her fee for services upon the results thereof. The AICPA has held that the performance of services for a contingent fee can be unethical; one exception is available, though, where (as in tax practice) the results are subject to third-party actions (here the government, in an audit setting). Several states are relaxing this restriction, allowing CPAs to mix the form of their compensation between fixed and contingent fees.

Correspondence examination An audit of one's tax return that is conducted largely by telephone or mail. Usually involves a request for substantiation or explanation of one or more items on a tax return, such as filing status, exemptions, and itemized deductions for medical expenses, interest, taxes paid, charitable contributions, or miscellaneous deductions.

Court of Appeals A federal appellate court that hears appeals from the Tax Court, Court of Federal Claims, or District Courts within its geographical boundaries. Organized into geographical circuits, although there are additional circuits for Washington, D.C., and for cases appealed from the Court of Federal Claims. Opinions are recorded in the *Federal Reporter,* various series, and in the AFTR and USTC tax case reporter series.

Court of Federal Claims A trial-level court in which the taxpayer typically sues the government for a refund of overpaid tax liability. Hears nontax matters as well, in Washington, D.C., or in other major cities. Opinions are reported in the Court of Federal Claims reporter, and in the AFTR and USTC case reporter series.

Criminal penalty A severe infraction of the elements of the federal tax law by a taxpayer or preparer. Felony or misdemeanor status for tax crimes can be accompanied by substantial fines or jail terms. Examples of tax crimes include tax evasion and other willful failures to comply with the Internal Revenue Code.

Cumulative Bulletin An official publication of the IRS, consolidating the material that first was published in the Internal Revenue Bulletin, in a (usually semiannual) hardbound volume. Publication alters the proper citation for the contents thereof.

Determination Letter An IRS pronouncement issued by the local IRS District Director, relative to the agency's position concerning a straightforward issue of tax law in the context of a completed transaction.

Direct history Case citations of only the lower or higher court decisions for the same case.

Discriminant function formula A means by which, on the basis of probable return to the IRS in terms of collected delinquent tax liabilities, the Service selects tax returns for examination.

District Court A trial-level court that hears tax and nontax cases. Organized according to geographical regions. Jury trials are available. Opinions are reported in the Federal Supplement series and in the AFTR and USTC tax case reporter series.

District director The chief operating officer of one of the IRS's functional districts. A District Director manages the district's resources and all of its examination, collection, investigation, and taxpayer service activities.

Effective tax rate The proportion of a taxpayer's economic income that was paid to the government as a tax liability (i.e., it is computed by dividing the tax liability by the taxpayer's economic income for the year). Economic income includes nontaxable sources of income, such as gifts and inheritances, and tax-exempt interest.

En banc When more than one Tax Court judge hears a case, the court is said to be sitting "en banc."

Enrolled agent One who is qualified to practice before the IRS by means other than becoming an attorney or CPA. Typically, one must pass a qualifying examination and meet other requirements to become an Enrolled Agent.

Ethical standards Boundaries of social or professional behavior, derived by the culture or its institutions. Tax ethics are described in various documents of governmental agencies or professional organizations. See, for example, Appendixes A–C of this text.

Fact issue A tax research issue in which the practitioner must determine whether a pertinent question of fact was satisfied by the taxpayer; e.g., was an election filed with the government in a timely manner? What was the taxpayer's motivation underlying the redemption of some corporate stock?

Field examination The review of a corporation or business tax return by an IRS agent. Typically involves more complex issues of law and/or fact than are the subject of a correspondence or office audit. Open-ended in nature. The agent who conducts a field examination reviews all of the taxpayer's business and financial operations, accounting methods, and means of internal control.

File memorandum A primary means by which to communicate the results of a research project to oneself, one's supervisor, and/or one's successor. Includes, among other features, a statement of the pertinent facts and assumptions, a detailed outline (and citations of) controlling tax law, a summary of the researcher's conclusions, and a listing of action recommendations for the client to consider.

Finding list An index to primary tax law sources, such as court cases or revenue rulings, typically arranged alphabetically, and referring to paragraph or division citations in the tax service's compilations.

Folio/Boolean syntax search A deductive logic search that allows for the intersection of terms by using connectors such as "or," "and," or "within # number of words".

Fraud In a tax practice context, a taxpayer action to evade the assessment of a tax. Criminal fraud requires a willful intent by the taxpayer. The IRS bears the burden of proof relative to fraud allegations.

Full text search A computerized version of a published index. A full-text search locates every occurrence of a word or phrase in every document available for the search.

General citation A citation that directs the researcher to the first page of the citing case.

***Golsen* rule** Tax Court decisions are appealed to the Court of Appeals for the taxpayer's place of work or residence. The decisions of the Courts of Appeal are not always consistent. Thus, when a taxpayer whose circuit has ruled on a given issue brings a case that includes that issue before the Tax Court, the Tax Court will follow the holding of the pertinent Circuit, even if the Tax Court disagrees with the holding, or if another circuit has issued a contrary holding. This can lead to contradictory Tax Court rulings, based solely upon the state of the taxpayer's residence.

Headnote Numbered paragraphs in which the editors of the court reporter summarize the court's holdings on each issue. These paragraphs appear in the court reporters before the text of the actual court case.

Hypertext A means of moving around within the documents of an electronic database by clicking on a mouse or keyboard where a special text color or character indicates that a related document is available. For instance, in reading a court case, the user might move to the opinion issued in another case cited in a footnote, or to a controlling Code section or Regulation that is cited in the document.

Independence The AICPA requires the CPA who renders an opinion relative to a client's financial statements to be (and to appear to be) independent from the client. This principle entails restrictions as to the CPA's direct and indirect financial dealings with the client.

Indirect history Cases other than lower or higher court decisions of the case of interest which are citing the case.

InfoTax Provider of a CD-ROM tax research service, including Code and Regulations, court cases, and administrative pronouncements.

Injunction The action by which the IRS or a court prevents (enjoins) a taxpayer, preparer, or tax shelter distributor from undertaking a specified action (e.g., preparing tax returns for compensation or offering a tax shelter for sale).

Interest-free loan The transfer of funds from a lender to a borrower at a stated interest rate of zero. Under current tax law, certain lenders and borrowers may be required to treat interest-free loans as gifts, dividends, or compensation, with accompanying gift and income tax consequences.

Internal Revenue Bulletin An official weekly publication of the Internal Revenue Service that includes Announcements, Treasury Decisions, Revenue Rulings, Revenue Procedures, and other information of interest to the tax researcher.

Internal Revenue Code The primary statutory source of the federal tax law, a collection of laws that have been passed by Congress and incorporated in Title 26 of the United States Code. The Code was last reorganized in 1954. It presently is known as the Internal Revenue Code of 1986. The chief subdivision of the Code is the section.

Internal Revenue Service A division of the Department of the Treasury, the federal agency that is charged with the collection of federal taxes and the implementation of other responsibilities that are conveyed by the Internal Revenue Code.

Internal Revenue Service Centers Locations at which the IRS receives and processes tax returns, distributes tax forms, and performs other specified functional activities in the administration of the federal tax laws.

Internet A means by which millions of remote computer stations are connected and can be used by individuals at any such station. Search engines assist in finding pertinent materials, and download features allow users to view and obtain files from the remote locations. The Internet is organized chiefly using the World Wide Web, bulletin board and newsgroup systems, and file transfer protocols. The Internet is useful to the tax researcher as a means of finding primary and secondary source documents in a timely fashion, sharing tax newsletters and spreadsheets, and transferring data to and from taxing jurisdictions.

In text   The method of updating Internet and CD ROM tax services. The text of the service is updated directly, and there is no use of supplemental files.

Insta-Cite   A powerful citator offered through WESTLAW. It provides a timely direct history of a court case, a negative indirect history of the case, and is useful for verifying the correct spelling, court of decision, date, and parallel citations for the case of interest.

Judicial sources   Certain federal court decisions that have the force of the statute in constructing the federal tax law. The magnitude of this authority depends upon the level and location of the courts that issued the opinions.

KeyCite   A WESTLAW citator that furnishes a comprehensive direct and indirect history for court cases. The indirect history includes secondary materials that have the cited case in their text. KeyCite allows the researcher to select a full history, negative history, or omit minor cases. This option is not available with the other citators.

Kleinrock Tax Library   Provider of a CD-ROM tax research service, including Code and Regulations, court cases, and administrative pronouncements.

Law issue   A tax research question in which one must determine which provision of the federal tax law applies to the client's fact situation. This entails the evaluation of various statutory, administrative, and judicial provisions with respect to the client's circumstances; e.g., is the client's charitable contribution subject to the 30 percent of adjusted gross income limitation?

Law reviews   Scholarly publications of law schools. These publications are edited either by faculty members or by graduate students under the guidance of the school's faculty. Most law reviews also use an outside advisory board comprised of practicing attorneys and law professors at other universities to aid in selecting and reviewing articles. The articles appearing in these publications are usually written by tax practitioners, academics, graduate students, or other noted commentators.

LEXCITE   A citator service of LEXIS. For the case citation entered, it ascertains parallel citations and then searches for all of the cites in the case law documents. It will find embedded references to a variety of documents such as cases, law reviews, journals, Federal Register, and Revenue Rulings.

LEXIS   An on-line database resource that allows the researcher to access a database consisting of the text of court cases, administrative rulings, and selected law review articles, and to search these files for tax (and other) law sources that may be relevant to the research problem.

Linking   A method of moving among the documents of an electronic database, as indicated by the controlling software. See hypertext.

Local citation   A citation that directs the researcher to the exact page where the cited case is mentioned in the citing case.

Marginal tax rate   The proportion of the next dollar of gross income (or other increase in the tax base) that the taxpayer must pay to the government as a tax. Thus, the marginal tax rate conveys the proportionate value of an additional deduction, or the cost of an increase to the tax base. Tax-effective decisions must take into account the marginal (and not the average or nominal) tax rate.

Memorandum decision   A decision of the Tax Court that, in the opinion of the chief judge, does not address any new issue of tax law. Accordingly, the government does not publish the opinion. Commerce Clearing House and Research Institute of America each publish annual collections of these Tax Court Memorandum decisions.

Mertens   See West Group *Mertens Law of Federal Income Taxation*

Negative indirect history Case citations that reduce the precedential value of the case of interest. Such cases would be those that criticize, limit, question, or overrule its logic or holding.

Negligence In a federal tax context, a (nonwillful) failure to exercise one's duty with respect to the Internal Revenue Code, or to use a reasonable degree of expected or professional care. Examples include the unacceptable failure to attempt to follow the IRS's rules and Regulations in the preparation of a tax return for compensation.

Ninety-day letter A statutory notice from the IRS that the taxpayer has failed to pay an assessed tax. An issuance of such a letter usually indicates that the taxpayer has exhausted all of his or her appeal rights within the IRS, and that the next forum for review will be a trial-level court. Strictly, the taxpayer has ninety days to petition the Tax Court to be relieved of the deficiency assessment. If no such petition is filed, the IRS is empowered to collect the assessed tax.

Nominal tax rate Determined by an inspection of the applicable rate schedule. The average nominal rate at which the taxpayer's total taxable income is taxed is computed by dividing the taxpayer's total tax liability by his or her taxable income. Tax-exempt income is not included in the denominator of this fraction.

Nonacquiescence An announcement by the IRS that it will not follow the decision of a regular Tax Court decision that was adverse to the agency. Notation is included in the proper citation of the disputed case. Announced in the Internal Revenue Bulletin.

Offer in compromise The means by which the government offers to reduce the amount of an assessed tax, usually because of some doubt as to the "litigation-proof" magnitude or collectibility of the tax. A legally enforceable promise that cannot be rescinded, an offer in compromise relates to the entire liability of the taxpayer, and it conclusively settles all of the issues for which an agreement can be made.

Office examination The audit of a nonbusiness tax return that is conducted at an IRS district office.

Usually requires some analysis and the exercise of the IRS personnel's judgment, rather than a mere inquiry or substantiation verification. Typically involves tip, rent or royalty income, travel and entertainment deductions, and income from partnerships or other conduit entities.

Online database In a tax research context, a collection of the text of court case opinions, statutes, administrative rulings, and selected law review articles. These text files can be searched by the practitioner in an extremely fast and efficient manner, to assist him or her in locating tax law sources that may be relevant to the disputed tax issue.

Open transaction A tax research issue is open when not all of the pertinent transactions have been completed by the taxpayer or other parties, such that the researcher can suggest to the client several alternative courses of action that will generate differing tax consequences.

Oral presentation A primary means of communicating the results of a research project to others by way of a telephone conversation or a more formal presentation system.

PH *Citator* The first series of citators formerly published by Prentice-Hall and now published by Research Institute of America. The first series, consists of three bound volumes that cover all of the federal tax cases dated between 1863 and 1953.

Practice before the IRS The privilege to sign tax returns as preparer for compensation and to represent others before the IRS or court in an audit or appeal proceeding. This privilege is granted by the IRS and controlled under Circular 230.

Practitioner journal Journals published by professional organizations and commercial companies. The objective of these journals is to keep tax practitioners abreast of the current changes and trends in the tax law.

PREMISE The software used to access WEST-LAW on-line.

Preparer One who prepares the tax return of another party. Other aspects of the definition, e.g., whether a preparer must receive compensation, and the educational and procedural requirements of a preparer, vary among presiding organizations. The Code levies penalties upon preparers who do not carry out their full responsibilities.

Preparer penalties A series of fines and other levies by which the IRS encourages taxpayers and preparers to fulfill their responsibilities under the Internal Revenue Code. Examples include penalties for failure to sign returns, keep or furnish copies of returns, and provide required information to federal agencies.

Primary authority An element of the federal tax law that was issued by Congress, the Treasury or Internal Revenue Service, or a federal court, and thus carries greater precedential weight than elements of the tax law issued by other parties.

Prime issues A series of disputed tax questions for which the IRS will not sign offers in compromise. Thus, the taxpayer's only alternatives are to satisfy the full assessed liability or to proceed with litigation. These issues are designated by the National Office of the IRS, as a policy matter, when it is believed that taxpayer abuse of the subject matter threatens the integrity or viability of the tax.

Private letter ruling A written determination published by the Internal Revenue Service relative to its position concerning the tax treatment of a prospective transaction. Strictly, it cannot be applied to any taxpayer other than the one who requested the ruling. Text or summaries thereof are included in various commercial tax services.

Problem Resolution Program An organizational means by which the IRS attempts to satisfy taxpayer complaints, inquiries, and disagreements, short of the appeals process or litigation. The taxpayer can employ the Problem Resolution Program when the usual agency channels do not produce the desired results. Typically, the program is used to resolve billing, procedural, computer-generated, and other problems that the taxpayer has not resolved after one or more contacts with the appropriate IRS office.

Proceedings The published versions of conference presentations. These proceeding are distributed to the participants at the conference and later to the general public in the form of a collection of articles.

Professional journals Synonym for practitioner journal.

Progressive tax rate If the marginal rates of a tax rate schedule increase as the magnitude of the tax base increases, the schedule includes progressive tax rates.

Proportional tax rate If the marginal rates of a tax rate schedule remain constant as the magnitude of the tax base increases, the schedule includes proportional tax rates.

Proposed regulation An interpretation or clarification of the provisions of a portion of the Internal Revenue Code, issued by the Treasury and available for comment (and possible revision) in a public hearing.

Query A means of searching an electronic database. Includes a definition of the scope of the search, and a specification of the targeted terms in which the researcher is interested, often employing connectors in the grammar of the query.

QuickCite A citator in WESTLAW that provides the most current citations. This citator uses the WESTLAW document search capabilities and permits date restrictions on the search.

Reasonable cause A means by which a taxpayer or preparer can be excused from an applicable penalty or other sanction. For instance, if the taxpayer failed to file a tax return on a timely basis because of illness, or if the underlying records were destroyed by natural cause, the taxpayer likely would be excused from the penalty (but not from the tax or any related interest) because of this reasonable cause.

Regressive tax rate If the marginal rates of a tax rate schedule decrease as the magnitude of the tax base increases, the schedule includes regressive tax rates.

Regulation An interpretation or clarification of the provisions of a portion of the Internal Revenue

Code, issued by the Treasury under authority granted by Congress. Legislative Regulations directly create the details of a tax law. Both general and legislative Regulations carry the force of the statute, unless they are held to be invalid in a judicial hearing.

Revenue Agent's Report Prepared upon the completion of the examination of a tax return to explain to the taxpayer the sources of any adjustments to the reported tax liability. If the taxpayer agrees to this recomputation, the associated tax, penalty, and interest become due. Lacking such agreement, other aspects of the appeals process are undertaken.

Revenue procedure A pronouncement of the Internal Revenue Service concerning the implementation details of a specific Code provision. Published in the *Internal Revenue Bulletin.*

Revenue ruling A pronouncement of the Internal Revenue Service concerning its interpretation of the application of the Code (typically) to a specific taxpayer-submitted fact situation. Published in the *Internal Revenue Bulletin.* Can be relied upon as precedent by other taxpayers who encounter similar fact patterns.

RIA *Analysis of Federal Taxes: Income* A condensed version of the *Coordinator.* Covers only income tax issues.

RIA CHECKPOINT The Internet tax service provided by Research Institute of America. This is one of the most authoritative and well known Internet tax services available. All services available from Research Institute of America may be accessed by subscription through CHECKPOINT.

RIA *Citators* The citator service published by Research Institute of America. It includes two series of citators, the *PH Citator* and the *Citator 2nd Series.*

RIA *Federal Tax Coordinator 2d* Comprehensive topical tax service published by Research Institute of America. The editors comments and evaluations of the law are the basis of the main text with footnotes used to direct researchers to primary sources. One of its strong points is its general background discussions summarizing the major issues.

RIA OnPoint CD resource that allows the researcher to access a database consisting of the text of court cases, administrative rulings, and selected tax treatises and analytical articles, and to search these files for tax law sources that may be relevant to the research problem.

RIA *United States Tax Reporter* The annotated service of Research Institute of America dedicated to federal income, estate, and gift taxation. Includes a weekly newsletter, topical index, tax calendar, rate tables and schedules, practitioner checklists, and case name, Code section, Regulation, and Revenue Ruling finding lists. This tax service has a unique and functional paragraph numbering system. All paragraphs pertaining to a particular Code section incorporate that section number into the paragraph number. A single digit is added to the end of the Code section number, indicating the nature of the material contained in the paragraph.

Seamless Ability to perform a function with little or no effort. For example, the ability to retrieve references full-text through the computer by double clicking on the reference's title.

Secondary authority An element of the federal tax law that was issued by a scholarly or professional writer, e.g., in a textbook, journal article, or treatise, and thus carries less precedential weight than elements of the tax law issued by primary sources.

Shepard's PreView A citator created to provide current case information with only a four to six week lag time.

Shepard's Federal Tax Citator A citator available through WESTLAW and LEXIS, organized by reference to the case reporter and volume number in which the case is found. Thus, to use the citator, the practitioner must know the court reporter citation for the case of interest.

Shepardizing The process of evaluating the validity of a case and locating additional authority via a citator.

Shepard's Citations The full coverage of Shepard's citators available through WESTLAW.

Small Cases Division The Tax Court allows taxpayers whose disputed tax liability does not exceed $50,000 to try the case before the court's Small Cases Division. Procedural rules of the division are somewhat relaxed, and taxpayers often represent themselves. The Small Cases Division decisions are not published, nor can either party appeal the holdings thereof.

Spine Scan A method of entering published tax services by scanning the volume contents listed on the spines of the tax service binders.

Statute of limitations Provides the maximum amount of time within which one or both parties in the taxing process must perform an act, such as file a return, pay a tax, or examine a return. Various time limits apply relative to the Internal Revenue Code, although both parties can, by mutual agreement, extend one or more of these time limitations, if desired.

Statutory notice of deficiency Synonym for a ninety-day letter.

Statutory sources The Constitution, tax treaties, and the Internal Revenue Code are the statutory sources of the federal tax law. They have the presumption of correctness, unless a court modifies or overturns a provision, in response to a taxpayer challenge. In this regard, legislative intent and history can be important in supporting the taxpayer's case.

Substantial authority A taxpayer penalty may be incurred if a tax return position is taken and not disclosed to the IRS where no substantial authority (generally, statute, Regulation, court decision, or written determination) supports the position.

Supreme Court The highest federal appellate court. Hears very few tax cases. Approves a writ of certiorari for the cases that it hears. Opinions are reported in the *U.S. Supreme Court Reports* (citation abbreviation, US); the *Supreme Court Reporter* (SCt); the *United States Reports, Lawyer's Edition* (LEd); the AFTR and USTC tax case reporter series; and, various on-line services.

Table of Authorities A service available through WESTLAW that lists cases that are cited within a case of interest.

Tax authority Any source of the federal tax law; in common usage, this term is used to refer to government agencies.

Tax avoidance The legal structuring of one's financial affairs so as to optimize the related tax liability. Synonym for tax planning.

***TaxBase*®** Electronic newsletter published daily by Tax Analysts. It covers federal, state, and worldwide tax news as well as court petitions and complaints and highlights of the daily tax news.

Tax compliance An element of modern tax practice in which a practitioner works with a client to file appropriate tax returns in a timely manner and represents the client in administrative proceedings.

Tax Court A trial-level court that hears only cases involving tax issues. Issues regular and memorandum decisions. Meets in Washington, D.C., and in other major cities. Formerly called the Board of Tax Appeals. Regular opinions are reported in the *US Tax Court Reports*. Memorandum opinions are published only by commercial tax services.

Tax ethics The application of ethical standards to the tax practice. See Appendixes A through C of this text.

Tax evasion The reduction of one's tax liability by illegal means.

Tax journal A periodic publication that addresses legal, factual, and procedural issues encountered in a modern tax practice. As a secondary source of federal tax law, analyses in tax journals can be used in support of a taxpayer's case before a government agency or, especially, before a court.

Tax litigation An element of modern tax practice in which a practitioner represents the client against the government in a judicial hearing.

Tax newsletter A weekly, biweekly, or monthly publication or electronic document, often furnished as part of a subscription to a commercial tax service. Typically provides digest-style summaries of current court case rulings, administrative pronouncements, pending or approved tax legislation, cross-referenced to the organization system of the tax service. Helps the practitioner to keep current relative to the breaking developments in the tax community.

Tax Notes A weekly collection of the latest regulations, written determinations, case opinions, congressional studies, policy analyses, and other items of interest to the tax practitioner. Available through the mail and on various electronic tax services.

Tax planning Synonym for tax avoidance.

Tax practice Meeting the tax research, litigation, planning, and compliance needs of a client by a recognized tax professional.

Tax research An examination of pertinent sources of the federal tax law in light of all relevant circumstances relative to a client's tax problem. Entails the use of professional judgment to draw an appropriate conclusion, and the communication of such conclusions or alternatives at a proper level to the client.

Tax service A commercial tax reference including statutory, administrative, and judicial sources of federal tax law. Structured to maximize the practitioner's ease of use via a variety of indexes and finding lists. Often includes the text of the pertinent tax authorities and relevant scholarly or professional commentary.

Tax treaty An act of Congress that addresses the application of certain Internal Revenue Code provisions to a taxpayer whose tax base falls under the taxing statutes of more than one country. Published, among other places, in the *Internal Revenue Bulletin*.

Taxpayer Advocate Empowered to achieve a temporary delay in the normal enforcement procedures of the IRS, as specified in a Taxpayer Assistance Order.

Taxpayer Assistance Order The taxpayer uses this request to engage an IRS Taxpayer Advocate to delay the implementation of an IRS action, such as a collection or seizure activity, where it appears that the taxpayer has received less than fair treatment through the administrative procedures of the agency.

Taxpayer Compliance Measurement Program A means by which the IRS develops its discriminant function formulae. The taxpayer's return is selected randomly for an extensive review, during which every item of income, credit, deduction, and exclusion is challenged by the government. The results of such reviews are used (other than to adjust the examined taxpayer's liability) to delineate criteria by which other taxpayers' returns will be selected for examination.

Technical Advice Memorandum A pronouncement of the National Office of the Internal Revenue Service stating the agency's position relative to the tax treatment of a taxpayer whose return is under audit. Text or discussion thereof may be included in the body of a commercial tax service.

Temporary regulation An administrative pronouncement of the IRS, typically concerning the application of a recently enacted or detailed provision of the tax law, especially where there is insufficient time to carry out the public-hearings process that usually accompanies the Regulations process. Temporary Regulations carry the force of law, although citations therefor differ from those for permanent Regulations with regard to the prefix.

Thirty-day letter A notice from the IRS formally notifying the taxpayer of the results of an examination of the return and requesting that the taxpayer agree to the proposed modifications to the tax liability. A taxpayer's failure to respond to the letter triggers the statutory notice of a tax deficiency, i.e., the ninety-day letter demanding the payment of the tax or a petition to the tax court.

Topical tax service A professional tax research reference collection, i.e., a secondary source of federal tax law. Includes Code, Regulation, and ruling analysis; judicial case notes; and other indexes and finding lists, organized by general topic. The most important topical tax services are published by the Research Institute of America, Callaghan, and the Bureau of National Affairs.

Treasury Decision A Regulation that has not yet been formally integrated into the published tax Regulation collection.

Treasury Department The cabinet-level government agency that is responsible for administering and enforcing laws that affect the currency. The Treasury has assigned its responsibilities relative to the Internal Revenue Code and the Internal Revenue Service.

Unauthorized practice of law A prohibited aspect of modern tax practice by nonattorneys, entailing, e.g., the issuance of a legal opinion or the drafting of a legal document for the client, for which the practitioner could be subject to legal or professional penalties.

USTC The citation abbreviation for the Commerce Clearing House reporter, *United States Tax Cases*. Includes most of the tax decisions of the federal courts other than the Tax Court.

U.S. Constitution Ultimate source of the federal tax law. Reproduced as Appendix D of this text.

Warren, Gorham & Lamont's *Index to Federal Tax Articles* An index to federal tax articles published by Warren, Gorham & Lamont. It provides citations and occasionally summaries for articles covering federal income, gift, and estate taxation or tax policy that appear in over 350 periodicals. This index has permanent cumulation indexes provided in paper-bound volumes and is update quarterly by paperback cumulative supplements. Both the topic and the author indexes contain full article citations.

West Group *Mertens Law of Federal Income Taxation* The topical tax service of the legal publisher West Group. This tax treatise service is designed chiefly by and for attorneys.

WESTLAW An on-line database resource provided by West Publishing Company. Allows the researcher to access a database consisting of the text of court cases, administrative rulings, and selected law review articles, and to search these files for tax (and other) law sources that may be relevant to the research problem.

WESTLAW *Federal Tax Citations* The computerized version of Shepard's *Federal Tax Citator* that is available through WESTLAW.

WESTMATE Software that is used to access WESTLAW via the Internet or from an on-line service.

World Wide Web A popular means by which to organize and present one's data to the Internet community. The IRS, various tax research services, and numerous law libraries offer World Wide Web home pages, such that tax professionals can find and search through the documents available on the computers of those hosting the Internet site.

Writ of certiorari Document issued by the Supreme Court indicating the Court will hear the petitioned case. If the case will not be heard, certiorari is said to be denied.

Written determination General description of IRS or Treasury pronouncements, including Revenue Rulings, Revenue Procedures, Private Letter Rulings, Technical Advice Memoranda, and Determination Letters.

TOPICAL INDEX

Credits

Westlaw pages courtesy of Westlaw and Shepard's. Reprinted with permission.

CCH exhibits reproduced with permission from CCH INCORPORATED, 2700 Lake Cook Road, Riverwoods, IL 60015.

Exhibits 6-1, 6-2, 6-3, 6-4, 6-5, 6-6, 6-7, 6-8, and 6-9 reprinted from *RIAG's Citator 2d Series*, with permission of the publisher, Research Institute of America Group.

Exhibits 7-5, 7-8, and 7-10 reprinted from *RIAG's United States Tax Reporter,* with permission of the publisher, Research Institute of America Group.

Exhibits 7-16, 7-17, and 7-18 reprinted from *RIAG's Federal Taxes: Income,* with permission of the publisher, Research Institute of America Group.

Exhibit 7-19 reprinted from *RIAG's Federal Tax Coordinator 2d,* with permission of the publisher, Research Institute of America Group.

Exhibit 7-20 reprinted with the permission of Tax Management, Inc., a subsidiary of The Bureau of National Affairs, Inc., Washington, D.C.

Exhibit 7-21 reprinted with the permission of Tax Management, Inc., a subsidiary of The Bureau of National Affairs, Inc., Washington, D.C.

Exhibit 7-22 reprinted with the permission of Tax Management, Inc., a subsidiary of The Bureau of National Affairs, Inc., Washington, D.C.

Exhibit 8-23 reprinted with the permission of LEXIS-NEXIS, a division of Reed Elsevier, Inc.

Exhibit 8-24 reprinted with the permission of LEXIS-NEXIS, a division of Reed Elsevier, Inc.

Exhibits 8-25, 8-26, 8-27, 8-28, 8-29, 8-30, and 8-31 reprinted by permission of Kleinrock Publishing. All rights reserved.

Exhibit 9-3 reprinted from *RIAG's Journal of Taxation*, with permission of the publisher, Research Institute of America Group.

Exhibit 9-4 reprinted from *RIAG's Journal of Partnership Taxation*, with permission of the publisher, Research Institute of America Group.

Exhibit 9-8 reprinted with the permission of Tax Management, Inc., a subsidiary of The Bureau of National Affairs, Inc., Washington, D.C.

Exhibit 9-9 reprinted with permission. Copyright 1998 Tax Analysts.

Exhibit 9-13 reprinted from *RIAG's WG&L Index to Federal Tax Articles*, with permission of the publisher, Research Institute of America Group.

Exhibit 9-14 reprinted with the permission of LEXIS-NEXIS, a division of Reed Elsevier, Inc.

Exhibit 9-15 reprinted with permission from Online Networks, Inc., publisher of AccountsLedger.com.

Appendix C reprinted with permission from the AICPA Code of Professional Conduct. Copyright ©1994 by the American Institute of Certified Public Accountants, Inc.